"Les Leopold has vividly brought to life an extraordinary man—an incorruptible fighter for the rights of labor—an historic figure who should never be forgotten. Whether leading the charge for the Occupational and Health Safety Act, protecting workers from toxic exposures, traveling the country to argue for health insurance, testifying before Congress, or inspiring a generation of student activists, Mazzocchi's fiery passion for social and economic justice was revealed in every action he took. And in Leopold he has found an equally passionate and dedicated biographer. This is an important work in the annals of labor history."

—Doris Kearns Goodwin, Pulitzer Prize–winning historian

"When a company comes and exploits natural resources, there are laws that say they have to replenish those resources. Yet when a company comes into a town and exploits our greatest natural resource, our workers, there are few laws that protect the people. Tony Mazzocchi spent his life fighting to protect workers like those who lost their jobs in my hometown and all over the country. We still don't have those laws. But maybe this book can inspire us to move a few steps closer."

—Bruce Springsteen, Grammy Award–winning musician

"*The Man Who Hated Work and Loved Labor* crackles with life—and it's hard to imagine a life better spent than Tony Mazzocchi's. He was a friend and an inspiration to me, as he will be to anyone who reads this riveting biography."

—Barbara Ehrenreich, author, *Nickel and Dimed*

"Tony Mazzocchi is one of the unsung, unnoticed heroes of the American working class, and Les Leopold's biography gives us the gift of his extraordinary life—from the battlefields of World War II to the present-day struggle for workers' rights. In that struggle, Tony Mazzocchi was brilliant, bold, imaginative, and fearless. He loved life, food, fun, and children, and I believe his story can inspire a new generation of activists to work for peace and economic justice."

—Howard Zinn, author, *A People's History of the United States*

"Tony Mazzocchi was one of the most visionary trade unionists in America. He wrote the book on building alliances between workers and environmentalists."

—Leo Gerard, President, United Steelworkers of America

"Tony Mazzocchi formed my understanding of the fundamental relationship between work and our environment. He always reminded me, 'Carl, companies don't eliminate jobs because of environmental standards. They fight environmental standards so they can degrade and eliminate jobs. It's a skilled, motivated workforce they want to get away from, not clean air and clean water. Workers are the environment's first line of defense."

—Carl Pope, Executive Director, Sierra Club

"Tony Mazzocchi expressed the highest purposes of the labor movement. He constantly reminded us why we needed to build a broad social movement to bring justice and equality to our society—a movement that could unite unions, environmentalists, and social justice organizations in the global struggle to tame corporate power. His commitment to single-payer health care and free higher education for all continues to inspire our work today. We hope his story will help fuel a new generation of movement activists."

—Richard Trumka, Secretary-Treasurer of the AFL-CIO

"Les Leopold's biography of Tony Mazzocchi should be required reading for anyone interested in the labor movement and social change. Mazzocchi is the real thing—a working-class hero who worked to build a democratic, progressive movement representing the interests of working people. Mazzocchi's life story is full of insight on organizing and democratic leadership. His example sets an inspiring path for union revitalization."

—Elaine Bernard, executive director of the
Labor and Worklife Program, Harvard Law School

The Man Who Hated Work and Loved Labor

The Man Who Hated Work and Loved Labor

LES LEOPOLD

Chelsea Green Publishing Company
White River Junction, Vermont

Developmental Editor: Russ Rymer
Project Manager and Copy Editor: Laura Jorstad
Proofreader: Eileen McNulty-Bowers
Indexer: Peggy Holloway
Interior Designer: Peter Holm, Sterling Hill Productions
Cover and Jacket Designer: Charles Kreloff

Printed in the United States of America
First printing, October 2007
10 9 8 7 6 5 4 3 2 1   1 2 3 4 5 6

Our Commitment to Green Publishing
Chelsea Green sees publishing as a tool for cultural change and ecological stewardship. We strive to align our book manufacturing practices with our editorial mission and to reduce the impact of our business enterprise on the environment. We print our books and catalogs on chlorine-free recycled paper, using soy-based inks whenever possible. This book may cost slightly more because we use recycled paper, and we hope you'll agree that it's worth it. Chelsea Green is a member of the Green Press Initiative (www.greenpressinitiative.org), a nonprofit coalition of publishers, manufacturers, and authors working to protect the world's endangered forests and conserve natural resources.

The Man Who Hated Work and Loved Labor was printed on Natures Natural, a 50-percent postconsumer-waste recycled, old-growth-forest–free paper supplied by Maple-Vail.

Library of Congress Cataloging-in-Publication Data
Leopold, Les.
The man who hated work and loved labor : the life and times of Tony Mazzocchi / Les Leopold.
p. cm.
Includes bibliographical references and index.
ISBN 978-1-933392-63-9 (hardcover)—ISBN 978-1-933392-64-6 (pbk.)
1. Mazzocchi, Tony. 2. Labor leaders—United States—Biography. 3. Labor unions—United States—Officials and employees—Biography. I. Title.

HD6509.M39L46 2007
331.88092—dc22
[B]

2007024185

Chelsea Green Publishing Company
Post Office Box 428
White River Junction, VT 05001
(802) 295-6300
www.chelseagreen.com

To Chester, Lilah, and Sharon, to sister Evelyn, and to the memory of Alice and Alex Leopold

Contents

Acknowledgments

This project was made possible by my colleagues at the Labor Institute and the Public Health Institute, in particular Paul Renner and Jim Young, who provided unwavering support and the time to write.

Special thanks also to David Dembo at the Council on International and Public Affairs for his world-class research. And I am deeply indebted to Mark Dudzic for his guidance and thoughtful suggestions.This project was greatly aided by three talented editors. Jim Young helped mightily, especially in the early going and during the endgame. Russ Rymer, our developmental editor, provided courageous guidance down the stretch. And I am forever grateful to the skill and heart of Laura McClure, who was there all the way. Clearly, she is among the most gifted editors, anywhere. Also, I truly valued the support, warmth, and good cheer from all the staff at Chelsea Green, especially Jonathan Teller-Elsberg and Editors in Chief John Barstow and Shay Totten. It was a delight to work with them.

A very special thanks also to Dan Berman, Carolyn Mugar, and Jim Young (again) for bringing Tony to Chelsea Green, and to Rose Ann DeMoro for linking the book to her prodigious network. And I am deeply indebted to my very special agent and friend, William Lee, who believed in this project and wouldn't rest until it found a home.

I would like to honor the memory of those who helped this project, but have since died: Robert Engler, Susan Mazzocchi, Ernie Rouselle, and Connie Tozzi.

My deepest appreciation goes to all those who gave so generously of their time and memories to make this a Tony-like collective effort: Geraldine Amitin, Joe Anderson, Stanley Aronowitz, Morty Bahr, Gail Bateson, Eula Bingham, Paul Brodeur, Bill Bywater, Barry Commoner, Molly Coye, Donna Dewitt, Bill Dodds, Pyser Edelsack, Rick Engler, Jerry and Ruth Fine, Stanley Fischer, Colin Greer, Bobby Guinta, Ken Heckler, Ruth Heifetz, Katherine Isaac, Sharon Itaya, Vern Jensen, Michael Kaufman, Sylvia Kieding, Dick Leonard, Cathy Lerza, Sam Love, Monica MacManus, Alejandra Martorell, Anthony and Kristina Mazzocchi, Stephen Markowitz, Michael Merrill, Richard Miller, David

Michaels, Rafael Moure, Ralph Nader, Linda Nagle, Phyllis Ohlemacher, Christine Oliver, Ed Ott, Glenn Paulson, Cecelia Perry, Adolph Reed Jr., George Roach, Linda Rudolph, Howard Saunders, Jack Sheehan, Sally Silvers, Jeanne Stellman, Doug Stevens, Jerome Summers, Rodrigo Toscano, Jean Urano, Baldemar Velasquez, and Bob Wages. And a special thanks to Steve Wodka, who pulled no punches in keeping Tony's story straight and true.

I am very grateful to Bernard Rapoport for his generous support and encouragement. And my love to my sister Evelyn Leopold, who taught me to cherish social justice.

While working on the book, I sometimes lost track of everything else, including our wonderful children, Chester and Lilah. But they usually forgave me because they, too, admired Tony. My lifelong partner and true love, Sharon Szymanski, made it all possible. Not only did she provide unwavering support, invaluable insight, and a constant reality check, but she loved me through it all. No Sharon, no book.

Prologue

The snow drifted thigh-high along the stone walls separating rolling farm fields from dense forest. Encrusted evergreens drooped with exhaustion.

On the ground, patches of red-tinted snow flagged the dead. Curiously, some corpses were not bloodied. These soldiers had been felled by concussions from exploding shells, leaving their bodies—and their greatcoats—whole, seemingly untouched.

You weren't supposed to do it; it was disrespectful to the dead. But soldiers fighting frostbite occasionally did it anyway: strip a coat from a dead comrade. The bitter chill in the Ardennes Forest excused a great deal. No one could remember a more frigid winter in Belgium than this one in 1944, when German Panzer divisions counterattacked ferociously against the Allies in the Battle of the Bulge.

As one soldier wrestled a coat off a limp body, the eighteen-year-old grunt still alive inside it was jolted by a spasm of consciousness: *Jesus, they're stripping me! Holy shit! If they get this jacket off me, it means I'm dead.*[1]

But the year wasn't 1944, it was 1975. And Tony Mazzocchi wasn't lying on the battlefield in the Ardennes, he was pinned upside down in his car beside a Virginia highway. The paramedics were struggling to get Tony's coat off to free him from the wreckage.

"I was hallucinating," Tony told me many years later. "When I came to, I heard this guy say, 'Take off his coat.'" And Tony's mind had slipped back to a searing memory from World War II, when he'd pilfered a coat from a dead soldier. He'd always felt bad about it.

Once Tony emerged from his soldier's flashback, he was puzzled by the pack of medics tending to him. "I was thinking, *What are they making all this fuss about?*" Tony said. "I felt okay." Then, as the medics stretchered him to the ambulance, "All of a sudden I turned and I saw the car laying on its side, totaled, the roof smashed down to the steering wheel. Next thing I knew I was in Manassas Hospital. I was bruised and I had a slight concussion. But I was lucky."

Lucky twice. Tony Mazzocchi had survived the Battle of the Bulge, the largest battle ever fought by American troops. And then in 1975, perhaps targeted in another epic American battle—this time against the nuclear industry—he'd cheated death again.

"I have no proof—not one iota of proof—that someone set me up," Tony said, sitting comfortably in my living room in 2002. He still didn't know what had caused the accident. He'd been driving home from a church-sponsored meeting on worker health and safety. He'd had two drinks after the meeting. But that didn't explain what happened as he drove east on Route 66: He blacked out before he hit the shoulder. The driver of an approaching car later said he watched the brand-new, two-tone Chevy coupe hit the grass median, flip into the air, roll, and land on its top. Thanks to the auto safety campaigns of Tony's friend Ralph Nader, this car wouldn't start until the seat belt was fastened. Inside the mangled chassis, that belt, along with Tony's sheepskin coat, had saved his life.

Mazzocchi and his colleagues had gone over it again and again. Yes, he'd been tired, given the breakneck pace of his crusading union work around the country during the previous five years. Was fatigue catching up with him? Or was something else at work?

He couldn't erase more sinister thoughts from his mind. Just two months before his 1975 accident, a woman working with Tony to expose deadly hazards at an Oklahoma nuclear facility also had suffered a mysterious automobile crash. She had been on her way to deliver damning evidence against her bosses at the Kerr-McGee Corporation to a *New York Times* reporter when her car went off the road and hit a concrete culvert. Tony Mazzocchi had survived his wreck. But his colleague, Karen Silkwood, had died.

I first met Tony Mazzocchi a few months before he met Karen Silkwood. I was a graduate student who had come to his cramped union office on 16th Street in Washington, DC, hoping to enlist in his radical occupational health and safety movement. Tony had other plans for me and for the movement. His idea was impossibly simple—and perhaps simply impossible. He wanted to build a new working-class economics crusade, and he wanted me to help.

"Look," he said, "I think the post–World War Two boom is over. Workers should be ready to learn about the problems of capitalism." All I had to do was follow the same steps Tony had taken to launch the health and safety movement. First we'd design a course. Then we'd write a popular book based on the course. "Just don't use a lot of Marxist jargon," Tony said. Presto, a new movement would be born! I tried to believe him.

That fall, David Gordon, the noted radical economist, piloted our new political economy course for members of the Oil, Chemical and Atomic Workers International Union (OCAW) at the Rutgers Labor Education Center in New Jersey. No surprise: We did not spark a mass movement. But it did lead in 1975 to the creation of the Labor Institute in New York.

I would work at the Institute for the next thirty-plus years, first as a staff member and later as its director, helping Tony with his countless schemes. During his period of exile from OCAW, Tony showed up on the Labor Institute's doorstep. And after his second marriage collapsed, he even moved in for a while with our family in New Jersey, pasta and canned tomatoes in hand.

I was drawn to Tony's intelligence and his unwavering commitment (as well as his anchovy sauces). Tony didn't just preach about the need for great social changes: He acted each day to create them. But as fiercely as Tony fought for his ideas, as tenaciously as he held on to his principles, he was a kindhearted soul with an earthy, self-deprecating sense of humor. Unlike so many people who rise to leadership, Tony did not have an ego you constantly had to tiptoe around. He almost never got angry, or blamed anyone, or felt slighted. He was brilliant but referred to himself as a "hoople-head" who got things done because he had just enough brains to surround himself with smart people.[2]

Tony was a big-picture organizer who couldn't sit still. All the time I knew him, he traveled the country incessantly, crusading for universal health care or a labor party—leaving too little time to spend with his six children from two broken marriages. He would start ten projects at once, tossing the details around like confetti while others swept up behind.

Yet he could be meticulous when it came to cooking, woodworking, home repairs, or cement work. He once spent three days taking apart a broken dishwasher piece by piece rather than call in a pro. And kids from all over (including mine) still have three-foot-long wooden fish he carefully cut out for them to paint at birthday parties.

Tony's method for radical social change was joyous and communal, involving stimulating conversation and lots of raucous meals with friends. Hopelessness and resignation were not in his repertoire. For inspiration he loved to read history, and his most forward-looking notions often owed a debt to the past. As an autodidact, Tony never recognized (or even noticed) the boundaries between different occupations and different fields of study. He eagerly collected information from everywhere. Then it all bumbled around in his unconventional mind, often producing ideas that catapulted him decades ahead of the curve.

As early as the 1950s, when the term *environment* was nowhere on the political radar, Tony learned about nuclear fallout and began integrating environmental concerns into his critique of capitalism and his union work. His environmental radicalism grew in the 1960s and '70s when he realized that corporations were willingly exposing workers to toxic, even lethal, substances to increase productivity and profits. In the late 1980s, Tony was arguing that global warming might force us to fundamentally alter capitalism. He believed that the struggle of capital against nature was *the* irreconcilable contradiction that would force systemic change.

For me, Tony conjured up a labor movement that didn't really exist, but just might. This movement would be militant and green. It wouldn't just fight to protect the workforce from toxic substances—it would *eliminate* them. It would bring about radical changes that would stop global warming. It would give workers real control over the quality and pace of work and over corporate investment decisions. It would champion the fight against militarism and for justice and equality. It would win life-enhancing social programs such as free health care. It would dare to create a new political party to counter the corporate domination of the two major parties. In short, it would make good on its potential to transform American capitalism into something much more humane.

When Tony talked about broad social programs, there were no sectarian overtones and no '60s hype. He poked through the accepted wisdom that our inequitable, unsustainable economy was the best system that had ever been and could ever be. He would continually ask why millions of people were stuck in low-paying, dead-end jobs—and why even good-paying jobs sentenced workers to so many occupational illnesses. He wanted every worker to have paid sabbaticals from work, a guaranteed income, and free access to higher education.

Tony's big ideas led to Tony's big actions—and both differentiated him from nearly every other modern labor leader. He built bridges from the often insular labor movement to all the other major movements of his time—feminism, environmentalism, antiwar, civil rights. He was instrumental in building the occupational health and safety movement, the environmental health movement, and labor-environmental alliances, as well as in creating a new generation of worker-oriented occupational health professionals. Thousands of workers' lives were spared as a result.

He was anti-corporate to the core. He thought that the drive for ever-increasing profits was in fundamental conflict with public health, worker health and safety, and a sound environment. He feared that growing corporate power could lead to authoritarianism. The antidote was growing democratic unions with an active rank and file. Most of all, he thought we had it all backward: The purpose of life was not to toil until we dropped to enrich someone else. Rather it was to live life to its fullest by working less, not more.

Then why didn't Tony Mazzocchi become a household name? Why didn't he succeed in turning the labor movement upside down? Maybe he was blocked by his fearsome enemies—including CIA operatives in his own union. The nation's most powerful corporate interests, from Big Oil to the nuclear industry, didn't like Tony very much, either.

Or maybe he was just too principled. His friends worried that he was too idealistic and pure to grab power when it was there for the grabbing.

But if Tony didn't reach the pinnacles of power because of his principles, perhaps he got as far as he did for the same reason. He was, as labor leader Ed Ott said, "the man who never sold out"—and many of us found this deeply inspiring. For Tony, the struggle for victory was also about how you got there.

When Tony was diagnosed with pancreatic cancer in 2002, I knew it would fall on me to tell his story. He agreed. But he really didn't want me to describe him as a "great man of history." He didn't believe he was a great man, and he didn't believe in the great-man (or -woman) theory of history anyway. Nevertheless, for the next nine months Tony allowed me to record countless interviews with him. He was very patient, knowing that he had an amateur at work. After he died on October 5, 2002, I was in shock. I was taken aback by the giant hole he left not only in my life, but in my labor movement. Without him to point the way, the pathway toward big-picture social change started to blur, at least for me. That's when the purpose of this book became clear. Maybe I could write Tony's story so that the catalyst within him could shine through. If I succeeded, then perhaps Tony could continue to inspire more of us to think big.

Tony viewed all of his work, especially his successes, as collective endeavors. So as much as this book focuses on his life, it is meant as a tribute to all those workers and allies who shared his fight for social justice, and who continue to carry it on.

Tony Mazzocchi hoped to lay out the stepping-stones to lead future generations to a healthier and more equitable society. I hope this book will help those generations, as they move along those uneven stones, to take courage from the audacious dreamer who put them in place.

—Les Leopold, May 2007

ONE

The Prince of Shallow Junior High

Tony Mazzocchi grew up to rebel against church, God, and the class system, and to help change the conditions in every workplace in America. And he did it with his native Bensonhurst, Brooklyn, schmeared all over him—a neighborhood set as far apart from the rest of New York as New York is from the rest of America. And yet Bensonhurst *is* America. Its comedians entertain us, its mobsters fascinate us, its outbursts of racist violence haunt us. Lying only a few miles from Manhattan, Bensonhurst links city and suburbs. It's as American as pasta and bagels.

Tony Mazzocchi had a lot in common with one of Bensonhurst's first British settlers: Lady Deborah Moody, daughter of a member of Queen Elizabeth's Parliament. Lady Moody startled her conservative Dutch neighbors by rejecting "infant baptism, the Sabbath, the office of preacher and the teaching of God's Word, saying that through these have come all sorts of contention into the world."[1] Moody had already been excommunicated in Britain for "ostentation" in the 1640s, then run out of New England, where the Puritan clergy demanded that she acknowledge "her evill [*sic*] in opposing churches, and leave her opinions behind her, for shee [*sic*] is a dangerous woman." Along with several other English expatriates, Lady Moody hoped to build, on land obtained from the Dutch West India Corporation, "a city by the sea." There, said historian David W. McCullough, the expatriates would enjoy "the unheard of right to pick their own form of government"—they chose collective town meetings, which would have been Tony's first choice as well.

Over the next three hundred years, Bensonhurst became a thriving community of 150,000 residents. It produced two kinds of celebrities in great numbers: Jewish entertainers and Italian mobsters. Among the entertainers were the Three Stooges, Buddy Hackett, Phil Silvers (Sergeant Bilko), Larry King (aka Larry Zeigler), opera star Robert Merrill, and, the pride of Jewish sports fans, Dodgers Hall of Fame southpaw Sandy Koufax. Later came actors Danny DeVito and Elliott Gould. Among the mobsters were the

Gambino, Lucchese, Colombo, Genovese, and Bonno families. The streets they inhabited held a collection of bakeries, small shops, synagogues, Catholic churches, crap shooters, opera lovers, mah-jongg and bocce addicts, and small Italian social clubs where men gathered to drink inexpensive wine and play cards.

"Life in Bensonhurst began around the El and then spread toward the ocean," wrote Anthony Valerio, a novelist from the neighborhood. "There was everything you needed under the El: a grocery store, a bread store, and a candy store. The Italians thrived amid noise and darkness, and enough beautiful women were born around the El to supply all the professional men who opened practices in Bensonhurst."[2]

The Mazzocchis were neither comedians, nor gangsters, nor professionals seeking beautiful women beneath the El. Their Bensonhurst centered on the dinner table, where hefty servings of pasta fazul fed discussion about the politics of the day and about a whole other set of infamous people—Mussolini, Stalin, Roosevelt, and John L. Lewis. Raised on this diet, Tony would for the rest of his life feel at home wherever he could cook big meals and talk big-picture politics.

II

The Mazzocchis thrived because of Tony's grandmother Teresa, an Italian villager who arrived at Ellis Island on September 6, 1901—the same day President William McKinley was shot. The family's first prayer on American soil was for the authorities not to blame an Italian. (Their prayer was answered—the killer was Polish anarchist Leon Czolgosz.)

The Mazzocchis had emigrated from Marigliano, Italy, ten miles northeast of Naples. The region's picturesque landscape hid a corrupt and tyrannical political structure. At the turn of the twentieth century, the people of Marigliano still serviced local estates and farms under a deteriorating feudal system. It was not a happy place for most. "Naples was 'a grotesque parasite,'" historian Harry Hearder wrote. "She lived on the back of a desperately overworked, desperately poor peasantry, who were given no civil rights."[3]

Teresa's husband, Saverio Mazzocchi, was a skilled tailor who occasionally moonlighted as a barber. In both roles, he was generous. "My grandfather was the dreamer," Connie Tozzi (Tony's older cousin) remembered. "He would make you a suit, but he would never come and collect the money. Sometimes he would say, 'Let me cut your hair the way I want, and you won't have to pay for it.'"[4]

This didn't sit well with Teresa. For her, said Connie, "A penny is a penny. She would have to go and get the money, because they had to eat. She was the one that thought of feeding the family and getting ahead." Teresa, an orphan, had grown up on a farm with her aunt and uncle, who "made her go out into the fields, and pick and work hard." The family owned a canteen where "the men used to sit around and get drunk. So my grandmother would have to go in there and serve, and be with all the men. You know, she was a very strong woman. But she used to always say, 'Oh, if I only had an education.'"

Teresa wanted out. But it took years to move the entire family to America. First she scraped together funds to send her son Giuseppi, who at age nineteen was an accomplished jacket maker. He found work as a tailor in Brooklyn and lived with an uncle who fleeced him—there would be no cash to send home. Teresa had to borrow money to ship the next Mazzocchi contingent: Saverio (who didn't really want to leave Marigliano, but couldn't match his wife's resolve), and their eldest daughter, Maria. Two years later, Teresa and her three youngest children finally got the money to follow—in steerage, in 1901.

They settled with Saverio, Maria, and Giuseppe in a neighborhood already colonized by others from their home region. "You always went to your paisans," Connie said. "They would give you a room. If they had an old couch or dresser, they'd try to put up a small apartment for you. So that's how so many of us ended up in the same area in Brooklyn. There were four families from our village living on the same block."

Teresa's husband Saverio and son Giuseppe (by then called Joe) ran a small neighborhood store that made custom clothes. Then Joe found work in Manhattan's turbulent garment industry. Mild-mannered, square-shouldered, and handsome, Joe was soon earning enough to make him a very eligible bachelor. After several years in New York, he fell in love with Angelina Lamardo, a young Italian woman with almond eyes, a round face, and a short frame bordering on voluptuous. "Yes, Angelina," said Connie. "A very beautiful woman. It was a real love match. All those beautiful love letters he wrote to her."

Joe and Angelina were married in 1913, and rented an apartment in Flatbush. Soon, with Teresa's help (and Joe's decent union job), they mustered the down payment on a home in Brooklyn's Borough Park. In 1914 a daughter, Tess, arrived—the first of their five children. Tony would be the last.

Tony often referred to his family as "illiterate peasants." He was wrong. Joe and his father, Saverio, knew how to read and write Italian (later, Joe would master English by reading *The New York Times*). As skilled tailors, Joe and his father were among the elite of Italian immigrants. Of nearly 1.5 million admitted to the United States between 1899 and 1910, only 15 percent were skilled craftsmen, like Joe, according to the Immigration Commission of 1911.[5] The Mazzocchis were people who, as labor historian Steven Fraser put it, had "room, however cramped, for some upward mobility." Among these immigrants, "fraternal associations thrived, literacy and voting were not unheard of, and an ethos of thrift, sobriety, and moral probity struggled against the more saturnine impulses of Italian peasant life."[6] For her part, Angelina came from a family that had owned land in the Old Country. "They were wealthy," Connie reported, "but not rich-rich."

III

Tony wondered how his father first became interested in unions and politics. "I don't know what the hell influenced him. That's the big mystery of my life—I don't have the vaguest idea." Joe may have been recruited into the union in the same year he married Angelina: 1913. It was the year of a mass strike of some sixty thousand garment workers led by the largely Jewish United Brotherhood of Tailors, whose members included the fiery young Fiorello La Guardia, then a union lawyer and later mayor of New York. The UBT joined with the Sons of Italy and other Italian organizations to discourage Italian strikebreakers and to enroll Italian workers into the union.[7] The strike led to the formation of the Amalgamated Clothing Workers, the union Joe Mazzocchi would belong to and aid for his entire working life.

By 1919, Joe's new union had grown to be the fourth largest in the country, with 138,000 members.[8] Every conceivable form of radical politics flowed through it. The Great War had ripped the old order to shreds, unleashing radical movements worldwide. Socialists, anarchists, and syndicalists argued their case for a worker-run state. In 1919, many of these radicals joined the Communist Party. While they fought for better wages and working conditions, the workers talked about controlling their shops, collectively owning their industries—maybe even running the whole country.

To many, the United States seemed on the verge of a revolution like the one that had seized Russia two years earlier. Western workers launched general strikes in Seattle, Portland, and Butte. In Boston, the police walked out. Industrial workers, including Slavic steelworkers led by William Foster (later head of the Communist Party USA), waged a colossal work stoppage against United States Steel. One out of every five American workers went on strike at some point during 1919. So pervasive was this radical activity that Supreme Court justice Louis Brandeis wrote to a colleague that the "wage system is doomed." He suggested that workers should eventually have "full responsibility" for running their industries.[9]

In 1920, Joe's union beat back a citywide lockout (employers barred workers from their workplaces to break the union). The Amalgamated also sent money to aid the striking steelworkers, and it dispatched its organizers to Paterson, New Jersey, and Lowell, Massachusetts, to bolster textile workers engaged in their radical-led strikes.

In 1918, Sidney Hillman, the Amalgamated's president, called for the recognition of the Soviet government and for public control of US industry.[10] In 1921, Hillman traveled to the new Soviet Union to visit his parents and to meet with the nation's new leaders, including Trotsky and Lenin. He reported back that Lenin was "one of the few great men that the human race has produced, one of the greatest statesmen of our age, perhaps of all ages."[11] In the early 1920s, the Amalgamated Clothing Workers launched a sizable joint venture with the Soviet government called the Russian-American Industrial Corporation, providing money and personnel to help establish a state-of-the-art Soviet clothing industry.

Later in the decade, however, Hillman and the union pulled away from both the Soviet Union and the American Communist Party. Although the union still believed in socialism and was active in third-party politics, it pushed for a more gradual transition through spreading unionism, managing destructive competition among owners, controlling and modernizing the production process, and securing decent wages and working conditions. The Amalgamated fought to steer a middle course between revolution and reform (though its moderate path would seem, by current standards, ultraradical).

Joe Mazzocchi was typical of most of the garment workers. While he "was friendly to the notion of socialism," Tony said, "he was basically a trade unionist who was caught up in the Amalgamated Clothing Workers. He had been involved in the big strikes after World War I, but he never belonged to any formal political organizations. He was just a union-conscious guy."[12]

Joe was shop steward at Rogers Peet, a prosperous Manhattan men's clothing store on 13th and Broadway off Union Square. He also "went out and did his work on Election Day," Tony said. "He was a Jimmy Higgins in the union." (Jimmy Higgins, a character invented by socialist Ben Hanford in the early 1900s, was "the anonymous devoted comrade who sold the party's literature, attended every meeting, performed all the humble chores that kept the organization going."[13])

The labor movement that had thrived during the Great War soon suffered terribly in peacetime. The steel strike of 1919 failed. American workers felt the whip of a vicious anti-union, anti-radical hysteria—a red scare unleashed by patriotic fervor, alarm about the Russian Revolution, and xenophobic fears of immigration. The government arrested thousands, and deported hundreds, of labor and political activists. Radical immigrants were targeted in what became known as the Palmer Raids after their impresario, US attorney general A. Mitchell Palmer. The attacks crippled many unions.

On September 14, 1920, at the height of the Palmer hysteria, two Italian American anarchists, Fernando "Nicola" Sacco and Bartolomeo Vanzetti, were arrested for allegedly killing a paymaster and his guard in Braintree, Massachusetts, during a failed effort to rob a shoe factory payroll. Their trial became a cause célèbre among liberals and radicals—including the Mazzocchis—who believed the two had been railroaded by prejudice.

Exonerating Sacco and Vanzetti became a workers' crusade, especially for union members who shared their "alien blood."[14] Joe Mazzocchi, who identified with the self-taught and well-read Vanzetti, "was very active in the Sacco-Vanzetti defense," according to Tony. For seven years, progressive unionists like Joe organized and marched on their behalf. Joe's union encouraged the demonstrations, hoping that its "staunch campaign on behalf of Sacco and Vanzetti [would] further strengthen . . . the ties between the Italian rank and file and the largely Jewish leadership."[15]

For Italian unionists like Joe, fighting to vindicate Sacco and Vanzetti was also a stab against stigmatization. Joe and Angelina had arrived in America at a time when racial hierarchy was taken for granted. Italians, especially those from southern Italy, had long fared poorly in this hierarchy. A wage chart for workers building the New Croton Aqueduct north of New York from 1861 to 1875 showed the following classifications:

Intelligent Labor	$1.50 to $1.60 per 10 hour day
Common Labor (Colored)	$1.35 to $1.40
Common Labor (Italian)	$1.15 to $1.25[16]

Such racist calculations were reinforced by the eugenics movement, which used modern science to define dozens of fictitious racial categories and to establish a self-serving pecking order among the world's populations. Conveniently, Anglo-Saxons occupied the highest rung of the ladder, justifying both their right to rule and their claim to the riches they had accumulated. In 1911, the US Immigration Commission published a *Dictionary of Races or People,* in which scientific and academic "experts" from a variety of disciplines carefully ranked immigrant races. Anglo-Saxons were on top; Hebrews and northern Italians were near the bottom. The lowest position was reserved for southern Italians, who were characterized as violent, undisciplined, and least capable of becoming good Americans.[17]

The Mazzocchis chafed at such prejudice, especially the striving Teresa, who required her children and grandchildren to shun all racial slang. "We were taught that we never said *wop* or *guinea* or *kike,*" recalled Connie. "My grandmother just wouldn't tolerate it." The family always referred to Tony as "Anthony," Connie said, because "you know, it was 'Tony the iceman,' 'Tony the wop.' It was always a slur. So he was Anthony to us."[18]

Vanzetti, in his famous, unscripted final words before he was sentenced on April 10, 1927, did not apologize for his identity:

> I am suffering because I am a radical, and indeed I am a radical; I have suffered because I was Italian, and indeed I am an Italian; I have suffered more for my family and for my beloved than for my self;

but I am so convinced to be right that you could execute me two times, and if I could be reborn two other times I would live again to do what I have done already.[19]

IV

Tony was born ugly—or so his sisters said—on St. Anthony's Day, June 13, 1926, on 40th Street between Fort Hamilton Parkway and 12th Avenue in Brooklyn. His cousin Connie (twelve at the time) said that the family had planned for Tony—unlike his older siblings—to be delivered by a doctor. But as it turned out, the Old Country method would prevail. "The doctor didn't come on time," Connie said. "And my grandmother delivered Anthony. We were all midwives."

Tony's grandmother Teresa "tied the cord and held it in her mouth until the doctor arrived, and the baby was almost strangled." The temporary garroting left the newborn discolored, to the alarm of his siblings and cousins. "We had another baby cousin in the house, and she was very beautiful," Connie remembered. "So Tony's sister Ethel kept saying, 'Can't we exchange babies?'"

The house was barely big enough to contain Tony and all his older siblings: Teresa (Tess), Maria (May), Otillia (Ethel), and Severio (Sam). Money was so tight in 1928, Joe Mazzocchi had to insist that his fourteen-year-old daughter, Tess, join him at the company as a buttonhole seamstress.[20] This decision did not come easily to the mild-mannered father: "Tess wanted to continue her education rather than to drop out and go to work. She always resented it," recalled Connie.

Soon the Mazzocchis' situation got much worse. Within a year of the 1929 stock market crash, clothing sales dropped by half, and 40 percent of New York clothing businesses closed. Jobs disappeared overnight. By 1931, half the industry's workers were unemployed, and most of the rest were employed only irregularly. Wages collapsed by 40 to 50 percent. Cutthroat competition returned to the garment industry, and with it the sweatshop conditions that the union had fought so hard to eradicate.[21] Unionized workers responded by waging fierce strikes, most of which failed because so many unemployed workers were desperate enough to cross picket lines. To succeed, strikers had to keep these strikebreakers—"scabs" to striking workers—out of the shops.

When workers struck Joe Mazzocchi's employer, Rogers Peet, Tony said, "All hell broke loose":

> My father was a supervisor, and when the union struck he said: "I better quit." And the union guys told him, "Don't quit. Stay there. We need you." So my father told me this story—I remember it because he told me about ten times. One night the steward came up to him and said, "Okay, we've got something for you to do." The cops were protecting the scabs, coming in and going out. So that night the union guys decided they were going to jump the scabs. But the police were out in front. So this guy got to my father and says, "You gotta tell the scabs that there's trouble out front—that they gotta go out the back door." And of course, the pickets were laying wait for them out in the back—beat the shit out of them.

Joe paid the price for his union loyalty. "My father lost his job—and got blackballed too," said Tony. Joe Mazzocchi, his daughter Tess, and his sister Autilia were all out on the street.

In the midst of this crisis, Tony's mother, Angelina, developed cancer in her stomach cavity. "In those days, you didn't go to the hospital unless you were really dying, because you couldn't afford it," Connie said. "We didn't have any kind of insurance." Nevertheless, Angelina endured many stays in Brooklyn's Maimonides Hospital during her yearlong illness; the bills mounted. Teresa Mazzocchi and Joe's sister Autilia provided periodic loans to help Joe feed the family and pay the mortgage. But without stable income from work, he could no longer make ends meet.

Tony, age four, began spending a lot of time at his grandmother Teresa's house in Bensonhurst. Sensing that his mother's death was near, Tony drew closer to his grandmother, refusing to leave her side during and after their visits to the hospital. Recalled Connie: "She would go upstairs to hang the clothes out and he would follow along, and make little men with all the clothespins, with this one fighting that one. When my grandmother finished and moved to another room, he'd pick them all up and go with her and set up again to play. He always stayed close to her." The little boy seemed able to erase the pain from his consciousness. In later years, said Connie, Tony "never talked about the Borough Park home or his mother—never mentioned her. And I remember that we thought, you know, that it was a little strange. I think he was frightened."

"He told me he had only two memories of his mother," said Tony's daughter Kristina. "The first was when he was about two or three years old and had been dreaming about a most amazing train set. The train kept circling him and he knew he was about to wake up. So he jumped on the train and hugged it to his stomach in order to bring it back with him when he woke up. When he woke up, he was hugging his arms to his chest but without the captured train. He said he cried, and he remembers his mother consoling him."

The other memory he shared with Kristina was sadder: "When his mother was no longer living at home, his aunt brought him to the hospital and they stood outside and looked up to his mother's window, where she was waving to him. . . . His aunt repeated to him over and over that his mother loved him. He was not allowed in the room."[22]

In 1930, Joe—jobless, broke, and a widower—was forced to sell his share of the house. Autilia, his sister, bought him out so that he could pay his debts. Joe and his five children moved in with Tony's grandmother Teresa, in the heart of Bensonhurst. "When Anthony's mother died, my uncle Joe didn't want to know nothing," said Connie. "He didn't even pack up his house or anything—my mother did all that. The whole family with five kids came to our house."

The Bensonhurst house at 1443 72nd Street between 14th and 15th Avenues was a joint venture. The primary partners (and residents) included Joe's brothers Michael, who had a stable assembly-line job at Ford Motor Company in Edgewater, New Jersey, and Lester, a service representative for a Manhattan credit company. Grandmother Teresa contributed by taking in boarders—a small apartment (no bath) on the third floor was occupied by a pair of Italian puppeteers and later by two political refugees from Ireland who, as Tony recalled, "didn't pay rent. My grandmother felt sorry for them."

The heavy financial lifting came from Autilia, Connie's mother, who had been widowed in 1919 at the age of twenty-eight. "My father had been a butcher," Connie said. "He made it big. He was across the street from an army factory, where the women made uniforms for the soldiers in the First World War. So when the women would go to work, they would drop off their meat orders, and then they would pick it up on the way home. My mother also helped and became an excellent butcher."

Autilia sold the business after her husband's death and continued to live well off several small buildings he had purchased. Connie recalled with a laugh, "My mother was the financier for the whole family. They all borrowed their down payments from her."

For Tony, the move to his grandmother's busy house represented a dramatic improvement. In the old, smaller house, he'd had to share his bed with two siblings. Here at Teresa's—despite a population of fourteen full-time residents—he slept only with his brother Sam. The Mazzocchis' three-story gray, white-trimmed residence had been a farmhouse before the land was subdivided. Its white picket fence still enclosed more than a quarter acre of land. A glorious garden bordered the front walk, which led to the stairs of the entry porch, where Saverio would take his daily nap in one of several rocking chairs. "We used to have beautiful displays of flowers," said Connie. "Every time the kindergarten teacher would walk their children around the neighborhood, it was one of the first places they would stop. My grandfather would be out there and he would cut some flowers and give them to the teacher to bring back to the classroom."

In a second lot next door, the family grew vegetables, Concord grapes, and cherry trees with "beautiful big cherries," said Connie. "And we also had a fig tree—everyone had one in those days." There was even a barn, which had been converted into seven garages that the family rented to neighbors, and stables for the neighbors' horses. "Yeah it was a big house. And it was a very exciting time, because my sisters and brothers had lots of friends who congregated there," Tony said. "I mean, New Year's Eve in my house was a big party—people from all over America."

It seemed like a party on most nights, or perhaps a Fellini movie in which every floor of the house had something going on. As Tony recalled:

> In the attic lived this couple, Ernie and Alita Giafrida. They were puppeteers—they had life-sized marionettes. It was an Italian tradition. They manipulated these huge things—150 pounds—with

> armor and swords. They would do all the classics—you know, Dumas, Shakespeare. Ernie couldn't read or write, but he knew all these plays by heart. He was brought up in the theater and played the piano. I'd go up and say, "Ernie, tell me a story." And he'd tell me *The Count of Monte Cristo.* He knew it line by line. And he had swords. He showed me how to duel.

Maureen Kelly, one of the third-floor Irish political refugees, was also a cello player and a graduate of Dublin's Trinity College. She had a powerful impact on the family: "She talked my brother into going to City College," Tony said. "He became an accountant—the first Mazzocchi to go to college."

Not only was Maureen cultured, intelligent, and politically aware—she was also a lesbian. "I don't remember what Maureen's politics were," said Tony, "but she was gay. She brought her girlfriend to the house all the time. And her girlfriend's name was Jan Gay, and Maureen adopted that last name—I don't think the word *gay* was used for lesbians in the 1930s. I didn't know anything about it at the time. I just knew this was Maureen's friend. It was accepted in the family. They all knew that Maureen was lesbian, and this was her girlfriend."

Tony's uncle Lester was also homosexual. Openly gay in 1930s Bensonhurst? "No, very quiet," Tony said. "I didn't know he was gay until after the war. My sisters knew."

The family life spilled out onto the neighborhood streets and back in again. "Nobody locked their doors," Connie said. Tony recalled that his sister May knew everyone. "The kids would come over after school all the time and May would make them meatball sandwiches." The children seized the streets to play stickball, punchball, or stoopball, tell stories, imagine sex, or even—if they were older and very lucky—have it. On summer days, they could walk west to swim at Poverty Beach, now the site of the Verrazano-Narrows Bridge. "The trick was to avoid the 'Bay Ridge flounders,' our own particular form of urban wildlife," recalled Tony. "At the time the Hudson River was the city's only means of sewage treatment. From time to time a school of used prophylactics would come floating by. You didn't want to come up with one on your head."

On special occasions like Christmas and New Year's, the Mazzocchi kitchen would explode into frenzy. Unlike most families at the time, "the men did lots of work" in the kitchen, Connie recalled. "They would clean and shop and cook, all of us together. I remember my uncle Mike when he came home from work on Christmas Eve, he used to go to the Fulton Fish Market, so the fish would be nice and fresh. He used to get eels. When my grandmother would cook them, they'd be jumping in the frying pan."

The kitchen was the center of the Mazzocchis' family life. To accommodate all the relatives, boarders, and friends, Teresa ordered the construction of a long white linoleum-covered table. When Tony would later refer to "learning my politics at the dinner table," this was the table he meant.

"We never suffered for lack of food," Tony said, because the family "always had enough people working to make ends meet." Uncle Mike held his auto job throughout the Depression. Autilia supplemented her income from rental properties with intermittent stints as a buttonhole sewer. Within a year of the move, Joe found work with Hedges Fifth Avenue tailors, makers of fine men's jackets, sewing clothes for celebrities including Rudy Vallee and Guy Lombardo.

Lester lost his job at the credit company, but that was just as well: "When the Depression came on, he couldn't stand doing debt collection," Tony said. Lester moved to rural Blairstown, New Jersey, to take over the management of the family's new venture, a boardinghouse on Maple Lane Farm. The 110-acre farm was Uncle Mike's brainchild. "My uncle, who worked at Ford, buys this place in 1931. I think he bought it for twelve hundred bucks," Tony remembered. Typically, the whole family pitched in on the purchase. "So somebody got the idea—why not start a boardinghouse? And my grandmother farmed a plot, a peasant from Italy, a whole acre of vegetables. Organic farming! Of course there was nothing else."

Connie recalled just what *organic* meant. "When my grandmother decided to grow potatoes, she gave us a can with kerosene in it. We had to pick the beetles off the plants and put them in it." There were cucumbers, broccoli, corn, all kinds of squash. And tomatoes, which the family canned in huge quantities to eat in the winter. "Grandma used to say to us, 'When I die, you'll still be using my tomatoes.'"

At first the guests at Maple Lane stayed in the old farmhouse. Then the family added two bunkhouses and even showers. According to Lester's brochure,

> Maple Lane Farm is in the foothills of the Poconos, ten miles from the Delaware Water Gap, and eighty-five miles from New York City. It is a modest resort, comfortably accommodating only thirteen families in beautifully landscaped surroundings. Every effort is made to prepare and serve meals that are both wholesome and varied. Italian specialties are included on the weekly menu. Only home-made pastries and cakes are served.

The Bensonhurst kids often spent weekends there, as well as the entire summer. The journey to the country began on the subway and ended with a drive in Uncle Mike's Model A down a mile-long country lane beneath maples and oaks, past a patch of daylilies and a low stone wall, to a white farmhouse with dark-trimmed windows. "The property had a little stream—it was this big," said Connie pointing to the width of her kitchen. "We used to go and sit on the rocks, and bring soap down." The children bathed in the stream, swam in two pristine lakes, and played under blooming fruit trees.

"It was paradise for us," Connie said. But Tony recalled at least one aspect of the visits with his face twisted into an expression of childhood disgust: "I had to raise the goddamn chickens in the summer, which I hated to do, and fed them grain and mash and leftovers from the table." When he was six or seven years old, he came down with scarlet fever, which threatened to condemn the whole family to a claustrophobic quarantine in Bensonhurst. "My mother asked the board of health if we could all go to Blairstown. And they agreed," said Connie. "So from May on we were there being taken care of by Grandmother. And I remember she used to make us homemade bread."

And the Depression? "Oh, we never really felt it," Connie said. "That was the best time in our lives."

V

Back in Bensonhurst, the Mazzocchi house overflowed with books, records, newspapers, and pamphlets. Uncle Lester's classical seventy-eight RPM records could be heard up and down the block. And there was a radio, a present to the Mazzocchis from themselves. "It had all these different knobs," Connie said. "We put little tags with all our names on them, because we gave it to each other. We made it one big gift at Christmas."

Tony remembered listening to *Jack Armstrong—the All American Boy* and other radio dramas. But the airwaves also brought politics. "There were some real liberal commentators and right-wing ones. H.V. Kaltenborn was a right-wing guy. He's the guy who later predicted the Dewey landslide over Truman. And he kept saying: 'The farm vote's not in yet!'"

The Mazzocchis were most taken by voices that reaffirmed their sense of justice, like this one.

> Stripped by the lure of profit by which to induce our people to follow their false leadership, they have resorted to exhortations, pleading tearfully for restored confidence. They know only the rules of a generation of self-seekers. They have no vision, and when there is no vision the people perish. The moneychangers have fled from their high seats in the temple of our civilization. We may now restore to the ancient truths. The measure of the restoration lies in the extent to which we apply social values more noble that mere monetary profit.[23]

This anti-corporate rhetoric came not from lowly radical immigrants, but from the very top of the Protestant elite—the new president of the United States, Franklin Delano Roosevelt. His first inaugural address ushered in the New Deal, and in short order the moribund workers' movement exploded.

When the Mazzocchis talked about the pitched battles for unionization as a class war, they weren't exaggerating. In 1934, the police attacked striking truckers in Minneapolis, wounding sixty and leaving two dead. In San Francisco, a virtual civil war broke out between the maritime workers and city police aided by vigilantes, leading to a general strike in which several workers died. In 1937, Ford's private police mauled strikers at the River Rouge plant in Michigan. Just four days later, in the Memorial Day Massacre, ten men died in battle at Republic Steel in Chicago. From textile workers in the South to tire workers in the North, laborers were walking out, sitting down, and occupying factories—all over the right to join a union.

Unions and class politics were in the air that Tony breathed. Although the Depression nearly sank the garment industry and produced almost unbearable economic strain, for a politically aware trade union family it was an era of great possibility. Labor was reawakening. In 1933, unions represented 11.3 percent of the nonagricultural workforce. By 1939, they had captured 28.6 percent. And by 1945, more than one out of every three workers (34.5 percent) was in a union.[24] (Today only 7.4 percent of private-sector workers are unionized, and 12 percent overall.[25]) Counting all those in union households, an enormous number of Americans were connected to labor unions. And in New York, especially Brooklyn, the percentages were huge. Unions were growing fast, and the Mazzocchis' optimism grew with them.

For Tony and his family, this uprising illuminated a special kind of unionism: social unionism. They believed that unions should serve the class as a whole, both in the workplace and in the community. Exactly how was a matter of much debate around the Mazzocchis' long white kitchen table. Connie remembered, "We used to go back and forth, discussing a lot of things—politics. Tony was always there. If there were three or four people arguing about anything, he always chimed in. Here's this little kid, you know, always there to tell them. He would just say: No, I believe it's this way—you believe it's that way. He would argue with them, too. But it was always Anthony with all the grown-ups."

The conversations continued as Tony's father, aunts, and uncles ironed and stitched their clothes. Part of Tony's political education was learning to press his own shirts and pants, something he continued to do with precision for the rest of his life. If the boy got a little too quarrelsome at times, no one seemed to mind, especially his father. Connie recalled that although spanking was common back then, "I remember Anthony did something at the table, and his father threw a napkin at him. That was the discipline."

"I consciously began to understand what was going on around the dinner table when I was seven or eight," Tony said. And in the process, he picked up one of his most powerful traits: the ability to tolerate—even enjoy—a diversity of working-class viewpoints and to have a friendly debate with those who disagreed with him. "My father and my uncle Lester are the progressives. The rest of the family is conservative," said Tony. Joe was the most political of the bunch. "By political, I mean *Vote for Roosevelt,*" Tony explained. "Uncle Mike was pretty conservative. But at Ford, he voted for the union when it came in." Uncle Lester was culturally refined, self-educated, and more radical. Over time, he moved more and more to the left. Tony soaked it all up. "We all lived in the same house. Family ties superseded everything. My sister went off—married this guy Cosmos who was in the America First Committee [headed by Charles Lindbergh, who was suspected of pro-Nazi sympathies and opposed US involvement in the growing war in Europe]. But we were all in the same place. You know, you sit around the dinner table, there's every view in the world."

But all the Mazzocchis shared deep beliefs about labor. They welcomed the birth of the Congress of Industrial Organizations (CIO), which in 1937 split from the American Federation of Labor (AFL), a federation largely of nonimmigrant craft workers. They supported the CIO's effort to organize unskilled and semiskilled industrial workers, especially immigrants, long neglected by the AFL. They thought that workers should be organized by industry rather than along narrow AFL craft lines, which they felt created harmful hierarchies and divisions. And the Mazzocchis valued the rank-and-file democracy that was springing up all around them as the CIO blossomed.

The Mazzocchis also believed that the labor movement should fight for a "social wage" for all workers: generous unemployment insurance, a livable minimum wage, free health care, pensions, education, and low-cost housing.

Joe agreed with Amalgamated Clothing Workers president (and CIO co-founder) Sidney Hillman that labor should support Roosevelt. Uncle Lester later argued for independent political action through a vehicle such as the American Labor Party in New York. The Mazzocchis agreed that social unionism required massive government intervention, including public ownership of key enterprises like railroads and utilities—perhaps along the lines of the vaunted Tennessee Valley Authority (TVA). But the family debated just how much of industry should be government-owned and worker-controlled.

As a matter of principle, the Mazzocchis' social unionism was multiracial and antidiscriminatory. They supported the rights of black Americans, upheld equal pay for equal work for women, and vigorously opposed anti-Semitism. "My father was antiracist," Tony recalled. "He saw that race divided the working class. He said, 'You know, the boss is going to divide you.' So that was pounded into everybody's head. That was just a constant in the house. I was exposed to racism by kids on the block, but I always had a different position because of my family."

And the Mazzocchis believed that there was more to life than work. They thought working people should liberate themselves from the confines of wage labor so that they could enjoy the finer things of life. The working class should have time to enjoy the music and books that they themselves loved so much.

In 1936, when Tony was nine, he and the family listened to the live broadcast of FDR's October 31 campaign speech at Madison Square Garden, in which the president questioned the very basis of capitalism. Pandemonium broke loose—and at home the Mazzocchis applauded—after the president blasted "business and financial monopoly, speculation, reckless banking, class antagonism, war profiteering . . . organized money. . . . I should like to have it said of my second Administration, that these forces met their master!"[26]

In households around the country, union families debated the depth of Roosevelt's radicalism. Did he really mean in his second term to shift the system toward public ownership? Or was he actually a reformer trying to save capitalism from the capitalists? On their Bensonhurst street, Joe and the Mazzocchis were mostly alone in their pro-FDR persuasion. After a Roosevelt victory, Tony remembered: "I think there was one other guy on the block that supported my father. I remember my father leaning out the window. The other guy was going to work, and my father opened the window and shouted out at him . . . 'Hey, we did it!'"

VI

"My dad was very gentle," Tony said. "He never lifted a hand against us. But he showed anger toward fascism. He was extremely anti-fascist." The Mazzocchis feared and detested the rise of fascism in Europe. In this, too, they were out of step with many of their Italian neighbors. Tony recalled that his father would "go across the street and play cards with the men. There was a candy store in front and a barber chair where we all got our haircuts. It wasn't even a barber chair—it was a regular chair. And in the back room the guys would play cards, and they'd buy stuff off the owner—you know, drink wine. They'd talk politics. They'd scream and everything, but it was a neighborhood, nobody got hurt. And you were defended because you came from the neighborhood, regardless of your politics."

Some of Tony's neighbors were proud of Italian fascism. Finally Italy—and Italian immigrants—had gained international respect. A common refrain was "Whatever you fellows may think of Mussolini, you've got to admit one thing. He has done more to get respect for Italian Americans than anyone else."[27]

Joe and his union, however, were having none of it. From the start, they proselytized against the anti-union content of fascism and the way it could undermine unity at work. The Amalgamated Clothing Workers helped found a new Italian American anti-fascist newspaper, *Il Nuovo Mondo*. And in 1928 the union called for the destruction of fascism and fascist organizations that vied for the allegiance of Italian union members. Tony recalled that his father would "never read the Italian press because it was so fascist. *Il Progresso*—run by a big political operator in New York—had a big circulation at the time."

In 1936, General Francisco Franco, supported by Hitler and Mussolini, directed a revolt of the army against the pro-worker and democratically elected government in Spain, igniting what social unionists in America saw as an epic battle pitting worker democracy against fascist dictatorship. In Bensonhurst, the neighborhood conversations heated up. Tony recalled, "During the Spanish Civil War, the church was really laying it on heavy—calling the Spanish Republicans atheistic communists."

Joe's union continued to resist fascism within its ranks, but fascists ignited what historian Steven Fraser called "a kind of guerilla warfare in the streets and shops of the garment industry."[28] In short order, fascism became a domestic, and local, issue.

Some in Tony's neighborhood, including the members of the Brooklyn Young Communist League, volunteered to fight in Spain with the Abraham Lincoln Brigade. None of the Mazzocchis joined, but when he was eleven Tony did enter the fray. When asked by his sixth-grade social studies teacher to name the capital of Spain, Tony shocked the class by saying "Barcelona" instead of "Madrid." Technically and politically, Barcelona was correct: The duly elected Loyalist government had moved their capital from Madrid to Valencia to Barcelona to escape fascist forces. The teacher did not take kindly to this cheeky, politically fraught response.

Some friends recalled that Tony's father became so outraged that he took off a day from work to tell Tony's teacher that whatever her views, she needed to acknowledge the accuracy of Tony's response. But Connie remembered otherwise—that it was the teacher who demanded to see Joe because of his son's show of disrespect. Connie said that Joe, having been called in many times before because of Tony's misbehavior, broke down in tears (as he would on such occasions), pleading for understanding for the motherless boy. In any event, all agree with Connie's conclusion: "That kid had nerve. He didn't care who you were, he would stand up for what he believed."

VII

At first, Mussolini went out of his way to say that fascism did not mean anti-Semitism. As late as 1937, he'd honored an Italian Jewish soldier killed in the Spanish Civil War. But in 1938, as Hitler advanced on Czechoslovakia and Austria, Mussolini issued decrees charging Jews with polluting the Italian race.

Tensions escalated between Jews and Italians in the streets, shops, and schools of Bensonhurst and in the Jewish-dominated Amalgamated Clothing Workers. Although most of Tony's pals on the street were Italian Catholics, Jews were not strangers in his home. "I mean, that's the one thing in our house that was clear," said Tony. "Anti-Semitism was the big thing, growing up in the 1930s. My family was really very strong on the fact that it was divisive—aside from the fact that everybody in the family had Jewish friends." As in many progressive labor households where socialism had replaced (or at least mitigated) religion, Jews and Italians mixed easily.

The Catholic Church increasingly viewed communism as a mortal enemy—and fascism, even with its anti-Semitism, as a lesser evil. For many church officials "communism" included not just the Soviets, but also America's radical trade unionists and even anti-communist socialists, especially if they were Jews. Just as Soviet communism inspired and activated American communists, European fascism inspired a virulent American offshoot. Soon the streets of New York saw hand-to-hand combat between

Irish Catholics (with strong backing from the Catholic hierarchy, especially the Brooklyn Diocese), on the one hand, and Jews and radicals on the other.

American fascism came through the airwaves into millions of homes, including the Mazzocchis', in the form of the Detroit radio priest Father Charles Coughlin. At first, he echoed Roosevelt's attack on economic royalists.[29] But by 1936, Coughlin had redirected his fire in a triple-barreled attack against economic royalists, communists, and Roosevelt himself, whom Coughlin said betrayed the working class. Soon the priest named the real demons behind them all—the Jews.[30] In November 1938, just after Germany was shaken by the murderous two-day anti-Jewish rampage of Kristallnacht, Coughlin came out in support of the Nazis. In radio broadcasts heard by the Mazzocchi household on the Christian radio station WMCA, Coughlin "explained and justified the Nazi persecution of Jews as a defensive response against Communism."[31]

Inspired by Coughlin's message, militant pro-fascist organizations formed in Brooklyn, including the Flatbush Anti-Communist League and the Flatbush Common Cause League. The latter held street-corner rallies at Flatbush Avenue and Albemarle Road in Brooklyn, and Kings Highway and East 17th Street, not far from the Mazzocchis' home. *The Tablet,* the Brooklyn diocese's official newspaper, provided favorable coverage. These groups soon morphed into the Christian Front, ready to do battle with the Jews and communists of New York—all with the blessing of Father Coughlin.[32] According to historian Ronald H. Bayor, the front's founding meeting addressed such topics as "Jewish involvement with Communism, the anti-Catholic position of the Jews during the Spanish Civil War, and Jewish control of labor unions and jobs." The group also set up the Christian Labor Front, designed to "infiltrate unions in order to oust Jewish-Communist leaders."[33] The organization, in fact, tried to provoke race war on New York's street corners, attacking Jews, harassing Jewish businesses, and breaking up Jewish community meetings.

This was a labor radical's worst nightmare, and Tony Mazzocchi would spend a lifetime combating it. Coughlin and the Christian Front were stoking an American working-class movement built on both class and bigotry—a movement that could divide and destroy militant unions by searching for scapegoats instead of root causes, by substituting hate for inspiration and vision. Sixty years later, when Tony warned progressives that "things could get ugly in this country," he knew, firsthand, that they could.

VIII

The Mazzocchis now felt betrayed not only by their native country but by their church as well. It was hard not to conclude that Catholicism stood against everything they believed in, and on behalf of everything they detested. Even worse, the church tried to instill its politics in the young. As Tony tells it, "You know we all went to Our Lady of Guadeloupe. I was in the Young Catholic Lay Missionary Society, and they proselytized to us about the godless Loyalists. Everybody was for the rebel—Franco."

Perhaps the church's betrayal stung less for Joe (whom Tony describes as agnostic and anti-clerical) and some other less-than-devout family members than it did for his more observant aunts and uncles. One of Tony's sisters was "very religious," he recalled, "but my oldest sister and brother were definitely atheists." Tony's own later rejection of God "wasn't a profound leap, where you woke up one morning and said 'Gee, there ain't no God.' I mean, I was doubting it since I was a kid, really. By fifteen, I just got to thinking: There was no such thing as God. It just didn't make sense to me."

But Tony, like the other kids on the block, went through the motions. "I didn't make my confirmation," he confessed. "That was sort of a no-no in the neighborhood. You had to at least make your confirmation. I didn't have the patience to do that."

Nevertheless, the church had its eye on Tony. Most churches in the area had drum-and-bugle corps, which Tony believed were designed to help them prepare for a fascist coup: "They figured, if it came, they were training." But Tony's church, Our Lady of Guadeloupe, didn't have a corps. Instead, said Tony, "they had the Young Catholic Lay Missionary Society through which they could 'educate' the most promising young leaders. So we'd go to these meetings where you'd have to be in debates all the time about the -isms. They were really in favor of Franco's victory at the time. They were cultivating me. And they figured: *Hey, this kid could be a leader.* I mean, I know that was in their mind. But I dropped out."

Tony's ability to lead had already been proven on the street, where he headed up a pack of neighborhood kids. "The kids really gravitated around me. In junior high I was always cutting school, playing ball, shooting craps, taking off for New York, screwing around. . . . And the kids always followed me. You know, they figured I was their leader. And they were tough kids. But you know they protected me, and I didn't have to get into any fights. My friends would belt them. I mean this guy, Miles—my best friend—his brother was a prizefighter, and he considered himself a prizefighter. After school, I used to have to hold his coat when he got into a fistfight. And he'd knock somebody out and then put his coat on and we'd go home."

By the time Tony reached Edward B. Shallow Junior High on 65th Street and 16th Avenue, he had established a spotty academic record. "If you failed math and English, you got left back. I always failed those two," he said. Yet, he recalled, "I loved reading *The Courtship of Miles Standish*. I was frozen to it. You were supposed to read it over the term. I had it done in days. And history, of course, I loved. My uncle had a lot of books at home, and I used to read a lot. I mean nobody pushed me or anything, I just picked up the books and read them and was really excited about them."

And he could orate with gusto. "Yeah that's the one skill I did have—and the teachers said, 'Someday you're gonna be a public speaker.'"

With the ninth grade came the moment of truth. The year was divided into halves, 9a and 9b, and Tony could not seem to get out of 9a. "The teachers didn't want to fail me," he recalled. "I really had caring, good teachers. I mean, the girls of the class who liked me went to the teacher and begged her. She said, 'I can't. The rules of the school are. . . .' It wasn't their fault." (It is possible that Tony suffered from dyscalculia, a form of dyslexia "in which numbers and formulas are as unruly as letters and words are in the more classic forms of dyslexia."[34])

So Tony was shipped out to "hammer and nails": the room where retarded children and those with behavioral problems were sent to pound nails as a dubious form of therapy. "There was 9a1—that's the smartest—then 9a2 . . . 3 . . . 4. . . . I was in something like 9a9," Tony recalled. "We had the toughest kids in the fucking school. And they liked me, you know, because I was smart—compared to them. But I wasn't showing off my smarts, like other kids—because I was one of them."

Tony twice failed 9a9. He was marking time, waiting to escape the misery. "Everybody was a year ahead of me, and I wanted to get the hell out of junior high school," he said. "So the equivalent was to go to this Metropolitan Vocational School in New York. It was a maritime school and one of the kids on my block was there in radio. So he says, 'Why don't you come?' I got in easy. The teachers were glad to get rid of me. They allowed me to transfer.

"We had a ferryboat," Tony remembered. "It was a crazy school."

How crazy?

> In one class a little elderly lady was going to teach us about table manners and proper service on board a ship. Her idea was for us to act out serving dinner for the king and queen of England. Can you imagine the bunch of us, trying to keep a straight face, with white linen over our arms serving each other with "Yes, Your Majesty," and "Pardon me, Your Highness"? We were rolling around in pain from laughing.

But in Tony's family, there was pride, not shame, in going to vocational school to become a skilled worker. When Ethel, Joe's youngest daughter, got married, the gifted tailors and seamstresses in the Mazzocchi family collaborated to make her the finest gown they could copy in New York. "I think they went to Saks Fifth Avenue," recalled Tony. "One of my cousins was a pattern maker. So she sketched it and they went and bought the material." What a gown! What a party! What a day to remember: December 7, 1941.

The news from Pearl Harbor that Sunday morning sliced through the celebration. The older boys immediately realized they would be the first to be called, since most had joined the National Guard to earn a few extra dollars during the Depression. "These were the 'apple blossom' soldiers from that song by the Andrews Sisters," Tony said. (The song—"I'll Be with You in Apple Blossom Time"—refers to soldiers' one-year hitches from June to June.)

Hitler had overrun Europe and invaded the Soviet Union. England was on the verge of collapse. And now Japan had attacked. Three days later, Germany would declare war against the United States. The Mazzocchi family responded to the outbreak of war with more than patriotism. As they saw it, this was the Spanish Civil War writ large, a contest that pitted worker democracy against fascism. And fascism was not simply the loss of freedom; it was the most evil expression of the bosses' state. It was a form of government that united dictators, big business, and the military to outlaw unions, enslave workers, and kill dissidents.

After one term at the maritime vocational academy, Tony was done with school for good. He'd turned sixteen and could now legally leave the public education system. Over the summer of 1942, he worked for a small defense contractor on Canal Street electroplating parts for military radios, and then at McGraw-Hill as a mail boy. "There was such a shortage of people due to the war that they couldn't even get mail boys," Tony said. "I went into the army from that job. And the guy begged me not to go. He was a World War I vet, he had been a captain in the infantry, and he said, 'Aw, listen. I agree with what you're doing but we need you.'"

Tony thought the war needed him much more. This was, after all, the ultimate battle of good versus evil. And so far it looked like evil was winning. Nineteen forty-two was not a good year for the Allies. In the Pacific, the Japanese advanced unabated, capturing Singapore, the Philippines, Malaya, the Dutch Indies, and Burma; they were poised to invade India.[35] Not until the end of the year at bloody Guadalcanal did the United States win a battle. The picture was even grimmer in Europe, which, except for an exhausted Britain, was either allied with or occupied by Germany and Italy. Only Sweden, Switzerland, Spain, and Portugal remained either neutral or out of the war. The Germans occupied western Russia from Leningrad in the north to the Black Sea in the south. German submarines off the US East Coast took their toll on American commercial and military ships.[36]

The military was so desperate for soldiers to fight this two-front war that it wasn't all that careful about checking the age of volunteers. When word of this laxness reached sixteen-year-old Tony Mazzocchi in early 1943, he headed to a Brooklyn recruiting station to enlist. He told the recruiters he was eighteen. No problem. "I asked for an expedited call-up. You could do that," recalled Tony. The navy rejected him because of his eyesight. "That was my first choice; all my friends were going in the navy." But the army said yes: his glasses-corrected vision was twenty-twenty.

Tony was so determined to enlist, said his cousin Connie Tozzi, that he had even threatened to join the French Foreign Legion. Nevertheless, Tony asked for his father's permission to go to war. Joe refused again and again, not wanting to see his young son in harm's way. "After I signed up and got in, I went home to tell him," said Tony. "He said he understood, but he was sad, very sad. He didn't want me to go. But he knew I was going anyway no matter what he said. I remember those sad eyes. He cried."

Tony's path for the next three years was set. A picture taken on the day he left for the war, May 1, 1943, shows him walking down 72nd Street wearing a nicely tailored light suit over a dark sweater, one hand in his pocket, the other carrying a small gym bag. A thatch of curly dark hair caps a very young, smooth face. He is walking with purpose, smiling and eager.

TWO

Basic Training

Mazzocchi's war had a Hollywood plotline. A young city kid boards the train for boot camp. Green and bewildered, he is thrown together with new recruits from all over the country, forming bonds that transcend class, ethnicity, region, and religion—a picture of a vital and united America. In the movies, the platoon, usually under the command of a tough but fair Protestant middle American, includes boys from the rural South, West, and Midwest, together with Italian, Irish, and Jewish soldiers from the urban Northeast. Rarely does a black person appear on this set.

In Tony's squad within the 563rd Anti-Aircraft Artillery Battalion, a protestant Ivy Leaguer, Lieutenant William E. Wylie, melded together soldiers named Woodward, Nelson, and Burgess with others named McIntire, Molanowski, Mosher, and Mazzocchi—and not a single person of color. In the movies and in Tony's battalion, the melting pot was conscious and deliberate: The idea was to overcome geographic and ethnic tensions through training, discipline, and combat. But when it came to skin color, there was no melting pot. Tony soon found himself in the middle of a race war, learning lessons that would shape the rest of his life.

As Tony's battalion began basic training at Camp Stewart, Georgia, in June 1943, racial tensions there exploded—a fact neatly omitted from an official account of the 563rd, a yearbook-like eighty-page retrospective written by an anonymous officer. The roots of the tension were obvious to Tony: The base was fully segregated. So was the town nearest the base, as well as the most popular "pass city" of Savannah, forty miles away. The white soldiers of the 563rd liked to entertain themselves at the Savannah and Desoto Hotels and at nightclubs and restaurants. Black soldiers were not admitted.

World War II marked a new stage in American race relations. During the mass immigration of the early twentieth century, science had viewed Italians, Poles, Irish, and Jews as distinct nonwhite races. However, the Depression, CIO organizing of immigrant industrial workers, and New Deal political coalitions and social programs tore down this racial ladder. The inferior "races" were transformed into "ethnic groups"—and Italians, Poles, Irish, and Jews miraculously turned white.

Even as Nazi scientists relied on American research to justify the superiority of the newly constructed Aryan race, the association with Hitler discredited racial eugenics in the United States. By the 1930s, when Tony was growing up, "southern Italian" was no longer included among the most inferior races. However, the socially constructed racial category of "Negro" was never transformed into an ethnicity. The unfounded notion of a biologically distinct "race" still applied, and despite small advances by the Roosevelt administration and the CIO, discrimination continued, especially in the South. The New Deal largely excluded blacks. Roosevelt's sweeping reforms depended on the votes of racist southern congressmen who thrived on one-party rule and disenfranchised black voters. They dominated the most powerful congressional committees and had no intention of allowing the New Deal to interfere with their region's pool of cheap black labor. They made certain that Roosevelt programs such as minimum-wage and maximum-hour laws did not cover farm and household workers, the vast majority of whom in the South were black. Blacks were also excluded from other critical government programs, from unemployment insurance to federal housing programs. Even the National Labor Relations Act of 1935, which gave workers the right to organize, permitted labor organizations to segregate black workers into separate local unions.

Nationally, black workers were challenging their exclusion. Sensing the wartime labor shortage, they pressed to end discrimination in the defense industry. A. Philip Randolph, head of the Brotherhood of Sleeping Car Porters, threatened a mass march on Washington, forcing Roosevelt to establish the Fair Employment Practices Committee to rectify employment discrimination.

The army seemed oblivious to such turmoil. The officers in Tony's unit were mostly concerned about integrating two rival white groups. According to the yearbook history, "The policy was set up originally of dividing the men evenly through the Batteries so that the Battalion was close to half and half, Rebel and Yanks." The officers were much relieved to learn that their policy worked: There was "no trouble on this score: we were too busy learning to get used to this Army life."[1] There was zero chance of black-white conflict in Tony's batallion: The history provides only one reference to nonwhite soldiers, when Company C "received three Chinese boys as fillers" (shoveling dirt into abandoned foxholes).

This was no accident. The army's leaders, according to historian Daniel Kryder, believed that segregation was "necessary to avoid irritating whites, who, it was thought, would fight to preserve the privilege of separate units."[2] Tony soon saw that black soldiers were also prepared to fight for their dignity. Black recruits, especially from the North, chafed at their treatment at Camp Stewart. Many whites were infuriated that black officers, from segregated units, outranked them. Credible rumors circulated of white soldiers refusing to salute black officers, and of confrontations between black recruits and white locals over such flashpoints as seating on buses.

By the time Tony arrived at Camp Stewart, in May 1943, black soldiers were openly defiant. In one nearby town, it was reported that civilian police had twice "jailed a black soldier for public drunkenness. In each case, shortly after the arrests, a truckload of black soldiers arrived at the jail and asked for the release of the soldier. One of the men in the truck had a Thompson submachine gun strapped across his back."[3] The soldiers were released without incident. When it was suggested that the local police allow black MPs to patrol the area, the police chief replied, "We ain't going to have any nigger police."[4]

On base, "white soldiers routinely harassed black soldiers and their wives and girlfriends, especially near its black-white frontier," Kryder reported.[5] On June 1, a rumor circulated that white soldiers had beaten a black woman and two black soldiers, killing the woman. No arrests were made.

The northern black press referred to Tony's base as "the Georgia HELL-HOLE," with "unspeakable conditions at Camp Stewart down in Georgia, where Jim Crow is riding, high, wide and handsome."[6] A black soldier wrote to the National Association for the Advancement of Colored People, "Please for God Sake help us. These old southern officers over us have us quarantined like slaves, come down and see. . . . They really hate colored. Please appeal to the war department about our treatment at once. We are no slaves."[7]

On June 9, four days before Tony's seventeenth birthday, Camp Stewart went to war—a civil war. The ejection of noncommissioned black officers from Post Exchange Number 8 touched off a gunfight between black soldiers and the military police. "One investigator reported that between five and six thousand rounds of .30 caliber ball and tracer ammunition were fired, while another estimated that six hundred rounds were fired," Kryder said. One MP died; several were wounded.[8]

No members of Tony's 563rd Battalion participated in the melee, perhaps because their barracks were on the other side of the base. But everyone knew about the insurrection, including the army's top brass. Their official investigation concluded that "the violence grew in part from a long-standing frustration and resentment within the black regiments. The surrounding communities mistreated the soldiers and Camp Stewart largely reflected and institutionalized that harsh discrimination."[9]

The army proposed reforms, but they were cosmetic and reflected prevailing racial stereotypes. The army's investigation stated that the "average Negro soldier's meager education, superstition, imagination, and excitability" made him prone to a "mass state of mind." So they tightened their security system to weed out agitators. Further, they concluded that "any further relaxation of segregation" would cause "continuous riots and disturbances." Latrines and post stockades remained segregated to prevent "constant irritation and disorder" among southern white soldiers. The most disruptive troops were quickly redeployed overseas.

The army hoped to "educate" black soldiers so they would better understand their role in the war. A new training manual advised black soldiers, "Any question about white people and black people will never be settled by barracks talk. *Let's forget about these things for the time being, buckle down to real soldiering, and win this war.*"[10] Training manuals explained that "if Hitler should win the war . . . blacks would be plunged into a new form of slavery far worse that that found in antebellum times."[11]

For Tony, the battle on the base reinforced beliefs he'd already absorbed from his family. Growing up, he'd viewed race through the lens of progressive union ideology. "We saw very few blacks," Tony said. "But in our family, opposing racism against blacks was a matter of trade union principles. My father made it clear to us that racism was used as a tool to divide working people. I internalized that. Seeing the conditions in Camp Stewart and the South brought it home for the first time."

The Mazzocchis learned about violent racism in the South through the progressive press. At least sixty-seven blacks were lynched between 1933 and 1935. The infamous trial of the Scottsboro Boys, nine black teenagers charged in 1931with raping two white women, dragged on for more than a decade with its convictions, appeals, reversals, retrials, and mistrials. Eight of the men were convicted by an all-white jury and sentenced to death, even after one of the alleged victims, Ruby Bates, testified that she and the other woman involved had made the incident up. The case was soaked in racial injustice—in closing arguments, one prosecutor asked the jury, "Is justice in this case going to be bought and sold in Alabama with Jew money from New York?"[12] It also provided a few glimmers of moral courage: The judge in the original case set aside the guilty verdict, anticipating correctly that his act of conscience would destroy his career. None of the defendants was executed, though their lives were ruined.

The case became as ardent a cause for many progressives as Sacco and Vanzetti. (The Communist Party represented the defendants in court.) But despite Tony's awareness of racial injustice in the South, "It was still a shock to see the segregated water fountains and bathrooms." He began to understand how structure and organization could make segregation appear routine, almost normal. Moreover, Tony witnessed a darker side of human nature. It wasn't only the bosses who promoted racism, but also the average GI, both northerner and southerner. "Except for a few, racism was the norm," Tony remembered. "I really didn't have any big ideas about what that meant, but I was developing the awareness that people would get ugly around race unless things were structured differently."

Yet Tony's upbringing had not completely immunized him to bias. "I'd rather be fighting in Europe than in the [Pacific]," the eighteen-year-old wrote home after surviving the Battle of the Bulge. "At least there are some cities and towns here, and white people, excluding the 'Germans.'"

II

The army taught Tony to be a good soldier. Basic training—the saluting, latrine swabbing, and drilling—lasted the summer, and Tony did well, despite his youth. "Yeah, I was a baby," he said. "But I had been going to my uncle's place in Blairstown, and the outdoors were nothing new to me. Being away from home was not a frightening proposition. A lot of these guys, grown guys, I heard them crying at night."

Solace, at least for whites, came from getting off the base. Thousands of soldiers flooded into Savannah from Camp Stewart and from the Marine Corps training facility on Parris Island, South Carolina. Navy men docked in Savannah harbor and Air Corps flyboys flooded in from nearby bases. It took ingenuity to avoid the crowds—and downright genius to find a date. Fortunately, Leonard Hacker, Tony's affable squad leader, excelled in the arts of leisure. Tony remembered Hacker as tough—pushing his soldiers hard through the trials of basic training—but fair.

Tony had a special in: Hacker came from Bensonhurst. The son of a Jewish upholsterer, he'd been the class clown in his high school, an overweight kid who forgot his lines in class productions and accidentally stuck his foot in a water bucket during his first football game. He'd gone on to become a comedian, breaking into the Borscht Belt in New York's Catskill Mountains. But at Camp Stewart he was just a GI with an eye for entertainment. "He told me to come to the synagogue in Savannah," recalled Tony. "He said I wouldn't be sorry. I said to him, 'What are you, nuts? I'm not Jewish.' But he said being from Brooklyn was good enough. 'Just say you're Jewish. They think everyone from New York is Jewish.' So I did and they did."

Genius at work. They joined the congregation (the oldest Reformed Jewish congregation in the country) and mingled during the refreshments, Oneg Shabat, that followed the Friday-night services. As Hacker predicted, their prayers were answered. "He sure knew what he was doing," Tony said. "He said it was a can't-miss place to meet girls, and he was right."

Unfortunately for Tony's career in Jewish studies, the army also noticed Hacker's talents and moved him into the entertainment corps. Soon Leonard Hacker changed his name to Buddy Hackett, the comedian whose rotund figure, sideways speech, and raunchy routines entertained the troops and the public for the next forty years.

III

By September 1943, Tony Mazzocchi's battalion had moved to the artillery range. They spent nights bivouacked among the mosquitoes, firing their M1 rifles and anti-aircraft guns, and days marching through the swamps. "Most of the guys from the city really had trouble with the swamps and the snakes," Tony said. "For me it was more familiar. I grew up playing in the woods."

With the swamp training and accompanying malaria prevention lessons, the troops assumed they were headed to the South Pacific. However, in November they moved to a camp near Lebanon, Tennessee, whose terrain resembled that of central-southern Germany. There they conducted two months of full-scale maneuvers, bivouacking in the woods, sleeping in pup tents, and becoming very intimate with the rain, mud, and snow. They figured they were off to Europe. Wrong again. Instead, they were sent back to Camp Stewart for "refresher training," which focused on learning the intricacies of their artillery—including the quad .50 mm anti-aircraft guns, a battery of four guns mounted on a lightly armored vehicle. They trained as a three-soldier crew—Tony was the one sitting between the two pairs of guns, rotating and elevating them to aim and firing with a trigger grip in each hand, while the others fed the ammunition. For a week, they practiced protecting their airstrip at the Waycross, Georgia, airbase.

According to the yearbook, they got a little time off to relax at a local cabaret called The Hayloft, which "had a nice dance floor and pleasant surroundings. One night this club put on as fine a show as could be found anywhere in the immediate vicinity, with 'Butch Hacker' as MC."[13] (Tony and Buddy Hackett did not locate the small worship center that substituted for a synagogue in Waycross.)

On June 19, 1944, six days after Tony's eighteenth birthday, two weeks after D-Day, and after fifteen months of training, Tony's battalion headed for Farmingdale, Long Island. The yearbook stated that "all the boys from Brooklyn roared their approval." The commanders reported, "Some of the Rebels were dubious about moving so far above the Mason-Dixon Line." But their worries disappeared as "the girls of Long Island were really raising havoc with our boys from South of the Mason Dixon line and vice versa.... Some of Southern boys had the civilian population amazed by their accent, music and adaptable manners of courtship"[14]

Mazzocchi used all of his pass time to visit family and friends for what he presumed would be the last stop before heading overseas to follow up on the invasion of Normandy.

And he would go as a grunt. The army measured achievement through tests. Tony had aced some and flunked others. But eventually the army noticed that Tony was in fact extremely bright and an ideal candidate for a specialized service such as communications, where his intelligence could be put to better use. To make a more accurate assessment of his abilities, the army gave Tony an intelligence test. Tony said he scored "moron."

D-Day—June 6, 1944—came and went. After a month of mock drills at the Farmington airfield, Tony's battalion was sent back south, to Camp Davis in North Carolina, where the training intensified. The soldiers found themselves stuck in mud and howling wind. They endured more than twenty inspections during their two-month stay, in preparation for a final inspection by the general in charge of Anti-Aircraft Artillery Command. They passed with flying colors. The training and the waiting were finally over. On September 30, 1944, the 563rd left for Camp Myles Standish, Massachusetts, embarking for England on the USS *Wakefield* on October 10.

During Tony's last leave, his family had a professional portrait taken of their boy. Tony faced the camera in dress uniform with a cap that dwarfed his thin, smooth face. He looked more like a sophomore in a high school military academy than a soldier going to war.

IV

Following a zigzag course to confound enemy submarines, the USS *Wakefield* took a week to reach Liverpool. The ship was a converted luxury liner now transporting more than seven thousand troops. The place to be on board, Tony and his compatriots quickly realized, was in the galley. Galley workers got three meals a day instead of two. Feeding so many troops took the form of an athletic contest: Companies vied with one another to see who could complete a meal in the shortest time. What struck Tony most was the level of organization. "It was amazing to watch that kitchen work round the clock. Imagine feeding seven thousand men on a ship made to hold maybe two thousand. One thing the army really knew how to do was to educate and organize people to do just about anything."

The more Tony soldiered, the more he saw that social transformation was not a utopian abstraction. It was happening all around him. After disembarking from a landing craft at Omaha Beach four months after D-Day, Tony encountered a French countryside turned upside down by war, and again by army reconstruction. The area now held hundreds of thousands of

Allied troops and the infrastructure to serve them. Roads, huts, and entire towns had been built overnight.

The 563rd Battalion's first task was to defend the Normandy coast from marauding German soldiers. Twenty thousand German troops had been trapped after D-Day on the Channel Islands with no supply lines. With only eight hundred men, Tony's battalion spread its guns up and down 120 miles of coastline, with Tony's Company A stationed at Vauville on November 28, 1944. On this westernmost front, all was so quiet that by December 9, Tony's battery was redeployed to sleepy Aywaille, Belgium.

For a week, the war seemed far removed. The soldiers enjoyed the hospitality of a liberated populace. They imbibed at a GI beer garden and took warm showers in Liège. The yearbook, sounding like a frat house publication, reported, "Most of us carry the memory of the women attendants in the shower rooms where we would be running around in our birthday suits and they would be weighing us or unlocking the door to our dressing rooms, quite unconcerned about it all."[15]

But on December 16, 1944, a cold, foggy day, the peaceful interlude was violently interrupted. The soldiers first heard shell bursts about twenty miles away, then suddenly German buzz bombs began falling on the gun positions of Battery B. "We were close enough to their target that they would pass low over our positions," reported an officer near Tony's squad. "Frequently, [their engines] would cut off just before they passed over us and we would never know whether or not they were going to drop on us."[16]

One officer in Tony's battalion reported the events by phone from the command post. A transcript made its way into the yearbook. "Here's another. . . . It's coming right at me. . . . It's getting real close. . . . It's coming right for us. . . . It's getting bigger. . . . Holy Mother, it's coming right at me. . . . It's getting real close. . . . It MIGHT miss us. . . . It's going by. . . . It's passed—jeez, what a night!"[17] For the rest of his life, Tony's sleep would be interrupted by terrifying dreams of war.

It was a big night for the entire European theater. The Battle of the Bulge, Germany's vast counteroffensive, was under way. Among the soldiers in Tony's battalion, confusion and fear spread quickly. Someone reported erroneously that English-speaking Germans in US uniforms had parachuted behind the lines within miles of Tony's Battery A position in Aywaille. As

Tony's battalion set up roadblocks along with the 143rd Gun Battalion, word spread of German executions of US troops in nearby Malmedy.

On December 23, the yearbook reported, the fog lifted; it was "a day with vivid blue skies and brilliantly clear air."[18] Unfortunately, the clear weather prompted the Messerschmidts to roar over Aywaille, attempting to blow out its bridge. Tony, in position behind his quad .50s, fired at the enemy for the first time. "The planes moved in so fast that each of us was given a certain quadrant to cover," he recalled. "We aimed toward one area of the sky and hoped for the best." Battery A was the first in the battalion to shoot down a German plane.

The outcome of the Battle of the Bulge was perilously uncertain. "We saw our own infantry retreating past us," Tony recalled. "We were that close to the front line"—in fact, the Germans came within five miles of overrunning his position. It was impossible to stay dry and warm. "It was bitter cold," said Tony. "We were told it was one of the coldest winters on record." One night, Tony broke the military code of conduct and stripped the coat from the body of a dead US soldier. For the rest of his life, he would feel guilty about it. Stealing that greatcoat was a recurring element of his sleepless nights and disquieting dreams.

As the soldiers shivered, the war flamed all around them. Far overhead, out of reach of their guns, a major battle for air supremacy raged as German fighter planes shot down US B-17s. On December 24, Tony's battery reported more German paratroopers falling near them. They spent Christmas burrowed in the snow.

"I guess you know by now what's happened here," Tony wrote home to his family that day. "'Prvt. Sauer Kraut' came out for a fling. They were trying to give us a rough time. It goes to prove there is still plenty of kick left in them. We were going to have a big Christmas party here where we are staying, but the 'Jerry' made us postpone it."

Two days later Tony wrote home again. "Well, it's the day after Xmas. I expected the 'Jerry' to bring us some presents yesterday but he surprised me. The Germans really came out this week, didn't they? I personally think it's their last desperate attempt to prolong the war so the Allies will settle with 'peace terms' instead of 'Unconditional Surrender.' They have a different guess coming though."

For the next two weeks, Tony's battalion faced repeated attacks from

German planes. Reading was Tony's refuge from carnage and fear. During his sleepless nights, he devoured all manner of great and trashy books. "They had all these paperback books, put out by the Army Information Education section. I think the CP had control of it," he said. "I read everything, mostly the classics, but anything I could get my hands on."

One day when the troops were under sustained enemy fire, "We went into this underground dugout. It was huge. The place was lined with books. It was incredible. It was like a library underground."

Tony read Dostoevsky, Maugham, Melville. "I was always reading because I was on a halftrack. I could carry a lot of books in the vehicle. . . . That was my way of relaxing," he recalled. "Novels, histories—they used to come in wooden crates. They'd be all over the place. You'd throw away the ones you read—and you'd look around, there'd be crates of new ones. The chaplain usually brought them out. One day he took out *Forever Amber.*[19] And he said, 'I don't think you guys should read this book.' Of course everyone wanted to read it, even guys who weren't reading anything else."

While it would take several more weeks for the 563rd to reach the Rhine River, the deadliest battle of World War II had finally ended. One hundred thousand Germans were killed, wounded, or captured. Nineteen thousand Americans were killed, and 23,554 were captured. Miraculously, Tony's entire battalion lost only one man.

In Malmedy, the Germans had executed eighty-six US soldiers, the worst atrocity against American troops in Europe. "I believe everything I ever heard about those bastards now," Tony wrote home. "They shoot plenty of our boys even when they surrendered. I'm enclosing an article about it. Just show it to those who think the Hun is just a peace loving citizen who just wants living room."

The 563rd entered Germany not as welcomed liberators but feared conquerors. They headed east toward the Rhine, behind the First Army Allied Infantry, traveling through a largely empty countryside that had been flattened by war. Villages lay in ruin. Tony was tormented by a soldier's most constant affliction, painful feet. "Since they always were wet, a fungus or something set in. But hey, I was on a vehicle and I was still breathing." Many thousands of others were less lucky. As Tony moved in his halftrack over icy gutted roads, his commander wrote that they "watched civilians dig dead Germans out of the snow, their bodies frozen in grotesque postures of death."

"The weather here is the biggest pain in the ass," Tony wrote to his brother Sam. "It has been snowing here lately, but last night it turned to rain. While the snow was disappearing other things were appearing. German bodies started to turn up. They were . . . grim reminders of the recent battle. I see the Russians have started their new winter offensive. I hope theirs with ours will be the last offensive of this war."

V

After surviving the Battle of the Bulge, Tony Mazzocchi found himself studying psychology—his own. He was beginning to discover the killer within. He'd gone from two years of preparing for war to three months of nonstop combat in one of the most hellish battles ever, during the coldest winter in memory. Now his unit was about to play a small, essential part in one of most improbable battles of the war—the fight for the Remagen Bridge.

The 563rd served within the Allied First Army, headed by General William M. Hoge, whose task was to move east and south to meet up with General Patton's Third Army. Together, the two armies would cut off the German divisions then retreating from the Bulge. On March 7, 1945, Tony's Battery A moved to Stadt Mechenheim, which had been captured only the night before by the Ninth Armored Division. There they set up their anti-aircraft guns to protect the growing number of nearby troops and command posts. Only a few people knew that a sortie of US tanks and infantry was headed south and east to capture Remagen, a small village on the Rhine, ten miles away.

After relatively light German resistance, this sortie discovered that the Lundendorff rail bridge, which spanned a thousand yards across the Rhine, still stood. This had startling implications. All bridges should have been destroyed, either from the air by the Allies to trap retreating German troops, or by the Germans to impede the Allies. Capturing an intact bridge would allow the rapid movement of Allied troops and matériel to the Rhine's east bank.

On the German-held side of the Lundendorff bridge was a small, ill-equipped group of local officers, wounded veterans, and civilians. They were under direct orders from Hitler, under penalty of death, to blow the bridge when the Allies approached, and toward that end they'd carefully wired it with explosives. Now they waited for trains carrying wounded German troops from the collapsing front to cross.

When the Americans approached, the Germans threw the switch. The electronic charges failed. A solitary German soldier was sent onto the bridge to light the primary cord for the emergency charge. According to historian Ken Hechler, the Germans "watched in awe as the huge structure lifted up, and steel, timbers, dust and thick black smoke mixed in the air. Many GIs threw themselves to the ground or buried their faces in their hands."

Incredibly, the bridge landed back on the pilings. "The sight of the bridge still spanning the Rhine brought no cheers from the [Americans]," wrote Hechler, "It was like an unwelcome specter. The suicide mission was on again."[20]

Braving gunfire, the American platoon made its way across the Remagen Bridge and secured a beachhead on the other side. General Hoge sent reinforcements before the Germans could mount a large counterattack. Knowing that failure would mean disgrace, the Germans tried again and again to destroy the bridge, but failed. Luftwaffe planes sent to finish the job were held off by American anti-aircraft battalions, including Tony's 563rd. For three days, according to the yearbook, the 563rd's "guns along the Rhine together with those of other units delivered the heaviest concentration of anti-aircraft firepower in the history of the war."[21]

Because the Germans now had deployed their new secret weapon, the jet, the army had to use "50 percent more anti-aircraft batteries than the American forces had at the Normandy beachheads."[22] When one of those jets, an Me 262, swooped down to attack Tony's convoy, according to the yearbook, one of the other gunners in the battalion, Chester Wear, "lined up his quad-fifties on the oncoming plane and opened up. In a matter of seconds, the enemy plane was sent spinning crazily into the earth," saving the convoy and possibly Tony as well.[23]

On March 10–11, Tony's Battery A hit another plane as it flew over at about a thousand feet, reconnoitering the network of roads. It disappeared over the ridge trailing smoke. Again, Tony had no idea whether his guns had hit the target: "There were so many guns firing at the same time, but I doubt I took down any plane."

One night, Tony was perched alone on his anti-aircraft gun, charged with protecting the river valley below. He spotted a German plane flying very low and relatively slowly. "I could see it perfectly through my sight," he said. "It was some kind of reconnaissance plane. I could even see the pilot, his face, his clothes. He seemed close enough to touch. He was dead in my sights. But I didn't fire."

Why not? "I don't know," Tony said, decades later. "I just didn't want to kill him. He wasn't firing. He wasn't attacking. It was too much like taking a life in cold blood."

The army, racing toward victory, didn't know and didn't care. Over the next week, the Americans moved the front toward the heart of Germany, hastened by their victory at Remagen Bridge. Eisenhower referred to the news of its capture as "one of my happy moments of the war."[24] For his part, Hitler was so infuriated by the loss that he ordered courts-martial and executed four of his officers.

When their brigade was disbanded a month later, Tony's commanding officer provided the troops with a summary of their accomplishments, including their role in turning "the Ardennes Bulge into the Ardennes Bubble." Brigadier General E. W. Timberlake wrote: "During the above campaigns the Battalion had 68 aerial engagements, destroying 9 enemy planes; had 16 ground engagements, destroying a score of enemy vehicles and killing or capturing over 400 supermen; while greatly facilitating the advance of assault infantry."

Tony took issue with this report. "It only mentions 9 planes," he wrote to his sister Ethel on July 23, 1945. "But I know damn well we got more than that. They are the confirmed ones and before you get one confirmed you have to go through so much trouble. As you see we did more ground fighting than anything else. I was on a half track and they always caught hell. The worst time we had was in the Bulge."

After Remagen Bridge, and until it was disbanded, the 563rd stayed behind to protect the Rhine, and the war passed them by. Tony and his battalion never fired their guns again. "We dropped out of the race and are now taking it easy," Tony wrote to his brother Sam on April 22, 1945. "I doubt we will ever see the front in this theater again. . . . I kinda hated being left behind at this stage of the game."

But his education in war was just beginning, and the next course would be unforgettable.

VI

After traveling 210 miles into Germany during five months of combat, the 563rd turned in its weapons in exchange for security guard uniforms. Tony became a military cop whose duties took him back and forth across the utter disarray of Central Europe. Entire populations were moving back to their homelands or away from their destroyed homes. Tony's job was to guard trainloads of liberated slave laborers and captured soldiers in need of transport. He was traveling east with sickly Russian prisoners of war on the day he celebrated his nineteenth birthday.

He grew wary of the Germans as he traveled through their war-ravaged land. "The more I see of these sons of bitches, the more it burns me up," he wrote to his brother Sam. "They are still arrogant as hell. . . . These Germans are smart in that respect. They see we aren't harsh and they do take advantage of the fact. They haven't learnt a lesson."

But Tony worried that the lesson might never be taught correctly, now that FDR had died (April 12, 1945). "Roosevelt's death," Tony wrote, "was the worst blow I believe has hit us yet. I can't see anyone who can compare with him. I'm just praying that Truman will carry out Roosevelt's foreign policy."

In between his guarding missions, Tony rejoined the informal political discussion groups organized by Lieutenant Wylie. "People from all sorts of political backgrounds were thrown together," Tony said. "We talked about whether a war like this would ever happen again, that sort of thing. Nothing profound."

Shortly after the Germans surrendered on May 7, 1945, two of Tony's COs entered Buchenwald. They subsequently arranged to have small groups of soldiers visit the camp each day. Lieutenant Wylie took his discussion group there. The experience shook Tony to his core: the scattered piles of teeth, the meat hooks where humans had been suffocated and hung like cattle, the mass-production crematorium with its mammoth chimney and dozens of ovens in a neat row. Here, at this facility in the very woods so beloved by Goethe, just outside Weimar, the historic capital of Germany's cultural splendors, the Nazis had killed fifty-six thousand Jews, Slavs, German Communists, Soviet POWs, other resistance fighters, homosexuals, and handicapped people—all viewed as hazards to the "Master Race."

Tony was stunned by the sophisticated industrial design and craftsmanship—the tall windows providing workers with ample natural light, the shower room's modern fixtures—and the red-brick ovens framed in sturdy black iron that were designed to burn bodies three at a time.[25] This wasn't a haphazard atrocity like Malmedy. Buchenwald was a factory whose workers performed on a piece-rate system. "It was like a job—the job of killing," Tony said. "Imagine, every day you came to work to kill. The next day you came to kill some more—a certain amount of people—a quota."[26]

It shook him to realize that "you could take a people and organize them into running a murder mill, right next door to a cultural center." And those cultured townspeople surely knew about these cruelties. "This was so close to Weimar—the trains ran right through their town. They had to have known."

Tony didn't need to see Buchenwald to reconfirm his atheism. "I had a guy in my crew who was always praying. I said, 'You know, Larry, these other guys, the Germans, are praying to the same God?' I thought it was ridiculous. But obviously, a lot of people didn't."

But Buchenwald shook Tony's secular religion—the one that believed in the basic goodness of the working class. Never a utopian, Tony was brought up to believe that workers turned bad when they were manipulated by a boss's divide-and-conquer tactics. He already believed that race and nationality could be used to trick workers into supporting fascists or racists, even against their own material interests. He'd seen it happen to kids on his block and to his fellow soldiers. Whether at Camp Stewart or in Germany, people could be anti-boss and racist or anti-union at the same time. Despite this, Tony still believed that people had an inherent humanity he could tap.

But it was very hard to understand the methodical destruction of life at Buchenwald. There was no escaping the fact that the average citizen—not just a few fascist fanatics or heartless bosses—could be organized to carry out mass murder, and comply with utter brutality. Workers could be organized to build a hospital or build a Buchenwald.

"I was just nineteen," said Tony. "I didn't know what it really meant. But I knew it was having a profound impact on me. Over time, I grew to understand that my work would have to take into account what I saw."

And he would leave on this battlefield any habits of mind that still viewed the world in terms of white, black, Jewish, and Asian races.

After Camp Stewart and Buchenwald, Tony saw the persecution of Jews or blacks as much more than individual acts of good or bad people. It was much more a question of organization, of routine, and of planning. He had spent three years in the army, the world's largest social planning machine. He had perceived the detailed social machinery behind Jim Crow racism, and he had seen the planning of the fascists. Everything was planning. Everything was organization.

He'd also seen how changeable the world could be. Houses were destroyed or thrown up overnight. People were dislocated, relocated, or fed by the thousands. Political institutions could build a society where killing factories seemed almost normal. Couldn't it also organize a world more just and equitable?

No university could have raised such questions more deeply.

The baby-faced boy who had rushed to enlist had grown into a veteran soldier. With his thick hair already beginning to recede, he looked as if he had aged a decade since the family picture taken two years before.

VII

After V-E Day, it looked like Tony was headed for mandatory graduate courses in the South Pacific. As he worked his way back from his train-guarding duties to meet up with his battalion in Brussels, President Truman readied the order to send more than a million troops for a final invasion of Japan. Thirty divisions, including Tony's, were preparing to travel to the Pacific from the European theater. Everyone heard the stories about the ferocious fighting abilities of the Japanese soldiers—how they preferred death over capture, how not one had surrendered. No one really wanted any piece of it. A great weariness was setting in.

"Well, VE has come at last," Tony wrote home on May 13, 1945. "I'm glad it's over. I guess the people went wild back home. If they did, I don't know why. It was just another event over here. The shooting has ceased but it doesn't mean coming home. We definitely will go to the [Pacific] or stay here. We won't come home."

But a few months later Tony learned that the United States had dropped its secret weapon, the atomic bomb, on Hiroshima. "One of my friends woke me up, coming off a leave, and told me about this bomb that had been dropped. I had no other thoughts than the Japanese would probably surrender now, and that we would go home. We didn't want to be in the invasion. We knew what had happened on Okinawa." Okinawa, the largest sea and land battle in history, had killed thousands. Then another bomb fell over Nagasaki. On August 14, Japan surrendered.

Tony and the entire 563rd rejoiced with the rest of America. He and his fellow soldiers worried little about the implications of the new weapon; nor did they question its use. As Tony recalled, "We were scheduled to be in the invasion in Japan, and nobody relished that."

Although Tony later would make a contribution to halting US nuclear testing, he never viewed the atomic bomb as categorically different from the conventional weapons that had destroyed entire cities in Europe and Japan: "Nobody thought about the enormity of the bomb. I still liken it to the stupid argument about what's the best way to kill people. The firebomb raids killed far more people in one night than Hiroshima or Nagasaki."

As the summer of 1945 turned to fall and then to winter, the troops wanted to go home and didn't understand why it was taking so long. Most enlisted men were exhausted. And they were fed up with the military. They'd witnessed for too long the privileges allotted officers and denied to them. As the army's own *Stars and Stripes* newspaper put it, "A caste system inherited from Frederick the Great of Prussia and the 18th-Century British navy is hardly appropriate to the United States. . . . The aristocracy-peasantry relationship characteristic of our armed forces has a counterpart nowhere else in American life."[27]

But the Truman administration still needed tens of thousands of troops to manage the surrender and occupation. Besides, some in the administration worried that a quick demobilization would lead to economic chaos at home—perhaps a recession or worse. They wanted to spread out the return over a number of years. The British were pressuring the United States to keep troops in Europe as a bulwark against the massive Soviet army that occupied all of Eastern Europe. If soldiers were demobilized too quickly, they argued, it could send a signal of weakness to the Soviets, who were still considered allies, although difficult ones. In the Far East, US troops also provided support for the Chinese nationalists led by Chiang Kai-shek against the advance of Mao Tse-tung's communist insurgents. And both France and

England hoped the US would help them regain or maintain their colonial holdings in the Far East.

To promote an orderly demobilization, the services came up with a points system that awarded credits to soldiers based on time of service, time overseas, number of battles fought, and number of children at home. Despite three battles and three years of service, Tony still didn't have enough points to get home.

"I've only got 55 points," Tony wrote to his sister from Belgium on September 8, 1945. "We may get a 4th battle star and that would be five more points."

Instead, for the next six months, Tony marked time. "I just got back from Paris tonight," he wrote his sister Ethel on February 7, 1946. "We took some prisoners there. . . . Our CO told us to stay because there wasn't anything for us to do. . . . We really did the town this time. . . . We also went to the Folies Bergère again. It still stinks."

When an order came from the War Department to slow down the demobilization process, two GIs with strong union backgrounds organized soldiers' resentment into a near insurrection. Emil Mazey of the United Auto Workers (in the Pacific) and David Livingston of Local 65, Retail, Wholesale and Department Store Union (in Europe), helped organize a movement called "Bring the Boys Back Home." (Mazey, who was considered left-wing, later became the UAW's anti-communist secretary-treasurer under president Walter Reuther. At this time, Livingston reportedly was in the Communist Party. Later he would leave it.)

During a visit to Manila by Secretary of War Robert Patterson in early January 1946, Mazey and company organized protests of ten thousand GIs on successive days. *Stars and Stripes*' headline read "Patterson Called Number One Enemy by Jeering Mob." As GI protesters marched through the streets, one colonel alluded to Mazey's background with the UAW (then engaged in a three-month strike against GM): "The colonel ordered them back to their barracks exclaiming, 'You men forget you're not working for General Motors. You're still in the Army.'"[28]

Soldiers also protested in Europe. During early January, "virtually every US command witnessed demonstrations against the 'slowdown' order. Soldiers booed their commanding officers at mass meetings and passed their service caps for money to buy ads in state-side newspapers. . . . Hundreds of GIs marched down the Champs-Élysées waving magnesium flares and shouting 'scab' at men who wouldn't join." In Frankfurt, two thousand soldiers chanted, "Service yes, serfdom no."[29]

As an MP, Tony Mazzocchi could not march with these protesters, but he shared their frustration. "Well Sis, I don't feel like even writing, that's how disgusted I am," Tony wrote on February 7, 1946, from Brussels. "Our orders have been changed again for the millionth time."

Back in the United States, a movement to "Bring the Boys Home by Christmas" financed largely by liberals and Communist Party (CP)-oriented unions bombarded President Truman with postcards. On December 17 alone, sixty thousand cards rained down on the White House urging the president to "press into service every ship flying our flag to bring back our troops by Christmas."[30]

The demonstrations both home and abroad focused on the military's plan to use American troops to prop up anti-worker, anti-peasant governments in Asia. Protestors in Seoul, Shanghai, Manila, and New Delhi asked, "Are we out here to protect Wall Street? Is this Yankee imperialism? Did you bring the 86th Division to suppress the aspirations of the Philippine people? Are we protecting the British Lion?"[31]

The army searched for evidence that communists had infiltrated the military protest movement. Classified intelligence reports claimed that by demonstrating, "Large numbers of American soldiers gave support to the Communist Party line and were not even aware of it."[32] But no secret counterintelligence operation was needed. The CP's American newspaper, the *Daily Worker,* openly argued in January 1946 that "The men who fought this war don't want to lose the peace. They don't favor the withdrawal of occupation forces from Germany and Japan. But they don't like the deal where we fight to free the Philippines and China and then keep troops there to enslave them."[33]

Conservative and liberal legislators alike jumped on the bandwagon. Emmanuel Celler, a liberal congressman from New York, wanted to know why American troops were still in India, which was struggling for independence from Britain. Arch-reactionary representative John E. Rankin wanted to know why we needed an army of occupation in the Philippines.

The pressure to bring the troops home became overwhelming, forcing

President Truman to accelerate his demobilization plans. Nevertheless, after the Japanese surrendered in August, it took another seven months before Tony and the 563rd returned and the unit that had been his home and family for three years disintegrated into the chaos of postwar America.

As they returned to Fort Dix, New Jersey, in March 1946, no one worried about postwar military weakness or conflict with the Soviets. No one worried about being duped by the Communists, least of all PFC Mazzocchi. He was coming home to Bensonhurst, to the guys on the block, and to his extended family. He had only thanks for those who had organized the Bring the Boys Home movement—especially his uncle Lester and his two oldest sisters, who had worked tirelessly for the effort. That they did so as members of the Communist Party was no cause for concern. Not then.

THREE

Running with the Reds

After the war, Tony Mazzocchi picked up where he'd left off—as office boy at McGraw-Hill, working at a publication called *Sweet's Industrial Tools Catalogue*. But the world around him had changed dramatically. America, like the movies, went from black-and-white to color as the drab of the Depression lifted. People had more money in their pockets. And if you were a GI, you could go to school for free or make a living even without working.

One veteran in the neighborhood told Tony how to register for the 52-20 Club under the Serviceman's Readjustment Act of 1944. The government provided GIs with twenty dollars per week for up to fifty-two weeks, which amounted to nearly two-thirds of the average worker's take-home pay. Not bad. What's more, vets could get it for a few weeks, work for a while, and then get back on it. They were entitled to a maximum of fifty-two payments. The average vet stayed in the 52-20 Club for about seventeen weeks. Tony stretched out all fifty-two payments over several years.

After his first stay in the 52-20 Club, Tony found a job at the American Can Company in Brooklyn. "One of the kids on the block had gotten a job there and got the rest of us in," he said. "It was at Bush Terminal, near the army base. I was on the night shift making containers, aluminum cans, and crap like that. It probably employed three or four thousand people. Steelworkers had it organized. I worked for about two months."

Then his uncle Mike got him one of the best union jobs in America—on a Ford assembly line in Edgewater, New Jersey. Here Tony learned the true meaning of work. "I worked on the trim line. I worked on the commercial line. Various jobs. Tough work. I said, *Boy, I don't want to work at this for the rest of my life.*" He also learned how others dealt with the production drill. "I remember we had this relief guy. He would take your job over so you could take a break. And he was like an artist. He would always work the job as slowly as possible so when you got back you had to work like crazy to get back to where you could keep up with the line without going crazy."

For Tony, the line induced a virtual coma. "One day I was starting to work and a little while later the bell rang and I said to the guy next to me, 'Hey, what the hell's the bell ringing for?' He said it was lunchtime. That was it for me. I didn't even know what happened to the morning. I was like a robot."

Eventually, Tony was assigned to a task he liked better. "I was laying down the floor mat with rubber cement," he said. "When the guy came under the chassis to put the spare-wheel rack in, it dripped on his neck. And every night I had to pull this ball of rubber cement off the back of his neck. I swear it was like that . . . *slurp,*" said Tony making a large sucking sound. "And he cursed at me. But it was a good job. It was dirty, but you could work ahead and not fall behind. Anytime I see autoworkers, I have a gut feeling how hard that work is. You can talk all you want about it being high paid, but it's hard work."

In the fall of 1946, Tony was laid off. "I said, 'Screw it, I'm not going back.'" Tony rejoined the 52-20 Club, then teamed up with his Bensonhurst pals to escape the cold winter. "Somebody said, 'Let's go to Florida.' I had never been there. A friend had a '38 Pontiac. We rebuilt the whole engine in this cold garage. I mean it was freezing. We did a ring job, the whole thing. In those days, you always had kids on the block who knew every part of a car. We took off in January for Florida."

For three months he bummed around the beaches on the GI version of "spring break"—and the longest vacation of his adult life. "There were a lot of vets who were just stretching out after the war on the 52-20 Club," Tony recalled, including an ex-marine who "got ambushed on Guadalcanal. He was the only one who survived. And every morning he went to the beach to ask *Why did God let [me] live?* And I was giving him, 'There ain't no God.'

"We had twenty bucks a week between the three of us," Tony continued. "We couldn't go to nightclubs or anything, but we had a good time."

By the time he got home at Easter, his family was worried about how their freewheeling vet would earn a living. Tony's older brother Sam—now an accountant—realized that manual labor and Tony were a bad mix. He advised learning a trade. "He was always trying to get me a job," Tony said. "The family thought I was going to be a gangster or something." After all, in Bensonhurst, the mob always had their eye out for street-smart dropouts who had the respect of the toughs on the block.

When Sam spotted an ad for a vocational program aimed right at vets like Tony, the family persuaded him to sign up.

II

In 1947, virtually every student at Manhattan's Kerpel Dental School on 70th and Broadway was paying tuition through the GI Bill of Rights and getting a monthly stipend of at least seventy-five dollars. The tuition, which was higher than Harvard's, paid for a rigorous, full-time, two-year program to become a dental technician. Four hundred students on two shifts learned how to make dentures. "There was carving, then waxing and casting," said Jerry Fine, one of Tony's classmates. "Then they had porcelain, partial dentures, and full dentures. You covered the whole of dental technology."[1]

Jerry, like Tony, found the courses absorbing. "Sculpting was the most interesting," he remembered, moving his hands as if molding clay. "We took things that looked like ice-cube trays with rubber sections, and we'd pour a very thin mix of plaster of paris. Then we'd get these cubes and start carving teeth out of that. . . . Just like a sculptor starts. And we did every tooth."

For the first time ever, Tony was enjoying a positive educational experience. His math and grammar learning issues didn't impede him, and his gift for visualization helped. He worked seriously and performed well. He felt a lifetime away from playing class clown at Shallow Junior High.

"There was not a lot of talk while we were working—or horsing around," said Jerry. "And some very fine technicians came out of that program."

But for Tony, Kerpel Dental School became the portal into an entirely different field. Jerry Fine opened the door. "One day we're taking a john break, and Jesus, there was an argument going on. This big guy, must have been six-feet-plus, like two hundred pounds—I think the term *redneck* would be appropriate. He was flushed and angry. There's this little guy, real thin, not even 140 pounds—Tony—going against the big right-wing guy. And he so deflated the big guy's arguments. Tony just laid him out, cool and calm. And this redneck guy was saying, 'You must be a fucking Communist. You son of a bitch.' And I think, I gotta meet this guy."

After work, Jerry Fine sought Tony out. They talked as they headed toward the subway at 72nd Street—and walked right past it. Jerry invited

Tony to meet Ruth, his young bride. In their two-room apartment in Brooklyn Heights, the three talked and ate and talked into the night. Ruth, still very new to the art of making coffee, offered Tony a cup. Tony took a sip and said with a straight face, "Oooh, this is. . . . I love it . . . It reminds me of the army. It burns all the way down," recalled Ruth through tears of laughter. "And he was the only one who ever finished a cup of my coffee—and asked for a second. I knew I loved him—right that moment."

The Fines invited Tony to spend the night, but they only had one double bed. To prevent complications, they had developed an unusual guest system. When a woman stayed over, Ruth slept in the middle. With a male guest, Jerry took the center spot. And so it was on this night. But Tony thrashed and bounced all over, fighting slumber all the way. Since combat, he hadn't slept very well, he explained. So Jerry and Ruth moved him to a small couch in the living room. That didn't work, either; they heard the couch shifting and scraping across their rugless floor. "We had to tie down the legs of the sofa in order to get a night's sleep," Ruth said. In the morning, they realized that Tony had spent much of the night reading.

But the Fines were grateful for their new friendship. Tony's coiled energy, big ideas, raucous humor, and high hopes supplied much-needed cheer for the couple in the fall of 1948. The Cold War had descended and a red scare was ripping through the nation. The Fines were beginning to feel the pain and isolation that came with being card-carrying members of the Communist Party.

III

Tony could no more fear the Communist Party than he could fear his uncle Lester or his sisters Tess and Ethel. Like Ruth and Jerry, they had joined the party during World War II—and they brought their politics to the Mazzocchi dinner table. Tony's father, Joe, while sympathetic to many of the CP's issues, had no interest in joining. Uncle Mike and Tony's sister May didn't like the party at all.

Tony kept an open mind. He valued many of the party members he'd met, and he agreed with many of the CP's positions on war, civil rights, and union democracy. He also admired the New York City unions that were "close" to the CP, like District 65 of the Retail and Distributive Workers, the Furriers, and the Transit Workers Union. An objective observer would probably conclude that from 1948 to 1950, Tony was "running with the reds."

Along the way he gained an excellent view of the party's strategy and structure, its discipline, its habit of hero worship, and its utter naïveté. Although Tony loved Jerry and Ruth, he chose a different path.

Jerry, whose dad made teeth for a living, had grown up in an apolitical middle-class Jewish home in Flatbush. During the war, he was assigned to make teeth for soldiers at Washington, DC's, Walter Reed Hospital. "I saw these young guys come back with legs off, arms off. I always pulled war duty. And on my watch I've seen guys die—young people. They were Depression kids, mostly, so their general health was terrible."

In DC he got a closer look at society's divisions. "The racism was pretty obvious—the back of the bus, the colored water fountains and bathrooms. I mean, I saw black kids jump on a trolley to get a free ride without shoes on in the wintertime."

After the war, Jerry, like Tony, came back to family and friends who had shifted to the left. "My sister had some friends in Flatbush, and she was more progressive than me. My brother was also moving toward the left. And it's like wherever you went, there were leftists."

His sister introduced him to a Communist Party youth group. As a vet, Jerry was accorded automatic respect by the group. But, he said, "They were so intellectual. I didn't feel I was getting anything out of this." Then he heard of another lefty group in the Red Hook housing project. "They were more down-to-earth. There were a lot of kids coming from poorer families—they weren't so intellectual. Yet they had a couple of brilliant leaders of the group and they were doing things."

One of the things they did was create opportunities for Jerry to see a young woman named Ruth whom he'd spotted at the first meeting. One day, the whole group went to the Museum of Modern Art to see a Russian movie. Afterward, Jerry, his brother, and Ruth stood around talking until Ruth realized that her friends had already left. She raced to catch them at the subway, as Jerry and his brother headed the other way. Then, Jerry said, "I hear this *click, click, click*—her high-heeled shoes running toward us. She had missed her friends and didn't have any car fare. . . . At least, that's what she told us. So she joined us for lunch." And as Ruth remembered, "That was the beginning of our romance."

For Ruth, falling in love and participating in the communist youth group at Red Hook were intertwined. Her father, a poor Russian immigrant, was a member of the International Workers Order, a left-wing Jewish organization that in its heyday provided insurance for more than 180,000 workers. He wasn't a communist, but he read the *Daily Worker*. At first, that embarrassed his daughter. "When I had a date with a guy, and my father's *Daily Worker* was on the table, I used to hide it under a couch cushion," Ruth remembered. After World War II, her own dating habits swerved to the left. "When I was a teen and we were looking for guys, we were attracted to this group of people in the projects. The most attractive guys were the ones in this political group." Ruth could not resist the lure of the Young Communist League. "They were wonderful organizers—they were great people. And they were very inviting—low-key—no pressure."

Jerry, enrolled at City College, was growing restless. "I wanted to make a living. I wanted to get married. So I decided to stop going to college." His father urged him to learn the dental trade while working in his lab. Jerry enrolled in Kerpel, with tuition paid in full by the GI Bill. A year later, in 1948, Ruth and Jerry married and moved to Brooklyn Heights. They continued work with the Red Hook group and became active in the Henry Wallace for President campaign, a major CP cause. The Red Hook group also helped the CP attempt to build an integrated union on the Brooklyn docks to oppose the segregated locals dominated by mob-connected Anthony Anastasia. And wouldn't it be great if that street-wise Italian kid from dental school would help them?

IV

Tony followed Jerry and Ruth into the chaos of waterfront labor strife—part of the strike wave that washed over the United States at the end of the war. The US Bureau of Labor Statistics reported 4,985 work stoppages in 1946 involving 4.6 million workers, the largest number on record.[2] Strikes nearly ground New York to a halt.

The waterfront conflicts were particularly difficult because the rank-and-file longshoremen were striking against their own union officials, who used violence and corruption to stay in power. On October 1, 1945, Manhattan stevedores struck to protest a contract with the New York Shipping Association that had been negotiated by the International Longshoreman's Association's "president for life," Joseph P. Ryan. Ryan dominated the thirty-five-thousand-member ILA. But not completely. When the rank and file saw that the contract failed to address their demands about workload and the hiring system, they spread their wildcat strike throughout the city.

Since the 1930s, Ryan's ILA had been viewed widely as a company union in which, as historian Joshua Freeman wrote, "corruption and thuggery were widespread."[3] When the CIO started to organize a union that united seamen and longshoremen, Ryan told a congressional committee, "We went to the [shipowners] and said, 'Give us money; we are going to fight them.' We got the money and drove them back with bats where they belonged."[4] According to historian Bruce Nelson, Ryan was utterly corrupt:

> Ryan maintained his long tenure by employing some of the nation's most notorious gangsters as officials of the union; and he was shrewd enough to utilize his hoods with careful attention to ethnicity. Anthony "Big Bang" Anastasia and his brother Albert patrolled the Italian sections of the Brooklyn waterfront, while Owney Madden's Irish underworld "serviced" the ILA locals in Chelsea.[5]

To fight Ryan's ruthless leadership, wildcatting workers needed the help of more seasoned organizers—which in New York meant the CP. "At first, the strikers had no organization, no spokespeople, not even formal demands," Freeman wrote. "But with the help of the Communists—a dock-side presence particularly in Brooklyn—they soon formulated demands and selected a leadership."[6]

In Elia Kazan's *On the Waterfront* (1954), longshore workers resisted mob corruption through the courage of Terry Molloy, a broken-boxer-turned-longshoreman, and Father Barry, the reforming priest. But until the late 1940s, the Communist Party, not the church, led the fight for democratic unionism and against mob control on the docks.

While the Communist Party's union section maintained a "dockside presence" in Brooklyn, the Red Hook Young Communist League helped with leafleting. In 1948, Jerry and Ruth invited Tony to come along. It was Tony Mazzocchi's first foray into political organizing. He was twenty-two.

Tony's job was to leaflet the docks for reforms aimed at opening up jobs for black workers. Tony realized immediately that he brought something valuable to this effort. "The kid leading the thing was Jewish. I'm Italian, and this is the Brooklyn waterfront where all these Italians are working. There weren't any Jewish longshoremen." When the Anastasia brothers unleashed their goons to pummel the communist kids from Red Hook, Tony's experience came in handy. "I was from the streets. I knew when to pass out the leaflets and argue, and I knew when to run."

Tony ran from the thugs but not from his new friends. Through Ruth and Jerry, he got a peek at life inside the party. He saw firsthand how the party's leadership cult and its doctrinaire lines alienated even those who respected its positions on issues such as civil rights and union organizing. Through Ruth and Jerry, he also witnessed the strains and embarrassments of party life. In meetings they attended together, the Fines quickly noted Tony's resistance. "He was always clear thinking," Ruth said. "There was a lot of stupid stuff going on, and he could see through it."

Jerry recalled that when they sang the labor song "We Shall Not Be Moved," the party members sometimes added a verse honoring CP leader William Z. Foster: "'Foster is our leader / we shall not be moved.' But Tony wasn't a hero worshiper—he was uncomfortable with it."

For Jerry and Ruth, party life involved meeting after meeting. It became all-encompassing and pulled them away from family and nonparty friends. Tony was different. "Even though he certainly was our intellectual equal, if not more so in his own way, he never left his old friends on the corner," said Jerry. "He wasn't going to leave them because he was a Marxist or whatever at the time. And I did. I left a lot of guys. I couldn't stand them anymore because they were so conservative."

"I don't think Tony was ever as close to the party as we were," said Ruth. "And just the way he operated even before we knew him—he was always friends with the guys on the street. That was more fun. He never left them."

Tony also didn't take to the party's assigned readings and study-group-like discussions. "I don't remember Tony doing any of that," said Jerry.

Tony certainly enjoyed the attention he received from the communist activists. If Jerry had star status as a vet, Tony, the Italian working-class vet, was a mega-star. Still, he felt distant from the group. "All the discussions were very intellectual," he said. "They were talking Marxist jargon and I'm saying to myself, *They ain't going to organize shit.* Just their manner of speech alone—it was like they came from a different planet." On the other hand, the party was also "a social place where you met women. That was fun. But they all were college graduates. I was the only one who wasn't."

Tony didn't share many party members' blind adoration of the Soviet Union, though he admired aspects of the socialist state and never viewed it as a threat. Tony's father had often questioned the lack of freedom in the USSR, and feared Stalin as a dictator. This gave Tony pause for thought. But in the late 1940s, most militant trade unionists believed that anti-communism and Cold War jingoism were Truman concoctions designed to protect Europe's colonies and thwart socialist worker movements in Europe. They believed the Truman administration had caved in to right-wing Republicans and old-guard AFL labor officials who still hated the CIO. The real threats seemed to be coming from the right wing at home, not from Soviet designs overseas.

Jerry and Ruth showed little ambivalence about Russia. As Ruth put it, "We were Russophiles. . . . We felt the negative things were lies and distortions. We dismissed a lot of things that we should have looked at more critically."

Tony also didn't like the way the party treated its rank and file. Ruth and Jerry told him that they had once been charged with "white chauvinism" because they had brought food to a black comrade who'd lost his job after continually oversleeping. They should have picketed the employer instead of supplying the food, party leaders told them. They were ordered to do extra community work in Harlem to cure them of their "shortcomings." Tony wondered why the Fines put up with such abuse.

Said Ruth: "It was our life."

V

Tony's life, and the entire post–World War II labor movement, were shaped by American communism and anti-communism, the Cold War, and the massive purges of leftists from the labor movement. Tony himself faced plenty of red-baiting. But the effect was much greater than that: Tony's feel for politics and his nuanced strategic skills were all crafted for a labor movement that was shredded and then pasted back together by anti-communism. It calibrated his political radar.

From the books he read and from his childhood kitchen-table conversations, Tony had absorbed a good deal of the Communist Party's history and intuitively grasped the party's value and shortcomings. On the plus side, he knew that the party, since its founding after World War I, was at the core of much industrial labor organizing, especially during the dark days of the anti-labor 1920s. He also knew that its tireless work had helped spark labor's upsurge during the Depression, and that party organizers were central to the CIO's infrastructure.

Tony admired the CP's unemployment councils and racially integrated organizations. He knew from his uncle Lester that the CP was the champion of minority rights in America. And its organizers had extraordinary energy, as even the harshest anti-CP historians, such as Irving Howe and Lewis Cosner, acknowledged. They wrote:

> The main and new source of the CP strength in the CIO was the participation of thousands of its members in the organizing drives of the late thirties. . . . If there was dirty work to do, they were ready. If leaflets had to be handed out on cold winter mornings before an Akron rubber plant or a New York subway station, the party could always find a few volunteers. If someone had to stick his neck out within the plants, a Communist was available.[7]

Tony's deepest political impressions developed during the party's Popular Front period. In 1935, the Seventh World Congress of the Comintern (the Soviet-dominated international organization of national communist parties) had declared a new policy to build a popular front movement in coalition with all anti-fascist groups. For Tony and his family, this was the glorious period of "big tent" progressive politics. The CP infused thousands of anti-fascist organizations with new vitality. It supported Roosevelt. The CIO, full of communist organizers, blossomed. And communists worked to minimize left fissures and sectarian fights in the interests of unity against Hitler, Franco, and Mussolini and for the New Deal at home. The Mazzocchi family celebrated these events around their long kitchen table, and Tony gobbled it up.

Tony and family understood the downsides of the party as well. None of them could justify the CP's backing of the Moscow purge trials during the late 1930s. Soviet leader Joseph Stalin's cold-blooded kangaroo courts destroyed the lives of many of the most beloved heroes of the 1917 revolution and led to the deaths of tens of thousands. It was even harder to explain away the June 1939 pact between Hitler and Stalin—and the subsequent dismembering of Poland and Russian invasion of Finland. At home, the Popular Front collapsed with the news of the Nazi-Soviet pact. The CP allied with arch-conservative isolationists in America to oppose US military support for Britain against Hitler. Thousands left the party.

On June 22, 1941, a few days after Tony turned fifteen, the CP did a 180-degree flip when Hitler invaded the Soviet Union. Overnight the party embraced the war, with a patriotic fervor second to none, helping to sell war bonds, organizing blood donations, collecting scrap tin, and helping with civil defense. As Tony learned from his uncle Mike, the CP also promoted the war effort by opposing all work stoppages and supporting industrial speedup measures universally hated by workers. To Uncle Mike and many other union members, war or no war, the CP seemed to be in bed with the boss. The Mazzocchis watched in disbelief.

Through all of this, Tony's uncle Lester remained a party member, and Tony understood why. It provided a special kind of family, a safe haven for this closeted gay man. Besides, the Soviet Union was still viewed as a workers' state, the one place on earth where workers weren't subject to capitalist exploitation. Lester did not trust contrary evidence from the capitalist press, which often lied about the party and the Soviet Union. Tony wasn't quite sure what to think. As he put it, "Sometimes the criticisms seemed true, sometimes they didn't. I kept an open mind."

But his mind was made up about one thing: Political organizing in America had to meet the needs of working people here, not the interests of an international organization or a foreign power. Tony was a homespun radical.

For all the CP's faults, Tony knew that in many unions—like the longshoremen's—the party was the lone rank-and-file voice for democracy. And because CP members were so disciplined, they often out-organized their opponents, setting the tone and determining the outcome of many issues. The party's tightly knit structure, in combination with its members' deep commitment, allowed the CP to fight long, hard, and effectively. When the CP used its organizational muscle to confront management, it gained enormous support from the rank and file. Tony knew this didn't come just from party-enforced discipline. It came from the selfless commitment of comrades such as Jerry and Ruth Fine.

Tony was in the army when the CP reached its apex. As its numbers grew during the war years, the party gained respect and influence. It was everywhere, especially in New York City. Several major New York unions and government agencies had large Communist Party cadres. Communists formed community groups in every borough and virtually every neighborhood. Communists mingled with entertainers and politicians, many of whom were communists themselves. In 1941, the communist candidate Peter Cacchione was elected to city council from Brooklyn. In 1943, he was reelected by a larger margin and was joined on the council by communist Benjamin Davis Jr. from Manhattan.

Even the CP's idealization of Russia was not completely out of step with mainstream American views. Nearly everyone, from Roosevelt on down, understood that the war could not be won without the Soviets. The Red Army and the Allies were comrades in arms. In New York, Russia was practically the sixth borough. New Yorkers flocked to Russian folk dances, movies, and art.

This was the Russia whose valor so thrilled Ruth, Jerry, Tony's two sisters, and other young communists. Oh, it was good to be young and communist, and in love with Russia.

VI

Then came 1948 and Henry Wallace's campaign for president, a watershed event for the left. It was Tony Mazzocchi's first political campaign, and a last national hurrah for the CP. The campaign provided a critical political lesson for Tony: Watch out for Cold War liberals—the most dangerous red-baiters of all. After 1948, Tony came to believe that liberals, more than the far right, were destroying the American left.

For many progressives, including Tony's father, Henry Wallace at first seemed the perfect antidote to virulent anti-communism. Wallace was as American as a cornfield. He had founded and owned a large part of Pioneer Hybrid, which earned millions selling new strains of corn, many designed by Wallace himself. His father had served as secretary of agriculture under Harding, and Henry had served as the dynamic secretary of agriculture under Roosevelt in his first two terms before becoming FDR's vice president in 1940. Replaced on the 1944 FDR ticket by the Democratic Party's insider choice, Harry Truman, Wallace nevertheless continued to serve under Roosevelt and then under Truman as secretary of commerce—until he was fired for advocating greater cooperation with the Soviets.

Wallace believed in God, enlightened capitalism, full civil rights for black Americans, freedom of determination for colonial countries, and in the United Nations. He opposed the Cold War, the Marshall Plan, and loyalty oaths. Until his run for the presidency, he was one of the most admired men in America. But the campaign coincided with a seismic shift in America's political culture. The red scare gained traction during the 1946 off-year congressional elections. American industry, the Republicans, and southern Democrats linked together against their axis of evil: New Deal = Unions = Communism = Russia. The Republicans easily captured both houses of Congress in 1946 behind the slogan of fighting "Communism, Confusion and Chaos"—*confusion* meaning the wartime price controls that were still in effect, and *chaos* referring to the massive strike wave that rocked the nation after the war.

The new Congress immediately stuck it to workers, enacting the infamous Taft-Hartley bill, which stripped labor of significant rights and took aim at left-wing unionists. The bill excluded groups such as foremen and contractors from unionization. It also robbed labor of invaluable strike tools like the secondary boycott of struck goods. It enabled the mostly southern "right to work" states to keep limiting or denying union rights. Most problematic for leftists was Section 9(h), which required that if a union wanted to use the National Labor Relations Board (NLRB) (to, say, conduct a vote for union representation), each union officer had to file an annual affidavit declaring that he or she was not a member of the Communist Party.

Truman vetoed Taft-Hartley, but Congress easily overrode the veto. Labor and New Deal liberals were on the run.

Truman and an increasingly conservative State Department believed that the Soviet Union could not be trusted and should be contained. But the country was in no mood for renewed tensions. In 1947, people were more in tune with Henry Wallace, who argued, "The only way to defeat communism in the world is to do a better and smoother job of maximum production and optimum distribution. . . . Let's out-compete Russia in the most friendly spirit possible, for we must realize that militarily speaking, there could be no final victor in any armed conflict between our two great nations."[8]

In a September 1946 speech at Madison Square Garden, Wallace warned, "Make no mistake about it, the British imperialistic policy in the Near East alone, combined with Russian retaliation, would lead the United States straight to war unless we have a clearly defined and realistic policy of our own."[9]

Truman fired him. To sell his new Marshall Plan for Europe to a war-weary public, Truman believed he had to pump up fears of communism at home—a feat he accomplished masterfully. In just a few months, Congress went from opposing nearly all foreign aid to opening up the tap in the name of stopping the reds. The president also tried to outflank the right by issuing Executive Order No. 9385, establishing the Federal Employees Loyalty and Security Program, under which federal employees could lose their jobs if an anonymous source said they were or had been communists. Accused employees could not confront their accuser, making a satisfactory defense almost impossible. The federal executive order was replicated by states, cities, universities, and unions throughout the country.

Wallace knew that through the executive order, government power was being abused to create hysteria, and hysteria was being used to enhance government power. "Communist," he wrote in his diary, "is used so loosely nowadays that no one can say what the truth is. Anyone who is further to the left than you are—and whom you don't like—is a communist."[10]

Wallace's words were music to the ears of the beleaguered CP. They hoped he could turn the anti-communist tide by rallying support from non-communists in the CIO and in the liberal community (who already found Truman wanting). And at first, liberals and leftists objected to Truman's pell-mell attack on civil liberties and peace. But Wallace went one step too far. It was one thing to be the voice of moderation and peace; it was quite another to run against Truman for president. As he moved toward mounting a challenge under the banner of the new Progressive Party, the noncommunist labor and liberal communities turned on Wallace with a vengeance. They gladly did the work for Truman—a fact that Tony would never forget.

VII

Tony's father and sisters were big in the Wallace campaign, as were Ruth and Jerry Fine. But not Tony. For him, it was a modest extracurricular activity coming after a hard day at dental school. Nevertheless, the liberal-versus-communist dynamics of the campaign would have a direct effect on his imminent emergence as a labor leader.

During the campaign's early months, Wallace attracted huge crowds; some actually paid to hear him. Fearing Wallace's growing popularity, many liberals soon turned the knife on him—and Truman was quite content to let them do the stabbing. Liberals in the Wallace campaign felt the heat and fled, citing "communist involvement." Auto Workers president Walter Reuther called Wallace "a lost soul" and said, "It is tragic that he is being used by the Communists the way they have used so many other people." Hubert Humphrey, the Minneapolis mayor who was about to become a senator from Minnesota, and FDR Jr., soon to be a US congressman from New York, issued statements saying: "Irrespective of Mr. Wallace's intentions, the goals of his sponsors are clear. They hope to divide progressives, create national confusion, and insure the triumph of . . . isolationism in 1948. They believe the achievement of these aims will serve the world interests of the international communist movement."[11] Repeatedly, they called for Wallace to disassociate himself from the communists. When on principle he refused to banish the CP from his campaign, they accused him of being an apologist for Stalin.

To oppose the Progressive Party, liberals and labor leaders—including Walter Reuther, theologian Reinhold Neibuhr, Hubert Humphrey, Eleanor Roosevelt, and Harvard professors Arthur Schlesinger Jr. and John Kenneth Galbraith—formed the Americans for Democratic Action. Their goal: routing communists and communist sympathizers from public life. The ADA's verbal rapiers sliced Wallace and his supporters to bits, setting the tone for harsher actions. In Evansville, Indiana, Wallace aides were slugged by surging mobs. A local college professor was fired for appearing on stage with Wallace. Wallace was barred from speaking at the University of Iowa, his home state. He was pelted with eggs; in Missouri his microphone was repeatedly cut off and hecklers drowned out his speech. In the South and in Michigan, Wallace supporters were arrested. Newspapers published the names of people who signed petitions to get Wallace on the ballot so that they could be hounded. A social studies book was banned in one school because it had a chapter on the former vice president. And even in liberal New York City, a judge ruled that during a child custody case, he would take into account whether or not the parent was a Wallace supporter.

The campaign opened up a destructive chasm in the labor movement. Truman and his anti-communist crusade depended on the support of the CIO, while Wallace depended on the CP and CP-led unions within the CIO. If the CIO destroyed those unions, Wallace would collapse. Ultimately, the Wallace campaign touched off a mass purge from the CIO of communists and alleged communist-controlled unions.

The opening salvo was fired at the CIO convention of October 1947, when its president, Philip Murray—who was also president of the United Steelworkers of America—urged the CIO to "operate only within the major political parties." Unions that violated Murray's edict could be expelled from the CIO. Murray knew that the CP was committed to Wallace, and his dictum was an attempt to isolate communists and then purge them from the CIO. An open season on communists ensued.

In January 1948, the CIO National Executive Council made support for the Marshall Plan and opposition to the Wallace campaign the litmus test for CIO membership. When CP-oriented unions and the CP continued to support Wallace, Murray moved to crush them. The CIO created an irresistible set of incentives to encourage the ouster of communists. Ambitious anti-communist union staff and elected leaders could quickly climb up the ladder by purging would-be communists above them or by starting new rival anti-communist unions. Tony watched as labor wiped out many of its most committed activists.

Truman was the enabler, par excellence. As soon as Murray began purging communists (and those accused of being communists), the Truman administration moved to persecute them under the new Taft-Hartley Act. If communist labor officials signed the act's anti-communist oath but retained party membership secretly, they could be prosecuted for perjury. If they refused to sign, their union would be denied rights and protections offered by the National Labor Relations Board. The union would not appear on the ballot during NLRB union recognition elections, enabling other unions to replace it.

Tony saw this unfold in New York, home of the most powerful communist-led unions. Mike Quill, the blusterous leader of the militant Transport Workers Union, broke from his communist allies and drummed them out of the union. Anti-communists and communists battled in the New York Newspaper Guild.[12] Joe Curran, the head of the National Maritime Union, switched sides to prevent being defeated by anti-communists within the union.

At the family boardinghouse in Blairstown, which Uncle Lester populated with leftists, Tony heard all about how New York unions twisted, turned, and fractured. National and local unions were breaking apart over the Taft-Hartley loyalty oath. Unions that had once worked together in the CIO now raided each other. Locals, fearing the loss of official recognition from employers, walked away from their left-wing parent unions. Mazzocchi family friends and relatives were hauled before government committees and blackballed from their jobs.

Stalin's geopolitical maneuvers only inflamed American anti-communism and further isolated Americans who pressed for cooperation and peaceful coexistence. First Stalin set off a coup in Czechoslovakia. Then, in June 1948, as Truman and Wallace geared up for the fall election, Stalin blockaded Berlin, which lay deep within the Soviet sector of Germany. Truman responded with the Berlin Airlift. By summer, hundreds of planes were flying food and fuel to Berliners in the city's French, British, and US-controlled sectors. Truman connected the dots for American voters: Stalin was the new Hitler, and Wallace was his enabler. As historians John C. Culver and John Hyde put it:

> Everything had turned on its head. The quiet son of Iowa soil had been transformed in the public mind into a wild-eyed fanatic bent on destroying the American way of life. . . . The ardent defender of World War II had become the Chamberlain-like appeaser. The

> deeply religious grandson of a Presbyterian minister had become an apostle of godless totalitarianism.[13]

On election night, Truman received 303 electoral votes, beating Republican Thomas Dewey in the popular vote by twenty-four million to twenty-two million. South Carolina governor Strom Thurman, running as a Dixiecrat (a split from the Democrats over civil rights), received thirty-nine electoral votes and 1.1 million popular votes. Wallace received no electoral votes and slightly fewer votes than the Dixiecrats. Nearly half of his votes came from New York, costing Truman the state. But it was a crushing defeat for the communist-oriented left.

According to pollster George Gallup, "As many as one-third of the people who said in late October that they were going to vote for Mr. Wallace shifted to Mr. Truman during the final ten days of the campaign."[14] At the dinner table on election night, Tony learned that his dad was among them. Joe Mazzocchi, who six months earlier had strongly supported Wallace, could not pull the Progressive Party lever. As Tony vividly recalled, "He told us he just couldn't do it. In the end he feared the Republicans more. He thought Truman was better. For him, Wallace was a wasted vote. I was twenty-two, and for me, it was my first vote for president. And I lost."

Tony lost and moved on. Wallace lost his good name but remained a multimillionaire thanks to his ever-expanding Pioneer seed business. The CP lost nearly all of its credibility, never to recover. All of this occurred before Joe McCarthy began his hunt for communists, before Chiang Kai-shek lost to Mao in China, before the Soviets got the bomb, and before the outbreak of the Korean War. Truman, the ADA liberal community, CIO leaders, and Stalin created McCarthyism before McCarthy himself had appeared on the scene.

For Tony, the up-and-coming radical organizer, the campaign held a lesson. At a time when daring to dissent meant facing threats against livelihood and reputation, you had to think very carefully about political strategy. From here on, Tony knew that he needed to be very smart about his left politics, or be crushed like Henry Wallace. Or like Jerry and Ruth Fine, who soon would be asked to lose their identities and go underground.

VIII

Even after Wallace's pummeling, Tony remained intrigued by third-party politics. Again, New York became his classroom. In the summer of 1949, after Tony had completed his two-year program at Kerpel Dental School, Jerry's father offered him a good job in his small Brooklyn lab. Although such jobs were scarce, Tony instead suggested that it go to his neighborhood friend Nicky, who had also just graduated.

Tony didn't want to make teeth. He wanted to become a political activist. So rather than continue the demanding technical work of denture fabrication, he took a mindless job that his brother found for him. "It was in a place called Airex in Queens—makes fishing reels," Tony said. "So I went there, working for some nut. I didn't know anything about fishing. It was a stupid job, and they had some racket union there. But there wasn't any heavy sweating."

With plenty of energy left at the end of the day, Tony again tried his hand at third-party politics. This time, his candidate was Vito Marcantonio, a radical East Harlem congressman who was running for mayor of New York City. The Mazzocchi family greatly admired Marcantonio because, like them, he was militant, pro-labor, and Italian. And he was as rooted in his community as they were in Bensonhurst.

A first-generation Italian, Marcantonio was a protégé of Fiorello La Guardia, the feisty labor lawyer who became an aggressive pro-labor Republican congressman and liberal New York mayor—another Mazzocchi family favorite. After serving as an assistant district attorney, Marcantonio in 1934 ran for Congress from the left, promising: "I will prove by my actions that the cause of the organized worker is the cause of Vito Marcantonio."[15]

His word was good, and then some. In his first term, Marcantonio became a champion of the unemployed and showed no fear of working with the Communist Party. This proved to be a major problem during his bid for Congress in 1936, however, when he, along with most Republicans, fell before the Roosevelt landslide. Marcantonio was saved by the creation of the American Labor Party, which provided a new ballot line for Roosevelt that was more acceptable to New York unionists than the Tammany Hall–tainted Democrats. The new party also provided Marcantonio a path back into Congress as he turned the ALP into his personal electoral machine. In

1940, he not only gained its nomination, but managed to run unopposed in the Republican primary as well. For good measure, he also challenged his opponent in the Democratic primary. He subsequently won his congressional seat every two years up through the 1946 elections.

As the anti-communist crusade mounted in 1947–1948, the New York State legislature passed the Wilson-Paluka Act, which forced candidates to get permission from party bosses to enter primaries of multiple parties. The measure was aimed at Marcantonio: It restricted him to the ALP line, which the press increasingly attacked as "Communist-dominated."[16] Nevertheless, in the anti-communist electoral year of 1948, Marcantonio won again.

Tony watched and learned. Most instructive was how Marcantonio carefully serviced his base while also staking out radical positions. Not only did he care for "workers" as a political category—he cared for his constituents personally. By some estimates he met one-on-one with more than twenty-thousand constituents each year. And he didn't just fix tickets or find jobs. He backed rent strikes. He battled to get his constituents immigration papers, welfare allotments, housing, legal help, veterans' benefits, and medical attention. He demanded that his staff follow up on every case—and pity the aide who let one slide.

The working-class Italian and Puerto Rican immigrants who made up the bulk of Marcantonio's district welcomed his service and—most of all—his respect. Marc, as he was called, earned their admiration day after day, and they would never turn their backs on him. Consequently, Marc's voters just didn't care about his relationship to the Communist Party. They didn't care that he opposed the Marshall Plan, promoted cooperation with Russia, and supported public control over housing, public utilities, and health care. They trusted that what he wanted, he wanted for them. And if he wanted to run for mayor blasting the two-party system and big business, more power to him.

And blast he did. Marcantonio called for an end to the "jungle law of atomic diplomacy." He decried persecution of CP leaders under the 1940 Smith Act, saying, "The price for free thinking for peace and against war is imprisonment." He charged that the two major parties were "in active partnership as the twin instruments of big business in the drive toward fascism and war." He concluded a massive Madison Square Garden rally with: "To hell with Wall Street and to hell with the politicians! Viva Il Popola Della Citta Di New York."[17]

As Marcantonio captured Tony's imagination, the American Labor Party captured Tony. As soon as he volunteered, he was promoted to be chair, at age twenty-three, of the Brooklyn Italian-American Committee for Marcantonio. The job wasn't quite as glamorous as it sounded, said Tony. "All we did was move around the sound truck and give leaflets out."

Tony saw that it was the worst of times for a left-wing campaign. The anti-communist atmosphere had only deepened since Wallace had been trounced. In the winter of 1948–1949 the communist Chinese offensive nearly destroyed the armies of Chiang Kai-shek, leading to the evacuation of US military forces and advisers. In the fall, Mao Tse-tung proclaimed his new People's Republic of China, confining Chiang to the island of Taiwan. And the four-year US monopoly on the atomic bomb ended with the detection of a successful explosion by the Soviet Union. The Republicans now saw a chance to regain control of the anti-communist agenda, which Truman had so masterfully manipulated. There were more congressional investigations, more state and city loyalty tests and oaths.

Enter Wisconsin senator Joe McCarthy, leading the hunt for communists under—and in—every bed.

Some of Tony's more doctrinaire Marcantonio co-campaigners were oblivious to the anti-communist hurricane. As Tony playfully recalled,

> I had this crazy Yugoslavian guy with me at a grocery store whose owner was very sympathetic to Marcantonio. And the Yugoslavian was arguing against the current mayor, and the grocery store owner says, "You got proof of that?" And the Yugoslavian says, "Yeah." And he pulls out the *Daily Worker*. The owner says, "That's the communist *Daily Worker*!" My partner responds with "Yeah, but it's true, you know."
>
> I took our guy aside and said "Are you crazy?" He was as politically dumb as all the party guys who were out there campaigning for Marc. So they threw us out of the store.

Marcantonio lost the election, though despite the red scare he managed a very strong showing of 356,423 votes—almost 14 percent of the total. For

Tony, the experience was sobering. It would take another thirty years before he seriously revisited third-party politics.

IX

Still in search of a political career, Tony stumbled into what became a famous anti-communist riot. For several years, civil rights organizations with strong CP ties had held summer concerts featuring Paul Robeson, the African American actor, singer, and former world-class athlete, who also was a prominent party member. In the summer of 1949, the concert, which also headlined folksinger Pete Seeger, was scheduled for picnic grounds in Peekskill, New York, about twenty miles north of New York City. Howard Fast, the novelist and CP journalist, would chair the event, a fund-raiser for the Civil Rights Congress.

A mob of enraged local vigilantes, many wearing American Legion hats, mobilized to pound those setting up the event. According to Fast, they yelled, "We'll finish Hitler's job. Fuck you white niggers! Give us Robeson! We'll string that big nigger up!"[18]

State troopers finally arrived in sufficient numbers to halt the riot, but not before many had been injured. The concert was canceled for that night. But the organizers, desperate for dignity, tried again. As historian Joshua Freeman wrote,

> Under pressure from its black cadre, the Communist Party resolved to return to Peekskill. Left leaders recruited hundreds of guards armed with baseball bats from the Furriers, Local 65 and other unions. On September 4 a crowd of twenty thousand gathered to hear Robeson at a golf course near Peekskill. The concert itself went off without a hitch, but as the concertgoers left the grounds along a narrow, uphill road, a rock-throwing crowd unrestrained by police, ambushed them. At the concert site, civilians and police attacked the remaining union guards. By the time the riot ended, dozens of cars and buses had had their windows broken or had been overturned and 150 concertgoers required medical attention.[19]

Tony was one of the recruited guards:

> I remember being approached by a District 65 guy, and they got me a ride up there. The legion could only turn out about a thousand people. We had a massive group, in three rows around the entire perimeter. And we had a lot of vets.
>
> After the concert, the legion got the bus drivers to leave without their passengers. When the drivers left, I jumped into a bus—I figured I'd drive it myself. And a cop says, "You got a license to drive this bus?' I said "No," and they dragged me out. They took away our transportation to leave after the concert.
>
> So Leon Straus, who was with the fur workers and who I think had been an attorney in the Air Corps during the war, decided everyone had better stay together. There was this camp about five miles away from the concert, and we told the cops that we were all going to go there together. The cops tried to stop us. And we said, "We're gonna go. And anyone gets in our way, there's going to be a fight." And the legion got scared off.

"For the Communists and their backers," wrote Freeman, "the concert had been a cathartic refusal to cower in the face of their enemies, a moment of brave determination remembered and recounted in the years to come. But it also demonstrated the frightening potential for violence and vigilantism by a Negro-hating, red-hating, Jew-bating citizenry led by respected organizations, unchecked by state authority."[20]

Tony understood that the Peekskill concert had been a CP event, but he noted that many of those attending—and standing up to the thugs—were unaffiliated rank-and-file workers from unions like District 65 and the Fur and Leather Workers.

By the end of 1949, it was the idea of building a strong union—not the party—that appealed to Tony. The apple had fallen not far from the tree: "My father was always talking union. I wanted to be involved in the union, too." Any union would do.

Tony's family supplied the contacts. His sisters still had friends in the party, and so did his uncle Lester. "It was all around me," he said. "My sisters were active. And there were always CPers up in Blairstown." In an all-white rural area of New Jersey, Lester did not hesitate to bring CP members, black and white, including interracial couples. "One guy was trying to get me a job in the Fur and Leather Workers," Tony recalled. "Good thing I never got that job, since the union disappeared."

Another leftist labor contact who vacationed there tried to get Tony a coveted job in the Brooklyn Gas Company. "But see," said Tony, "I had to take a test to get hired. The questions about electrical wiring were no big deal—but the mathematics test I flunked. The guy said, 'I can't help you. You have to pass this fundamental test to get the job.'"

It became clear to Tony that the only way into the labor movement would be through a shop that had the same entrance requirements as the hammer-and-nail classes in Shallow Junior High. As he put it: "I needed to find a place where I didn't have to take a test—where they'd take you as long as you were warm."

X

To District 65, Tony was more than warm.

District 65 had started as a local union of wholesale and warehouse workers within the Retail, Wholesale and Department Store Union (RWDSU). But in August 1948, the national union ordered all its locals to comply with Taft-Hartley. Several New York locals responded by disaffiliating. In 1950, thirty thousand workers formed District 65, making it the largest left-leaning union in New York City, with a union headquarters so big it even had its own nightclub. For a twenty-four-year-old bachelor eager to join the labor movement, this was the hottest spot in town.

The union's leaders wanted Tony to be a "colonizer"—get into a shop, form a cadre of progressive workers, and then bring the shop into District 65. "Milt Reverby, one of the vice presidents of District 65, thought he could tutor me," Tony recalled. But they weren't talking about organizing the unorganized. Rather, they wanted Tony to help raid an anti-communist CIO union, the United Gas, Coke and Chemical Workers, which had a local at Helena Rubinstein Cosmetics Company in Long Island City, Queens. They hoped Tony would take over the local and bring it into District 65.

On May 1, 1950, precisely seven years after he had enlisted in the army,

Tony went to work at Rubinstein. He figured if he could make it through the company's thirty-day probationary period, he'd have the chance to build the kind of union the Mazzocchis could be proud of.

But Tony also wanted to stand up for peace and against the Cold War. So on Memorial Day 1950, he joined Jerry and Ruth one last time in a harmless political prank for peace—one that almost cost Tony his job, his personal freedom, and his career in the labor movement.

The year 1950 was another bad one for US-Soviet relations and American communists. Joseph McCarthy, who had recently been voted the worst senator by the press corps of his home state of Wisconsin, found a new issue to rescue his career. On February 9, the senator delivered his infamous speech charging that the State Department was harboring communists. He waved a piece of paper while declaring that he had "here in my hand" the names of 205 "known communists" in the State Department, a list he never revealed. Soon Joe McCarthy took over the witch hunt and magnified its destructiveness.

Already Alger Hiss, formerly a well-respected State Department officer, had been accused by Whittaker Chambers of being a communist and convicted of perjury in a New York court. Klaus Fuchs, a scientist who had worked to help build the first atomic bomb, had been arrested in London on charges of conveying high-level secrets to the Soviets. Two of Fuchs's accomplices, Harry Gold and David Greenglass, were arrested in New York.

Tony's political radar should have warned him that this was not an auspicious time to paint peace signs on public property.

It was the eve of the Memorial Day parade in Brooklyn. "We met in someone's basement," Ruth Fine said. "I remember talking about this plan—of painting PEACE on the line of march." The target would be the small version of the Arc de Triomphe that stands at Grand Army Plaza on the edge of Brooklyn's Prospect Park. The plan was part of the CP's coordinated effort to promote the Stockholm Peace Pledge, which called for the end of the use of nuclear weapons. (It had collected more than two and a half million pledge signatures nationwide.[21]) The party provided guidance for the PEACE-painting effort. Said Ruth, "There was this plan. You didn't have to go along with it if you didn't want to or anything like that. But it sounded like the right thing to do."

Around midnight, four carloads of people arrived at Grand Army Plaza.

After writing PEACE on the statue and on the sidewalk, the graffitists went to Jerry and Ruth's apartment. Later, some in the group, including two Italian immigrants who had been partisans during the war and two New York City teachers, wanted to go back to see the completed job. Tony asked the four to drop him off at the subway station. "They had to go back to admire their work?" Tony said later. "No street smarts."

Unfortunately, a late-night dog walker had spotted the protesters as they painted and had ID'd the car now being driven by the returning party. The police stopped the car and arrested the passengers. Tony had already been left at the subway.

"It killed their lives," said Tony.

Part of the problem was timing. On June 25, 1950, just before the protesters' court hearing, the Cold War turned hot: Communist troops from North Korea charged into South Korea to capture Seoul. By June 30, the United States was fully committed to the war.[22]

A week later, a super-patriotic judge who presided over the protesters' case treated the charges as though they constituted treason. The two partisans, who had fought against the Germans during the war, were deported immediately. The two teachers, George and Rose Daitsman, were fired. They, along with a third American from the Brewery Workers Union, were charged with a felony—malicious mischief—and jailed for one year.

Once again, Tony had been saved by his education on the street. As he put it half a century later, "If I'd been caught, we wouldn't be having this conversation right now. I'd probably be selling used cars."

Jerry and Ruth were never implicated in the caper. But later, they would suffer greatly for their loyalty to the Communist Party. Leaders asked Ruth and Jerry to give up their identities and become part of the network of anonymous safe houses for fugitive party leaders who had been targeted under the Smith Act. Jerry and Ruth would have no part of it.

"It was the worst scenario that I could think of," Jerry said. "Changing your whole being and setting up somewhere in an apartment so that second-string leaders who weren't in jail could come and stay."

Instead the couple moved to Schenectady, New York, where Jerry could work in the giant General Electric facility represented by a CP-friendly local of the United Electrical Workers. "The party was then turning its face to the working class, and they wanted people to get involved in industry," Jerry said. The Fines reasoned that if Truman propelled the world into a nuclear war over Korea, they and their newborn might be safer in Schenectady than in New York City. "I remember *The New York Times* had a drawing of bodies piled up along the Hudson River, if a nuclear war broke out," said Jerry.

Going to work in a big shop like GE was considered prestigious in the CP. "It's like most people today talk about money," said Jerry. "Back then, being a labor organizer was a high calling."

But the anti-red crusade was more intense in Schenectady than in New York City—especially at GE. Shortly before the Fines arrived, government investigative committees had held public meetings aimed at ousting the communist leaders of the local United Electrical Workers union at GE. Also before the Fines arrived, the FBI had marked them. Jerry was blacklisted, and GE refused to hire him. Instead, he went from factory to factory, always fired before the end of the probationary period. "I filled in the gaps with dental work," said Jerry. "Good thing I had that training."

FBI agent Robert Murchison periodically visited the Fines. His men would take pictures of the family from parked cars. The Fines were afraid to be seen with party members, and so became increasingly isolated.

"Ruth had an especially hard time," Jerry said. "I tried bringing some friends home from work, but I hardly made friends at work, since I'd only be there a month at the most."

After a year of job-hopping, the siege seemed to lift. "I got a job over in Rensselaer at a chemical plant, and by that time things had mellowed out." Finally Jerry began to realize some of the dream that had lured him north. His co-workers elected him steward. "They put me up—and I actually won. So that was like everything I wanted to do."

But things were not going so well for Ruth. The party was falling apart and, she said, "I felt tainted. I was contaminated." She was asked to run for the board of the local NAACP. She tried to decline, knowing that the FBI would intervene. But "I was prevailed upon to run, so my name was on the slate. And then I get a call from the guy who had pressured me to run asking me to decline. He'd been visited."

Even more sadly, Ruth learned that her taint could spread and hurt others. A friend from the local League of Woman Voters, who knew nothing about Ruth's CP background, was married to a GE worker. One day, said Ruth, the couple "came bursting into our house, distraught. Her husband's department was being transferred to the South. Every time they were transferred, they had to undergo another security clearance. But this time they were denied clearance because of their association with us. Imagine how I felt. I was always afraid of hurting other people's future. But I'm glad it didn't hurt Tony."

XI

Tony would not be hounded like the Fines, in part because conditions in the labor movement had already begun to change. As he went to work at Helena Rubinstein in May 1950, left-leaning unions like District 65 were moving toward reconciliation with the anti-communist CIO. The anti-communists were in full command of the labor movement, and the CP unionists had little choice but to accept that primacy.

Still, Tony's association with known communists and his work for Wallace, Marcantonio, and District 65 would later lead some of his critics to question whether he himself was a communist. Tony flatly denied that he ever joined the CP or had any interest in doing so.

After repeated Freedom of Information requests, the FBI claimed unequivocally that it did not have now, nor did it ever have a Tony Mazzocchi file. But perhaps this begs a larger question. Was Tony, at age twenty-four, nevertheless a communist with a small *c*?

Tony would laugh at any effort to put him in such a tidy box. Although he would never turn his back on his CP friends and relatives, he said he didn't want any part of "all these sectarian groups hassling each other." Asked in his later years if he still believed in socialism, Tony would reply, "Socialism's a great idea—somebody should try it sometime." For him, none of the forms of state socialism in existence met his ideals for openness, freedom, and democracy. Besides, he argued, any kind of "socialism" won in the United States would have to be uniquely American. And that was something that hadn't been invented yet.

Tony, like so many CIO activists, believed in the ideal of socialism. But formal Marxism and its terminology were far too doctrinaire for him. "We did have a lot of discussions about what a just society would look like," he said, "and whether it would be a socialist society or otherwise. I don't think any of us thought that was even in the cards. I think most of us thought we would democratize this society—you know, social democracy. I don't think there was any secret about that."

By today's standards, both the communists (big and little *C*) of the 1940s and 1950s as well as most of the CIO's anti-communists would look like Marxists. Marxism provided unions with a framework for understanding destructive features of laissez-faire capitalism. During the 1930s, people frequently questioned whether capitalism's production for profit could fulfill basic human needs and avoid devastating depressions. You'd need ideological blinders to ignore the possibility that our economic system might be fundamentally flawed.

To correct those flaws, many reformers wanted to experiment with publicly owned utilities, like the Tennessee Valley Authority. Many wondered if basic industries such as oil should be nationalized. Most Americans wanted (and may still want) universal public programs to provide affordable housing, free higher education, and universal health care. These beliefs were shared by a much wider slice of the population than the CP roster, or even the roster of those who called themselves socialists. The New York of Tony's youth was alive with these possibilities.

By the time he began working at Rubinstein in 1950, neither the CP unions nor their anti-communist foes planned to challenge the basic system of production—at least not anytime soon. The CP unions, according to historian Freeman, "shared with . . . liberal opponents a commitment to increased productivity and hierarchal workplace relations, unlike the World War I era left, which challenged the fundamental social structure of industry." As a result, reconciliation was easier. "Popular Front unionists could be welcomed back to the House of Labor after often-superficial rituals of renunciation because of a shared belief in progress through rationality, technology and production."[23]

Mazzocchi, as it turned out, would become far more radical than the CP, rejecting the "shared belief" about the inherent desirability of modern production techniques and ever-increasing productivity. His brush with heavy manual labor convinced him that the good life required something beyond traditional work. Slowly, that sense would crystallize into a stinging critique of the left's obsession with "jobs, jobs, jobs." Mazzocchi would later apply his version of radicalism to anticipate a different kind of contradiction of capitalism: He believed the clash of capital against nature (as in global warming or environmental health)—not just a clash over economic resources—would force systemic change.

Tony was not a communist, but he did share one trait with them, which Freeman described well: "Far more than their labor and working class rivals, the reds considered themselves capable of anything and everything."[24]

For Tony, the world could be shaped, like clay teeth. Always, he believed that profound social change was possible: "After the war, I was conscious that big things could change," he said. "A lot of us thought that major changes could take place in a relatively short time. We thought that it could be a much more democratic society. It could be a society that would live in peace, and that people's lives would be enhanced: that people could be housed, people could be fed, people could have their health care taken care of. That vision of society was foremost in our minds. We thought it was achievable—and not in a long period of time."

Those goals and the confidence to achieve them would never leave Tony. He began his trade union life at Helena Rubinstein convinced that labor could become again a transformative movement.

Communists were often accused of being unpatriotic—of caring more about the Soviet Union than about the United States. Their critics charged that they showed too little respect for democratic rights and freedom. And communists often were depicted as manipulative and deceitful.[25]

Perhaps Tony largely eluded the "communist" label because he bore no resemblance to this image of a communist. Not only did he fight for his country in World War II, but, more importantly, he was profoundly democratic. He would never veer from his strong belief in, and practice of, rank-and-file democracy in the workplace and the country at large. And in every way, he was in love with freedom, both personal and political.

Unlike many middle-class radicals, Tony could not be seen as a pretender. He never had the slightest need or inclination to reject his family and friends, and he never had to purge himself of class privileges or bourgeois attitudes or racism. He never had a shred of doubt about which side he was on, and for whom he would fight. His connection to working people was innate, natural, immediate, and unstudied. He was them.

The precocious kid who loved to talk politics with the grown-ups; the dropout who became a natural leader for the toughs; the army private who voraciously read, and witnessed the Holocaust; the manual laborer who hated monotony; the vet who learned how to fix teeth; the Henry Wallace supporter with a feel for debate; the chairman of Italians for Marcantonio who learned the real meaning of servicing your base; the Peekskill guard who (despite his small size) would never fear picket duty; the boy who knew when to fight and when to run—Tony would use all this experience and more as he sought to build a model union at Helena Rubinstein.

FOUR

Infiltrator

On May 1, 1950, Tony Mazzocchi hopped on the subway in Brooklyn, rode through Manhattan and over the East River on the Queensborough Bridge to the 23rd and Ely Avenue station in Long Island City, Queens. He walked two blocks toward the river to the two-story white brick Helena Rubinstein factory on 43rd Avenue. He filled out a form in the personnel office and was sent up to the second floor, where a young man with piercing blue eyes handed him a new work uniform.

The history and future of American labor converged in that quick transaction. The uniform was an artifact of successful class struggle—in 1944, the War Labor Board had ruled in favor of the union and ordered that Helena Rubinstein had to supply and launder one shirt a week for each male employee.[1]

The blue-eyed man was Richard "Mac" McManus, a twenty-year-old worker who would become Tony's lifelong friend and top lieutenant. As he escorted Tony to his workstation in the finishing department, Mac gave a quick tour of the plant. The facility ran multiple production lines. Rubinstein shampoos in sixteen- and fourteen-ounce bottles sped along one conveyor at better than a hundred per minute. Other lines carried Rubinstein cologne, rouge and lipstick, face cream, hand cream, and their best-selling Town and Country cream—which came in small, flat-shaped bottles with the heft of solid glass.

The shop employed four hundred union members, whose jobs were defined by gender. Approximately three hundred women worked on the assembly lines, while a hundred or so men did the heavy lifting, since the company did not yet have forklifts. Most of the men worked in receiving and shipping, where raw materials entered and finished product left the facility. A handful worked loading bottles onto the line and moving the product after it came off. That's where Mac escorted Tony, who for the next year would mindlessly lift the loaded boxes of new cosmetic products away from the end of the line—eight hours a day, five days a week, plus overtime. Neither math nor grammar required.

The workers who ran this ordinary assembly line (and were run by it) had no idea they were about to embark on a grand voyage into radical unionism. Most of the workers were white Catholics. Rubinstein's management thought they would be more respectful of authority and less likely to wage a strike—like the bitter one in 1941 that had brought the union in.

At first glance, strikes and workforce profiling seemed at odds with the liberal reputation of Madam Helena Rubinstein, the woman who had built the company from the ground up. Born of Jewish parents in Poland in 1871, she moved at age eighteen to Melbourne, Australia. Within two years, she had started a cosmetics business around one simple product—face cream. At a time when women were a rarity in business, she adeptly expanded her company to London, Paris, and, in 1912, New York. She became a multimillionaire and a major patron of the arts, and in 1953 set up a foundation to support women in going to college and pursuing nontraditional careers. "My fortune comes from women and should benefit them and their children, to better their quality of life," she said.[2] She favored liberal reformers like FDR and Fiorello La Guardia, and liked to believe that her workers were treated with respect. It pained her when they claimed otherwise. When "her" workers joined United Mine Workers District 50, the John L. Lewis/CIO catchall union, Madam Rubinstein was shocked. When they actually struck in October 1941, biographer Maxine Fabe claimed:

> Helena fumed at their "ingratitude," and turned a deaf ear on their demands as long as she could. But not all *that* deaf an ear. "What are they chanting?" she would whisper to her secretary, her "Little Girl," as she called her. "Run down and see."[3]

Madam and her managers brought in strikebreakers and created a company union to undermine the real one. But the strikers, led by Fred Hamilton and Jack Curran, blocked "the scabs" from entering the plant. George Roach, who later became one of Tony's key aides, remembered it vividly: "My two aunts worked at Rubinstein when the strike broke out. They would greet the scabs in the subway station and swing their purses at them. The purses were filled with rocks."[4]

Rocks flew around the picket line as well. But although mounted police monitored the line to protect the strikebreakers, Mayor La Guardia had barred the police from carrying clubs or guns. The strikers held out for seventeen long winter weeks. Eventually they secured union recognition and a contract, much to the chagrin of Helena Rubinstein.

United Mine Workers president and CIO leader John L. Lewis was enormously satisfied. The victory gave District 50 a major presence in the growing cosmetics and chemical industries in the New York area. But soon Lewis, like Madam Rubinstein, would lose his grip on these workers, setting in motion a drama of betrayal and revenge that had everything to do with the arrival at the company of a young Italian American vet. So how did Tony Mazzocchi land a job at Rubinstein? And why was he really there?

II

Tony's entry into the Rubinstein local union was intimately connected with the rise and fall of the communists within the United Gas, Coke and Chemical Workers Union (called Gas-Coke). Gas-Coke had broken away from United Mine Workers District 50 after Lewis, a vehement isolationist, opposed Roosevelt and the US involvement in the war in Europe. But the CIO leadership as well as the Communist Party (eventually) backed Roosevelt and the war effort, forcing Lewis out of the CIO. At that point Gas-Coke, which included the Rubinstein workers, received a new charter from the CIO and started its own union.

Charles Doyle, the popular Gas-Coke leader from the Buffalo area, was a major hero of this new union and an outspoken leftist either very near or actually in the Communist Party. In the dark days after the German invasion of Russia, many unions worked closely with CP-friendly activists who zealously supported the war effort. In Gas-Coke, leftists like Doyle and Fred Hamilton, who helped organize the Rubinstein local, were key to the union's organizing efforts—and its survival. That Gas-Coke held its 1942 founding convention in Doyle's home area of Niagara Falls signaled the left's prominence in the new union. Convention delegates passed resolutions condemning racial discrimination; supporting Roosevelt's Fair Employment Practices Committee; praising the Pittsburgh Pirates for hiring

Negro minor-league baseball players; and urging that women be promoted to labor leadership. Another resolution called on the Allies to open a second front in Western Europe, echoing the plea from the beleaguered Soviet Union.[5] Not only did the CP/left platform prevail at the convention, but several CP-friendly leaders, including Doyle, were elected to the national executive board.

To survive, Gas-Coke needed to win a series of battles against John L. Lewis's well-financed District 50. The most ferocious and significant battle was in Doyle's own Niagara Falls: Which union would represent the three thousand workers at the Carborundum Corporation, a maker of abrasives? After a series of brawls, the issue was settled with two NLRB elections: Workers rejected Lewis and stayed with Gas-Coke. Doyle was the hero of the hour.

Doyle's star rose even higher with the rapid growth of Gas-Coke's District 2 in western New York. The new union expanded from fifty-five hundred in 1942 to more than forty-two thousand dues-paying members nationally in 1946, and Doyle's area alone accounted for eleven thousand.

During World War II, all was well between the communists and anti-communists who together led the Rubinstein local. But by 1946, the anti-communists within Gas-Coke began plotting to eliminate the communists. Fearing that a major split would destroy the union, Allan Haywood, the national CIO vice president and organizing director, appeared before the 1946 Gas-Coke convention in New York City to demand unity—and indeed, the convention then formed a slate that carefully balanced communists and anti-communists. As part of the deal, Doyle became one of the union's two vice presidents.

In April 1947, however, the slim anti-communist majority of the Gas-Coke national executive board passed a vicious policy statement, which said, in part:

> Today the nation is aroused at the threat to our government and our democratic freedoms from communism. . . . Communists in the trade union movement have been insidious in their tactics . . . They are ordered to spare no effort to gain control of trade unions. Endowed with a psychopathic zeal, they will labor long and hard, deceiving workers that such labor is for their benefit when in reality it is to gain control. The communists will not hesitate to sabotage,

> spy and create discord to gain their ends or those dictated by foreign forces.[6]

When Doyle spoke out publicly against this statement, the Gas-Coke president, Martin Wagner, removed him from the union's payroll, effectively shackling the union's most dynamic leader. However, Doyle was still an honorary member of the Carborundum local and secretary of the District 2 Gas-Coke Council—and would remain vice president at least until the next convention in 1948. This irked the anti-communists, who wanted Doyle's head on a platter. They were stuck, though: Doyle had rock-solid support in upstate New York. It seemed that the only way to get rid of Doyle was to scuttle union democracy, which the anti-communists proceeded to do, with help from the Truman administration.

Soon friends and comrades in the Rubinstein local would be knifing one another in the back in plain view. And this would lead to Mazzocchi's entry into the local, stiletto in hand.

III

The stiletto belonged to Fred Hamilton, Doyle's left-wing ally, who was (almost certainly) a CP member. Hamilton had nurtured the Rubinstein local from its first CIO organizing committee right through the purges of 1946 and sat on the Gas-Coke international executive board, representing New York City. As the union's New York district director, Hamilton shared office space with the local at 24-20 Jackson Avenue in Queens, only a few blocks from the Rubinstein plant.

Hamilton wanted Tony to get even with the Gas-Coke anti-communists who had gone after Doyle and other union leftists. Hamilton was especially eager to get rid of Jack Curran, the president of the Rubinstein local, who had become an anti-communist. Perhaps Tony could knock Curran out of office.

The contest between Hamilton and Curran was more bitter for being personal. Curran had worked closely with Hamilton for five years; the two had been the best of friends. With avuncular guidance from Hamilton, Curran had served as chairman of the strike committee during the brutal

1941 recognition strike and then as president of the local. Together the two developed the basic mechanisms of the new union—committees, a grievance structure, and support activities for other unions. They created a system for collecting dues worker by worker, since membership was voluntary and there was no payroll dues deduction. They issued small fines against members who didn't show up regularly for meetings. "I liked him very much—a good guy, a strong guy," recalled Curran.[7]

When Curran was serving his two years in the army, Hamilton held the local together. The war over, Hamilton gave control back to Curran. He also rose to Curran's defense whenever he ran into trouble with quarrelsome rank-and-file members. At the local union's October 1, 1946, membership meeting, Hamilton shored up support for Curran and his negotiating committee, urging the union to "have confidence in this committee and not believe any rumors."[8] In other union meetings, the pair jointly admonished members who gamed the overtime system by staying home on a weekday and then working on the weekend (thus gaining the 50 percent premium allotted weekend and holiday work). After the bargaining committee accepted a contract that permitted paid overtime only after forty hours of work, Hamilton again backed Curran, saying, "In our contract, we gained everything and lost nothing. [The new forty-hour rule] was brought on by the people themselves by staying out one day a week and then getting time and a half on Saturday."

In this relationship, Hamilton was the wise mentor and Curran the young up-and-coming leader. In minutes of local meetings Curran called Hamilton "Mr. Hamilton," while Hamilton called Curran "Jack."

In 1946, the local functioned like any other progressive CIO union. When Hamilton suggested at a May membership meeting that the local provide financial support to the CP-dominated United Electrical Workers during its difficult Phelps-Dodge strike, the local voted to take up a collection. When Hamilton asked it to make a donation to a progressive city council campaign, the membership voted twenty-five dollars from their treasury. The leadership marched in the May Day parade. And in May 1946, when it was time to commit delegates to the national Gas-Coke convention to select national officers, the local nominated and supported Hamilton for national executive board member and as New York district director. At that same convention, the local unanimously voted to send a letter to Truman protesting the firing of Henry Wallace as secretary of commerce.[9]

But behind the scenes at the 1946 Gas-Coke convention, a new anti-communist caucus formed with the express purpose of eliminating communists and pro-communists from the union—especially Hamilton and Doyle.[10] "The Commies were taking the control," Curran recalled. "The Russian Ballet entertained us. It wasn't Kosher to me. I made some contacts with people who felt the same way. I found out Hamilton was the head of the Commie cell of chemicals workers."[11]

The tensions erupted as soon as Curran returned home from the convention. What should have been a minor matter, hiring lawyers for the local, turned into the first open battle between Hamilton and Curran. In January 1947, as anti-communism spread nationally, Hamilton wanted the local to drop its humdrum lawyers and instead support a firm deeply committed to the left, Newberger, Shapiro and Rabinowitz. Curran opposed the move, publicly challenging Hamilton for the first time. According to the minutes, "Mr. Hamilton assured him that the change was important to our local." Since "Mr. Hamilton" still had sufficient respect and standing with the membership, the motion to hire the new lawyers carried.

Curran tried again at the October 1947 meeting of the local's executive board. This time, he prevailed: The board voted six to one to fire Hamilton's lawyers. The general membership then rejected that motion, but Curran refused to quit. At the November executive board meeting, he again pushed the motion through.

At the next general membership meeting, Curran moved that the local's officers sign the Taft-Hartley anti-communist oath. He also distributed the national union's rabid anti-communist statement of policy, which Doyle and Hamilton opposed. What the membership did not know was that behind the scenes, Curran and his anti-communist allies were plotting to destroy the union's leftist vice president, Charles Doyle—with Hamilton thrown in for good measure.

IV

Curran said he wanted to get rid of "the stain attached to our union."[12] But patriotism also paid. Anti-communism offered dividends: upward mobility, extra income, status, and prestige. Curran had his eye on Fred Hamilton's job as district director, which would net him an extra $340 a month (more than twice his pay at the plant). If he showed sufficient zeal and finesse during the witch hunt, he might land Doyle's job as national vice president as well. Gas-Coke officers could hold multiple positions at the same time, with the salaries, pensions, and expense reimbursements accumulating.

Arranging all that would take great ingenuity. Although Curran had gained control of the local's executive board, Hamilton still retained enormous influence in the local and towered over him in the union's chain of command. To ascend, Curran needed to tear down the respect Hamilton had built over years of service. A direct attack, however, would not work as long as Doyle retained power at the top of the union. So Curran's future required that one way or another he eliminate the militant forty-three-year-old Doyle from national office. But Doyle was so popular that defeating him through elections was out of the question. It would take an enormous dirty trick. The anti-communist caucus came up with an ingenious idea: How about getting Truman's Justice Department to deport Doyle? The plan was as simple as it was cruel, a brutal act of red-bashing.

Someone in the union or FBI knew that Doyle, a Scot who'd arrived in the United States in 1923, had never bothered to become a citizen. They also knew that the Truman administration, in its quest to help labor purge the left, would be willing to use the Immigration and Naturalization Service (INS) to make trouble for Doyle. (It deported twenty-five so-called subversive aliens in 1947 alone.) All they needed was a pretext to lure Doyle across the border; the government would do the rest.

So a national executive board meeting was scheduled to be held in Windsor, Ontario, on January 10, 1948. It was an unobtrusive move, since the union had a Canadian district. Tony Sabatine, a member of the anti-communist camp from Buffalo but also an admirer of Doyle, claimed that he warned Doyle not to cross the border. But Doyle could ill afford to miss a national meeting, given the power struggles on the board between the right and the left. On January 11, when he attempted to return home to his wife and three children in Buffalo, the INS stopped him at the border claiming he was an undesirable alien—a foreign communist. Doyle found a way to smuggle himself back into the United States, and went into hiding. Six weeks later he surrendered himself to the INS, facing deportation hearings.

As with so many anti-communist attacks within labor, the rank and file suffered. At the time he'd been barred from the country, Doyle was the chief negotiator in a strike at Carborundum. The *Union Leader* (published by the Greater Buffalo Industrial Union Council, CIO) reported on February 26, 1948, that Doyle's "forced stay in Canada disrupted negotiations" at Carborundum. The resulting settlement, some argued, was poorer because of Doyle's absence.

Doyle's first deportation hearing exposed the frailty of the government's case. The chief witness against him, Frank W. Eleey of Buffalo, admitted that between 1926 and 1941, "He was paid in time of peace by an officer of the National Guard for 'spying on Communists' in the labor movement." Eleey testified that he was "'planted' in the Communist Party of Erie County to supply information to the military, the Buffalo police, industrial concerns and the Secret Service." Also, Eleey claimed to have "kept tabs" on Doyle for private industrial spying services including Pinkerton and the Standard Service Bureau in Buffalo. (At the time, Doyle had been part of a CIO team that had successfully organized the steel industry despite violent opposition from the mill owners and labor-spying services such as Pinkerton.) When the defense asked Eleey whether he knew that the Wagner Act of 1935 had outlawed industrial spying, he said, "I was not spying on labor. I was spying on an organization which even at that time was considered un-American." After being forced to admit that he had done work for labor-spying companies, he declared, "I am proud to spy on Communists."[13]

Next, the government trotted out two "former high officials of the Communist party" who testified that they knew that Doyle was a party member because they had heard him give a speech at a New York State Communist Party convention in 1938. Under cross-examination, though, "the witness was unable to identify the authors of other speeches in the convention record."[14]

Due to the weakness of the case, the hearing was adjourned subject to recall. But Doyle was still detained on Ellis Island without bail.

The anti-communists began generating a drumbeat of horrendous publicity. On April 4, 1948, the *Union Leader* reported that Doyle had joined a hunger strike to secure bail with three other people, including "Gerhart Eisler, alleged No 1 US Communist" and Irving Potash, whom the *Leader* identified as a Russian citizen and a member of the Communist Party national committee.

A Scottish alien, a Russian alien—a bunch of communists starving themselves? They must be guilty of something! Union members heard again and again in the *Leader* that the government would try Doyle "as a subversive alien advocating the overthrow of the United States by force and violence and as an illegal alien who gave false and misleading statements at the time of his latest entry into the country."[15]

Rapidly, the union stripped Doyle of his power. The national union took away his paid job as director of organization. Then the anti-communist-controlled District 2 Council of Gas-Coke in western New York removed Doyle from his position as treasurer and editor of the newspaper.[16] In a final slap, the Carborundum local revoked his honorary membership, leaving Doyle with only his unpaid position as national vice president.

V

After Doyle's arrest, Curran moved vigorously to take the local away from Hamilton. At a general membership meeting on January 16, 1948, only days after Doyle was trapped at the border, Curran was ready for a new skirmish over the radical lawyers. But he feared that the members still might be too sympathetic to Hamilton. So Curran subverted the local's democratic rules and declared that "it was the privilege of the executive board to hire whom they deemed fit." The executive board decision avoided the test of a rank-and-file vote. Hamilton's lefty lawyers vanished.

Within a month, the anti-red publicity surrounding Doyle's arrest had discredited both Hamilton and Doyle within the Rubinstein local. At a meeting on February 18, the executive board recommended that the local pull out of the New York District Council, which they said was dominated by "followers of the party line (communism)." There followed an overtly xenophobic discussion about Doyle, who was "suspected of being a communist and being foreign born." Curran declared that he opposed a recent vote by the members to send a telegram to the immigration board calling for Doyle's release.

And then Curran stuck the dagger deep: "Jack Curran made a motion to keep Fred Hamilton out of Local 149 affairs." Motion carried.

At the next meeting, on February 27, Curran read to members the letter that the executive board had sent Fred Hamilton severing all connections. The membership had this one last chance to save Hamilton by rejecting the executive board's report. But they didn't. The report was seconded and approved. There was no record of a strenuous debate or a divided vote. Hamilton became persona non grata in the local he had built from scratch. Curran had done the dirty work for the great cause of anti-communism, God, and country. Would he now get his earthly rewards, as well?

VI

The bloody showdown between left and right now moved to the national stage. At the July 1948 national Gas-Coke convention in Milwaukee—a meeting marred by catcalls, fistfights, and anti-communist purges—the leadership pushed through resolution after resolution against the communists. The Rubinstein local did not endorse Doyle for vice president, and in the contest for the international executive board member, it voted for Curran over Hamilton. Hamilton's job as district director now was within Curran's reach.

The convention marked the end of one era and the start of another. Anti-communism had so penetrated trade union consciousness that the CIO's radical tradition crashed to a halt. The moment came when the anti-communists presented a resolution reading: "This convention condemns and forever damns those who spread chaos, confusion and disruption by their traitorous sabotage of the [anti-communist] Statement of Policy."[17] The resolution literally parroted the anti-left and anti-labor Republican campaign mantra of two years earlier against "Chaos, Confusion and Communism." After another flurry of fistfights, the resolution passed.

The main purpose of the gathering was to dispose of Doyle and other leftists and divide up the spoils. Doyle received only fifty of six hundred votes cast for vice president. And from the delegates in his own upstate New York district (where news of his trials and imprisonment gained the greatest publicity), he received no votes at all. Surfing along on this great wave of anti-communism, Curran easily defeated Hamilton. Finally, the New York directorship, with its extra pay, ample office, and prestige, was his.

After the convention, Doyle's suffering continued. The federal court in

New York's western district convicted him of illegal entry into the United States and sentenced him to a five-hundred-dollar fine and one year in jail. A federal appeals court overturned the decision, saying that the jury had erred, but INS officials soon succeeded in deporting him. Like Henry Wallace, Charles Doyle had been destroyed by a deadly combination of trade union and Truman administration anti-communism.

VII

Jack Curran now served as an international executive board member, salaried New York district director, and unpaid president of the Rubinstein local. He was cruising comfortably along the new CIO anti-communism path. Under his guidance, the local threw its support to Truman in the 1948 elections. It bought ads in the journal of the Association of Catholic Trade Unionists (ACTU), which vehemently opposed communists in unions. It rejoined the New York CIO Political Action Committee, now purged of communist-oriented unions. It also continued to provide funds for other unions on strike—though again, most had already expelled their communists.

The membership paid a price for the purge, as management reclaimed more and more control from the union at Rubinstein. The company reneged on agreements and failed to resolve grievances. Rubinstein also hardened its positions during contract negotiations, skimping on wage and benefit improvements. The local's minutes of March 18, 1949, noted that the company would no longer allow the union to collect money for political action or strike support during working hours.

While Curran struggled to confront management about these power grabs, he took more and more power into his own hands within the union. A dangerous dynamic developed: As the most active members grew frustrated and quit, they ceded greater power to Curran. Even Harold Phillipsen, the elected chief steward (the only paid union position inside the plant) and Curran's right-hand man, resigned, upset at the loss of control by his rank-and-file bargaining committee. His departure inflicted little damage on Curran; it emphasized a new leadership principle: "Jack will take care of it." And Jack did, replacing Phillipsen quickly with the popular but ineffectual Agnes Hesslin.

Meanwhile, Curran profited. Out of nowhere, a motion appeared calling for the local to provide for the first time a generous Christmas gift to its president for all his hard work: a five-hundred-dollar US savings bond. It cost the local union treasury $375—the equivalent of more than two months' pay for many Rubinstein workers. Not everyone could stomach this tribute, but after "discussions were held pro and con," according to the minutes, a vote showed "nine-tenths of the members in favor of the bond."

To management, Curran gave the most precious gift of all—a retreat from union militancy. No longer did workers talk of withholding overtime to press contract demands. No longer did they contemplate strikes. Under Hesslin's tenure as chief steward, grievances piled up. The purge that succeeded in establishing Curran's power also crippled the national union. And now that its anti-communist leaders had succeeded in destroying their most committed, idealistic organizers, the union ceased to grow. By 1954, even the anti-communist CIO leadership placed Gas-Coke on a short list of unions that it called "small, impecunious, ill led and lacking in energy."[18]

But the union's potential still resided in the workers. They had lived through the early strikes and now bristled at the deteriorating working conditions. What Jack could not "take care of" was the possibility that someone might arise with the power to release workers' pent-up energy.

Even as Curran was busily taking care of himself and enjoying his new power and prestige, a young, articulate, energetic vet was about to appear on his doorstep. And not by chance. He was planted there by the very victims of the union's anti-communist purge. The foes Curran thought he'd vanquished were readying a counterattack. And they'd found just the weapon they needed: Tony Mazzocchi.

VIII

The Gas-Coke anti-communists gloated extravagantly over their purge of Charles Doyle. The caper at the Canadian border became legendary as the anti-communists boasted about their clever trap, the unsuspecting prey, and the delicious victory meal enjoyed at Doyle's expense. For years, Wesley Hilts from the Carborundum local would brag about how they'd set up the meeting in Canada and tipped off INS. He gleefully described the support the plotters had gotten from the Association of Catholic Trade Unionists. "We would go to Monsignor's house in Niagara Falls to plan," he said to Mark Dudzic (who became president of Local 149 in 1985). "We decided who would sit where at the union meetings, and who would say what. The communists thought they were the only ones who knew how to organize? We showed them."

But Doyle's leftist friends, especially Fred Hamilton, still ached over the humiliating defeat. They hungered for justice, but could only hope for revenge.

By early 1950, several purged leftist organizers and officials had found refuge in another union: the left-leaning District 65. From there, they decided to teach Curran a lesson—and rescue the workers from his grip. Hamilton and his allies saw clearly that Curran had broken the militant spirit of the union, and they wanted to resurrect it. They planned to snatch Local 149 at Helena Rubinstein away from the anti-communist Gas-Coke and bring it into District 65. Hundreds of other communist purges nationwide were combining at that time to suck the life out of the labor movement. It would be uplifting to see the anti-communist Curran rejected by his own members. The move made sense for bargaining as well: District 65 represented cosmetics workers at Revlon, a major Rubinstein competitor, and workers could leverage more power if both companies were represented by the same union.

The District 65 leftists believed Tony Mazzocchi could deliver the blow.

Getting Tony the job at Rubinstein wasn't hard. A contact at the plant alerted them when Rubinstein was hiring. With a name like *Mazzocchi,* Tony would pass safely through the company's screening system, which viewed Italian Catholics as safely conservative. The fix was in. If Mazzocchi showed up for the job, it was his.

Fred Hamilton and Milt Reverby, a prominent District 65 organizer in or close to the CP, thought Tony was still wet behind the ears and in need of careful coaching. They met regularly with him to discuss strategy and tactics, both before and after he started working at Rubinstein in May 1950. Hamilton knew the ins and outs of Local 149 and its contract, so Mazzocchi arrived with plenty of information.

But from the start, Tony harbored serious misgivings about the political advice he was receiving from Hamilton and company. In a matter of days, he'd realized that Helena Rubinstein workers were deeply connected to Gas-Coke's militant history. "They fought a big strike to win their union in 1941. Seventeen weeks, police breaking up pickets. They were proud of that," Tony recalled. "I don't think another union had a chance of pulling them out. I saw that right away. They wanted to fight to make the union do the right thing, but they were not about to go out. I don't even think they knew who District 65 was."

Tony also questioned the political judgment of his mentors, who urged him to raise contentious foreign policy issues on the shop floor, opposing the Marshall Plan and the Korean War. "Hamilton and Reverby were trying to tutor me," Tony said. "They'd give me good tips. But then they'd say, 'You gotta go in the local and talk about the Marshall Plan.' I said, 'Are you nuts?'"

> That was the craziest position they ever had. That's what wrecked a lot of the CP-oriented unions. It was a straight CP line of: The Marshall Plan was bad. It made Europe captive to American capital—blah, blah, blah. And you're going to argue that in the plant? First of all, people didn't give a shit about the Marshall Plan. And it was an indefensible position. How do you oppose the Marshall Plan to the average person? They thought I could bring that shop into 65 based on the Marshall Plan stuff. But I knew that was bullshit when I got into the shop. These Rubinstein members weren't going to be involved in that crap.

Hamilton tried hard to maintain a grip on Tony. "He had a good history," Mazzocchi recalled. "He organized for John L. Lewis. There was no question that people supported his trade union principles and tenacity and ability to win economic gains. But anti-communism prevailed over anything else. They'd say, 'Great guy, but he was a communist and he had to go. . . .' But he talked to me a lot, always telling me what to do, and I'm saying to myself: *Well, they knocked your ass out of here.* So when I got to the shop, I said, *Man, this has gotta be a step-by-step process, and I need allies.* I held my own counsel. I had to do it my way, on my own. And that's basically what it boiled down to."

The wet-behind-the-ears organizer turned out to have a hidden source of experience. "Look, basically I learned to organize from the streets of Brooklyn. We had a very close-knit group of kids. And to do anything, you have to learn how to work with people. We organized ourselves to play ball against the other blocks. And then in the army, we had a big group of guys who were as tight as we could be. I had a lot of friends. I was never the one other guys left out. And I guess people thought that at least I was smart."

So at age twenty-four, while he respectfully listened to the advice of seasoned, albeit defeated, organizers, he charted his own course: "If I had followed their advice, this thing would have collapsed. I had to follow my own instincts. I mean, my co-workers were like the people I knew all my life. I knew what they were and weren't prepared to do. I was either going to rise or fall on my own instincts."

IX

Mazzocchi's instincts told him that Curran's power base resided with the women. Curran went out of his way to get the women's grievances solved, and of course the local's chief steward was a woman, Agnes Hesslin. Meanwhile, the men in receiving, shipping, and the warehouse felt ignored and poorly represented. According to Tony, Curran "was a very clever guy who divided the men against the women. He had no support among the men, but he had 85 percent of the women in the shop."

Tony's strategy was simple enough—win over the men, and then make inroads into Agnes Hesslin's base among women.

Tony bonded with two young workers who quickly became his chief organizers—Mac McManus and George Roach. Mac, two years younger than Tony, came from the Greenpoint section of Brooklyn (but was a Yankee fan). Though a good student, he was forced to drop out of high school to support his mother and three younger siblings after his father died. With his work clothes always carefully pressed and creased, Mac struck Tony as thorough and precise. He was also a worrier. In later years, Mac would get upset stomachs and headaches during negotiations, prompting Tony to remark, "Mac, we're supposed to give *them* the headaches, not us."

Mac's good friend George Roach, who worked at the warehouse several blocks from the main facility, came from the hardscrabble Hell's Kitchen neighborhood on Manhattan's West Side. As George saw it, Tony was the brains of the operation, Mac was the conscience, and he, George, provided the brawn. When he was a kid, George and his gang did gymnastics, practicing in the early mornings on the high bar and horizontal ladders in Central Park. Instead of mats, they learned to do their flyways and layouts onto the concrete. In the navy, George boxed with several Golden Glove contenders, though he was five foot ten and 140 pounds.

At twenty-two, George already served as a steward in the warehouse and commanded respect from the workers. Later he would become the local's vice president, a key organizer, and one of the best strike captains in the labor movement. For now, his job—and Mac's—was to round up the Rubinstein men to vote for Tony as chief steward, and unseat Agnes Hesslin.

The men often groused about Hesslin and talked about voting her out of her half-time union job. But because she tended to her base of women on the lines, she seemed invulnerable. Tony, however, believed correctly that the gender divide reflected an overall weakness in the union that Hesslin could not rectify: "She was a nice woman, but heavily influenced by Curran and was not capable of standing up to the company."

Thanks to Hamilton's tutelage, Tony knew more about the contract than any worker in the plant, including Hesslin. And he was not shy about pointing out its deficiencies at a meeting only two weeks after he was hired. "I wasn't afraid to get up and talk, which really helped. There would be four hundred people in the hall and the officers were in front. The guys were always moaning about them, but they were afraid to challenge. And I got up, and it was very effective."

Tony spoke out about the need for an "escalator" clause providing for automatic wage increases. "And all of us looked at each other," said George. "The only thing we knew about an escalator was like maybe in Macy's they had this escalator. We didn't know what the hell he was talking about, but it had to be something thrilling."

On September 15, 1950, Tony Mazzocchi appeared for the first time in the local's official minutes when he "spoke on opening wages and stopping speedup in the plant." At the October 21 meeting, "Anthony Mazzocchi requested to have more Labor-Management meetings." At the next monthly meeting he "spoke on safety of machines."

Tony's questions about the contract filtered into the plant, where workers gnawed on them for days—often during coffee breaks, especially in the alley behind the plant where the younger men and women displayed their plumage. The men from the warehouse, especially George, joined them. Tony was always around explaining the ins and outs of contracts, chatting up everyone.

George remembered clearly how easily Tony made friends: "I was from Hell's Kitchen—a dropout from school, worked all over, knew the streets. I was pretty tough. And for me this guy was for real. I just plain liked him. He was a good guy. You talked to him, you had to like him."

For one thing, he was entertaining. "In those days we all wore hats—and Tony would go around the locker room, putting on everybody's hat and doing a little routine on that person," George recalled. "He would have everyone lying on the floor, crying, laughing." Tony's amiability had a purpose. "During the breaks, he suggested to us that maybe we should think about forming a committee to talk about improving the contract," George said. "He was very clever. He didn't push too hard or too fast. He took his time."

If the men were Tony's base, he was also well positioned to draw in women. "They put me in the main production area, which was also the largest department," he remembered. "That's where all the women were. There were only a few men in there. You know, you worked at the end of the line. Stuff would come down and you'd package it. That was a 'man's' job. And I was able to talk to women, day in and day out."

Tony's charm and skill radiated through the rouge and lipstick lines and helped speed his advancement. The women in shampoo and face cream heard nice things about him. And the hand cream and face cream women liked him, too. Although Tony did not have the handsome raw features of a Jack Curran, his sparkling energy, self-deprecating humor, and quick mind made him a hit.

Tony did favors, and enjoyed it. Occasionally, he'd fix an older worker's dentures for free at Fine's dental lab. Like Marcantonio, Tony never directly sought repayment at election time for all the favors he'd done. Just doing the favors projected the image of a concerned guy who would go out of his way to help solve your problems—exactly what a union leader was supposed to do.

It didn't take long for the men to realize that Tony might be their salvation. As Tony recalled, "When they saw how I worked with the women, these guys said, 'You're the only guy these women are going to listen to.' Because, you know, I wasn't treating them like crap."

He talked. He charmed. He showed respect. He played on the baseball and bowling teams. He spoke up at every meeting. "Sometimes I said good stuff, sometimes I didn't. But basically, I got up and talked at union meetings about the shortcomings of the contract. I mean, they were obvious, and a lot of people felt them but couldn't give voice to it."

Rumors added luster to Tony's reputation. "A guy named Artie Brown said that Tony had this uncle or father or something—really a big shot in the union—who knows all about unions and what to do," George said. Bobby Guinta, who was hired on the same day as Tony, recalled that Mazzocchi's war record enhanced his aura. "Most of us young guys were in the service after the war," Bobby said. "Tony seemed a lot older and experienced since he had been in the war, and been in battle. We respected that."[19]

And people could not help but be drawn to his self-confidence. As George put it, "My first impression is, he was a speaker. He got up there and he was gonna be somebody in our union. Most of us didn't know what the hell we were doing and we *knew* we didn't know what the hell we were doing, and he stands up and he has direction. He had all his ducks in a row.

"As soon as Tony spoke up at that first union meeting, we knew we had a leader."

X

Compared with Tony, George and Mac were kids. But despite the best efforts of the company's personnel department, they were not hardwired for anti-communism and fear of authority. They had already absorbed much of New York's trade union culture. George had gotten a job at age sixteen as an elevator operator and joined the CP-oriented United Office and Professional Workers of America: "Because in my neighborhood, that's what you do—you join the union." George and Mac would form the backbone of Tony's drive to build a progressive union at Rubinstein.

Tony had already raised his profile by getting elected to a committee that would represent the local at the Gas-Coke District Council (which had been shattered by the red purges). At its first meeting, in February,

Mazzocchi became the council's recording secretary and spokesperson for the council committee at Local 149 membership meetings. He was positioned well to unseat Hesslin as chief steward.

After only nine months on the job, Tony was nominated by Mac for the job of chief steward—much to the shock of Curran, Hesslin, and even Hamilton back at District 65. But the nomination proved to be a stumble. For all of Tony's homework—and Hamilton's guidance—they hadn't read the bylaws' fine print: To run for chief steward, a member had to have at least one year of seniority. Curran knew this, and at the March 8, 1951, executive board meeting, he pointed it out. Tony was disqualified, and Hesslin ran unopposed.

The misstep was costly: Tony lost the element of surprise. Until the aborted challenge, both Curran and Hesslin had not viewed him as a serious threat. Now they knew better. Rubinstein's management no doubt took notice as well. Recovering quickly, Tony ran to be delegate to the national Gas-Coke convention. He received the third highest vote total, only fifteen fewer than Curran. At the May 18, 1951, membership meeting, Tony again spoke about speed-up. Workers hated the line's increasing pace, which had gone unopposed in the Curran era. Hesslin weakly defended herself: "If machines are run too fast, report it to supervision."

The Curran-Hesslin team proposed forming a contract committee of all shop stewards. Mazzocchi followed up with a motion that the contract committee be elected by the full membership—providing for more rank-and-file democracy. When elections to the contract committee were held, Tony received the highest number of votes—one more than Agnes Hesslin, the sitting chief steward.

Curran was no fool. He realized that Tony might pose a serious challenge to his power and sought to co-opt him. Curran was covering his bets, just in case Mazzocchi defeated Hesslin for chief steward next time around. At the October 1951 executive board meeting, Curran and the board recommended—and the membership later agreed—that Tony become chair of the local's political action committee. This new position allowed Tony a regular spot on the agenda at each membership meeting. Without objection, Tony was also chosen to attend the national CIO convention in New York. And in February 1952, Curran asked Tony's political action committee to join the deliberations of the executive board.

Soon the showdown for chief steward was reenacted: In February 1952, Mac McManus again nominated Tony; he would face both Agnes Hesslin and Lillian Casey. Tony nominated Mac for the local union's recording secretary and for steward from the general finishing department.

Hesslin played the youth card, implying that Tony, twenty years her junior, was just too young to be chief steward. But Tony's youth and dash worked to his favor. He had continued to make friends, do favors, and raise issues since the last election. He'd repaired more dentures, told more jokes, flattered, flirted, and spoken up at more meetings. Most of all, he'd had more time to convince the women workers that he really would fight to improve conditions on the line. And he called for reducing the pay gap between male and female job classifications.

Despite hard campaigning by George, Mac, and Tony, the chief steward election in March 1952—three months before Tony's twenty-sixth birthday—was not a done deal. "A lot of the guys didn't even come out to vote because they were in a separate warehouse," Tony said. But he had sufficiently penetrated Hesslin's base of support among women to eke out a cliffhanger victory—he won by only twelve votes out of nearly four hundred cast.

XI

Tony wasn't the only one making moves. Madam Rubinstein had a whopper of her own in store: She was moving the plant out of New York. For more than a year, the workers had heard rumors. Curran had reassured them that the plant would stay in the metropolitan area. While that was technically accurate, workers were shocked when Rubinstein announced in June 1952 that production would move to a new facility in Roslyn, Long Island—more than twenty miles from midtown Manhattan and nearly a sixty-mile round trip from Tony's home in Brooklyn. Thus Rubinstein joined a long list of employers fleeing high-priced New York City for the open spaces and cheaper labor found in more conservative suburban and rural areas.

The move would set the clock back for the union. Although no one would be forced to resign, many would leave the company, choosing to take a modest severance package rather than suffer the long commute. At first,

Curran hoped to set up carpools with workers who owned vehicles. That proved impractical. Next, Curran worked with Rubinstein to set up charter buses that would run daily to transport 250 workers from a collection point in the city to Roslyn. (The August 5, 1952, minutes reported, "Smoking and singing permitted.")

As Tony recalled, "I think the company figured the people would get dissuaded from using the buses. Also, the company knew that the regular bus companies would fight us because we didn't have a franchise to run charter buses over their routes. The company figured our bus company would collapse under the pressure."

During negotiations over the move, Curran fell into a common management trap: He reopened the contract to permit a two-tier wage structure. "Everybody who worked at Rubinstein at the time of the move and made the commute would get a wage increase," Tony said. "Everyone hired after that started at a lower rate of pay." The workers who ratified that contract would get the higher rate. "Of course the people were going to vote for it. None of them were negatively affected," Tony said. "But I knew that was divisive and that it would haunt us."

If Tony chose to stay with the local, he would have to start all over building his influence. The new workers would increasingly come from the Long Island suburbs, far removed from New York's militant labor culture. Many were Irish Catholics; many were Republicans. According to Tony, "None of the new hires came with a union background." They would have no memory of the solidarity and struggle that had brought the union to Helena Rubinstein in 1941.

Tony's personal circumstances also were changing. He had met a fiery Sicilian beauty named Rose Alfonso. In 1950, they'd gotten married and planted themselves in Brooklyn near their families and friends. Moving to the suburbs was out of the question. Given the loss of many union members, the long commute, the inevitable strain on family life, and the divisive new two-tier wage structure, it would have been natural for Tony to look for a new job nearer to Brooklyn. But Rubinstein's new chief steward took in the daunting new landscape and welcomed it. In fact, he upped the ante. Once the plant moved to Roslyn, the race for local president would be on—and Tony Mazzocchi planned to run.

XII

Jack Curran barely seemed to notice the impending election. He was still trying to co-opt Tony. At a membership meeting in April 1952, Curran moved to send Tony to Penn State College for a union training program. He also appointed Tony to the new bylaws committee. When it was time to select a bargaining committee in June 1952, Curran nominated Tony. Curran made Tony a delegate to the district council. He also wanted Tony to chair the new newspaper committee—and of course the dance committee! Further, by missing several meetings due to his job as district director, Curran gave Tony all the time and space he needed to hold forth. He might as well have been Mazzocchi's campaign manager.

Tony quickly turned the chief steward position into a full-time company-paid union position. He even persuaded Rubinstein to provide the union with an office inside the new Long Island facility. He could wander through the plant and talk to anyone at will while Jack Curran, the president, worked out of his district director's office in faraway Queens. What's more, to his great relief, Tony didn't have to work the line anymore.

Advantage Mazzocchi.

Tony's first task was rebuilding the steward system so that grievances no longer languished as they had in Hesslin's tenure. The stewards needed to form a system for communicating to and from the shop floor. And they needed to know their contract front to back. For the first time, each steward received a copy. "We ran a tight union grievance system. We really addressed people's problems immediately," Tony said. "I used to meet with the stewards as a group every week."

But what leverage did they have to solve problems? Rubinstein's management obviously preferred the Curran-Hesslin team, who acquiesced to their authority. Normally, the company would have made life difficult for the new chief steward, delaying grievances and working to convince members that they'd be better off with someone else.

But management was desperate for worker cooperation in getting the new plant up and running. "The company had moved, and it was really in a state of disarray," Tony said. "When they moved from a multistory Queens plant to a single-floor, brand-new facility on the Island, it took our cooperation just to get it to run properly." In return for that cooperation, Tony made the company pay for stewards' meetings. They now met every week for thirty minutes on company time.

The chaos of the move and continual changes on the line meant more grievances and more chances for Tony, Mac, and George to solve them. "We would review each grievance at the weekly meetings and then decide how to deal with the ever-changing situation on the shop floor," Tony said. "We insisted that the stewards all go back to their sections and report what the union position was on various things. They would stand on top of tables, talk to groups of people."

Overtime was a big issue. It was gold for workers, who got a 50 percent pay premium for each extra hour of work over forty hours. Overtime was the easiest way to transform an okay-paying job into a good one, so it was a difficult offer to refuse, and management knew it. For management, overtime provided enormous flexibility. The company could exploit it to expand and contract work time without hiring and firing workers. Paying time and a half for the extra hours was a terrific bargain—especially during peak seasons or during the transition to a new facility.

Refusing overtime was therefore a powerful weapon for the union—provided that the members were willing to sacrifice a significant amount of extra pay. Each worker had to understand from the stewards why the union was asking them to forgo all that money. At Helena Rubinstein, the union's position on overtime became a mantra. "You had that constant interaction between the stewards and the people," Tony remembered. "And everyone understood what the union line was—like why we weren't going to work overtime—which was our most effective weapon."

The charter buses offered a powerful means of communication. The "old" workers who made the hour journey each way formed a captive audience for Mazzocchi's communication system. Each bus had a captain, and every day that captain would go over the union's key issues. As a result, Mazzocchi said, "We had extremely good discipline."

Knowing that the election for local president would be close, Mazzocchi came up with a promising organizing lead through the women workers. Many of the women's husbands worked at a five-hundred-member tungsten facility nearby (owned by a different employer) that was desperately in need of a union. If Local 149 could organize the plant, those five hundred workers would double the membership of the local and give Tony an enormous edge in the election.

There was a problem, though. Unbeknownst to the tungsten plant workers, they already had union—a mobbed-up one. It was run by Tony Castalado, who also represented ten contract janitors at Helena Rubinstein. Racketeers like Castalado would approach an employer and propose a deal: If the employer provided the racketeers with "dues," the racketeers promised to keep any real union out. Workers would be deprived of wage increases and decent benefits, and often never even knew they had a union.

Tony forced a confrontation with Castalado over the tungsten plant: "Castalado comes in and he says, 'Hey, you can't raid that plant! I got their charter!' Guy reaches into his pocket and goes through all these charters. He says, 'I got a friggin' charter!' I said: 'I don't give a crap about your friggin' charter.'"

Castalado, a small-time operator, had no recourse against Tony. But Curran did. He refused to allow the new workers to join the local. Instead, he turned the organizing drive over to the Steelworkers. "So it went to the Steelworkers, because Curran didn't want the local to be amalgamated," Tony said. "By then he knew I was going to run against him, and he figured if we organized this five-hundred-member plant, we were gonna beat his ass."

In the end, the Steelworkers gained the new members but were so ineffectual that Tony had to run their recognition strike for them. That was okay by Curran, so long as the tungsten workers didn't vote in his local.

At a February 1953 membership meeting, Tony declared his candidacy for president. According to the minutes, "Jack Curran and Anthony Mazzocchi spoke pro and con on the state of the union." Curran remained confident that he could defeat the young upstart. So did Tony's radical mentors, including Hamilton. They thought Tony was making his move too soon and would jeopardize their careful plans. Tony continued to meet with these advisers, but "most of the time," he said, "I was just doing it out of friendship—especially for this one really well-meaning guy named Harold Phillips who worked at a shop in New York. He sort of thought he was the guy who nurtured me."

Tony defined his campaign for president around one central issue: eliminating the two-tier system that Curran had negotiated. Tony believed the two-tier system divided the workforce and greatly weakened the union. He could hear the divisiveness as workers talked about "new girls" and "old girls." And he worried that at some point, the new workers would vote to eliminate the union entirely. The wage difference—though it was only a dime an hour less—was more than enough to breed resentment. "A dime an hour in those days was big stuff," said Tony. "But it was also just the whole idea of it. It broke down relations between the new people and the old people."

Tony started to hear what he feared most: "A lot of the new people had never been in a union before. And they were saying, 'What the hell do I belong to the union for?' I thought they might get the union decertified. And that's why I ran on wiping out the two-tier."

Curran, only ten years older than Mazzocchi, found it useful to argue that Mazzocchi was still too green to run a union. Mazzocchi countered that the union needed a full-time president who worked in the plant, not one who spent most of his time as regional director at the district office. But the election turned as much on Mazzocchi's ability to read accurately the informal networks on the shop floor. He understood what scientific management had uncovered decades earlier—that workers naturally formed work groups and group leaders. If you could identify and win over those group leaders, you could control the shop.

Tony did so intuitively.

> I knew who the women leaders were, and I immediately went after them to win them over. This woman named Ann Sherman was a big leader during the '41 strike, and she never wanted to run for office. A very strange woman—her whole life was strange. But when she said something in that plant the women listened—they looked to her. She became a follower of mine and she hated Curran—she thought he was a sellout. She was a strong Catholic but she supported Fred Hamilton, the known commie. She thought he was the best thing that ever happened to the union. He was the one who had led her through the strike.

Tony connected with one group leader after another—Katilia Rose, Anne McKenzie, Vinne Hyman. He fused these new supporters with the small army of men that George, Mac, and Bobby had built. And to win an extra friend or two, Tony continued to repair dentures.

The election came. If Tony Mazzocchi won, the besieged leftists would finally have their revenge: Curran, the man who'd helped destroy Doyle and Hamilton, would be out. And, Tony's mentors assumed, the local would be rescued from the red-baiters of the Gas-Coke union and nestled safely into the arms of District 65, one of the few remaining left-leaning unions in the country.

The turnout was massive. More than 95 percent of the five hundred eligible members voted. (Years later, local lore claimed that these workers lined up in the rain for hours in order to cast their ballots.) Tony Mazzocchi won by sixty-five votes—sweeping his buddies into office as well. Mac became chief steward. George Roach won the steward position in receiving, and Pat Duffy, another Mazzocchi loyalist for the next twenty years, joined the executive board. Curran was through.

"The night I won the presidency, in the middle of the night, I got a phone call from this guy Harold Phillips, in the District 65 group that coached me," Tony remembered. "He says, 'God, I've lived all my life for this! You beat Curran.' He was going nuts, you know? I called Fred Hamilton the next morning, and his son said he had left for England to flee McCarthyite persecution. I was shocked."

In fact, the entire CP was in disarray. Few party members were around to savor Mazzocchi's victory.

Curran spoke with emotion and pride as he handed over the reins of the union to Mazzocchi at the March 20, 1953, meeting. He described what the local had won during his decade-long tenure: "The benefits such as company paid holidays, sick leave, work clothes, premium pay for overtime, company paid life insurance, disability insurance, hospitalization, surgical and medical insurance for members and their families, increased wages . . . [as well as] rest periods, vacations of one week for one year, two weeks for two years and three weeks for five years, job security through seniority and the right to have grievances heard through the grievance machinery."

And the minutes reported that Curran, a mainstream unionist, called for "a shorter work-week . . . and a guaranteed annual wage"—positions far to the left of today's labor movement.

Curran recognized that Mazzocchi's campaign strategy had worked. He "heard that the people wanted the president in the plant and now they have gotten their wish," Curran said. As he turned over the gavel, Jack Curran gave his successor the traditional tip of the hat, saying that Tony should "be honest and fair to the membership and they would give him their full support."

Curran had no idea how right he was. The members of Local 149 would provide rock-solid support for Tony Mazzocchi for years to come and together with their president would build one of the most dynamic local unions in America.

XIII

But the communists were still waiting for their final act of revenge: Soon, they assumed, Tony would disaffiliate his local from the anti-communist Gas-Coke and bring it into District 65.

Tony betrayed the avengers. His loyalty now was to his workers, not his handlers.

> There was no way they were going to raid this shop. The people had roots. They'd fought a huge struggle ten years before. Besides, District 65 was going to be red-baited, and the people had no affinity to it anyway. I knew where I wanted to go, and I knew the people. I had their support.

Hamilton and the scattered remnants of the CP would be bitter for years to come. When Hamilton returned to the country a few years later, Mazzocchi recalled, "He got pissed at me," for failing to pull the local into District 65. But by then getting angry was all Hamilton could do. Tony refused to take revenge on Curran. In fact, he went out of his way to help him. Tony was broadening his base of support, not narrowing it through sectarian warfare. According to Mark Dudzic, who later became president of the local, "Curran remained a local member right up until his retirement and would occasionally attend union events. He never badmouthed Tony to me or to other local leaders."[20]

In the afterglow of victory, Mazzocchi understood he would live or die by his campaign promise: He had to get rid of the two-tier system at Rubinstein. And to do that, he would have to build a militant local union in the heart of the growing American suburbs, the alleged graveyard of class consciousness and radical politics.

FIVE

Subversive Suburbs

Tony embarked on a suicide mission: building a radical, militant trade union in the heart of the American suburbs—Long Island, New York. Common sense said that he'd picked not only the wrong place, but the wrong time—the McCarthyite 1950s.

Historians have argued that New York City was the home turf of militant unions, while the suburbs were their tomb. In their view, the mass migration from the cities to the staid and stultifying suburbs helped explain why CIO militant unionism collapsed after World War II. Historian Joshua B. Freeman said New York City was the "laboratory for a social urbanism committed to an expansive welfare state, racial equality and popular access to culture and education." But during the 1950s, workers "rejected this vision, preferring suburban-style, single-family home living, racially exclusive neighborhoods and low taxes."[1] And there went the labor movement as a radical agent of change.

Tony was perhaps foolish to buck this trend, particularly on Long Island, home of Levittown, the planned community that was the prototype for postwar suburban living. William J. Levitt and family took a thousand-acre plot of potato farms near Hempstead, thirty-three miles from Midtown Manhattan, and turned it into a swath of low-cost, cookie-cutter, mass-produced homes just perfect for World War II vets. Levitt offered "$1,000 down, $70 monthly for a three-bedroom house with a log-burning fireplace, a gas range, Venetian blinds, a gas heater and a landscaped lot of 75 by 100 feet, all for a total price of $9,990."[2]

After constructing a thousand nearly identical homes in Levittown, Levitt cloned the development; by 1949 he was putting up more than four thousand little boxes per year. Other builders quickly followed suit, dotting the postwar landscape with clusters of nearly identical houses. The Cape Cods of Levittown, so evenly spaced across the barren landscape, seemed a fitting expression of 1950s capitalism and the resulting consumerism, conformity, and commuter trains.

Even back in 1953, many people felt that this new working-class suburbia would be the last place on earth to embrace militant trade unionism. Tony didn't buy it. He also ignored the prevailing messages coming from the new and wildly popular medium of television. The suburbs and TV were born and raised together, with each created in the other's image. Together they disseminated a rightward-tilting value system for the 1950s, a vision of suburban families engaged in conformist pursuits, surrounded by material goodies, set within pleasant grounds far from the city's grime—and light-years from Tony's radical vision.

TV didn't mix with Mazzocchi-style worker militancy. In some cases, it even made work disappear entirely. Did Jim Anderson (Robert Young) in *Father Knows Best*—the caring, middle-class patriarch—ever work? In *The Life of Riley,* Chester Riley (William Bendix) actually carried a lunch pail from his single-family home to his blue-collar job. But the focus was still on his cloistered suburban 1950s household that consumed, but never produced.

Then came *I Led Three Lives,* which brought the issue of communist infiltration deep into the nuclear family. Aired from 1953 to 1956 during the peak of the red scare, this drama was based on the true story of Herbert Philbrick (played by Richard Carlson). After tucking his wife and precious children to bed, Philbrick worked late into the night microfilming communist documents for the FBI. Almost always on the verge of blowing his cover and violating nearly every civil liberty of the communists he spied upon, Philbrick risked his life to protect the American Dream from the likes of—well, Tony Mazzocchi. By purging America of dangerous Moscow puppets, he safeguarded befuddled workers from communist union infiltrators—like Tony's mentors in District 65.

Riley, Anderson, Philbrick—all shared an unlimited, yet anxious, American optimism. They believed with religious certainty that they would prosper so long as they worked without complaint, defended family values, and kept an ever-vigilant eye on those who sought to destroy their way of life. Tony's radical dreams were their nightmares.

II

If the suburbs and TV weren't enough to thwart Mazzocchi, then surely McCarthyism would do the trick. By the time Tony hit Long Island, the anti-communist enterprise included Hoover's FBI, the military, right-wing politicians, the House Un-American Activities Committee, the Senate Internal Security Subcommittee, bitter former communists, liberal anti-communists, anti-communist unionists, professional informers, the media, and even the CIA, in violation of its charter. These institutions and individuals attacked reds and their sympathizers for allegedly ceding Eastern Europe to Stalin (Alger Hiss), sending atomic secrets to the Soviets (the Rosenbergs), weakening US military might by questioning nuclear weapons (physicist Robert Oppenheimer), and losing China to the communists (scholar Owen Lattimore and East Asia experts in the State Department).

When the Korean War broke out, the anti-communists went on a feeding frenzy, devouring thousands of reds, fellow travelers, independent leftists, and civil rights advocates. Millions of federal, state, and local public employees were investigated through a process by which the accuser—and often the specific charges—were hidden from the accused in the name of national security. The red-baiters destroyed the careers of scientists, professors, schoolteachers, union leaders, actors, and writers. Tony knew plenty such people.

As Tony tried to build his local union into a progressive fighting machine, a noose of anti-communist informers was predictably tightening around him. FBI surveillance of the left, especially in unions, was extensive. By 1954, J. Edgar Hoover had compiled the infamous Security Index, a secret list of twenty-six thousand supposedly dangerous radicals who were to be arrested within one hour of a national emergency. The FBI, according to Ellen Schrecker's exhaustive history of the era, "had also compiled separate lists of slightly less dangerous individuals, mostly intellectuals, professionals and labor leaders who, it believed, 'in time of national emergency, are in a position to influence others against the national interests or are likely to furnish financial or other material aid to subversive elements.'"[3]

The FBI especially targeted labor in the defense industry—Long Island's economic engine—because these workers potentially could sabotage military production. "In June 1953," Schrecker discovered, "the FBI had 109,119 informants at over 10,745 defense plants, research centers, and other installations like bridges and telephone exchanges that the Defense Department had identified as 'vital facilities.'"[4] The bureau commonly employed illegal entries and wiretaps, perjury, counterespionage, and agent provocateurs against American communists and their friends and allies.

But Tony did not show up on the list of CP members, subversives, or even maybe-reds. Instead, he was judged by the ever-popular "Duck Test": If you walked like a duck, quacked like a duck, and looked like a duck, you were a duck. If you read Marx, Lenin, or God forbid Stalin, you thought like a duck. If two decades earlier, you had been a member of a popular front group that opposed fascism, or if you had given support to the Loyalists in Spain, you quacked. And unless you repented and named names, you were duck soup.

Anti-communism had ripped the heart out of the progressive movement. As Schrecker eloquently wrote: "Gone was the Popular Front mindset with its glorification of the little man and its celebration of labor and cultural diversity. Gone, too, was the class consciousness and the emphasis on collective struggle that had pervaded so much of the American culture during the 1930s and 1940s."[5]

Tony Mazzocchi was supposed to be extinct, a member of what Schrecker called "the missing radical generation"—leftists so defeated by witch hunts that they had "little useful political experience to pass on to the next generation of radicals."[6]

Fortunately, someone forgot to tell Tony about this as he set out to build a vibrant "city-style" union smack in the middle of all those boxy little houses.

III

Rubinstein's new plant was nestled in the rolling, leafy hills of Long Island's North Shore, on the undeveloped eastern edge of Roslyn. It looked more like a junior college campus than a chemical factory. If a well-lit, beautifully constructed and situated workplace could produce happy workers, then the Rubinstein workforce was destined for bliss. It was so bucolic that in the summer, workers could pick wild berries behind the building. As Bobby

Guinta, put it, "We went into God's country when we came out here. To us it was a paradise."

The Roslyn area also met Helena Rubinstein's standards for progressive culture. According to real estate lore, early settlers gave the town its name because it reminded them of the area near Roslin Castle in Scotland. In the mid–nineteenth century, Roslyn became an artists' and writers' community, drawing the likes of poet and journalist William Cullen Bryant, who later donated a library-meetinghouse to the town for "their intellectual and social improvement." In 1885, the philanthropist Ellen Ward built a clock tower for Roslyn, which sat on a grassy island in the center of town. The block-long downtown boasted fifty buildings built between 1693 and 1850, including an ancient gristmill, which served as a tea shop during the 1950s. A freshwater duck pond hid behind the art deco movie theater; across the street was a small inlet edged with marsh grasses leading out to Long Island Sound.

Across from the clock tower was a pretty two-story stucco, stone, and wood building that reflected the town's refined ambience—but housed one of the brashest local unions on Long Island. From here, Tony Mazzocchi would build a cadre of worker radicals who would transform working conditions in the plant, fight the mob, and organize new unions in dozens of other plants. This office would become the hub of Democratic politics for Long Island, as well as activity against nuclear bomb testing. And it would become the launching pad for Mazzocchi's campaign to become the Marcantonio of the suburbs.

IV

After Mazzocchi took the gavel from Local 149 president Jack Curran on March 20, 1953, at St. Mary's Hall in Roslyn, he requested graciously that "the membership give a rising vote of thanks to the past officers."[7] With their heartfelt applause, the rank and file thanked Curran for his years of service—and cheered their new president, from whom they expected great things.

Starting with that first meeting, members began to see subtle but significant changes—little boring details that expanded union democracy. There were more people at executive board meetings because Tony invited stewards and members of other committees to attend. Tony also insisted that all new committees be selected by rank-and-file members rather than by the executive board, reversing top-down controls instituted by Curran. The composition of the labor-management committee, which met weekly with Rubinstein managers to discuss grievances, grew to include not only the president, vice president, and chief steward, but also three shop stewards and an executive board member.

Thanks to another Tony reform, more of Local 149's members started attending political and labor forums and conferences in places like Albany, Washington, or Philadelphia. Recalled Bobby Guinta: "The local union allotted a certain amount of funds for accommodation and for eating per diem. But instead of having each individual put a certain amount of money into their own pocket, which they were authorized to do, Tony said: 'They're giving us enough money for three guys—if we pool it, we can take five.' And that way we exposed more people to various kinds of activities."

Tony built on the local's militant past.

> The 1941 strike was one of the outstanding strikes in New York City. When I got there, there was still a memory of it. A lot of the strikers were still there. They knew the value of the union. But the union began to roll under the company, and I needed to turn it back into a militant union that extracted economic concessions from the employer. And I had to create a rank-and-file-run union so that people understood what the union was about on the shop floor.

The first task was to deep-six the two-tier wage structure. Tony recalled: "I told everybody to prepare for a major strike. I said, 'If we don't overcome this two-tier, we ain't never gonna build this union, and the company's gonna dump us.' And we worked for a solid year preparing people for a strike."

Tony knew that the company would prevail unless the local demonstrated its militancy. They had to convince the company that to eliminate the two-tier system, members would do what they did in 1941: strike indefinitely over a matter of union principle. A full year before the contract was to expire, Tony asked the members to assess themselves special dues to establish a strike fund. The stewards went to each member every week and asked for a quarter. The fund would only provide modest help during a strike, but Tony recognized that the act of collection sent a militant signal to both members and management.

"The company at first laughed at it," he said. "But they started to take us more seriously when we rented a strike headquarters about two months before the contract expired. I made sure we rented a very visible one."

Tony also revived the CIO tradition of intensive strike support for other unions. The common approach was to donate money, support a boycott, or show up at a picket line once or twice. But Tony thought that if he could get his members to more actively support other workers' strikes, it would stiffen their backbone in confronting Rubinstein—and make the company think twice about two-tier wage rates.

And so the members of Local 149 marched into the maelstrom of strikes—at industrial facilities like Reeves Instrument, Arma, Sperry, and Republic—that sprang up all over Long Island in the supposedly placid 1950s. The mass picketing and police violence in these strikes were reminiscent of the 1930s. Always the unions needed more hands to keep strikebreakers and suppliers from crossing the picket lines.

"It would be nothing to see five hundred cops out there in a phalanx in one of these strikes," said Tony. "We'd run our buses in early. We had a lot of elderly women—and we'd bring them, too. I'd bring out two to three hundred people."

George Roach remembered driving out to Roosevelt Field to block scabs at the 6 AM shift change during a strike by several thousand members of the International Union of Electrical, Radio and Machine Workers (IUE) against Reeves Instrument. When he arrived, Roach said, "You could see this field of blue. *What the hell is that?* I thought. . . . And you get closer and closer and there were cops with helmets. All these cops and their big vans, and we're gonna walk the picket line and hold out the day shift?"

Picket-line duty could get rough. As Tony recalled:

> The IUE fought very militant strikes in those days. A lot of the guys came out of the UE [United Electrical Workers Union] when all the red-baiting took place, and they had a militant tradition. There was a guy named Fitzgerald who was getting beat up every day on that picket line. He was a prizefighter. But the law was that

> if you hit somebody outside of the ring you'd go to jail. So when Fitzgerald rapped a cop, they started dragging him away. His friends yell out, "Don't let him get arrested!" Because once they book you, they're going to know who you are. So the cops are dragging Fitzgerald one way and our guys start pulling him the other. It's a tug-of-war with this guy's body. They had all these cameras on the roof filming this. They used it to try to get an injunction against the strike.

In the next few years Tony and the members turned their local into a strike support machine. "We were persistent," Tony said. "We were there in countless strikes, and we were bringing out large groups of people. We developed a reputation as a militant group on Long Island. And our women were just as tough as our men."

In the IUE strike at Reeves, in 1957, Tony Mazzocchi's local sent scores of workers to the picket lines for more than thirty-five days in a row. In an extraordinary show of thanks, IUE president James Carey, who had served as the first secretary of the CIO and was a staunch anti-communist, sent a letter to the convention of Local 149's national union (no longer called Gas-Coke, but now the Oil, Chemical and Atomic Workers Union). In it, Carey praised Local 149 members for picketing day after day in the face of police brutality and for their weekly strike collections and food collections. Carey called Local 149's solidarity "an inspiration to all organized workers."[8]

"That letter made us," said Tony.

As intended, the barrage of strike support sent a clear message to Rubinstein's management. So many workers showed up late for work after serving on these picket lines that sometimes management had to shut down the lines for the first hour. "We were still coming in on the buses from New York, and we wouldn't let our folks go to work until they went out to the IUE picket lines," said Tony. "The company was going ape about it."

Not only were the Local 149 members late, but they had an attitude about it as well. Rubinstein's managers could read the defiance on their faces as they straggled into work. "The company was scared shitless," Tony said. "They knew we were having a pitched battle with those Nassau County cops every day. The company figured, if you're going to do this on somebody *else's* picket line, what are you gonna do when it's your own?"

Rubinstein didn't want to find out. Negotiations began. Management was willing to remove the two-tier system—but only after several years. "We said, 'No. It's got to go now,'" Tony recalled. "Management was saying, 'Why do you want to negotiate for people who don't even have a job here?' That was the old line." But along with the old line came the old memory—the 1941 strike. Rubinstein managers who had been responsible for that fiasco had been fired. The new negotiators did not want a replay: The two-tier wage system was eliminated.

For the next twelve years, Tony Mazzocchi and his members would continue to win enormous gains without ever having to strike.

The local won a standard-setting health care plan. "We were the first in the nation to win dental coverage," Tony said. "And our reputation spread all over Long Island. The women who worked in our shop—and it was maybe 85 percent women—had husbands who worked for super-profitable defense companies. And yet they knew that we'd won a benefit plan that was better than anything that existed."

V

Of course a model health plan wasn't all Tony had in mind. "I needed people's support before I could talk about anything more radical," he said. "We had to produce. We couldn't go with a lot of empty rhetoric."

Still, "The union had to be more than a shop-floor institution. It had to have a broader political understanding. I mean, I understood that corporations dominated the political scene. And that if you were going to fight effectively, people had to understand, ideologically, the need to deal with this huge corporate sector. I knew when I became president of the local, it was a fight for the minds of the people."

Tony needed a core group of "minds" within the local committed to radical unionism. He created this cadre deliberately. His blueprint included sending his young aides to political meetings in the city and having them report back to the membership on pressing issues of the day. He sent George Roach to hear legendary UAW president Walter Reuther. Bobby Guinta went to meetings featuring the fiery Transport Workers Union president Mike Quill. George and Mac were sent to Cornell University in Ithaca for a weeklong labor program in which they learned how to produce a punchy union newsletter.

As Bobby Guinta recalled, "There were so many meetings to go to, you never got home. Little wonder our marriages fell apart."

Tony had soon hooked his lieutenants on a life of round-the-clock activism. But the random meetings weren't enough. Tony wanted his local activists to know about social movements, the history of progressive unionism, and the struggle for black civil rights. While he could send members to schools to learn how to design a newspaper or process a grievance, there was no school that taught about labor as a cause. He needed to transform McManus, Roach, and about twenty others into radical activists who saw militant unionism as part of a social movement, a cause that extended far beyond the union and its immediate interests. And the only way to do that, Tony believed, was through books.

"Unless I had a group who, politically and ideologically, understood the meaning of trade unionism—that it was more than just winning a grievance in the shop—we'd lose people," Tony said. "People had to have a vision of a different world, and then you could talk about socialism and everything else."

So Mazzocchi, the ninth-grade dropout, launched an informal book club. There wasn't a single high school graduate in the bunch. Despite that, Mac, George, and Bobby were already voracious readers. Though, as each confessed, they'd only read "trash" until they met Tony.

It started out casually among the activists who stayed after work to help at the union office. It was a "guy" thing. In the male-dominated nuclear family of the 1950s, the men could hang out at the union hall after work while the women went home to their second jobs as wives and mothers. So although the books traveled to some of the women, the core group included only men.

Tony's informal book club did a number on George. "Like everything else he did," George said, "Tony was subtle. One day Tony gave me a book by Howard Fast, *Freedom Road*. He thought I might like it. And I really did. He gave me another, then another, and I was hooked."

Tony loaned books to Mac and others as well. Soon the book exchange became a weekly institution. "We would get together on Monday nights at the union office to put out the local's newspaper," Roach said. "The local gave us each a buck for food, and we pooled it to buy some meat and potatoes for dinner. As we worked on the paper, Tony would cook up the food on a hot plate. At some point he suggested that we each chip in a quarter a week to buy some books to circulate. Since I lived in Manhattan, they would send me to the used-book stores to find the old stuff. And we just kept circulating the books."

There were no formal study groups or meetings. They talked at the local bar or over dinner in the office. Soon there were more than twenty people in the klatch. It was the University of Mazzocchi. The introductory "curriculum" packed a political wallop. It started with Howard Fast, then an avowed communist whose historical novels were considered brilliant by some and cheap communist propaganda by others. During World War II, when *Freedom Road* first appeared, it was a literary hit hailed by the elite press. But during the late 1940s, anti-communists denounced the book, a devastating account of racism and the collapse of Reconstruction. Fast's books were removed from public library shelves. His publishers, who had handsomely profited from his early works, refused to touch his new ones. He served time in jail for refusing to name names during the McCarthy witch hunt. Finally, after a decade of unsuccessful self-publishing, Fast's American star rose again—after he had left the Communist Party, disgusted by Khrushchev's 1956 revelations about Stalin's atrocities.

Later, Fast's *Spartacus,* about a slave revolt in ancient Rome, turned into a best seller and a Hollywood blockbuster. During the 1950s, books such as *Freedom Road, Spartacus,* and *Citizen Tom Paine* were still considered subversive, which greatly added to their charm for Tony and his young militants.

Then the group turned to the history of American class struggle through such works as *Labor's Untold Story* and *The History of the Fur and Leather Workers*. For some, the reading group opened the door to more traditional literature as well. George remembered how they passed around the *Iliad* and the *Odyssey.*

Reading Howard Fast and Jack London was one thing, but was it really possible that this collection of dropouts read *Homer*? They all said yes in separate interviews. Clearly, these unionists did not conform to the stereotype of "workers" as people who shuttled back and forth from job to mall to TV. They read the *Iliad.*

Tony's group saw itself as part of a working-class culture that encouraged self-education through literature. Tony had come from a tradition that held common people in high esteem. Workers were the ones who made the industrial world turn around. But they were also endowed with transformative power—they had the potential to take over and run an economy, a nation, the world. Every worker had an inalienable right to education for its own sake (not just training) and the right to enjoy high culture. Workers could appropriate the humanities as well as the means of production. So Tony was not surprised that his cadre of dropouts could read these books and become leaders in the struggle.

First, though, their casual racism had to be uprooted. As Tony recalled, "I looked around the plant and I saw it was an interesting place, but backward in many ways. There was a lot of racism. Only two blacks worked there, and they were janitors."

Bobby Guinta remembered a similar atmosphere: "We used foul language—no doubt about that. Being in the infantry, you learned foul language. We used ethnic slurs, anti-Semitic comments, anti-black comments."

"Well, it's a working-class-type thing," George Roach confirmed. "You know, like when you come in, someone's a kike, someone's a spic, someone's a mick."

How bigoted were they? "Racist as hell," Tony said. "Gradually, I introduced them to these books. And *Freedom Road* transformed them."

Fast's novel told of an effort by freed slaves and poor white farmers to unite to win land and education for all in the aftermath of the Civil War. The plantation owners, devastated by the war, plot their path back to their aristocratic lifestyle. If the Local 149 activists were going to understand divide-and-conquer tactics, then they first had to look at their white skin in a new way, which was precisely what Fast made them do. In this passage, for instance, southern elites discuss their plan for regaining power by giving poor whites "their white skin."

> This business of white nightshirts and burning crosses is tomfoolery, but it has its use. The weasel type, the timid, they become bolder when they hide their faces. . . . There'll be enough men, the scum we used for overseers, the trash that bought and sold slaves and bred them, the kind who were the men with the bullwhip and filth without one, the kind who have only one virtue, their white skin.

> Gentlemen, we'll play a symphony on that white skin, we'll make it a badge of honor. We'll put a premium on that white skin. We'll dredge the sewers and swamps for candidates and we'll give them their white skin—and in return they will give us back what we lost through this insane war, yes, all of it.[9]

The activists read the book in the early 1950s. Afterward, said Tony, "We went to the company and said, 'You've got to hire blacks.'"

At the time, Tony was certain he could push this through, since, as he put it, "We were kicking the shit out of the company."

But Rubinstein's managers refused at first to change its hiring practices, fearing that Tony's group was too far out in front and that the workers would object. And management was largely correct. As Tony recalled, "One of my big supporters, a steward, came to me and said, 'Look, the people said, if we have to share lockers with them, we're gonna refuse to do it.'"

But with the backing of his readers, Mazzocchi stood firm: "I said, 'If you don't like the policy, you can give up your job. It's a union policy and it's a union shop and we made the decision because it's the right thing to do.'"

In the end, "The company started hiring blacks. No one quit their job and after a while, the whites accepted them. And we crossed that bridge long before the civil rights revolution broke out into the open."

Mazzocchi's reading program also strayed beyond the socialist canon. The group read a book by Franz Werfel, a Jew who'd escaped death in the Holocaust with help from a French convent. After virtually converting to Catholicism, he gave thanks by writing *The Song of Bernadette,* which was nominated for twelve Academy Awards. Mazzocchi learned about a different Werfel story called *The Forty Days of Musa Dagh*.

In that 1933 novel, Werfel described the extermination of the Armenians by the Turks during World War I, and the valiant struggle of resistance by the Armenians high in the Musa Dagh mountains. Werfel expertly revealed the patterns of thought that in a few short years would lead to the Nazi Holocaust. And he called into question the entire notion that technical progress was automatically good. It was a heavy book for the dropouts, but they loved it.

Spartacus, which George Roach called "my bible," seemed to be written with the Rubinstein workers in mind. This saga of a slave rebellion ends with a description of Crassius, the Roman general who put down the Spartacus slave rebellions, leading a tour of his perfume factory—the ancient equivalent of the Rubinstein factory. Fast has Spartacus reveal the secret of his wealth and the wonders of free labor:

> "They gave me the Servile War which paid me small profit indeed. So I have my own small secrets, and this factory is one of them. Each of those silver tubes of quintessence is worth 10 times its weight in pure gold. A slave eats your food and dies. But these workers turn themselves into gold. Nor am I concerned with feeding and housing them. . . ."
>
> "Workers revolt?" Crassius smiled and shook his head. "No that will never be. You see, they are not slaves. They are free men. They can come and go as they please. Why should they ever revolt?"[10]

As Rubinstein's perfume workers read their books, they hoped to prove Crassius wrong. And no one read more or tried harder than Bobby Guinta.

VI

Bobby had always been a good student. But like so many kids in his neighborhood, he got restless, dropped out, and joined the military. Little did he know that in a few short years, he would become the University of Mazzocchi's valedictorian. He grew up on 11th Street in Long Island City, only a few blocks from the original Rubinstein plant. His father drove trucks and helped organize a Teamsters local. Like everyone in their Italian neighborhood, the Guintas were devout Catholics whose lives revolved around the local church—St. Mary's.

Bobby made excellent grades, and a city college should have been his next stop. But he dropped out. Bobby said he was a "typically neurotic kid of that era. I was leaving school with an average in my classes of close to ninety. My teachers didn't want me out of school. But my father signed me out because I was so damn insistent. I didn't know what the hell I was doing. I joined the army. Then after I got in I was looking to get out. So you're talking about a very confused young man."

After Bobby did well on an intelligence test, the army sent him to typing school. Three years later, he was out on the street looking for a job. He was offered two or three positions at the phone company. "But all started at about thirty dollars a week. My sister was a secretary of one of the managers at Rubinstein and she said, 'You know, Helena Rubinstein pays pretty good—thirty-nine dollars a week.'" At the time, said Bobby, "I really didn't think of my future or my working life as a career. It was only to get a job."

Bobby and Tony were natural compatriots who both hired on at Rubinstein on the same day. But Bobby worked at the warehouse twenty blocks from the main facility, so at first he only saw Tony at union meetings. He was impressed when Mazzocchi rose to challenge Curran.

"Tony was very nondescript. You would underestimate him." And Curran: "Good-looking, well-spoken, the man had a command of speaking, no doubt about that." But then, "Nondescript Tony got up and said something about the five-hundred-dollar bonus and how giving candy to the executive board was inappropriate. Tony spoke with a measure of authority. I didn't know him very well at all. I just knew that he sounded good when he spoke."

After Tony became president, he sensed that Bobby wanted to get more involved, so he sent him to represent the union at political meetings. "He'd say to me, 'There's going to be Mike Quill speaking at the New York City Labor Council. You want to go?'" Bobby recalled. "Like, in the beginning, to just give you something to do. And I said, 'Yeah, I'll go and see what it's like.' I went there and it sounded interesting. And Mike Quill was full of shit as usual. I'd come back and tell him about it."

Bobby moved closer to the inner circle. And in 1953, Tony started the local's newspaper, *The Militant*.

> I was a typist in the army. . . . "Hey Bob, we need somebody to type the friggin' *Militant*!" "Oh, okay. Good." So I'd go do that, and you'd hang around with interesting people. There was a Gestetner mimeograph machine. And we typed up the damn things and what a pain in the ass that was. Make one friggin' mistake and you had to use that white-out. I knew how to type, and I had a fairly decent command of language, too.

Bobby was hooked. The line and the sinker came when Tony fed him books—knowing full well that Bobby liked to read. "You never saw me without a book. From the age of twelve, I always had a book in my hand."

But Tony's books were different. *Spartacus, Tom Paine* . . . "Well, you can well imagine if you were a twenty-two-year-old and started reading that stuff—it's enough to make you want to go out and get a gun. Then it started to be a brain-buster to read some of the stuff that Tony talked about [like Werfel]. And I said, 'Yeah those books are good.' Then it started this whole education. I would go to the Strand Bookstore to buy books for a buck. . . ."

Bobby described how Tony would lead him, like a dope peddler, to more and more ecstasy. "Tony would say, 'Well, did you ever read anything by Jack London?' 'Oh yeah, sure, the dog stories.' Well, how about reading *The People from the Abyss,* or the *Iron Heel,* or *Martin Eden*? I mean, if you're ready to learn, if you're thirsting for something in your life—you read these books, and your whole mind opens up."

Guinta went on a reading binge. "We read all the classics. Tony started a burst of intellectual development that was astonishing. McManus read just about the whole history of Native Americans. We read all of Dickens. Not much of Shakespeare. Tony wasn't too big on Shakespeare. I don't know why. Oh, Victor Hugo, Emile Zola, *J'Accuse,* Anatole France, *Penguin Island*."

Tony seemed to come from a more cultured intellectual milieu that greatly attracted Bobby. "A couple of times my wife and I went to visit Tony at his home," he said. "And he had a big monaural system at the time. And he played some music; naturally, he liked Beethoven. And Arturo Toscanini because he was anti-fascist. And from then on, I was kind of emulating him. I wanted to be like him. But I didn't realize until many years later that he was my mentor in life. . . . I must admit, there was a time when I never questioned anything he said. Whatever he said was gospel. Which I'm sure was not his intent, but it might have been something I needed at the time."

Mazzocchi invited his readers and activists—as well as their spouses and children—to his uncle Lester's place in Blairstown. Was it some kind of left-wing camp where trade unionists could be indoctrinated? "No," Bobby said, "this was not a CP camp. We played bocce, Ping-Pong. I discovered that Tony could have been an Olympic champion in Ping-Pong, he was that good. Lester was there. Tony's sisters were there. Even his aunt and his father came up there, too—old Italian guy, a very nice man."

But politics were never far away. "I remember talking to Tony alone one evening, and that was the first time that he spoke about socialism. And he didn't say the Soviet Union, he just said socialism in general and that capitalism is an exploitative process."

Oh, was Bobby ever ready for this! "And then when Tony started telling me about the difference between the people owning the means of production and not owning it, we must have sat two or three hours. And we talked about the fading away of the police state. What are the police for? What's the army for? This was a very typical discussion of Marxist ideology. And he described this to me and it sounded interesting. And I said, 'Yeah, you know, it sounds right.' And naturally I started spouting a lot of things Tony said. You know, it was new knowledge."

Tony "didn't proselytize too much," Bobby continued. "Tony never got up and made speeches about things. Maybe if we're sitting around, maybe him, me, Mac, and George, he'd be talking about things, like how instead of cowboys and Indians as kids he used to play Loyalists and the fascists against each other."

Bobby started attending more meetings. "I would go to the NAACP in Brooklyn. Speakers like A. Philip Randolph. We saw Sidney Poitier. He wasn't even a famous actor yet. He had given speeches about some kind of civil rights and we'd go."

It was only a matter of time before Bobby experienced a first-class identity crisis. First to go was his self-image as a devout, anti-communist American, which Bobby had picked up as a kid tracking his uncle's travels in East Asia as an enlisted man during the 1930s. "My idols were General Patton, Omar Bradley, Douglas McCarthy—that fascist bastard! We were not a military family, but there was that connection to the whole Orient, especially China. And Chiang Kai-shek was another hero. When he was defeated, that was terrible. . . . You know, 'The communists are taking over.' And I tell you we were violently, rabidly anti-communist. Rabid."

But like the thousands of students who colorfully rejected their parents' teachings a decade later during the 1960s, Bobby became a convert to a new way of thinking. "My whole religious upbringing, my patriotism, my jingoism. Every time I saw the American flag, I'd have a lump in my throat. All the books that I had read, all the entertainers, the singers, the music, every single thing that I'd loved up until that age—I was twenty-three years old—all of it was thrown the hell out. A complete 180-degree turn."

Hardest of all for Guinta was the death of God. Bobby can't recall exactly when it happened, but "it probably started up at Lester's place. Tony said he didn't believe in God, didn't believe in a hereafter, nothing. And then naturally he gives me another book, *Tolerance* by Hendrik van Loon. One of the most profound books I ever read. It gives you a whole history of all the different religions that were pleading for tolerance, until they became the majority. Apparently Tony recommended it all the time. And he recommended *The Seventh Cross*. They made a movie out of it with Spencer Tracy. Oh and naturally, *Johnny Got His Gun* by Dalton Trumbo. And Christ, *The Grapes of Wrath*. That changed my mind completely."

So how about Tony's atheism? "That son of a bitch caused me to lay awake every night, six months straight. I could not sleep every night of the friggin' week because I didn't realize that I was becoming an atheist. Because I believed that I was gonna live forever. I mean I was so friggin' sure of it, nothing could shake that belief. It was a monumental change."

The change was tumultuous. It was, said Bobby, an "emotional state we were in at the time. Not Tony, because Tony was never in any emotional state. He was always pretty clear, I think. He seemed to me to have led his life in a straight line all the way. I can't say that about myself. Do you remember Eric Hoffer's book *The True Believer*? There were a number of true believers. I have to put myself in that category."

Tony encouraged Bobby to explore the far edges of radical literature and figure out if any of the traditional Marxist texts—most of which were too dense and polemical for Tony to stomach—could offer any guidance.

"Oh, the Little Lenin Library," said Bobby. After Tony and Bobby had worked together for three or four years, Bobby became the group's unofficial theoretician. "Yeah, I guess every CP cell needed their theoretician. . . . And Tony was probably conflicted about this—how much should you follow the Soviet Union's line?"

Were they really in a secret CP cell? "No. We never had any thought about joining the CP, there's no doubt about that. At least I am not aware that he was ever a member."

Bobby, the new militant, sometimes got too exuberant. Tony's street smarts were a counterbalance. "He used to send me to demonstrations. He said, 'Don't get yourself arrested. It ain't gonna do you any good. Just go there and report back.'"

This admonishment pertained especially to New York demonstrations against the "duck-and-cover" air raid drills designed to prepare the population for nuclear war. Although Bobby said he wanted to be arrested at one of these protests, Tony cautioned against it. Perhaps Tony saved Bobby from commitment to a mental institution. According to one account from 1955, a New York City judge "sent an actress to the psychiatric ward of Bellevue Hospital for having defied an air raid drill."[11]

Bobby also was tempted to take a stand on the Taft-Hartley loyalty oaths that they all had to sign. "I said 'Tony, what are we gonna do?' 'Cause I was shop steward then. 'We gonna sign these?' He said, 'Sure, you gotta sign them. So what?'"

Still, why weren't they run out of town for being communists? "We didn't get red-baited," Bobby said. "Because Tony kept it quiet. We kept it among ourselves. We didn't talk about the books we were reading to everybody. You certainly wouldn't give Jack Curran a book."

In effect, Tony taught them to quack quietly. What saved them, Bobby said, was their steady focus on being good trade unionists, on building their union—and their complete avoidance of Marxist catechisms. "Tony never spoke in radical terms, never used any of the radical terminology. It was just the normal practicing of real good trade unionism which altered people like me, McManus, George Roach, and a number of others. That's what got us to understand that these injustices were built into the system," recalled Bobby. "And once you realized that, like, why do you need unions? What's the premise? If capitalism is so great, why is it that you had to scratch for every nickel and dime that you got? See, one of the things Tony taught us, and by exactly what process I'm not sure, is to deal with the causes, not with the effects. And you gotta do this on everything. But once you start understanding that, there's no going back."

Especially not for Guinta. The more he developed politically, the more responsibility Tony placed on him. Tony drafted Bobby to create and run the local's credit union, a cooperative enterprise that had somehow survived the dawning Cold War. Under a New Deal provision built upon an old German guild tradition, groups with a common association could run a bank-like entity where members could save their money and take out small loans. When the operation worked well, members would get a dividend instead of interest on the savings. "For every dollar of money you put into your account, you would have one dollar's worth of insurance, too," said Bobby. "So that if you died, your money would double at no charge to the members."

For some unions during the '50s, running your own credit union was the ticket to personal wealth. In mobbed-up unions, the rules might be bent a little so that funds could be siphoned off for risky loans to dubious characters or small diversions into the pockets of family and friends. Tony was not above bending the rules, but his motive was entirely different. He wanted to put money into the pockets of the members to demonstrate that the credit union was a viable institution. As Bobby recalled, "He says, 'You know, we gotta pay a dividend this year.' I says, 'They're ain't no fuckin' money to pay a dividend.' He says, 'We gotta figure out some way.' And he could be a prick, too, if he wanted to. I said, 'I'll play stupid that I don't know anything about accounting.' I paid the dividend."

When the fiscal examiner came, Bobby continued to play stupid. "'Oh gee,' I said. 'I'm very sorry that I did that. Well, we'll correct it next year.'"

Bobby slaved over his unpaid work for the credit union. Its success reflected well on the local's leadership, perpetuating the mystique that whatever they touched worked. Bobby yearned to work side by side with Tony every day through a full-time union job. By the 1960s, the local had organized so many shops that it could afford another full-time position. Bobby hoped that job had his name written all over it.

But Tony wanted to develop female leadership and would not give Bobby Guinta the job. This precipitated a difficult break between mentor and student. Bobby thought he saw the colder, calculating side of Tony, and it made him bitter. "After all the time and energy that I spent on the credit union, he really pissed me off," Guinta said. "I was the logical choice, but Tony said, 'No, we gotta give it to one of the women.' Because, you know, we needed their support. I thought that was a lot of bullshit. I said, 'You made a mistake.' And from that day on I decided to leave the labor movement."

Guinta stumbled through another year of work, then quit Rubinstein and union organizing. He found work in computer programming at a large bank. The next step might have been to reject his own blind devotion, recant the beliefs that bound him to Tony, and embrace the corporate order he was now part of. But Bobby was never able turn his back on the political consciousness he and Tony had shared. Nor could he lose his affection for Tony.

Trained to look for root causes, Bobby had to find something fundamentally wrong to explain his soured relationship with Mazzocchi. It didn't take him long: It was the whole damn labor movement! Tony was a good man in a bad movement. Guinta developed a scathing critique of trade unionism—not because it was too anti-corporate, but because it wasn't anti-corporate enough. For Bobby, the union movement missed the boat forever when it failed to embrace the radical '60s movement, which, he believed, embodied the revolutionary spirit.

"You know, Tony was involved with the labor movement during its utter demise. If anyone can name one thing that the American labor movement contributed to the advancement of mankind in the last forty years, I'll kiss their ass on Times Square. And I believe in labor unions!"

But the former chief theoretician for Local 149 also looked for philosophical differences with his mentor. He came to question the value of his University of Mazzocchi degree. "We were so young and uncritical. Lack of formal education deprived us of an introduction to people like Albert Camus and the philosophers" and to a "well-rounded critical, analytical kind of approach to things." But Bobby never ceased to value Tony's vision of change. "He always said—and he said it long before Bobby Kennedy did—'Every person you meet in your life you will have an influence on, and they will influence others. And that's how the whole world changes.'

"There's one thing about Tony, and this is the first time I ever thought about using this word. He had this magnetism that affected men as well women. I don't mean in a sexual way, but the fuck was charismatic."

More than thirty years after his abrupt departure, Bobby heard Tony speak at a forum in New York.

"We threw our arms around each other," Bobby said. And to his amazement, it only took moments before Tony started to pull him in again. "I hadn't seen him for like fifteen years, and after listening to him for ten minutes, I was ready to take up the fuckin' gun again. Seductive, the bastard was seductive. He had a way of explaining things."

Bobby seemed genuinely puzzled by this. As if staring at his imaginary and worthless University of Mazzocchi degree, he asked, "... where the hell does he get it? It can't all be from books."

VII

There was also the school of hard knocks. No amount of reading could prepare Tony Mazzocchi for what greeted him after only two months in office. His militant dreams for the labor movement were nearly stolen away. Just as Tony stepped into office, Helena Rubinstein revealed an elaborate sting operation to catch workers who pilfered products from the company. Rubinstein's elite wares came in small containers that easily found their way into pockets. And of course they could be sold on the street for good money.

The company hired undercover agents as employees to ferret out major offenders. Many people stole, and many were caught. One Rubinstein employee operated a small business out of her basement for neighbors and friends. Another had set up a stall among the carts on Orchard Street on Manhattan's Lower East Side. It was said that everyone stole at one time or another. Except Mazzocchi.

Tony didn't know what to do. The rock-solid sureness that had guided him to victory abandoned him. On what progressive grounds could he defend the thirty workers who had been caught with goods? But what kind of leader would he be if he let the company fire them or send them to jail? Those who saw him wrestle with this said that for the first time he seemed lost, unsure of himself.

The sting left little room for doubt about the thefts. Once the company had accumulated the evidence, it brought the perpetrators into the personnel office and confronted them, encouraging confessions. The deal was simple: Confess and resign, or we'll press charges. They confessed and were seen to the door.

When the union stewards met to discuss what to do, Tony didn't have much to say. They could feel his uncertainty. And they sensed what he sensed—that the company meant business on this one. It would take a Herculean struggle to keep the company from firing or prosecuting the thieves. The union and its members would have to put everything on the line. Would the members stay solid in such a battle?

Tony recommended nothing, and the local did nothing. They didn't write leaflets. They didn't mention it in *The Militant.* The only written record was a veiled reference in the local union minutes on May 19, 1953, when Tony "said a good policy is to stick to the cash sales," a reference to the weekly company store sales at which workers could buy products for 40 percent off.

Buy wholesale and don't steal from your capitalist bosses: That was the essence of Tony's position. He also told workers to leave their lockers unlocked so they could not be accused of theft. If company goods were found in their lockers, they could say that anyone might have put it there. At a labor-management committee meeting, the union told managers that now that they had their thirty victims, the operation had to stop. Management agreed, but in fact the fight wasn't over.

With the advantage shifting their way, managers decided to press their case, hoping to recapture control of the shop floor from this increasingly aggressive union. They said they wanted to eliminate the conditions that had allowed theft to take place in the first place. One manager had a stroke of genius: Sew up the pockets on hourly workers' company work clothes. No pockets, no theft.

Tony may have temporarily lost his confidence, but his base knew how to handle this one. They didn't need his leadership. Tony had already helped ignite the members' imagination and willpower, and now they would save him from his indecision. One Monday morning when workers came to get their overalls (for men) and smocks (for women), a sheepish supervisor acknowledged that the pockets had been sewn shut to prevent stealing. Workers were shocked and angry.

"Where am I going to put my tissues?" one woman sniffed.

Workers grumbled as they walked to their work areas. By the mid-morning coffee break, the griping turned into action. "We didn't do a lot of planning, maybe ten minutes' worth," remembered George Roach. "We wrote numbers across the pockets of our uniforms—like prison numbers. We made out little signs that said GUESTS and gave them to the visiting deliverymen, asking them to join us."

"We started to chant real loud, 'Yeah! Yeah! Yeah! *Yeah!*' We said it in kind of a menacing way. We started to walk toward personnel. Lots of folks followed, everyone chanting *'Yeah! Yeah! Yeah!'* The security guards locked themselves into their room. I mean, the walls were shaking."

Two hundred chanting workers sat down in front of the personnel office. The company's lawyer, known to the workers more for his inflated ego than his legal skills, walked down the corridor to a loud Bronx cheer. Enraged, he demanded that several workers be fired on the spot for showing disrespect. But soon, sensing defeat or worse, he retreated.

Tony happened to be inside the human relations office when he heard the roars. He was clueless about the protest, but sensed an advantage. A wry grin crossed his face as he suggested to managers that they take a look outside. As Tony walked out with them and viewed the chanting masses on the floor, his grin widened. Now he knew what to do. He escorted management through the illegal sit-down strike to determine the nature of the grievance. Sewn pockets? And then his smile got even bigger.

Management had overreached—they knew it and so did Tony. As the bell rang signaling the end of the break, Tony gave an almost imperceptible nod and George asked everyone to return to their jobs. George followed the workers closely to make sure they didn't tear anything down on the way back.

The negotiations didn't take long. Working into the night, managers used razors to remove the stitches on every pocket in every article of clothing. Management hubris and worker direct action had reclaimed the union's honor, and Tony's confidence to lead.

VIII

In 1953, around the time of the Pockets War, the local started a Tuesday-night bowling league. It would become infamous, a weekly orgy of flying pins and illicit liaisons, a warm-up for a long night of carousing. The bowling league was the graveyard for young marriages. It strained traditional 1950s family values, but it also helped the union wrest workers' social lives away from the company. Bowling, dances, picnics, baseball teams, parties, blood drives: All could contribute to class struggle so long as the union, not the company, sponsored them.

Rubinstein tried to compete with its own picnics, bowling league (for white-collar workers only), and charitable drives, but they were no match for Local 149. The union bowling nights became such a hot attraction that the white-collar workers soon abandoned the company's league, preferring the intense partying that followed an evening of union-sponsored bowling.

Even the increasingly popular TV failed to dim the intensity of the union's social life—including barn dances at the Polish Hall, sports teams, and impromptu celebrations for holidays, birthdays, and engagements. Mazzocchi's members loved to party. Tony thought it fulfilled a deep need. "We injected something into people's lives that was missing: a sense of excitement, a sense of confronting a company, organizing." And a sense of deep camaraderie people can only get after they've had a lot of good times together.

Beyond entertainment, the local, at Tony's prodding, provided free medical checkups for each member. Said Bobby Guinta: "One of the most significant things he started was medical screening. We went to the HIP center [a clinic], and they'd set aside an entire evening for all the people in our local union. They'd take your blood, x-ray. That was the first time we all got the pipe shoved up our behind. And we did it at least annually." In another coup for the local, Mazzocchi also arranged for all members to get the new Salk polio vaccine.

The Salk vaccine, the bowling league, the credit union, the blood bank, the checkups—all enhanced the local's prestige and made Tony seem invincible. As George put it: "We felt there wasn't anything he couldn't do. If he set his mind to do something like that, it was gonna be done, and we felt it would be done to the affirmative. And when I use the word *we,* I'm speaking of a whole lot of people."

The Militant pulled it all together with accounts about local bargaining, grievance issues, broader social themes, health education, sports, and local gossip. It was important enough that Tony struggled through his learning disabilities to write a periodic column. These two- to three-hundred-word essays form almost the entire sum of his written works. Because writing was difficult, Tony had no choice but to make *The Militant* a collective enterprise, drawing on the local's would-be writers, poets, and artists. The first edition hit the shop floor on September 10, 1954. It wasn't much, just a few articles about what the union provided, how the new welfare fund worked, and how to use the optical plan.

An issue produced the next year included cartoons from an aspiring artist in the local. One depicted a robot grabbing a young woman. The caption read, "Cut it out Buster: There's some ways in which automation will never replace the man." It ran with articles attacking automation and layoffs, and extolling the virtues of eating unprocessed foods. An anonymous writer penned an ode to the tune of "My Gal Sal" for the local's baseball star. They even took aim at one of their own: "Bobby Guinta denies he's egotistical. Says Bob, 'I don't think I'm half as smart as I really am.'"[12]

If gossip was social currency, then *The Militant* was the mint, with three gossip columns: "Shop Talk," "Office Chit Chat," and "Confidential Chit Chat." These included notes such as: "It's heard that a comely young lass in the shipping dept. (initials J.G.) expects an engagement ring this September."

In its earliest years, *The Militant* focused on local issues and strike support for other unions. At first, it reported primarily on petty gripes about management—the time it failed to provide refreshments during a heat wave, or kept the plant open during the hurricane, or doubled the price of vending machine sodas. Then the gripes escalated into complaints about layoffs caused by automation. By early 1956, the gripes stopped entirely as the local won more and more grievances.

The Militant launched a barrage of articles aimed at organizing Rubinstein's sixty office workers into the local. They pointed out the false pride that kept office workers from gaining the benefits of unionization: "The same laws that protect Production Workers—also protect White Collar Workers if they want to shed the fear complex and does not mean just a clean collar, or a pretty dress—but the dignity that makes one feel free of domination—free to come to work without the fear of dismissal or discipline at the whim of a supervisor—yes—a freedom that will permit your conscience to speak out."[13]

Tony's early "Reports from the President" were uncontroversial and boring, though they could draw letters from those who felt stung. ("Your President's column is a hunk of childish babble," sputtered one boss.) Tony urged help for flood victims of Hurricane Diane, welcomed new members, stressed the importance of participation and solidarity, and called for organizing the unorganized and political action to protect collective bargaining gains. When the national AFL and CIO merged in 1955, he listed the merger's pros and cons, then came out firmly in support.

In late 1955, the first sparkle of ideology emerged in *The Militant* when

Tony used George Meany, the new AFL-CIO president, to make the case for the possibility of a labor party. Knowing full well that Henry Wallace's third-party foray had fed the anti-left labor purges of 1949, Tony quoted the anti-communist Meany to full advantage: "Meany also stated that we would continue to work through the two major political parties, but if labor is rebuffed . . . we would start a labor party of our own."[14]

Even Tony's most the mundane columns were infused with a clear sense of class. He described what he saw as constant pressure by corporations to roll back unionization and defeat labor-friendly politicians. He decried union busting and urged support for strikes. It was as if Tony were carefully explaining the basics of unionism to the guys and gals back in 9a9 at Shallow Junior High.

At least five editorials focused on the highly publicized McClellan Senate hearings on labor racketeering. Because the hearings made all of labor look crime-ridden, Tony rose to the movement's defense. He used a class struggle angle: "The fact is that wherever racketeers exist in the unions, they do so with the cooperation of the bosses."[15] Tony criticized proposed anti-racketeering legislation because it let management off the hook: "I'm all for legislation that will keep welfare funds protected from racketeers whether they are from labor or management," argued Tony. "The one drawback is that the legislation Eisenhower proposes does not cover management-run welfare plans. About 92 percent of all welfare plans are management run."[16]

But Tony also tied mob penetration to a lack of rank-and-file participation. "Too many times apathy on the members' part about the affairs of their union lets the racketeers get in by default."[17] Later he wrote, "Racketeering and sellouts cannot occur where an informed rank and file exists." He added that "the same rule applies to political action. Bad legislators are elected because of the apathy of many unionists."[18]

The Militant distinguished itself on civil rights. In stark contrast with much of the labor movement during the mid-1950s, it championed the rising civil rights movement—even though the local's membership was 95 percent white. The first thirty issues of *The Militant* included no less than *twenty* articles and editorials supporting civil rights struggles.

The newsletter's first such article in August 1955 addressed that most contentious issue for unions—jobs. Under the headline of "Put Up or Shut

Up," it described a campaign by the American Newspaper Guild to shame management into hiring more minorities given that "there are only 21 Negro news-editorial workers (none in advertising) out of some 80,000 persons staffing the 1,784 general dailies and 9,770 general weekly newspapers in the US."[19]

The Militant also addressed the 1955 slaying of fourteen-year-old Emmitt Till, a Chicago native who was visiting relatives in Mississippi when he accepted a dare to talk to a white woman. For the effrontery he was kidnapped, mutilated, and killed. An all-white jury acquitted the killers. Under a headline that read "Reuther Blasts 'Mississippi Justice,'" *The Militant* quoted UAW president Walter Reuther's statement, which said in part, "Fair minded people all over the world are properly indignant over the efforts by some residents to strangle the democratic way of life."[20] (Tony would often use Reuther to legitimize his own progressive positions.)

In 1956, the local backed the Montgomery bus boycott. Heeding a call by Martin Luther King Jr., the local raised money for a station wagon to transport blacks during the boycott of segregated public transportation. In May 1956, *The Militant* called on members to attend a civil rights rally at Madison Square Garden featuring Eleanor Roosevelt, Martin Luther King Jr., Adam Clayton Powell, Roy Wilkins, and A. Philip Randolph.

Unlike Walter Reuther, Tony refused to use Cold War ideology to support civil rights. While Reuther presented racism as a blot on US democracy and its image around the world as it competed with the communists, Tony used class struggle to connect civil rights and labor rights. "By relying on irrational prejudices the bosses—with the help of the Ku Klux Klan, and an organization known as the White Citizens Council—are keeping the workers divided and out of unions," he wrote. "The resultant low wages and poor working conditions are an open invitation for Northern industry to move South." Tony likened raising money for bus boycotters to raising funds for strikers: "Our local has always been in the forefront against injustice, whether it be in relation to a strike or an attack on democracy." *The Militant* also noted that "Montgomery authorities dragged out an antilabor law to arrest these leaders. Labor's rights can never be protected while attacks on individual civil liberties go on."

Again and again, *The Militant* in 1956 and 1957 attacked discrimination as a moral and as a labor issue. On the second anniversary of the Supreme

Court's prohibition of "separate but equal" schools, one worker passionately pleaded in his article, "Let each of us evaluate our thoughts, past actions, and functions in helping first to educate ourselves and then to educate people whose unfounded prejudices constantly make the road a rougher one."[21]

The most soul-searching article didn't come from Tony. In 1957, John McCarthy, editor of *The Militant,* expressed outrage over an incident in a nearby town: "We found out over the weekend, that these so called 'cranks' are not confined to the South but are here in this area as well, as a Negro family was harassed in Bayside. The facts that these 'idiots' present us, with their violent acts, do not have to be analyzed, but our own thinking does."[22]

Without using any guilt-laden lingo about white chauvinism, the working-class dropouts of Local 149 learned to talk freely with one another about racism and social justice.

The local's newspaper, credit union, the vast array of social activities—all combined to create a remarkable new spirit at work. A new consciousness and a defiant attitude became the norm. Conditions at Rubinstein dramatically improved as grievances were solved and wages and benefits increased. Equally important, rank-and-file workers began reacting to management and to one another with more confidence and a greater sense of equality. To borrow Marxist lingo, Tony changed the social relations of production by adding a new layer of political excitement to work. Even though the jobs themselves were still drudgery, the plant was alive with debate and discussion. To hear Tony, George, and Bobby describe it, they transformed the dullest of assembly lines into Plato's *Republic.*

Tony, who had so quickly escaped manual labor to become a full-time union officer, said, "Life became exciting. The job was more than just the job. Everybody waited till the day was over, so we could go out and do something else, and then come right back in. It was a fight. You know, people were proselytizing all the time."

Bobby Guinta recalled there were "constant debates on every friggin' subject under the sun":

> Once they were awakened, you couldn't get them shut them up. . . . It was astonishing. We would be packing away, we wouldn't be thinking about what we were doing. We would be arguing about

> something or other that was going on in the country, or with the Cold War. It was always discussions. Everyone, I don't know, honing their skills for what? Debates. It became a debating society. Supervisors used to come around and say, "Hey, a little less debating and a little more working." I said, "I know. But we gotta talk about this; it's very important." Because no one wanted to be packing boxes. You know, we were more interested in talking about these interesting things.

For George Roach, it was a mind-bending experience: "What did Mazzocchi do? For most of us he changed the world. You know, everything was quite different from what it had been."

SIX

From Bombs to Broadway

During Tony Mazzocchi's twelve years as president, members of Local 149 got used to the union's innovative projects. In Local 149, they could bowl, fight the mob, enjoy their fabulous dental plan, rally behind Martin Luther King Jr., go to a barn dance, plan for the reconstruction of Long Island's defense industry, and wage a congressional campaign. The members came to expect this activity, anticipate it.

But just how unusual was Tony Mazzocchi's local? Tony's own assessment fluctuated between modesty and pride. Did he think there were other local unions with so much activity? "Who knows?" he offered. "There are about eighty thousand locals in the country."

How about on Long Island during his tenure as president? "No," Tony stated. "On the Island, there was nobody like us."

Tony took pride in the union's vigorous strike support, its organizing acumen, and the many social causes it supported. But his aims were higher. Could he and his allies fundamentally change the conditions of work and the culture on the shop floor? Could they make the razzle-dazzle of "social unionism" translate into a change in boss-worker relations as well as improvements in wages and benefits? Could Tony and company pry open the iron cage of production enough so workers developed a taste for freedom at work? Could the union become the center of people's lives, a source of excitement, a cause so great that workers would see themselves as a wellspring of power, rather than the victims of it?

A partial answer to these questions came from author Barbara Garson. In *All the Livelong Day: The Meaning and Demeaning of Routine Work*, Garson examined and compared several different assembly-line factories during the early 1970s. One of her case studies was Local 149. Her instructive account ignored the community activities, concentrating only on shop-floor attitudes and behavior. She interviewed workers and union officials at Local 149 several years after Tony left, and concluded that it was "one of the best union locals in the country. It's militant, it's democratic, it has the highest pay in the industry and it has never given up the daily struggle on the shop floor."[1]

Unlike the other assembly-line workers she visited, the Rubinstein workers rotated jobs every two hours. When they shifted temporarily to lower-grade work, they were paid the higher rate. "Overtime is also distributed with absolute equity," she wrote. "The stewards go around the plant offering it out according to a strict rotation system. Again there's hardly any way that either the company or the union can play favorites."[2]

Garson also noted the results of Mazzocchi's long effort to achieve wage equity between men and women. "More striking than the average pay," Garson wrote, "is the high pay at the lower end of the scale. The union has deliberately kept the wage differences low."[3]

Perhaps most telling, Garson saw signs that Tony had achieved his deepest desire at Local 149: to humanize the lives of workers, if not the work itself. "The most important benefit from the past struggles in this factory, and from the impartial rotation system, has no official recognition," Garson wrote. "There is no clause in the contract that says that the workers shall have the right to laugh, to talk, and be helpful to one another. Nor is there a formal guarantee that the workers can shrug, sneer or otherwise indicate what they think of supervisors. . . . The right to respond like a person, even while your hands are operating like a machine, is something that has been fought for in this factory. And this right is defended daily, formally through the grievance process and informally through militantly kidding around."[4]

Tony greatly enriched the lives of these workers, especially the women, and had helped build one of the finest local unions in America. Now he intended to use it.

II

During the 1950s, the nation trembled from an onslaught of nuclear bomb tests, civil defense drills, and fears of espionage. The decade opened with a hot war in Korea during which the military considered using nuclear weapons. As progressives ran for political cover from McCarthyism, their children learned to "duck and cover" under school desks. Every day, it seemed another massive nuclear test exploded somewhere around the globe.

Between 1945 and 1963, the United States conducted eighteen series of tests, each with multiple atmospheric nuclear explosions. In 1953, during the first three months of Tony Mazzocchi's tenure as president of Local 149, Operation Upshot-Knothole exploded eleven thermonuclear devices in Nevada.[5]

Mazzocchi deeply opposed nuclear testing and wanted to protest it. He found very few labor allies. The overwhelming majority of officials in the purged labor movement now supported the growth of the national security state. Yet the stalemated Korean War was unpopular, with climbing casualties and unclear objectives. Back in 1952, Eisenhower had run as the peace candidate, while Democrat Adlai Stevenson had played the hawk, hoping to protect his right flank against charges that he was "soft on communism." Jack Curran, then still president of Tony's local union, wanted the local to support Stevenson. But Tony, as chief steward, prevented the endorsement. "We had qualms about the war," Tony said. "We didn't endorse Stevenson because he was pretty much of a hawk in '52." Four years later, after Stevenson had startled the country by calling for an end to atmospheric nuclear testing, Tony warmed to him.

By 1956, Tony and Local 149 had become the driving force in Democratic Party politics on Long Island. "It was virgin ground," said Tony. "The Republicans totally dominated the island, and we became known as the most active union." Local 149 members worked hard to identify unionists, register them, and get them out to vote. George Roach remembered the union office being wallpapered with voter lists from unions all over the island. Said Roach, "We had it broken down from the congressional district to the block level."

Tony resurrected the Long Island CIO Council, which had been destroyed during the anti-communist purges, and was named vice president in charge of political action. After the CIO merged with the AFL in 1955, Tony became the director of Long Island's Committee on Political Education (COPE). In front of the union's office in the heart of Republican Roslyn, Tony defiantly hung up a large Stevenson campaign poster. "People stopped in the office and said, 'Hey, this is the first Democratic Party sign we've ever seen in this town,'" he recalled.

The signs lured a supportive local TV commentator named Judy Levitan into the office. "We got to talking about what to do next," said Tony. "I had just read about Stevenson's statement on nuclear weapons testing and I said, 'Why don't we have a meeting about it?' And Judith said she knew a physicist who had just returned from the Bikini Island tests. She thought maybe he could bring along a few other people."

Sensing an important political opening, Tony arranged a symposium at Roslyn High School where the public would hear about the impact of nuclear fallout from a geneticist, a physicist, and a pathologist who had participated in the Bikini tests. Local 149 conducted a massive leafleting campaign. "We had an ancient mimeograph machine," Tony said. "It looked like an old sewing machine with all that fancy wrought-iron stuff. But it had a motor on it, and we ground out thousands of leaflets and distributed them all over."

The turnout was overwhelming: More than eight hundred residents packed the auditorium. But the presentation from the stage was inconclusive and equivocal, and people left the meeting somewhat confused and dissatisfied. Nevertheless, the popularity of the event alerted Mazzocchi and Local 149 to an opportunity. "Everybody was amazed that that many people came out," said Tony. "We all said, 'This is an issue that can move people.' I mean, who the hell comes out to political meetings?" Tony assumed that similar meetings were in progress around the country. Not so. Anti-communist hysteria had effectively shut down the debate. "We later learned that this was the only meeting held anywhere in the US devoted exclusively to nuclear weapons testing in response to the Stevenson campaign," Tony said.

Stevenson was buried by an Eisenhower landslide in 1956. But Tony remained captivated by antinuclear issues. After hearing scientists refer repeatedly to the "BEIR Report" (Biological Effects of Ionizing Radiation), Tony tracked it down and read it. What he discovered truly scared him. "I had a child, Geraldine, and I said, 'Oh my God,'" Tony recalled. "I suddenly realized that nuclear weapons testing was really fearsome."

He also read the National Academy of Sciences' 1956 "report to the public" on "The Biological Effects of Atomic Radiation." The report summarized a litany of fallout dangers:

> Any radiation which reaches the reproductive cells causes mutations . . . that are passed on to succeeding generations.

> There is no minimum amount of radiation which must be exceeded before mutations occur. . . . The more radiation, the more mutations.
>
> The harm is cumulative.
>
> Radiation from fall-out inevitably contaminates man's food supply. Radioactive elements in the soil are taken up and concentrated by plants. The plants may be eaten by humans, or by animals which in turn serve as human food.

This report also contained the famous lines that would make parents blanch the next time they exhorted their children to "Drink your milk!"

> Probably the most important potential food contaminant is strontium-90—a radioactive element that concentrates in bone tissue. Already, detectable although biologically insignificant traces of it have turned up in milk supplies thousands of miles from the site of atomic explosions.[6]

In other words, testing atomic weapons, even in faraway oceans and deserts, could kill or cripple our children with leukemia and other bone diseases. Tony knew he could run with this issue, but he had no firm idea of how to go about it. So in December 1956 he tramped around New York, visiting his contacts, looking for leads. Someone suggested he visit Polykarp Kusch at Columbia University, who won the 1955 Nobel Prize in Physics.

Tony didn't realize that this was a particularly bad time for scientists to risk a public stance against nuclear weapons. Literally thousands of them—and the universities and research institutes employing them—received government funds to research, build, test, and deploy nuclear weapons. At Caltech, for instance, scientists were reprimanded for signing a letter in support of Stevenson's statement. The penalties got worse for prominent scientists. Physicist Robert Oppenheimer, who had spearheaded the Manhattan Project, had lost his security clearance after his right-wing former colleague Edward Teller had questioned Oppenheimer's motives for opposing the development of nuclear weapons. Imagine the anxiety that greeted Tony when he showed up out of nowhere to ask Polykarp Kusch about the hazards of nuclear fallout.

"Kusch was probably the first scientist I ever met in my life, aside from the guys who spoke at the meeting." Tony said. "And he says, 'Yeah, there might be a problem. But, you know, I'm really busy. Why don't you see so-and-so?'"

So on Tony trudged. Everywhere he went, he got the same response: "Nobody wanted to get involved." He couldn't make sense of it until he learned about the government grants. "I finally ran into someone who explained that these scientists all got money from the Atomic Energy Commission—which I knew very little about. And I didn't even know what a grant was."

Tony abandoned the hunt. And then: "One day I get a call from Stewart Meacham, a Quaker from the American Friends Service Committee. He said, 'I hear you've been interested in this nuclear testing issue.' I said, 'Yeah, but nobody's interested in telling me about it.' And he said, 'Look, I've picked up your trail.'"

Finally, Tony had a live lead from an activist with a strong pedigree. As a minister ordained by Union Theological Seminary in New York City, Meacham fought for civil rights, civil liberties, labor rights, peace, and disarmament. According to Tony, in the 1930s, "Meacham got tarred and feathered in Alabama as a minister because he was supporting the Mine Workers' union organizing." By the mid-1950s, Meacham wanted to do something about nuclear weapons and was looking for union contacts. He approached Paul Jennings, regional director of the International Union of Electrical Workers, who knew of Tony from the massive strike support Local 149 had provided his union on Long Island.

Meacham immediately invited Tony to the Woodrow Wilson Foundation in New York for a small meeting of leaders interested in the nuclear testing issue. And so Tony, the ethnic from Bensonhurst, was introduced to the WASP world of Manhattan.

"I go to this meeting and there's nothing but ministers," Tony remembered. "And they're Protestant ministers in the middle of New York City, which is full mostly of Jews and Catholics." Baptist evangelist Billy Graham's personal representative was there. So was Ralph Sockman, pastor of the United Methodist Christ Church, and Algernon Black, leader of the New York Society for Ethical Culture. "These were people I would never have met in a million years," said Tony. After several meetings, this cautious group set itself up as the New York Committee Against Nuclear Weapons Testing. Tony served as its first treasurer and only union representative. "I went back to my local and got 250 bucks, which was the first donation to the group."

Tony believed this august group could make a real difference, if only it could overcome its agonizing propensity to meet and talk, talk and meet. He found an ally in Robert Gilmore, the committee's chair and regional director of the American Friends Service Committee. "A golden-haired boy, a very charming guy, very bright and very articulate," Tony said. "He was a bombardier in the war."

Together Mazzocchi, Gilmore, and Meacham prodded the group toward action. "These people had all sorts of contacts." Tony said. "This was the Protestant hierarchy of New York. No one was going to red-bait this group."

But Tony grew increasingly frustrated by the group's slow pace. What was holding them back? "One time they said, 'No, we can't hold a meeting in July or August. Everybody goes to the Cape or to the Hamptons.' I said, 'What? There are eight million people in the city who don't go to the Cape or the Hamptons. Look, I think this is a subject we ought to talk to people about.'" Meaning, now!

Shamed into unpacking their Bermuda shorts, these religious leaders finally agreed to support an ambitious Mazzocchi/Gilmore/Meacham plan for a meeting to protest nuclear weapons at Town Hall on August 7, 1957—the twelfth anniversary of the Hiroshima bombing. The program would feature speeches from leading scientists and peace activists including Quakers like Gilmore and other Protestant clergy. Norman Thomas, perennial socialist candidate for president, would also speak. Wouldn't a public connection with such a noted socialist as Thomas taint the cause? Tony laughed. "He was a big red-baiter, too. He had a great reputation, but he was vociferously anti-Soviet. And the Quakers were more or less an anti-communist shield, as were the Protestant clergy."

Perhaps the riskiest invitee was Walter Selove, a prominent scientist who had returned just a month earlier from the first Pugwash Conference in Nova Scotia. The conference, which had drawn twenty-two leading scientists from ten countries (including China and the Soviet Union) to discuss nuclear disarmament, was conceived by philosopher Bertrand Russell and endorsed by Albert Einstein shortly before his death. McCarthyites viewed the participating scientists as communist dupes or worse. And yet the conference's chief financial backer, Cyrus Eaton (who hosted the meeting at his estate in Pugwash, Nova Scotia), was a capitalist of the first order. Eaton was founder of Republic Steel, which had fought CIO organizers viciously in the 1930s. That he supported a diplomatic rapprochement signaled another crack in the Cold War edifice.

The New York Times reported that nearly one thousand people turned out for the Town Hall event. Although the *Times* didn't overtly red-bait, the coverage focused exclusively on Norman Thomas. Under a small headline that read, "Would End Bomb Tests, Norman Thomas Urges Step as Start of Disarmament," the *Times* wrote that "the Socialist leader said he is 'interested profoundly' in stopping nuclear weapons tests, but only as a first stage on the road to completely controlled international disarmament under a stronger United Nations."

The crowd, which included several Rubinstein workers, also heard Tony Mazzocchi make his first major address on nuclear testing. The mere sight of Local 149's president speaking at this high-powered gathering thrilled George Roach. "I was born and raised in Manhattan and this is Town Hall. And who's up there?" said Roach. "I was so proud. I mean I had goose pimples that high on my arm."

After this success, the New York Committee Against Nuclear Weapons Testing reconstituted itself as the Committee for a Sane Nuclear Policy (SANE). Norman Cousins, the liberal anti-communist editor of the prestigious *Saturday Review,* served as chair.

The New York Times didn't mention Mazzocchi's role in all this. But Tony didn't mind. Again and again, he encouraged those with prominent egos and reputations, like Cousins, to bask in the sunlight while he worked behind the scenes. Tony knew precisely what he brought to SANE. "I didn't try to play scientist," he said. "I always thought competing with people was a big mistake. I had great respect for their scientific ability. But at the same time, I knew that they had no ability to communicate with the people I represented. It was very apparent that I could talk to my people, and I could deliver them because they were rooted to the union. And I think there was mutual respect with the leaders of SANE."

Through conferences, pamphlets, interviews, and speeches, SANE became the leading voice against the nuclear arms race. But the Cold War was not over, nor was McCarthyite red-baiting—as SANE would learn the hard way. Senator Tom Dodd (a Cousins neighbor in well-heeled Connecticut) accused the group of "communist infiltration," pointing to Henry Abrams, arguably SANE's most effective organizer, who'd been a leader of the American Labor Party and the Henry Wallace campaign twenty years earlier. Rather than defending Abrams, Cousins forced him out and passed an internal anti-communist resolution that alienated many. Dodd went after SANE anyway, attacking Nobel laureate chemist Linus Pauling, another SANE leader, and threatening more investigations of SANE's alleged communist infiltration. Cousins and the board stood up for Pauling, but it was too late. The outside pressure and internal purging cracked SANE, driving away progressives including Gilmore, Meacham, and Mazzocchi, as well as thousands of students, who soon progressed to the student peace movement.

Although SANE was later credited with leading the struggle for the treaty banning atmospheric testing, which President Kennedy signed in 1963, it abdicated any leadership of the broader peace movement. In 1961, the House Un-American Activities Committee finally reported that SANE "is not a Communist front." And the FBI did not find "any indication of any substantial Communist infiltration."[7]

For the next three decades, Tony Mazzocchi would not quit on nuclear issues—and the issues wouldn't quit on him. Although he felt proud of his contribution to SANE, he never exaggerated his influence. He was glad that SANE had involved "the most unlikely union around—oil, chemical, and atomic workers." SANE had introduced Tony to leading scientists, environmentalists, and activists who would soon join him in building an occupational safety and health movement—and a movement against the Vietnam War.

III

If Tony was going to build a real peace movement, then the Local 149 rank and file needed to understand why. In 1957, Tony urged *The Militant,* the local's newspaper, to break its self-imposed silence on foreign affairs and national security issues. *The Militant* soon ran three guest articles by Stewart Meacham, Tony's colleague from SANE. Meacham slammed away at the wasteful space race, praised the brave anti-nuclear protesters who sailed into a Pacific nuclear test site, described the perils of fallout, and argued for a ban on nuclear testing. Quoting Dr. Selove, Meacham wrote, "It is not correct to believe that there is a 'safe' level" of nuclear fallout. "There is good reason to believe that even small doses of Strontium 90 can cause leukemia or bone cancer, in proportion to the dose."[8]

In its July 31, 1957, issue, *The Militant* finally got militant on nuclear weapons.

> *The Militant* staff feels that the following article is the most important and sobering one that has ever appeared in *The Militant*. In view of the fact that there seems to be so much light headed talk about war and the fact that many people seem to think that if war comes it will be something that takes place far, far away, we urge you to read the article through because its content deeply affects you.

What followed was the infamous congressional testimony by Rand researchers given on May 27–28, 1957, about the awful impact of a full-scale nuclear war. *The Militant* devoted five pages to the testimony, including the chilling remarks of dispassionate scientists estimating the body count from a nuclear attack on the United States—deaths that could not be prevented with fallout shelters or miracle drugs.

1st day	36 million dead	57 million injured
by 7th day	51 million dead	42 million injured
by 14th day	61 million dead	31 million injured
by 60th day	72 million dead	21 million injured

Sensing the impact of this information on his members, Tony searched for a way for them to act on it.

Tony Mazzocchi, the former dental technician, thought of teeth. He'd read about a study led by Dr. Barry Commoner at Washington University, which examined the effects of nuclear testing on children by measuring the amount of strontium 90 in their bodies. Strontium 90, a by-product of nuclear explosions, bonds with calcium and collects in children's bones. Commoner's clever and dramatic approach was to collect baby teeth from residents of the St. Louis area before, during, and after nuclear tests, and measure them for strontium 90. His findings confirmed parents' worst fears: Their children's bodies had indeed absorbed strontium 90, in levels that rose and fell with the bomb tests. The radioactive isotope accumulated in bones, putting the children at risk of leukemia.

Mazzocchi jumped on the study. He urged his members to bring in baby teeth from their children and grandchildren. Commoner was unable to use the teeth collected by Local 149 and other groups around the country. "We were inundated with them," he said. "Unfortunately, we could only use those from our local area" near St. Louis. Still, even the act of collecting the teeth had provided an education on nuclear fallout that the union members would never forget. Local 149 became part of the peace movement.

IV

How could a local with only five hundred members lead a new militant labor movement? It couldn't, Tony concluded. "We had to get bigger. We wanted to be a presence in our own international union, and we didn't want to depend on the company for growth. If the company hired, you grew; if the company laid off, you shrank. We wanted to organize the unorganized Long Island shops. We knew their low wages were a threat to us. So we engaged in a great deal of organizing."

But if your name is Mazzocchi and you're organizing small shops in the New York area, you're either in the mob or you're fighting it.

The region's thousands of small shops were the mob's snack of choice. In some cases, a business owner would pay a corrupt local union a certain sum per worker each month, bogus "dues" that were deducted from workers' paychecks. These were paper locals with sweetheart contracts providing lousy pay and working conditions and no benefits to speak of. It could be seen as a sort of shakedown, but the owners were far from helpless victims: They used the mob to keep real unions out. It was much cheaper.

Organizing in these corrupt shops was dangerous. Take the case of Halben Chemical Company, which made mothballs and para blocks for urinals. Owners Hal and Ben employed fifteen workers at a polluted loft on Bond Street near the Bowery in Manhattan. By 1957, when Local 149 came along, Ben was dead. Tony called Hal "a low life" who paid the minimum wage and got his kicks spying on his workers in the ladies' room. The atrocious working conditions finally provoked Halben's black and Hispanic workforce to reach out to the Association of Catholic Trade Unionists, who referred the workers to Local 149 because they knew it was squeaky clean.

ACTU and Local 149 made for an unlikely alliance. After all, ACTU had coached the anti-communist caucus in the old Gas-Coke union to destroy leftists like Doyle and Hamilton. In New York, however, ACTU had two wings—the anti-communists and the Catholic Workers Movement, led by Dorothy Day. Day, according to one account, started as "a Communist seeking religious truth and ended as a Catholic influenced by Communist ideals." She was credited with anticipating "liberation theology by some thirty-five years."[9]

George Roach believed that Day's allies had a natural affinity for the progressivism of Local 149. And it helped to be connected with her. "I didn't have any trouble with the cops because they knew we were wired to Dottie Day," Roach remembered. "That was a big deal."[10]

If Local 149 was going to come to the rescue of the workers at Halben, it was going to have to cross a very scary guy named John Dioguardi, aka Johnny Dio. Dio became the poster child for the rackets when a UPI photographer captured his snarling portrait seconds before Dio slugged him at a Senate hearing on racketeering. As a made man in the Lucchese family, Dio did not take kindly to criticism. In 1956, the labor columnist Victor Riesel tore into Dio in the press. Shortly afterward, Abe Telvi, a small-time hood, tossed acid in Riesel's face, blinding him. Dio was indicted for hiring Telvi, but the charges were dropped when Telvi was murdered and the witnesses against Dio refused to testify.

Dio had his hooks deep into Teamsters Union Local 284, which in turn had its hooks into the unfortunate workers at Halben. According to Tony, Dio "would go to a small employer and say, 'Hey, we're gonna give you protection against a real union.' Most unions walked away when they found out a shop had a Dio contract. The guy had a big business. You know how many thousands of members he had who didn't even know they were members? The boss was paying their dues and the workers didn't even know they had a contract."

Local 149 had more pluck than other unions. "We went to Halben, and the workers signed our cards," said Tony. The mob union and Halben then went to the National Labor Relations Board to complain that they had been raided by Local 149. According to Tony: "We said, 'Stick it up your ass. We're gonna strike.' And that's when I called on KN."

KN, a tall, well-dressed, rugged man, serviced shops for a corrupt union. Like Tony, he was self-taught and extremely bright. In fact, he would later rise in the Teamsters to become a chief researcher and columnist for the union. By the late 1960s, he was respectable enough to lecture at elite colleges. But he was hardly an idealist. KN could discuss with nuance a range of alternatives to the Landrum-Griffin Act for ridding unions of corruption and in the next breath grab his crotch while recounting a memorable mother-daughter sexual escapade.

Tony had met KN in an earlier foray into a racket shop. "We raided this jewelry plant, up in the Bronx," Tony said. "It was a racket union. KN was working for them. So he calls me and he says, 'Hey I need this job.' He says, 'You know, I'm gonna be leaving but if you guys raid it, my job is lost.'" Tony, sensing that KN might be useful down the road, decided to help. "I told him we'd back out, but only if we could have our guy sitting in on their contract negotiations. I sent George." And George Roach proceeded to negotiate a strong contract for the jewelry workers.

"KN, we saved his ass," Tony said. "And he never forgot it. He went on to be a bigwig in the Teamsters union. And he always said, 'We owe you. And I don't give a shit what it is you need.'"

Often Teamster truck drivers would drive right through workers' picket lines with supplies or to pick up garbage. So when Tony launched a strike at Halben, he called KN. "I said, 'We're gonna have a damn strike. We don't want your guys crossing our picket line.'"

On December 10, 1957, *The Militant* reported:

> The [Dio] Teamster local, which came under close scrutiny by the McClellan Committee . . . boasts criminal records, including narcotics convictions, extortion, bribery, and Sullivan violations. After extensive hearings at the National Labor Relations Board, both [Teamster Local] 284, and the company [Halben] refused to produce any contracts. The workers were seeking to decertify the Teamsters and join [our local]. Last Friday, the company fired five of the shop leaders in an obvious attempt to coerce the workers into

the maintenance of "labor peace" Dio style. The workers' answer was to strike Monday morning.

George Roach led the effort along with the shop-floor leader at Halben, Jose Cardinal, a former calypso singer from Puerto Rico. Roach recalled that as he walked the picket line with the workers, a sparkling new Buick approached carrying two thugs in expensive suits. And just like in the B movies, they said, "Kid, why don't you leave before you end up with the fishes?"

But after adding up the number of baseball bats in the hands of the picketers, the mob messengers demurred before anything could happen to their silk suits or new car. It wasn't hard to understand their annoyance. One of the picket signs read, MY BOSS IS PLAYING FOOTSIE WITH JOHNNY DIO. Another warned, JOHNNY DIO IS A DRUG PUSHER. THAT MAKES MY BOSS A DRUG PUSHER TOO. Dio was used to commanding a bit more respect.

The first strike didn't succeed in forcing the company to allow workers to join Local 149. But the fight continued. Hal developed a new scam that both undermined Local 149's organizing drive and turned a buck. He contracted with the employment agencies on Worth Street, where for a forty-dollar fee, a worker could get a job guaranteed for thirty days—the exact number of days before a worker had union representation. On the thirtieth day of employment at Halben, Hal would fire the new worker and get a kickback from the agency, which in turn would send a new victim to Hal.

To counter the move, Local 149—in deliberate violation of labor law—would sign the worker up on the first day, then file an unfair labor practice charge on the dismissals, throw up a picket line, and shut the operation down.

It took three years of strikes, hearings, and haggling to bring the Halben workers into Tony's local. Finally, though, they came. All fifteen of them.

Tony's tussle with Johnny Dio continued as Local 149 went on to raid one mob shop after another. Who the hell did that punk Mazzocchi think he was? A business agent from Dio's sham union and his ominous-looking sidekick decided to deliver a message to Tony personally. The hoods came dressed to the nines; the suit on The Ominous One fit snugly enough to highlight both his bulging muscles and his gun. "Silent Sam. The guy always carried a gun," said Tony. "He used to come in with the union rep. He was supposed to intimidate us. Fuckin' walks into *our* union office; *he's* gonna intimidate us."

One day, the two hoods called on Tony while he was eating his breakfast at a diner across from the local. "They say, 'You're raiding our shops'—blah, blah, blah." And I said, 'Fuck you guys, you're not a union.'"

George Roach and Bobby Guinta remembered a slightly different scene that became legendary in the union. As the hoods approached, they recalled, Tony slowly looked up from his plate, almost bored, and then looked down again casually to take another bite of his bacon and eggs. As Bobby put it, "Tony was so cool and collected. He didn't even flinch."

Tony then looked up again, swung his fork, dripping with runny egg, around the diner, and said loudly, "Do you think you'll get out of this place alive if you touch me? These are all my men." And about twenty men, also eating their breakfasts, looked up. It wasn't clear how many of them were even in the local.

"Get the fuck out of here," Tony said calmly. The mob boys slowly complied, eyeing each table carefully as they backed out of the diner.

Some time later, as Mac was getting into his car after an organizing meeting, two thugs approached him and asked if he was Dick McManus. One guy grabbed him from behind, and the other slugged him. Mac woke up in the hospital with his jaw wired shut. But the union continued to organize mob locals.

Dio and his fellow mobster Benny the Bug decided to up the ante. A discussion of their plan found its way onto a wiretap of a mob meeting in Manhattan. The DA's office then called Local 149 with a warning: Dio and company were plotting to bomb the union's Roslyn office. The notice caused hearts to thump any time a tire squealed or an engine backfired, but the local hands tried to carry on undaunted. One cold winter day, Tony and several others in the union office tensed as tires peeled around the corner. An object came hurling into the office, shattering the big picture window that faced the street, and landing at their feet. It was only a brick.

After that incident Dio gave up, apparently preoccupied with his federal court cases. Local 149 kept raiding mob-controlled shops.

KN wasn't Tony's only unlikely ally in these battles. Tony also developed a relationship of sorts with Bernie Adelstein, the corrupt Teamster leader with ties to the Gambino crime family.[11] Adelstein made KN look like a Boy

Scout. He ran a union of Long Island private garbage truck haulers (Local 813) as well as a second catchall local that included cemetery workers, barbers, and almost anyone else who could breathe and pay union dues.

"Now Bernie, he was really in the friggin' mob," Tony said. To get Bernie and his Teamsters to honor the Local 149 pickets, Tony was willing to support him on legitimate union issues. For example, during a garbage strike, Adelstein asked the local to keep scab trucks from picking up garbage. "So we helped him. And he says, 'I never forget my friends.'"

Local 149 ran into Uncle Bernie's gang again at a chemical plant they tried to organize in Brooklyn. Tony sent George Roach in to sell the union to twenty-five tough workers. Three well-clad "organizers" from Adelstein's paper local showed up to pitch their racket union to the same workers. With Roach's guidance, the workers dismissed the Teamster organizers from the scene. But as Local 149 was preparing to demand recognition, Adelstein's local petitioned the NLRB for an election, saying they had cards from the workers asking for Teamster representation. The NLRB scheduled a hearing. Roach brought along one of the chemical workers, Ernest Wright.

"The Teamster guys with their nice suits showed up with one signed card," said Roach. "During a break, I asked to take a look at it. It says 'Ernest Wright,' who was standing right next to me. It was a left-handed card, a forgery. That was a violation of labor law which could get Adelstein's gang in big trouble. I mean, the feds were looking for anything they could find to put him away. But I was not about to snitch to the government on them. I said, 'Okay, you walk away from the plant, and I forget this card.' And they jumped at the deal."

Local 149 was on a roll, and they felt invincible. But they soon got their butts kicked, not by organized crime, but by organized capital. Scientific Design was a small plant, with only eleven workers. *The Militant* boasted about its ten-to-one victory in the NLRB election, which it called "a culmination of many months of intensive work on behalf of the organizing committee which had to cope with two NLRB hearings before the proper unit was decided upon."[12]

The problems began when the union tried to bargain for its first contract. The bargaining unit was composed entirely of PhDs who worked on processing the last molecule of carbon to form xylene. They had assured

Tony that they were invaluable to the company and could not be replaced while on strike.

"We were stupid. We didn't do any research," admitted Tony. "Who the hell ever heard of Scientific Design? Well it was the second largest builder of oil refineries worldwide. So the guys said they can't operate without us? The company had five hundred PhDs."

To make matters worse, the workers insisted on going on strike in quest of a union shop, where union membership is a mandatory condition of the job. "What a bunch of fucking nuts," said Tony. "I told those PhDs, 'You don't go out over a union shop.' There were only eleven guys. I said, 'If you can't organize anybody that comes into this place, forget it.'" No, they wanted a union-shop clause. "We struck and they beat our ass after—I don't know—seven or eight weeks. These PhDs weren't used to long strikes."

As Tony tasted his first defeat, he also received his first bribe offer. He got a call from a manager at Scientific Design, who told him that the eleven-person shop was just a "pilot plant" that would be shut down in several months. "But he says, 'We don't want to deal with a union. What will it take for you to walk away?' I said, 'Man, we organized these guys. We ain't walking away.' And then June came and boom, the plant went down."

Another kind of bribe—a legal one—came Tony's way. According to Bobby Guinta, "Helena Rubinstein offered Tony a job in the company—as their public relations guy," Guinta said. "They probably were offering him twenty-five thousand dollars a year. I mean, that was a time when we were earning, maybe, $115 a week. But you could have offered Tony ten million. He was totally, completely incorruptible."

Bribed, battered, but ever optimistic, Mazzocchi prodded Local 149's organizing campaign forward. They won shop after shop. "Our members themselves were our best organizers for leads," said Tony. "They'd say, 'Hey, my husband's working in this lousy shop. Or my friend.' And we got into a lot of living rooms that way. The best way to get into an unorganized shop was through a neighbor. It was never easy, but people trusted their neighbors."

By the late 1960s, the local represented workers at more than thirty plants. Membership peaked at nearly fifteen hundred. Finally, Tony commanded a base big enough to rock his national union and maybe even the labor movement.

V

As Local 149 grew, so did its income from union dues. And with more funds came the capacity to experiment. The combination of money, imagination, and Mazzocchi was explosive. Anything could happen—like a Broadway play.

"I read this play," Tony said. "I don't know who gave it to me. It was by Barry Stavis, called *The Man Who Never Died.* It was about Joe Hill. I don't think I'd ever been to a Broadway play. But I said, 'I'd like to see this play.' So I called the publisher. He gives me the name of the playwright, and I go out and meet this guy."

Stavis, no dummy, immediately arranged for Tony to attend a meeting of financial backers. "They were thrilled to have a union that was willing to invest in this play," Tony said. They were, in fact, desperate for money, and Tony's local seemed to have deep pockets. "We also tried to raise money from other unions, like the ILGWU [International Ladies Garment Workers], because they had produced *Pins and Needles* in the 1930s." No go. Local 149 was the only union putting up cash.

Producing a working-class play flowed directly from Tony's idea "that we would capture every part of people's lives." It was a natural extension of the local's bowling league, barn dances, ball teams, and Salk vaccine shots. Tony also believed that books, art, music, and theater were more important to the lives of Rubinstein workers than stuffing eye shadow into jars fifty weeks a year. He believed that workers should get more time off to enjoy culture. In fact, in 1956 he set a first in collective bargaining by calling for paid worker sabbaticals, an idea he picked up from academics at SANE.

"I always thought that work is pretty shitty in our society," Tony said. "People should be able to get away from it for a time and rejuvenate themselves and pursue things that you normally don't get to pursue—theater, music—that evoked, or portrayed, their own life experiences."

While Tony did not, as yet, have the power to win sabbaticals for his workers, he could give them a night on Broadway—or right next to it, at the Jan Hus Auditorium on 47th Street. Naturally, the union was utterly naive about Broadway. For starters, the investors—that is, the workers who would have to approve any union expenditures for the production—had never heard of Joe Hill. So it was up to *The Militant* (on June 17, 1958) to reclaim him as a labor hero for the local. As usual, it did so with gusto, devoting an entire page to the subject.

Not only did Tony expect the local's investment to produce good working-class culture, he thought it would generate a surplus that could fund other good deeds. He even pledged to spend the profits before they were earned. As *The Militant* reported, "A scholarship program for the children and grandchildren of Local members was instituted at the General Membership meeting. The scholarship will be known as 'The Joe Hill Scholarship.' It will receive its initial financing as a result of the local's investment in the off Broadway production of 'The Man Who Never Died,' a play about Joe Hill. . . . Local 149 is making labor history by being one of the principal backers of a play about labor's greatest martyr."

Tony thought the local's magical string of success would transfer onto the play. It was certainly encouraging that the union's investment made mainstream news. A week after *The Militant* broke the story to the membership, *The New York Times*, under the headline "Union to Be 'Angel,'" devoted two paragraphs to it.

But turning a buck on an off-Broadway play about a labor radical was next to impossible. Tony had hoped that in New York, where more than one in three people still belonged to a union, workers might fill the house once word got out through union newspapers and meetings.

Word did get out through theater critics. Euphemia Van Rensselaer Wyatt, who reviewed the play for the *Catholic World,* wrote that "The play's action is tersely direct and tense and is played with simple sincerity by an unexpectedly good cast of thirty-six directed by Robert Mayberry."

But the far more influential Donald Malcolm in *The New Yorker* wrote that Barrie Stavis "scorns such late embellishments as plot. To him the trial, not the play, is the thing and he has traced with infinite care the judicial process by which Joe Hill . . . was framed, tried, condemned, and executed. The resultant evening of theatre, from the viewpoint of the post-Babylonian spectator, is more peculiar than agreeable." After the tedium of the court case, said Malcolm, Joe Hill's "execution came [not] a moment too soon. Ten minutes more of stage legality and a restive audience might have taken the law into its own hands."

The *New York Times* review by Brooks Atkinson could make or break such a production. Without overtly red-baiting the play, Atkinson tossed it into the dustbin of radical history, calling it "a literal transcript of the agit-prop plays that popped up here and there in the Thirties when the virtuous workers were shaking their fists at merciless capitalists on a number of excited stages. . . . It repeats all the stencils—labor solidarity, milk for the children, down with the bosses, police brutality, vicious judges and strike, strike, strike. . . . The form and the temper of his play seems naive and maudlin in the world of [mafia-linked union leaders] Dave Beck and Jimmy Hoffa, Mr. Stavis writes as if he did not realize that the rabble-rousing labor play died a long time ago."

Panned by the reviewers, the play never developed an audience. Not only did the local lose its initial investment, but it had to keep on paying because Tony, uncharacteristically, failed to grasp the contract's fine print. "We learned something about the theater, which is a call-in," he said. "You put up twenty-five thousand dollars. And if the play starts going broke, they can call in additional money. Man, we almost went broke."

Tony tried to fill the theater by reducing ticket prices for union members to a dollar. It didn't help. The play closed after a few months under a pile of debt.

But, said Tony, "We got the members to go to the theater. They had a good time. Everybody loved the play. . . . It lost its shirt—but it was our experience. And people always talked about it afterward." Yes, he confessed, he'd been "ragged on it once or twice. But the membership was doing anything we asked them to do. We were winning a lot of big victories and people were loyal to anything we did."

Tony remained committed to the project of working-class culture. But a bigger stage with brighter lights beckoned him. He'd set his sights on Washington.

VI

Tony Mazzocchi wanted to be the next Vito Marcantonio. Almost as soon as the factory moved to Long Island, Tony decided to make a run for the US House of Representatives. He knew it would take years to build an electoral base. In the 1950s, the Democratic Party barely existed on Long Island. This was Republican country, and a fierce conservative, Steven

Boghos Derounian, ruled the roost, making a Democratic nomination for Congress from the district virtually meaningless.

"We got involved with rebuilding the Democratic Party," Tony said. By the time of the anti-nuclear town meeting in 1956, Mazzocchi understood that the composition of the North Shore district was changing, and that core elements of Derounian's support were vulnerable. "The Republicans relied on big working-class support in Glen Cove," he said. "But it was an Italian community. With all the members and support I had up there, and my prominence in the Democratic Party, I thought I could win. I was going to be the type of congressperson who would champion all the most controversial issues of the day."

Tony had continued to commute to work from his beloved Bensonhurst. But like the Dodgers who fled Brooklyn for Los Angeles, Tony realized he had to move, too. "All my activity, my identification, was on the Island. By 1960, I knew that I had to be a resident there. Frank Barbaro, a longshoreman [who later ran for mayor, served as a state assemblyman, and became a New York State judge] and I loaded the truck up for my move. Just the two of us."

By this time, Tony already had a strong political base. "Anybody who ran for office, the first thing they did was head for our local," said Tony. "We put a lot of work in various campaigns. We were building the size of the local; we were involved in the community, and deeply involved in the Nassau-Suffolk CIO council, which then became the Long Island Federation of Labor. We had a couple hundred thousand people in that council and we started to become a force in politics and in the issues of the day on Long Island."

Rather than tack to the political center to prepare for his run, Mazzocchi pushed toward the radical edge with a series of policy proposals for Long Island. First was his plan to convert Long Island's defense industry to peaceful uses, an effort inspired by his conversations with Seymour Melman, a Columbia economics professor involved with SANE. Tony liked the notion because it was practical and struck at the heart of the Cold War.

Long Island's defense industry, the area's largest employer, was on the decline. Military production was being relocated, primarily to the South, wreaking havoc on workers and the regional economy. Tony, through the Long Island Federation of Labor, developed a detailed plan to use defense industry workers' vast skills to build public buses and subway cars for New York.

Tony argued that national defense actually justified this conversion. "We had all these engineers and machinists who could build military goods, and we had all these facilities," he said. "We made the case that we should keep them intact in case there is a new military emergency by having the government take over the closed plants and build subway cars."

In February 1964, Tony managed to get a hearing for this idea with President Lyndon Johnson at the White House. "I brought the presidents of all these locals to present this proposal to convert. It was all over the newspapers," said Tony.

Long Island's *Newsday* carried a picture of the labor leaders with LBJ as they proposed "that Nassau and Suffolk counties . . . become a pilot area for a government program of converting defense-based local economies to consumer-based economies . . . converting the plant's machines of war into tools of peace."[13]

LBJ listened politely but nothing happened, except that Tony Mazzocchi became known as an innovator.

Tony's strongest political bonds were in the civil rights movement, including with Dr. Martin Luther King Jr. The growing liberal community on Long Island provided King with legal services and a great deal of money. King visited the Island regularly, and Tony introduced King at several meetings and rallies. Local 149's early support for the civil rights movement in the South, and its championing of open housing and school integration in the North, now commended Tony to black and liberal constituencies.

Tony methodically worked every local Democratic club in the district. As the 1964 election approached, "I had the endorsement of every single club," he said. "When it came time, I practically had the nomination locked up." His prospects looked even brighter as the presidential race tilted strongly toward LBJ and the Democrats after Senator Barry Goldwater, an ultraconservative, won the Republican nomination. A Democratic landslide was in the making.

Congressman Mazzocchi was starting to sound real.

Then realpolitik took over. In 1962, for the first time ever, a Democrat, Eugene Nickerson, had won the job of Nassau County executive, a position that came with hundreds of patronage jobs and millions in legal fees and construction contracts for the party faithful. The party desperately wanted Nickerson to win reelection in 1964.

This was the business of politics. And since the Island's party leaders, topped by Jack English (a prominent attorney and Kennedy confidant), were all loyal to the reigning Kennedy clan, keeping control over Nassau County had national as well as statewide implications. After all, Bobby Kennedy, who had recently left the Johnson administration, was running for US senator from New York in 1964 and had his eye on the presidency. He needed a stable henchman running Nassau County. The party leaders viewed all issues, nominations, and politics through a simple lens: Would it help or hurt Nickerson's reelection?

To the machine, Mazzocchi looked vulnerable. So English sat down with Tony to explain the facts of life. "Jack English said, 'We think you're gonna hurt the slate because of your position on nuclear weapons testing.' Jack thought that if I ran for Congress against Derounian, who was a vicious red-baiter, I could bring down the ticket. They thought I was too radical. They thought Derounian would love to run against me because I'd be the easiest one to beat."

The message was blunt. If Tony chose to run, the party would run someone against him in the primary. Tony was stunned. The party he had helped to resurrect from oblivion was turning on him. He realized this was more fallout from Senator Dodd's attack on SANE. Democratic Party leaders thought that anti-nuclear activists were too pink to hold public office. "They didn't have any candidates," Tony said. "They brought out a guy who'd never even registered to vote, Lester Wolf."

It was obvious that the Democratic Party didn't really care about the congressional seat. They just didn't want Mazzocchi's politics to endanger Nickerson's reelection bid. Tony was in a fix. He was thirty-eight. He'd spent nearly ten years building his labor base and the Democratic Party on Long Island. He'd run labor's COPE effort. He had helped define the party's platform. All of this signaled that he was a team player, not a renegade. Yet he could only become the next Marcantonio if he was willing to buck the Democratic leadership and fight it out in a primary.

Surprisingly, unlike his mentor Marcantonio, Mazzocchi backed away from the fight. He didn't want to be divisive, he explained. If he ran in a hotly contested, no-holds-barred primary against the party's chosen candidate, he could lose his standing among the Island's Democrats. Tony worried that if Nickerson lost, he would be viewed by labor and political insiders as a spoiler.

His biggest fear was the damage a vicious red-baiting campaign might do to the labor movement, his union allies, and his family. When English warned Tony that Derounian would go after him because of his stand against the bomb, Tony knew where that could lead. Tony might be dragged through the mud, not just within the Democratic Party, but within the labor movement as well. Someone might know or might find out about his uncle and sisters' work in the CP and the fellow travelers his uncle invited to Blairstown. Maybe they knew about his close friendship with CP members like the Fines. Maybe they knew he had participated in CP-sponsored events in the late 1940s. Or about his early meetings with CPers in District 65, which led to his entry into Helena Rubinstein. Had the FBI captured a list of leftist books he passed around Local 149? Could there be an informer in his ranks?

As the Dodd hearings had shown, none of this was out of the question. And with the Berlin crisis, the Cuban Missile Crisis, and the US anti-communist foray into Vietnam, red-baiting again was in full bloom.

But if Tony was vulnerable, so was Derounian, as a right-wing extremist. *Newsweek* (June 27, 1966) wrote that the Republican candidate had "impeachable credentials as a vintage archconservative. In Congress he stood unflinchingly against such programs as the 1958 aid-to-education bill, the poverty war, the Peace Corps, public-welfare, and water pollution controls." After the Kennedy assassination, such conservatives were out of sync with the country's politics, especially in the Northeast. The hawkish Derounian was firmly tied to the soon-to-be-nominated Goldwater and his extreme right faction of the Republican Party. He was estranged from the more liberal Nelson Rockefeller, the New York governor who had just lost the presidential nomination to Goldwater. Rockefeller lost no sleep when he pushed through a redistricting plan that undercut Derounian's formerly safe Republican district.

Would red-baiting really work? Although Mazzocchi was viewed as progressive, he'd won the affection and respect of his moderate peers. Morty Bahr, a fervent anti-communist who later became national president of the Communications Workers of America, remembered Mazzocchi fondly during this period. "We met frequently," Bahr said. "I used to just go by his office, even if it was a little bit out of my way, before I would go to the city. We liked each other as individuals. We became fast friends. And I looked at him not only as an aggressive trade unionist—because, you know, he really did a good job for his union—but I used to wonder how he had time to think about all these things like laws to protect health and safety."[14]

In describing Tony, Bahr used the exact word that had been used to depict Henry Wallace—and Tony's own grandfather—*dreamer.* Bahr's picture was at once flattering and critical. "People saw him as a very progressive thinker, but they thought he was dealing with things that weren't doable."

Was Tony too idealistic? "Absolutely," replied Bahr. "Absolutely. He dreamed about things that most of us weren't thinking about." And yet, said Bahr, "Everybody took him seriously."

Tony had learned from the Wallace debacle that the real threat came not from the right but from liberal and labor anti-communists. They had crushed Henry Wallace and purged the ranks of labor. The Kennedy clan could easily turn on him, and fracture the labor movement on Long Island in the process.

Tony's decision to back out of the 1964 congressional election revealed both his Achilles' heel and an unusual strength. The cause, not Tony's ego, always came first. He could lead only by projecting idealism. He and everyone around him had to be committed to the cause and act as exemplars of progressive change. And in 1964, Tony felt that dividing the party and the labor movement over the issue of *his* congressional run would undermine the common cause.

Besides, Mazzocchi had other political irons in the fire. He was a member of his union's national executive board and believed he could eventually win top office. As president of his national union, Tony believed he would be in a stronger position to lead a broad social movement.

The election probably could have been his. Even Lester Wolf, the unregistered Democrat, found a way to win, albeit in a very close contest. And nearly every other Democrat in the country was swept along in Johnson's landslide win over Goldwater.

The closeness of the Wolf-Derounian race didn't hurt Nickerson in the slightest: The Democrat rolled over his Republican opponent, John Burns, 354,358 to 263,434.

Hand-wringing and lamentation ensued. "All the labor guys came to me the day after and said, 'Oh God, you could have been in Congress. You should have never quit,'" Tony said.

Never again did Tony run for public office. For years to come, his supporters urged him to consider other openings, including Nassau County executive (after Nickerson managed to lose it) as well as a Long Island congressional seat during the 1970s, but Tony refused. Instead, he concentrated on the longer and more difficult path to high office within the union. Tony forever claimed to have no regrets about his capitulation to the Democratic kingmakers. He would always say, "Good thing I didn't go to Congress, because I got a lot more done outside of it."

SEVEN

From CIO to CIA

Tony Mazzocchi, the anti–Cold War militant, soon entered a union teeming with Cold War deceptions and intrigue. In 1955, Tony's union, the United Gas, Coke and Chemical Workers, merged with the Oil Workers International Union to form the Oil, Chemical and Atomic Workers (OCAW). And with the Oil Workers came the CIA.

The CIA was all over the labor movement during the Cold War, and US labor didn't resist. In fact, it embraced its role as a major Cold War player. After World War II, a cohort of labor leaders led by George Meany and his assistant, Jay Lovestone (the former head of the Communist Party USA, turned anti-communist), willingly enlisted as international crusaders to "guide" labor movements abroad away from communism. American unions helped anti-communist unions worldwide through training, exchange programs, and support for collective bargaining. And when no one was looking, they also served as bagmen for the CIA, delivering funds to make sure the right people won union elections.

For many, fighting on the front lines of the Cold War seemed an idealistic cause amid the dying embers of CIO unionism. It was a lot sexier to work at the foreign desk than to attend to the dull chores of collective bargaining. As Tony would learn, some people thought it was thrilling to hop on a plane to help topple a government or two, especially when all expenses were paid.

Even UAW leaders Walter and Victor Reuther, whom Tony admired, became postwar advocates of American interests overseas, providing considerable financial support for American-friendly, progressive, but anti-communist labor movements in Europe. According to CIA operative Thomas W. Braden, some of that support came clandestinely from the CIA. At Victor Reuther's request, he said, "I went to Detroit one morning and gave Walter $50,000 in $50 bills. Victor spent the money, mostly in West Germany, to bolster unions there. He tried 'undercover techniques' to keep me from finding out how he spent it. But I had my own 'undercover techniques.'"[1]

Oil was pivotal in the US geopolitical struggle with the Soviets. From the Middle East to Latin America, US unions collaborated with the CIA to make certain that control of oil did not fall into the hands of communists or even social democrats. The CIA and American labor joined hands in Iran, Venezuela, Mexico, Lebanon, Jordan, Greece, Indonesia, and Brazil. Tony's new union was at the epicenter of the intrigue. Its president, O. A. "Jack" Knight, was a prime example of a CIO-progressive-turned-liberal-cold-warrior. He was precisely the kind of leader Tony wanted to replace. Knight, a member of the Hammond, Indiana, Oil Workers local, led the strike committee that successfully shut down the Amoco refinery there in 1934. In 1936, when the oil workers set up a national rank-and-file executive board, Knight ran from his district and won. He then was assigned by the union to organize in California, where, OCAW historian Ray Davidson reported, he "quickly made a name for himself as an organizer of extraordinary intelligence."[2]

In 1940, when he was thirty-eight, Knight rose up as an insurgent to win the presidency of the Oil Workers International Union, CIO. As Davidson recounted:

> A small wiry man, he bounded up stairs two at a time—then and for twenty-five years to come. He was ambitious. He had a quick mind and an engaging personality. He was rapidly developing into a compelling speaker in an era when oratory skill was a major component of leadership.[3]

For a time Knight went along with the CIO trend of using communists and radicals as organizers. But by 1949, he had joined the anti-communist juggernaut.

The CIO purges had created a stifling atmosphere in most unions. The oil workers were so desperate to show their patriotism that they banned the use of pink mimeograph paper at their headquarters. Perhaps it was a relief, after such pettiness, for Knight to join with the CIA and become a shining hero in the great international crusade against communism. He'd apparently developed a taste for the cause after being sent by CIO president Philip Murray to several Latin American conferences. Davidson recounted that Knight "enjoyed the change of pace and the touch of color and romance provided by his trips south of the border."[4]

Knight and company traveled to the world's hottest spots. In 1953, his confidant and assistant Lloyd Haskins took a "fact-finding" trip to Iran at a particularly propitious moment. Even as he was meeting with Iranian oil workers, the CIA was leading a coup that removed the democratically elected government of Mohammed Mossadegh. Under Mossadegh's leadership, the Iranian parliament had dared to nationalize the British-owned oil company that controlled Iran's entire oil supply. Haskins later bragged to Tony that during the coup he'd entered Mossadegh's office even before the CIA arrived.

Knight and Haskins soon established the International Federation of Petroleum Workers (IFPW), with Knight as president and Haskins as secretary-general. Tony didn't realize until later that the CIA had invented the federation and served as its generous investment banker, arrangements eventually confirmed by Philip Agee, the former CIA agent and whistleblower.[5]

So while American oil workers were being shackled by Taft-Hartley labor restrictions at home, their union received a blank check (or at least a very large one) to promote "free" anti-communist trade unions around the globe. The more the US trade union movement partnered with the Cold War planners, the more money they got to develop massive exchange programs with "free" trade union leaders. According to OCAW's official union history, the union "played a role far beyond its size in these foreign exchanges. Its staff members and local leaders devoted thousands of hours of time hosting foreign union visitors," most of which was paid for by US government funds "by roundabout methods."[6]

In two feature articles in the early 1960s, *Business Week* wrote of a new breed of unionists who had put aside Mazzocchi-style CIO militancy as they cruised comfortably around the globe. The overseas representatives of Jack Knight's International Federation of Petroleum Workers were "typical of a whole new generation of unionists—calm, committed tacticians rather than knockdown battlers, many of whom have chosen to work in international unionism."[7] *Business Week* followed the IFPW workers as they leapt miraculously from country to country with endless good cheer, all on a modest budget. *Business Week* proclaimed, "Today, 10 employees, including the secretaries and translators, keep IFPW humming on a yearly budget of less than $100,000. It has a European office in Paris, an Asian office in

Karachi and plans to open an office in Bogotá shortly. 'We wear out a set of luggage a year,' says a staffer, emphasizing the outfit's 'trouble-shooting' nature."[8]

Henry Louis, Mobil Oil's personnel director in Lebanon, loved these cooperative American unionists. "IFPW has helped unions here understand their position better," he told *Business Week*. "It has taught them not to ask for the moon, and how to work with management, not against it."[9]

For *Business Week* readers, it didn't get much better than that. For Tony, it couldn't get much worse. These union patriots, he believed, were blind drunk on US global power. The last vestiges of CIO class consciousness were wiped from their souls as they joined corporate and government allies in Cold War intrigue—gaining prestige, influence, and CIA cash along the way.

The 1955 merger that formed OCAW also brought to the new organization ten thousand atomic workers, people employed in the epicenter of the national security state. These workers manufactured nuclear weapons and enriched uranium at places like Paducah, Kentucky, and Oak Ridge, Tennessee. For them, every new bomb and every new nuclear test meant more job security. It would be hard to imagine a more difficult environment for Tony Mazzocchi's militant brand of unionism, or for his protests against the insanity of the arms race. Tony's plan to rise to high office in such a union was perhaps a fool's errand. But turning this union into one that would lead a class war . . . *that* had to be impossible.

II

By 1955, the United Gas, Coke and Chemical Workers Union was such a mess that Tony actually *welcomed* the merger with the CIA-led Oil Workers. He knew that Gas-Coke would never recover from its crippling purges, decaying finances, and stifling bureaucracy. Reuther, then the head of the CIO, wanted the unions merged, and even offered (but never delivered) vast sums for new organizing in the growing energy and chemical sectors. As Tony recalled, "The chemical workers felt they couldn't survive anymore, although we had almost as many members as the oil workers. In those days they wanted to put like unions together and these two unions—Gas-Coke and the Oil Workers—shared jurisdictions."

While Tony was repelled by the Oil Workers' global politics, he was attracted to the union's long tradition of rank-and-file democracy. The Oil Workers union was among a handful with rank-and-file members making up its executive board, which held ultimate power. This board checked the power of the national union officers. In more centralized unions, the district directors, vice presidents, secretary-treasurer, and president made up the executive board. Once these officers were elected, they ran all aspects of the union, including patronage, creating a political machine that was rarely challenged from below. But under the Oil Workers' constitution, board members could not be national officers or employees of the international union. (US unions are often called *international* because they include Canadian workers.) Instead, each of the union's sixteen regional districts elected one "rank-and-file" member to the executive board. This person could be either a full-time worker or a full-time local union officer. No other union had such grassroots control. Tony liked the looks of it.

The Industrial Workers of the World (IWW) or "Wobblies" could be thanked for this unusual tradition. The Wobblies were famous for denouncing written contracts with employers, whom they considered, one and all, class enemies. Instead they relied on quick strikes to achieve gains on the job. Attracted to this direct action, many oil workers signed up with the Wobblies in the early 1900s and carried two cards—the AFL Oil Workers blue card and the IWW red card. The Wobblies also distrusted union leaders, whom they called "pie cards."

Over time a Wobbly-inspired democratic union culture developed among the defiant and independent oil workers, especially in Oklahoma, Texas, California, and Missouri. As the oil union grew during the 1930s and became one of the founding unions of the CIO, rank-and-file members and national leaders began vying for control of the Oil Workers. After a disastrous strike against Mid-Continent Oil Company in 1939–1940, the balance shifted to the restive rank and file. The union's constitution was amended in 1940 based on a "workers' control" program developed by District 5 in Oklahoma, which had strong Wobbly roots. As historian Harvey O'Connor noted, "The president was stripped of his power to remove other officers and to fill vacancies and this was placed in the hands of the [rank-and-file] executive council."[10]

To lead them under this new constitution, the workers chose an energetic and articulate young organizer: O.A. "Jack" Knight, the very man who would eventually partner with the CIA and turn away from the rank and file.

Tony desperately wanted to preserve the union's democratic structures, especially its directly elected executive board. "My local understood it." Tony recalled. "I don't think anyone else gave a shit about the rank-and-file board."

Tony had no use for the Gas-Coke union's system of electing district directors. While in principle electing these officers (rather than appointing them) seemed democratic, Tony thought this structure fragmented the union into regional fiefdoms, allowed union leaders to hold multiple jobs, and blurred the distinction between staff and local elected leaders. He'd seen enough of it in Local 149, where Jack Curran had once served as both local union president and district director. By monopolizing multiple positions, the union's staff became a self-perpetuating machine, making a democratic insurgency difficult.

Furthermore, the Gas-Coke structure had included a unique procedure aimed at snuffing out rebels like Charlie Doyle or Tony Mazzocchi. If one district got too radical and elected a director that the union president didn't approve of, the president had the power to call for a vote on that position by the entire union. This virtually guaranteed that the president could block the election of a radical insurgent. In fact, this clause already had dissuaded Mazzocchi from running for district director. As Tony recalled, "Most of us wanted to get rid of the old director setup. In Gas-Coke, I could have won the election in my district. But the minute that happened, the president would have said, 'No, you're unacceptable.' And then they had the rest of the union to beat me."

What drew Tony most toward the Oil Workers Union was that good old Wobbly rank-and-file executive board and the spirited rebelliousness it represented. Through it, he saw a path for rank-and-file power.

Thanks in part to Tony's influence, the Oil, Chemical and Atomic Workers' constitution, hammered out in the 1955 merger convention, retained the rank-and-file board, with one member to be selected by convention caucus from each of sixteen districts. In the new union, the president would appoint district directors with "due deference" to the board, which could remove officers. If a top officer position became vacant, the president could nominate a replacement, but the board could reject the nomination.

It was curious that Knight and his CIA allies let this happen. Surely, by 1955, they were powerful enough to silence the faint echoes of Wobbly democracy. The merger presumably provided a perfect opportunity to centralize the union and adopt bureaucratic structures more like those of other unions. Perhaps Knight, who saw himself as a world leader in promoting "free trade unions," didn't want to be the one to squelch democracy in his own union at home. Mark Dudzic, an OCAW local leader, suggested a structural reason. "The oil industry never really accepted the union as a junior partner," he said. "The union was never able to win the union shop and all the other accoutrements of class peace. As a result, the culture of militancy was deeply embedded in the union."[11]

Whatever the reasons, the union's rank-and-file board gave Tony his stepping-stones to power.

III

But at best, they were slippery stones.

At the founding convention, Tony's supporters, enthralled by his rise as local union president, urged him to run for the powerful national executive board. "But I did some nose counting," said Tony. "I knew I would get beat. I was close, but I didn't yet have issues to run on. So I decided to let it go."

A year later, he was ready. "I had built my strength by forming a district council of locals in our area. So I decided to take a shot at it. I figured I had the votes."

To win, Tony was relying on an international representative (a "rep," on the union's national payroll) who believed in Tony and promised he would get certain delegates into the Mazzocchi camp. But as the vote neared, the rep began to fret about how his union bosses would view his support for an insurgent. As Tony put it, "He was one of our friends, but he was chicken."

Tony had been so confident of victory that he left the convention even before the vote to attend an important bargaining session back on Long Island. Unfortunately, the rep fried him. "He pulled his delegates, and I lost by that margin," said Tony. "That taught us a lesson. We didn't get caught in that trap again."

Tony couldn't stomach union leaders who sat in their office like a black hole, sucking the life out of the union. In fact, after corruption, Tony's sharpest critique was often leveled at unionists who *didn't want to do anything.*

In Tony's view, this perfectly described W. J. Trombley, the director of Tony's own OCAW District 14. "We had to get rid of him," said Tony. "He and I were really at loggerheads. He was very bureaucratic."

Tony planned to challenge Trombley at OCAW's August 1957 convention—which began one day after Tony had addressed the seminal anti-nuclear-testing event at Town Hall.

In a union representing workers whose jobs were tied to weapons production and the Cold War, it might have been prudent for Tony to downplay his opposition to nuclear weapons testing, at least until *after* he'd won his seat. But Tony believed the entire point of getting elected was to raise bold issues, not play it safe. So he made his nuclear concerns a centerpiece of his convention activity: He called on union leaders to hold a workshop on nuclear health and safety. He also distributed a thousand copies of Albert Schweitzer's call for an end to nuclear weapons. He wanted to make this debate accessible to the entire union, including its weapons workers and the union's CIA operatives.

It was a hell of a way to run for national office in a union representing atomic workers at the height of the Cold War. He might as well have walked through the convention waving a red flag that read, I'M A BAN-THE-BOMB RADICAL FROM BROOKLYN. Several factors protected him. First, Tony knew that the fear of nuclear fallout was so widespread, he could bring workers along. He had already witnessed the outpouring of interest during the Stevenson campaign and at the Town Hall meeting.

Second, Tony let outside expert speakers present the issue. By arguing that "we ought to listen to all points of view," he was able to introduce union members to new and sometimes subversive ideas. Over the years, Mazzocchi used this methodology again and again, opening up provocative debates on everything from the Vietnam War to global warming.

Tony appealed to what he believed was a genuine rank-and-file interest in knowing more. He aimed high. He wanted workers to hear and evaluate sophisticated points of view. By not selling them short, he showed respect toward his constituency, and they responded in kind. While sometimes workers disagreed with the radical perspectives Tony paraded before them, they valued the opportunity to hear those views. He put his members into the eye of the storm, and they grew to love the turbulent political winds.

Tony's district council had passed a resolution calling on the 1957 convention to hold an educational plenary on the health effects of fallout, knowing full well that the union would invite pro-nuclear-testing speakers vetted by the Atomic Energy Commission. Tony brought with him "the other point of view" in the form of reprints of Albert Schweitzer's April 28, 1957, international radio broadcast from Oslo, entitled "Declaration of Conscience." The five-thousand-word declaration was a carefully constructed primer on radiation that would help workers understand the perils they faced on the job and as citizens.

Schweitzer cited a study of radioactivity from the Hanford Nuclear Reservation (which employed more than one thousand atomic workers who later would join OCAW) about how radioactive materials accumulated in the food chain in the Columbia River region surrounding the plant. Tony knew the presentation would captivate a membership fond of hunting and fishing. Schweitzer said,

> The radioactivity of the river was insignificant. But the radioactivity of the plankton was 2,000 times higher, that of the ducks was 40,000 times higher, that of the fish 15,000 times higher. In young swallows fed on insects caught by their parents in the river the radioactivity was 500,000 higher, and in the egg yolks of water birds more than 1,000,000 times higher.[12]

No one at the convention, reading this, could dispute that Tony had the health of workers and their families in mind when he raised the nuclear issue. The Schweitzer primer set the pattern for the next twenty-five years of Tony's work as he fought to protect the health and safety of nuclear workers and uranium miners while at the same time challenging the Cold War politics that gave rise to these industries.

For the Atomic Energy Commission and its allies inside OCAW, Tony's distribution of the "Declaration of Conscience" was a declaration of war. Elwood Swisher, the former president of Gas-Coke, and then vice president of OCAW, ably represented the interests of the Atomic Energy Commission and the national security state within the union. While Swisher could not cancel the fallout forum, he did have the power to move the Mazzocchi debate away from prime time.

"Swisher wouldn't allow the discussion to be on the formal agenda," Tony recalled, "so we did an evening meeting. A number of the nuclear workers came and talked about what they were beginning to observe in these facilities. But Swisher got the AEC to send people from Argon National Lab to shoot us down. They dismissed our concerns about health and safety in the plant."

Fortunately, Tony got significant political cover at the convention from none other than James Carey, the powerful (anti-communist) president of the International Union of Electrical Workers—a union that the CIO had founded explicitly to destroy the more radical United Electrical Workers. Carey had sent around the convention an unprecedented open letter of thanks to Tony and Local 149 for their tireless support of IUE strikes on Long Island. Said Carey: "President Mazzocchi led an average of from 40 to 50 rank and file members of his local on the Reeves Picket line for four solid weeks every morning from 6 AM to 8 AM. . . . That . . . kind of fraternal spirit, that kind of fighting trade unionism is. . . . what made the American Labor movement. . . ."[13]

The praise from this prominent anti-communist greatly bolstered Tony's position and left no doubt about his commitment to solidarity. As many would say over the next decades, "he may be a little pink, but he's our kind of fighter."

Tony's candidacy might not have survived a red-baiting attack by the union's CIA forces. Luckily, OCAW president Jack Knight did not allow a witch hunt, perhaps because Knight knew what it was like to be on the other end of one, not once, but twice.

In 1951, Knight was subjected to a routine government investigation to clear him for participation on the National Production Authority. According to the official union history, on December 31, 1951, "he stumbled out of his office pale with shock and almost speechless" after opening a letter noting "that a reasonable doubt exists as to your loyalty to the government of the United States and that you therefore are unsuitable for federal employment." The loyalty board of the Commerce Department believed Knight "was a member of, affiliated with, or in sympathetic association with the Communist Party."[14] Of course, under Truman administration rules, Knight was not allowed to see the sources for that claim, nor to appeal.

The experience may have accelerated Knight's subsequent move into the CIA fold, where he could prove his patriotism. But it certainly did not make him fond of McCarthyism.

McCarthyism struck Knight again after he joined a delegation of industrial unionists in a meeting with Khrushchev, in defiance of George Meany and Jay Lovestone's boycott of all contacts with the Soviet leader. To get even, Meany engineered a smear on Knight by Victor Riesel (the same man who'd been blinded by Johnny Dio's acid attack). Riesel, a vicious anti-communist and longtime Meany collaborator, wrote in his syndicated column that Khrushchev had called Knight a "stupid SOB," prompting the press to further ridicule Knight.

Several years later, Knight told OCAW members: "Unfortunately, publicity has gone out throughout the nation, instigated by an individual who has my sympathy, an individual who recently lost his eyes but is still doing his best to help mold public opinion through the medium of a column that he puts out. I don't know what caused him to do it. This gentleman printed an absolute lie, a false statement about myself."[15]

After the abuse he'd taken from red-baiters, Knight had no stomach for going after Mazzocchi.

And so in August 1957, Tony Mazzocchi was elected to OCAW's executive board representing OCAW's District 14—elected with his politics on his sleeve.

IV

It was only a matter of time before Mazzocchi and his opponents in OCAW would square off over the union's CIA connections. But this issue was not the one that fueled Tony's rise in OCAW. Instead, he rose because he offered an alternative to the kind of business unionism promoted by Knight, his International Federation of Petroleum Workers, and *Business Week*. In fact, the more Knight labored to sell American business unionism abroad, the less he was able to deliver for his workers at home.

Although the oil industry welcomed the union's help overseas, it showed no inclination to halt its drive to streamline its domestic workforce. With a vengeance, it cut the number of union employees and broke down craft distinctions. Working conditions deteriorated. At the same time, the oil industry increased wages for the remaining workers, so that those who still had jobs formed an elite tier among industrial workers. This industry could well afford to do this, because labor costs represented—and still represent—a tiny fraction of the costs of oil production. Big Oil was the first industry to use automated, continuous-flow systems. It strike-proofed its facilities not only by reducing its unionized workforce, but also by maintaining a large supply of supervisors who could run the refinery indefinitely through a strike.

While Knight labored overseas, his union at home was too weak to counter these moves. Oil workers' declining power was clear in the brutal yearlong Shell strike that started in Pasadena, Texas, in August 1962. Management, which over the four previous years had reduced the number of workers from thirty-one hundred to twenty-one hundred, provoked the strike by asking for unlimited power to assign work and cut more jobs. When the strike began, seven hundred supervisors crossed the lines to work twelve-hour shifts. AFL building-trades workers also crossed the picket lines to do maintenance work to keep the plants functioning. (The official union history reported, "It was a sorry sight. Since 1918, workers had struggled to establish effective industrial unionism but were handicapped again and again by their half brothers in the building trades."[16])

Knight got Secretary of Labor Willard Wirtz to assign a mediator and pressure Shell. But the union buckled and was forced to accept an agreement that provided management with more flexibility in assigning work. By 1964, another six hundred workers had been cut from the Pasadena refinery.

The union watched helplessly as the oil companies outsourced nearly all major maintenance work, removing thousands of OCAW workers from their payrolls. Job classifications blurred so that workers were forced to handle a variety of jobs, making more of them redundant and reducing the quality of work life. Many oil companies also resisted new union organizing at home, even while welcoming anti-communist organizing overseas. For the first time since its founding, OCAW membership declined.

Angry workers sought ways to express their discontent. Business-as-usual unionism could not deliver in OCAW. But Knight and his fellow officers did not offer an alternative direction. Instead, Knight took the path traveled by so many union leaders: He began to scorn his own members. They were growing too fat from the good contracts he had negotiated for them. They didn't appreciate the grand mission he was leading overseas. And now, through their apathy, they were reaping what they had sowed. If their union wasn't fighting hard enough anymore, they should look in the mirror.

In blaming the rank and file, the OCAW leadership was in tune with the latest trends in political theory. Sociologists and political scientists of this period, led by Yale's Robert Dahl, argued that modern democracy needed to contain, not expand, mass participation. The masses could not be trusted to govern directly, since they were too easily captured by charismatic demagogues like Joe McCarthy. Instead, these theorists argued for a pluralistic democracy run by elites. They believed that America worked well because elites from a variety of interest groups—including labor—conducted rational negotiations with one another. Only the elites from labor, management, government, and other interest groups possessed sufficient knowledge and skill to protect the public good and contain mass hysteria.

Knight relished his role as one of these elites. But to play at that level, he needed a freer hand within the union, which meant stripping his rank-and-file board of its power. In response to his members' rising discontent, Knight and his allies pushed for a constitutional amendment that would give them, the union officers, a vote on the board. They had no idea that they faced a man who would soon become one of the era's greatest defenders of rank-and-file democracy. As labor sociologist Stanley Aronowitz put it, "What Reuther was to building centralized bureaucratic unionism, Mazzocchi was to democratic unionism."[17]

As a new member of OCAW's executive board, Tony said, "I wanted to move the union. I didn't think in terms of winning national office. I thought I could be an important spokesperson on the board for progressive views. The union had a progressive past. Jack Knight couldn't be considered a right-wing guy. The union was rank-and-file run, so my position on the board was to push for more rank-and-file control."

At first, Tony's voice carried little weight. His District 14 was the smallest of the union's sixteen districts, and the oil-worker-dominated districts in California, Texas, and Canada often voted together. "These larger districts beat us every time on the board," said Tony. Clearly, Tony and his allies had to build coalitions with other progressives who were coming onto the rank-

and-file board. And of course they needed to defend the power of the board against Knight's attempts to dilute it.

An opportunity to do all this came at OCAW's 1961 convention, a contest that would prefigure all future battles for power between Mazzocchi insurgents and OCAW's business unionists. Mazzocchi knew that Knight would propose drastically reducing the size of the executive board. Tony saw the logic of this: "Some of us had always talked about combining the districts. It was very expensive to have sixteen administrators and staffs. My own district had only twenty-six hundred people. And then we had some director from New York City who was resting on his laurels and provided no leadership at all."

Tony also knew that the way the districts were reshaped and who was elected to lead them would determine the union's future. Fortunately, he had found a new progressive ally: Al Grospiron, an oil worker and secretary-treasurer of a Texas local that was part of District 4, the largest district in the union, representing oil workers along the Gulf Coast. At the 1961 convention, Grospiron would vie for the executive board member slot from District 4.

"I found out that we viewed the union the same way. And that was incredible," said Tony. "Here was this Texan guy who could move this union." For Tony, Grospiron passed several important litmus tests. He was a fighter and could stand toe-to-toe with any company. During a tough strike against Standard Oil in 1959, Grospiron emerged as the key leader in Texas City. Tony believed that Grospiron was also fully committed to rank-and-file control of the union. Grospiron wasn't an anti-communist; radicalism didn't bother him. Al was "good on civil rights," said Tony. "He was a southerner. He understood. And this period was the heart of the civil rights movement. He had all the right instincts and would always support my positions on civil rights. He had guts."

For progressives to gain control of the union, "I knew that there had to be an alliance between the southern sectors and our sectors in the Northeast," said Tony. "We could never do it with the Northeast alone. So Grospiron and I began to go into long and extensive discussions about all this. And we thought the first move had to be to combine the districts."

But first Tony had to upend Knight's convention proposal to diminish the executive board's power and enhance their own by adding the union's four officers as voting members of the board. If successful, they would easily capture control of the entire board. Their proposal would mark the beginning of the end of the rank-and-file board, and Tony's hopes for leading a successful rank-and-file revolt.

When Knight's motion to add the four officers to the executive board reached the convention floor, Mazzocchi rose to challenge it:

> You would no longer have a proper check and balance. You would more likely have a sort of stacked executive board. . . . So I maintain if we are to retain the rank-and-file executive board, it should be a rank-and-file executive board that fulfills its proper responsibility of checks and balances and I urge my fellow delegates to support [its retention].[18]

It wasn't even close: OCAW members voted overwhelmingly to save their rank-and-file board.

Next, the convention considered whether to reduce the number of districts from sixteen to eight, plus Canada—a move Tony supported. If this passed, each rank-and-file member would have much more power. "We'd gotten the executive board to approve this plan," said Tony. "And it was a courageous thing for them to do, because they were eliminating their own positions and their chief political supporters, the directors. We brought it up on the convention floor. We had to carry it by two-thirds. And we rolled it in. The union was shocked."

Tony's District 14, the smallest in the union, was now combined with several other districts to make the new District 8—by far the largest district in the union. And, said Tony, "Because of the way the district lines were redrawn, we had five previous board members contesting for one position" on the new executive board. One of the five was Tony. Beating the other four candidates became a life-and-death struggle for his union career.

"The convention passed the merger of districts on Thursday evening," said Tony. "I had from Thursday evening to Friday afternoon to campaign. We had five board members, and we were all over the lot. Everybody was scrambling to emerge."

To be elected to the executive board, the candidate needed to gain a majority. But with so many candidates running, the election would involve runoffs until one candidate received a majority. In each round, the person with the lowest number of votes would be dropped off the ballot. To survive, Mazzocchi had to find a way off the bottom. So he cut deals with his friends and allies, trying to position himself to hold on to a spot. "It was uphill. I don't think anybody could have predicted what happened. Everybody was in such a state of disarray. But we put all the deals together. And I delivered on every one of my commitments."

Tony recalled the scene: "We start voting around five in the evening. And it ended at three o'clock in the morning. Each round was a roll-call vote. It was incredible. The guy who swung it was Nelson Lawrence, who was president of the Merck local in Rahway, New Jersey. He got up on the floor and said, 'I cast my vote for the only guy who can really do this job right.'"

Tony won, to the utter surprise of Knight and many others. "Here we are, the smallest district in the union, and I end up board member for the largest district in the union," said Tony. "The president never wanted me to be the board member. He didn't think the merger of districts was going to come off. They were shocked because the power equation changed overnight."

Grospiron won his bid to represent District 4, the union's second largest district. "My most powerful ally was Grospiron," said Tony. "So we had District 8, District 4, and the Canadian who gets elected becomes my best friend, Tommy Towler. That's three districts starting off. It was just a matter of time."

V

How much time would depend on unforeseen events. The Knight faction saw no need to panic. Although the board was slipping out of their control, they still held the top spots in the union with no serious rivals in sight. But the fates turned when, in 1963, Tom McCormick, then the union's secretary-treasurer and a strong Knight supporter, suddenly died. "McCormick was this huge guy," Tony said. "The doctor always warned him about his weight, but he'd go on these eating binges. He'd lose weight, then go on another eating binge. And then he dropped dead suddenly in Canada while on vacation. And I moved right away."

The union constitution gave Knight the power to appoint a temporary secretary-treasurer until the next convention, giving that appointee a huge leg up in the next election. But the ghosts of Wobblies past came into play. The rank-and-file board had to confirm Knight's choice. So McCormick's successor would become a matter of struggle between Knight's faction and Mazzocchi's.

"I called Grospiron to say we had to convene the board," said Tony. "And I said, 'Al, you ought to be secretary-treasurer.' Now, that was unheard of, to take a rank-and-filer and elevate him to an international officer."

President Knight was not about to appoint a board member who was part of the Mazzocchi opposition. Further, the union's nine district directors and staff did not want such a plum job to go to someone outside their ranks. But by now, Tony knew how to play politics. Already he'd turned his three votes on the board of nine into five. Knight could not appoint anyone without those votes.

Grospiron had a chance to win, although a slim one, made even slimmer by his unusually large ego. As Tony recalled, "Grospiron got stubborn and said he wanted it to be a unanimous vote. I said, 'I can't get that.' The administration had two board members locked in."

Mazzocchi put his political imagination in gear. He knew that if the executive board did not meet soon to decide on the new secretary-treasurer, the union's district directors would "start moving among themselves and come up with their own candidate."

So he found an excuse for a hasty gathering of the executive board: McCormick's funeral in Denver, where OCAW was headquartered.

The vacancy provided an opportunity for Knight and company to consolidate their grip on the union and line up a successor for president. After Knight's twenty-three-year tenure, his CIA friends did not want some unfriendly leader in the union's number two position. They wanted one of their own, someone who understood how critical the union was to national security and to winning the Cold War. They wanted someone who would lie if necessary to protect the union's special relationship with the intelligence community. In fact, *they wanted a full-fledged CIA agent:* Lloyd Haskins, the general secretary of the IFPW. Haskins could replace McCormick and then succeed Knight. Haskins became Knight's candidate for secretary-treasurer.

Was the CIA really seeking to take over one of the country's most democratic unions, in violation of its charter, the law, and its stated belief in "free" trade unions?

Philip Agee, the former CIA agent and author of *Inside the Company: CIA Diary,* left little doubt that IFPW was a CIA-created and -funded operation, and that Haskins was a CIA agent. In his appendix listing CIA front groups and agents was the following entry for "Haskins, Lloyd":

> Executive Secretary of the International Federation of Petroleum and Chemical Workers (IFPCW), q.v. CIA agent in charge of this union.[19]

In his detailed diary notes for "Washington DC, November 1960," Agee wrote that while he was receiving secret training for a CIA assignment to Ecuador,

> I had to take a special course in labor operations. Much emphasis was given to the advantages of using agents in the different International Trade Secretariats in which, in Latin America at least, the Agency has considerable control. Lloyd Haskins, Executive Secretary of the International Federation of Petroleum and Chemical Workers, gave us a lecture on how he can help in organizing Latin American workers in the critical petroleum industry. . . . Overall the course emphasized that Agency labor operators must seek to develop trade unions in underdeveloped countries that will focus on economic issues and stay away from politics and the ideology of class struggle.[20]

Is it possible that Haskins simply served as an "outside" guest lecturer? Perhaps. But Agee's account places him in a room full of prized CIA agents whose identities would be highly classified. The facts strongly suggest that Haskins was part of the CIA—whether paid or unpaid.

This was the man Jack Knight wanted to succeed him as president of OCAW.

Tony Mazzocchi and his allies didn't know it at the time, but they were the only thing standing between the CIA and their beloved union.

VI

Tony did know, however, that Haskins was a business unionist who relished his involvement in the Cold War:

> Haskins himself told me that he was in Iran when Mossadegh was overthrown. He told me the race was on to beat the British to Mossadegh's office, because the American oil interests wanted to jump the British, and they did. Haskins said he and the other Americans got there first and seized all of Mossadegh's documents. So he was in the middle of things. He told me this long before this other shit [about Haskins' CIA links] came out.

For Tony, the idea of Haskins becoming secretary-treasurer and then perhaps the president was simply too much to bear. "So I said, fuck this guy. He wasn't even an OCAW member."

As Tony had arranged, the executive board assembled in Denver at the time of McCormick's funeral. At the meeting to fill the vacant position, Knight proposed Haskins. Said Tony: "We were deadlocked. I had five to four board members in favor of Grospiron. But we didn't have the power to nominate, only to approve or reject. Jack refused to accept Grospiron as a candidate. He wanted Haskins and we said no. He kept submitting the nomination for Haskins and we kept voting against it."

Tony finally told Knight directly: "We're never going to approve who you come up with."

Knight and his allies encouraged the union's district directors to pressure the board members in the Mazzocchi-Grospiron camp. Tony protected his flock and fortified them with free lodging and some of his excellent Italian meals: "I had a fully furnished apartment we used to rent in Denver a week at a time, and I had my five board guys bunked there for a week. We were holding solid, despite the phone calls from directors and everything. But I knew if something didn't happen soon, I would lose some of them."

When the executive board met again, Tony, the math dummy, came up with a scheme.

> I said, "Look, let's have a straw vote. Whoever wins the straw vote, we all support." So they agreed to it—which was crazy. Some of these guys couldn't count. They saw we had five votes but they figured they would prevail? So we do the straw vote and we win five to four. So I move Al. He gets all the votes, the president finally accepts him, and he becomes secretary-treasurer in '63.

VII

Now only a very tired and discouraged President Knight stood in the way of a total coup by the Grospiron-Mazzocchi progressive alliance. Even the Knight-friendly official union history painted a sorry picture: "There was widespread concern about Jack Knight's weakening grasp of his duties, his forgetfulness, his obvious weariness with the frustrations of the job."[21]

The CIA needed a new script to keep Knight in office until they found a replacement. But time was catching up with the agency. And so was Cuba. After Castro's revolution in 1959, the CIA had been castigated for allowing a communist government to be set up only ninety miles from Florida. But the botched Bay of Pigs invasion only worsened the agency's image in the American mind. Until that failed attack on Cuba in 1961, the little that was known about the CIA was generally positive. Some intellectuals even considered the CIA to be a liberal alternative to the FBI and McCarthyism, an agency that cared about democratic freedoms at home and abroad.

The mid-1960s was a tipping point. During the mounting chaos in Southeast Asia, the CIA became associated with TV images of bloody regime changes and burning Buddhist monks. Soon the agency would symbolize for many a betrayal of American ideas, a runaway clandestine organization that murdered foreign leaders, overthrew governments, and manipulated public institutions at home and abroad.

A few congressional leaders for the first time began to question the CIA. Even Congress members with no ax to grind, such as Representative Wright Patman, a liberal Democrat from Texas, were rankled by the CIA's manipulation and stonewalling. This led to unexpected consequences for the anti-Mazzocchi forces.

In early September 1964, Patman, a tax populist, conducted hearings on charitable organizations with tax exemptions under IRS code 501(c)(3). Patman believed that the wealthy were using this status to illegally shelter money from federal taxes. Patman scanned IRS returns from foundations that reported large contributions from unaccounted sources or that gave unexplained grants. The review uncovered the Kaplan Foundation in New York, whose stated purpose was "to strengthen democracy at home and abroad through a general program of assistance to benevolent charitable education/scientific and literary activities."[22]

Headed by Jacob M. Kaplan, chair of the board of the New School for Social Research and former president of the Welch's Grape Juice Company, the Kaplan Foundation normally donated to organizations that supported free Shakespeare plays in Central Park, a waterfront park in Brooklyn, or the Henry Street Settlement. According to *The New York Times,* what caught Patman's attention was "an unexplained grant of $395,000" in 1963, which was exceptionally large for Kaplan, accounting for nearly 40 percent of its giving. And the recipient seemed a bit strange as well: the Institute of International Labor Research, Inc., on East 37th Street in Manhattan. The *Times* reported that the institute's secretary-treasurer, Sacha Volman, a naturalized refugee from Romania, had for years "headed a group called Free Trade Unions in Exile that worked underground with anticommunist forces in Eastern Europe."

When Patman asked his intelligence sources about this suspicious grant, he got the runaround. Infuriated, he decided to go public with the information he had. In a *New York Times* front-page article on September 1, 1964, Patman disclosed that the "Central Intelligence Agency gave money to a private foundation that, he said, served as a 'secret conduit' for the agency. . . . The Congressman said he was disclosing the agency's payment to the fund because he thought he had been 'trifled with' in connection with the case."

Quickly the Johnson administration and the CIA engaged in damage control. Only two days after his revelation, Patman announced that he was dropping the CIA phase of the investigation, saying, according to the *Times,* "The CIA does not belong in this foundation investigation."

But on September 4, 1964, *The New York Times* editorial page writers sounded the alarm:

> Its [the Institute of International Labor Research] continuation permits the Communists and the cynical everywhere to charge that American scholars, scientists and writers going abroad on grants from foundations are cover agents or spies for the CIA. All scholars—especially those involved in East-West exchanges will suffer if the integrity of their research is thus made suspect. . . . The use of Government intelligence funds to get foundations to underwrite institutions, organizations, magazines and newspapers abroad is a distortion of CIA's mission on gathering and evaluating intelligence. It means operating behind a mask to introduce governmental direction . . . where it does not belong—at least not in a democracy like ours.

The *Times* also noted that while Patman discovered that the CIA "is giving money to and working through at least one private foundation . . . if [there is] one, there must be others."

And there *were*. Before LBJ had put the lid on, Patman had fingered eight other mysterious foundations that contributed $923,950 to the Kaplan Foundation between 1961 and 1963. One of them was the Andrew Hamilton Foundation in Philadelphia, which also lavishly funded the International Federation of Petroleum Workers for its good deeds overseas.

Without knowing it, Patman had just made a significant contribution to Mazzocchi's effort to knock Knight and the CIA clique from power. "We had always suspected the IFPW was getting money from the State Department," Tony recalled,

> But we had no idea of CIA involvement. OCAW had a pretty shitty office on California Street in Denver. It was a one-story building that was falling apart. But the IFPW rented a building a couple doors down from us, and it was fancy. The OCAW board used to meet in their office because they had a really nice boardroom and everything else. And they had a good income. We used

> to say, "Where do you get this money from? It must be the State Department." It was a joke among us.
>
> Knight says, "There's this foundation in Philadelphia, called the Andrew Hamilton Foundation—they think the IFPW is a good thing, and they're the main financers."
>
> So when we saw that the *Times* listed the Andrew Hamilton Foundation in its story about the CIA, we said, "Holy shit!" So we go to Knight and ask him what's going on here. He had some crazy, convoluted response. But we figured: We ain't meeting in *that* office anymore, that's one thing.

Tony knew the CIA revelation would not be enough to defeat Knight at the 1965 convention. The trick was to encourage him to resign beforehand. Tony sensed that Knight no longer had the stomach for a convention fight, even if he could win it.

Again, Tony carefully chose the setting to maximize his chances for success. He thought he could get Knight to retire gracefully if he could just speak to him alone.

> I got us to have a board meeting in Vegas away from all the palace guard in Denver. That was the first board meeting ever held out of Denver. We used the pretense that we were going to examine facilities in Vegas for a convention.
>
> We said to Knight, "Look, you're sixty-three. It looks like there's going to be opposition at the convention. We'll have the union pay you until you're sixty-five, and then you can get your pension." He took the deal and made a formal announcement then and there.

Knight wrote, "If I did succeed in getting elected at the next convention such reelection might not be in the best interests of OCAW as it would cause a period of extensive political activity with consequent disruption of our efforts in behalf of the membership of OCAW."[23]

But the decisive battle over the union's future was still to come at the 1965 convention in Miami. Mazzocchi called it "a dog-down fight"—a wide-open clash between Grospiron and his challenger for president, Bill Forrester. Tony characterized Forrester as "a staid oil worker from California, an old stuffed shirt." The official OCAW history didn't flatter him, either, calling him "an unobtrusive participant in International union affairs. He was considered competent but not [a] spectacular staff employee. . . ."[24]

With Grospiron running for president, it seemed like a good time for Tony to take on Elwood Swisher, the former president of Gas-Coke, for one of the two vice president spots. "He was an enemy of mine," said Tony. "He hated me because of all my pro-worker positions and my stands on nuclear testing and health-and-safety stuff. He was always defending industry's positions. He kissed the company's ass. He was on the tit of the nuclear industry, totally."

Was he in the CIA, too?

"No," Tony guessed. "He was just a Cold War guy, but he never was involved with them officially. Sympathies? Sure."

But once again, Tony decided not to stand for office. He was acting out of realpolitik. He knew he couldn't beat Swisher or Ben Schafer, the popular OCAW vice president. They had much more delegate support. Tony also understood that although his own popularity was growing, he had not made his mark on the union. Unlike Knight, Swisher, and Schafer, he had never been responsible for national bargaining, working round the clock to get a national contract. He had yet to visit local leaders around the country. He had led no national strikes. He was still green, and in large areas of the country he was unknown. Besides, he was only thirty-nine years old. He had time to make his move. It was far wiser to work for the Grospiron ticket as its campaign manager, secure an appointed position where he could make a difference, and earn his shot at the top spot later on.

VIII

The August 1965 convention in steamy Florida, at the Bal Harbour Americana Hotel, was straight out of a Graham Greene novel. The International Federation of Petroleum Worker staff arrived from all points of the globe, ready to use their technical talents, contacts, and perhaps a little cash to prevent a Grospiron-Mazzocchi coup. They rightfully feared that a Grospiron victory would spell the end of the CIA-OCAW-IFPW ménage à trois. In fact, Mazzocchi and Grospiron had already agreed they would "knock it [the IFPW] out the minute he got elected," Tony said.

Did the IFPW crew really bring cash with them to swing the election to Forrester? "I think they funneled money," said Tony. "See, that wasn't covered under Taft-Hartley, so there was no way of us knowing whether they contributed."

Tony knew some of the IFPW staffers who showed up in Bal Harbour. "I said, 'So how come you guys are at the convention?' 'Oh, we're taking our vacation.'"

In any case, they certainly did not apologize for their doings abroad. Stanley Aronowitz, then an OCAW staffer, recalled how an IFPW representative at the convention boasted to him about being "dispatched to Nairobi, Kenya, with a bag of $300,000 to buy the daily newspaper for Tom Mboya, head of Kenya's Oil Workers Union. The money undoubtedly was supplied by the CIA." Stanley continued, "Mboya, a darling of US liberal anticommunist intellectuals, became a major politician in Kenya, bringing its politics in line with the US."[25] (Mboya was linked with the CIA by a variety of sources; he was assassinated in 1969 in Kenya.)

With the stakes so high and the pressure mounting, the convention turned ugly. Steve Depew, a Grospiron loyalist, defected and decided to run as an independent for secretary-treasurer. Under pressure from the CIA-linked faction, Depew backed off and agreed to become its campaign treasurer. Then, confused and depressed, Depew took his own life. Mazzocchi remembered vividly, "The second day of the convention, Steve Depew leapt out of the window at lunch hour, right near the crowd that was gathered outside the Americana Hotel for lunch. He was ripped apart on the rocks. I mean just splat. I'd been there in Denver when his wife committed suicide two years before. They had seven kids. We got blamed for driving him to jump. That's what kind of convention it was. It was bloody."

Shrewdly, the anti-Grospiron alliance tried to link the Grospiron slate with another clandestine organization, the mob. They began persistent whispers in the hallways about Tony Sabatine (who was running on the Grospiron ticket for vice president), Tony Mazzocchi, and East Coast mob money.

The mob accusations cut more deeply than any revelations about OCAW-CIA connections. Quickly, Mazzocchi's team found itself on the defensive. "I had to get up and make this speech on the last day just before the voting," said Tony.

The speech printed in the convention proceedings revealed a desperate defense—and no overt attack on the opposition's CIA connections. Tony was forced to defend a testimonial fund-raising dinner for Sabatine "to honor twenty-six years in the labor movement . . . the only monies expended were those necessary to carry out the testimonial reception."

And, Tony said, "We are prepared to make a disclosure from A to Z on every single cent spent on this particular campaign, every cent detailed and documented in bills."

Was this the time to blow the lid off the CIA faction's grip on the union? To point out all the spies who'd come to take their vacations together in muggy Bal Harbour in August? Perhaps to read from the podium the *New York Times* editorial about CIA corruption of domestic institutions?

No, Tony decided, it was too late to sling more mud, with so much already clogging the convention. This was not a teachable moment. Tony sensed that instead of more slimy accusations, the delegates longed for someone to help them climb to higher ground.

"I am not interested in what the other side did," Mazzocchi exclaimed with a straight face to the convention delegates. "I know them, the people on the other side. I have no question as to their integrity, from Brother Forrester on down. I have no question as to where they raised their money; I trust their integrity. I trust that their money came from proper sources. I have no questions whatsoever."

Tony followed this dubious statement with a defense of Tony Sabatine:

> I am dismayed, though—and I don't accuse the other candidates of this—I am dismayed that one would question our integrity. I thought as Oil, Chemical and Atomic Workers, the one thing we had in common regardless of who we are for, the one thing was a sense of purpose, a sense of unity, a sense of being right, that I share with every brother in this union. . . . And Anthony Sabatine represents integrity; District 8 represents integrity, and the Oil, Chemical and Atomic Workers represents integrity. . . . I say to you, let's elect our officers based on facts and issues, not innuendoes or insinuations. Let's talk about facts. The very thing we stand for is the fact that we have the capability to listen to both sides of the questions and make up our own minds, regardless of where we stand on an issue. . . .[26]

Would it work? That depended on outgoing president Jack Knight, who was to give his swan song after twenty-three years as president.

In keeping with his reputation as orator and statesman, Knight dutifully dipped into poetry, reading from Thackeray's "The End of the Day" to express his melancholy upon leaving OCAW. ("The play is done, the curtain drops. . . .")

After Knight had floated upward on the wings of his muse, it would have been difficult to bring his audience back down into the gutter by launching an attack on his opponents. Instead, after Tony's plea for integrity, Knight was moved almost to defend Sabatine's honor:

> So I say in this final day of the convention, sure there are political contests and sure there will be political heat, but let's keep them within perspective and decency and in line with the oath that we have all taken—never knowingly wrong a Brother or see him wronged if it is in our power to prevent it.[27]

The vote quickly followed. "When my district finished voting we were still thousands of votes behind," Tony said. "But when that Canadian walked up—the president of the district council in Canada, Neil Reimer, a good friend of mine—I knew we were going to win by about two thousand votes. They voted the entire Canada vote for Grospiron, and we carried our whole slate through, just barely."

Grospiron received 75,633 votes to 72,910 for Forrester. The popular Ben Schafer (who ran on Grospiron's ticket) won the race for secretary-treasurer by nearly thirty thousand votes. And Sabatine, who had needed 74,079 votes to gain the vice president's seat, squeaked by with a margin of 334 votes. Mazzocchi's team was in.

IX

The 1965 convention that established Tony's political fortunes had another dramatic effect on his life: It ended his marriage. Tony's personal life had already become almost as tumultuous as his political one. His family started with promise and pain. Tony and Rose Alfonso had met at Uncle Lester's retreat in Blairstown through friends of friends with left political pedigrees. Everyone agreed that Rose was gorgeous. Both she and Tony were known as wild and gutsy, never backing down from anyone, being out on the edge, being out much of the night. Sparks flew between them, but, at least at first, they were often the best sort of sparks.

The family whispered about an unwanted pregnancy, a hasty marriage proposal, a car accident on an icy night leading, maybe, to a miscarriage. Or maybe nothing happened to account for the short engagement and sudden wedding. But they didn't elope and no shotguns were present at their sumptuous neighborhood ceremony on September 10, 1950, complete with well-tailored Mazzocchi-made outfits.

The pair moved into their own apartment in a two-family house in Bensonhurst, and Rose continued at her office job while Tony spent most of his waking hours at work and at the union hall. Occasionally, she would join Tony on picket lines, where she would literally pound away on any scab who dared to cross.

They socialized with family and friends, took a few short vacations to upstate New York with other young couples, and enjoyed inexpensive nights out in Manhattan. They waited six years for their first child, Geraldine, born the day after Christmas in 1956. Rose, following the 1950s pattern, quit her job to take care of the child. Carol was born on July 5, 1958. They waited a long time before Linda arrived on May 5, 1964.

For years, Tony had continued his maniacal commitment to building the local union, running for Congress, and moving up the national union ladder. And at home, his wife and growing family missed him. Despite his politics, Tony's lifestyle paralleled that of an ambitious young 1950s executive with a wife and family at home. Rose suspected infidelity, especially given all the time Tony spent away from home. She surely sensed how women gravitated toward him. It had to get lonely and confining. Her bitterness grew.

Perhaps to help cope with family tensions, Tony turned to home improvement projects. Fulfilling the Italian stereotype, he seemed married to cement. "Cement, always mixing cement. Those are my most vivid and early memories of Tony," recalled his daughter Geraldine. "Our ranch house was on a steep driveway with a big dirt slope in front. I remember he was always mixing cement in a big wheelbarrow, him and those union guys, but mostly him. He built a brick patio around the whole front of house, big long brick walkway. And a huge brick patio in the backyard, and sort of a privacy wall behind us. He loved to brag about it. He was always working with cement, and eating fish out of a can—anchovies, or sardines."[28]

How many generations of Mazzocchis in Naples had escaped family tensions with canned fish and cement?

Tony and Rose's piece of the American dream was on 51 Hammond Road in Glencove, a three-bedroom ranch house with a den and a basement for Dad's tools, all financed through the GI Bill. Perched on a hill, it snuck a view of Long Island Sound in the distance. The neighborhood was mostly the working-class Italians whom Tony had hoped to represent in Congress. But it wasn't monochromatic. At the end of the block was a low-income housing project. And in an era of more compressed incomes, a professor lived up the hill, an architect next door; another neighbor acted in commercials.

While most of the Italians went to parochial school, Tony and Rose sent their kids to the integrated public school: "In fact I was the only white kid in my kindergarten," Geraldine said.

For the most part Geraldine recalled family tranquility: "I remember lots of family outings. Going to the beach with Aunt May, Aunt Tess and Connie, Uncle Sam and Nina. Going with suitcases full of Italian foods. I remember George Roach and Pat Duffy from the union always being in the kitchen—smoking cigarettes, a navy tattoo on George's arm, always bringing stuff from the bakery. I remember my dad eating corn-on-the-cob, the juice squirting from the corn, and the beer squirting from the can; he was almost peasant-like when he ate. And always there was family events and cooking."

Tony and Rose thought that maybe the girls should get some ethical education, so they sent Geraldine and Carol to attend a Friends Sunday school on Long Island, an experiment that floundered after a year. More typically, however, Tony was oblivious on this question, as when he scandalized his religious sister, May, during a family dinner by using her Holy Bible as a makeshift high seat.

And of course there were the many causes. Said Geraldine: "I remember marching with my dad somewhere in Glencove for desegregation of the schools, me sitting up on his shoulders. And I remember standing on the kitchen chair, giving speeches for my mom and dad—'If you vote for me, I will . . .'"

In fact the only family political tensions came on Halloween. "My mom would get annoyed with him because he wouldn't come out with us for trick-or-treat," Geraldine said. "But it was always close to election time and he was always on the phone."

Her father's growing notoriety more than made up for these lapses. "We drove with him, during the LIRR railroad worker strike, so he could give a Democratic Party reply on television," Geraldine recalled. "We took a picture of him on TV. And one time in 1964 he came home with a big campaign truck. Bobby Kennedy was actually supposed to stay at our house that night. But it didn't happen. The next day, Dad campaigned with Bobby on that truck."

Some of that notoriety rubbed off on Geraldine in school. She remembered, "Anything you asked him, he would do. He gave a speech to my fifth-grade class on atomic energy. Everyone in the class wrote back thank-you letters to him. And the teacher, Miss Smiley, was really beautiful. She was smitten by him."

It was easy to be smitten by Tony. Rose suspected that her husband was unfaithful, and she was correct. At the 1965 OCAW convention, he shacked up with a journalist. Rose found out about it, and she didn't take the news lightly.

"It was the night before Thanksgiving," recalled Geraldine. "Dad had been out all night. They had this huge fight. Mom knew he was cheating on her. They were killing each other. I mean she was hitting him. I don't think he hit her back. He never hit anyone. And I was trying to get in the middle of them, clutching my teddy bear, trying to get them to stop. That's when they separated."

The extended family rushed in to protect the kids, whisking away Rose and the three girls to live with Uncle Sam, Tony's brother, and his wife, Irene, in Ridgewood, New Jersey. There they remained until the end of March. Several times, Tony and Rose tried unsuccessfully to reconcile. In fact, things deteriorated as Tony spent more time with the journalist at her home in Bayside, Long Island.

Rose had no intention of making the separation easy on Tony. In a desperate rage, she was not above using the kids to pry him loose and back into the marriage. Geraldine painfully remembered:

> Did you ever see *Goodfellas*? When I saw it, I couldn't believe it—it almost word for word described when my mom took us to the house where Dad stayed. My mom takes us to this lady's house, walks up, and bangs on the door screaming, "I have three kids! Leave my husband alone!" And then Mom would make me call her and say, "We hate you, leave my father alone."

Tony knew he needed a big change. He accepted the union's appointment to live in Washington, DC, as the union's national legislative director, leaving behind both his family and the local for which he had worked for fifteen years.

It was "tough," said Tony. "I had grown up in the local. I had been there so long. It was sad to leave it."

It was also hard to commute back and forth by car each weekend to see the kids on Sunday as part of the agreement for the couple's legal separation. Every Sunday, he found ways to entertain his three little girls.

For Geraldine, at least, it was joyous—like being with a loving but tired Santa with a phone stuck in his ear. As she recalled,

> To get cash from his credit card, in those days, he'd have to take us to the airport. Then he'd get on a phone while we ran around. He would take us to Central Park, the Empire State Building, Coney Island, the Statue of Liberty—he carried Linda all the way up the Statue of Liberty. And when Aunt May would take cruises, he would take us down to the dock to watch the ships. And once when I was reading *Misty of Chincoteague,* he arranged to take us there to see the wild horses. Sometimes we'd visit an aunt, and Dad would spend most of the time asleep on the couch. But usually, he'd find his way to a phone. I remember he always said, "Operator, I'd like to make a credit card call. . . ." He'd take us to diners and make up names for them—*Let's go to the Gobblygook diner*—that one was near the union office on Willis Avenue. Then we'd go to the office. The main room had a big long table where

> we could play. He'd go sit in Mac's office [Mac had succeeded Tony as president of the local], where on the wall were pictures of JFK and LBJ. For hours and hours we'd play there, and he'd be on the phone.

Didn't she resent the inattention, the hours he slept on a couch or talked on the phone? "No, we loved going to these places, having the freedom to fool around. One of the best was when he'd take us to the Gilmores' house in Greenwich Village [home of Robert Gilmore, the man who worked with Tony to build SANE]. Their brownstone had an enormous kitchen and backyard like you would never know you were in the city, a garden, floors full of beautiful rooms. The top floor had a glassed-in patio. We must have gone there ten or twenty times. We played all over that house. We were there Christmas and New Year's. They had a Rolls-Royce and a house upstate. The family owned Publishers Clearinghouse."

In stark contrast, the Mazzocchis soon owned next to nothing. The Glencove house was sold. The cost of Tony's commute and his room in DC, plus a rental for the family, dried up their cash. For the first time in his career, Tony accepted a political plum from the Democratic Party. Apparently somebody in the Kennedy-Nickerson machine had heard of Tony's difficulties and appointed him to the Nassau County Planning Commission, which paid seventy-five dollars per month plus travel to the meetings. Although he made the best of it by pursuing progressive causes, he told his old leftist friends the Fines that it was a sellout he didn't feel good about.

Still, the extra money made it easier for Rose and the girls to move into an apartment complex in more upscale Jewish Great Neck, which offered them a new kind of suburban family life. As Geraldine observed, "There were so many single mothers—and the fathers would all come visit on the weekends."

Did Geraldine resent the breakup and Tony's move to DC? "Actually," she offered, "living in Great Neck made us seem more normal. We weren't the only ones. We [the children] never took sides. But growing up was shitty. My mom was crazy with bitterness. She hated him. All we heard was how bad he was. It was miserable. She didn't become happier until she went to work again. In a way, both of them were negative, like about pushing us to go to school. I mean Dad didn't encourage us at all. I guess he thought he made it on his own without school, why not us? But here we are in Great Neck, a town full of parents who really push their kids hard, and we didn't get any of that support. Neither of them told us anything positive about getting an education."

But Geraldine, in fact, learned a good deal. As she recalled,

> I didn't hate my mom. It was hard. I grew to realize that she was a product of the '50s. At the time, you were supposed to give up your job and take care of the kids and be a housewife. Her family was traditional. As a divorced woman she was an outcast—embarrassed around the family. When you're an adult, you can see how hard it was for her. It was hard for us, too, living through all that, but it's really up to you later on. You can't let how you were brought up hinder you. I learned something important. I was never going to be totally dependent on somebody else. Even when my ex-husband owned all those furniture stores, I would always have a job.

Geraldine was not alone: Millions of women were beginning to break out of their 1950s constraints. A rebellion was about to sweep the country, radically altering the assumptions about the role of women and the nature of family life.

As Tony left his shattered family for Washington and a new job, the great wave of the 1960s was about to crash over him.

EIGHT

Masters of War

In the winter of 1965, Tony Mazzocchi headed to Washington as the union's chief lobbyist, with only one goal in mind: to "put the union on the map."

"We thought our legislative department was crap," Tony said. "I mean, nobody knew us. The legislative guy would make a speech about the importance of COPE [the union's Committee on Political Education] every once in a while. The guy had been there for twenty-five years by the time we knocked him out in '65. Al Grospiron [OCAW's new president] gave me carte blanche to do what I needed to do in Washington—that was the deal. I was given free rein to put the union on the map."

All around him, the country was exploding. Each year packed in a decade of turmoil. A whole generation now seemed afflicted with the same frenetic pace Tony had maintained all through the 1950s—the all-day, all-night organizing, the total commitment to movement building. The horror of the Vietnam War created a cacophony of domestic rebellions breaking out like psychedelic pox on the body politic.

Could Tony contribute to this rapidly evolving social movement? Or was this just political chaos and no movement at all? Tony was raring to go, but didn't know where he was headed.

Two worlds shaped Tony's work in Washington: the labor movement and the student movement that was emerging out of the campus upheavals. One he knew like the back of his hand. The other was foreign. Labor, he believed, was trapped in a bureaucratic cage. Perhaps the student movement was a cudgel to help break it free. While Tony viewed labor as far too staid, the student movement seemed too much in flux. Also, as Tony could sense, the two were on a collision course.

Most labor leaders were not happy about the rising chaos. Led by cigar-chomping George Meany, business unionists waddled into the 1960s fattened on Cold War dividends, plump with postwar prosperity, and stripped of any vestiges of anti-capitalist ideology. Union bureaucracies were bursting with tens of thousands of staff members who had escaped the shop floor. Armed with credit cards and union car allowances, many of these labor bureaucrats acted like a domestic occupation force, keeping workers in check and committed to Cold War corporate capitalism. Prosperity, past victories, and Kennedy-Johnson liberalism had made them absolutely secure in their role as full partners, builders, and defenders of the American dream against all comers—including Tony, if he wasn't careful.

Vietnam? Many union leaders viewed it as just another place to teach the commies a lesson.

Tony saw the liberal side of Cold War unionism as well. Many unions lent considerable support to the civil rights uprising in the South. Unions large and small formed much of the organizational muscle for the 1963 March for Civil Rights and Jobs that drew more than two hundred thousand white and black Americans to Washington. Labor supported all manner of civil rights legislation, as well as the vast array of social welfare legislation that became Johnson's Great Society and War on Poverty. The Cold War rhetoric in support of "free" labor abroad reinforced labor's case for equal rights at home.

Anti-communism still prevailed, especially as tensions increased in the early 1960s with the construction of the Berlin Wall, the Cuban Missile Crisis, and the possible "loss" of Southeast Asia to communism. When Kennedy sent "advisers" to Vietnam, labor's Cold Warriors were on board. When Johnson, with a wink and a nod, asked for full authority in the 1964 Gulf of Tonkin Resolution to increase US involvement, the AFL-CIO didn't flinch.

Meanwhile, Tony struggled to make sense of the makeshift student movement. In fact, the very category of "college student" had no political meaning in his class struggle lexicon. He'd never been one, and he rarely visited a campus. But he appreciated the nation's dramatically changing demographics: The average age in America dropped from thirty-four in 1960 (exactly Tony's age then) to only seventeen in 1965. More than forty-five million kids turned eighteen between 1960 and 1972.[1]

Tony felt a strong connection with the southern black students who had borrowed labor's sit-in tactics to protest segregated Woolworth's lunch counters in the early 1960s. He shared the rising sense of optimism as the sit-ins spread from segregated state to segregated state. He saw the potential of a much larger social movement erupting when, over the next two years, more than seventy thousand students participated throughout the South. Perhaps that crusade, Tony thought, could help reignite the labor movement.

Tony also understood the sacrifice of students who took part in the Freedom Rides and the 1964 Freedom Summer, when hundreds of northern students joined with the Student Nonviolent Coordinating Committee to set up Freedom Schools and to register black voters. He was horrified when that summer racist vigilantes beat eighty civil rights workers, shot at thirty volunteers, and killed four; and bombed or burned black homes and businesses.[2]

The murders of civil rights workers Michael Schwerner, Andrew Goodman, and James Chaney, two of whom had just arrived in Mississippi from the New York area to help register voters, became emblematic of that summer. The local connections to Schwerner and Goodman were palpable to Tony and his civil rights contacts.

He also had his eye on a new movement of radical, mostly white students called Students for a Democratic Society (SDS). These student activists, inspired by the courage of southern black students, questioned the hollowness of the affluent society. They rebelled against its constraints, its devotion to consumption, its hypocrisy toward blacks and poverty, and its blind commitment to the Cold War and the nuclear arms race. Although SDS then consisted only of about five hundred students on a handful of campuses, it was charting new territory. Like Tony, SDS wanted to leave behind the baggage of Old Left politics and its divisive sectarian debates. Nor did it have any sympathy with anti-communist liberals who still defined themselves in virulent opposition to the nearly defunct CP. And most importantly, it questioned whether bureaucratic political institutions, including staid unions, would combat growing corporate power. In short, SDSers sounded a good deal like Mazzocchi, but they had never heard of him.

As Tony was moving toward a radical vision of worker control over health and safety, these student radicals developed a call for participatory democracy. They wanted more direct involvement by the poor and the disempowered outside the confines of party politics and bureaucratic structures. Although *participatory democracy* defied precise definition, it expressed powerfully a shared belief that American needed great changes. With a founding cadre that included several of the most astute and committed student visionaries of their generation, SDS became the head, heart, and soul of the emerging New Left.

Few in labor were listening. With more than seventeen million members in 1965 covering nearly 30 percent of the workforce, labor could afford to ignore the eloquent critique of a pesky campus organization like SDS. And labor's assessment might have been dead on, were it not for Vietnam.

Tony already knew a great deal about Vietnam, having received his education in the late 1950s from his civil rights friends on Long Island. He opposed Kennedy's support for South Vietnam's dictators and his counterinsurgency efforts. He was even more appalled when in 1965 LBJ ordered the first major air strikes, Operation Rolling Thunder, against North Vietnam in response to a Vietnamese attack on a small US base at Pleiku. And serious alarm bells went off when LBJ changed the mission of the twenty-five thousand US advisers so that they could conduct combat missions.

In those early days, Tony could do little in the labor movement to oppose the growing war. So he was pleased to see SDS, along with pockets of students and peace activists around the country, step up their protests. At the University of Michigan, SDS leaders organized Vietnam teach-ins that involved more than three thousand students and professors. At Berkeley, twenty thousand participated over a thirty-six-hour period. Then in April 1965, SDS organized the first major demonstration on Washington, surprising itself and everyone else when twenty thousand people turned out to march to the Washington Monument, singing antiwar songs.

But LBJ and the labor movement would not sing along. Backed by advisers held over from the Kennedy administration, Johnson in 1965 increased the number of troops from 25,000 to 125,000, and then, without announcing it, upped it to 200,000 as the United States replaced the South Vietnamese as the army of choice to fight the Vietnamese insurgents. Except for the pesky students and a few labor leaders like Tony, the country continued to applaud. As a *Time* magazine headline put it during the summer of 1965, it was "The Right War and the Right Time."[3]

But not for many draft-aged baby boomers. In the mid-1960s, a joyous party of defiance against traditional authority erupted, joyous because most activists still believed that America would listen, the established powers would yield, and America could keep its promise of equality, peace, the end of poverty, and fulfillment through participation and community. Many students found protesting personally fulfilling and festive as well, in contrast to the world of obedient work offered by the 1950s generation of gray flannel suits. It was a madcap celebration of being young and alive and not in Vietnam. Here was a generation that hated traditional work as much as Tony did.

Yet there was Tony Mazzocchi as if from outer space, wondering what all the fuss was about. "The campus revolt? I was nowhere near it," he said. "I really didn't know anything about was going on at college campuses."

Clearly. He didn't have enough hair to grow it long. He liked wine, not weed. Rock sounded to him like factory noise. Dylan, the Beatles, the Stones? Tony was oblivious, only catching them by accident on the car radio, and almost purposely getting their names hopelessly confused. He liked opera, especially if it was Italian, and from classical anti-fascist composers and conductors.

As for the growing looseness around sex—it didn't seem all that different from the Local 149 all-night bowling league. And while Tony certainly welcomed the assault on traditional work, he knew absolutely nothing of hippies. He was no more of the '60s New Left than he had been of the '30s Old Left. He was more like a ghost of what SDSers called "the missing generation"—the genuine radical who neither blindly followed the Kremlin line nor degenerated into the blind anti-communism of the labor movement. He either should have sold out by now, or have been drummed out of the labor movement.

But there he was, and unlike the New Left students, he did not struggle with personal authenticity. He didn't need to find political meaning in Appalachia or in the urban ghettos. He didn't need to define himself though connections to the underclass.

Tony was connected all right, tied firmly to the workers who formed the very heart of labor's pro-war consensus.

II

In late 1965, the vast majority of OCAW members were hawks—like so many well-paid, mostly white unionists who had profited from the Cold War. The oil workers earned among the highest blue-collar wages in the country. The atomic workers, also well paid, pumped out nuclear fuel and weapons by the thousands. OCAW workers worked overtime to produce ordnance, chemical feeder stocks for napalm, and jungle defoliants for the Vietnam War.

These workers could easily have joined the growing backlash against the increasingly militant civil rights and antiwar movements. OCAW members' children were more likely to go to Vietnam than to college, and many were dying for their country. "My local had more of our members' kids killed in Vietnam than in World War II," Tony recalled. "I remember the chief steward at the Merck local—his kid had just been killed. I'd brought Senator Mike Gravel to a district meeting to speak against the war, and the Merck guy got up and said, 'Look. My son was just killed.' You know, they fly these flags above the Capitol. I went to a congressman to get one, and we donated it to the local in honor of this guy's son."

In the summer of 1967, Tony went to Radford, Virginia, to dedicate a new union hall. "Bernie Emrick was the district director down there. I'm pissing and moaning about the war, and Bernie said, 'No, I don't agree with you.' He said: 'My son is now off to Vietnam.' I said, 'Well, Bernie, I think that you should think more about it.' He said, 'No, I'm proud of the kid.' I mean, Bernie was a friend, and he was a supporter, but we disagreed. And his kid got killed three weeks later. That was a real blow."

Teach-ins were the rage on campus. Tony organized teach-ins on the war for workers, but he didn't call them that. As before, Tony let others make the critique, creating room for discussion. "I started bringing in outside speakers the minute I got to DC," he recalled. "I'm not going to get up there and rant about the war. I'm bringing in people and saying, 'Look. You guys have got to listen to both sides of this question.'"

But not the pro-war side, because, as Tony put it, "the other side was everywhere. Most people were hawks."

Tony arranged presentations by antiwar senators George McGovern and Eugene McCarthy. He also brought Bobby Kennedy and Senator Hubert Humphrey to appear at the 1967 OCAW convention in New York, as they were squaring off to run against each other for president. He invited Senator Wayne Morse, who opposed the Gulf of Tonkin Resolution. On occasion, Mazzocchi arranged for special briefings on important war stories before they hit the news. "I was doing something at every meeting," he remembered. "I always had somebody there at these legislative conferences. . . . So the directors were sitting there with [investigative reporter] Sy Hersh, and he said to me: 'The My Lai thing is gonna break.' This was the day before the story broke, and he came into the meeting and talked to our guys about the massacre in My Lai."

But despite the teach-ins, Tony learned in the summer of 1967 that in his union the war was still too hot to handle.

III

The lesson was delivered by proxy—via Stanley Aronowitz.[4]

Ten years younger than Mazzocchi, Aronowitz bounded into the union movement after getting bounced out of Brooklyn College in 1950 for protesting its anti-communist policies. The precocious son of cultured working-class (and active union) parents, Aronowitz headed for the life of a labor agitator. After six years on the shop floor in a New Jersey wire mill organized by the Steelworkers, Aronowitz joined the staff of the Amalgamated Clothing Workers and soon became its organizing director. He and Mazzocchi met in the small but growing circle of New York area socialist-minded unionists who worried about nuclear arms, peace, and union democracy.

They appreciated each other's ability to think broadly and deeply about labor and social issues. Like Mazzocchi, Aronowitz was articulate, smart, extremely well read, and incredibly confident. Both were independent socialists who subscribed neither to anti-communism nor Stalinism. Both had quickly concluded that the growing US involvement in Vietnam was not simply a mistake, but the result of global capitalism's need to contain communism. When they looked at society and labor, they saw similar features. When they talked, they used common symbols and constructs.

Mazzocchi also saw Aronowitz as a crackerjack organizer who'd won a string of organizing campaigns for the Amalgamated Clothing Workers in Pennsylvania during the early 1960s. In 1963, Mazzocchi pushed the OCAW to hire Aronowitz as an international representative and organizer serving the New York area. This was an extraordinary move, since in OCAW such jobs were reserved for those who came up through the ranks. But Tony persisted, and Stanley Aronowitz became the first outside person hired for a coveted rep's job.

Tony needed an infusion of organizing talent and energy to arrest the union's declining membership. Perhaps more importantly, he needed a unionist with a radical imagination, someone deeply committed to building an insurgent rank-and-file movement. Someone who would never become a labor bureaucrat. Aronowitz was that person: There wasn't the faintest bureaucratic twitch in Aronowitz's bubbly persona. In fact, with his shirt-tail sticking out and his necktie usually off to the side, Aronowitz exuded deeply anti-bureaucratic vibes.

While this was all to the good, Tony failed to see that Stanley would be, more or less, a one-man bureaucracy wrecking crew. The man said whatever he felt needed to be said. Wherever Aronowitz went, bureaucrats would shudder. Deadlines, time lines, and appointments seemed to come in and out focus as his mind and interests drifted. He could brilliantly negotiate a difficult contract almost without effort, and with this same brilliance alienate key members of the local's bargaining committee. Without trying, Aronowitz collected enemies just waiting to get even.

But Aronowitz's anti-bureaucratic style wasn't his most controversial quality. It was his outspoken opposition to the Vietnam War. Aronowitz was one of labor's few productive links to New Left. In fact, Aronowitz himself nurtured and helped define the New Left. Not only did he work with Tony to raise funds for the Long Island Democratic Party and the civil rights movement, but he also spoke often at public meetings and teach-ins against the war. Unlike Tony, however, Stanley didn't use *other* public figures to address controversial war issues. Instead, Aronowitz himself was often the only labor speaker at antiwar events. He lectured all over the city. He toured colleges. He was far ahead of the OCAW members who employed him.

Unfortunately for both Stanley and Tony, Stanley's efforts did not go unnoticed by those itching to red-bait the antiwar movement. He was a sitting duck for Victor Riesel, the mob-blinded labor columnist who had smeared OCAW president Jack Knight. In his popular syndicated column, Riesel accused Stanley of leading a communistic, antiwar contingent within labor.

But why target Aronowitz? He wasn't an elected official and didn't have a particularly high profile in the movement. He wasn't even a communist. Aronowitz, reflecting back, reasoned that "Riesel went after me as a proxy for Tony. Riesel knew I was his guy and that by red-baiting me he would make life very difficult for Tony, which in fact he succeeded in doing."[5]

But why not go after Mazzocchi directly? "They just didn't have anything on him," Aronowitz explained. "He had not yet come out against the war. He was too good at building his base. A groundless attack like that might have made Tony even more revered in the union."

Riesel's column caused a firestorm of protest within the union, putting Aronowitz on political life support. Tony stuck with him. "He did everything he could do," Aronowitz said. "He arranged a District 8 council meeting and secured a unanimous resolution of support. He backed me to the hilt with Grospiron. It was principled solidarity, and I greatly appreciated it."

But Grospiron struggled under the wave of protest against Aronowitz from anti-communist union members. Finally, Grospiron asked Stanley to accept an organizer's job in Puerto Rico, far from Riesel's reach and from those in the union calling for his head. Aronowitz understood these realities and accepted the transfer, working there for eighteen months before leaving the union.

In the next few years Aronowitz wrote *False Promises,* arguably the most penetrating critique of the postwar labor movement. He would leave the movement, finish college, earn a doctorate degree in sociology, and become a noted sociology professor, public intellectual, and author of twenty-three more books. In 2003, Aronowitz ran for governor of New York as the Green Party's nominee.

In *The 60s Without Apology,* he candidly summarized how he differed from Mazzocchi on the war:

> I was critical at the time of his cautious, even conservative approach to the war, but he had his ear to the ground. Given the deep-seated anticommunism of American workers and their conviction that war work was needed for full employment, given George Meany's open hostility to any criticism of U.S. foreign policy, Mazzocchi stepped just far enough out on the limb to keep his legs intact. I, of course, got mine cut off because by 1966 I had gone public in my anti-war activities inside and outside the trade unions.[6]

Mazzocchi got far enough out on the limb to hear it cracking. At OCAW's convention in New York City in August 1967, he and Aronowitz conducted a poll on the war. Mazzocchi believed that OCAW members were harboring doubts after the United States bombed the densely populated port of Haiphong. A poll that highlighted workers' antiwar opinions, Mazzocchi thought, could convince other unions to speak out against the war. After all, if national security workers like these opposed the war, anyone could.

Mazzocchi got delegates to fill out the questionnaire by resorting to a combination of sexism and gambling. "I said to Stanley, 'I need an attractive young woman who can be a lure for the guys to come over to the table to fill out the questionnaire.' Also, in my old local we had this shop that made the fanciest watchcases. So I said to one of the guys, 'We need a watchcase,' and he got us one. Between the case and the guts of the watch I spent a hundred bucks for a beautiful watch. So we said to the delegates, 'If you fill out the questionnaire, you could win a Longine watch.' And the guys start coming over to the table, not only to win a watch, but to try and make this young woman."

The brazen effort failed: The poll unexpectedly made a case for the other side. As Tony painfully recalled, "I counted the things. The majority of the people said: Bomb Haiphong Harbor. And by the way, the resolution authorizing the poll said that we would publish the results in the union newspaper! So I'm sitting on it, because I don't want to release the results. I said, 'Oh, shit, what do I do?'"

If he shared the results at the convention, he would provide ammunition for hawks both within the union and in the labor movement at large. He stalled, hoping that the other convention activities would distract the delegates. Luckily, no one seemed to notice or care that the poll results were not forthcoming.

After dodging that bullet, Mazzocchi proceeded to shoot himself in the foot. He could rarely resist telling a good story, especially when he was the butt of the joke. In this case, he told and retold the poll story to all of his antiwar union colleagues in DC, including one who retold it to Al Barkin, the AFL-CIO's hawkish political action director.

> So I get a call from Al one day. He says: "We're gonna have dinner with the president tonight, about twelve of us. Meet us at the back

> door of the White House at 7 PM." I get there, and there are all the legislative directors. We have dinner with Lyndon and his wife, the whole thing. We all had our photographs taken with Lyndon. Then Al Barkin turns to Lyndon, who was being dogged in the press on the war, and he says, "Hey, Tony. You did a poll at your convention. Tell him what the people said about the bombing of Haiphong Harbor." And I had to divulge the poll results. My friends never let me forget it.

A small but vocal core of OCAW local leaders would not let Mazzocchi forget Aronowitz, either. Long after he left, Aronowitz continued to serve as a political scapegoat for conservative members who adored Tony personally but worried about his radicalism. Many shared the opinion of the red-faced OCAW official who barged over to Tony at a fund-raiser for Mazzocchi's 1979 campaign to upbraid him, "I'm supporting you this time, but I'll always hold Aronowitz against you."

IV

While OCAW may not have been in sync with the student movement, in 1967 it had a most unusual connection to National Student Association (NSA), an organization of campus leaders. Again it involved the CIA.

Three years after Wright Patman uncovered CIA money laundering through domestic organizations, *Ramparts* magazine broke a story about CIA involvement in the NSA. It led to a media feeding frenzy as investigative journalists tracked CIA funds all over America.

It was the kind of story that nearly justified the paranoia sweeping through the student antiwar movement. It shook even more moderate Americans to learn that the National Student Association had been corrupted by a clandestine operation. Since the 1950s, the NSA had been the home of clean-cut student leaders, the movers and shakers on campus and the leaders-in-waiting for the liberal establishment. NSA supported civil rights before most of its constituent schools had dared to act. NSA's national staff contained the kind of students that Americans wanted to believe in.

NSA's international affairs staff played a crucial role overseas during the

Cold War. As NSA noted in letters to draft boards to get deferments, "NSA is largely responsible for the creation and maintenance of the International Student Conference, which was established in 1950 to combat the communist controlled International Union of Students. More than 50 countries—almost every state with a national union this side of the Iron Curtain—now participate in the International Student Conference."[7]

In fact, the NSA was the student version of OCAW's International Federation of Petroleum Workers. Both saw themselves as idealistic groups that carried forth the torch of freedom and justice against totalitarian communism. And just as US unions stood for "free" labor movements independent from government domination, the NSA's motto was "a free university in a free society." Unfortunately, the CIA controlled both.

Ramparts magazine reported (and congressional investigations later confirmed) that the NSA international affairs department was a CIA shop, unbeknownst to the thousands of students involved in the organization. CIA operatives, several of whom were former NSA officers, perpetuated the CIA's grip by recruiting new NSA officers into their covert circle.

Hundreds of thousands of CIA dollars poured into the organization, which worked out of a rent-free building in DC. Its leaders, like the IFPW staff, roamed the globe connecting with counterparts abroad and reporting back information to the CIA. These students lived well, traveled far, and talked to important people at home and abroad. And they got one more important perk: a draft deferment. Every national officer and staff person received one almost automatically due to their service in the fight against global communism.

Members of the CIA-NSA inner circle were called "witty." A new student recruit to the inner circle would be taken out to lunch by a witty staff member, along with a representative of Covert Action Division Five of the CIA's Plans Division. Prospective witty members were told at lunch that their work would make them privy to information affecting national security, requiring them to sign an official loyalty oath. New recruits who signed the oath would then be told about the CIA relationship and be asked to cooperate fully.

But Phil Sherburne, the NSA president in 1965–1966, grew uneasy with the CIA tie and needed someone to talk to about it. He then broke the cardinal rule. He told a nonwitty person: Michael Wood, an ordinary

NSA staffer. Wood, who had not signed the CIA's loyalty oath, leaked the story to *Ramparts*. All hell broke loose. Reporters followed the money and found CIA funds going to the National Council of Churches, the National Education Association, publishing houses, scholars, and several unions.

On February 22, 1967, *The New York Times* reported that between 1959 and 1964 the international affairs department of the American Federation of State, County, and Municipal Employees (AFSCME) "was actually run by two intelligence agency aides who operated out of the union's former headquarters in Washington with the knowledge of the union's leadership." The *Times* reported that AFSCME had used CIA money to help oust Dr. Cheddi Jagan, the leftist prime minister of Guyana, in 1962. According to the *Times,* the AFSCME operatives helped the pro-American Forbes S. Burnham faction instigate a campaign of "riots, racial strife and strikes, which brought down the duly elected leader of Guyana."[8]

The trail of hot money also ran into OCAW. The story hit the front page of *The Denver Post* with the screaming headline, "CIA Money Use Linked to 2 Denver Labor Units."[9] The report described how the CIA used OCAW and the International Federation of Petroleum Workers "to pump hundreds of thousands of dollars into undercover activities in Latin America and the Middle East." Again the Alexander Hamilton Foundation, the mysterious CIA benefactor, "was identified as the prime link between the CIA and the federation."

The paper further described how OCAW president Al Grospiron had started the process of "disengagement," feeling that "it was improper for a labor organization to be used as an instrument of government policy."

Lloyd Haskins, who still ran the IFPW, denied everything: "I don't know where you got such a report," he told *The Denver Post* and *The New York Times*, "It's completely false."

As the *Times* reported, most politicians also feigned ignorance of these CIA plots. Vice President Hubert Humphrey described the CIA infiltration into the National Student Association as "one of the saddest times our government has had in terms of public policy."[10]

But Bobby Kennedy, then the Democratic senator from New York, admitted that the highest levels of the Kennedy administration had approved of the CIA infiltration. He said it was unfair to let the CIA "take the rap for secretly financing groups," because the decisions were made by "the executive branch in the Eisenhower, Kennedy and Johnson Administrations. . . . If the policy was wrong, it was not the product of the CIA, but of each Administration."[11]

The labor establishment showed far less candor. AFL-CIO president George Meany said "he had no knowledge of any affiliated union's having received any funds, directly or indirectly, from the agency."[12] Meany also denied that the AFL-CIO's director of international affairs, Jay Lovestone, was a spook, despite much evidence to the contrary. It got even more embarrassing for labor when UAW leader Victor Reuther revealed that the CIA had deep links with the AFL-CIO. A former CIA officer then came forward to say that Victor himself had served as a CIA bagman to European anti-communist unions after World War II.

Why did labor leaders so brazenly lie even after the facts were revealed? Meany, Lovestone, and Haskins may have believed that the worldwide battle against communism required that they lie to protect their country's national security assets. It is also possible that some of these CIA-linked labor officials signed oaths pledging them to silence and feared they would be committing a felony if they spoke up.

In any event, their bald-faced denials contributed to the growing distrust of established institutions and their leaders. From the president on down, everyone seemed to be lying. And when they got caught they lied some more.

V

Tony Mazzocchi, of all people, should have been paranoid. After all, he was in the heart of what Eisenhower called the "military-industrial complex."

But it was actually the atomic-industrial complex, not the CIA, that pushed its tentacles most deeply into the Oil, Chemical and Atomic Workers. This complex comprised a network of government agencies, facilities, and corporations so vast and murky that few knew its entire extent. It included uranium mining and milling facilities in the Southwest; enormous research complexes at Los Alamos, Idaho Falls, Lawrence Livermore, Fermi, and Brookhaven; and atomic weapons plants in Hanford, Paducah, Rocky Flats, and Oak Ridge. Oak Ridge was so large that during World War II it used as much electricity per day as the city of Los Angeles.

Tens of thousands of people worked in secrecy on the latest weapons. Thousands of corporations large and small lined up at the public trough to profit from the work. Added to the mix were the companies, government officials, and military personnel involved in producing and managing missiles and long-range bombers, spy satellites, and tracking systems, as well as espionage and counterespionage. The research component alone was mind boggling: Planners were exploring atomic rocket ships, atomic cars, and even atomic explosions to excavate canals. Then in the 1960s came the construction of atomic reactors that would supposedly generate unlimited power, making electricity "too cheap to meter."

Tony had stirred nuclear controversy ever since his work with SANE in 1957. Now, as the union's national legislative director, he was duty-bound to represent the interests of ten thousand atomic workers who actually made nuclear weapons and enriched uranium. How could he do it? The trick was to find ways to help atomic workers without calling for more job-creating nuclear production. Finding this path would require an unusual guide: the only mentor Tony would ever acknowledge, Leo Goodman.

"Oh, Leo! There's the unsung hero of a lot of this stuff," Tony recalled fondly. "Leo was this incredible guy who came from MIT into the CIO during the Depression. He got involved with the shoe workers in Maine."

Later, in the mid-1930s, Goodman served on Walter Reuther's staff as executive secretary of the CIO's housing committee. Goodman's efforts to secure public affordable housing for workers during and after World War II led him to discover the dismal living conditions of the scientists and technicians in the Manhattan Project. He argued that "we had thirty concentration camps [for nuclear workers] as a result of the atomic program in the United States."[13]

Goodman soon joined the CIO's successful effort to unionize atomic bomb production workers into Gas-Coke. In 1955, Reuther sent him to facilitate the merger between the Oil Workers and Gas-Coke. And that's when Leo Goodman met Tony Mazzocchi. As Tony recalled,

> He was at the merger convention with the oil workers, and I was on the resolutions committee. He kept yanking me out to get me to put

> *atomic* into the title of the new union. He was against the weapons program, yet he was a fierce anti-communist. But he thought there was a great future for peaceful uses of atomic energy, which I also believed. You know, we let the genie out of the bottle. But back then we thought it had this great potential. At that time we were only making nuclear weapons. But we thought that you could use this technology for science to advance the public welfare. Our position was: peaceful development, not military development, of the industry. And although we were aware of problems with radiation, we thought they were resolvable. We believed that if workers had the power to fight for their health and safety, we could advance this industry. But it was pregnant with problems. We understood that.

Most progressives still had unbounded faith that new technology led to progress. If properly used, "atoms for peace," the Cold Warriors' velvet glove, could not only make endless power, but also show off the strength of US civilian technology. The prospect of using nuclear technology for a peaceful purpose also helped calm a nervous public that both revered and feared the awesome power of the bomb. Some Orwellian atomic cheerleaders even floated the idea that the units measuring radioactivity should be changed from "rads" to "sunshine units." The left-right debate was restricted to whether the military or civilians should control atomic development.

In the early 1960s, even consumer advocate Ralph Nader still believed in "atoms for peace." As did SDS radicals, who referred to "peaceful uses of atomic energy" in their Port Huron Statement. SDS was unaware that the massive fast-breeder nuclear reactor being built in Detroit, only thirty miles from its headquarters in Ann Arbor, had enough fissionable material to kill an estimated 133,000 people.

On this issue, the gawky Goodman would soon switch sides and move far to the left of SDS. He would become the first within labor, and perhaps in the country, to take on the budding nuclear industry after realizing that the latest power-generating atomic technologies were too dangerous for domestic use. "He is the father of the anti-nuclear movement," Tony said. "He's the one who got me involved."

It was a baptism by fire. Goodman was the kind of activist who wouldn't let go. As Tony put it, "I mean, he was a real tiger on a lot of issues. He's the guy who used to go through the garbage on Capitol Hill. Always looking."

In 1956, Leo Goodman declared war on the fast-breeder reactor. He soon convinced Walter Reuther that Detroit Edison's effort to build a reactor, named the Enrico Fermi Power Plant, at the Lagoona Beach site near Detroit, would pose an enormous threat to autoworkers and the auto industry. This wasn't the normal kind of reactor that used water to transfer heat from the uranium core to make steam for generation. The fast breeder would use highly experimental technology to create atomic power from uranium while at the same time breeding plutonium that could be used later for more power or for weapons.

As in an alchemist's dream, the fast breeder would make more nuclear fuel than it used. But the process was extremely complicated and volatile. The reactor core used liquid sodium to transfer heat from the nuclear fuel rods to water to make steam to drive the turbines. Liquid sodium itself is highly volatile: It ignites when it contacts air or water. If for any reason the sodium did not flow properly around the many uranium fuel assemblies in the reactor core, the fuel rods might overheat. This could lead to two potentially lethal releases: The fuel rods could catch fire, emitting deadly fissionable products, or they could melt down and re-form into a different shape. If this new geometry permitted a fissionable event, the base of the reactor could explode, causing a "rapid critical assembly"—a euphemism for an atomic explosion.[14]

The plutonium that could be spewed through the air during a fast-breeder meltdown is the most deadly substance known: "It has been estimated that 1/30,000,000 of an ounce of plutonium could bring on cancer if inhaled."[15]

As Leo Goodman pored through government documents, he discovered that several nuclear disasters and near disasters had already occurred at smaller test reactors in Canada, Scotland, and Idaho Falls, Idaho. He also dug into the workings of the Atomic Energy Commission, which had been assigned the awkward task of both promoting and regulating atomic development. Leo soon discovered that the AEC's own safety committee had severe reservations about the plans for the Detroit facility, finding that "there is insufficient information available at this time to give assurance that [the reactor] can be operated at this site without public hazard."[16] The committee was overruled by the AEC, however, which issued a construction permit on August 4, 1956.

Goodman, through his boss Walter Reuther, forced the first-ever congressional hearing on nuclear safety. Still, the AEC was determined to issue an operating permit the moment construction was completed. But while safety studies may not have mattered to the AEC or the nuclear industry, the insurance industry cared a great deal. No reactor could operate without insurance, and a Brookhaven study estimated a potential liability of the Fermi 1 plant to be seventeen billion dollars (then a hefty 4 percent of the GDP). A collection of insurance companies agreed to put up only sixty million into a pool to insure nuclear reactors. If the government did not finance the remainder, the civilian nuclear industry as well as the Fermi reactor would be stillborn.

For the atomic hawks in Congress, this would be an unmitigated disaster, for they, along with the AEC, believed that building civilian nuclear plants would perpetually hook the country to the atomic-industrial complex. The solution to the insurance problem, strongly opposed by Goodman and Reuther, came from Senator Clinton Anderson and Representative Melvin Price. Their measure, the Price-Anderson Act, provided a maximum of $560 million of public money to insure the Fermi plant and removed all liability from the utility industry. Should a nuclear incident do more damage than that, too bad for the injured and the affected property owners.

Reuther and Goodman sued to stop the construction permit in July 1959. While the International Union of Electrical Workers and the United Paperworkers of America joined the UAW in the brief, OCAW refused. Tony, who was serving on OCAW's executive board at the time, tried to get his union to join the suit, but Swisher, the vice president in charge of the union's atomic worker section, shot him down. "The board said, 'Yeah, why don't we join that suit?'" Tony recalled. "But Swisher said, 'Well, you know, we should represent *all* our workers.'"

On June 10, 1960, the court of appeals ruled that the construction permit for Fermi was illegal. All construction was to halt immediately. But reactor builder Walker Cisler, the head of Detroit Edison, backed by the Eisenhower Justice Department and the AEC, appealed immediately to the Supreme Court. The appeal's approach was simple: "Don't worry, this is not a license to operate. It is only for construction. Fermi will have to meet all manner of safety conditions before we allow it to operate."

While the Supreme Court deliberated in January 1961, a small research reactor in Idaho malfunctioned as three men attempted to shove a stuck control rod back into the reactor core. All perished. One worker had to be pried off the ceiling, where he had been impaled through the groin on a control rod that had blasted out of the reactor core. It took another twenty days for the radioactivity to subside sufficiently for the bodies to be buried. This test reactor was tiny compared with the planned Fermi plant.

Nevertheless, on June 12, 1961, the Supreme Court ruled in favor of the atomic-industrial complex, seven to two. In their dissent, Justices Black and Douglas reasoned:

> They presuppose . . . that safety findings can be made after the construction is finished. But when that point is reached, when millions have been invested, the momentum is on the side of the applicant, not on the side of the public. The momentum is not only generated by the desire to salvage an investment. No agency wants to be the architect of a white elephant. . . .[17]

On August 6, 1966, about eight months after Tony had settled into DC, something went very wrong at Fermi. As the reactor was moving up to half power for the first time, it was releasing radioactive particles, setting off alarms. No one knew why. The temperature of several of the fuel elements had climbed, signaling that the liquid sodium coolant had not reached them. Was this the beginning of the worst-case scenario that Cisler had said could not happen—a meltdown, possibly to be followed by a nuclear explosion?

Not quite. It took four months for investigators to figure out that fuel did indeed melt down, but not sufficiently to touch off an explosion. It took another five months to remove the damaged fuel assemblies.

Despite the company's strenuous efforts, in August 1972 the AEC finally denied it a permit to operate. By 1974, a second reactor that Cisler had started to build in Detroit using more conventional technologies also died for lack of funding.

Goodman had won this battle against nuclear white elephants. Along the way, he trained Mazzocchi in the art of fighting the atomic-government complex, protecting the health and safety of workers and the public alike.

But as Tony Mazzocchi and Karen Silkwood would discover, the other side played hardball.

VI

Soon Tony found himself testifying before the Joint Atomic Energy Committee, trying to defend the most vulnerable victims of the atomic-industrial complex: Navajo uranium miners. Their occupational-related sicknesses would shame the nation.

"A group of women approached Leo called WAR—Widows Against Radiation," Tony said. "They were the wives of men who mined in Colorado—mostly non-union—who had been denied workers' comp for their lung cancer. They were all sorts of folks, not just Navajo. Leo introduced me to them, and they told me their story. Leo wanted me to testify in their behalf, and I agreed."

Goodman, by then a well-known anti-nuke troublemaker, wanted these widows to be defended by someone other than himself. Tony seemed like the perfect choice, except that he was new to the issues.

"I really didn't familiarize myself with that testimony," Tony said. "Leo's assumption was that I had grasped all this information. And I could grasp it. But the minute someone began to question me, I didn't have a wealth of information to defend our position. Leo had that, not me."

The AEC's disregard for health and safety was the underlying issue. Although the Public Health Service had warned as early as 1950 that southwestern uranium miners and millers were being exposed to enormous amounts of radiation from radon and uranium, the federal government refused to act. It didn't take a nuclear scientist to figure out why. The government wanted to maximize production of nuclear weapons. And industry wanted to maximize its profits.

No government entity was willing to take responsibility for uranium mine safety. The states in which the mining took place said it was the AEC's job, since it controlled production, prices, and distribution. The AEC said responsibility belonged to the Bureau of Mines, which in turn said the Department of Labor should be in charge. The Department of Labor demurred, saying it had neither the mandate nor the technical staff to do the job.

Meanwhile, studies showed that miners were dying, with extraordinary high rates of cancer and lung disease. With no government enforcement, the grim statistics mounted. More than one thousand miners would be killed from excess exposure. But when workers tried to file compensation claims for their work-related diseases, their employers testified against them, claiming their injuries were due to non-job-related factors.

Finally, in 1967, after more than fifteen years of official denial, J. V. Reistrup of *The Washington Post* broke the story. Willard Wirtz, LBJ's secretary of labor, read Reistrup's article and decided to move forcefully. Furious at the government's failure to act, he proposed dramatically reducing the amount of radon permitted in the air in mines. "Industry officials and politicians who considered the AEC their personal domain were incensed," wrote historian Peter Eichstaedt.[18]

The powerful Joint Committee on Atomic Energy was full of such irate politicians. As the virtual executive committee of the atomic-industrial complex, it rightly viewed Wirtz's proposed mine regulations as a critique of its work and an infringement of its powers. The committee decided to hold hearings on Wirtz's plan. Co-chair Representative Chet Holifield (a California Democrat), known as "Mr. Atomic Energy," used the hearings to challenge the science underlying the new regulations.

Wirtz appeared before the committee in May 1967 and showed little respect for Holifield's charges. "After 17 years of debate and discussion regarding the respective private State and Federal responsibilities for conditions in the uranium mines, there . . . were . . . no adequate and effective health and safety standards[s] [or] inspection procedures for uranium mining," Wirtz said. "There is unmistakable evidence of a high incidence of lung cancer among uranium miners."[19]

The industry trotted out witnesses to blast Wirtz, including M. F. Bolton, a vice president of the Kerr-McGee Corporation, who asserted that more safety actually meant less safety. "We believe that the means which would have to be followed to comply with that directive would unnecessarily greatly increase the hazards to the uranium miners," Bolton said.[20]

Goodman countered by lining up labor representatives to back the Wirtz standard, even though few of the miners were unionized. An array of union leaders sent letters of support; several testified. Goodman sent Mazzocchi in to testify first, hoping he would frame the issue in the best possible manner.

After a year and a half in DC, this was Tony's first appearance before any congressional hearing. It was a high-profile debut. He explained,

> There were only two joint committees—economic and atomic energy. And atomic was the most powerful committee. Whatever they approved would pass. It was shrouded in national security, and it dealt with such an esoteric subject. Holifield had an anti-nuclear record before. But when he got the chair, they told him: "You're either going to promote this industry or you're out."

The site of the hearing "was rather foreboding," said Jack Sheehan, the Steelworkers legislative director, who also testified that day. "You could only get there from one elevator near the rotunda guarded by an armed soldier."[21]

Tony read from a text written by Goodman. As soon as he uttered the first words in defense of Secretary Wirtz's new regulation, Holifield shoved them down his throat. "Why do you make a statement like that? 'There has been much talk but no action on any of the various issues,'" mocked Holifield. "There has been a great deal of action. There has been constant improvement and constant care, and millions of dollars have been spent in research and development to try to control the hazards of atomic energy which applied to workers in the plants that are under the control of the Atomic Energy Commission. I think if you will reconsider that sentence then you will withdraw it from the record, because it is absolutely false."[22]

What did I say that was so bad? thought Tony. He hadn't come to fight the chair of the committee. He only wanted to do his duty and get out of there, like giving blood to the Red Cross. But Tony knew he had to defend Leo's text. So he held his ground—or, more precisely, he shifted the ground to an area he knew something about.

"I would consider withdrawing it only if my own experience had demonstrated otherwise. I was a president of a local union that represented—" Tony began.

"I don't care what your experience is," Holifield interrupted. ". . . So when you say there is no action on any of the various issues, I say you are making a false statement."[23]

What a disaster! Only moments into Tony's testimony, the chair of one of the most powerful committees in Congress had called him a liar in front of the press, Leo, and Tony's labor movement peers. And every word would be published in the *Congressional Record*!

Realizing that it was already too late to placate Holifield, Mazzocchi tried to shield himself with compound sentences. "I have never made false statements to my knowledge," Tony offered. "My concern, as I said before, grows out of the fact that I did represent workers in an atomic energy installation and I was confronted many times with the type of hazardous situation that dealt with expressions representatives of my union have made before this committee in asking for action by the Congress or other responsible agencies."

Tony drifted into a discussion of the need for more health and safety protection for OCAW workers in Idaho Falls, especially after the infamous 1961 nuclear meltdown at its research reactor.

But Holifield only baited Mazzocchi with a classic blame-the-worker defense for government neglect. As if washing his hands of any responsibility for the worker who had been nailed to the ceiling by a control rod at the Idaho reactor incident, Holifield said:

> There is absolutely no protection that you can put around a man violating a regulation. With any use of any dangerous substance, whether it be chemicals in a chemical plant or moving machinery in industrial plants, if the rules and regulations regarding the following of safety procedures are not followed, either accidentally or deliberately, there is going to be an accident.[24]

Inadvertently, Holifield had moved the discussion back onto Mazzocchi's turf. Mazzocchi agreed with Holifield's description of human fallibility, but drew the opposite conclusion: The hazards needed to be eliminated to protect workers from their very human propensity to make mistakes. Again Tony fell back on his own experiences, this time at the Sylvania plant in Long Island.

"I organized a plant of atomic energy workers [who] were manufacturing nuclear fuel elements," he said. "I found out they knew practically nothing. We organized a training program to teach them the meaning of criticality. . . . We had to teach them the fundamentals they should have been taught. A proper effort was not made in the plant regarding this hazard. The plant was located in the midst of a [growing] community."

Holifield momentarily took the bait. "Where did this happen?"[25]

Instinctively, Tony had walked Holifield into a logical trap. If, as Holifield claimed, AEC regulations and training programs offered no protection from worker error, and if the Long Island plant was involved in highly radioactive work, then why on earth did the AEC give it a license to produce fuel rods in the middle of densely populated Long Island?

"Hey, this isn't so hard," Tony began to think. In fact, once you had control of the debate, it was kind of fun. But his ordeal wasn't over. Conway, the committee's leading staff person, challenged Tony's credentials. "You represent yourself as being the Washington representative of your union. Would you explain for the record how long you have represented your union here in Washington?"

"About a year and a half," said Tony, watching in slow motion as Conway proceeded to swing a two-by-four at his head.

"Will you tell us how many times you have been in contact with me or any member of the committee? I don't know you. You have never seen me before to the best of my knowledge."[26]

"This is the first time I felt we had a chance to express our concern on a very specific item we were dealing with," Tony said. It appeared that while he claimed to have had a problem in 1961, he'd waited until 1967 to even mention it to the AEC.

Tony was embarrassed in front of his union peers waiting to testify. "There was George Taylor from the AFL-CIO and Jack Sheehan from the Steelworkers, and they're climbing under their chairs."

"There has never been a time when a letter from a representative of a labor union to this committee asking to be heard or asking for conferences with the staff or the members has been turned down," Holifield said. "So my friend, if you have—"

Shouts from the audience cut Holifield off in midsentence. A demonstration? A sit-in? Guerrilla theater? No, it was Leo Goodman, jumping up and down, coming to Mazzocchi's rescue. He bounded up with a pile of books in his arms and yelled at Holifield, "You yourself turned me down several times."

"Sit down or leave the room," Holifield said.

"This committee will be in order," Senator Price demanded. "We will have no more demonstrations from the guests of this committee."

"I said, 'representative of labor,'" Holifield told Goodman.[27]

During the commotion, Tony staggered back into his corner, gasping for air.

"Leo knew all these guys and they knew Leo," said Tony. "And they're spitting all over themselves: You better be seated, Leo, or we're gonna have you forcefully ejected! In the meantime, during the interruption, I'm thinking I gotta get out of this thing."

Leo bought Tony just enough time to hit upon a promising line of defense: What about the widows and orphans?

"I have been dealing with widows," Tony somberly offered after the room settled down, "and I have been dealing with members of families of radiation victims."[28]

Tony continued to read, from Leo's text, a minefield of accusations that could blow up in any direction. "We would hope that this committee would commend the Secretary of Labor [Wirtz] rather than harass him."

"Was he harassed when he was before this committee?" Holifield interrupted. "Wasn't he treated with the utmost politeness? Was there any harsh thing said to him when he was before the committee?"[29]

Tony backed down, apologizing for the use of the word *harassed*.

Holifield didn't notice: "The committee must exercise its judgment, its background of knowledge on some of these technical matters which are beyond the competence of Secretary Wirtz or any other layman . . . keep that in mind. . . . Because this committee does not go along with a layman's opinion and a muddled and ambiguous directive, you said you think we are harassing the Secretary?"[30]

When Tony tried feebly to enter the scientific debate by defending the Public Health Service's study that had backed up the Wirtz regulation, Holifield countered, "Did you know that [the PHS doctor] has since acknowledged that he did not testify in accord with the facts?" snapped Holifield. "Did you know that? . . . that he acted upon improper computations. . . ?"

Tony had no idea what Holifield was talking about. "Mr. Holifield, I am aware that miners are dying and have died in this industry," said Tony.

"Let us not get off into the emotion of miners dying," Holifield replied. "We are aware that miners are dying. We are aware that people are dying on the highways as a result of automobile accidents but we are not closing down the automobile plants. . . . Don't retreat into a defense of humanitarianism in front of this committee, because this committee is just as humanitarian as you are, just as much concerned with humanitarian principles. So when you run from a scientific fact into maudlin sentimentality, it does not impress me."[31]

Mazzocchi, stunned, said, "I did not profess to be a scientist or to deal with the scientific questions involved."

"But you are making accusations against this committee because it did not go along with regulations that were improperly written, which were ambiguous and which have been admitted to have been improperly written," Holifield said.

Tony responded, "I am saying when there is a bone of contention that deals with a scientific question, as a worker I say that the burden of proof should be on those who would call for a higher exposure level in the mine rather than a lower exposure." (Today this is called the Precautionary Principle.)

Tony went on to read his testimony, which included Leo's bombshell: The charts Holifield's committee had prepared for the hearing contained PHS data for white miners only! Taking Navajos out of the statistical presentation greatly lowered the death and disease rates, since white miners usually were managers working above ground while Navajos worked below, where exposure was high.

Tony read, "I for one think the figures, which have been presented before this committee are incomplete. Shakespeare had Shylock say, 'If you prick us, do we not bleed? If you tickle us, do we not laugh? If you poison us, do we not die?'[32] I say, 'If a Navajo Indian breathes radon gas in the mines, he is injured just as much as a white man.' It seems that the information we have is incomplete. The atomic worker, the atomic peaceful soldier, is in the front line of the advance of atomic energy. His battle with the invisible enemy, radiation exposure, calls for armaments much more powerful than the present equivalent of a flintlock rifle."[33]

Having finally finished reading his prepared text, Tony stood unarmed before the committee. "I am sorry I have to get emotional at times," he said. "I react forcefully when a widow gets me by the scruff of the collar and is talking to me about this problem. I admit then that the emotional switch in me does react and I guess it happens to all of us."

"I don't criticize you for that," said Holifield.

At last the ordeal was over, or so everyone hoped. But after a few concluding civilities, Holifield asked, "Have you ever been down in a uranium mine?"

Mazzocchi: "No sir."

Holifield. "I have."

Conway: "I have too!"[34]

What could Tony say? Nothing, except that he appreciated "the fact that this hearing has been held and that the dialogue has occurred."

And thank God it was over!

"Man, I walked out of there clobbered!" said Tony. "And word got all around town that I was clobbered. . . . I was never going to go before a committee unprepared again. Either I understand the subject matter inside and out, or I ain't going. But that's part of your baptism of fire. It's better that you learn it that way so that next time you're really super-cautious."

J.V Reistrup didn't make it sound so bad in his *Washington Post* editorial titled "Industry Attacks, Labor Defends New Limit on Radiation in Mines":

> Another labor witness, Anthony Mazzocchi of the Oil, Chemical and Atomic Workers Union, also defended the Wirtz order. He prompted an angry exchange when he said, "There has been much talk but no action on any of the various issues which we have raised repeatedly before this committee." . . . Mazzocchi said his organization had been, 'frustrated' in achieving radiation safety and argued that miners are dying. Holifield said, "maudlin sentimentality" didn't impress him and called Wirtz's order scientifically unsound.[35]

Tony chalked up the good coverage to luck. "Look, the reporter had a thing against Holifield. If you read the record, you'll see I was killed in there. But who the hell reads the *Congressional Record*?"

Tony was profoundly affected by the shellacking. He realized that if he was going to take on the big boys, he needed his own experts in tow. Perhaps those rebellious students, with their vast technical skills, would be itching to join him in the fight.

NINE

Stars in Their Vision

The New Left saw red, not green. Radicals, or at least many of the serious ones, viewed the environment as a soft liberal concern. SDS's twenty-five-thousand-word manifesto, the historic 1962 Port Huron Statement, was eloquent about alienation, the deadliness of a suburban bureaucratic life, the lack of true democracy, and the insanity of the nuclear arms race, but made no mention of pollution, radiation, fallout, or toxic chemicals.

Later that same year, Rachel Carson published *Silent Spring,* which passionately portrayed the disastrous impact of toxic chemicals on nature and on people. But most New Left radicals ignored her acclaimed book. For serious '60s radicals, environmental issues conjured up flower children and back-to-nature hippies trying to escape war and racial oppression rather than fight them. Many in the New Left believed that liberals were using the issue as a fig leaf, like Lady Bird Johnson campaigning for fences around junkyards while her husband littered Vietnam with bombs, defoliants, and corpses. To *real* radicals, the environment was '60s Lite, not the serious stuff of revolution.

Many in the New Left also did not warm at first to Ralph Nader and his consumer protection movement. They saw Nader's muckraking classic on the auto industry, *Unsafe at Any Speed*, as a call for minor reforms rather than a radical attack on the wasteful system of overproduction and overconsumption. They didn't think Nader had the vision to see beyond capitalism or the guts to speak out against the war.

Besides, the New Left didn't identify with *the consumer,* a term that conjured up plastic slipcovers, TV dinners, manicured lawns, and scrubbed cars. This generation was looking for meaning, not material goodies. For radicals, the quality of consumer goods was an utterly trivial concern compared with the evils of a system that produced meaningless products for people living meaningless lives in a world gone mad with war and racism. Why focus on the needs of shopping-mall patrons as if they were the new oppressed proletariat? With millions of Americans too poor to consume much of anything, no self-respecting 1960s radical could worry about suburban consumer rights. The Beatles had it right again, thought the New Left, when they eulogized the consumer as a "nowhere man, sitting in his nowhere land, making plans for nobody."

Tony Mazzocchi did not agree.

II

In the wake of his work with SANE, Mazzocchi's interest shifted to Barry Commoner's Science Information Movement, which sought to inform the public about radiation and pollution. As a representative of tens of thousands of chemical workers, Mazzocchi took note of what Commoner and Rachel Carson had to say about chemical hazards. If Carson was correct about the growing chemically induced cancer crisis, then nearly every member of the Oil, Chemical and Atomic Workers Union was in jeopardy. But although Carson beamed a bright light on the spread of harmful chemicals into homes, plants, animals, and people's bodies, her brilliant beam grew dimmer as it approached the factory fence.

Silent Spring, Mazzocchi realized, made very few references to workers at all. In describing the bioaccumulation properties of DDT in the human body, Carson wrote, "According to various studies, individuals with no known exposure (except the inevitable dietary one) store an average of 5.3 parts per million to 7.4 parts per million; agricultural workers 17.1 parts per million; and workers in insecticide plants as high as 648 parts per million! So the range of proven storage is quite wide and, what is even more to the point, the minimum figures are above the level at which damage to the liver and other organs or tissues may begin."[1]

But what about workers who suffered the *maximum* figures? Carson didn't say.

In discussing the hazards of the insecticides Dieldrin, Aldrin, and Endrin, Carson mentioned workers, but only to provide historical perspective. "As long ago as the mid-1930's a special group of hydrocarbons, the chlorinated naphthalenes, was found to cause hepatitis, and also a rare and almost invariably fatal liver disease in persons subjected to occupational exposures."[2] Invariable fatal liver disease? How many died? When? Where? How many workers were still at risk?

It seemed to Tony that Carson viewed the concerns of production workers as a private matter. In warning consumers about the dangers of pesticide residues on food, she started the chain not in the factory where the pesticides were manufactured, but with those who sprayed the chemicals. "The hazard [of synergistic combinations of chemicals] exists," Carson wrote, "not only for the man who may spray this week with one insecticide and next week with another; it exists also for the consumer of sprayed products."[3]

Carson's prizewinning narrative never mentions the black hole of production, where thousands are sickened or killed by multiple exposures.

Carson's blindness, Mazzocchi recognized, was fundamentally rooted in class. Perhaps she—and much of the reading public—thought workers willingly *elected* to work in chemical factories, and so the hazards they faced lay outside the bounds of general public concern.

Carson, no left-winger, may have lacked a sense of class politics, but the same could not be said of Dr. Barry Commoner, who at first also did not connect the dots between environmental health and the workplace. Mazzocchi and Commoner had both come of age in New York's vibrant left political culture of the '30s and '40s. (Later, both worked against nuclear weapons testing, and both became concerned about the impact of capitalist production on the environment and public health.) What linked them most strongly were habits of mind developed in New York's progressive culture.

Some of the very best organizers in America learned how to think and work strategically during that period. Unlike so many left sectarians, the best CIO-era organizers knew how to build support for the long run. As independent socialists, they refused to allow the Soviet Union's policies to jerk them around. And rather than scream from the sidelines, they channeled their idealism and boundless energies into causes they knew would take a lifetime or more to achieve. The best of them—Mazzocchi and Commoner included—always looked to widen their base of support.

Mazzocchi's mission was to radicalize the labor movement, while Commoner organized within the academic community. Tony was kept back in the ninth grade; Commoner entered Columbia University in 1933, before his sixteenth birthday. There, according to Commoner, a "lefty" professor recruited him to work on radical causes. While Mazzocchi dropped out of school to become an army private, Commoner, after earning his doctorate in biology from Harvard, conducted research as a US Naval Air Force officer. In the late 1940s, Commoner secured a tenured position at Washington University in St. Louis.

In both their realms, left-wing connections helped. Mazzocchi got his start at Helena Rubinstein through his mentors at District 65; Commoner said he "got assigned to the military affairs committee because the guy who led the staff was a lefty also."

Like Mazzocchi, Commoner searched for ways to build a social movement without getting red-baited—at this, both men succeeded remarkably well. But while Mazzocchi wanted to transform the social relations of production, Commoner focused on what he called the "social relations of science"—the role science and scientists played in production and reproduction of capitalism. Commoner, like Mazzocchi, gained the respect of his peers, enabling him to move on issues ranging from civil rights to nuclear weapons.

Both men had to confront the pervasive nuclear-industrial-academic complex. Just as Mazzocchi's union had deep ties to the nuclear weapons establishment and the CIA, Commoner was part of an academic community highly dependent on military-related grants. Therefore, both men had to carefully craft their political organizing strategies to avoid becoming marginalized. While Mazzocchi worked steadily to make his union a hotbed of political action and provocative debate, Commoner promoted his views within elite scientific organizations, especially the American Association for the Advancement of Science (AAAS), which published the respected journal *Science*.

Both men searched for a *breakthrough,* an idea that would mobilize progressives without provoking a polarizing backlash.

Commoner, nine years older than Mazzocchi, made his breakthrough first. Realizing that the resistance to progressive political work within AAAS was insurmountable, he hit upon a powerful idea. "In 1958, I invented the solution: that we don't take sides but that we take the responsibility to educate the public about what the scientific background of the issue is," he recalled. "This was the beginning of what we called the Science Information Movement. The position was very simple. The scientist was no more equipped than anyone else to make the judgment about what was moral and political. That's not scientific. But what we can do, and have an involuntary responsibility to do, is to educate the public."[4]

Forsaking the recalcitrant AAAS, Commoner proposed a "citizen-scientist committee" to address the issue of nuclear fallout: the St. Louis Committee for Nuclear Information—CNI. In 1958, CNI focused on the baby teeth study at Washington University, which proved that radioactive strontium 90 from atmospheric tests had penetrated children's bones. As CNI publicized this information through its journal, articles, and public speeches, the public began to turn against atmospheric nuclear testing.

"In 1963, there was a test ban treaty, and we got a lot of credit for it," Commoner said. Since the organization had fulfilled its original mission, "Everybody said, *Let's disband.* So we had a big discussion and my position was that we were really doing environmental work. And this was right after Rachel Carson."

Commoner prevailed, and the group changed its name to the Committee for Environmental Information, which soon put out a new journal for the public called *Environment.* Commoner encouraged people around the country to form local scientific committees for public information, and he helped develop a new national organization called the Scientists' Institute for Public Information. "It was a lefty group, but very well respected," said Commoner. It included Nobel laureates Edwin Tatum, Margaret Mead, and renowned environmentalist René Dubos, author of the famous quote "Think globally, act locally."

But like Carson, Commoner parked his arguments at the factory gate. Commoner's first political book, *Science and Society,* published a year after *Silent Spring,* forcefully detailed the effects of pesticides and detergents, but didn't refer to the people who manufactured these products or had to use them at work. His discussion of the risks of nuclear deterrence did not mention the health effects on uranium miners and the thousands who manufactured and tested the weapons. (In fairness to Commoner, his focus was on the utter futility of nuclear deterrence and the corruption of science on both sides of the Iron Curtain.)

Commoner simply missed the connection between workers and environmental health. And he missed for a time the possibility of enlisting workers as agents for environmental change.

Mazzocchi realized that in pushing scientific information into the community, Commoner was on to something big. He listened carefully as

Commoner argued for a new role for scientists: to *inform the public about the facts* so that citizens could make wise decisions about technologies.

Through Commoner and Carson, Mazzocchi got a first glimpse of his own colossal breakthrough soon to come. He saw an entirely new arena for labor organizing: His union could become one of the largest environmental organizations in the country. All Mazzocchi needed to do was to tear down the factory fence that separated Commoner and Carson from workers.

So while much of the New Left still scorned environmental concerns as trivial, Mazzocchi grasped their radical potential. Commoner and Carson had aroused the public with a systematic indictment of the chemical industry and nuclear-industrial complex, had linked growing chemical production to environmental degradation, and had educated people to distrust industry scientists, company doctors, and government officials who minimized chemical and radiological dangers. Mazzocchi didn't expect them also to champion the cause of worker health. That was his job, and it would become his most enduring contribution to America.

When he looked at modern capitalism's addiction to harmful chemicals, Mazzocchi saw an irreconcilable conflict between private profit and public health. If he could mobilize the workers, their "widows and orphans," their communities, and public health and environmental advocates, perhaps the entire system could be challenged. It was Mazzocchi's chance to radically change corporate capitalism, and he knew it.

"It was the workers in these industries who taught me that there was a systematic conflict between profits and health," Mazzocchi explained. "They said: 'You know, it's production that's causing all these problems.' When you start thinking that, when you start to interfere with the forces of production, you're going to the heart of the beast, right?"

III

Mazzocchi's new awareness did not come on suddenly. "At first, I didn't focus on it. All this stuff was coming in, like a huge funnel: strikes, the war, a hubbub of activity. The universe was speeding up. I was hearing this stuff about health and safety and it wasn't clear in my mind how to approach it all.

"The nuclear weapons stuff led me into occupational safety and health. I figured there must be problems in the manufacture of these weapons," Tony continued. But mostly, "I hadn't given thought to the chemical problems at all. I remember there was a guy at Rubinstein who was studying to be a chiropractor. And he would say, 'Look at this stuff. You know, this could be toxic.' And we sort of pooh-poohed it—laughed about it, actually. We had absolutely no reason to believe that it was dangerous. But a lot of it later was found to be nasty stuff."

In the booming '60s, increased chemical production enshrouded OCAW workers in a fog of smoke and dust. The shop floor was a colossal mess, and Mazzocchi realized that appalling work conditions were the norm. He became increasingly aware that corporations not only tolerated such conditions, but consciously calculated them into their cost structures. This callousness later would be revealed by *New Yorker* writer Paul Brodeur, who quoted an asbestos plant manager's chilling account of a conversation with representatives from asbestos manufacturer Johns Manville: "We asked them if they knew of any way we could improve the dust situation in our factory. My God, they were brutal bastards! Why, they practically laughed in our faces! They told us that workmen's-compensation payments were the same for death as for disability. In effect, they told us to let the men *work themselves to death*!"[5]

Mazzocchi's *aha!* moment came through his job as OCAW's legislative director, as local unionists began calling him about their concerns. Mazzocchi was positioned perfectly to see new interconnections—and equipped with a mind that recognized them. As he put it,

> In 1966, I started getting phone calls from locals on particular health and safety problems—because when people encounter a problem, they think there's a law to protect them. And I said, "Yeah, there must be something"—and I started calling around. I couldn't find out anything. Gee, there's no law. And it starts to dawn on me that there's a pattern to this stuff. People have problems and there's no place to turn.

Mazzocchi found a weak federal law passed in the 1930s, the Walsh-Healy Act, which offered meager health and safety protection for workers in industries doing business on government contracts. The Department of

Labor, charged with enforcing the law, had little technical expertise. And, said Mazzocchi, "They had twenty inspectors for twenty-three million people covered by the act. So I called up some people that I'd met through SANE, and nobody knew anything. I could mention a chemical to them, and they didn't know much. It was beginning to percolate in my mind that there was a major problem out there."

But Mazzocchi's focus still remained elsewhere. "All these issues were coming up in the union—the war and a zillion other things." But by the summer of 1967, Mazzocchi finally realized he needed his union's mandate to build a national health and safety campaign and to reach out to the environmental movement.

If he could get such a mandate, it would mark the first time in history that a union systematically sought to ally with environmentalists.

IV

To be empowered directly by the OCAW membership, Mazzocchi needed a resolution passed at the union's 1967 national convention—the same one that had generated his disastrous Vietnam War poll.

In producing and directing union conventions, Tony had no peer. They were his political theater, the set for his political imagination. He created spectacles to elevate the delegates' collective sense of purpose and inspire militancy. Sure, the delegates needed the nice hotel, the booze, and the hospitality suites. But they also needed to be treated to something politically stimulating. So while other unions luxuriated at their conventions, Mazzocchi piled on the major political players of the day, putting his delegates on the cutting edge.

Mazzocchi hoped the August 1967 convention at Manhattan's Americana Hotel would provide top-notch political theater. The delegates were not disappointed. The hall was less than two miles from Harlem during America's summer of urban unrest. Since the massive upheaval in the Watts section of Los Angeles in 1965, American inner cities had been burning. More than two hundred riots—racial rebellions—exploded in 1966–1967. The July 1967 upheaval in Newark, New Jersey, just across the river from the convention, had become such a maelstrom that the National Guard and local police were firing at each other. A week later an even larger conflagration ignited Detroit: Forty-three died, seven thousand were arrested, thirteen hundred buildings were destroyed, and twenty-seven hundred businesses were looted, leaving the city looking, in the words of Detroit mayor Jerome Cavanagh, "like Berlin in 1945."[6]

Just coming to New York City felt risky for many OCAW delegates. Protests had escalated, as had the war. In 1967, the number of US combat troops in Vietnam topped half a million: An average of twenty-six soldiers died per day. More than five hundred thousand people rallied in Central Park in April 1967 in protest, and two hundred burned their draft cards. It was a hell of a time for OCAW delegates from places like Beaumont, Texas, and Mandan, North Dakota, to visit the city.

One of the convention's first speakers, AFL-CIO president George Meany, addressed urban unrest from a decidedly liberal perspective. Rather than calling for law and order, he focused on the AFL-CIO's strong opposition to discrimination, which he believed was the root cause of the unrest. He described how unions had purged themselves of discriminatory bylaws, Jim Crow contracts, and segregated locals—and how they now fought for housing desegregation, aid to education, Medicare, and a higher minimum wage. Meany's speech was well received by this overwhelmingly white male audience in this summer of urban discontent.

The highlight of Meany's speech was a demonstration by OCAW delegates who were on strike against Shell Oil in Texas. Marching through the convention hall, they called on Meany to force building-trades workers to stop crossing their picket lines. Meany, a former plumbers' union leader who held sway over the building trades, had been ignoring the Shell workers' plea for months.

Mazzocchi welcomed this drama and greatly enjoyed Meany's steadfast performance. "All these pickets are marching around the entire convention hall, and Meany didn't bat an eye," Mazzocchi said.

He admired even more OCAW president Al Grospiron's nerve in allowing the protest. "What other international president would invite the president of the AFL-CIO and then allow a local to picket the son of a bitch?"

The delegates also heard from prospective presidential candidates Hubert Humphrey and Robert Kennedy. Humphrey, like Meany, ducked the war and focused entirely on the riots lighting up the urban skies across the river. He railed against discrimination in housing and education, which left ghetto dwellers feeling like "second-class citizens of this rich and fortunate nation."[7] OCAW members cheered when the vice president insisted that all of this could be solved. "You know what I think we can do? Anything we want to. . . . When we Americans make up our minds that we want to do something we get it done."[8]

Kennedy by contrast was a halting and chilly tragic prince. Rather than echo Meany's and Humphrey's joyful odes about past and future American glory, he confronted the obvious—that the war and urban riots were ripping the country apart. "Even as we meet," Kennedy lamented, "we hear the sounds of war in a land 10,000 miles away, and the crack of gunfire in our cities."[9]

Kennedy also sought to raise worker environmental awareness. "We have revolutionized our lives with electricity, but our power plants pollute the air," he charged. "Our industry has grown . . . but has turned our rivers into sewers and our lakes into swamps. We have built new homes and products with lumber from our forests, but we have destroyed three-quarters of our virgin redwoods. . . ."[10] If his points seemed perfect lead-ins for environmental unionism, that was no accident: He had been briefed by Mazzocchi.

RFK touched on urban renewal ("We have rebuilt our cities with gleaming stores and new housing, but we have destroyed the neighborhoods of the poor and imprisoned them in ghettoes. We have split the two Americas further and further apart, feeding the fires of despair which have exploded today into violence"[11]) and foreign affairs ("We built a foreign policy on the rhetoric of anticommunism; and found ourselves imprisoned in that rhetoric when the Communist monolith began to crumble"[12]). He closed his sobering account of America gone wrong by returning to the themes Mazzocchi needed for his health and safety resolution:

> We and you, must ask what a new product or a new factory will do to our environment; whether it is safe as well as profitable to build it; whether what it will destroy is worth more than what it will create. . . . We must remember there is no constituency for our rivers, and our forests, nor for the purity of the air we breathe, nor those who look up to us for help in building their new lives. . . . We

> know the kind of world we mean to leave for our children, but if you and I, if we do nothing to help build them, who will?[13]

Mazzocchi realized how far Kennedy had come. Bobby was no longer the red-baiting hatchet man on Joe McCarthy's staff. He no longer attacked union corruption while remaining silent about corporate crime. He was no longer a cheerleader for counterinsurgency and the Green Berets. But although Kennedy was perhaps now the nation's best hope for ending the war, Mazzocchi saw that the delegates greatly preferred Hubert's happy talk and unabashed enthusiasm over Kennedy's insightful intellectualism.

Mazzocchi wanted his health and safety resolution to be prefaced by a speech from his good friend, the young consumer crusader Ralph Nader. Over the preceding two years, Mazzocchi and Nader had teamed up to protest the hazards of natural-gas pipelines and the weak or nonexistent state regulations governing them. OCAW represented thousands of workers who produced and distributed natural gas. The safety issue emerged nationally after a government study had found that over the previous fifteen years, gas pipeline accidents had "caused 64 deaths and 222 injuries, almost half of them involving persons who were not gas company employees."[14] (As in *Silent Spring,* the statement implied that it was one thing to kill a worker, but quite another to blow up an innocent citizen.)

A month after this report, Nader, already a famous consumer advocate, argued in *The New York Times* that "although pipeline safety affects all of us and although the consumer pays for this service, the decision as to how much safety to afford the public is made unilaterally by the pipeline companies whose primary motive is obviously profit-maximization."[15]

"Beneath our feet lies troubled earth," Nader said.[16]

Senator Gale McGee of Wyoming warned the industry that "a single dramatic accident or a series of accidents may be sufficient to unleash the forces of regulatory fervor in Congress."[17]

And then it nearly happened. On Friday the thirteenth, January 1967, a natural-gas explosion rocked Queens, New York, destroying nine buildings housing nineteen families. According to *The New York Times*, the explosion and ensuing fire were "traced to natural gas escaping from the Union Gas Company's distribution network."

Miraculously, no one was hurt. But the press immediately turned to Nader for a statement, and the *Times* again headlined him.

On February 16, LBJ hopped on Nader's bandwagon, calling on Congress to enact a package of consumer protection laws that would do everything from ensuring the safety of X-ray machines to eliminating hazardous household products. The package also included what would be come the National Gas Pipeline Safety Act of 1967.

Mazzocchi brought the union into the fray. In August 1967, the *Times* quoted him saying that "corrosion and disrepair of the natural gas system serving St. Louis were causing millions of cubic feet of raw natural gas to flow unrestricted under the city's streets." He told a Senate commerce subcommittee there was "reason to believe that the situation is probably similar in other major cities."[18]

Ralph Nader noted that a gas company worker Mazzocchi had brought to testify "showed the startled lawmakers pipeline sections whose gaping holes were patched over, sometimes with cloth, in the most primitive way. The risks of greater explosions from old or un-repaired pipes became very real that day on Capitol Hill."[19]

Tony and Ralph formed a potent tag team: While Nader commanded the public stage, Mazzocchi hooked in workers from the very industries Nader was talking about. At the OCAW convention, Nader knew his mission well. He needed to convince the delegates to help lead the growing fight against corporate abuse of workers and consumers. He wanted to make them proud that their union was already the leader in health and safety. And he wanted to urge them to do much more: for starters, pass Mazzocchi's resolution.

Nader began his talk by describing how health and safety now went much farther than worrying about slips and falls at the workplace. "Industrial hazards have been diversified . . . moving from the simple forms of trauma to toxicity," he said.[20] He warned the delegates about the deadly long-term effects of chemicals and radiation exposure, "far more insidious inflictions [than trauma] that show their effect five, ten, fifteen, or twenty years after the original exposure."[21]

Nader wasn't shy about attacking unions that failed to challenge these corporate crimes. "Too often there has been silence. Too often there has been lip service—lip-service resolutions, lip-service congressional testimony—instead of muscle service. Too often unions have supported safety reform for the record, but not on the ramparts."[22]

Nader urged delegates to use Mazzocchi's resolution as "an igniter for action," not "a substitute for action."[23] He wrapped up with a warning that reflected both Mazzocchi's view of labor and Nader's hope for Mazzocchi. If organized labor was "to survive as a creative force instead of a defensive force," he said, it would have to "stake out broader roots in its social role. . . . If I have any grounds for hoping that labor will recover its nerve, it rests substantially on the often unappreciated and dedicated union representatives who still have stars in their vision . . .

"Your union's advocacy in Washington for greater safeguards against pipelines and radiation hazards is an extremely promising development, because it's more than lip service and more than resolutions," Nader concluded. "It's day-to-day and while immediate beneficiaries may be those closest to the hazards, the full beneficiary will be those yet unborn . . . Such is hopefully a bright omen for the future."[24]

Nader had broken with the common etiquette at such events by offering praise for Mazzocchi and none at all for union president Grospiron. Tony no doubt sensed that Grospiron's ego would be bruised. Someday there would be hell to pay.

Nevertheless, Nader was leading a parade that later would include thousands of workers, journalists, scientists, and students—all seeking out Tony Mazzocchi, the man with "stars in his vision."

V

The final act of Mazzocchi's convention extravaganza was a moment he hoped would lay the basis for a new movement. "I got Humphrey there. I got Kennedy there. I even had Reuther, but he had to cancel at the last moment," said Tony. "It was all carefully designed so that we would pass the resolution mandating me to build community support for an occupational safety act. It was going to allow me to go all over North America dramatizing the horrors of toxic production."

The health and safety resolution that was about to be read to the delegates jumped forty years ahead of the labor movement. In the tradition of union resolutions, it opened with a string of *Whereas* statements that described the problem, starting with the most obvious: "Whereas new hazards to health and safety have developed in industry in recent years, but measures of protection against these hazards have lagged."

> . . . Whereas new chemicals, the dangers of which are not fully known, are being handled not only in chemical plants but also in many other industrial operations.
>
> . . . Whereas in its zeal to apply new technologies and to reduce labor and maintenance costs, industry has seriously undermanned many operations and preventive maintenance is a thing of the past.
>
> . . . Whereas all of these hazards threaten not only the people working in the plants and operation involved, but also the residents of surrounding communities.

Then came the mandates:

> To this end, THEREFORE BE IT RESOLVED by the 9th Constitutional Convention [that the] Oil, Chemical and Atomic Workers International Union endorses the following action:
>
> That the International Union shall develop a health and safety program, covering all segments of the union with such a program to be implemented by educational, collective bargaining and political action processes.

The resolution gave Mazzocchi permission to build alliances, calling for the union to work "with the labor movement and other sympathetic organizations in the support of legislation and regulations. . . ."

Then came the measure's most revolutionary clause: The union mandated that "each local union develop a relationship with the press and with community leaders so that the public may be fully informed of health and safety hazards which may develop."

For the first time in American labor history, a union was calling on its own local unions to protect the community's environment. "In this and all other health and safety activities," the resolution said, "full consideration must be given to hazards to the community as well as to hazards to the workforce."[25]

Wasn't this threatening to OCAW members whose livelihoods depended on poisonous production? Wouldn't workers be afraid to inform the public about toxic hazards when the warning might lead to a call to shut down hazardous facilities? How did Mazzocchi avoid a rebellion from delegates over this jobs-versus-environment conflict?

Neither Mazzocchi nor the union was quite ready to square up to this problem. Fortunately, in the late '60s, they didn't have to. The war economy was booming; blue-collar jobs were abundant. At the same time, the growing demand pressed managers to speed up production and cut preventive maintenance. With jobs plentiful, yet dangerous, this was the perfect time to build alliances between workers and health-minded community members.

Mazzocchi didn't hesitate. Neither did Grospiron. "You know, Grospiron said, 'Cut loose.' And I did," said Mazzocchi.

There was only one problem: 1968, the most turbulent year of a turbulent decade.

VI

With half a million ground troops committed to Vietnam, 1968 began much the same as the previous year—with US commanders promising the imminent defeat of the enemy, dutifully reported by a compliant media. Then, on January 30, at the start of the Tet holiday, America watched on the nightly news as the National Liberation Front and the People's Army of Vietnam simultaneously attacked every major US stronghold in Vietnam—six major cities, thirty-six provincial capitals, and sixty-four district capitals, as well as nearly every military base.[26] Television showed live battles raging in Saigon and the American embassy under siege. Although American forces repelled the attacks and inflicted enormous harm on the insurgents, over the next several weeks many Americans finally realized that the Johnson administration was misleading them.

The Tet Offensive created an insurmountable credibility gap for the government. Walter Cronkite, the nation's most respected TV anchor, reflected both the public's previous naïveté and new mood of distrust when he remarked on the air to millions of people, "What's going on here? I thought

"He threatened to join the French Foreign Legion if his father didn't let him go." Tony, at age sixteen, leaving home for World War II, May 1, 1943.

"I learned my politics at the dinner table." The Mazzocchis' former home in Bensonhurst, Brooklyn, 2003.

"He got up there and he was gonna be somebody in our union . . ." Tony addresses a 1953 New York CIO shop stewards' meeting. In the same row to the far left are his two lifelong lieutenants, George Roach and Dick McManus.

"I knew the two-tier wage structure . . . would haunt us." Tony at the Helena Rubinstein bargaining table circa 1953. Seated on the right are Jack Curran, whom Tony defeated for president of the local in 1953, and Agnes Hesslin, whom he defeated for chief steward in 1952.

"The company was scared shitless. . . . The company figured, if you're going to do this on somebody *else's* picket line, what are you gonna do when it's your own?" Tony leading Local 149 in support of IUE Local 460 on strike against the Arma Corporation (1953).

"We drove with him, during the LIRR railroad worker strike, so he could give a Democratic Party reply on television," said Tony's daughter Geraldine. "We took a picture of him on TV" (1960).

"Anybody who ran for office, the first thing they did was head for was our local." Tony and Mac (seated) campaigning on Long Island for Senator John F. Kennedy (1960).

"'Hey, Tony. You did a poll at your convention. Tell him what the people said about the bombing of Haiphong Harbor.' And I had to divulge the poll results. My friends never let me forget it." Tony with LBJ and Lady Bird after the 1967 dinner at which he had to give Johnson the results of an OCAW poll revealing that the members supported the bombing of North Vietnam urban areas.

"All the labor guys came to me the day after and said, 'Oh God, you could have been in Congress. You should have never quit.'" A Long Island electioneering meeting, circa 1964. Stanley Aronowitz is on the far left. Henry Murray, AFL-CIO New England–New York COPE director, is leaning over the table. Tony is in the center with John Eagan, Long Island Federation of Labor vice president, to the right. Third in from the right is Rocco Campanaro, Long Island Federation of Labor president.

"One time in 1964 he came home with a big campaign truck. Bobby Kennedy was actually supposed to stay at our house that night." Tony and New York senatorial candidate Bobby Kennedy, circa 1964.

"There are these pictures of me with my friggin' hair down to my shoulders. I'm standing around a table, negotiating with the clean-cut company guys with crew cuts." The twenty-two-year-old Steve Wodka at the Kawecki Berylco bargaining table (1970). From the left: Herb Sterling, Robert Corrigan, Richard Chamberlin, Steve Wodka, Frankie Fellin, Joe Leahy, and Bob Petruce.

"The lesson was that you had to organize a broad public-interest community—because you don't defeat a company like Shell Oil alone on a picket line." Shell strike, 1973.

Tony Mazzocchi in 1976 wearing a SUPPORTERS OF SILKWOOD button.

Karen Silkwood shortly before she was killed, fall 1974.

"I felt okay, and all of a sudden I turn and I see the car laying on its side, totaled, the roof smashed down to the steering wheel." Mazzocchi wrecked car which took place in January 1975, one month after Karen Silkwood's fatal car crash.

"Our business is America's concern. The trade union movement is the only hope America has." Tony on the campaign trail for his second attempt at the OCAW presidency.

"It was time to put the union together." Tony joins Bob Wages and other OCAW activists and allies just before getting arrested in a protest against BASF during the five-year lockout (circa 1987).

Tony and Susan Mazzocchi.

Tony with one of his premature twin girls, 1976.

Tony with his son Anthony, 1976.

Tony with the twins (Elizabeth and Kristina) and Anthony, 1977.

The Mazzocchis, circa 1982. Back row, from the left: Carol, Geri, Susan, Tony, and Linda. In front are Elizabeth, Anthony, and Kristina.

"My friends kept saying 'Look, Mazzocchi, Al did not want you to become president, because you would have outshone him.'" Mazzocchi, retiring OCAW president Al Grospiron, and Robert Goss before the 1979 race for the presidency.

Tony, "defeated in his bid for the presidency, collects his thoughts before congratulating OCAW president, Bob Goss on his victory. Mazzocchi told the delegates, 'Those of us who fought this long fight . . . will support any effort to unite the union against its only foe—corporate America . . .'" (OCAW *Union News,* September 1981).

we were winning this war."[27] Support for the war collapsed. In one of the most rapid shifts ever recorded, polls showed public opinion going from 60 percent hawk/24 percent dove before Tet, to 42 percent dove/41 percent hawk after.[28] LBJ was a goner.

Mazzocchi saw new political possibilities. Before Tet, polls showed peace candidate Eugene McCarthy with only 6 percent of the New Hampshire primary vote, with LBJ winning 76 percent. On primary night, after the Tet offensive had sunk in, McCarthy won a startling 42 percent, gaining twenty of the state's twenty-four delegates to the Democratic National Convention. Not since 1912 had a sitting president been so challenged.

Four days later, Robert Kennedy declared his candidacy. While Mazzocchi believed Kennedy could reach deeply into the working class, his delay in entering the race hurt him badly among the college students already revved up to defeat Johnson. When Kennedy spoke at Brooklyn College, he was greeted with a poster that expressed the prevailing antiwar student mood: BOBBY KENNEDY: HAWK, DOVE OR CHICKEN?[29]

When LBJ addressed the nation on prime-time TV to say, "I shall not seek, and I will not accept, the nomination of my party for another term as your president," Tony was stunned. Could those students actually knock out a sitting president and install a dove? Was the system Mazzocchi so wanted to change finally cracking?

VII

As the Tet body count rose, Mazzocchi concentrated on casualties of a different kind, at the National Lead Company in New Jersey. "The local union guys called me," Mazzocchi said. "A guy had died of carbon monoxide poisoning. I wanted to know what the hell carbon monoxide was used for in that facility." He learned that the company had recently started a new process to produce titanium dioxide, an ingredient in unleaded paint that required carbon monoxide and chlorine gas. Both were deadly. One worker died when, without warning, a valve opened in a room with no ventilation. Two others passed out and required hospitalization; one of these suffered severe brain damage. As in Vietnam, the victims were young: the oldest was twenty-five. All had young children.

In his earlier years, Mazzocchi might have immediately publicized the story. But after his public humiliation before the Joint Atomic Energy Committee, he knew he needed to do his homework before turning a spotlight on the widows and orphans. "These guys needed help, but I said, 'I can't go in there without some expertise.' So I called Commoner in St. Louis." Commoner recommended that Mazzocchi get in touch with two students at Rockefeller University who were active in Scientists' Institute for Public Information—Glenn Paulson and Max Snodderly.

Paulson's thesis adviser was René Dubos, whom Commoner considered a trusted progressive. Dubos (with others) had inspired Paulson to join the public information movement to publicize facts about strontium 90, napalm, and dioxin-tainted Agent Orange. "We also became interested and worried about the proposal to build a nuclear reactor across the East River from Manhattan," Glenn recalled. "We even explored the issue of global warming."[30] In 1966–1967, Paulson served on the New York Scientific Committee for Public Information's national board, along with Margaret Mead and Commoner.

Then, Paulson recalled, "I got this call from Mazzocchi, who said, 'You don't know me but I got your name from Commoner. Can you help us?' I then invited him and the local union president from National Lead to meet with us in that cafeteria at Rockefeller University. I don't know, but it may have been the first time union officials had eaten there. I always wondered how Tony felt about coming to a place named *Rockefeller.* After meeting with them, Max and I did some research and learned more about high levels of exposure to carbon monoxide. I had only known about the relatively low levels involved in urban air pollution."

Did Paulson realize that he had fallen into Commoner's left-wing network of scientists? "No," said Paulson. "Among this faculty, there was no talk of socialism like there was when you were around Mazzocchi."

Mazzocchi invited Paulson and Snodderly to tour the plant in Sayreville, New Jersey. "There would be a meeting with one shift of workers, then the plant tour, then a visit with another shift," Paulson recalled. "At our first meeting with the workers, we were received coolly. They were suspicious of us. Both of us had beards. Clearly we were white collar. But Mazzocchi stood by us. He said, 'Look, these are our guys. They're here to help us. I want you to give them your full cooperation.' But they were still cool to us."

Then the bearded ones, Mazzocchi, and the local president went to the plant entrance. "I became involved in my first labor dispute," Paulson said. "It was a cold spring day. We were at the gate, and some of the top management people came out to tell us that we could not go in. Mazzocchi basically put them up against a wall, telling them that if they didn't let him bring in his experts, 'I'll shut the place down right now.' Management huddled momentarily to consider that threat and then agreed to let us in."

The tour was an eye-opener. As Paulson recalled,

> We entered this very large room that contained the process to separate the titanium needed for the paint. Carbon monoxide and chlorine were used to bond with the titanium, transform it into a gas, and separate it from the impure mixture. They showed us all the monitoring devices and where they were located. At this time, the maximum level was supposed to be fifty parts per million. I'm kind of curious about machines, so I started to look around . . . and I found one where the alarm was set to go off at 100 ppm. The management people got very embarrassed by that and they immediately changed it. Mazzocchi looked around. He found one that was set to go off at 200 ppm. And I think it was the safety officer at the time, he started to look around at them. He found one that was set to go off at 400 ppm. If somebody breathes that for a few hours, they'll fall unconscious.

It was a killing zone.

Fortunately, Paulson knew his chemistry and put his knowledge to good advantage during the plant tour. "At one point during the visit, we felt that we couldn't really make sense of the process with all the pipes and tubing around unless we looked at the blueprint," Paulson said:

> So they brought us to a conference room with a twenty-foot table and rolled out a blueprint that covered nearly all of it. . . . I pored over it as several managers watched. It was clear that the process started with raw material—a type of sand—that was 96 percent titanium, 3 percent vanadium, and 1 percent other metal oxides. . . . With my eclectic background in chemistry, it was clear as a bell to

> me that the process left behind very rich vanadium ore, and vanadium used as an additive for steel products is very valuable, much more valuable than titanium. It's used for shielding of missiles and rockets. Seeing that the process left behind a substance that was 75 percent vanadium, I said something like, "Do you realize that you have left the richest vanadium ore in the world?"

At that point, side discussions within the room halted. Like a herd sensing danger, the silence spread from the management side and across the room. "I realized that I had hit upon their trade secret—the fundamental profitable aspect of the process," Paulson said. "It was the vanadium. It was obvious from their silence and from their expressions. From that point on they got real respectful. In subsequent discussions, we were treated as equals. Management now realized that Mazzocchi had scientific backing to be reckoned with. They realized they had to address the serious health and safety problems and that they should talk seriously to us about how best to protect these workers. They agreed to fix and maintain the monitors and reduce the CO and chlorine exposures. In exchange, we agreed to maintain their trade secret."

The next shift meeting between the workers and the bearded ones was very different: "At that second meeting," Paulson said, "instead of hostility we were warmly welcomed. Word had spread that these were the guys who had nailed the bosses. It was a day-and-night difference."

This was about the last success for Mazzocchi in that awful spring of 1968.

VIII

That spring, the presidential campaign of Gene McCarthy had unraveled in the face of Robert Kennedy's growing appeal. After Martin Luther King Jr. was gunned down in Memphis, Kennedy had walked the ghetto streets, appealing for calm. His leadership emphasized the black community's loyalty to the Kennedy clan, a dynamic that McCarthy couldn't fight, and that his student supporters couldn't ignore. Kennedy's appeal grew among working-class whites as well—even as independent candidate George Wallace's overtly racist message won over working-class voters in the North and South.

Then, as Kennedy walked from the podium after claiming victory in the California primary, he was shot dead by Sirhan Sirhan.

Whatever Mazzocchi hoped to build was put on hold. The nation was reeling. Campus demonstrations grew more intense and violent, and the SDS shutdown of Columbia University lasted months. The police became more aggressive toward potheads and peaceniks and downright lethal toward black activists, who were under siege by covert law enforcement agencies. The country was gearing up for a major catharsis, a ritual of bloodletting that would release the despair and hopelessness.

It was called Chicago.

Kennedy had been Tony's candidate, as well as his colleague. After the assassination, Mazzocchi turned to McCarthy, even as McCarthy turned inward and lost heart. Although McCarthy's campaign won in New York and gained delegates in other states, the candidate vanished. Mazzocchi could not stop OCAW from endorsing Humphrey. Mazzocchi headed to the Democratic National Convention in Chicago as a guest of labor, to do what he could for McCarthy—which wasn't much. Instead, he would witness one of the darkest weeks in American history.

Like the radicals descending on the convention city, Chicago mayor Richard Daley was itching for a fight. He was determined to teach the long-haired, pot-smoking, unpatriotic rabble a lesson, even if it meant jailing them all. State and federal agencies sent out several thousand undercover agents in preparation for the demonstrations. To further heighten the tension, the mayor refused to provide permits for marches, making protest "illegal."

Chicago turned into a war zone, an unrestrained police riot. Police tear-gassed and slugged and billy-clubbed protesters, journalists, and spectators. For the police, if you were there on the street, you were a traitor. For those unaccustomed to police thugs on picket lines or to vigilante justice in the South, it seemed as if fascism had sprung up in the heart of America. Inside the convention hall, McCarthy delegates took punches to the gut and clubs over the head for sitting in the wrong seat. Outside, they got clubbed for watching a demonstration or while walking down the sidewalk to their hotels. A Daley goon socked CBS journalist Mike Wallace in the face. Dan Rather took one to the stomach.

From the convention podium on prime-time TV, Senator Abe Ribicoff, the liberal Democrat from Connecticut, referred to Daley's "Gestapo tactics."

From their front-row seats, Daley and his commandants shouted insults at Ribicoff. Looking like a grotesque caricature of himself, the red-faced Daley screamed out, "Fuck you, you Jew son of a bitch, you lousy motherfucker. Go home!"[31]

The city was put under virtual martial law; federal troops with machine guns mounted on jeeps surrounded Mazzocchi's hotel. From his window, Tony watched as the police charged the demonstrators in Grant Park, teargas canisters arcing through the air. He avoided the police clubs, but not the gas. "I was close to the McCarthy people," Mazzocchi said. "My friends had gotten elected as McCarthy delegates from Long Island. We got gassed—you know, the whole fucking thing."

Yet Mazzocchi really couldn't help McCarthy's cause much because "I had to be careful of my own union, which had endorsed Humphrey."

Humphrey's only chance rested on his willingness to accept a mild peace plank, a smart move given that more than 80 percent of the Democratic primary voters had supported antiwar candidates. However, Johnson, who controlled the majority at the convention, refused. As the innocuous peace plank went down to defeat, Mazzocchi witnessed the end of the liberal coalition that had held power throughout the '60s.

That fall, OCAW worked hard for Humphrey against Nixon. But Mazzocchi had no stomach for it. Nixon was benefiting from a growing backlash that blamed the antiwar kids for Daley's riot in Chicago. Nixon also hinted that he had a secret plan to end the war. Humphrey finally made a few dovish statements in a desperate effort to resurrect his campaign. But it was too little, too late. Nixon was soon at the controls.

Like a vast firestorm, these political disasters—King, Kennedy, and Chicago—sucked the air out of moderate peaceful protest. SDS was torn apart, with an armed faction going underground, another creating a sectarian party, and many former members moving into community groups and other forms of activism. The gun-toting Black Panthers, heavily infiltrated by police provocateurs, were gunned down. And Mazzocchi, Mr. Democrat from Long Island who only five years earlier had almost become its Democratic congressman, lost faith in the Democratic Party.

Thousands of progressive activists were now looking for a new direction, a connection, a home. Mazzocchi would soon build one for them.

IX

Glenn Paulson's visit to the National Lead plant made him the first of many young scientists whom Mazzocchi would escort across the line separating civil society from factory work.

At first, Paulson thought he had come across an isolated case of factory pollution. Surely such conditions weren't the norm. A few months later, Mazzocchi invited him to give a report about National Lead to OCAW's District 8 council in New York. Paulson said he was shocked when these workers "unleashed a flood of problems, which made me believe that, if urban areas are bad for air pollution, chemical plants are much, much worse."

After that meeting, Mazzocchi knew for sure that he was on to something big. Until the late 1960s, people did not clearly understand the health problems caused by toxic production—other than radiation and miner's black lung disease. As one Texas public health official said about asbestos, "How can there be a serious danger if it doesn't hurt you right away?"[32]

No wonder an OCAW asbestos worker could report that "no one ever told me or anyone else I know that asbestos could harm you. Why, I can remember some of our supervisors saying it not only wouldn't hurt you, but was *good* for you! They even used to tell us you could *eat* it!"[33]

To understand the risks, workers needed to place their faith in science and embrace the concept of latency—that a disease might turn up ten to thirty years after they'd been exposed. The debates over nuclear fallout had already introduced the idea that mysterious substances could kill us over years. But only scientists could "prove" it or credibly explain it. Only scientists could confirm the connection between cause and effect over decades. A layperson such as Mazzocchi would be howling in the wind unless scientists and doctors backed him up.

So Mazzocchi came upon a simple idea that would change America: Take the New York meeting on the road. Why not hold district council meetings on the workplace environment in every district in the United States and Canada? What would happen if workers all around the country could discuss with scientists and doctors their many workplace health issues? This road show—a traveling circus of scientists and doctors—would "ventilate the issue," as Mazzocchi liked to say, among workers. He could frame and moderate the discussions; scientists could learn about toxic substances from workers; and workers could get answers from scientists.

The focus would be on collecting evidence to win a strong new national bill to protect worker safety and health. To win that law, Mazzocchi thought, labor had to go far beyond traditional lobbying. That approach had failed repeatedly to force such a bill out of committee during the Johnson years. The problem, Mazzocchi thought, was that the public didn't know the extent of factory-floor pollution. Labor had focused on Capitol Hill, where too many politicians conveniently bought industry's line: "Don't worry; we take care of our workers." Instead, labor had to tap the public's growing concern about environmental dangers.

Mazzocchi opened new terrain by fundamentally reframing the environmental question. It was deceptively simple. Before Mazzocchi, pollution was viewed largely as a problem of dumping and emissions, of where the bad stuff ended up—in the air, the water, the soil, in our food.

Mazzocchi's conceptual breakthrough was that *pollution always starts in the workplace,* and then moves into the community and the natural environment. Workplace pollution, therefore, was the *source* of environmental degradation, and only strict workplace controls on pollutants and toxic substances could adequately protect us from hazards. Mazzocchi tied the environment to the workplace by calling his road show "Hazards in the Industrial Environment."

There was another reason Mazzocchi wanted to go on the road rather than schmooze on Capitol Hill. Tony, the union's chief lobbyist, hated lobbying. Let labor lobbyists with less restless temperaments spend their time in quiet conversations with congressional aides. He had a different theory of political change: that social movements, not quiet conversation among elites, made history. "We had enough union lobbyists around town. I wanted to build a mass base," Tony said.

Mazzocchi had been extremely upset by how the oil industry had "knifed" the earlier worker safety and health bill. "This was a Democratic Congress, a Democratic president. And we got hosed, of course, because of the oil industry, which always dominated the Democratic Party—contrary to popular myth." What offended him most was "the bill got killed in committee and *nobody even knew about it!* I mean the public, the workers; the impacted people never even knew it happened," he said. "I was determined to make sure that wouldn't happen again."

X

The road show debuted on March 29, 1969, at the Holiday Inn in Kenilworth, New Jersey. More than two hundred local union leaders from OCAW's District 8 attended, as well as workers from independent chemical unions. The event featured presentations from Glenn Paulson, and from ubiquitous troublemaker Leo Goodman. Mazzocchi also brought along several doctors, though none, unfortunately, had much experience in occupational medicine.

Much of the knowledge the experts shared came from the "bluebook" of occupational standards, *The Documentation of Threshold Values*. This guide was the basis for federal workplace exposure standards under the weak Walsh-Healy Act.

But the guide testified to the sorry state of workplace regulations. It was published by the American Conference of Governmental Industrial Hygienists (ACGIH)—a governmental-sounding organization that was in fact sponsored by private industry. And ACGIH committees, not the government, had created the exposure limits, with no outside review or avenue of appeal. These private committees included management representatives, but no one from labor. If a management person felt the exposure limit was too burdensome, it would be raised until everyone could agree to it. Not only were the ACGIH standards weak, they covered fewer than five hundred chemicals. Mazzocchi and Paulson would soon discover that there were more than twenty thousand chemicals in use for which there were no standards.

When Mazzocchi tried to get copies of the guide for each OCAW local, ACGIH did all it could to stop him. First, the group said the book was out of print and no copies were available. When Mazzocchi offered to pay royalties to reprint the old book, ACGIH refused, saying the book would only become available after it was updated, which would take two years. Finally Mazzocchi purchased a reprint from the University of Michigan's microfilm archives, the only public source available.

The law was even more inadequate than the ACGIH reference book. The Walsh-Healy Act only covered workers in facilities with government contracts worth more than ten thousand dollars per year. On the rare occasion when inspectors visited a facility, management was given advance notice, and the problem often disappeared miraculously before the inspection. Results of an inspection were shown only to the company, not the union. When the union filed a request under the Freedom of Information Act to see the inspection report, the government denied it, citing an FOIA clause that barred the release of information gained through "enforcement" investigations.

In short, the regulatory regime was a hoax. There were no effective standards. There was no enforcement. The corporations ruled as absolute monarchs over chemical production, exposure, and regulation. They decided if and when to monitor conditions. They decided how much exposure was too much. In truth, they decided whether you died before your time.

"This morning we're embarking upon what I consider to be an historic undertaking," Mazzocchi said in his opening remarks. "Though we've talked about health and safety for a long time in the trade union movement, the emphasis had been on the safety aspect of it—whether a fellow gets his hand caught in a machine, or a whether a gal gets her hair caught. . . . But the industry we work in had a danger that most people are unaware of, and it's insidious. It's the danger of a contaminated environment, the workplace; something we don't feel, see or smell, and of which most of us become contemptuous, simply because it doesn't affect us immediately. And then, when we do become ill, we attribute it to something other than the workplace.[34]

"Now I have sat before a congressional committee," Mazzocchi continued, "and I must admit that I was chewed and torn limb from limb, with Brother Goodman, by our old friend, Chet Holifield, for what he characterized as an emotional approach to this problem, because I expressed Leo's and my concern about having to deal with widows. He wanted scientific facts. "That's why we want to document our case. So that we can go again before these committees and say, 'Mr. Congressman, Mr. Senator, this is what's happening in the plants. This is what's happening to our people. We need a law.'" Mazzocchi added: "I can tell you that most congressmen who sit on those committees feel that your bosses are looking after you, and there is really nothing wrong. And they've got to hear the stories that are being told."[35]

The stories reported on that day in 1969 revealed that chemical workers were literally dying for a law.

Steven Lawrence from the American Cyanamid plant in Linden, New Jersey, said that he "came here today to find out . . . what the crippling effects of acrylamide might be. We've had six or seven people that have suffered strokes, paralysis. One of the men became blind a year ago. . . . I have labels here of many of the products what we handle which are very toxic: malathion, parathion, thiamide, xanthade, and maybe fifty more. But what I'm interested in now is finding out exactly what the crippling effects of this acrylamide are. Because everybody in this plant is exposed to this due to the faulty equipment that management has installed there. They're only concerned with production yield, not a safety standard."[36]

Unfortunately Glenn Paulson, armed only with the ACGIH bluebook, had to report that "Acrylamide is one of the 5,600 chemicals not in this book."[37]

This gave Mazzocchi a chance to demand what later would be called the Precautionary Principle—that workers' health, not chemicals, should be given the benefit of the doubt. As Mazzocchi explained, "We're struggling for legislation that will say that unless a chemical or product has a standard established for it, it should not be used in industry. Right now you're going to be the [casualty] statistic that someone writes about in the development of a standard. Because ultimately, these chemicals will be understood after all the case studies [about disease and death] are analyzed. And our members will probably be part of those case studies."[38]

Thanks to the carbon monoxide incident at National Lead, Pete McIntyre, the local union president, came fully prepared. Although the intervention by Mazzocchi and the scientists had led to "some improvements," at the plant, he reported, the place was still a hellhole. McIntyre and his safety committee had conducted a survey of the problems workers faced.

"There's a man named Stanley Wollana, his clock number is 930," McIntyre reported. "He's a mechanic in the Chloride Department. He's been on the job for three years. Now the question we asked them all is, 'Have you ever been overcome by gas at the chlorine plant?'" McIntyre read the mechanic's response in full:

> Yes, chlorine, carbon monoxide and aluminum chloride on numerous occasions. . . . Prior to my admittance to the hospital, in this particular instance, I was overcome by inhaling on numerous occasions. The usual effect left the throat very irritated and a feeling of pressure on the chest, sometimes remaining for two or three days afterwards. In this particular instance, because of malfunction [of the machine] I was recalled three times, within three

> hours, to [fix] the automatic valve emitting fumes. The fumes in the reactor were from aluminum chloride. After completing the job, I was subjected to the same feeling: scratchy throat, pressure on my chest and difficulty breathing. On hitting the outside air, I passed out completely. Admitted to the hospital . . . I developed a blood clot on the wall of my heart. As a result of this I was confined to the hospital for four weeks. A total of five months elapsed before I was able to return to work. I have limitations I previously have not experienced. . . . In general my strength is completely exhausted within the course of a day. One thing luckily, I can tell it myself instead of having it written about me.[39]

McIntyre methodically read case after case:

Asked if he had ever been overcome by gas at the chloride plant, Dan Stanley, who had been on the job only a month, replied. "Yes, July, 1967, was the date. I was sitting outside the conversion building. I had just finished eating lunch . . ." He required three months of medical treatment.

Richard Elliot was overcome by titanium tetrachlorine. "He was doing his regular operating job. His treatment [from the foreman] was cough syrup . . . still has sore throat, chest pains, under doctor's care occasionally." After Robert Hawkins was overcome by emissions, he, too, received cough medicine.

Robert Frazer, who also passed out on the job, said, that his "nose should have been cleaned afterwards . . . Clothing should be removed and changed. Clothing carries fumes and causes severe headaches, tightness of chest, sore, raspy throat . . . very easy catching cold."

Floyd Garen got knocked out by CO and spent five days in the hospital. Chris Michaelson became "chlorine fumed November 15th 1968 . . . have not been feeling too well after this incident."

Twice chlorine fumes overcame Charles E. Check. "He still feels pressure in his chest."

As McIntyre's barefoot epidemiology continued, a sickening pattern emerged. Again and again the workers who tended the leaking machinery went down. As one put it, the "fumes were so bad that other operators could not get to me to help me. I managed to get down, trying to hold my breath and proceeded to cough and throw up in the street."

Again and again, "The foreman went inside and brought out some cough medicine."

To add insult to injury, the company blamed the workers for being sickened. As McIntyre put it, "Some people [managers] say that the operators and mechanics, they're not paying attention; they should be doing this; they should do that. Now these are strange words to me, because every time I talk to the company they tell me they have a right to run their plant—until it comes to health and safety. All of a sudden, it's our job. . . . This seems to be the one part that management does not assume is its responsibility in running the plant. . . ."[40]

Union Carbide wasn't any better. Bob Diehl from an independent union in Bound Brook, New Jersey, described how Carbide informed workers that allyl alcohol "gave off a harmless gas . . . and that, although it might be obnoxious to smell, and a little bit irritating to the eyes, it was harmless."

But the workers had a hunch that it was dangerous. On their own, they researched the chemical at a nearby Rutgers University chemistry library where, Diehl said, they "found out some very interesting things on it. First of all, that it was a very harmful chemical when turned into fumes; that it did irritate the eyes, and the mucous membranes; that permanent damage could arise, and that, if used in any type of fairly high concentration in the air, it could result in convulsions, coma and death, within a very short period of time. We confronted the company with this information; of course, they were all surprised about it."[41]

Even exposure to well-known substances like mercury failed to draw management's attention. According to Harold Smith from Woodbridge Chemical, exposures were routine. "We have three furnaces where we run reactors of nitric acid and mercury. . . . When I first went to work in this department, I used to run in and out of this building all day long, trying to get away from the fumes."

As for the even more dangerous mercury dust, Smith reported: "We turn it into powder and we have to pack it. . . . The dust from this powder gets into our lungs, even though we have a mask on."

Smith continued, "Every time the doctor comes in to test me for the mercury that I inhale from this powder, they always tell me that they should take me down to the still instead of sending scrap mercury, because I have more mercury in my system than we collect in the scrap container."

Sadly, Smith reported that he took it home as well: "When I go home at night, I have roast beef and the fumes. I can taste it, still taste it when I get home. If I have dessert, I can still taste some of the chemicals."[42]

Smith's family may have noticed the fumes, too (and might have been sickened by them). Barry Commoner recalled meeting with OCAW workers in 1980. "It was a hot day in Washington. It was hot in the room and I could smell the phenol coming from the perspiration of these workers."

Why did any of them keep going to work in the morning? Was the pay really that great?

Mazzocchi understood: It wasn't just the money. This was what working-class people did. They went to work. They supported their families. They endured, or at least tried to.

As Smith said, "My father worked in a chemical plant right next door to the one I worked for for about twenty years. He's dead now. I had an uncle; he worked in a chemical plant; the same plant right next door to me. He died of cancer, this cancer in the throat, and it was a result of working in this chemical plant; he didn't have it before he went there. But a certain chemical that he inhaled got in his throat and his throat was a mess and he died. I mean, I don't use the expression, but he died like a dog."

And then Smith made the saddest plea of this day: "Maybe you can help me, because I just came from the hospital too."[43]

Mazzocchi believed this working-class fatalism masked a pent-up rage at bosses who used them up and tossed them away. Unleashing that anger required answers, lots of them, and quickly. These workers needed doctors and scientists to shine some light on their dark, dangerous world. But at least at first, the doctors simply could not answer most of the questions. As Dr. Jampol (whom Mazzocchi invited from the Group Health Insurance Company) reported to the group, "There's really a crying need in this field for long-range, longitudinal studies on individual workers in plants where they're exposed to chemicals, some of which we don't even know. . . ."[44]

Glenn Paulson concurred, "You can usually say flatly that there's almost no studies checking what are the effects of a combination of two [chemicals]. . . . They rarely, if ever, try to duplicate in the laboratory what actually happens in the world, where somebody is not only breathing one chemical; he's breathing half a dozen, some of which you might not even know, and he's also got lots of noise, and he's also working under stress. . . ."[45]

At this first road show, all the workers really got from the experts was a willingness to listen. But Mazzocchi believed he was igniting in them a passion to find out more and to act rather than to accept their fate. Sharing their misery and asking questions broke these workers out of their isolated, silent anger and grief. In many ways, the sessions echoed what women were doing in their new consciousness-raising groups: gather to affirm themselves and assert that it was up to them, not others, to define their needs and interests.

In Mazzocchi's version of consciousness raising, workers were discovering their shared suffering. They were starting to declare that they, not their boss, needed to define health and safety. And just as thousands of women's groups fueled a national women's movement, the Kenilworth conversation, repeated in communities across the country, would lay the foundation for the modern health and safety movement.

Mazzocchi also wanted workers to understand that they were the heart of a larger environmental movement. Leo Goodman challenged them "to serve as a force in the entire community, because it's clear that, not only do we have these pollutants on the job, but we also have some of the pollutants affecting the neighborhood, the community, and the consumer."[46]

As it turned out, many workers didn't need convincing. As Harold Smith from Woodbridge Chemical put it, "Not only do we suffer from these fumes in the plant, but the people in the community around our plant suffer. That means that somebody else's kid is inhaling these fumes when he wakes up in the morning."[47]

With so much fear in the air, Mazzocchi had to provide a sense of direction. He did it using the only framework that made sense to him—class struggle. He explained that health and safety legislation had been blocked by supposedly labor-friendly members of Congress who feared the power of the chemical and oil industries. "We have a lot of good friends here in New Jersey," Mazzocchi reminded the group. "But when the oil company barks, every congressman here—and I don't care what his party or identification is—he shakes. . . . When you talk about specific problems involving chemical and oil, you've got to dig real deep for our friends."[48]

Mazzocchi wanted the union's political "friends" to hear workers' living testimony about the horrors they faced at work. Tony stated that he wanted the Kenilworth meeting to say to legislators: "This is what's ailing us; these are the documented facts. We want you to do something about it, because we don't intend to tolerate, one moment longer, the murder of ourselves and our families"[49]

And Mazzocchi meant murder—not accident or neglect or laxness or stupidity. The murder weapon was concealed in the latency period. And Mazzocchi planned to prosecute.

"Now we've all been on picket lines; we've all been in struggles," he explained to the Kenilworth workers. "We can identify the boss on the picket line; we can identify the cop who beats our heads in on the picket line. But we just can't seem to identify the enemy when it comes to health and welfare. We all seem to fall under the spell of that expert who comes forward and says, 'Fellas, there's really nothing wrong.'"[50]

Mazzocchi was in effect agreeing with his nemesis Chet Holifield that the time for "maudlin sentimentality" had passed. From now on, he would use hard, cold facts to prosecute transgressions before Congress and the jury of public opinion. He would marshal a small army of experts and workers to offer concrete examples, medical reports, and scientific studies, building an irrefutable case.

"We've got to document every single item," he urged these workers. "You can't be shunted off by the boss. . . . We're going to make available to the group instruments for air sampling. We've got to train a safety guy in the plant to use that type of sophisticated equipment, to understand how to make that air-sample reading."[51]

And as for the traditional joint labor-management safety committees:

> I wish you'd all abolish your safety committees. I know you are very proud of your safety committees, but they're nonsense because no matter how well-intentioned your safety guys are, they only know what the company lets them know. You have to make every worker a safety chairman in the plant . . . in the area of health and the environment of the plant, every man's got to be a shop steward, every woman.[52]

Together, the workers would form a posse that would bring the murderers to justice—and perhaps in the process they would also wake the union movement from its stupor. But the posse needed new allies. Said Tony:

> I'm going to solicit the help of some of our friends—guys like Ralph Nader—who has been consistently on our side. He has recruited a bunch of young kids out of the universities, who've done more work on this subject in the last year than any thousand guys like myself and other people that I know. . . . They're bright, they're forceful, they can't be bought off, at this point in life, anyhow, and they're willing to go forward with the facts.[53]

It was time for the labor movement to catch up with the 1960s, said Mazzocchi. "We in the labor movement have been missing out. I tell you that this summer, when Nader develops his 'Raiders,' [they can] get in on the pollution question, the plant question. . . . We've got to get behind guys like this."[54]

Mazzocchi concluded: "If the contribution we're going to make to our children is a society and an environment that's not worth living in, then we should not be proud. Because when those kids grow up . . . If you think that kids are alienated today, you wait till your children are old enough to say, 'Is this what you left us?' And if they're not in a position to reverse the trend, because the atmosphere is polluted and the plant is not worth working in, and the food is not worth eating—that is a burden none of you want to bear. I know none of you do."[55]

Modern organizers might wince at Mazzocchi's barrage of negative images. But he wouldn't sugarcoat the truth. Workers had to see that a colossal struggle was ahead. Workers across the country were dying on the job, not by accident, but by design. And they were about to begin a life-and-death struggle to change the corporate world that profited by that design.

So rather than ending with the usual singing of "Solidarity Forever," Mazzocchi issued a warning. "Now, we've been through many fights," he said. "We've sung a lot of songs. We've written a lot of songs about moving the union on. But this one's a big, big obstacle to overcome and we need your assistance."

XI

Tony was still struggling over his broken marriage—and so was his estranged wife, Rose. Tony thought of himself as liberated, and especially after his separation, he veered toward libertine. The lefty gloss on sexual liberation was that marriage was bourgeois and patriarchal, subjugated women, and repressed healthy desire. But to Rose, Tony was simply a lying, cheating womanizer who broke up the family and left her to manage three girls on her own.

So which was it—progressive lover or incorrigible scoundrel? Was Mazzocchi a womanizer feasting on newly liberated '60s women or a decent, caring, politically progressive, liberated male? Some in the emerging women's movement weren't so sure there was a difference. Many radicalized women felt used and discarded by movement men. They resented being relegated to menial support chores as their men gave speeches and took all the leadership roles. They felt unfulfilled sexually by men who didn't even notice. As a result, many would have agreed that Mazzocchi's libertine ideology was nothing but a smokescreen for plain old philandering.

As one sympathetic observer put it, "Anyone who knew Mazzocchi was aware of his relationships. I am inclined to view them less ideologically and more related to his very intense and mobile life style. He was human and not necessarily a model of human perfection, or a paragon of virtue."[56]

And yet he was not a typical male chauvinist—that's why women liked him. As Tony put it, "I didn't treat women like crap."

He didn't need to flirt overtly. When he walked into a room, he spoke to men and women in much the same way. Many women, maybe even most women, found him interesting. In fact, he was particularly attractive to "liberated" female activists—young women in science, medicine, journalism, and politics who formed the backbone of the new women's movement. Part of this charm was his bright, engaging, and positive attitude. Part was the power he wielded.

Men were drawn, too. As one local OCAW union president put it, "One thing I really respected about him was not only that he was really intelligent and that he believed in the cause, but also that he could deal both with really tough, hard, nasty men as well as being incredibly kindhearted and sensitive toward his friends, especially women."[57]

Mazzocchi inherited from his gay uncle Lester a strong dose of the CP's egalitarian culture, which considered chauvinism a movement sin. And from the streets of Bensonhurst, he learned that sex was wonderful and should be relished as often as possible, just like breathing fresh air or eating Junior's cheesecake in Brooklyn.

Of course Mazzocchi had enough street smarts to know that he held a minority position better kept to himself. Nevertheless, he acted out his liberation theology on the sly as if the revolution already had arrived. In the late 1960s, it was easy to pretend that it had. The student movement, the women's movement, the antiwar movement, and the war itself blasted a gaping hole through the fortress of monogamy. Experimental lifestyles abounded—communes, collectives, group marriages, open marriages, no marriages, free love, multiple partners, same-sex couplings, no-sex couplings, and on and on in endless permutations.

The women who seemed most attracted to Mazzocchi, however, were those who experimented more cautiously and with mixed emotions on questions of monogamy, family, and gender roles. Those who loved Mazzocchi suffered some shattered illusions as they realized that their relationship to him did not preclude others. Although not all of his partners would leave laughing, for his sake and for the cause he held so dearly, they tried.

Despite his unconventionality, Mazzocchi was nearly twenty years older than the '60s generation, and he seemed straighter in form, if not content. He had no intention of joining the kids in their grand collective sexual experiments. He had enough problems. He lived in the world of broken working-class marriages.

XII

On his legislative director's salary, Mazzocchi could afford a place in Washington, DC, but certainly not another in New York, where he returned each weekend to see his three daughters. He was often a vagabond on the couches of relatives and friends, and in the beds of his lovers. It was an exhausting haul.

Frequently, he took comfort at the home of his anti-nuclear ally Robert Gilmore. Thanks to the family fortune, the Gilmores lived in a lavish town house in Greenwich Village. But a price was exacted for such visits. Over the Christmas holidays, Mazzocchi had to endure dinner parties that featured the liberal and artistic elite in the Gilmores' orbit. He was the lone working-class dropout in the room—a curio.

At one such gathering, a tall, attractive, dark-haired young woman sought him out for small talk. "I don't know. He looked so awkward there," she recalled. "Here was this nervous, shy guy off in the corner—a union person, completely different from anyone else around. And I didn't know anything about unions or politics. I was a blank slate and I was intrigued."

It was part of Susan Kleinwaks's new job as Gilmore's assistant to organize parties like this one.[58]

For reasons she never fathomed, Gilmore had selected her from a bevy of applicants. As a painter and art major, Susan had drifted toward the Gilmore job via Greece. She had been part of the Athenian art scene, working with the editor of *Greek Heritage*. From her penthouse overlooking the Aegean and the Acropolis, she'd savored the good life while meeting the likes of Prime Minister Andreas Papandreou, Gore Vidal, and Tennessee Williams. After returning to New York, she found work in the Greek Tourism Bureau. But after the Colonels' Coup of 1967, Kleinwaks's conscience drove her away, leading to her interview with Gilmore.

Clearly she cut quite a figure. "I was a clueless child," she said. "I remember bouncing in there for an interview in a miniskirt and bowler hat."

Gilmore was smitten. "They called me back for a second one," she recalled. "It seemed like an endless process. So I took another job with a film company. Then Gilmore called to insist that I take the job since he had chosen me from a field of three hundred applicants. I was certainly flattered and finally took it. I was supposed to write a brochure that described his Center for War/Peace Studies, an impossible task since they really had no idea what they wanted to do. And part of the job was helping him plan his lavish dinner parties."

A few weeks after that first encounter, Tony and Susan met again at another Gilmore party, each with their own date. "I had on a ball gown and Tony wore a tuxedo with a blue ruffled shirt," she recalled. "He found his way over to me and said, 'You look exquisite.' I was pleased."

A few days after that, Tony turned up unexpectedly at Gilmore's office near the end of the day, claiming he needed some clerical help. "It was getting late and he offered to drive me home to the Upper West Side since he was going there anyway for a meeting," she said. "It turned out there was no meeting."

After suffering through an awkward dinner, he asked her out—Mazzocchi-style. Susan remembered him saying, "I'll come by on Saturday night and we can go to a late dinner and a movie."

That Saturday, Susan dressed and then waited and waited. She had failed to grasp what Tony meant by *late.* "He was coming from seeing his kids on Long Island," Susan recalled. "I got ready at 7 PM. He showed up at about eleven. And then he comes in and starts to take off his clothes saying, 'Mind if I take a shower before we go out?' Here was this guy I hardly knew, some labor guy walking around my apartment in a towel. I wanted him out of there. It was a dinner date and nothing more."

Out they went. After dinner, Tony, both for romantic and practical purposes, wanted to know if it would be okay for him to crash on the couch.

Susan declined.

Over the next several months, the romance began in earnest, and Tony eventually moved in. With the new relationship came renewed pressure for Tony to divorce Rose. The messiness of Tony's lingering marriage wasn't easy for Susan, the good Jewish girl from suburban New Jersey. She could not continue much longer as mistress to a married man with three children. Although it seemed like the last thing Mazzocchi wanted was another marriage, he deeply wanted to continue his romance with Susan. He wanted her enough to go through the enormous hassle of ending his first marriage and letting the bourgeois state sanction a new one.

The couple's class and cultural differences intrigued both of them. "Here I was the high school dropout with this very educated, artistic, and refined woman," Tony said.

Maybe Susan fulfilled an embedded childhood wish that grew from a household steeped in classical music and books. Susan took Tony up to the high culture that he and his family so valued. And of course, he also liked her miniskirt and bowler hat. If it took a second marriage to continue the romance, so be it.

But not if Rose could help it. Knowing that Tony and Susan badly needed her to grant a divorce only intensified her resistance. Tony tried everything, including a Mexican divorce, which Rose refused to recognize. Finally, his lawyer succeeded—by drafting an agreement whose terms would punish Tony harshly for years.

"I wanted out," Tony said. "So my lawyer went over the top to be generous and put in a cost-of-living escalator in the payments. And this was just as inflation began to hit. I really paid for that. Years later at a hearing, a judge told me that my lawyer should have been disbarred and I should flee the state because the terms were so bad."

But for Tony, it was well worth it. He and Susan would share twenty-three years of marriage and raise a son and twin girls together. She also became a vital part of his work, starting with the original health and safety conferences.

Like nearly everyone who spent more than five minutes around Tony, she saw up close how this lively catalyst ignited chaos. His hectic lifestyle begged for someone to bring order, anchor his dreams, and enable his brilliant schemes. When he was president of Local 149, Dick McManus had played that role. Now it was Susan to the rescue. When Mazzocchi mentioned that he wanted the new worker health and safety conferences taped, transcribed, and turned into a historic document that would transform the nation's consciousness, Susan naively asked, "Who's going to do it?"

Not Tony, that was certain. Of course, Susan immediately filled the breach with the next question, "Why don't I do it?" And off she went, tape recorder in hand.

Like everyone else at these seminal meetings, Susan immediately perceived the glaring problems they had uncovered. Even the experts knew little about the health hazards of chemicals. As she grew more familiar with the subject matter, Susan joined the research effort, seeking out additional experts to provide information.

And like many who listened carefully to these workers describe their appalling workplace conditions, Susan began to change.

"I was really moved," she said. "I remember one of the workers who just learned about the toxic nature of the chemicals in his shop. He asked with such tragic sincerity, 'Doc, are we gonna die?'"

TEN

The Mad Rush

As the 1960s crashed to a conclusion, America came unhinged. Gone was the Kennedy optimism. Gone was trust in institutions—the government, the military, the police, marriage, and traditional gender roles. Gone, too, was the view of America as a righteous global defender of liberty and justice. Americans were confused and angry. And just when it seemed it couldn't get worse, the stench of burning bodies from My Lai wafted over us.

Seymour Hersh, a friend of Mazzocchi's, broke the story of the massacred village in December 1969. Many Americans just couldn't make sense of the fact that our boys raped women and slaughtered children in Vietnam. My Lai made many antiwar activists feel that extremism was now justified. As antiwar protests became increasingly violent, Mazzocchi charted a more positive path for social change that would attract, if not rescue, many otherwise disillusioned young progressives.

Mazzocchi saw events in Vietnam through the lens of corporate power. Preventing Vietnam from becoming socialist, he believed, stemmed from the imperative of keeping markets safe for capitalist expansion. Tony kept on his office wall a map of offshore oil leases in Vietnam. Pointing to it, he would say, "That's the reason we're there: To protect the leases of the oil companies."[1] So for Mazzocchi, protecting workplace health at oil refineries and stopping the slaughter in Vietnam were connected. As long as unfettered corporate power ruled, working people would die both in Vietnam and on the job at home.

II

Mazzocchi hoped that My Lai might finally crack open George Meany's prowar lockdown of the AFL-CIO. After all, five years had passed since Stanley Aronowitz was red-baited out of OCAW for opposing the war. Surely the labor movement was now ready for serious debate about Vietnam.

But Meany held on tighter than ever. Mazzocchi watched the federation and most unions walk away from any leadership role in the antiwar movement. The vacuum was filled quickly by ersatz young revolutionaries (like the Weathermen, named for a Bob Dylan song Mazzocchi had never even heard) who believed peaceful demonstrations and electoral work were for the weak and fearful. Mazzocchi could hear these kids taunt the moderates: "We're going to elect a bunch of opportunist politicians to stop the killing? We're going to have a big parade on the Washington Mall and pray for peace? We're going to sign a petition and hope *that* will stop the killing and raping?"

But playing at revolution without the faintest hope of mass support, Mazzocchi knew, was worse than useless. He believed it drove working people farther away from antiwar protest and ripened them for right-wing appeals. Nixon had skillfully defined a "silent majority" that longed for an explanation of what had gone wrong in America. Nixon's answer: By coddling (mostly white) students, we got immoral sex, dangerous drugs, and violent protest. By coddling blacks we got crime and riots. No more coddling!

In the spring of 1970, the New York building trades heeded Nixon's call. Two hundred unionists in hard hats, chanting "Kill the commie bastards," beat up seventy students at an antiwar protest near Wall Street. The union leaders, far from being reprimanded for their brutality, soon staged a much larger pro-war march.

If this kept up much longer, Mazzocchi could kiss good-bye any hope of a progressive working-class movement.

Fortunately, thousands of radical students did long for a connection to labor. They differed noticeably both from the self-proclaimed revolutionaries and the hippie countercultural dropouts. Many of them protested by day and studied by night. Many believed in socialism as an ideal; most hoped in the immediate future to change the world by serving the disadvantaged and the working class with their skills in science, medicine, film, education, and journalism. They valued meaning over money. They formed work "collectives" and cooperatives to practice law, publish alternative newspapers and magazines, produce movement films, found alternative schools, revamp oppressive social service agencies, and provide alternative medical care, among other things.

They saw in Mazzocchi a creative, radical unionist, self-taught, up from the ranks, and committed to workers' control, democracy, and socialism. Not only did he offer them a connection to the socialist dream, but he also offered access to what was for many of these young people an unknown world: the modern industrial workplace.

And because Tony genuinely needed smart, technically skilled people who were willing to work round the clock to stand up for workers, he welcomed these young radicals:

> I knew we couldn't conduct these struggles alone, especially struggles requiring technical help. Whether it was industrial health or a political issue like nuclear weapons testing, we needed people who had credibility and credentials, and who could give legitimacy to our work. After all, what we knew about toxics and disease, we learned from them. I mean, we didn't come up with this shit ourselves.

Many of the young people who joined Mazzocchi hadn't yet found their politics. "A few of the people we were bringing into the fray were left-wing intellectuals," said Mazzocchi. "But most of them were just scientists concerned with health and safety and environmental issues and who then came to their own radical conclusions not so much politically, but by virtue of their science. They started to say, 'Hey, this shit is bad.' Many learned their politics from us, or interacting with groups like ourselves. I understood that this was an opportunity."

Interns had started to trickle into Tony's office in the late 1960s. The first doctor was Jim Keogh. "He volunteered his services because the hospital had released him to do an elective on occupational health and safety," Tony said.

Immediately he sent Keogh to ICI America, Inc., a maker of explosives and medicinals (an interesting combo) in Tamaqua, Pennsylvania. The local president, Mazzocchi said, had reported that his members were dying of heart attacks—"but only on weekends. The local president thought there was some association between what they were doing and elevated blood pressure levels."

Keogh followed up on the hunch and uncovered an association between nitroglycerin, used in ICI's process, and the heart attacks. During the week, workers were exposed to nitroglycerin, which reduced their blood pressure.

On weekends, when they no longer inhaled those emissions, their blood pressure shot up, and their hearts seized.

"It was quite an experience for us: An MD goes in to look at a problem, assesses it, and comes up with a remedy," Mazzocchi recalled. "It was incredible. After that, I said, 'If we could get docs in, great.'" Unfortunately, he didn't have the resources.

But in 1976, Pyser Edelsack of Montefiore Hospital's Department of Social Medicine and the Albert Einstein College of Medicine told Tony he wanted to set up summer internships in occupational medicine.

Edelsack, a former Peace Corps volunteer, a community organizer, and a passionate opponent of the Vietnam War, connected easily with Mazzocchi. His many years as a community organizer also taught him to respect legitimate, elected leaders. Edelsack instinctively understood what the interns could and could not do. They needed to stay out of local union politics and couldn't wear their leftist ideologies on their sleeves.

Edelsack also knew he had to do the heavy lifting. As Mazzocchi recalled: "I told them that I could provide the places for the students to go, but Pyser would have to create the structure so that it had value for the students."

The first group of students included not only medical interns but also a radical economics student invited by Mazzocchi. They were sent to the Merck pharmaceutical complex in Rahway, New Jersey. Mazzocchi hoped they'd uncover why so many workers suffered from elevated serum enzymes, an indication of liver damage.

After eight weeks of investigation, the students produced a classic of the internship program: *Merck Is Not a Candy Factory,* a sixty-four-page catalog of the Merck workers' exposures and their impact, ranging from lung irritation to heart disease. They also proposed collective bargaining demands, suggested a worker education program, and called for further research.

The student radicals Mazzocchi unleashed onto the Merck local had begun the summer believing that the root cause of worker illness was capitalism, and they'd finished the summer even more convinced of it. Their report concluded:

> Our study this summer has confirmed our belief that unhealthy and unsafe working conditions are the end result of management's drive to maximize profits, and not an inherent feature of industrial

> or chemical production. The experience at Merck has served to sharpen for us the fundamental question: Can industry that is privately owned and organized for the profit of a few, establish as its first priority the well-being of working people?[2]

It was a ballsy move for the students to present such a report to the local union—and for Mazzocchi to approve it. But for Tony, the radical interns weren't radical enough. He took exception to their assertion that unsafe working conditions were "not an inherent feature of industrial or chemical production." He thought toxic chemicals *were* inherently dangerous, no matter who owned the means of production. Certainly, production for profit made it worse, but Mazzocchi believed that producing poisons would inevitably expose workers, the community, and the environment to long-lasting harm. Mazzocchi wanted poisons removed from production and use because, as he put it, "What's in gets out, sooner or later—always."

He pointed out the correlation between the rise and spread of cancer and the rapid rise of the postwar petrochemical economy. He was certain that if the government set up a national cancer registry, it would show elevated levels of the disease in areas with many chemical and petrochemical plants. To stop cancer, he believed society needed to forgo toxic chemistry entirely. "Civilization existed for five thousand years without these chemicals and plastics," he said. "We can do so again."

In the summer of 1977, another crew of medical interns took on the Union Carbide facility in Boundbrook, New Jersey, a mammoth plastics complex that produced Bakelite, the heavy-duty plastic used in standard telephones and radio cases of the era. During the Vietnam War, it also made the material for body bags. The president of the fifteen-hundred-member local, Vern Jensen, worked with Edelsack to structure the internships.

At first glance, Jensen seemed to be part of the anti-Mazzocchi opposition. He had supported Barry Goldwater, admired Ayn Rand, and for years opposed affiliation with OCAW. To beat back an OCAW organizing drive, Jensen distributed the slanderous Victor Riesel column accusing Stanley Aronowitz of being a communist plant. "I put together a leaflet with the article and passed it out to the John Birchers in Building 105 who at the time supported the affiliation with OCAW," Jensen said. "The effect was immediate. They dropped their support of OCAW."

But Mazzocchi won him over. "I admired his intelligence," Jensen said. "I knew he truly believed in his ideals even if I didn't agree with them. He was totally committed, not self-aggrandizing. I knew he was willing to sacrifice for his cause. And he just wouldn't lie or equivocate and had not the slightest degree of phoniness."

Vern Jensen became a fierce Mazzocchi ally. Edelsack recalled a meeting at Jensen's local where "a guy in the back yelled, 'Oh, that Mazzocchi, he's a communist.' And I remember Vern's response was, 'Well, if that's communism, then I'm a communist, too,' and they all applauded."[3]

Jensen, whose distinguished shock of silver hair and well-spoken ways made him resemble an MD himself, enjoyed working with the interns. "We were getting a new generation of industrial doctors to better understand the workplace. There was stuff they learned from us that they couldn't possibly have learned in a classroom."[4]

And industrial doctors were badly needed: At that time, fewer than four of the roughly ten thousand medical students graduated in the United States each year went on to specialize in occupational medicine.[5]

Said Mazzocchi, "Here I was—one single person. I was trying to do something, and all these folks, these soldiers came out of nowhere. And they had talents that none of us possessed."

III

In late 1969, one such soldier, only twenty, marched into Mazzocchi's office with a perceptible swagger. His brown-eyed, handsome face sported a substantial mustache, and his unruly mop of curly dark hair cascaded down to his shoulders. He was Steven Wodka, already a veteran of the SDS wars at Columbia University and the United Farm Workers' struggles in California. He'd been raised in a middle-class Jewish home in suburban Philadelphia; his high school social activism revolved mostly around the National Federation of Temple Youth. But by the time Wodka became president of his Temple Youth chapter in the mid-'60s, the group was engaged in civil rights activism. He'd registered as a conscientious objector to protest the war. During his first week at Columbia, he'd protested against a job recruiter from Dow Chemical, maker of napalm.

Wodka was among the SDS militants who in April 1968 occupied Columbia's administration building and held the dean hostage. The SDSers, led by Mark Rudd, wanted the university to halt construction on a new gym that would displace Harlem residents, discontinue war-related research, and grant all protesters amnesty from prosecution and university discipline.

"I was right behind Mark Rudd when he picked up the walkway directional stand and smashed open the side door of Low Library, the administration building," Steve said. "I was right there when they were sitting with their feet on the desk of President Kirk, smoking his cigars and leafing through his stack of *Playboy* magazines."

After the occupation, police violence, and mass arrests, the university closed for the remainder of the semester. Wodka considered his options. "I couldn't stand Columbia anymore," he said. "The curriculum was uninspiring. The school had so much complicity in the war. My girlfriend and I decided to go to Antioch in Ohio."

Antioch ran an unusual work-study program—students engaged in classroom study for three months then worked or interned away from campus for the following three months. In the fall of 1968, someone from Cesar Chavez's United Farm Workers Organizing Committee visited Antioch looking for volunteers to help farmworkers in California. Wodka and his girlfriend signed up.

"I ended up with the lawyers," Wodka recalled. "They had me work on a lawsuit against the county agricultural commissioners, which gave out permits to spray pesticides over the farms. The workers would be sent out into the fields too soon after the spraying and they would get sick. They lent me this 1960 Corvair station wagon and I would drive out to these little airstrips and take pictures of what they loaded into the crop duster. Then I would follow the plane as it flew over and dusted the fields. Next they sent me up to the University of California–Berkeley medical school library to look up everything I could find about these pesticides. I stayed with the United Farm Workers for three months. It was the most meaningful work I had ever done."

It was also excellent preparation for the work he would soon be doing in spades with Mazzocchi.

Having heard about Nader's Raiders, Wodka approached Nader to request a spot for his next work-study period in the summer of 1969. Nader told Wodka that "given my interests in labor and pesticides, I should work with a good union person." Nader called a couple; Mazzocchi called back. "He told me he could give me a hundred dollars a week for three months," Wodka recalled. "I took the offer."

So while Wodka's SDS pals argued about the future of workers' revolution, Wodka was about to become the primary field lieutenant in a war to win worker control over the workplace environment. He had sauntered into one of the most exciting social change jobs in America.

The Mazzocchi-Wodka show opened in early 1970 when Herb Sterling, an OCAW rep from Pennsylvania, called with questions about beryllium hazards at the Kawecki Berylco facility in Hazelton, Pennsylvania, deep in northern Appalachian coal country.

"Sterling was a dapper guy, always dressed to the nines, drove a Cadillac," Tony said. Sterling wanted Mazzocchi to meet with the workers to discuss the beryllium problem. Mazzocchi wouldn't go without an expert to take along. Harriet Hardy of MIT, the world's leading expert on beryllium, was his first choice. Hardy said she doubted the workers' charges because she had helped Kawecki Berylco develop the safety design for this very facility. Nevertheless, she sent a doctor from Philadelphia to join Mazzocchi at the meeting.

The Philly doctor was a disaster. Although trained by Hardy, he was wedded to the old theory that beryllium problems reflected worker susceptibility: It was like an allergy—not a problem of overexposure. But after listening to the tapes of the session with the Philly doctor, Hardy realized that these workers were in serious danger. This time she provided Mazzocchi with a more expert industrial hygiene engineer, Richard Chamberlin.

Mazzocchi assigned Wodka to work on the case, and soon, Tony said, Kawecki Berylco "became his baby."

"I drove up there and back, again and again—stayed in motels and called Mazzocchi each day to talk strategy," Wodka recalled.

After touring the plant, Wodka eagerly relayed his findings to Mazzocchi and Hardy. "I told them that, literally, I was walking through so much beryllium dust in the plant that I could see my footprints in the dust," he said. "It was pure, 100 percent beryllium."

Hardy's response took Wodka by surprise. Instead of just worrying about the workers, she instructed Wodka himself to get a chest X-ray that same day. Wodka recalled, "They take me over to the hospital, and they shoot a chest X-ray of me to get a baseline because they were fearful that I had been overexposed. We didn't have respirators during the inspection. We just went through it. And that's when we decided that things had to change."

Wodka had to negotiate with the company to make sure the union's experts had free access to the plant. What were the plant managers thinking as they faced the twenty-one-year-old across the bargaining table? "There are these pictures of me with my friggin' hair down to my shoulders," Wodka said. "I'm standing around a table, negotiating with the clean-cut company guys with crew cuts."

According to Andy Soltis of the local union's health and safety committee, "Steve was something else. He'd come into those negotiations, throw his feet up on the table and start demanding. Those management guys didn't know how to deal with this punk kid. He kept them off balance from the start."[6]

Mazzocchi and Wodka soon arranged for a health study to be conducted by Dr. Homayoun Kazemi, a protégé of Hardy who headed the pulmonary unit at Massachusetts General Hospital. "He was in charge of running the beryllium-case registry at that time," Wodka said. "Since the 1950s, Harriet Hardy had gotten the industry to agree that every case of beryllium disease that was diagnosed should be entered into this registry—so they could be followed and you could understand the disease."

Kazemi's study found that many workers had signs of beryllium-related diseases. The company refused to address the problem. But workers insisted—with a six-month strike at the end of 1972. Their demands were groundbreaking: They wanted the union to have full control of the facility's industrial hygiene program. The union, Wodka said, wanted the power "to monitor the facility and jobs whenever it wanted—with its own equipment, with its own people. If beryllium was above a certain level, the operation would be shut down and the workers would be paid."

Wodka said the union also demanded that the company "stop burning beryllium-contaminated scrap out at the landfill—rags and all kinds of stuff that was polluting the air. Beryllium doesn't burn, it doesn't decompose, in a fire. So they were releasing it all out into the community. This wasn't an occupational health and safety issue—it was an environmental issue." Again, OCAW was breaching the wall between worker health and community health.

Mazzocchi enticed Homer Bigart, the famous *New York Times* war correspondent, to cover the strike. Under the headline, "Lung-Disease Problem, Traced to Beryllium Refinery, Plagues Hazelton, Pa.," Bigart skillfully presented the union's case. OCAW, he wrote, "contends that the company has done too little, too late and that it has no confidence in the state and Federal agencies that enforce standards for the workers' health and safety. The union wants the right to monitor the air in the plant and quit work whenever beryllium dust reaches unacceptable levels. . . ."[7]

Industrial hygienist Richard Chamberlin, Bigart wrote, was brought in by OCAW members who were "skeptical of air samplings taken in the plant by the company. The Federal Government has set the maximum permissible level for airborne beryllium dust at an average of two micrograms per cubic feet of air in any eight-hour period. Mr. Chamberlin's measurements in September, 1971 showed beryllium concentrations as high as 1,310 micrograms in one plant location. . . ."[8]

Bigart also reported the union's most visionary demand: "The union will also seek automatic retirement at full pay plus medical benefits when a worker is found to have berylliosis. . . ."[9]

With Mazzocchi's prompting, the *Times* ran additional pieces and the local *Hazelton Standard* wrote a lengthy feature in 1972. According to the paper, the union wanted to "give the afflicted not only automatic retirement with full pay plus medical expenses, but also would award them all pay increases won in future negotiations. . . . 'We want to bring some sense of justice to the situation,' Wodka said, claiming the company should be financially responsible to those whose capacity for earning a living has been 'permanently destroyed.'"[10]

In the end, said Wodka, "We didn't win the right to shut down the job with pay, but we certainly won a great deal more than any union had won before. We did get union people to do monitoring of the plant. And they were trained not by the friggin' company, but by MIT—by Chamberlin—on how to do industrial hygiene monitoring. MIT analyzed the samples. And the company paid for the training and for the analysis."

By then, Wodka said, "We all knew from Mazzocchi that worker control of health and safety was the only way to solve these problems."[11]

The beryllium battle set the pattern for how Wodka and Mazzocchi would work together for the next decade. "The main thing we learned was, the minute there was a problem, Steve was on his horse, into the plant," Tony said. "Because if you let the issues fester for a while, the local union leaders would start chickening out."

Did it really work, sending this acerbic longhaired kid out on his white horse?

"At the end of the day I didn't have anyone else to send," Mazzocchi said with a laugh. "He was smart. Our workers got over their reservations right away if somebody was there to help them. Steve always had good rapport with the union rep—because if you didn't, you were out. And Steve was very thorough. I mean, the guy was meticulous."

And when it came to tackling workers' problems, Wodka was a bulldog. Over the next ten years, Mazzocchi could always count on his undivided loyalty, lawyer-like craftsmanship, and ferocious tenacity.

IV

As the 1960s collapsed, Mazzocchi shifted into high gear. His workplace environment road show toured the country with remarkable success. After its debut in New Jersey, the show moved from Montreal to Baltimore, Fort Wayne, and Tulsa. By then it was quite polished. Everyone knew their lines. Glenn Paulson walked the workers through the basics of chemical exposures, and workers poured out their toxic horror stories.

Thanks to Susan, Tony could now send transcripts along with his questions to dozens of scientists. Why was there a cluster of early deaths at the Phillips Petroleum facility in Texas? What problems were caused by the new and expanding use of enzymes in detergents on Staten Island? Why were there so many cancers at Texaco?

Of course, the conferences also mobilized workers to pressure their congressional members for a new occupational health and safety bill. And Mazzocchi also knew he had to reach the general public—which meant working the press. He helped spur dozens of local and national reporters to investigate workplace hazards.

He even had the *Today* show in tow for an OCAW workplace environment conference in Atlanta in January 1970. Under the glare of TV cameras, Mazzocchi told workers that to win, they had to build a profound connection with the emerging environmental movement—which was just then organizing a day of teach-ins around the country. The event's prime organizer, Dennis Hays, dubbed it Earth Day.

As the *Today* cameras rolled, Mazzocchi told workers, "We're getting involved in the environmental teach-ins around Earth Day. We think we have a real stake in the teach-ins." He wrapped his movement around the environmental cause:

> I received many letters in my office when I first became legislative director from our union members saying, "Listen, don't complain about air pollution or water pollution because you're going to have the plant closed down." And frankly, this had a retarding effect as far as my doing anything about these environmental problems. . . . Now everyone is concerned about the environment, and we're making the point that you can't be concerned about the general environment unless you're concerned about the industrial environment, because the two are inseparable. After all, we create the pollutants. Let's face it, fellows, we are responsible for most of the pollutants being introduced into the total environment. We make them. We put them into the water. When you read these conference transcripts and see what we're putting into the water, which we ultimately have to drink and depend upon for life, and what we introduce into the air, you have a very frightening picture. . . . We've got to control the plant environment and we've got to tell the truth about what we're doing to the plant environment.[12]

Only days after the Atlanta conference, Mazzocchi was asked to serve as chair for the centerpiece Earth Day rally held in New York City's Union Square. Other participants included actors Paul Newman and Dustin Hoffman, conductor and composer Leonard Bernstein, the cast of the hit Broadway show *Hair,* Mayor John Lindsay, and folksinger Pete Seeger.

"They didn't make me the chair because of my looks," said Mazzocchi. "It was because I talked about the link between the inside of the plant and the community. It was because the union was leading this fight."

Mazzocchi didn't realize that he was in the middle of a "be-in"—a '60s-style festival of music, protest, street theater, dancing, and drugs. Some hundred thousand people drifted through Union Square that day, many of them high as a kite. The largest of hundreds of such gatherings across the country, New York Earth Day mixed hippie counterculture and serious political protest. As *The New York Times* reported on April 23:

> At mid-afternoon, the full range in mood of protests was reflected in a musical counter point: On 14th Street the folk singer Odetta was singing "We Shall Overcome" while at the other end of the square a rock group was chanting, "Power to the People." . . . The Environmental Action Coalition sold a "New York Pollution Survival Kit" with a list of 40 actions that individuals could take to fight noise, waste and dirt. A quotation from Pogo on one of the booths caught this side of Earth Day: "We have met the enemy and they is us." . . . On Fifth Avenue, a youthful group of demonstrators called attention to the utility company's connection with fish kills in the Hudson River by displaying several dead fish. "You're next. People! You're next!" they cried, . . . Each visitor to the Square had to improvise his own Earth Day. Some resolved the range of choices by taking part in a nonstop Frisbee game, . . . Thousands crowded into a block-long polyethylene "bubble" on 17th Street to breathe pure, filtered air; before the enclosure had been open to the public for half an hour the pure air carried unmistakable whiffs of marijuana.[13]

But events overseas partly overshadowed the festive mood. In his speech at Union Square, Mayor Lindsay warned, "Pure water will not wash away the stain of an immoral war."[14]

V

Mazzocchi faced a choice. His strategy for getting Congress to pass a new worker safety law was paying off. Labor was united in its support. Rank-and-file evidence from Mazzocchi's road shows flooded congressional offices. The media was picking up the issue. The environmental movement lent its support, as did Ralph Nader and experts of all kinds. Even Richard

Nixon seemed interested in throwing a bone to blue-collar workers—especially those who supported his war efforts.

Maybe Mazzocchi should keep his mouth shut about the war until after the bill was passed and Nixon signed it? Not a chance.

By now, union offices all over DC were filled with staff and elected officials who hated the war, but feared reprisal if they openly declared dissent. Apart from the UAW, which had split from the AFL-CIO in 1968, no major national union had dared to challenge AFL-CIO president George Meany's pro-war stance. But failing to challenge it only increased the public perception that labor was unified in support of the war.

In fact, antiwar sentiment had been building in the labor movement since the mid-1960s. Billy Dodds, the UAW political director, recalled, "Before Walter Reuther came out against the war he was getting a lot of antiwar heat from members of the executive board, especially Emil Mazey, the secretary treasurer. That gave me room to also take antiwar positions."[15] (This was the same Mazey who had led "Bring Home the Boys" demonstrations among the troops in the Pacific at the end of World War II.)

Bill Bywater, a leader of the International Union of Electrical Workers, recalled how hard and lonely it was to stand up against the war at national AFL-CIO meetings. "I remember the 1967 gathering in Bal Harbour," he said. "I was one of two or three delegates who spoke up against the war. Afterward I almost came to blows with pro-war union people who were harassing me."[16]

In the fall of 1967, a handful of labor leaders gathered in Chicago to set up the Labor Leadership Assembly for Peace. In addition to Mazey, the sponsors included left-leaning labor leaders like Pat Gorman from the Meatcutters and Frank Rosenblum from the Amalgamated Clothing and Textile Workers Union. Al Hartung, from the small, left-wing International Woodworkers of America, was the only national union president.

According to Albert Lannon and Marvin Rogoff, who attended, "While the delegates to the founding meeting may have been members of many unions, few of them could speak for their organizations; while they individually were for an end to the war, their unions remained part of the labor-hawk consensus." The group's plan to form a significant antiwar labor organization "quietly faded away."[17]

Rogoff, a staffer for the American Federation of Government Employees in DC, encouraged locals in his union to adopt antiwar resolutions, and several did. Immediately, the union's top leaders sent out a ludicrous memo explaining that the peace symbol was really an "anti-Christ broken cross—the mark of the beast—designed by Emperor Nero."[18] Those locals that didn't revoke their peace resolutions were disbanded and eventually given away to other unions.

Rogoff's luck changed when he ran into Tony Mazzocchi, who was quietly mobilizing against the war. "When I got to DC, I started to host a series of brown-bag lunch meetings about the war," Mazzocchi said. "I would get the antiwar guys together to see if we could move our unions more against the war."

Even as his workplace health campaign was taking off, Mazzocchi was expanding his antiwar effort. In November 1969, he invited union representatives to hear Senator Alan Cranston and Victor Reuther speak about the war. Tony also spoke. "About fifty people came," he said. "And Vic Reuther—it was the first time he stepped out. A lot of people came out of the closet."

In a follow-up meeting, Mazzocchi urged the closeted labor peaceniks to sign their names to a full-page ad in *The Washington Post* protesting the war. He recruited Rogoff and Roy Morgan to draft the ad and tried to pay for it by getting ten dollars from each of the five hundred Washington-area unionists he expected to sign. Victor Reuther kicked in an extra five hundred. But Mazzocchi could only find about a hundred signers, so he persuaded a wealthy patron of peace to donate the remainder.

Enter Bernard Rapoport, the Texas insurance tycoon.

The Mazzocchi-Rapoport relationship would develop into one of the most unusual and warm friendships either would ever experience. Bernard, the son of a Jewish socialist refugee from pre-Bolshevik Russia, grew up in small Texas towns where his father, a traveling salesman, peddled goods and preached against capitalism. "My father would get up on a little wooden crate and speak in Spanish to the local residents, urging them to cast off their capitalist yokes and join the revolution," Bernard said.[19] (Rapoport proudly has saved his father's Socialist Party of America membership card, Local 18, San Antonio, Texas, dated June 7, 1914.)

His father was active in labor struggles in the 1930s South and took Bernard with him on his visits with key CIO organizers. The senior

Rapoport settled down long enough to allow his son to attend the University of Texas during the Depression. To pay his way through, Bernard worked in a local jewelry store. He quickly realized he possessed a gift for business. While Bernard had inherited his father's passion for justice and his striving restlessness, he differed when it came to socialism. "I believed in the dream of socialism but didn't think it would work," said Bernard. "Capitalism, done right, seemed to be the best system."

The conflict between ideology and earning a buck resolved itself when Rapoport became arguably the most radical businessman in the country—and one of the most successful. After finishing college and spending more time in the jewelry business, he moved into insurance. But he had no intention of working his way up the corporate ladder. "I realized that I could never compete with the big boys. But I saw something that they were missing—a worker niche."

He realized that working-class people needed small, affordable insurance policies that allowed them to pay only a few dollars per month. He also knew they needed coverage that continued while they were on strike or unemployed—even if they missed some payments. And he understood that the best way to reach these working people was through their unions, where he was already known thanks to his father's efforts.

So Bernard Rapoport set up an insurance company in Indianapolis, Indiana. (He moved to Waco, Texas, in 1955.) He put together a sales team—the only unionized one in the country—that visited union families door to door.

He approached union presidents with a simple proposition. He would offer each union member a small but not trivial amount of life insurance for free. Union leaders were only too happy to write a letter to their members offering this great benefit. To get it, all workers had to do was write back; one of Bernard's sales reps would then make a home visit to do the paperwork and explain the free policy. Of course, once in the door, the rep also would pitch additional policies designed for working-class budgets. It worked in two out of three homes.

As working-class incomes grew during the 1960s, Rapoport's niche turned him into a multimillionaire. He donated generously to civil rights causes, the antiwar movement, and liberal Democrats.

When Rapoport met Mazzocchi, it was political love at first sight. "I think I was introduced to Bernard in '66 by a mutual friend," Mazzocchi said. "We hit it off right away. He was antiwar. I was in the middle of building the Labor for Peace group."

Bernard remembered fondly their encounter at the 1968 Chicago convention: "I was there with my son Ronnie, a junior at Oberlin, who passionately wanted McCarthy to win," Bernard said. "Tony was at the same hotel, the Drake, I believe, and we watched the carnage below. Tony tried to console my boy, who was devastated by the outcome of the convention."

Bernard saw in Tony a labor leader who believed in justice and socialism with all his soul. In short, he saw the spirit of his father. And perhaps he saw the kind of person his father always hoped Bernard would become. As Rapoport put it after Mazzocchi died, "I had never met another like him in the modern labor movement. He was absolutely straight ahead for the cause. He couldn't be bought. He wouldn't sell out—he was pure for the cause like no other."

So when Mazzocchi needed money for the antiwar ad, Rapoport came through. The ad appeared in *The Washington Post* on February 25, 1970, with 110 names from twenty-two unions. It was the first major labor statement against the war. As Mazzocchi put it, "I finally got my labor progressive friends to say, 'Fuck it.'"

Mazzocchi titled the ad "A Rich Man's War and Poor Man's Fight," a phrase borrowed from a Civil War protest poster that chastised wealthy men who bought their way out of service. The headline was superimposed over the famous photo of a GI whose haunting dark eyes peered from the shadow of a combat helmet on which the soldier had written WAR IS HELL.

The ad's text was a direct appeal to rank-and-file workers:

> **Hawk or Dove, We are all Clay Pigeons.**
> The greatest horror of Vietnam is its cost in lives . . . 40,000 young Americans so far, and hundreds of thousands of Vietnamese. No amount of American money, or material, or good intentions can buy back the lives lost. Nor assuage the agony of thousands of our families. This is horror enough. But Vietnam creates a second horror: The disfigurement of our society and our economy.
>
> We are active trade unionists who are convinced that every dollar spent in Vietnam inflicts a scar on our nation and our economy. We

share a common determination that the war in Vietnam must end . . . NOW.

Compelling economic facts convince us that the Vietnam War is a threat to the American people and to the kind of society we, as trade unionists, are trying to establish.

VIETNAM EATS UP WORKERS' WAGES

VIETNAM CAUSES INFLATION

AS LONG AS WE ARE IN VIETNAM, WE WILL NOT ACHIEVE TAX JUSTICE

AS LONG AS WE ARE IN VIETNAM, WE WILL PAY SKY-HIGH INTEREST RATES

AS LONG AS WE ARE IN VIETNAM, WE WILL HAVE INSUFFICIENT HOUSING, EDUCATION AND HEALTH CARE; OUR CITIES WILL ROT

Readers were urged to join a new organization, Labor for Peace, "to demand an immediate withdrawal of troops and cessation of hostilities in Vietnam, and to begin putting our money where it counts . . . at home."

The 110 names that followed were listed in two columns in no discernible order. Each name was accompanied with a home-city address and no union affiliation, making it clear that the signers represented only themselves and not the unions they served.

Labor for Peace quickly followed up on the ad with a vigil and fast in Lafayette Park that drew about four hundred antiwar laborites. However, the coverage paled in comparison with the media circus created a few days later when two hundred construction workers pummeled antiwar demonstrators near Wall Street and then organized their own pro-war demonstration.

To further spread the ideas behind Labor for Peace, Mazzocchi spurred the creation of an eighty-page booklet, *A Rich Man's War, A Poor Man's Fight: A Handbook for Trade Unionists on the Vietnam War.* Released on Labor Day, 1971, it made some of the same arguments as the ad, but also primed workers on how to answer such questions as:

- What about the prisoners of war?
- Don't we have an obligation to help Vietnam?
- But doesn't the President have more facts than we do?
- Don't we have to resist aggression?

- Isn't "Vietnamization" and the "Phased Withdrawal" of American troops really ending our involvement?
- Why should the United States lose a war for the first time?
- Isn't the "Peace Movement" just a bunch of freaks and subversives?
- Why should I care if a bunch of "crazies" gets busted?

"I had a printing press I had brought down with me from my local on Long Island, an offset press, and we actually printed this book," said Mazzocchi. "Guys from the OCAW research department put it together. And it was the best piece I had seen on the war. We put out the line that workers had no real interest in the war. They were gonna fight it, and they were gonna be punished economically. It forced people to take a stand."

VI

Mazzocchi's antiwar organizing did not distract him from his quest for national health and safety legislation.

The workers who had been drawn to Mazzocchi's road shows across the country had provided poignant congressional testimony in support of the new legislation.

"Our contribution was making the issue public through the conferences we had" and through bringing in workers to testify before Congress, said Mazzocchi. "I said to the labor lobbyists: 'You guys know Capitol Hill, but in the absence of public pressure, you're not gonna get anywhere.'"

The lack of public pressure, Mazzocchi believed, had allowed a previous bill proposed by President Johnson to get bottled up in committee in 1968. The war had also pulled Johnson's attention away from the bill. And the outdated pictures of hazardous workplace conditions that the Department of Labor presented in hearings and booklets didn't help the cause, either.

After Nixon's election in 1968, the Democratic-controlled Congress had again pushed forward a bill. This time the combination of intense congressional lobbying and Mazzocchi's road show and regional congressional hearings kept the bill before the public. "The heavy lobbying," said Tony, was done by Jack Sheehan, the environmentally aware legislative director of the Steelworkers—as well as George Taylor from the AFL-CIO and Howard McQuiggen from the AFL-CIO's Industrial Union Department.

Ralph Nader was also involved. "I went over the proposed legislation paragraph by paragraph with Phil Burton [a Democratic congressman from California]," Nader recalled. "The only unions really in play were the Steelworkers, OCAW, the Meatcutters, and the Textile Workers."[20]

The swirl of public activity made some kind of bill seem inevitable. Nixon proposed an industry-friendly version that would have relied more on self-policing by private industry and state government than on federal enforcement. But Sheehan and other labor lobbyists pushed hard for the Johnson bill, which called for federal standard setting and enforcement by the Department of Labor.

In the end, they compromised: The Occupational Safety and Health Act (OSHA) gave the secretary of labor the power to set health and safety standards and to enforce them through workplace inspections. A separate commission would act as a kind of court of appeals. The National Institute of Occupational Safety and Health (NIOSH), lodged in another agency, was charged with conducting workplace health studies, while OSHA focused on regulations and enforcement.

The Clean Air Act of 1970 established the framework used for OSHA, said Sheehan: "Without the Clean Air Act, there would be no OSHA. All the legislative constructs, terminology, and technical expertise required for the OSHA legislation were learned from our work on the Clean Air Act."[21]

The Steelworkers' focus on air pollution started in 1948 when a temperature inversion and the fumes from a smelter in Donora, Pennsylvania, combined to kill twenty residents and sicken six thousand. Clearly, the Steelworkers realized, they had to address the problem of fumes both inside and outside the mills. In 1963, it supported the first Clean Air Act; in 1969, with Sheehan's prompting, it held an unprecedented national union legislative conference on air pollution in steel-producing communities, which helped lead to passage of the Clean Air Act of 1970. (The union convened another national conference on the smelting industries.[22])

Steelworkers president I. W. Abel made it clear that the union would not shill for the polluters. "We refuse to be the buffer between positive pollution control activity by the community and resistance by industry," he said.[23]

So the union's central role in passing OSHA was no aberration. "OSHA was never high on the AFL-CIO priority list, and it was willing to let a weaker bill pass," said Sheehan. "But we made it a priority and worked hard with Senator Harrison Williams of New Jersey and Jacob Javitz of New York to get a much better bill than Nixon had proposed."

One of Mazzocchi's contributions to the OSHA effort, according to Sheehan, was his "particular charisma with the press. Mazzocchi, with his abrupt, strong, anti-industrial language, gave them very good quotes."

During the signing ceremony on December 29, 1970, Secretary of Labor James D. Hodgeson referred to "a new national passion . . . for environmental improvement. And when you think of it, what environment is more important to 80 million working Americans than their workplace?"[24] (He had previously proclaimed at a Steelworker convention that the bill would be passed only over his dead body.[25])

As Nixon signed the bill, he was flanked by labor and industry heavies: George Meany, I. W. Abel, Frank Fitzsimmons (the president of the Teamsters), as well as the presidents of the chamber of commerce and the National Association of Manufacturing. Mazzocchi was nowhere to be found.

The new law contained several remarkable advances for worker safety. First, it established a "general duty clause," which required that each employer "shall furnish . . . a place of employment which is free from recognized hazards that are causing or are likely to cause death or serious physical harm to his employees." Second, it gave unions and other interested groups the right to petition the secretary of labor for new or stronger health and safety standards. Third, it allowed unions to call for immediate inspections in the case of "imminent danger." In addition, it set up a regime of record keeping, unannounced inspections, and federal enforcement.

The new law also established the Occupational Safety and Health Review Commission (OSHRC), an independent federal agency that would determine contested citations or penalties resulting from OSHA inspections.[26] Finally, the act created NIOSH to conduct research and education to promote workplace health and safety.

While Sheehan and the Steelworkers deserve much credit for OSHA, the US Department of Labor's legislative history left little doubt about Mazzocchi's role. In fact, he was the only labor leader quoted: "Unions felt that strong action was needed to deal with the hazards of the workplace, especially alarming new chemical dangers. As Anthony Mazzocchi of the Oil, Chemical and Atomic Workers union put it: 'The mad rush of science has propelled us into a strange and uncharted environment. . . . We grope in the dark and can light only a few candles.'"[27]

By organizing under the new law, Mazzocchi hoped he and his allies could shake up labor's complacent bureaucracies and turn unions once again into leaders of a great cause. Tony wanted to use the fight for a safe workplace to help fuse together the antiwar movement, the young people inspired by Nader, and the growing environmental movement with the millions of workers exposed and injured on the job. He hoped these forged movements would fundamentally challenge corporate power.

But why make workplace health—of all issues—the centerpiece? Mazzocchi believed that corporate capitalism could not contain, let alone solve, the occupational safety and health crisis. In his view there was a fundamental conflict between profits and productivity on one hand, and health on the other. In fact, Mazzocchi believed that cancer and other workplace-related diseases were the unavoidable by-products of the drive for profits in the petrochemical industry.

Tony's not-so-hidden message was, "If we want a healthy society, then we'd better find another way to organize oil and chemical production." The beauty of workplace health struggles was that once engaged, workers could see for themselves how reckless companies could be in the pursuit of profits and productivity. In worksite after worksite, workers were learning the hard way that their employers' insatiable drive for profits would kill them unless they challenged the fundamentals of corporate power and control. For Mazzocchi, this contradiction gave health and safety transformative power to change capitalism.

And by linking worker health and safety to the rising "green" movement, the challenge to corporate power would be more potent still.

VII

Unfortunately, the Occupational Safety and Health Act fell far short of Mazzocchi's dreams. It failed to establish the Precautionary Principle, which would have required that chemicals be tested *before* they were foisted on workers and society. It didn't give workers the "right to know" about the ingredients and health effects of the chemicals to which they were exposed. Corporations that violated OSHA regulations incurred only minor fines.

But Mazzocchi's team jumped on the language that allowed unions and other groups to petition the secretary of labor for new and stricter exposure limits.

"We were vigorous in using every remedy provided by the law," Mazzocchi said. "OCAW went before the review board more times than all the other unions put together to make sure the government enforced its citations. And we petitioned for new standards."

As soon as OSHA opened its doors, Mazzocchi filed the first complaint, leading to the first OSHA citation. The employer was the Allied Chemical Corporation in Moundsville, West Virginia. The complaint: unregulated worker exposures to mercury. The struggle to force this company to stop its evident poisoning of workers showed both OSHA's limits and the union's determination.

Starting in 1965, the members of OCAW Local 3-586 had sought protection from exposures at the Allied Chemical chlor-alkali facility. The plant produced chlorine through the interaction of mercury in electrolytic cells. The local did what most unions did back then: It asked management to reduce the obvious mercury hazards. And Allied Chemical did what most such companies did: It denied there was a problem and did very little to clean up the mess.

Facing a profit squeeze, the company had cut its maintenance crews. This led to more mercury dripping from many of the 104 cells in the building. On May 26, 1970, after five years of deteriorating conditions, the local union president, Tom Riggle, wrote to Mazzocchi's office for help.

Mazzocchi's interns supplied Riggle with details on the dangers of chlorine and mercury. The local again complained to management about exposures in the cell building, citing their new information. This time, management tried job blackmail. According to a detailed report written by Susan Mazzocchi, the workers "were told that business was bad and there was no money to buy the necessary equipment for repairs or to add to the maintenance crews. According to Riggle, on several occasions the workers were warned that their efforts to achieve safe work conditions could result in closing down the plant."[28]

During this pre-OSHA period, the local union took what it viewed as a very bold step—it wrote another letter. This time it went not only to Mazzocchi (on November 1, 1970) but also to Allied Chemical; the US Department of Health, Education and Welfare; the US Department of Labor; the West Virginia Labor Federation; the West Virginia Department of Labor; the governor of West Virginia; the state's two senators; and its congressional members. And President Nixon, just to be sure. The letter provided a detailed technical account of the source and extent of workers' exposures: "The South Plant uses the mercury type cells to produce chlorine, caustic soda and hydrogen. There are 104 cells of this type, each cell containing approximately 3600 lbs of raw mercury or a total of around 187 tons. . . . At present there are five employees . . . with high mercury in their urine (500–700 mg/liter). We have several others in the so-called danger point of 500 mg/liter. . . .[29]

"We have exhausted our means of combating these hazards locally," the letter explained. "In 1965 this company quelled any further investigation by giving twenty-eight employees that work in this cell building a complete physical examination. No one ever heard or received any results of this examination."[30]

The letter set in motion a tragicomedy of inspection and enforcement. During the pre-OSHA phase, state inspectors came for a look-see. But in keeping with tradition, they informed the company before they arrived. Of course, Allied cleaned up what it could and cut back production to a meager 10 percent of its normal capacity to minimize the mercury and chlorine releases during the inspection. Even so, state inspectors found excessive exposures and wrote a detailed report on how the company should remedy the situation. They refused to give the union a copy or inform it of their findings and recommendations.

Fortunately, times were changing. Nader's Raiders had an outpost in West Virginia, where a few brave souls investigated unsavory cases of corporate–government collusion. According to Susan Mazzocchi's report, one of those Raiders, Willie Osborne, just happened "to see the survey report on the desk of the State Labor Commissioner during a visit to his office. He asked for a copy and the Commissioner complied."

Once Osborne had the goods, he immediately sent copies to the Moundsville local and to Mazzocchi's office. With the report in hand, Mazzocchi unleashed Steve Wodka on Allied Chemical.

Almost immediately a pissing match ensued—literally. The War of the Urine Samples pitted the company and its testing laboratories against those of the newly formed National Institute of Occupational Safety and Health. Allied Chemical took urine samples from the Moundsville workers and split each one: Half of each sample was tested by a lab hired by the company, and half was tested in the NIOSH lab. Lo and behold, the company lab detected 275 percent less mercury in the samples than NIOSH did.

Allied Chemical proclaimed to the media and its workers that the government tests were wrong. The company argued that the urine must have been improperly split, leading to the high mercury readings in the NIOSH results. NIOSH responded with a scathing attack on the company. "If we assume that the urine specimens were improperly split (by Allied Chemical staff) so that the NIOSH aliquots were excessively heavy in mercury content, how can one portion be accurate and the other portion be inaccurate? Is it not logical that, if the portions analyzed by NIOSH were excessively high in mercury content, then the other portions, analyzed by Allied Chemical, were excessively low? . . . In our opinion, the significant point is that . . . about 50% of the people in your plant still exhibited absorption of mercury. Therefore, all efforts must continue to be directed toward expediting the reduction of these excessive exposures."[31]

In short, workers were being poisoned. But Allied continued to deny and obscure that plain fact.

Then Wodka and Mazzocchi deployed another weapon in the form of Dr. Sidney Wolfe, a public-interest physician in Washington who later became director of the Nader-linked Health Research Group. Wolfe wanted to get a definitive study of the workers' health. He turned to Dr. Fred Hochberg from the Public Health Service Center for Disease Control, who was known for his work on mercury poisoning. Hochberg was interested in conducting the study, but he required a written invitation from West Virginia's director of health.

State Director of Health Harvey Roberts at first responded: "Mercury poisoning went out in the 1920s with Alice in Wonderland and the Mad Hatter."[32] But with Wodka applying the screws, Roberts finally relented and issued the invitation. Hochberg then led a medical team to Moundsville to examine workers. It was the first week of May 1971—only days after OSHA had opened its doors. As Hochberg moved forward on his study, the company found its own expert, whose research had been funded by the industry's Chlorine Institute. This researcher concluded that Allied Chemical was "extremely health and safety conscious."

A few weeks later, Hochberg's results came in: The evidence showed "a persistent degree of contamination of individuals working in the cell areas. Blood levels bordering on those at which one would expect to find neurologic signs and symptoms have indeed been seen . . . a chronic exposure pattern."[33]

The news was so bad, one of the Public Health Service researchers told Wodka "that an imminent danger situation existed in the plant."

Imminent danger had very specific regulatory meaning in the new OSHA legislation. If such a danger existed, workers and their representatives could petition for an immediate inspection. OSHA was supposed to act quickly. Mazzocchi and Wodka used the Allied Chemical case to test that provision.

Wodka and Sheldon Samuels, director of occupational safety and environmental health for the AFL-CIO's Industrial Union Department, walked a letter of request to the Department of Labor on May 13, 1971—fifteen days after OSHA opened. OSHA officials agreed to investigate. They also agreed not to inform the company before they arrived. But there was a catch: They wouldn't tell the union, either. Wodka found this outrageous. He argued that "for the inspection to be effective, the knowledgeable local union president had to be present and prepared."[34]

But the OSHA officials wouldn't budge. They were clinging to what Mazzocchi believed was a warped notion of impartiality, which insisted that those who were doing the poisoning and those who were being poisoned should be treated equally.

The inspectors certainly did not rush to the scene. "It took them two weeks to get into the goddamn plant," Wodka said.[35] However, two inspectors from the Department of Labor finally arrived unannounced as promised, to inspect for mercury exposures. As soon as they walked into the cell room, they smelled the heavy odor of chlorine.

The *smell* of chlorine? The inspectors were no dummies. They knew that if you could smell it, the amount of chlorine in the air was at least three and a half times the level then considered safe.

Should they sound the alarms? Evacuate the plant? Demand that the company immediately provide respirators to each worker—and to themselves?

One of the inspectors, Charles Benjamin, whipped out his own respirator (which he had wisely brought along, just in case), donned it quickly, and hurried through the plant with his partner, hoping not to cause a stampede for the exits.

It was quite a picture: a federal inspector walking through the plant in a full-faced respirator, while all around him every worker continued to labor (as they'd been doing for countless hours) with no protection at all.

"Our workers were saying,'What are you guys doing with a self-breathing apparatus?'" Mazzocchi said. "The inspectors said there was a chlorine problem there—but we hadn't even put a complaint in on chlorine, or mentioned that the chlorine atmosphere was dangerous."

Would OSHA actually *do* something about the mercury poisoning and chlorine exposure? Under threat of a lawsuit, Nixon's assistant secretary of labor for OSHA, George Guenther, agreed to meet with Mazzocchi, Wodka, Samuels, and Dr. Wolfe to review the case. Guenther's subsequent ruling: There was no imminent danger, because the case did not involve an acute hazard like an explosion or a building collapse.

Of course this flew in the face of the imminent danger section of the OSH Act, which was "intended to include the restraining of specific industrial operation in which lethal substances or conditions are present and exposure to these will cause irreversible harm, *even though the resulting physical disability may not manifest itself at once*" (emphasis added).

Mazzocchi recalled telling Guenther, "You know, we're not that dumbass. We don't need to call you if something's gonna explode. We'll just run. We need you in nonexplosive situations when the exposures are harmful."

Sidney Wolfe then conducted a symptom survey of twenty-two employees, finding that "sixty-seven percent experienced numbness and tingling, positive signs of mercury poisoning. Seventy-six percent had memory difficulty . . ." and so on right down the list of the symptoms of mercury poisoning.[36]

Two weeks later, OSHA—after receiving air samples from the plant—cited the company for a "serious" violation—the very first OSHA citation.

So new was OSHA that this citation was written on a makeshift fill-in-the-blank form—Citation # 1, Date Issued May 28th 1971, with lines and boxes created by hand and ruler.

In its "description of violation," OSHA validated OCAW's complaint:

> Visible pools and droplets of mercury have been allowed to accumulate and remain on the cell room floor, in the basement, and in other working areas and working surfaces, contributing to airborne concentrations of mercury which significantly exceed levels generally accepted to be safe levels of such concentrations. Employees are being exposed to such concentrations. Instances of excessive airborne concentrations of mercury had been made known to the employer on occasions prior to the date of this inspection. This condition constitutes a recognized hazard that is causing or is likely to cause death or serious physical harm to employees.

The order called for the problems to be corrected by June 2, but the company appealed the ruling. Eventually, OSHA rapped Allied Chemical lightly on the knuckles with a thousand-dollar fine. Allied wrote the check and hoped to moved on.

But the three-way confrontation continued. OCAW would report to OSHA that the company had not adequately cleaned up the plant. OSHA would conduct a surprise inspection (although sometimes the company would find out and do a quick cleanup). Test results would show excessive exposures. OSHA would tell the company to remediate. The company would make cosmetic changes. The exposures would continue, and the cycle would start all over.

Mazzocchi and Steve Wodka believed they had scored an important victory by forcing OSHA to act on a chronic exposure case. However, they had no illusions that OSHA would ever solve the problem on its own. At best, the agency was another tool in the struggle to force companies to protect worker health and safety. Most importantly, OSHA established basic rights for workers: The company had a duty to provide a safe workplace, and it was the job of government to enforce those rights, however feebly.

But it would take years for significant change to reach the shop floor. In 1976, five years after OSHA's first contact with Allied Chemical and despite incessant OCAW pressure, the workers still suffered from "poor ventilation due to inoperative basement cell fans and roof vents, caustic header and cell casing leaks throughout the basement area, lack of rapid cleanup of mercury droplets, escape of mercury vapors from disconnected degasser lines, and escape of hydrogen and mercury vapors from leaking hydrogen cooler jumper lines."[37]

It was better than before—but still bad.

Mazzocchi knew that if workers wanted to live healthfully—or in some cases at all—they had to fight back on a larger scale. They would have to call for new principles and ideas like the "right to know" about the chemicals that poisoned them and the "right to act" to protect themselves at the workplace. They would even have to consider the ultimate protection: getting rid of the dangerous chemicals entirely.

None of this could succeed local by local or through OSHA. It would take a much larger movement, powerful enough to buckle the knees of the world's largest industries—starting with Big Oil.

ELEVEN

Catalytic Converter

Mazzocchi was hot. He'd helped get OSHA passed and now was using it aggressively to protect workers from toxic exposures at company after company. His attacks on polluters made him a darling of the growing environmental movement: He was prominent at the New York Earth Day rally in 1971, and the newly formed Natural Resources Defense Council put him on their board. Gifted students and medical professionals were joining his cause. His vigorous support for local union health and safety struggles was winning him allies in OCAW and other unions. A new workplace health movement was emerging with Mazzocchi as its founder and undisputed leader.

But Mazzocchi had an unusual definition of leadership. He didn't accept the "great man" notion of social change. As he put it,

> History presents circumstances, and if the circumstances aren't there I don't care who you are, you're not going to make change occur. When I came into the workplace, there were certain conditions that existed. I'm not going to deny that I was skillful in organizing it. Somebody had to organize it, but the conditions were there. I couldn't create those conditions. And I think that's always the case.
>
> Individuals have to organize within the context of a particular situation. And individuals do become personifications of historical forces. But if you zero in on those individuals, I think you can lose your focus on what you're trying to change or what you're trying to do.

Pushed to describe himself as a leader, he said,

> I was a catalyst. The talented people were out there, but they lacked political consciousness, simply because they were never exposed to it. I think my contribution was to be able to organize these profes-

> sionals, the scientists, the docs. I recognized that early on we could use these people. Their political consciousness had developed to the point where they knew the boss screwed people, but they didn't know the specifics.

In a 1972 *Washington Post* piece (actually titled "Long Live Mazzocchi!"), columnist Hal Willard made a similar observation: "Mazzocchi's theme was that it is time for ordinary workers and citizens to stop being polite to industry and other sources of environmental pollution. . . . The Mazzocchis of this world act as catalysts to the rest of us."[1]

As a catalyst (an appropriate label for a former chemical worker), much of Mazzocchi's effect was hidden from full view. He created chain reactions among hundreds of individuals and dozens of institutions. Usually, others got the recognition. The catalyst could only savor the satisfaction of knowing that the entire movement progressed. Didn't that bother Mazzocchi?

> Blowing your own horn? It's a waste of friggin' time. Your horn can be blown much better for you by virtue of what you do, by being recognized for that. And you know, I think that the more people who get involved, the better. Most union leaders don't share anything. They're always looking at everybody as a threat to their position. I viewed it the other way around, that my colleagues and allies out there were a strength, not a weakness. In other words, I wasn't worried about being replaced by anybody. In fact, I was hoping we could clone a hell of a lot of people to do what needed to be done.

Mazzocchi had realized that he needed to clone writers to help him build a national movement. He wanted someone to record the movement's history to date and make the case for uniting labor, environmentalists, women, and minorities against the purveyors of poison.

Mazzocchi certainly wasn't going to write it. In fact, he couldn't write a lick. The basic tools of grammar weren't accessible to him. Mazzocchi could absorb complex concepts from the stacks of books he read each year; he could innovate and form new ideas; he could give moving speeches. But when he tried to write, the words, the paper, and the pen pulled in different directions, leaving nothing much behind. Until his death, he believed that his grammatical deficits were of his own making—he was a "dumber," he often said, a ninth-grade dropout who'd been too lazy and impatient to learn.

It was hard enough to keep up with correspondence in the legislative office. He relied heavily on dictating to his secretary. For longer pieces, Mazzocchi turned to his college-educated interns and staff, especially Steve Wodka, who wrote the bulk of Mazzocchi's health and safety testimony.

But the fledgling health and safety movement needed an author who could transform the local workplace outrages Mazzocchi had helped uncloak into a national scandal.

Where was this movement's Rachel Carson?

II

Jeanne Stellman, a precocious doctoral student in physical chemistry at City University of New York, met Tony at a community meeting about Agent Orange at Columbia. "It was about 1971," said Stellman. "Tony Mazzocchi was also speaking, and he started talking about benzene and health. I had pretty much spent the day in a lab wallowing around in benzene. And I went up and volunteered. 'I'm a chemist and maybe I can help.'"[2]

It was not a whimsical offer. Stellman, born in a refugee camp in Poland, grew up in a left-leaning family. Her father was a union machinist; her mother helped to unionize Gimbels department store in Manhattan. Little wonder that during the 1960s, Jeanne became a vocal antiwar academic.

Mazzocchi and Stellman decided to do something entirely new—to create a union-sponsored occupational health and safety course for workers. Mazzocchi would arrange for a pilot test in his home district. "We always used District 8 to introduce our new programs," Mazzocchi said. "So we set up this course. I think it was a ten-week thing at Rutgers with Jeannie and other docs and scientists."

At the time, Stellman said, "I realized that I didn't know very much. But I was a good researcher, and I looked things up. I think one of the earliest plants we dealt with was Boyle-Midway, which has since been bought up. They made a lot of the household pesticides. I learned how pesticides would inhibit cholinesterase activity and cause nervous system stimulations so that people's eye pupils would stay open. It became very clear to me very soon that not only did I not know anything, but there was no information for *anyone* out there on occupational health and safety. And the problems were so enormous."

Stellman tapped the talent pool of progressives hungry for a constructive cause. "I realized I couldn't do this all by myself," she said. So she formed the Scientists' Committee for Occupational Health. In her new position as a professor at the Rutgers Labor Education Center, she began recruiting scholars to help her with the course and an accompanying guide on occupational health and safety. "Tony Vega, a wonderful man and a teacher there, facilitated things," Stellman recalled. "Jim Weeks, an industrial engineer, he wrote a chapter. Mike Green, who is in the chemistry department at City College—I think we made him learn about ventilation. And Dave Kotelchuck prepared the work on ionizing radiation because he was getting a degree in nuclear physics. Susan Daum, who was chief resident in hematology at Mount Sinai, also contributed."

Mazzocchi felt confident about the team's technical skills. But, he said, "I always had problems finding people who could talk to ordinary folks. After they got into these meetings with workers, they could pick up the sense of where people were at, and then they started to modify their presentations. That happened with Jeanne Stellman and her whole crowd. I mean, I took them right out of an academic setting. It took them time to learn, but they wised up."

No one learned better, Mazzocchi believed, than Stellman herself. Not only did she put on the course, but she also authored an accessible, practical guide. Still, Mazzocchi feared that the book would languish at a tiny left-wing press.

> They came to me and said: "We're gonna get this published with Pluto Press." It's a socialist press in London with a circulation of about forty-nine. So I said: "Look. I know a guy—Andre Schiffrin from Pantheon Books. He might be interested." Schiffrin had come to me one time, and said that if somebody ever writes a good book on health and safety, let him know. I just put it in the back of my mind. So they go to Schiffrin, and the book took off.

The book, *Work Is Dangerous to Your Health,* sold tens of thousands of copies in the first year—well over a hundred thousand since 1972—and was translated into more than twenty languages. For over a decade, it was the most important popular guide to occupational safety and health among both professionals and workers. But while the book served as an excellent reference, it was not intended as a stirring narrative to stimulate public outrage. Carson's spot remained unclaimed.

III

Paul Brodeur, a novelist and writer for *The New Yorker* magazine, developed an interest in worker health after meeting Dr. Irving Selikoff, a doctor at New York's Mount Sinai Hospital. Selikoff had uncovered an epidemic of lung disease among asbestos insulation workers and their families. The asbestos industry responded by smearing Selikoff and his work. In 1968, Brodeur wrote "The Magic Mineral," a defense of Selikoff, for *The New Yorker.*

Brodeur became fascinated by the intersections among government neglect, corporate greed, and moral corruption. He also learned firsthand how corporate carrot-and-stick tactics were used to stifle criticism. At one point, he discovered that a PR firm working for Johns Manville (the largest asbestos producer) was investigating his own marital life, telling those they questioned that Brodeur was being nominated to the Overseas Press Club. There was no such nomination. Manville later tried the carrot, offering Brodeur a PR job that paid more than three times what he earned at *The New Yorker.*[3]

As Brodeur grew more interested in the workplace environment, he inevitably fell into Mazzocchi's orbit and catalytic process. Soon he became the muse of occupational safety and health.

The two men met over laundry detergent. In the '60s, detergent manufacturers tried to boost sales by adding powerful new cleaning agents. One of these was a stain-eating protolytic enzyme, which the commercials depicted as hungry Pac-Man-like creatures that would "just eat away those hard-to-get-out stains." Unfortunately, the enzymes also ate away your lungs and were associated with worker pulmonary disease and skin rashes.

"Workers, not scientists, are always the first to uncover the connections between disease and chemical exposure," Tony noted. In the enzyme case, the first inkling came at a small health and safety meeting Mazzocchi held in New York City in 1968. There, workers from an OCAW-represented Staten Island detergent plant complained about new allergic-like reactions.

Mazzocchi called a districtwide health and safety conference on enzymes in Baltimore on June 14, 1969. The meeting, like his other "Hazards in the Workplace Environment" conferences, included both workers and experts.

One of Mazzocchi's student researchers discovered that a Dr. Muriel. L. Newhouse of the London School of Hygiene and Tropical Medicine had conducted a study suggesting that enzyme exposure posed acute dangers to detergent workers in Britain. Mazzocchi wanted to bring Newhouse to the United States. He persuaded Selikoff, then president of the New York Academy of Sciences, to host a one-day meeting in New York on November 22, 1969, at which Newhouse would discuss her preliminary findings.

The meeting drew thirteen scientists, thirteen representatives from government and regulatory agencies, twenty-six representatives from industry (of whom seventeen were scientists working for detergent companies), and sixteen union representatives. Brodeur reported that "One of the chief accomplishments of the meeting was to make the scientific community aware of the intricacies of the enzyme problem."[4] But, he continued, scientists "were dismayed by the intransigence of the soap companies even to admit that such a problem might exist."[5]

By now, Brodeur was on the case. He recalled sitting at Tony and Susan's kitchen table on the Upper West Side talking it through. And in January 1971, he broadcast the problem nationwide through *The New Yorker*. The article created a public relations crisis for the detergent industry. Brodeur later wrote that it "produced an immediate outcry of concern from one end of the nation to the other, and within a few weeks the three leading detergent manufacturers—Procter and Gamble, Colgate-Palmolive, and Lever Brothers—quietly withdrew the enzymes from their products."[6]

IV

In spring 1971, Mazzocchi gave a speech at the Harvard School of Public Health. The class included "a lot of conscientious objectors, commissioned officers who were going to work in the Public Health Service in the newly founded National Institute for Occupational Safety and Health." And, said Tony, "They were very skeptical."

> My pitch was, "Look, I'm a workers' advocate. I'm biased. I'm not going to give you an objective picture. I'm here to give you a picture of how workers see the problem. If you don't believe me, and you shouldn't, then you've also got to be skeptical about what you're hearing from the industry. . . ." Because they were only hearing from the industry side.
>
> Five days later I got a call from this guy, Bill Johnson, a captain who had been in the course, and he told me he'd been skeptical of what I'd said. But he'd just gotten to NIOSH, and he'd found all that Tyler, Texas, stuff in a drawer.

That "stuff" was a study by the industry-friendly Bureau of Occupational Safety and Health (NIOSH's predecessor), which revealed enormously high levels of deadly asbestos fibers in the air in several plants, including one in Tyler represented by OCAW. In fact, one of Tyler's air samples had so many fibers that it was "too dusty to count."[7] Johnson also learned that the man who coordinated the study, Dr. Lewis Cralley, "refused to release any data from his studies to anyone except the management of the companies involved."[8]

When Johnson approached the plant owner, Pittsburgh Corning, about protecting workers, its medical consultant, Dr. Lee B. Grant, told him "there really wasn't much of a problem at the Tyler plant, because the place was so dusty that people didn't stay around long enough to get sick."[9]

Dr. Johnson blew the whistle: He informed Mazzocchi and Wodka.

They soon found Selikoff's studies of an almost identical plant in Paterson, New Jersey. Those studies made it clear that an alarming percentage of the exposed Tyler, Texas, workers would probably get lung disease, cancer, and mesothelioma (a rare cancer caused only by exposure to asbestos). Mazzocchi and Wodka immediately contacted the Tyler local union. Together they developed a set of demands on the company to monitor the workers and clean up the plant.

Contract negotiations at Tyler began in October 1971. Faced with workers' stringent demands, the company threatened to shut down the plant. In an internal union report, Wodka surmised that "the company wanted to see how far the union would sacrifice its health and standard of living to keep the plant going."[10]

The union didn't flinch: It called on NIOSH to restudy the plant and make recommendations on how best to protect the workers' health. The new NIOSH study, conducted in late October 1971 and released in early December, was devastating. The plant was a hellhole of asbestos exposures; seven out of eighteen men with ten years of employment showed signs of asbestosis. "In conclusion," wrote the NIOSH investigators, "an extremely serious and critical occupational health situation exists at this plant. Immediate corrective action is necessary. . . ."[11]

OSHA inspected the plant and fined Pittsburgh Corning all of $210!

In January 1972, Wodka and the local union leaders discovered a dump about one mile north of the plant that, according to Wodka, was "about half the size of a football field and was filled to a depth of at least one foot with asbestos tailings." Also, Herman Yandle, a local union officer, told Wodka that "the burlap bags in which the raw asbestos was shipped to the plant were resold to garden nurseries throughout the southeastern United States."[12]

OSHA inspected the plant again on January 13, found that the company had not complied with the previous citations, and fined Pittsburgh Corning $6,990. As the union continued to demand protection, the twenty-three-year-old Wodka wrote to OCAW president Al Grospiron on January 28, 1972, that "the company would like to see the plant shut down, the men quietly fade away, and the Tyler pin removed from the corporate map."[13]

On February 3, Pittsburgh Corning did just that. Not only did they shut the plant down, but they buried the entire asbestos facility piece by piece to prevent more contamination. Yet Mazzocchi, Wodka, and soon Brodeur would not drop the case.

> Mazzocchi believed that the Administration's people were hoping that if they slapped Pittsburgh Corning lightly on the wrist with some non-serious violations the whole affair would blow over. That it did not, as so many other occupational-health scandals had, was largely the result of the efforts of Mazzocchi who was determined to make it a *cause célèbre*.[14]

"Mazzocchi," wrote Brodeur, "voiced the fear that many of the men who had worked in the factory [more than 890] would one day be afflicted with lung cancer or other malignant tumors."[15]

Brodeur's powerful five-part series, called "Annals of Industry: Casualties of the Workplace," ran in *The New Yorker* during 1972–1973. (*Expendable Americans,* the book version of the series, was published in 1974.) In it, Brodeur backed up Mazzocchi's and Wodka's claims about what had happened in Tyler and substantiated Mazzocchi's entire critique of the government-medical-industrial complex that made workers' health a callous cost of production. Brodeur understood perfectly why workers were dying:

> That the company should be placed on the defensive over some dumps and burlap bags, and not because of the awful jeopardy in which it had put the health of hundreds of workers and their families, seems ironic. It should not, however, come as any surprise. Much of industry in the United States has long operated on the assumption that it could endanger the lives of its employees with relative impunity—and without embarrassing publicity and possibly damaging repercussions—so long as it did not overtly threaten the health and safety of the community at large. Underlying this assumption is the further assumption that workers are not so much a part of the community as part of the equipment and machinery of production. As such, upon being proved defective they become expendable. They can be replaced or transferred, or, if worst comes to worst, given workmen's compensation (which in most states is minimal) and retired. At that point, they cease to be anyone's responsibility. Like the eight hundred and ninety-five men who worked in the Tyler plant over the years, they are out of sight and out of mind. In a sense, therefore, like much of the factory itself, they are buried.[16]

Brodeur movingly recounted his visits with the men who once worked in the Tyler plant. He turned them from statistics into raucous living characters who coughed and laughed together as they recalled how the company had obfuscated the dangers of asbestos. Many of the workers he interviewed would die of asbestos-related disease. Even the mother of one of the workers,

Herman Yandel, would die from mesothelioma in 1983. Her only exposure had come from washing her son's work clothes.[17]

In painstaking detail, Brodeur showed how the asbestos industry had gotten OSHA to adopt a standard so lax that millions of workers would suffer the deadly effects of asbestos exposures for years to come.

Brodeur quoted at length Mazzocchi's congressional testimony on the failings of OSHA, the ubiquitous use of asbestos around the country, the criminality of the proposed standard, and the collusion between corporations and bought-off medical professionals who belittled worker health hazards. Brodeur also cited Mazzocchi's radical policy solutions. Permissible asbestos exposure levels should be reduced to zero. Hazards needed to be engineered away, not accommodated by forcing workers to use personal protective equipment, like respirators. Workers' annual physical exams should be performed by "doctors of their own choice, but at the employer's expense." Further, said Mazzocchi, "the records of these examinations should not be sent to the employer but to a central record-keeping facility at NIOSH, where such records could be kept intact and confidential. . . . It has been our sad experience in case after case, that as soon as management finds out how badly it has injured the health of a worker, management does its best to get rid of him. . . ."[18]

Wrote Brodeur: "Mazzocchi concluded by declaring that a deficient standard for protection from the hazards of asbestos would legislate sickness and an early death for thousands of people. 'Faced with this prospect, I would seek no new rule at all, rather than be held responsible for the cases of asbestos disease that will surface thirty years from now,' he said."[19]

The final episodes of Brodeur's account followed Wodka's fight over beryllium exposures in Hazelton and substantiated claims about company-paid researchers serving as government advisers. He interviewed Jeanne Stellman (then an assistant to OCAW's president responsible for occupational safety and health) about how corporations had corrupted the process of setting standards for the carcinogen benzene.

Brodeur ended his exposé by describing his final attempt, on a conference room dais, to secure an interview with Pittsburgh Corning's elusive chief doctor, Lee B. Grant, who had continually downplayed the asbestos problem at the Tyler plant.

When I reached the platform, I introduced myself to Dr. Grant, who was standing above me, at approximately knee-to-eyeball level, and reminded him I had telephoned him in March in the hope of being able to talk with him about the Tyler plant. . . .

"I wonder if there might be some time in the next day or two that I could talk with you," I said.

Dr. Grant appeared to hesitate. Then, glancing quickly over the ballroom, which was emptying, he shook his head. "I'm afraid I can't," he replied. "In this instance, it's a question of the patient's rights."

For a moment I thought I had not heard him correctly. Then it dawned on me that he was talking about the company. "Do you mean Pittsburgh Corning?" I said.

"Why, yes," Dr. Grant replied. "If they don't want me to talk with you, there's nothing I can do."

"But, isn't the patient all those men who worked in the Tyler plant?" I asked.

Dr. Grant straightened up and looked down at me from his full height on the platform. "Well, in the larger sense, of course, that's probably true," he replied. "And now, if you'll excuse me, I have some business to attend to."

I stood at the platform and watched Dr. Grant, who, as he moved away, put a cigar in his mouth, lit it and exhaled a cloud of smoke into the air. A moment later, I saw him throw an arm in greeting around the shoulders of a colleague. Then I turned away, and found myself looking straight into the face of Anthony Mazzocchi, who, as it turned out, had been invited to speak at one of the convention's sessions on occupational health.

"Did you hear that?" I asked him. "Did you hear what he said?"

For a long time, Mazzocchi looked at me without a trace of expression on his face. Then, very slowly, he nodded his head up and down. And then, just as slowly, he shook it from side to side.[20]

"What I will always remember are the eloquent and angry words of Anthony Mazzocchi," Brodeur wrote in 1997. "A blunt-spoken man, Mazzocchi had long brooded over what he considered to be the gross immorality that attended the plight of men who were either dying or being disabled early in life as a result of exposure to toxic substances such as asbestos, whose adverse health effects had long been known and ignored by the members of the medical-industrial complex. This is how he explained his reasons for making a *cause célèbre* of the Tyler factory:

"'I wanted the whole country to know in detail what had happened at that factory, and to understand that what had gone on there—the fruitless Bureau of Occupational Safety and Health Inspections, the lack of enforcement by the Department of Labor, the whole long, lousy history of neglect, deceit, and stupidity—was happening in dozens of other ways, in hundreds of other factories, to thousands of other men across the land. I wanted people to know that thousands upon thousands of their fellow citizens were being assaulted daily, and that the police—in this case, the federal government—had done nothing to remedy the situation. In short I wanted them to know that murder was being committed in the workplace, and that no one was bothering about it.'"[21]

The New Yorker magazine made Mazzocchi's defiant words the centerpiece of a full-page *New York Times* ad for the Brodeur series on October 23, 1973. The ad, a blank mock-up of a *New Yorker* page, featured Mazzocchi's quote, alone, in twenty-point boldface. At the bottom of the page in small type, it read: "From a series of articles by Paul Brodeur, beginning in this week's issue (October 29) of *The New Yorker*. . . ."

Tony Mazzocchi's name was nowhere on the page. (Did *The New Yorker*'s marketing people fear that its readers would associate Tony's surname and title with *union mobster*?) Brodeur had nothing to do with the ad, and there is no record of Tony mentioning the omission. In fact, Mazzocchi was proud of it: He reproduced and distributed the ad widely. What mattered was that Brodeur had written an outstanding series and *The New Yorker* was promoting it—and that it would change the intellectual landscape for occupational safety and health.

V

Meanwhile, Mazzocchi had to change the oil industry.

Years of jobs cuts, especially in maintenance, coupled with dramatically rising production, had increased toxic releases and other hazards faced by refinery workers. In 1972, Mazzocchi convinced the union to make health and safety the primary issue in negotiations. The union demanded periodic health and safety inspections of oil facilities by independent consultants jointly approved by labor and management. OCAW also wanted union-approved doctors to examine workers at company expense, and access to all morbidity and mortality records. In addition, OCAW demanded paid time off for workers to conduct union inspections and participate in health and safety meetings.

And, said Mazzocchi, "We wanted the 'right to know' about what we worked with, and the 'right to act' on what we knew. We were raising a whole host of breakthrough questions."

To many of these demands, the oil industry said yes.

Except Shell Oil. "Shell said that safety was not the business of workers—it was the business of business," said Mazzocchi. "They said our demand was illegal under the National Labor Relations Act. They maintained it wasn't a mandatory subject of bargaining."

And so, said Mazzocchi, "We decided to strike." On January 21, 1973, more than four thousand Shell OCAW members from five oil refineries and three chemical plants around the country put their livelihoods on the line, trying to hold Shell to the union's new high standard for workplace health. The union also launched a nationwide boycott of Shell.

Mazzocchi knew they couldn't win a traditional strike: Oil companies like Shell were so automated, they were virtually strike-proof. Said Mazzocchi, "We didn't stop an ounce of gasoline from being produced. There were two supervisors working in the industry for every worker, and they would run the plant during the strike. The industry ran Pullman cars into the plant so that their scabs—the supervisors—could sleep in those cars. And they used helicopters to fly in food and supplies. We had no way to intervene to stop the refining process."

So, said Mazzocchi, "We decided to take the industry on in a different way." He asked community and environmental allies to join the union in a high-profile assault on the industry's public vulnerabilities.

And vulnerable they were. For environmentalists, Big Oil meant spills like the one in 1969 that had slimed wildlife and the pristine shores near Santa Barbara. For the left, Big Oil was the embodiment of imperialism, subverting nations around the world. And middle American populists saw a sinister monopoly that manipulated government to pile up obscene tax breaks, drilling rights, and immense profits.

Mazzocchi believed he could shape the public's distrust into a powerful labor-community alliance.

But to build it, the union would have to win the allegiance of young activists like Cathy Lerza. The daughter of a conservative-libertarian engineer and a liberal stay-at-home mom, Cathy was raised in a gilded Los Angeles suburb. Even though she attended the University of California–Berkeley during its radical heyday, she admitted that "I didn't know about unions. I didn't know about the working class. I thought autoworkers were like poor people."[22]

At Berkeley, she said, "The 'real' radicals thought environmentalism was a ruling-class effort to siphon off energy from the antiwar movement." Ignoring this critique, she studied with the fledging Environmental Studies Department, which looked carefully at the connections between corporate power and environmental degradation. After graduation, she got a job as an intern with the newly formed Environmental Protection Agency, working on noise abatement. "I got disillusioned in a hurry," she said. "There I sat with posters of John Muir on my wall, but I was meeting real bureaucrats for the first time. I discovered the one I was working for was a dirty old man."

After running into the executive director of Environmental Action (EA), a new advocacy group that had grown out of Earth Day, Cathy escaped the EPA to become co-editor of EA's newsletter. Her group, like thousands of other movement organizations at the time, governed its affairs collectively and took pride in being anti-capitalist. Unlike the more established "hook-and-gun" environmental groups, EA developed an interest in health and safety because, as Cathy put it, "we were concerned about the impact on people, not just the environment."

This was just the kind of group Mazzocchi needed for his fight against the oil industry. He approached them: Could the union enlist Environmental Action to organize community support for the strike? After all, as he said to the press, "It's not a bunch of workers going out on strike for a dime an hour." The strike against Shell was a cause—a fight for worker and community health.

The EA collective had to deliberate on that one. They sent Cathy Lerza on a fact-gathering visit to Mazzocchi.

"There I was: long, straight hair, granny glasses, long dress, the women's movement stereotype," Cathy said. "I went to interview Mazzocchi and I was stunned. I had never met anyone like him. Here was this tough guy who challenged all my stereotypes about labor. He was tough but he supported civil rights. He confronted corporate power and authority every day. There was passion in his voice, and anger about what his members needed. It was clear immediately that he wanted to make serious change. But as I interviewed him, he never played working-class hero—like saying, *You don't know what it's like to be a worker because you're from a privileged class.* He didn't guilt-trip me. Instead he saw me as a resource—as someone with skills who could help.

"He never treated me in a sexist way," Cathy continued. "Believe me, I could tell the difference. I had met with some of his young aides, and the air always was loaded with sexual vibes—like *Are we here to talk about the strike or is this a pickup?* It was always awkward, but not with Mazzocchi. He treated me professionally. He wanted me to understand the issues and be able to write good articles about them. I felt as if he saw something valuable in what I could contribute. My dad always made me feel stupid about technical stuff, like I couldn't get it. Mazzocchi made me feel competent and useful."

Environmental Action decided to get fully involved and accepted an OCAW grant to support organizers. They set up the Committee to Support the Shell Strike. According to Sam Love, EA's director at the time, "Barry Weisberg, an organizer Mazzocchi had enlisted, coordinated the work on the West Coast, and I more or less worked the rest of the country."[23]

Cathy was assigned to write the key piece on the strike. The experience changed her life.

"It was like a light went on," she said. "I saw a bigger framework that included the connections between class and the corporate system of power and decision making. I started thinking about workers. Hello-o! They make this crap, they get exposed, they get abused. I never lost that framework."

Lerza's March 3, 1973, piece, "Environmental Issues Reach the Bargaining Table," published in *Environmental Action,* called for a new blue-green politics. Lerza argued that "the strike is important to forward-looking environmentalists because it is the realization of a long-dreamed-of alliance: workers and environmentalists working together to reach a common goal. It's been long claimed that environmental activists are elitists who are more interested in conserving pretty vistas and saving wildlife than in helping working people; conversely, it has been asserted that workers gladly condone pollution if it means higher wages for them. The OCAW strike marks the beginning of a new awareness of the scope of environmental issues by both organized labor and environmental activists. . . . The strike against Shell may well be the turning point in the environmental movement."[24]

In fact, the strike turned some environmental organizations inside out—especially the Sierra Club. Mazzocchi recalled that the oil industry sent a representative to a Sierra Club board meeting to steer them away from backing the strike. "They had a lot of members saying that supporting this strike was not really the business of the Sierra Club. But the club had an internal discussion, and they arrived at the point where they said: This *is* our business. This is a crucial environmental struggle. And what these strikers are striking for is integral to our own goals."

Mazzocchi recalled a newspaper headline at the time: "'Archie Bunker Meets the Sierra Club.' Talk about class and the perception of it!"

Meanwhile, Environmental Action's organizing was paying off. On January 1, 1973, *The Washington Post* carried a UPI story, which noted, "Eleven environmental protection organizations aligned themselves with labor yesterday and announced support for a strike against Shell Oil Co. refineries and a nation-wide boycott against Shell products."

The *Post* quoted EA's Sam Love: "It is the first time a major labor union has struck on what is fundamentally an environmental issue, and the strike is a first-time alliance between labor and environmental organizing."[25]

Mazzocchi commissioned a national ad in which twenty-nine leading scientists and doctors, including several Nobel laureates, expressed their support for the Shell strikers. The signers, rounded up by Sam Epstein, then a toxicologist with Case Western Reserve University, included Barry Commoner, Linus Pauling, Irving Selikoff, George Wald, Sid Wolfe, and Eula Bingham.

"Workers have long served as unwitting 'guinea pigs', providing useful toxicological data which helped to protect the public," read the ad, which was drafted by Epstein. "The effects of most environmental pollutants, such as carbon monoxide, lead, mercury and also of most human carcinogens were first detected in workmen." The signers concluded, "The success of the OCAW strike is critical both to labor and the public. . . . The demand to participate actively in protecting health and safety of workers is basic and inalienable and cannot be sacrificed to narrow economic interests."[26]

In March, Mazzocchi got *The Washington Post*'s Stuart Auerbach to cover the strike. Auerbach set the tone in the lead paragraph: "For the first time in American labor history, a major strike has started over the potential health hazards of an industry—the long-term dangers of a constant exposure to poisonous chemicals in oil refineries and chemical plants." After quoting Mazzocchi, Sid Wolfe, and Irving Selikoff, Auerbach concluded with a quote from Sam Epstein: "The worker, the most vitally concerned individual in the health area, is the individual with the least input. This is totally unacceptable and it is about time unions realized it."[27]

With workers and environmentalists staging rallies near Shell gas stations and refineries, the pressure mounted. And finally, four months after the strike began, the company gave in to some, though not all, of the union's demands. The strike officially ended on June 1, 1973.

The lesson of this surprising victory, Tony argued, was that "You don't defeat a company like Shell Oil alone on a picket line. The other oil companies forced Shell to settle, because they were getting embarrassed. We were publicizing their misdeeds all over the place. We were detailing exactly how the company pollutes. And when the Sierra Club formed this alliance with us, the industry told Shell, 'You better settle this thing, because we're being dragged through the mud with the revelations coming out about the industry.' So our members learned that you can't win these fights alone."

VI

Historian Robert Gordon isn't so sure the Shell strike ended in victory. Writing in 1998, he claimed that "the four-month-old strike had quickly drained the union's financial reserves and weakened its resolve."[28] Gordon reported that at the Deer Park, Texas, Shell Oil facility, "a group of younger employees rejected the union's insistence upon inclusion of the health and safety clause and moved to form an independent union."[29]

By negotiating a separate deal with the Deer Park unit, he continued, "Shell exploited these internal divisions. On the surface, the deal met all of the union's demands, including the creation of a health and safety committee. Upon closer examination, however, . . . [it] was in fact a major defeat for the union since the recommendations of the health and safety committee would not be binding." Further, said Gordon, the company refused to pay for regular plant inspections by independent health professionals.[30]

Gordon said that Grospiron admitted "that the agreement was considerably less comprehensive than the 300-plus contracts signed with other companies in the industry."[31]

However, the toothless joint health and safety committee didn't bother Mazzocchi. "I never was for joint health and safety committees. I wanted safety committees that contained only union members." Tony believed that joint committees operate on the erroneous assumption that management wants to make serious changes. He believed that managers instead used such committees as a ruse to deny, stall, and then fix as little as possible. What Gordon called a loss was actually a relief for Mazzocchi.

According to Gordon, "Grospiron and others in the union put a positive spin on the deal labeling it a 'compromise' and pointed out that Shell agreed to provide the union with mortality and morbidity statistics it had demanded for years."[32]

For Mazzocchi, access to mortality and morbidity statistics was not "spin." In fact, access to this data was much more important to him than were feel-good joint committees. With company statistics in hand, he believed, the Selikoffs, the Wolfes, the Commoners, and the Epsteins might provide the union with many epidemiological smoking guns aimed directly at corporate culpability. No company, Mazzocchi knew, willingly gave up such data.

It was also clear to Tony that the strike had helped build a stronger anti-corporate movement. While it did little harm to Shell economically, the labor-environment alliance had embarrassed the company into a settlement. And that settlement protected the gains won from the other oil companies. Had the strike been lost, the oil companies that had already signed contracts would have backed away from their deals. Even a "compromise" win at Shell set in place the basics of Mazzocchi's health and safety regime throughout the industry.

Gordon himself conceded:

> The importance of the 1973 Shell strike does not stem from OCAW's failure to secure all of its health and safety demands, nor from the failure of the environmentally backed boycott to bring Shell to its knees. From a broader perspective, in fact, OCAW has made remarkable progress. Almost all of the union's contracts with other oil companies were renewed with the strict health and safety clause. . . . In addition, OCAW's efforts heightened public awareness of health hazards confronting millions of American workers. . . . Perhaps most importantly, the Shell strike solidified the tentative labor-environmental alliance.[33]

VII

Mazzocchi's budding blue-green alliance immediately sailed into a howling gale of economic woe as the prosperous 1960s war economy gave way to inflation and Nixon's wage and price controls. In the fall of 1973, the Yom Kippur War and resulting OPEC oil embargo caused major price shocks in the West. For the first time since the late 1950s, chronic job insecurity reappeared, and with it increased tensions for a new labor-environmental alliance.

The United Mine Workers, under the corrupt leadership of Tony Boyle, had already cast its environmental lot with management, sanctioning massive strip mining that leveled mountains, polluted streams, and, because of new technologies, destroyed jobs.

West Coast building-trades unions accused environmentalists of being anti-growth and anti-jobs. In fact, the same issue of the *San Francisco Chronicle* that featured an article on the Sierra Club–OCAW alliance also included an article in which John Henning, the progressive antiwar head of California's AFL-CIO, claimed: "Thousands of workers throughout California have been displaced by environmental proposals well-intentioned but not related to the economic and social needs of the working people of this state."[34]

Washington Post columnist John Herling put it more graphically in a February 24, 1973, op-ed piece in support of the Shell strike's labor-environmental alliance: "Some trade unions have regarded ecology as economic pornography, a dirty concept that threatens their jobs and in the process may shake up their labor-management relations."[35]

It might be expected that OCAW, a union so entwined with the oil industry, atomic energy, and the national security state, would be the epicenter of the anti-environmentalist backlash. Wall-to-wall, OCAW dealt with poisons and weapons of mass destruction, most of which a saner society would ban. OCAW members might well have been hanging environmental activists in effigy.

Instead, OCAW invited Sierra Club executive director Mike McCloskey to address its two thousand delegates at the union's August 1973 convention. (The union and the Sierra Club later turned the speech into a booklet to distribute to workers and environmentalists.) In his presentation, McCloskey expressed puzzlement that environmentalists "are being singled out for special criticism on the job issue." In fact, he argued that the Sierra Club was out in front of the battle against "environmental blackmail." He declared its support for "proposals to force disclosure of the facts whenever a company threatens to close a plant because of pollution requirements to see whether this is the true reason or is simply a threat or whether it is being closed because it is obsolete."[36]

McCloskey was also troubled by the Mine Workers, which he said was "automating itself out of business" by endorsing strip mining. The Sierra Club hoped to help the Mine Workers' new reform leaders "to save jobs and the surface environment by curtailing strip-mining, which devastates the land for short-term profits."[37]

To tackle the jobs issue, McCloskey aligned the Sierra Club with one of Mazzocchi's pet proposals (which Mazzocchi first called Superfund for Workers and then Just Transition). McCloskey called on the government "to indemnify workers who are displaced in true cases of plant closures for environmental reasons. Workers should not be made to bear the brunt of any nation's commitment to a decent environment for all. Society should assume this burden and aid them in every way possible."[38]

However, the Sierra Club was on the defensive. McCloskey was stung when the California building trades joined the chamber of commerce to fight environmentalists. He told the OCAW delegates, "I can't help wondering how far down the line unions that can work hand-in-glove with industry like this have moved toward becoming company unions. They are not only taking their jobs from industry, but their cues on strategy, and even their political rhetoric."[39]

It's hard to imagine that McCloskey could have made such comments before any other American union audience. How was it possible to do it here?

Tony knew that the union had a choice: It could join management in resisting environmental regulation in the hope of salvaging jobs. Or it could ally with environmentalists to challenge corporate power.

Mazzocchi believed if the union took the pro-corporate fork and worked to protect industry from environmental regulations, there would be no going back. The union and workers would be caught in a negative cycle: The more jobs they lost, the more workers would feel compelled to support industry against environmental regulation. Management would perpetuate the cycle by continually driving home the wedge: either loosen environmental protections or lose your job. If union leaders tried to tack back toward an alliance with environmentalists, the company would encourage the ranks to stop them. Taking the wrong fork now, Mazzocchi believed, would lock the union into an anti-environmental culture that would be nearly impossible to change.

Mazzocchi thought the construction unions already were a lost cause: "They'd pave over the Atlantic Ocean, if given the chance," he quipped. But he was more disappointed when later his progressive allies in the Mine Workers and the United Automobile Workers adopted the corporate framework on global warming.

Mazzocchi's OCAW, like the United Steelworkers, took the other fork. They bombarded union members with education campaigns on the workplace environment and other environmental issues, from air pollution to nuclear safety. Gradually, the rank and file developed a deeper understanding that workplace environment and the community environment were of a piece.

Along the way, Tony and his union brothers and sisters created a glow around the union. As OCAW gained visibility for its pioneering workplace health struggles, union members earned a reputation as fighters for the cause. The Shell strike only enhanced this image. It was something special to be an OCAW member.

The Shell strike had been a turning point. Oil workers saw with their own eyes environmentalists out on the streets demonstrating in common cause. The hard-boiled oil workers, in fact, had to rely on environmentalists during the strike—they couldn't have succeeded any other way. As a result, Mazzocchi helped create in OCAW *an obligation of reciprocity:* They were in debt to the environmental movement.

But something even more remarkable happened. Not only did OCAW members feel beholden, but they also began to take pride in seeing their union as an environmental union.

The anti-corporate framework did it. For decades, Mazzocchi had preached that an unchecked drive for profits was the root cause of the problem in both the workplace and the environment. That framework gave workers a powerful defense when their employers tried to drive a wedge between them and environmentalists. In the wake of the Shell strike, many workers could see for themselves that workers and environmentalists needed each other.

TWELVE

Crash

A delegation of three arrived in Washington, DC, on September 26, 1974, eagerly seeking Mazzocchi's help. Jack Tice was shop chairman of the OCAW local union at the Kerr-McGee nuclear facility in Cimarron, Oklahoma, and Jerry Brewer was second in command. With them was a woman in her late twenties who recently had been elected to the bargaining committee. Her name was Karen Silkwood.

A Texas native, Karen had dropped out of college after marrying young. A few years later, she'd set off to Oklahoma in search of work, leaving three kids behind with her ex-husband. She soon landed a good-paying job as a laboratory analyst at the Cimarron plant—just before a strike. The granddaughter of a Texas oil worker and OCAW member, Silkwood threw herself into picket-line duty, taking up the union's cause. Bright and spirited—a child of the rebellious '60s, Texas-style—she walked into Mazzocchi's office in search of a cause.

She'd come to the right place.

But it was unusual that Silkwood and her two colleagues had come to meet with the union's legislative director at all. OCAW vice president Elwood Swisher, who was responsible for the union's atomic sector, did not approve of Mazzocchi's anti-corporate politics. So he kept Mazzocchi away from OCAW's atomic sector.

In fact, many atomic workers, and especially their leaders, didn't trust Tony's politics or his friends—like Ralph Nader and all those environmentalists. As civilian-soldiers of the national security state, most atomic workers were selected for qualities that put them at odds with the likes of a Mazzocchi. They had little use for his health and safety crusade. They were more inclined to unite with their employers against all critics.

But by the 1970s, dozens of civilian atomic power plants had come online, and hundreds more were in the works. More and more of OCAW's nuclear workers—people who mined and refined uranium and made nuclear fuel rods—came from the civilian side of the industry, where the work culture was less militaristic. They were more open to Mazzocchi's ideas. And they needed all the help they could get from the union, since they faced harsh conditions, ruthless employers, and lax government oversight.

Nowhere were conditions crueler than at Kerr-McGee's facilities in the Southwest, which employed mostly Mexican American uranium miners. Steve Wodka glimpsed these conditions during an epic struggle in Grants, New Mexico, in 1973:

> In '73 there was this long, horrific strike by Kerr-McGee uranium miners in New Mexico. OCAW ran big spreads in the union paper. And to me—you know, I was twenty-two, twenty-three years old—it looked just like *The Salt of the Earth*. The same Chicano workers, up against the big company, under terrible conditions. I mean, Kerr-McGee was brutal. It was a violent, brutal strike.[1]

The seven hundred workers at Kerr-McGee's uranium mines and mills walked out after the company tried to break the union by removing the grievance procedure, seniority rights, and job security protections. Eighty percent of the strikers were Mexican Americans; another 7 percent were Native Americans.

The local union president, Margarito Martinez, believed that Kerr-McGee's attack was payback for the union's drive for better health and safety conditions. Martinez himself had testified at government hearings calling for stricter radioactive exposure limits to halt the growing epidemic of lung cancer among uranium miners. Others speculated that the company forced a strike over workers' seniority and job security protections so it could rid itself of older, overexposed workers before they were diagnosed with cancer, saddling the company with their expensive health care costs.[2]

A year before the Grants conflict, Kerr-McGee had instigated another strike at a small, isolated plant that Mazzocchi hadn't heard of—a new facility in Cimarron, Oklahoma. The Cimarron plant produced fuel rods containing plutonium pellets for use in an experimental fast-flux (breeder) reactor. Proponents hoped such breeder reactors would produce endless quantities of plutonium for both nuclear devices and civilian atomic power plants.

Kerr-McGee planned to take advantage of this bonanza, and did not want a union at its new fuel rod production plant to get in the way. So the company tried to rip up the contract with the 150 Cimarron workers.

The company's founding partner Bob Kerr, who died in 1963, had been a governor and influential US senator from Oklahoma. Kerr was infamous for having his hand in every conceivable government and industry cookie jar and for cheerfully channeling money and contracts to his state, his friends, and himself.[3] Along the way, he and his partner, Dean McGee, known for his prowess in finding oil, turned their little exploration company into a mammoth energy combine with interests in coal, uranium, natural gas, timber, and chemicals. By the 1970s, Kerr-McGee was the largest private-sector uranium producer in the world.[4] In sparsely populated Oklahoma, it *was* the world. And yet there in the middle of a "right-to-work" state (where workers did not have to join the union even if a majority voted in favor of it), workers unionized. In 1972, 100 of the Cimarron plant's 150 workers voluntarily paid dues to the union. And in that year, they decided to strike over poor working conditions. Unfortunately, the company had no problem finding farm boys and girls willing to cross the picket lines. By the end of the strike, the union was barely breathing: Only twenty dues-paying members remained under contract, a contract literally written by Kerr-McGee.

For the company, busting the strike was only a first step. Managers began working behind the scenes to entice workers to sign a petition calling for a decertification election to eliminate the union.

In 1974, Swisher reversed his long-held policy of keeping Mazzocchi and Wodka at bay. "He paid for this committee from the Cimarron local to come to DC—and that began the episode," Mazzocchi said. "Swisher must have figured it was a loser. Otherwise, he would never let us get near a nuclear plant."

II

When the three-member delegation from Cimarron sat down in his cramped offices on 16th Street, Mazzocchi could sense defeat. Tice, Brewer, and Silkwood told Mazzocchi their story of woe: the broken strike, the gutted contract, the company's push to decertify the union.

"I said, 'Look. I'll send you up to the Atomic Energy Commission tomorrow,'" Mazzocchi remembered. "But in my mind I'm saying, *There ain't a fuckin' thing we're gonna do here. There's gonna be a lost decert election.*"

As Wodka worked with the threesome to shape their complaints into precise demands to the AEC, it became clear that Kerr-McGee was running a plutonium pigsty in rural Oklahoma. It was also clear that the company encouraged workers to think that assembling plutonium pellets into fuel rods was little more dangerous than assembling curtain rods. Yes, plutonium was radioactive, and alarms did go off regularly at the plant. Of course workers received small doses of radiation now and then. But according to Tice, Brewer, and Silkwood, the company had never mentioned the C-word—cancer. Workers didn't know that plutonium was the most carcinogenic substance ever discovered.

Even many of Kerr-McGee's local managers genuinely believed there was no cancer link. Company-oriented consultants repeated the mantra, "Plutonium has not been found ever to have poisoned a single employee or a single member of the public at large"—though hundreds of uranium miners had died of similar exposures caused by alpha radiation.[5] The Cimarron plant's health and safety director had a degree in poultry science.[6]

Cutbacks and speedup created such horrific working conditions that production workers turned over at a rate of nearly 60 percent a year, according to the local unionists. On the plus side, this meant that most workers soon got out of harm's way. But with such rapid turnover, it was predictable that accidents would happen. And they did.

Mazzocchi learned quickly that Tice, Brewer, and Silkwood themselves didn't have a clue that the plutonium processed at their plant caused cancer. He arranged for two nuclear scientists to conduct educational sessions for workers back at the Cimarron plant as soon as possible. Maybe this would disrupt workers' company-induced complacency and win a majority back to the union.

But while the move might boost the union's vote in the decertification election, it wouldn't keep workers from being crushed again come bargaining time. Mazzocchi thought that Kerr-McGee would force another strike and again replace the OCAW strikers with local scabs. The union workers needed more than an education session. But what? The press would hardly be interested in a tiny Oklahoma struggle over wages and working conditions, unless a pile of bodies appeared or plutonium threatened the community.

Without a hook, Mazzocchi was pessimistic. He returned to work, letting Wodka finish up with the visiting delegation.

Then, as the three Cimarron unionists were preparing to leave, Silkwood drifted into Mazzocchi's private office—and offered him a potent lead.

> Karen said: "You know, there's some other problems that I'd like to talk to you about." I said, "What are they?" She said, "I work in a quality-control lab, and I noticed the lab technician would use a felt pen on the X-ray to cover over that little thin line that showed a crack in the control rod welds." And she told me there was some fooling with the computer data, too. I said, "Look, Karen, if you could prove that, I think we could use it to beat the company and improve the conditions in that facility."

Mazzocchi then told Silkwood about his good friend David Burnham, a writer for *The New York Times*. Burnham had broken the Serpico case (about corruption in the New York City Police Department) and was now researching atomic energy issues. As Tony explained it later:

> My idea was for Karen to steal X-rays and other data and deliver it to us. Then we'd deliver them to the *Times*. Dave could get us a front-page story. We would then get his piece to the workers to convince them they should keep a union, that the union could protect them. I also thought that if the company had a front-page *New York Times* story, the nuclear industry would jump their ass and say to Kerr-McGee, "Hey, you better resolve this union problem before we get smeared further."

The strategy had worked on Shell Oil, which had been pressured to back down by an embarrassed industry. With the public already jittery about nukes, an exposé of possible faulty control rods for the controversial fast-breeder reactor might well send the industry running to the phone to tell Kerr-McGee to settle this tiny labor squabble.

Mazzocchi's aggressive game plan assumed certain unwritten rules of engagement. The union's job was to inform the members and empower them to fight intensely against unsafe conditions—by finding community allies, embarrassing the company through the media, and any other smart tactics the union could think of. It expected the company to retaliate by threatening workers' jobs, suspending or firing activists, and otherwise violating labor law. In a strike or lockout, the company would rely on scabs, get injunctions to cripple picket lines, cut off strikers' health benefits, get finance companies to harass strikers who fell behind on their mortgages and loans, and perhaps even instigate physical attacks on picketers.

But usually a large company like Kerr-McGee would go only so far to win its war with labor. While the company might see a show of force as necessary, its primary goal was to get back to quiet production. Major corporations did not like public exposure, so they often chose to settle rather than wage a protracted war.

By 1974, Tony was seasoned. He'd seen organized crime, mass strikes, red-baiting, police violence, political corruption, and dozens of union bargaining campaigns. He had no reason to believe that Kerr-McGee was different from any other company. Mazzocchi didn't believe in good and bad corporations or executives. The logic of capitalism, he was convinced, would force any company, no matter how good or bad, to place profits before worker and public health, and to give in only when their profits or reputation were sufficiently threatened.

A company like Kerr-McGee might be a little more pigheaded than average, but in the end it was just another giant to be confronted. And with luck, guile, and union workers courageous and tough enough to put their jobs on the line, it could perhaps be defeated. The keys, as always, were building a base among workers, appealing to the community, and finding the company's vulnerabilities—a Mazzocchi-style corporate campaign.

But although neither Mazzocchi nor Wodka would ever acknowledge it, they were in over their heads. At Kerr-McGee, it turned out the usual rules of engagement did not apply.

Kerr-McGee's little plutonium venture in Oklahoma formed a critical element in a very large fight about the future of atomic energy. The battle had begun with the building of a fast-breeder reactor on the Clinch River in Tennessee. The Atomic Energy Commission and large corporations such as Westinghouse and Kerr-McGee placed considerable bets on it, with the AEC providing much of the financing. The AEC undermined anyone who argued that plutonium was just too dangerous for use in civilian reactors.

The agency buried its own safety study, which had found that a single mishap could contaminate an area the size of Pennsylvania and kill hundreds of thousands. The commission repeatedly fought against improved safety standards for workers, arguing that the danger was minimal. Billions of federal and corporate funds were at risk.

The nuclear-industrial complex needed the Cimarron plant and its plutonium-packed fuel rods for its new breeder reactors. National security was at stake. While oil was critical for defense and the economy, plutonium was defense itself. The "oil weapon" was a metaphor. Nuclear weapons were the real thing.

Mazzocchi did not grasp at first how powerful this government-military-corporate compact was. Nuclear weapons production and atomic fuel production were shrouded in secrecy, not subject to normal congressional oversight. This made it easier for the weapons establishment, the atomic industry, and Kerr-McGee to operate outside the law. Investigations in 1975 would reveal that the AEC regularly cheated on its budgets to promote projects such as the breeder reactor. Nuclear supremacy justified all manner of public deceit.

This industry also rewrote the laws of the marketplace. It demanded and received huge public subsidies and guaranteed profits. In fact, without government insurance, civilian nuclear power plants could not exist.

In Oklahoma, things were worse. Kerr-McGee was king, and what was good for the company was by definition good for the state.

As he geared up for a fight, Mazzocchi did not fully appreciate the qualitative differences between the oil bosses and the plutonium bosses—the degree of corporate-government collusion and the extremes to which the plutonium industry and its government allies might go to protect their interests. Mazzocchi assumed the other side would play by the unspoken rules of the game. They would cheat, lie, intimidate, and manipulate. But never did he entertain the notion that this fight might lead to murder.

III

Mazzocchi knew from experience that Kerr-McGee would probably catch wind of Karen Silkwood's efforts. If management found out too soon, the scheme would collapse, and Silkwood would be fired. Mazzocchi told her that under no circumstances was she to tell a soul—not Tice, not Brewer, not even her best friend. She would report only to Wodka.

Tony put a great deal of trust in Karen. She was "forceful," he said, and very smart. The later depiction of Silkwood as a wild child did not do her justice. Mazzocchi and Wodka saw immediately that she was levelheaded, conscientious, and tough. Mazzocchi felt that if Silkwood had "the goods," they just might turn around this loser of a struggle.

Wodka also sensed these qualities in Silkwood—and more. She had an attractive, alluring edge. After that first conference in Washington and a working dinner with the group, he showed her the town. They hit it off and began a clandestine relationship. It was heady stuff for Silkwood. She had come to Washington as the lowly third wheel of a delegation representing only 20 of 150 workers at a little-known plant. In a matter of hours she was working with the best minds in her union—and being wooed by one of them. And she was being enlisted as a secret source for *The New York Times*.

But first she had to return to hell in Oklahoma: Management was applying the screws to the union as the decertification election neared.

Silkwood prepared for the educational meetings with scientists that Mazzocchi had set up for the Cimarron plant workers. And on the sly, she continued to collect evidence on the company's faulty fuel rods. Her lifeline was Steve Wodka, whom she called regularly. With her permission, Wodka recorded Silkwood's detailed reports about conditions in the plant. On October 7, 1974, Karen let Steve know that there were "no repercussions from the trip to DC," but that the workers were "still a little scared of us. They think we're trying to shut down the plant and take away their jobs."[7]

As she itemized a string of incidents and grievances, Silkwood displayed an acute analytical understanding. She knew, for instance, that the company violated the law when it refused to allow the union to talk to workers during lunchtime and breaks. And as for quality control: "We're still passing all the welds [on the control rods] no matter what the pictures look like," she told Wodka. "I've got a [bad] weld I'd love for you to see."

That was the smoking gun. Kerr-McGee was cheating on their quality-control tests, and if those faulty rods failed inside an experimental fast-breeder reactor, it could spark a nuclear nightmare.

Silkwood also described to Wodka extremely dangerous conditions in which "people were walking into hot rooms" where plutonium had been released without protective gear. "We've got eighteen- and nineteen-year-old boys. . . . They didn't have the schooling. They don't understand what radiation is." She told Wodka that the company monitored workers through nasal tests, then told them, after the numbers went down, that the radiation "all came out in the nasal smear."

Silkwood herself worked in the quality-control lab, not in production. She was most concerned about those who were regularly exposed to plutonium when pipes leaked and gloves ripped. "What about those other boys?" she asked Wodka. "It works on their genes? It accumulates in their genes?"

"It sure as hell does," he said.

Silkwood said she was worried about what would happen to them over time as they "breathe [plutonium] in once a week, every week. You're out there and you're goddamn well gonna have something," she said to Wodka.

Wodka had just returned from visiting Dean Abrahamson and Donald Geesman, the two atomic scientists from the University of Minnesota who soon would speak to the Cimarron workers. He responded to Karen bluntly. "The whole point is that plutonium is so carcinogenic, so potent . . . that the conditions you work under . . . you don't have to work there for five years. You might only have to work there for one friggin' month and you've got enough of a body burden to cause cancer."

In a flash, Silkwood realized that not only were all those unschooled farm boys in danger, but so was everyone in the plant—including her. With a hint of panic, she shot back, "Steve, don't tell me that shit!"

"That shit" was the main weapon in Mazzocchi's strategy to win the decertification campaign. The unionists had to prove to Cimarron workers that their health was in danger and that they needed the union to protect them.

Silkwood arranged for the workshops with the scientists to be held near the facility—one session before work and another after. The workshops were public, and management would know every word that was said. On October 10, Silkwood and one hundred of her co-workers came to hear Abrahamson and Geesman talk about the toxicity of plutonium. Tapes of the workshops revealed that Silkwood had quickly absorbed the gravity of the situation. She asked key questions and offered useful comments.[8]

But the tapes also revealed how clueless other workers were about the dangers they faced. They were stunned to learn that plutonium could cause cancer. Once they realized the severity of their exposure, nearly every question they asked focused on possible cures. Could chelated compounds clear out all the plutonium from their bodies, as management had told them? No. Could they get the plutonium out of their lungs? No. When the company gave them a few days off until their readings went down, did that mean the problem was gone? No.

As the questions cascaded, it started to dawn on these workers that the company had done everything possible to downplay the problem. As Professor Geesman later stated on ABC TV's *Reasoner Report:* "You've got a management that just manages to be aware that plutonium is different from soybean meal. You've got a weak local union plant situated in a dirt-poor area of the state with basically a captive labor force. The labor force is highly transient with a substantial turnover every year. . . . It's not my image of the nuclear priesthood."[9]

For workers, two worlds of authority had collided. The paternalistic company, which had assured everyone they were safe and protected, had been challenged by the scientific experts, who told them that inhaling a microscopic grain of plutonium could cause lung cancer.

As Mazzocchi envisioned, the briefings gave workers a new framework for comprehending the lax safety conditions at the plant. For the first time, many of them realized the company would not protect them, but the union just might.

Support grew.

Just one week after the presentations, workers voted against decertifying the union by a margin of eighty to sixty-one.

Karen continued to secretly collect data for her upcoming meeting with *New York Times* reporter David Burnham. She sensed that the company was on to her. In her conversations with Wodka and others, Karen said she also feared for her own health, as she realized how much she had been exposed to lethal substances at Kerr-McGee. She wanted to have more children but now was afraid her reproductive organs might already be damaged. One more severe plutonium exposure, it seemed, could send her running from the plant for good.

As if on cue, just as she was preparing for her first meeting with the

Times, Silkwood was contaminated—repeatedly. On November 5, her arm, neck, and nose emitted high levels of radioactivity. She learned from Abrahamson that high nose readings were extremely dangerous because they signified that plutonium had already entered the lungs. The company then put her through a decontamination shower using a wire brush dipped in a mixture of Clorox and Tide. The readings went down.

The next day, after only one hour in the plant, her readings increased again. This time she scrubbed down with stronger chemicals: potassium-permanganate and sodium-bisulfate. She called Abrahamson in tears. On November 7, Silkwood returned to work with urine and fecal samples to be tested, and took another nasal smear. The results were more than three hundred times higher than the day before. Her hands, arms, chest, neck, and ear were red hot.[10]

The company searched for the source and could not locate it inside the plant. It checked her car and several other places where she had traveled. Still negative.

Kerr-McGee then sent a team in full protective gear to search Silkwood's home. They discovered extremely high readings in her bathroom and in her refrigerator—especially in a baloney sandwich. They tore her house apart, put all her belongings in drums, and carted them away. They brought lawyers to the scene who grilled her. They cordoned off her home but did not offer her alternative accommodations.

Silkwood was in serious distress. She believed someone had deliberately contaminated her and her house. For the first time, she thought the exposures she received might kill her.

The timing of the contamination and the locations all indicated that she had not poisoned herself, but had been poisoned deliberately, and more than once, by someone else. "They put something in her refrigerator, contaminated the baloney," Mazzocchi said. "She was eating baloney with her hands, it got all over the house. Under AEC regulations, you could get into the house if it was contaminated. It was a perfect setup for them. But they didn't find the evidence. They knew she had it. They had been tapping her phone."

Mazzocchi wasn't paranoid. James Smith, a Kerr-McGee manager, later said in a sworn affidavit that a special Kerr-McGee inspection team had read Silkwood's personal letters, notes, diaries, and other documents. Then they gave the papers to James Reading, Kerr-McGee's chief of security and a former lieutenant in the Oklahoma City police. According to Smith, they wanted anything that could incriminate Silkwood.[11]

Kerr-McGee officials wanted to interview Silkwood more fully. They implied that they suspected her of deliberately taking plutonium home with her. (Their accusation was self-implicating. Were their security procedures so lax that employees could walk right out of the plant with plutonium? Yes. Investigations would show that any number of employees, corporate officials, agents, or security personnel could have taken the plutonium from the plant and placed it in Silkwood's home.)

When Karen called Steve Wodka after the search, her calm, analytical demeanor was eroding. She feared the worst.

Wodka told her to refuse to meet with the company unless he was present. Mazzocchi suggested that she immediately get tested by doctors with no connection to Kerr-McGee.

"I was in Reno, Nevada, at the time," Mazzocchi said. "Steve called me and said, 'Karen's been contaminated.' I said, 'Demand that they fly her to the whole-body counter at Los Alamos,' which I figured was the nearest place she could get a whole-body scan. It's similar to a CAT scan. You go through this dark tube, and it measures your radiation."

At Wodka's persistent urging, the company agreed to fly Silkwood, her boyfriend Drew Stephens, and her roommate Sheri Ellis, to Los Alamos on November 10, 1974, for testing. The results, they were told, showed small but statistically insignificant readings for Sheri and Drew. Karen had higher readings, about a quarter of what the AEC then allowed for a lifetime of exposure. Nevertheless, the Los Alamos doctors assured Karen that she had nothing to fear. Karen tried hard to believe them.

What they didn't tell her was that there was little evidence that these standards were safe even for healthy, nonsmoking males—let alone a ninety-four-pound female with asthma who smoked heavily. But Karen had desperately needed some good news. She and Sheri, leaving Drew behind, went out partying on that cool November night, a small respite from the plutonium plague.

Mazzocchi realized that time was not on their side. Silkwood no longer was working quietly behind the scenes. *She* was the scene. The sooner she handed over her evidence to the *Times,* the better.

"I thought we needed to push up our time line," Mazzocchi recalled. He wanted Wodka to make sure that Silkwood had documentation. If she didn't, "I'm not going to send Burnham down there. We can't deal with allegations, only facts."

During a series of conversations, Wodka gave Silkwood every opportunity to back out. She assured him that she had real evidence and was ready. The Burnham rendezvous was moved up to November 13, 1974, at the Holiday Inn in Oklahoma City, only thirty miles from Cimarron. Drew would pick up Wodka and Burnham at the airport and take them to the hotel. Karen had a union meeting to attend that day; afterward she would drive to meet them.

In violation of Mazzocchi's gag order, Karen had already confided in her friend and co-worker Jean Jung about her undercover mission. Later, in a sworn affidavit, Jung recounted that Silkwood "told me . . . she had photographs of defective welds on sample fuel pin claddings taken from lots which were passed by quality control. She once told me about a particularly bad batch of rods . . . which she said should never have been allowed to leave the plant."

Jung reported that after the union meeting, Karen had come over to her, crying quietly, to let her know that she was contaminated and that she was frightened. Despite the good news from the Los Alamos tests, Karen believed she would die of cancer.

According to Jung, Karen then pointed to documents in a dark brown folder she was carrying and said "there was one thing she was glad about. That she had all the proof concerning falsification of records. As she said this she clenched her hand more firmly on the folder and notebook she was holding. She told me she was on her way to meet Steve Wodka and the *New York Times* reporter. . . ."[12]

Then Silkwood got into her white 1973 Honda to complete her mission.

Steve Wodka, Karen's boyfriend Drew Stephens, and reporter David Burnham had arrived at the Holiday Inn around 8:30 PM and ordered take-out food. They hoped Silkwood might already be there, but they knew being late wasn't unusual for her. By 10 PM, however, they began to worry. Wodka called the café where the union meeting had been held, but everyone had left.

He then reached Jack Tice at home and got the jolt of his young life.

Karen had been in a bad accident on Highway 74. She was taken to Logan County Hospital, where they pronounced her dead on arrival.

IV

Mazzocchi had prepared himself for the worst imaginable outcome at the Cimarron plant. "I had promised her a job in New York, at Group Health Insurance," he said, "and I had that nailed down for her. I thought she was going to get fired. Who thought she was going to get killed?"

After receiving the news, Wodka, Burnham, and Stephens rushed to the crash scene in search of evidence. The car had already been towed, but they snooped around looking for tracks and skid marks, finding nothing except some detritus from the crash.

They scrambled to locate Karen's car and to get a report from the Oklahoma Highway Patrol. Trooper Rick Fagen, who investigated the accident, told them that he believed Silkwood fell asleep at the wheel. Her car had crashed into a concrete culvert, and Karen had been impaled by her steering wheel. When Wodka suggested the possibility of foul play, Fagen forcefully dismissed the notion.

Wodka and Drew Stephens convinced Silkwood's parents to allow the authorities to release the vehicle to Stephens so that it could be further examined.

The next day, Fagen interviewed workers at the plant, especially those who saw Karen at the union meeting. He also examined evidence from the car, finding what he believed were two marijuana joints and some sedatives. His report insinuated that Silkwood crashed after passing out while under the influence of drugs.

Fagen reported that he found no documents in Silkwood's car.

Mazzocchi seriously considered the idea that Silkwood's death may have been purely accidental. Yes, her death did represent a stroke of good luck for the company she had been targeting, but it was entirely possible that while traveling down that dark road, Silkwood ran into the culvert by accident. Burnham suggested the union hire a crash investigator, and Wodka convinced Mazzocchi to do it

Wodka located A. O. Pipkin, a former cop who had investigated more than two thousand cases and testified in over three hundred trials. Pipkin, who demanded no interference from the union, meticulously examined the car and the scene of the accident. He would later bring in another expert to go over his findings as well. What Pipkin initially reported to the union directly challenged the Oklahoma Highway Patrol report.

Pipkin said Silkwood hadn't fallen asleep or passed out at the wheel: The steering wheel was bent back on the sides, proving she'd been wide awake and hanging on tight as she tried to maintain control.

Pipkin also questioned how it was possible for someone who was asleep or in a drugged stupor to leave the road at a forty-five-degree angle and then drive along the grassy shoulder in a straight line until flying over the culvert and crashing into the wing wall.

What's more, Pipkin's microscopic analysis of a dent in Silkwood's back bumper showed that it was new and could not have been caused by either the crash or the towing of the wreck. Silkwood's death, he concluded, was no accident.

"It is my opinion," wrote Pipkin in his report, "there is enough circumstantial evidence present to indicate that V-1 [Silkwood's vehicle] was struck from the rear by an unknown vehicle, causing it go out of control, due to either the initial impact or to the combined impact and driver over-reaction."[13]

He put it more bluntly to Burnham and *The New York Times* on November 19: "I am not accusing any particular person of murder. Based on an independent investigation, however, it is apparent that someone forced Karen Silkwood from the road, therefore causing her death. I'll leave it to the Federal authorities to determine who and why."[14]

Did Mazzocchi and Wodka have a murder on their hands? Perhaps. Over and over, they tried to fit the facts into a more benign framework. Maybe someone from the company, or associated with it, wanted to scare Karen and bumped her car to get her to pull over and give back the documents, not realizing that the culvert was up ahead. Almost thirty years later, both Mazzocchi and Wodka still viewed it that way:

> **Wodka:** Looking back, people did know what she was up to. . . . The word did get out. And somebody put two and two together and realized that that night she was going to meet

with the reporter—and was, I think, just trying to get whatever papers she had—not to kill her, or drive her off the road—but, basically . . .

Mazzocchi: . . . Scare her. You know, in retrospect, you get involved in these things. You don't think somebody's gonna murder somebody. And I'm sure they didn't set out to murder her. Whoever drove her off the road that night set out to scare her. I mean, the chance of her hitting this cement culvert was remote. I mean, how many are there out in the field? . . . I don't think somebody went out to kill her that night—'cause on that road, to try to kill somebody, was serendipity. I mean, I think the guy was bumping her car—I think we have good evidence of that. And that culvert was there. And the car hit it—and, you know, it leaped over this thing, and she got impaled on the steering wheel. . . .

Wodka: I mean, she's driving a Honda Civic. . . . They were tiny, tiny cars. . . . And I've driven up and down that road. It's a dark, two-lane highway. I mean, you go for miles and miles. There's nothing but farms and fields. . . . So it was a good place to do it.

I remember asking her—she had been contaminated; she had lost all her possessions; she had lost her home. And she had gone out to Los Alamos. She had gone through the whole body counter. . . . She had come up with a count—the whole thing. I remember talking to her. I said, "Do you still want to go ahead, or not?"—Like "I got to chill out for a while" or "I gotta get my life back together." She said, "No, I want to go ahead." So we went ahead.

Were Kerr-McGee employees directly or indirectly involved? Mazzocchi thought the company's behavior after the crash was suspicious. For one thing, when Kerr-McGee heard that the union had hired Pipkin, it promptly hired the notoriously anti-union Pinkerton Detective Agency to investigate not Pipkin's findings, but Pipkin himself.[15] When OCAW released Pipkin's results, Kerr-McGee leaked stories about alleged problems with Pipkin's credentials, suggesting he was a shady operator. None of these allegations turned out to be true.

Then Kerr-McGee flexed its raw corporate power to crush the controversy. From depositions, Mazzocchi later learned that Kerr-McGee was briefed regularly by the state police and the FBI about the Silkwood investigation—just as it had been informed in advance of "surprise" health and safety inspections. As Wodka noted, "Kerr-McGee had so much control and influence with the Atomic Energy Commission, they didn't need to influence any investigation through the media."

To Wodka, the most terrifying thing was the lie detector test Kerr-McGee required workers to take when the company interrogated them about Silkwood. "They just forced the workers to take it. If they refused, they could be fired. If they took the test and it showed inconsistencies, they could be fired. If they told the truth about how they were helping the union, they could be fired as well."[16]

The questions Kerr-McGee asked workers were outrageous: According to union affidavits and filings with the National Labor Relations Board and the Nuclear Regulatory Commission, on December 23, 1974, Kerr-McGee asked the following:

- Did you know or ever talk to Steve Wodka?
- Do you belong to the union?
- Did you know or ever speak with Karen Silkwood?
- Have you recently seen or talked to Drew Stephens [Silkwood's boyfriend]?
- Did you ever do anything detrimental to Kerr-McGee?
- Did you ever have an affair with a fellow employee?
- Did you ever talk to the press?[17]

Although the union urged its members not to participate, many who feared for their jobs succumbed.

Union officer Jerry Brewer was fired for an unproven time-card irregularity, going to his car during break time, and "his attitude." Shop chair Jack Tice was transferred to a remote area of the facility, and a manager was assigned to watch him constantly, even following him to the bathroom.[18]

And in case any of the farm boys were still too thick to get the anti-union message, Kerr-McGee abruptly shut the facility down (with no pay) for two weeks during the holiday season.

As Mazzocchi said on ABC's *Reasoner Report,* "Workers have been fired, fingerprinted, and given lie detector tests. The plutonium police state has arrived."[19]

Mazzocchi and Wodka used every tool at their disposal to keep the heat on Kerr-McGee. They pressured the Nuclear Regulatory Commission to rule on the union's health and safety complaints. They asked the National Labor Relations Board to reinstate Brewer and Tice. They urged the FBI to investigate of the crash. They called for a congressional investigation. And Mazzocchi worked the media hard.

David Burnham wrote seven stories over the next month in *The New York Times,* giving the union ample opportunity to air its case. On November 19, Burnham revealed Pipkin's initial findings in a story headlined, "Death of Plutonium Worker Questioned by Union Officials." The next day, in an article titled "Plutonium Plant Under Scrutiny," Burnham reported that the AEC would investigate allegations that "an Oklahoma plutonium factory had been falsifying the inspection records of fuel rods to be used in an experimental reactor."

The controversy that erupted over whether or not Karen was asleep at the wheel continued. The Oklahoma police had said Silkwood was exhausted from her long drive back from Los Alamos the night before her crash. Burnham reported she actually had flown back a day earlier.[20] The Oklahoma medical examiner said that Silkwood was under the influence of "a sedative-hypnotic drug, methaqualone, associated with traces of ethyl alcohol."[21] But ABC's *Reasoner Report,* using Pipkin's findings, forced the Oklahoma State Police chief to admit on the air that Silkwood had been wide awake at the time of the crash, because the steering wheel was pushed back on its sides.

There was also the controversy about how the plutonium got into Silkwood's house and into her body. Rumors circulated that she smuggled plutonium out of the factory in her vagina, and then poisoned herself to embarrass the company and help the union. Others alleged she was part of a plutonium smuggling ring. In early January, the AEC released a report revealing that Silkwood did not have ready access to the specific type of plutonium found in her in body (AEC isotope studies can detect differences in each lot of plutonium pellets). The AEC also concluded that someone had spiked two of her urine samples with plutonium. The report could not explain how the plutonium got into her house and food.[22] In "AEC Can't Say How Worker Swallowed Plutonium," Burnham wrote that AEC officials had told Wodka there was "absolutely no evidence to suggest that Miss Silkwood had been smuggling plutonium."[23] No smuggling evidence against her ever surfaced.

The blame-the-victim corporate offensive continued. In December, three plutonium accidents occurred at the Cimarron plant in one day, prompting the AEC to investigate. Kerr-McGee told the *Times* it had "evidence that some of the incidents have been contrived."[24] No evidence was forthcoming.

But Tony and the press couldn't find the original smoking gun: The papers and photographs Silkwood had planned to deliver documenting the faulty control rods had vanished.

A backlash started to build. When National Public Radio's Barbara Newman and Peter Stockton visited the Cimarron area, they found a great deal of hostility toward Silkwood: More than a few referred to her as "that bitch" who had threatened their jobs. Even Tice and Brewer had become critical of the union after learning that Silkwood had done undercover work without their knowledge.[25]

Mazzocchi also could feel the pendulum inside the union swinging not only against Silkwood, but against him as well. OCAW officials wanted him to back off. The union had already paid for Pipkin and for the hundreds of hours that Wodka and Mazzocchi had spent pressing public agencies and the media to investigate. The Kerr-McGee workers were becoming increasingly hostile, and some unionists worried that the Silkwood publicity was harming the interests of all atomic workers.

OCAW vice president Swisher arranged a quiet meeting between the union's top officers and Dean McGee to patch things up. As Mazzocchi recalled:

> I got called to Denver to meet with McGee himself. Because Swisher got to Grospiron, who says: "You know, this publicity is bad stuff for us." So when I got in the room with Dean McGee, I said, "First of all, you tried to decert the union." He denied that. I

> took a fuckin' leaflet out that the company had put out. He said, "Well, I didn't know anything about that." I said, "Well . . . the place is a bloody mess. You did nothing to clean it up." He said, "Well, we want to cooperate—we want to turn over a new leaf." I said, "Fine. But we're not gonna lay off following up on who killed Karen Silkwood."
>
> Grospiron said, "Yeah, we're not." The company just wanted to get us off the Silkwood thing. So McGee left, and I left, and we continued to do what we did. I give Grospiron credit. There was a lot of pressure on him.

Grospiron's resolve had limits. Union officers soon ganged up on Mazzocchi and told him to stay away from the press. But Mazzocchi worked incessantly behind the scenes, talking about Silkwood to reporters, to movement activists, to anyone who would listen. The murkiness of the Silkwood case invited innuendo, hearsay, and paranoia; Mazzocchi was determined to stick to facts and plausible theories. It felt to Tony as if "nobody knew about what happened to Karen—nobody cared. She was dead. I tried to get people interested in it, and I couldn't."

With Burnham running out of leads and top OCAW officers growing impatient, Mazzocchi was left virtually alone in his dogged quest for the truth about Karen Silkwood. He never considered that Silkwood's killers might come after him.

Then, on, the night of January 17, 1975, Mazzocchi blacked out while driving home from an AFL-CIO health and safety conference in Warrenton, Virginia. His car hit the grass median, flipped into the air, and landed upside down. Its roof was smashed to the steering wheel.

Miraculously, Mazzocchi survived.

The accident, coming just two months after Silkwood's, alarmed the famously unflappable, practical-minded union leader. Mazzocchi couldn't help thinking about how much the nuclear industry would have benefited from his death. "If they knocked me out, the union would have shut up about Silkwood," Mazzocchi said. "There was a lot of pressure in the union to get off it. If I had died, it would have been over with. There wouldn't have been a story."

After his crash, Mazzocchi redoubled his efforts. He convinced Ronnie

Eldridge, the editor of *Ms. Magazine,* to cover the story. Eldridge assigned B. J. Phillips, who wrote "The Case of Karen Silkwood" for the magazine in the spring of 1975. Mazzocchi also worked with Howard Kohn at *Rolling Stone,* who in March wrote a more provocative piece titled "The Nuclear Industry's Terrible Power and How It Silenced Karen Silkwood." Barbara Newman did a March segment for National Public Radio, updating her December report.

The *Ms*. connection ignited two feminist organizers, Kitty Tucker and Sarah Nelson, from the National Organization for Women (NOW), to pick up the Silkwood story. "It would be terrific if the women's movement does something about this," Mazzocchi told them.[26]

Tucker and Nelson set up Supporters of Silkwood (SOS). They made November 13, 1975, Karen Silkwood Memorial Day, and put her front and center in NOW's "Stop Violence Against Women" campaign. They mobilized local chapters to write to their senators asking for a congressional investigation. They circulated petitions. They notified the local press and held rallies and candlelight parades in several cities to the cry of "Who Killed Karen Silkwood?" Their superb organizing, coupled with increasing interest in the women's movement, drew the media.

When NOW leaders visited the Justice Department in August 1975 to demand a thorough investigation of Silkwood's death, according to one account "nearly 100 reporters and TV crew members were waiting in the corridor and on the stone steps."[27]

The activists shepherded Silkwood's cause through congressional hearings and into a 1979 civil trial pleaded by Danny Sheehan, an idealistic young lawyer, and the more seasoned and famed attorney Gerry Spense. After the longest civil trial in Oklahoma history, the jury awarded Karen's father and children a $10.5 million verdict against Kerr-McGee.*

Soon Hollywood producers and others were vying for the movie rights. As Mazzocchi recalled:

> Gloria Steinem popped into my office with B. J. Phillips, and they wanted exclusive rights to the Silkwood stuff. I said, "I'm not going

*Kerr-McGee appealed, and in 1985 the Tenth Circuit Court ordered a new trial. Kerr-McGee then offered the family $1.38 million; the case was settled out of court.

> to give you exclusive rights. This story belongs to everybody. If anybody wants to make a movie of it, they should."
>
> They start jumping up and down. B. J. Phillips said that she wrote the first article. So I said, "Yeah. So? It was a lousy article to start with. Hey. Just because you wrote one story, it doesn't give you exclusive rights." So they stormed out of the office.

Soon after, Mike Nichols directed the movie *Silkwood,* starring Meryl Streep as Silkwood; Cher as Silkwood's roommate Sherri Ellis; Kurt Russell as her boyfriend Drew Stephens; and Ron Silver as Steve Wodka.

"Mr. Nobody played Mazzocchi," said Wodka with a chuckle.[28]

"It was ABC, of all people, that did *Silkwood,* Tony said. "We told them we wouldn't give them any information unless they named Kerr-McGee and the union. And they did it. Cher said that Streep asking her to play the role of Sherri resurrected her career."

> We gave Streep the tapes of the union's conversations with Silkwood, because we had taped Karen every time she called us. And we described Karen to Streep. And then, when I looked at the movie, Streep had all Karen's body motions. And for you to describe another human being, and how they move, and then see the actor move in exactly the same way—it was incredible.

And yet physically, Mazzocchi said, "It was Cher who was the dead ringer for Karen."

By 1983, when the movie was released, thousands of activists had already turned Karen Silkwood into a genuine American heroine. Mazzocchi was thrilled by these events, but he also wanted to set the record straight. As he told the OCAW convention in 1979:

> I have nothing against feminism, but Karen wasn't a feminist. She's been adopted by the feminist movement. . . . She has been portrayed as an anti-nuclear activist. She wasn't. She was involved in one simple activity; it was to save a local union at Kerr-McGee where the company was hell bent on destroying it. . . . Karen was solely a trade union martyr. . . . She made the supreme sacrifice.[29]

V

Had someone really tried to kill Mazzocchi to keep the Silkwood story buried? No one knows (or is telling). Stranger plots were rumored in the 1970s. In 1975, *The Washington Post*'s Bob Woodward reported that the Watergate special prosecutor's office was investigating a bizarre plan by E. Howard Hunt, a Nixon operative, to kill columnist Jack Anderson after he had published sensitive national security information. According to the article, "Hunt said one plan involved placing on the steering wheel of Anderson's car a substance that would enter the body through skin contact." Hunt had allegedly been looking for, and may have found, "a drug that would take effect when Anderson was driving home at high speed. . . ."[30]

Mazzocchi readily admitted that he had no evidence that he had been drugged before his accident. He had his suspicions, but saw no point in pursuing what would look like a narcissistic conspiracy theory. It was enough that he survived the wreck and was able to keep the Silkwood story alive.

One day more than a year after the accident, Susan Mazzocchi was packing up the house in preparation for a move. As she removed a clock from the kitchen wall, something fell to the floor and broke apart.

"It's a bug!" she exclaimed to Tony.

"I was looking for a roach to smash," Mazzocchi said. But what Susan had found was the other kind of bug.

Mazzocchi's ally (and Silkwood family attorney) Danny Sheehan took the find to a contact who worked for the CIA. "He called it 'the most sophisticated bugging device,'" said Mazzocchi. "It was sending a radio signal that somebody was picking up, maybe blocks away from the house."

Were the spying, the accident, and Silkwood connected? Sheehan tried to trace the bug through dark alleys of the surveillance underworld. He gave the device (still broken from its fall from the kitchen wall) to David Waters, a former CIA electronics expert. Reportedly, when Waters saw it he just smiled, and in less than a minute had the two-inch-long, three-quarter-inch-wide device back together again. Then he asked Sheehan, "What are you doing that the NSA is so interested in?"[31]

The suggestion that the National Security Agency was involved in the bugging of Mazzocchi's house seemed extravagant. But someone had been listening, and Tony always believed it was someone with an interest in thwarting a serious investigation of the Silkwood case—someone who feared its impact on the huge financial potential of nuclear power.

Through their dogged efforts, Mazzocchi and activists around the country had ensured that Karen Silkwood's sacrifice would never be forgotten.

Now, in looking ahead, Mazzocchi looked up. If he was ever going to liberate OCAW from the business unionists, the CIA, and the atomic establishment, he needed more authority. Mazzocchi wanted to become president of his union.

Karen Silkwood would have welcomed that.

THIRTEEN

The Heart of the Deal

Mazzocchi for president!

It was about time. Tony's rank-and-file allies had wanted this ever since he rode them up the escalator clause at the Rubinstein plant. But Mazzocchi took it slow. He viewed his run for the OCAW presidency as "an expression of a resurgent rank-and-file movement," not a personal quest. It was a mass "crusade," he said, for a dramatically different direction for the union and for the entire labor movement. His anti-corporate organizing had paved the way—the health and safety wars, the Shell strike, and the Silkwood battle.

Mazzocchi was determined not to make the usual cynical compromises—the payoffs, the promised jobs, the watered-down platform planks. He didn't see himself as a purist. But he believed he could only transform the union into a mass movement by winning a clean, clear mandate. He would hide nothing, running unabashedly as a militant, just as he had in his successful campaigns to be chief steward, local president, and executive board member.

This time, Mazzocchi would face more formidable opponents, both inside and outside the union, all determined to bring his winning streak to a halt. The OCAW was packed with influential officers and staff who were seasick from Tony's incessant boat rocking. They preferred a smooth ride with full union perks—extra pay, car allowances, the respect of their management "peers," and continued insulation from their own rank and file so they could stay comfortably in power. The last thing they wanted was Mazzocchi's class war.

The established leadership started with a big edge: the union's indirect method of electing officers, which favored wheeler-dealer incumbents. Instead of a rank-and-file vote, each local union selected delegates in a number proportionate to the local's size. At union conventions, about fifteen hundred delegates cast the votes of 168,000 union members to select the top four national officers. Under OCAW's rules, these delegates were free agents with no obligation to vote the preferences of their local's rank and file. Usually the delegation included the local's officers, who often voted in alignment with their international representative, the union staffer on whom they depended to help them negotiate contracts and solve grievances. Many delegates aspired to be appointed a rep themselves. So incumbent officers often made deals and promised jobs in exchange for delegate votes. With the system so rigged, OCAW's conservatives had good reason to think they could crush Mazzocchi.

Anti-Mazzocchi forces amassed outside the union as well. Oil executives did not appreciate the way he had whipped up public sentiment against them during the 1973 Shell strike. Dozens of corporations also had been bloodied by Mazzocchi-Wodka health and safety assaults—including Shell, Amoco, Texaco, Gulf, the Ethyl Corporation, Standard Oil, American Cyanamid, BASF, 3M, Carborundum, and Goodyear Atomic. Kerr-McGee was hardly fond of Mazzocchi, and the nuclear establishment as a whole did not relish the atomic workers' union being run by a founder of SANE and a friend of Ralph Nader.

And then there were the AFL-CIO's Cold Warriors, who knew that Mazzocchi would become a very loud voice within the federation, opposing all ties to CIA operatives and front groups. They knew Mazzocchi was disgusted with the AFL-CIO's training of Chilean unionists to help overthrow President Salvador Allende in 1973 and with the federation's massive support for the American Institute for Free Labor Development (AIFLD)—the big-business–AFL-CIO-CIA alliance that subverted left-leaning unions in Latin America.

In fact, the OCAW bureaucrats, the oil industry, and the Cold Warriors all yearned for the same kind of candidate—someone who was thoroughly dedicated to the nuts and bolts of American-style business unionism. Someone who would collaborate with industry through quiet collective bargaining, grievance handling, and arbitration. They already had such a person in tow.

II

Bob Goss first appeared on the national OCAW stage in 1965, after Mazzocchi maneuvered President Jack Knight into resigning. Goss tossed his hat into the race for OCAW president against Al Grospiron, Mazzocchi's candidate. Actually, he tossed his sombrero. For the previous nine years, Goss had worked for ORIT (Organizacion Regional Interamericana de Trabajo), an organization of the Western Hemisphere's "free" labor unions based in Mexico City.

ORIT was an offshoot of the International Confederation of Free Trade Unions, a consortium of national labor federations formed at the dawn of the Cold War to compete with World Federation of Trade Unions (which contained communist unions from the Soviet bloc as well as progressive unions from nonaligned and Western countries). ORIT worked in Latin America to encourage pro-capitalist trade unions and to oppose communist and socialist unions—which also included other unions that were, as one historian put it, "simply uncooperative."[1]

When it was based in Cuba in the early 1950s, ORIT first opposed the 1953 military coup that brought dictator Fulgencio Batista to power, then accommodated itself to his brutal regime. When the Castro-led revolution prevailed in 1959, ORIT fled to Mexico City to set up its new headquarters and chose one of Batista's former cabinet members as an assistant to ORIT's general secretary.[2] It was common knowledge among Latin American unionists that ORIT fronted for the CIA. As one US State Department official put it, "ORIT was bought and paid for by Uncle Sam."[3]

Philip Agee, the former CIA agent and whistleblower, fingered ORIT as "a principal mechanism for CIA labor operations in Latin America."[4] Its purpose, said Agee, was to subvert radical Latin American unions and help the CIA "divide the victims and neutralize their leaders."[5]

Bob Goss could hardly miss the CIA connections. Agee reported that, as of 1963, Goss's ORIT bosses—its secretary-general and assistant secretary-general—were CIA agents.[6] According to OCAW's official history, two years later Goss had become ORIT's assistant secretary-general.[7]

The CIA apparently viewed ORIT as incompetent. Agee, in a 1960 diary entry, wrote: "Officers in the WH Division [the CIA's Western Hemisphere Division] were practically unanimous in condemning ORIT. . . . They said ORIT is hopeless, discredited and completely ineffective for attracting non-communist labor organizations in Latin America."[8] At that time, Goss was hard at work for ORIT in Mexico City.

Goss also did odd jobs for the International Federation of Petroleum and Chemical Workers (IFPCW), where, according to a 1960 *Business Week* article, he "on one occasion jumped from Pakistan, to Greece, to Africa in order to lend a hand in strike settlements."[9] Congress would later expose the IFPCW as a CIA front at the time Goss was aiding it. While Goss was at ORIT, the IFPCW also served as a conduit for the CIA to channel money to Brazilian oil unions—part of the agency's successful effort to topple the democratically elected government of Joao Goulart in favor of a military dictatorship.[10]

It took chutzpah for Goss to run for OCAW president in 1965 while he was still working at ORIT's Mexico City spy center. He hadn't worked in an oil refinery since the 1940s, and he hadn't worked for OCAW since 1955, when he'd served as an international representative in California. Even the union's official (anti-Mazzocchi) history admitted that Goss "stood on a strange springboard from which to attempt the great leap to the top of the union."[11] Goss was doing what ORIT had trained him to do—"neutralize" yet another militant labor leader. Only this time he had to come home to do it.

The Grospiron-Mazzocchi alliance proved too tough for Goss to crack in 1965. When it became clear that Grospiron would win on the first ballot, Goss withdrew. He was no tactical dummy. After the election, Goss left Mexico and returned to his old job as international representative in California. This put him among the tribe of reps who most feared a Mazzocchi presidency, and who had the most power to block it. Within only two years, Goss had climbed his way up to become Grospiron's assistant, a highly coveted job. Mazzocchi, now living in DC and busily building the health and safety movement, didn't take Goss very seriously.

Goss quietly played yin to Mazzocchi's yang. While Mazzocchi was igniting grassroots health and safety wildfires all over the country, Goss, sitting in the office next to Grospiron, worked the union from the top down. As a keen student of power, he saw that Grospiron's inflated ego needed constant pumping. He also realized that Grospiron harbored a latent resentment of Mazzocchi's growing fame—a resentment Goss would fan.

Goss used his nuts-and-bolts skills to make his boss's job easier while also doing favors for as many reps as possible. Goss played the competent, ingratiating Grospiron lieutenant; Mazzocchi was the daring field general who created headaches for his boss. Goss was always there to point out Mazzocchi's excesses and suggest ways to rein him in.

Goss's good-old-boy personality also served him well. Genuinely personable, he was the kind of politician who remembered everyone's name, their spouse's name, and their birthdays. Mazzocchi, by contrast, was cooler. Small talk was not his specialty. While he relished addressing large audiences, Mazzocchi often avoided one-on-one eye contact. His dead-fish handshake didn't help, either. Mazzocchi built loyalty through his work, his vision, and his incredible commitment to the workers' cause. Goss built support by making friends and getting people comfortable with him.

Yin and yang moved into the starting gates when the union's two vice presidential spots opened up. Grospiron appointed Goss to the first opening in 1975, and then Mazzocchi and Goss both ran unopposed for the two vice presidential spots at the 1977 convention.

While the positioning seemed equitable, in fact Goss got the better deal. Grospiron put him in charge of oil and chemical bargaining, which would allow him to build alliances with the majority of the union's local leaders. It also allowed him to benefit from Grospiron's strong oil bargaining program. Mazzocchi, on the other hand, was stuck with health and safety, which he already led. He was also assigned the most difficult task in the union: organizing. In an ironic twist, Mazzocchi also inherited the atomic sector from Swisher, who had retired. But this sector was not fertile ground for votes.

Mazzocchi accepted the division of duties for two reasons: because he knew the union desperately needed a creative overhaul of its lackluster organizing program; and because Grospiron had promised to switch Mazzocchi's and Goss's assignments in 1979. With the cards so dealt, everyone anticipated the race to be decided at the 1981 convention, when Grospiron was expected to retire.

So while Mazzocchi had been out defending uranium miners, conducting dozens of health and safety campaigns, supporting the Shell strike, and trying to bring Karen Silkwood's killers to justice, Goss had moved from his CIA sinecure in Mexico to become the establishment favorite to succeed Grospiron.

III

When Tony became vice president, he, Susan, their six-year-old son Anthony, and their baby twins, Krissy and Lizzy, moved to Denver. With a mortgage financed by the GI Bill, they bought a home in the economically mixed Park Hill area.

"I got my ass kicked on a regular basis," recalled Anthony. "My parents didn't believe in busing and chose to send me to the neighborhood school. Finally my dad, who wouldn't hit a soul, bought a punching bag and taught me how to box. After that I held my own."[12]

The combination of the neighborhood and his father's incessant travel led young Anthony to harbor some strange beliefs. "I really thought my dad lived on an airplane. I told that to everyone. A teacher finally told my parents," he said. "Also, one day after I came home from a tough day getting beat up, I burst out, 'I hate black people—except for Daddy.' I thought he was black—you know, the darker Mediterranean complexion."

When Anthony acted up, Susan wanted Tony to exert some manly discipline. "My mother told him to spank me. I remember he had his tongue sticking out of the side of his mouth as he raised his hand," Anthony said. "But he could not do it. He never struck us. Instead my mom stepped in and did it. But it was bad enough if he looked disappointed in you."

Did Anthony feel neglected with a father on the road so much? "There was tons of love from my dad. If ever there was a crisis, he got there immediately, no matter where he was. And between the two of them, I felt lots of support and a lot of communication. But with my dad, I learned early on that you couldn't talk about heavy emotional stuff. It made him very uncomfortable, so we saved that for my mom.

"It's not like I had an epiphany, but I'm doing it differently with my baby son, Luca. I want to raise my own son: to be present and to be there emotionally as well."

IV

As Mazzocchi crisscrossed the country in his home in the sky, he launched a new organizing experiment that would make OCAW bureaucrats even more determined to deny him the presidency.

Tony believed the union was failing to organize new members because too many of the union's staff had little or nothing to do with recruiting. To close that gap, he declared an "organizing week" during which *all* full-time union officials and staff as well as rank-and-file volunteers would leaflet workplaces all over the country. Many reps were miffed: This seemed like unpaid compulsory overtime.

Mazzocchi commissioned original artwork and a new folk song, "Share Your Courage," to inspire the troops. For one spring week in 1979, the entire union went into the field, music blaring, leaflets in hand. Mazzocchi thought it was a breakthrough. Addressing the 1979 convention, he said:

> This was the first time we had mobilized this union or any union in behalf of a single effort. . . . We distributed over one-hundred-fifty thousand leaflets at plant gates from the Mexican border to the Arctic Circle, from the Atlantic to the Pacific Ocean, and it was a uniform scene and a uniform response. We said, "Join us." And workers responded, "Where the hell have you been?" And it's true, where have we been? We cannot organize people if we do not talk to them. We can't organize them if we do not go out to them.[13]

For Mazzocchi, this was a dress rehearsal for greater mobilizations. Once he became president of OCAW, he wanted to marshal the entire bureaucratic structure of the labor movement.

> We learned something else that week. We have the opportunity to mobilize around any issue. There are forty to fifty thousand fulltime union officials of all unions and locals in the United States and Canada. Can you imagine any given week or any given day when there is a total mobilization of this fulltime force, not counting the volunteers . . . ? It would be a message to corporations and the government that the trade union movement is awakening.
>
> I've been approached by a number of unions to join us in an effort of this sort and I would hope that in the next organizing week we are able to take the fifteen international unions who are geared to this [into] one single dimensioned effort of being at plant gates, or if it's around energy prices or the price of food. . . . This was a practice run. It was successful. It's a key to how we have to work in the future.[14]

Mazzocchi would send young radicals out into the field as well—like Carolyn Mugar, a law school graduate. "She said she wanted to work in the labor movement and understand what happens from a grassroots level before she became active as an attorney," Mazzocchi told the convention delegates.[15] Mugar volunteered to go work in a shop—just as he had done in 1950 at Helena Rubinstein.

Before she met Tony, Mugar, a talented photographer, had traveled to North Vietnam on a peace delegation and captured on film the pain and joy of the civilians during wartime, especially the children. In 1973, she was part of the activist support team for the American Indian Movement's seventy-one-day capture of Wounded Knee, South Dakota, site of an 1890 massacre of Sioux Indians by US troops.

Then Mugar heard Mazzocchi speak at Harvard. "He made you think you could be part of it. You felt invited. It was nonexclusionary. The 'it' for me was organizing. You thought there was a place you could do something—everybody did."[16]

The OCAW constitution did not make it easy for outsiders to become organizers. Those jobs were reserved for the rank and file. As Mark Dudzic, a local OCAW leader and Mazzocchi ally observed, this policy "was an important remnant of the CIO that helped OCAW maintain much of its unique character. While there was a certain amount of careerism in maintaining this policy, it also helped build a union that was not run by technicians and lawyers. It respected and nourished really smart local union leaders."[17]

But that rule didn't stop Carolyn Mugar. "I wanted to be a union organizer," she said "I was hell-bent on it."

That persistence was Mazzocchi's first impression of Mugar. He met her after making a speech in Cambridge. His group retired to a bar. "I really was just paying half attention. She said, 'I'd like to organize.' I knew nothing about her. And she bugged me and bugged me and bugged me with phone calls."

Mazzocchi finally relented. Although he couldn't hire Carolyn as an official organizer, he set up a new category of "organizing intern." Mugar was sent to Fair Play, South Carolina, where she worked with Mazzocchi's lieutenant, George Roach, to recruit atomic workers. A quick study, she soon became the coordinator of the new OCAW Boston Organizing Project working with Dick McManus, then Tony's assistant in Denver, to draw more young radicals into organizing. The project successfully pulled in a substantial number of new shops, but some in OCAW's bureaucracy worried about the young radicals.

V

Bob Goss built on these suspicions. He was the ultimate insider, the leader of the oil sector, the reps' good friend, and the defender of nuts-and-bolts unionism against Mazzocchi's left-wing militancy. As *The Washington Post* put it, "By conventional standards, Robert Goss, a popular union vice president with years of broad experience in the OCAW, should be a shoo-in to succeed Al Grospiron. . . ."[18]

What's more, Goss had learned a trick or two south of the border about how to discredit and defeat left-leaning labor leaders. He had no qualms about impugning Mazzocchi's motives, morals, and patriotism.

Or playing hardball, as Rafael Moure, OCAW's health and safety director, would learn on the day he received his marching orders. "Goss said to me, 'I understand that you people in the health and safety department are supporting Mazzocchi. I would like to warn you that there will be consequences if staff becomes involved.'"

Rafael, however, could not contain himself. He campaigned for Mazzocchi. Goss noticed. "He says to me, 'Look, I fucking hired you,'" Rafael said. "'A key value in the labor movement is loyalty. I thought we had an understanding about maintaining neutrality.' I said, 'You are right. But I want to tell you that I am not neutral.' At that point Goss saw red and said, 'You do as you see fit. But remember that all of it will have consequences.'"

Rafael, who had grown up in Colombia and absorbed liberation theology, didn't back down. "Before I met Mazzocchi, my socialist ideals had run their course," he said. "I knew we needed radical social change and revolutionary unions, but that it wasn't going to happen in America, not in my lifetime. And then you meet this man who shows you that there is so much that can be done and that we can fight politically to make change. And he gives you hope because he shows how as a professional you can contribute."

Goss had a different vision. A grand anti-communist accord uniting labor, capital, and government, he believed, would deliver an ever-rising standard of living to OCAW members. Yes, there would be conflicts, but management and labor could settle them. That was clear just from looking at oil workers' wages. From 1966 to 1979, their average hourly rates (after taxes) increased from $3.02 per hour to $9.95. The workers were solid middle-class Americans—most with a house and a couple of cars, maybe a boat, and enough left over to send the kids to college. Anyone who wanted to rock *that* boat had to be crazy, Goss believed. He proudly proclaimed to *The Washington Post* that he was an "internal nuts and bolts union man . . . with broad experience in the day-to-day operations of the union." And if you have a problem with management, he said, "you sit down and work it out."

If you have a problem? In Mazzocchi's view, unions were on the *Titanic*—and bureaucrats like Goss were belowdecks tightening a few loose screws. Goss and most of the hawkish AFL-CIO leadership lived in a make-believe world, Tony argued. There was no grand alliance among labor, management, and government, and if ever there had been, it was over. As globalization accelerated, corporate America was fleeing to cheaper labor markets. Soon all of Goss's nuts and bolts would be produced overseas. Mazzocchi called Goss the "business as usual candidate" with "his feet firmly planted in yesterday and no vision or strategy for the future."[19]

Mazzocchi's charges struck a chord with workers who were increasingly frustrated by labor's "impotence," as Tony called it. Even highly paid oil workers felt betrayed by a Democratic president and a Democratic Congress that had caved to Big Oil. Now that they'd finally earned their way into the middle class, their gains were being eaten away by inflation as the government pressured wages, but not profits. As Mazzocchi pointed out, the wage gains Goss touted amounted to a total increase of only sixteen cents an hour over fourteen years, after inflation was taken into account.

And by now OCAW workers understood better than anyone else that their health, their family's health, and their community's well-being were severely compromised by toxic exposures at work. "Business as usual" was hazardous to their health.

Mazzocchi also tapped into the rank and file's long-festering anti-bureaucratic instincts. Workers of all ideologies had seen their union leaders turn into collective bargaining managers with nice cars and clothes. "Too many labor leaders have forgotten where they came from. Too often they act more like corporation executives than the elected representatives of working people," Mazzocchi said. "If we are to survive, then the gap between leadership and membership must be closed."[20]

Mazzocchi also offered hope. At the very least he would try new strategies. He called for a broad community-labor alliance against the oil industry, for more worker and public input into corporate investment decisions. He wanted to implement a global union strategy to tackle multinational corporations. And he wanted to end labor's dependence on the Democratic Party by opening up a debate on the need for a new independent political party like Canada's New Democratic Party.

In the end, the OCAW election would come down to a contest of dreams—Goss's dream of a grand alliance between labor and capital that was no more versus Mazzocchi's dream of a workers' social movement that might never be.

VI

As far as Mazzocchi knew, this contest of dreams would be deferred until 1981, when Al Grospiron was scheduled to retire. When the time came, Mazzocchi expected Grospiron's support. As a civil rights populist from Texas, Grospiron was much closer to Mazzocchi ideologically than he was to Goss. But Grospiron felt Mazzocchi's shadow creeping over him.

Mazzocchi's growing fame—and his merry band of loyal young allies—surely grated on Grospiron's nerves. To soothe them, Tony made sure Al received as much credit as possible for OCAW's growing reputation. Because of Mazzocchi's health and safety work, the AFL-CIO chose Grospiron to lead its first national health and safety committee. When reporters sought statements and insight from Mazzocchi, he made sure they also spoke to Grospiron, sometimes with comical results. After being interviewed by a CBS crew at the union's Denver headquarters, Mazzocchi urged them also to interview Grospiron. When the producer complained that he didn't have film to waste, Mazzocchi got the crew to conduct the Grospiron interview with an empty camera.

By 1981, Grospiron would have served as president for sixteen years. "Al did a good job at OCAW," Tony maintained. "Nobody could have done what Al did. I understood that. He was a tough son of a bitch with the oil industry. But by then, he was tired." To happily step down, Grospiron needed a new position that would be at least somewhat gratifying to his ego. Mazzocchi thought he knew of the perfect job—Grospiron could lead the health and safety program of the AFL-CIO and of the International Chemical and Energy Federation (ICEF). ICEF, a worldwide association of chemical and energy unions, was run by Mazzocchi's progressive friend Chip Levinson. It was based in Geneva, "and Al wanted to travel," Tony said. "I told him, 'Al, it's the perfect thing for you. When you retire, we could organize worldwide, and you'll be our spokesperson.' We had this whole thing planned."

The wild card in Tony's presidential plan was the logarithmic growth of Grospiron's ego. Al preened at what he saw in the mirror. He was dashing and fashionable. He believed he had remade OCAW into the crown jewel of the labor movement, making him the nation's greatest labor leader. Grospiron could be crude. To his less-than-fulfilling marriage, he'd added a consort, rumored to be a model/hooker who distributed a menu and price list for her favors. No one was surprised when, during a negotiation with government officials, Grospiron made his point by pulling down his pants and mooning his opponents. Grospiron's outsized ego alienated even his allies, like Tony's Texan insurance company friend Bernard Rapoport, who told Tony that "I see Al coming, I cross the street. I'm tired of hearing about the greatest labor leader who ever lived."

"I was always pulling his chestnuts out of the fire," said Mazzocchi.

"Al was problematical. And the Goss people pumped his ego constantly. You know, 'You're the guy. You shouldn't be letting Mazzocchi do this or that. He's always in the paper. . . .'"

Over time, Goss helped Grospiron see that if Mazzocchi became president, history would view Grospiron as a faded footnote. With the patience of a skilled undercover agent, Goss waited for that demeaning notion to metastasize. By early 1979, Grospiron began spreading the word that he thought Mazzocchi did not have enough oil bargaining experience to successfully lead the union.

As late as three months before the August 1979 convention, Grospiron showed no signs of abandoning the presidency. In May, he took personal charge of oil bargaining, holding one-on-one meetings with Gulf Oil, the lead company, to work out a settlement that would set the pattern for bargaining in the rest of the industry.

Mazzocchi finally caught wind that something was up:

> The rumor was out that Al was gonna jump. But I discounted it because Al and I used to have real discussions. I said, "Al. You're gonna retire and go home and live with your wife? You ain't gonna do that." He was always getting in trouble with women, which I had to bail him out of. And I was the only guy that could talk to him straight up and down. But you know, Al had this palace guard whispering in his ear. And he must have been telling these Goss guys all the while that he was going to step down.
>
> My friends kept saying "Look, Mazzocchi, Al did not want you to become president, because you would have outshone him, and he wanted to be the best president that OCAW ever had."

The inevitable puncture of Al's ego occurred by accident during a May 1979 visit to the union by Wayne Glenn, the president of the Paperworkers union. Grospiron had invited Glenn to a board meeting to pitch a potential merger between their two unions. But Glenn's presentation did not go well: Board members tore into the merger idea. Grospiron took it personally. Furious that his honored guest had been so rudely received, Grospiron exploded and stormed out of the room, telling his aide-de-camp, Bob Wages, a sandy-haired young lawyer from Kansas City, to come with him. According to Wages:

> I remember the night that Al pulled the pin. . . . Al got pissed, went into his office, and told everyone to stay—that he wanted to have an executive session. He got up to leave and he said, "Come with me." So I went into his office and he said, "Fix me a drink." He had this little bar in his office, so I fixed him a drink. He says, "Fix one for yourself," so I fixed myself one. He said, "I'm getting the fuck out." I said, "What?" And he downed his drink, Dewar's on the rocks, and walked back in the board meeting and announced his

> fucking retirement, that he wouldn't stand election at the convention in August.
>
> What he wanted to happen—he didn't say it to me, but I knew the bastard as well as my own father—he wanted everyone to fall prostrate on the ground begging him not to do that—and they didn't. There was stone fucking silence.[21]

Mazzocchi was stunned. Just the night before, he and Al had talked about jobs for Al after 1981 and what they could do to line them up:

> I remember we went to this fancy French restaurant with the board. And afterward, he and I got together. And we're having this big conversation about the future. The very fucking next day, Al says to the board, "I want it be made known that I am not a candidate for reelection." Everybody's fuckin' in shock.
>
> What Al wanted, I think, was the board to rush out and say, *Don't do it Al. You can't leave.* But the board *hated* him because he got into squabbles with people. Drinking, fistfights, and every fuckin' thing else.

After Grospiron's startling announcement, the meeting quickly broke up. Said Mazzocchi:

> You know what happened? Goss goes out one door, I go out another, and Al's left alone. And that night there's a cocktail party for Wayne Glenn. And there's Al, in the fucking corner. He's the president of the union—normally with every sycophant up his ass. Now they were all maneuvering around my group or Goss's group. Al was a nonentity from that moment on.

VII

As the race took off for national office, a Portsmouth, Ohio, gaseous diffusion local and an atomic facility in Tennessee had the guts to go out on strike. Led by Denny Bloomfield, an ardent Mazzocchi supporter, workers walked out during bargaining, demanding better wages, working conditions, and seniority rights. In consultation with Mazzocchi and Wodka, their strike turned into a major health and safety struggle.

The health and safety focus helped workers gain national attention for their strike. They picketed the Nuclear Regulatory Commission and other government officials demanding that they instruct the employer, a private contractor, to settle with the union. Said Lonnie Tolley, president of OCAW's Erwin, Tennessee, local, "We got attention in Washington. People there listened to us. They were concerned and I think they got on some people's hides for us."[22]

Three months after the walkout began, on July 18, 1979, two hundred striking workers demonstrated in Washington. A few days later, the strike ended on terms much more favorable to the union. Mazzocchi's star finally rose among the atomic groups. Unexpectedly, it seemed that votes from the large gaseous diffusion locals in Portsmouth and Paducah were coming his way.

Then, out of nowhere, appeared an anti-nuclear leaflet in which Mazzocchi supposedly expressed anti-nuke sentiments. The four-page leaflet had been produced, it seemed, by the California-based Labor Task Force of the Alliance for Survival, one of many groups that had sprung up after the March 28, 1979, Three Mile Island nuclear incident in Pennsylvania. The pamphlet described the potential deadly impact of nuclear power accidents, the problems associated with storing nuclear waste, and the inefficiencies of nuclear power. Only a handful of local unions were listed as allies, showing the paucity of labor support for the anti-nuclear cause.

Neither Mazzocchi nor the OCAW was mentioned at all, except in a prominent quote on the first page. Under the headline "Labor's Stake in the Fight Against Nuclear Power" was an excerpt from testimony that Mazzocchi supposedly gave to a congressional subcommittee on energy in 1978:

> The nation should be *creating,* not *destroying,* jobs through energy policy . . . employment is of little use to a worker sick in a hospital or dead in the graveyard. . . . If an energy source is found to be ultimately unsafe or highly destructive of the natural environment, then that energy source should be abandoned.

The flyer made Mazzocchi look like the labor hero of the anti-nuclear movement. Someone had passed the leaflet out at a large OCAW refinery local in the Los Angeles area—Goss's home local. Goss supporters then circulated it throughout the OCAW, especially among the atomic groups. It was the smoking gun that proved Mazzocchi was anti-nuke.

"The enviro guys killed me," Mazzocchi said. To make it even more galling, the quote had been a distortion. "This guy actually snipped my speech to come out making comments that I didn't intend to make. Goss used it. I wrote a letter in protest. But Goss's argument was, 'Well, I didn't write it—the enviro group wrote it.'"

In fact, Mazzocchi had read before Congress a statement from Grospiron, who'd had to cancel at the last minute. And most surprisingly, the testimony was not about nuclear energy at all, but rather the Carter administration's national energy plan. The administration wanted to give incentives to the oil industry to develop oil shale and coal slurry, and OCAW feared this would cause a shift away from refineries, costing OCAW jobs while damaging the environment. OCAW argued that new sources such as shale and slurry should first be proven "safe for the health of workers and the public, and that they impose minimal disruption on the natural environment, beginning with its extraction from the earth." The union warned against these unproven technologies that might turn out to be as dangerous to workers and the environment as coal had been to coal miners and uranium extraction had been to uranium miners.

How did this testimony, which never even mentioned nuclear energy, become a banner headline for an anti-nuke leaflet?

It took scissors and some serious literary license that involved rearranging sentences and adding words. Mazzocchi's campaign responded with a detailed letter to all the leaders of the atomic locals that included both his original testimony and the damning leaflet.

But nothing Tony said could change the fact that he was a founder of SANE and was allied with anti-nuke activists like Ralph Nader. He couldn't say what they really wanted to hear—that nuclear power was safe or that he supported continued production of nuclear weapons—because that's not what he believed.

Mazzocchi always thought the leaflet was the product of some clueless anti-nuke activists. "I met the guy who did it. He said, 'I thought I was helping you.' I said, 'How could you be so stupid, to go in front of an OCAW hall with those anti-nuclear remarks?'"

But Bob Wages, who had been part of Goss's inner circle, did not think the leaflet came from the environmentalists. "I think it came from Goss and was a setup," he said. "I thought Goss kind of crowed about it," he added. "I really don't think it was some innocent dupe."[23] It was odd that the testimony had found its way to the California anti-nuke activists, especially since the hearing was not one concerning nuclear power. Very few people in the union even knew about the testimony. Among those who did was Bob Goss.

VIII

For Goss, Mazzocchi was not only too green, but too flaming red. Goss's people started a whisper campaign that Mazzocchi really was a communist and that, as an Italian from Brooklyn, he surely had ties to the mob.

Sharon Itaya witnessed the hatchet job. Itaya was one of the gifted medical doctors whom Tony had drafted to intern in OCAW's health and safety campaigns. He assigned her to inspect plants for hazards. "I was obnoxious," she said of her professional approach. "But I had some pretty good training and could ask hard questions."[24]

The local unionists Sharon worked with were "really friendly"—and yet they didn't exactly trust her. "I was a woman. I was Asian. One guy asked me 'Where did you get your degree—on a boat on the way over here?' They assumed that I was some kind of communist for doing a job like this."

She found Mazzocchi "brilliant. I worshiped him. He was so smart. He had so many good ideas. For example, he understood immediately the implications of genetic testing—what companies would try to do with it to eliminate 'susceptible' workers and to remove women of childbearing age from the workplace rather than to make it safe. He could bring together these ideas and make them relevant politically. But also, he made such a difference in us. He brought us into this real world and gave us something politically important to do."

Itaya wanted Mazzocchi to be elected union president. "All the docs wanted Mazzocchi to win so badly," she said. "But he made it clear that we should keep out of union politics, that we were not paid to be political 'hackies.' I guess that's a combination of being a hack and a lackey."

But working from her base in Houston, Sharon also saw that Tony had enemies. He was seen as an intellectual who lived apart from their tough westerner culture. "I mean, when there was an important union meeting, they all would come packing," Itaya said. "It was a little intimidating. They had a rough side. It would be hard for them to cotton to Mazzocchi. He was something else, something different altogether."

She remembered a tense campaign stop deep in the heart of Goss country: "I accompanied Tony to a large meeting at the Port Arthur local. They were ready for him. After he gave his speech the first question was, 'Are you a communist?' The second question was, 'Are you connected with the mob back East?'

Bob Wages spoke in much the same way: "He was red-baited all over the fucking country. Every southern oil worker was doing it. The head of the Port Arthur local got up in front of his membership and said we're not going to support a fucking communist."[25]

Given the chance to speak, Mazzocchi usually won over a majority of the rank and file. Traveling from local to local, he urged workers to reject "business as usual" and help him recapture the spirit of CIO militancy. He also raised funds from his supporters inside and outside the union for mailings to each of OCAW's 168,000 members. The mailings repeated his basic theme: "Forward or Backward? Mazzocchi or Goss?"

But in a delegate election, the final outcome would be determined by strategic lobbying, deals, and luck.

IX

As the delegates gathered at the Diplomat Hotel in Hollywood Beach, Florida, on August 13, 1979, Goss's forces immediately drew attention to the many "outsiders" Mazzocchi had invited to the convention. There were at least two dozen docs, interns, grant staff, and other allies who showed up to help their working-class hero take power. This elite crew could hardly melt into the blue-collar crowd. Although many delegates were grateful for the efforts of these young people, plenty of malicious rumors floated around about what Mazzocchi's docs and interns—mostly young women—were really up to.

In fact, they were there because of Tony's long-term strategy of connecting scientists with workers. The strategy had kicked into full gear with the help of an important ally, Professor Eula Bingham, a noted biologist from the University of Cincinnati who later became director of OSHA.

As an occupational health activist, Bingham had supported the 1973 Shell strike, and Tony believed her experience with that strike had helped transform her into a "great worker advocate." But Bingham noted that she didn't really need converting. "My dad was a railroad man," she said. "My God, I supported strikes."[26]

At the College of Medicine at the University of Cincinnati, Bingham worked closely with scientists from Standard Oil, Mobil, and other large oil companies trying to determine which petroleum fractions were the most carcinogenic. In the early 1970s, Dr. Irving Selikoff invited her into the "Group of 100" at the New York Academy of Sciences—the collection of scientists that would become the Society for Occupational and Environmental Health. At one of their meetings, she met Mazzocchi.

In 1977, President Carter appointed Bingham to head OSHA. She wasted no time opening her office to Mazzocchi. "I invited him up as soon as I got there," she recalled. "I wanted to make a statement to the rest of the building."

Tony appreciated this access, and Bingham appreciated Mazzocchi's ideas. "Oh, he was so smart, so insightful, so well read," she said. "He was very intuitive. He was really impressive as a scholar, quite frankly. He always would come up with the bottom line, how it would impact workers and their real world."

The two conferred on how best to gain for workers the "right to know" the toxic properties of the substances in their workplaces. "Tony and I discussed how to structure the labeling bill," she said. "We agreed that it was important, but Mazzocchi insisted that we also gain the right of every worker to have access to his or her corporate medical records. The federal labeling got blocked and didn't become law until the 1980s. But we succeeded with the medical records."

As they worked together to win stricter standards for a series of highly toxic substances, Bingham focused on the importance of worker training. "I was an educator and of course I believed in training," she said. "I saw what the OCAW and the UAW were doing with their excellent efforts. I told people on the Hill that I would like some money for a worker education program."

She got it. And soon she launched the New Directions Program, which funded worker training and paid for doctors and interns to work for unions. After winning a major New Directions grant, Mazzocchi wasn't shy about broadcasting it during his convention address as he ran for president in 1979:

> We have forced the government to trickle back a bit of our taxpayers' money. We have received a five-year grant, $225,000 a year to institute the most innovative and I think imaginative program. OSHA has one MD to take care of 55 million workers covered under this act. OCAW now employs five MDs under an OSHA grant and we have an additional MD through a Robert Wood Johnson Fellowship. We now have six times more MDs than the federal government [has for the whole country], working for this union on your behalf.[27]

And work they did—for the union, for Tony and for their ideals.

X

Among the OCAW docs in attendance at that watershed convention in Florida in 1979 was Christine Oliver. Oliver came from what had been a long line of poor white North Carolina farmers until her grandfather became a successful doctor in Raleigh. Her father was also a physician, and the two men's example led Oliver to med school. The antiwar, civil rights, and women's movements led her to social activism. She chose an internal medicine residency in the impoverished South Bronx and then helped start the Chelsea Health Center in Boston, where she practiced preventive medicine for the poor.

Oliver heard Mazzocchi speak at a 1977 meeting in Washington on the safety issues surrounding recombinant DNA. She remembers him saying "to all the health professionals present, 'The only time you think about workers is when they turn up on a mortuary slab.'"[28] The following year, after a residency at the Harvard School of Public Health, she was interning with him, courtesy of an OSHA grant and funds Mazzocchi raised. She later was hired by the union.

Oliver went to work producing high-quality health hazard evaluations for the union. These were eye-popping experiences. Oliver toured the Reichhold Chemical plant in Elizabeth, New Jersey: "The pits," she said. "Resins dripping everywhere." She inspected Velsicol in Memphis, which produced heptachlor and chlordane, two highly toxic pesticides that have since been banned. "The union rep picked me up in a big Cadillac and wore a pink leisure suit," she said. "After my tour, he asked me to give a presentation of my findings at their labor-management banquet being held that night. I had to sit at the head table with the Velsicol officials. When I realized that the local was in bed with management, I was a little less strident with my report."

In 1979, at the Goodyear Tire and Rubber Company in Niagara Falls, Oliver helped the OCAW local investigate the prevalence of chest pain, heart disease, and heart attacks among workers in one area of the plant. "It was really quite an experience from start to finish," she said. "A classic worker-initiated epidemiology. Here's the problem: chest pain. What are the exposures? Carbon disulfide and methemoglobin formers—both of which could cause chest pain for different reasons. Next step, check it out, which we did. And we could never have done it without a union—a union tuned in to health and safety."[29] Oliver's study of chest pain in chemical workers would be published in the *British Journal of Industrial Medicine*.

Another of the doctors at the 1979 convention was Ruth Heifetz, a red-diaper baby from New York. Heifetz went to medical school in the mid-1950s, when it was still extremely difficult for women, especially married women, to gain admission. Tufts Medical School rescinded her admission when she got married; Temple University Medical School demanded to know how she planned to prevent getting pregnant. "I attended," she said. "but there were two women and 120 angry men who felt we had taken two spots from their buddies."[30]

At a family medical clinic in East Harlem, she began seeing women in unconventional blue-collar trades as patients. "They would come in and say, 'This stuff I'm working with is making me dizzy. Can it harm me? Will it hurt my pregnancy?' That got me looking into occupational safety questions."

She joined OCAW through a one-year grant from the New Directions Program and worked primarily in California, where she got an earful from the Los Angeles–area leadership, who "really hated Mazzocchi with a passion. They referred to him as Bozo the Clown, even in my presence," she said.

Ruth's notion of unions and working-class politics matured. "I guess I came into the situation with a great romantic notion of the union movement," she said. "I became disillusioned on some level. I saw a great reluctance on the part of many of the officers to develop new leadership from the rank and file. Perhaps because the work was so dangerous, people really fought hard to get and keep their union jobs and get off the shop floor."

Ruth did what she could to help emerging rank-and-file leaders. "I organized a health and safety film series in LA," she said. "We showed *Song of the Canary,* which had just come out and featured OCAW workers who had become sterile from workplace exposures to DBCP at a plant in California. Sometimes seventy to a hundred workers would attend along with their families, and this would create a forum for those who wanted to challenge the leadership."

During her sophomore year at Johns Hopkins medical school, Molly Coye attended a presentation by the National Institute for Occupational Safety and Health aimed at encouraging medical students to consider occupational health. Mazzocchi was one of the panelists. "I saw a poster announcing the event and I talked a girlfriend of mine at medical school—Linda Rosenstock, who later became the head of NIOSH—into coming with me," Molly said. "Mazzocchi was mesmerizing. I thought, *This guy is so different.* I had been all over the world, and Mazzocchi was more foreign to me than those I met abroad. He was so fascinating—so blunt. And it turned out he was also accurate about what he described about the workplace and health—painfully accurate. He was not full of bluster or ideology. He had a hungry intellect and quickly became very sophisticated about technical and scientific issues. I was inspired and fascinated."[31]

Coye said to herself, *"Okay, that's what I want to do."*

After the talk, she approached Mazzocchi and asked how she could help. His response was simple: "Come work with us."

Mazzocchi asked her to join him at the bargaining table representing gas pipeline workers who were being contaminated with mercury when they entered pipeline shacks to read meters and make repairs.

"I remember being terrified," said Molly. "I knew the union was counting on me, and I was just a junior in medical school. The company had this big-name expert from Duke, a leading researcher in the field. So I went to the library and copied all this stuff he had written. At the session, he denied that the levels of mercury were high enough to cause health problems. And I was just incredulous. I had his very own words that contradicted everything he now was saying. I was flabbergasted. I whispered something about it to Tony and he said, 'So say it!' So I said that I had his reports right there that said these levels of exposure were dangerous. The expert hemmed and hawed and said something about how there had been more research since then. But he was caught off guard. It was a very defining experience for me."

Coye would go on to establish the first workers' health clinic at a hospital in the Bay Area, and in 1986 to become the New Jersey commissioner of health.

Perhaps the only doc who joined OCAW without a Mazzocchi conversion experience was Linda Rudolph. While she was at University of California–San Francisco medical school and San Francisco General Hospital learning acute pediatric care, she had become friends with Rafael Moure, OCAW's health and safety director. "In 1979, Rafael called and asked me what I was doing with my life," Rudolph recalled. "He said he had a job for me."[32] After some initial training at the Centers for Disease Control, OCAW sent her to work on health and safety issues with uranium and hard rock miners, refinery workers, and chemical workers.

Her most critical work, she believed, was building a community–union coalition to win "right to know" legislation in Contra Costa County. "I helped bring together unions, faith-based groups, and community organizations to win a law that forced companies to publicly report what chemicals they used that might be harmful to workers, the community, and environment," she said. "It was very satisfying when Governor Jerry Brown's administration picked up the idea and turned it into a statewide law."

What did it mean to work with Mazzocchi? "It opened up a whole new world to me, and I'm still in it," she said in 2007 as the chief public health officer for the city of Berkeley.

To admirers and critics alike, it seemed as if Mazzocchi had recruited quite a collection of exceedingly bright women. They even called themselves Tony's Angels.

It was a powerful partnership. "Mazzocchi's greatest contribution may have been linking labor with scientists," said Ralph Nader. "No one before or since has done so. The education obviously went both ways, and it was a strategic relationship. He brought together two power centers: knowledgeable scientists whom society held in great esteem and a mass labor organization which had the power of numbers and votes."[33]

Or as one teasing worker put it: "Mazzocchi, I know you're a dummy just like the rest of us, but you sure have a lot of smart friends."

XI

Rather than running on his own like Goss, Mazzocchi put together a ticket for three of the four top union positions. Bernie Emrick, the director from District 3 in the South, and Ernie Rouselle, a popular international rep from Louisiana, would run for the two vice president positions. But Bernie, Ernie, and Tony (as the ticket was fondly or derisively called in Three Stooges fashion) all came from the chemical sector. Mazzocchi didn't think he could do much to dent Goss's base among the oil workers.

Bernie, whose son had died in Vietnam, was a decent man and a capable administrator. And as district director, he would—Mazzocchi hoped—have great influence on the delegates from District 3, whose votes could put Mazzocchi over the top.

But as it turned out, Bernie was a poor politician and a less-than-charismatic speaker. He admitted as much at the very start of his convention speech: "I've been told I should be more forceful when I speak, but what you hear here today will be me, because to do otherwise would be phony."[34]

It didn't get any better. On and on went Bernie, taking many good positions on important issues that no one would remember ten seconds later. "Emrick was a nice guy and a good friend," said Mazzocchi. "But he was a bomb. I thought he had control of the southern locals, and he didn't. It was a wrong choice."

Ernie Rouselle, however, proved to be a strong campaigner. Born in Luling, Louisiana, near New Orleans, Ernie was the kind of southern unionist—integrationist, anti-corporate—who gave hope to the movement. After leaving high school in 1952, he signed on with American Cyanamid (in what is now called Cancer Alley) as a clerk-typist before getting a job in production. He was active in his town's politics and soon worked his way up the local union ladder as well. By the time he met Mazzocchi in 1964, he was his district's alternative executive board member. They had a long talk about chemical bargaining; Rouselle recalled that "I was impressed by his sincerity and his ability to get things done."[35] Goss, on the other hand, "was lousy," said Rouselle. "I had no respect for him."

Ernie's profile rose after he led the fight against a forty-four-month lockout from 1975 to 1979 at American Cyanamid. In the end, workers received one of the largest back-pay settlements in labor history.

Both camps saw the election as a cliffhanger. With every vote tipping the balance, it was rumored that Goss's side deployed its own fallen angels to service lonely delegates. Rafael Moure believed it was more than a rumor:

> The Goss campaign did things that were amazing—like recruiting prostitutes. I had been on assignment to work with a local in New Mexico. I had established a friendly relationship with the local president—we would have dinner when he was in Denver as well. During the convention, he called me drunk one night and said, "Can you set me up with a good woman?" I said, no, I don't think so. And he said, "Well your opposition is very good at that." I did not believe he was joking.[36]

One of the few reps in Tony's corner was Percy Ashcraft, who came from the Ohio–West Virginia border. After working his way up through his local in the Ohio River town of Marietta, Ashcraft became a rep covering Columbia Gas groups in Clendenin, Columbia, Boomer, and Clarksburg,

West Virginia. Together these locals would cast 3,302 votes, with the largest block—846—coming from Ashcraft's home local.

Ashcraft was drawn to Mazzocchi's militancy, and he planned to deliver all those votes. There was every reason to think he could. Like most reps, he had great influence over the locals he served. A strong, competent rep could make local union officials more effective and popular—and lighten their workload. If you wanted to stay in local office, it paid to have cordial relations with your rep. So if a strong rep like Ashcraft wanted to steer your votes to a particular candidate, you listened.

With Ashcraft's votes in tow, Mazzocchi came into the convention with a small lead. This was great news for the docs and interns. Afflicted by infectious optimism, the five Mazzocchi docs at the convention decided to skip the mob scene at lunch on the first day. Instead, they took off together to the supermarket to pick up supplies. It was a fateful decision.

Ashcraft collapsed in the middle of the convention floor with a massive heart attack. By the time medical help arrived, he was dead. Sharon Itaya, one of the doctors on the food run, felt terrible about not being there. "I knew CPR like the back of my hand," she said. "Had I been there I might have saved him."[37]

Without Ashcraft there to bind the locals together, his troops were open to enormous pressures from other reps, most of whom supported Goss. Mazzocchi mourned both Percy and his votes: "As long as he was alive, he was holding his locals. The minute he died, the other reps swarmed in and pulled them to Goss."

At the very least, Ashcraft's death meant the loss of his home local—a shift of 1,692 votes.

XII

Union convention speeches seldom matter, since most elections are decided before the delegates arrive. But the Mazzocchi-Goss election was so close that a shift of just one delegate could prove decisive. As Goss walked to the podium, he faced a simple task. He had to stick to the main message that Bob Wages, his campaign aide, had concocted for him: He was "steady Bob Goss, Mr. Reliable, the guy you know and trust." The power of that message was how it conjured up the opposite about Mazzocchi: the wild man who would turn the union upside down.

But, Goss didn't stay on message. He couldn't resist defending himself from Mazzocchi's "business-as-usual" charge. Said Goss, "I'd like to clarify from the very beginning that the other slate are not running my campaign. They've gone to extensive trouble to talk to you about what I'm saying: 'business as usual.' Those are their words. Those are not my words.[38]

"I have no fears of the challenges of the '80s," Goss continued. "I have been around long enough that I worked on the challenges of the '60s, I worked with you in the challenges of the '70s. And we're going to handle the challenges of the '80s."

He sounded just like what Mazzocchi said he was: a bureaucrat committed to stacks of paper, not action. With prose that could knock out an insomniac, Goss intoned:

> Because of our diversity within our union, special programs to meet the special problems unique to each of these groups must be developed. . . . The programs of our union must be the result of a study of the problem, or problems, the establishment of a direction, the ultimate solution we see and the complete implementation of the union's resources, resources of the union to bring about the solution that we are trying to attain. . . . Our union must have a total program in all of the activities that we are engaged in and that total program must be in total balance. Certainly, we have priorities in our programs, and those program priorities can vary from time to time depending upon the priorities of the challenge in a given week or a given month. . . .

Inside this mental cubicle, Goss continued to play defense. No, he would not, as Mazzocchi claimed, be weak in the upcoming oil bargaining. He would negotiate, "not capitulate," but "we have to have a realistic approach to it." No, he was not really devoid of new ideas; "I intend not only to offer new ideas but I will accept your new ideas."

Eventually, Goss got back to the theme Wages had urged: "We want to make sure we don't turn the organization upside down, that's a direction we don't want to go. . . . My programs are basic: organize, educate, legislate around the bargaining process. Success lies with the people who do the basic things better than anyone else. . . . I offer you a basic trade union approach to basic trade union problems." He should be elected, Goss said, because he understood "the nuts and bolts of this union, what it's all about."

Mazzocchi was up next, and he faced a more difficult task. He had to sell his action-packed leadership style and get the delegates to join him in building a new labor-led social movement. In short, he had to give a speech like no other in the postwar union era.

Tony lived for such moments. Limbering up like an athlete, he would ever so slightly roll one shoulder, then the other, while rocking from side to side. When addressing a thousand workers, he had extra zing and confidence. His listeners soon saw that he was tapping a deep flow of history, of social movements. This convention speech was his best chance ever to open the labor movement to his vision. He began:

> The labor movement is in trouble. We've lost three million members; but more important we've lost the faith of our membership. . . . Union members no longer truly believe in the trade union movement as a cause, as a social commitment, as a crusade. The gap between the leadership and the membership has widened. . . . I've grown disappointed as I watch George Meany drive to work in the morning with a chauffeur-driven Cadillac . . . that's not the symbol that I thought should be the image of the labor movement. . . . Too much of the labor movement has forgotten where they came from.[39]

And Goss's prescription wouldn't right the wrong:

> Bob did suggest that he will continue to do what he's been doing and will solicit ideas. We are on the brink of a crisis. . . . More of our members complain about the union than they do about the company. They've lost their consciousness about who the enemy is. . . . We cannot just bargain around the tables of America. We have to be bargaining within the total context of all of American lives. We've got to organize the community behind our desires and our concerns.

It wasn't just a matter of how to bargain, it was what to bargain for:

> We are going to seek and insist upon demands that go beyond what traditionally has been collective bargaining. Our Western European brothers have left us far behind. They've handled the question of plant moves. They've handled the question of investment decisions, which goes right to the corporate heart. . . . Instead, we have confined ourselves. We have let the other side set the rules. . . . We've got to carry these struggles nationwide. You have to organize outside your ranks in order to win. . . .

Tony wanted it clear that this wasn't just some abstract discussion. It also was about how to fight the oil industry based on "a program that says to this industry we are going to mobilize the American public behind our demands."

Mazzocchi had no choice but to confront Goss's strongest suit, his congenial personality:

> Bob interrelates better than any man I know, but this is not a social club, it's a social movement. I've been accused of being militant. I think that's a sad reflection of where we are. I thought we would wear proudly the fact that we are militant. I don't intend to bow before any . . . unjust company, unjust government or tyranny in any form; that's my role to the last breath of my life. That's what trade unionism is all about.
>
> I propose that . . . a signal go out from this hall on Friday morning that says we're tired of the old way. We're tired of losing our membership. We're for a rebirth of idealism. We want to mount a new crusade that will win the hearts and minds of American workers. We want this crusade to move across borders, and we want to build a new labor movement.
>
> There is no comfortable road. You cannot choose comfort, and I know that comfortable is to choose what you're familiar with. Brothers and sisters, the time has come to lay aside comfort. Our survival is at stake. . . . I hope it can be said that it started in this hall, that OCAW was the spot that brought back a labor movement to life.

> I urge that you don't succumb to some hysteria about where I possibly may lead you. I can only lead where you're willing to go. But I have the responsibility to point the direction that I think we must go in. And I see the future. I've analyzed the past. I understand the present. I offer you a choice. . . . I ask that you join in this fight and in this crusade.

XIII

But as it turned out, Mazzocchi's fate would be determined behind closed doors, not through the convention speeches. And once again his fate turned on the question of nukes, which sat like a devil on his shoulder, offering him the presidency in return for his soul.

To win, Mazzocchi didn't need to sweep the atomic groups. He knew he had the support of the Portsmouth, Ohio, strikers. Rouselle had made a few inroads into the Paducah, Kentucky, gaseous diffusion plant as well. But the grand prize was Oak Ridge and its 2,590 votes, more than enough to swing this tight election.

As a vital part of the Manhattan Project, Oak Ridge was the world's largest public works project. Designed to enrich uranium for the first atomic bombs during World War II, it drew more than forty-five thousand workers to construct and operate a set of mammoth uranium separation facilities on fifty-nine thousand acres twenty miles west of Knoxville.

Enrichment—the separating of tiny amounts of fissionable U235 in mined uranium U238—was the monumental task assigned to Oak Ridge. During the Cold War era, gaseous diffusion became the preferred method to produce U235. Oak Ridge's Y25 facility, the original diffusion plant, became a vital part of the military and civilian nuclear establishment.

Working at Oak Ridge was a life-shaping experience. You were making fuel for the most destructive weapons ever conceived. You needed high-level security clearance and were sworn to secrecy. You became part of the national security state. You worked in a facility that made the Great Pyramids look small. As Doug Stevens, then the vice president of the OCAW Oak Ridge local put it, "We saw ourselves as national defense workers. We enriched uranium that could be stockpiled to help us win the Cold War and to keep Russia from running over us."[40]

Oak Ridge represented a curious nexus of public and private power. The government owned the facilities, but some of the nation's largest private corporations operated them. Oak Ridge workers always had two bosses, the contractor and the government. And sometimes, if union officials colluded with the national security apparatus, they had a third boss—their own union officials—who could expedite or delay action on their concerns. But because of the shroud of secrecy, it was hard for workers to go public with their grievances.

Some frustrated atomic workers wanted help from a bold leader such as Mazzocchi. But most feared him and preferred Goss, who would maintain the status quo. The complicated lines of authority also generated complicated politics and ambitious labor leaders. Because these locals controlled many votes, their leaders often were in line for staff jobs. The field was wide open for those with large egos and skill.

In 1979, Charlie Baker ran the Oak Ridge local with an iron fist. John Williams, the area's international rep, worked closely with him. Together they decided on which candidate would get the Oak Ridge votes. Sensing a close election, they put their votes up to the highest bidder.

Both the Mazzocchi and Goss forces pounded the convention delegates for pledges until the very last moment. Doug Stevens recalled, "We got calls and visits all night long. But in our delegation we voted as a bloc. What Charlie said, we did."[41]

Stevens heard that "Mazzocchi was anti-nuke and that was our livelihood. Some of the Mazzocchi folks were telling us that he was just fighting for our health and safety, but mostly we heard that he was anti-nuke."

But that didn't bother John Williams. Like Plunkett of Tammany Hall ("I seen my opportunities and I took 'em"), rep Williams wanted to grab Bernie Emrick's job as District 3 director. If Bernie became vice president, the job would be vacant. All Williams needed was for the new president to appoint him and the executive board to approve him. But everyone knew Bernie Emrick was going to lose the vice presidency and would still be the District 3 director. Therefore, Williams was asking Mazzocchi to dump Emrick, his running mate and friend, to make room for Williams.

Williams's offer to Goss and Mazzocchi included about five thousand votes:

the Oak Ridge votes plus another couple of thousand from other locals he serviced. John Williams had the union by the short hairs and he knew it. As Stevens put it, "With Big John, it was one for John and all for John."

"No," said Mazzocchi. "I won't make the deal."

As Wages explained, "Mazzocchi was in no position to make the deal because of the Emrick situation. Bernie was the incumbent director. Could Mazzocchi make a deal to dump him?"

No, he couldn't do it to this brokenhearted guy whose son had died in Vietnam. Mazzocchi was boxed in by his own integrity. Besides, Mazzocchi saw Williams as the archetypical union opportunist, and his entire campaign was about taking back the labor movement from such careerists. How could he in good conscience appoint one in order to get elected?

"Once I do that," Mazzocchi said, "every other hack in the union would be holding me up to do the same for them." Mazzocchi saw the move as a slippery slope to business unionism, and as a betrayal.

Yet virtually all of Mazzocchi's close allies wanted him to make the deal. In their eyes, Mazzocchi had such a surfeit of integrity that sacrificing some of it to Williams wouldn't be so bad. One of Mazzocchi's staunchest staff supporters, Sylvia Kieding, had tears in her eyes twenty-five years later when she said, "We could have found something for Bernie."[42] Mazzocchi, after all, was a genius in creating new programs and new opportunities.

But Mazzocchi said, "What am I gonna do? Have the guy come out and stick his neck out, and then reduce him to a rep?"

Mazzocchi refused to even ask Bernie to okay the deal—perhaps because Bernie was already crestfallen about his poor performance in the campaign and would have agreed to anything Mazzocchi asked. Mazzocchi had to find another way to win. Some of Mazzocchi's aides suggested, why not make the deal and then break it later? It happened all the time. Mazzocchi could say he couldn't pull it off and offer Williams some lesser appointment.

"That's cynical politics," he warned. "You get involved in that type of cynicism, you're just like the other guys. You can't do anything after you win." Mazzocchi had accused Goss of doing just that—promising jobs to everyone even when he knew there were none to give.

But . . . was this a replay of 1964 when Tony let the Kennedy machine bump him out of a congressional seat? At that time, Tony demurred, fearing a nasty fight that would split labor. This time he feared the slippery slope.

What did he really fear?

You could burrow through Tony Mazzocchi's early home life and perhaps construct a personality that lacked the ruthlessness to prevail in morally ambiguous battles. But a more fruitful place to look might be on the streets of Bensonhurst, where you were only as good as your word, and the neighborhood was too small to backstab your friends. Your standing was your only capital and you never gave it up. Mazzocchi's politics transferred these neighborhood values onto a national stage. Whether they enabled him or hamstrung him is a matter of debate. But screwing his buddy, making an unprincipled deal, did not seem to Tony the correct path to power, as every kid on the old block would have known.

Mazzocchi would never concede that not making the deal was a mistake—even though it may have killed his deepest dreams for the labor movement.

XIV

The voting started on Friday, August 17. It was far too close to call. Mazzocchi, a no-nonsense vote counter, knew that closeness meant trouble. The sequence of the voting made the situation even worse, since it started with Goss's home base in District 1 on the West Coast, then proceeded to District 2 in the Rocky Mountain states, which also was expected to go heavily for Goss. District 3, Emrick's district in the South, was split, and District 4, encompassing mostly Texas and Louisiana oil workers, again heavily favored Goss. By the time District 4 voted, it would look like a Goss landslide. This could be devastating to the morale of the Mazzocchi forces, especially for those delegates new to convention politics.

Bill Perry from District 1 was the first delegate to report his votes: "Brother Chairman, . . . I'm speaking on behalf of District 1. District 1 Ferndale Local 590 casts 205 votes for Tony Mazzocchi. District 1 casts 13,250 votes for your friend and mine, and the next president of the international union, Robert F. Goss."[43]

Next up was Delegate Newman, president of the District 2 council, who cast 7,211 votes for Goss. The only dissenting votes came from Climax Molybdenum workers in Colorado, who had worked closely with

Mazzocchi on health and safety issues. President David Jones cast his local's 537 votes for Mazzocchi.

In a matter of minutes, the count was 20,461 for Goss and only 742 for Mazzocchi. An apparent rout was on. Goss needed a total of eighty-four thousand votes to win.

In hotly contested District 3 (including Alabama, Virginia, West Virginia, and Tennessee, plus the Portsmouth atomic local), every local union came to the microphone to cast its votes.

The collapse of "the deal" was apparent as Williams delivered Oak Ridge's 2,590 votes to Goss. Denny Bloomfield made sure his Portsmouth, Ohio, local cast all 1,551 votes for Mazzocchi. But then Paducah's gaseous diffusion plant cast its 1,459 votes for Goss. As Mazzocchi put it, "I kept bad company—Ralph Nader. All that could not be shunted off. That was a reality."

The morale of Mazzocchi delegates was plummeting. Delegate Riggs from Local 3-523 in East Ashland, Kentucky, announced his union's votes by reporting, "We cast 477 for Tony Mazzocchi. It was a good try anyway."[44]

With District 3 split down the middle, Goss was up about nineteen thousand votes heading into District 4, which again was Goss oil territory.

But it didn't all go to Goss. The giant Port Arthur local, where Mazzocchi had been asked if he was a communist or a mobster, gave 1,104 of its 6,629 votes to Mazzocchi. The other large Texas oil locals in Port Neches, Houston, Beaumont, Pasadena, and Texas City cast more than 12,000 of their 13,500 votes for Goss. Although Mazzocchi picked up a few large locals in Louisiana, he lost District 4 by more than fifteen thousand votes, leaving Goss up by thirty-five thousand.

District 5 (Missouri, Oklahoma, Kansas, and Arkansas) and District 6 in the north-central states canceled each other out. With only three districts to go, Mazzocchi still trailed by thirty-five thousand votes.

District 7 (in the heavily industrial areas of Illinois, Indiana, Michigan, and Ohio) cast nearly twenty-five thousand votes, most of them for Goss, leaving Mazzocchi more than forty-six thousand votes behind with only two districts to go—District 8, Mazzocchi's home base, and District 9, the Canadian district.

To have any chance at all, Mazzocchi needed every one of Canada's sixteen thousand votes. The Canadians were engaged in their own high-stakes politics: They were about to leave OCAW and join with other Canadian branches of US-based unions to build their own union in Canada. They wanted to break free from AFL-CIO organizing rules, American business unionism, the Democratic Party, and the CIA. (The Canadian OCAW supported Canada's New Democratic Party, a third party formed by progressive unionists, farmers, and others.)

If, as expected, Canada cast all its votes for Mazzocchi, District 8, Mazzocchi's home base, would prove to be the kingmaker. The reorganization of OCAW back in the late 1950s had turned the district into the union's largest, stretching from Maryland to Maine. Over the years, Mazzocchi had soaked the district in education programs and piloted new initiatives on everything from health and safety (with expert docs at unionists' service) to radical economics. As a result, Mazzocchi's base was wide and deep. But it would take a virtual sweep of the district's thirty-two thousand votes—plus the Canadians—to put Mazzocchi into the presidency.

Optimism increased as the District 8 voting began. With a few minor exceptions, local after local cast their votes for the man that one voting delegate called "the conscience of this international union and a progressive leader and a man who will be the president of this international, brother Anthony, Tony, Mazzocchi!"[45]

The insurmountable Goss lead began to crumble. If it fell below sixteen thousand votes, then Mazzocchi, with massive support from the Canadians, would win.

A sweep depended on the massive Carborundum local in Niagara Falls and its 2,173 votes. This was the local that had first been organized and led by Charlie Doyle, the radical Gas-Coke leader who later was run out of the country by the union and the Truman Justice Department. Now the local was run by Angelo Augustino, a tough leader who adored Mazzocchi. But it was a fractious local with several factions vying for power.

Augustino, stuck in strike negotiations back home, had sent three delegates—instead of the usual eighteen—to represent the local at the convention. Traditionally, delegates decided among themselves by majority vote whom to support and then voted as a bloc.

But unbeknownst to Augustino, one of the three delegates the local had sent—Harold Edwards, a six-foot-two, two-hundred-pound hunk of a chemical worker—had decided to go his own way. As chief steward of the local, he believed that Augustino and his team didn't support him enough and gave up too easily on important grievances. Edwards sent out feelers to Goss. "I had nothing against Mazzocchi," Edwards said twenty-five years later. "I just felt the district needed a change from the clique that was running it."[46] Besides, Goss seemed "likable and very cooperative." Goss also promised to reward Edwards with a rep job after the election.

Fearing that Edwards might be physically prevented from voting—or persuaded to rejoin the Mazzocchi forces—Goss's campaign operatives stuck to him like glue at the convention. "I guess I was too dumb to be scared," recalled the affable Edwards. "But they gave me this bodyguard from District 4 anyway. He followed me wherever I went."

Traditionally, only one person from a delegation was recognized to cast the delegation's votes. In the case of Carborundum local, that was Delegate Farina. Only with the cooperation of the convention chair, Al Grospiron, could Edwards be recognized at a different mike. If Grospiron chose to ignore him, there was no recourse for Edwards, since the chair's decision during a roll call could not be subjected to a floor vote.

When Carborundum's turn came, Farina cast the local's 2,173 votes for Mazzocchi. Edwards, carefully coached by Goss's team, went to a different mike flanked by a platoon of District 4 heavies. He asked to be heard and was recognized by Grospiron, who had been tipped off in advance.

"Mike 8, why do you rise?" said Grospiron.[47]

Edwards then had his moment in the sun. "I rise to make a correction of the total amount of votes for Tony Mazzocchi. My name is Harold Edwards, Local 8-12058. I cast 725 votes for Bob Goss."

According to Mazzocchi, it was the first time in OCAW history that a delegate cast his votes from a physical location outside his own delegation.

Farina, rising in protest, was recognized at mike 3: "I'm chairman of this delegation. We always came down here non-mandated, and we took a vote among the delegates that were here, and we always go by the majority rule. We have in the past and we contacted the president [Augustino] of the local back home who was on strike. He told us to go by majority rule. That's why I vote 2,173 votes."

Grospiron, gavel in hand, could now tip the votes either toward Goss or Mazzocchi—and his decision could not be challenged.

"May we have a little order, please?" said Grospiron. "As I understand the question, the local says it's subject to a unit rule?"

Farina agreed.

"And one of the delegates wants to vote separately?" continued Grospiron, playing it out slowly even though he had decided on the outcome long before.

"Apparently, that is the case," Farina said.

Grospiron finally had Mazzocchi by the balls.

"This may cause you some problems when you get home," Grospiron opined to Edwards, "but this convention has to recognize the voting of votes as allocated to each delegate by the credentials committee." Goss supporters began applauding.

"Therefore," said Grospiron, "Delegate Edwards is entitled to vote his vote. . . ."

Quickly, Farina challenged the ruling of the chair. Grospiron, well prepared, played his trump card: "There are no challenges in order during a role call. . . . The appeal is out of order."

In fact, Edwards was not morally entitled to all of those votes since the vast majority of the Niagara Falls members favored Mazzocchi. It would have been easy for Grospiron to rule that Edwards was out of order in the first place. Or he could have ruled in favor of Farina and then overruled any objections with the same line he had used to overrule Farina—"there are no challenges in order during a role call."

But by this time Grospiron might as well have been wearing a Goss button. He handed Goss a crucial 725 votes for a swing of 1,450 votes. Later, Goss did offer Edwards a job—but he knew full well that Augustino as board member would block it.

Mazzocchi's supporters were devastated. Even the Canadians' subsequent vote—they dumped all of their sixteen thousand votes into the Mazzocchi column—was not enough. After nearly sweeping District 8 and gaining all the votes of District 9, Mazzocchi came up 3,500 votes short out of 168,000 cast. A swing of just 1,751 votes would have unleashed a radical militant upon the labor movement, Big Oil, and the nuclear establishment.

Instead, Goss and his CIA allies were in.

XV

As the convention ended, Mazzocchi provided a postmortem on KPFA, a Bay Area public radio station. He went over the obvious: Grospiron's unexpected resignation, Goss's better union assignments, Mazzocchi's association with anti-nuke activists like Ralph Nader, the conservatism of the well-paid oil workers, the death of Percy Ashcraft, the defection of Edwards, and the sequence of the voting that made it seem like a landslide instead of a cliffhanger.

Many of the delegates, Mazzocchi said, identified with his call for reinvigorating the labor movement. But it was very frustrating, he said, that "many of the people who voted against me came up after my speech and said . . . 'Look, we agree.'"[48]

With a soft voice sagging from sadness, Mazzocchi described the sorrow of the supporters who had come to his campaign suite after their defeat. "I've been around a lot of conventions," he told KPFA. "I've been in this movement thirty years. I've seen more tears this time than I've ever seen before—real tears." These workers, Mazzocchi said, "felt that they were really fighting for something that meant something."

Gathered in Tony's campaign suite had been militant unionists like Mac, George, and Denny Bloomfield, and a crowd of other blue-collar Mazzocchi delegates. And then there were the beautiful interns, the Phi Beta Kappa docs, and the talented staffers. It was a room full of radical technicians and worker-leaders. Mazzocchi had hoped that they would be the new OCAW, prefiguring a new movement that would break labor free from its insular, self-defeating culture. But the old culture had beat them back.

KPFA's mike captured a mix of hope, sadness and energetic defiance as Mazzocchi's motley crew sang "We Shall Not Be Moved."

"People understood that we lost more than a candidate," Mazzocchi said. "We lost a *real* opportunity to move things. And we were so close."

FOURTEEN

Round Two

If there are dominant genes for bitterness, for sulking, or for revenge, then Tony Mazzocchi was a mutant. He'd been betrayed and red-baited; he'd been called unpatriotic and a gangster. His opponents had promised jobs that didn't exist to get votes. Grospiron had knifed him, and he'd been deprived by a CIA flunky of what was perhaps his best chance to rekindle a militant labor movement. But while some of Mazzocchi's aides seethed at the opposition and dreamed of getting even, Tony didn't. "Well, I never went after my opposition personally. It was political," Tony said mildly. "I was nice to them."

Tony's allies, he confessed, sometimes asked him, "How can you talk to those guys?" Tony replied: "Listen, you don't know where somebody's going to be tomorrow. A lot of guys just like them came over. And if you alienate them just because they voted against you, it's crazy. Ultimately, we need them. I mean, where are the votes going to come from?"

Besides, said Mazzocchi, "To get into that type of mode, personally, is debilitating. It destroys you."

This wasn't just an exercise in emotional repression. Mazzocchi actually did not *feel* anger. As a result, he had a huge advantage over his opponents who took slights and defeats personally, flew into rages, burned bridges with their opponents, wore out the allegiances of their supporters, and turned friends into enemies.

When asked by the author how he felt about one of his opponents' devastating moves, Mazzocchi demonstrated a total lack of bitterness:

> **Mazzocchi:** What are we going to do? I mean, there might be satisfaction in burning somebody at the stake. But after they're burned, then what do you do? You're still left with the same set of circumstances.
>
> **Interviewer:** So you don't have even the slightest desire to hit him over the head with a two-by-four?

Mazzocchi: That's a waste of energy.

Interviewer: But you don't even feel that impulse?

Mazzocchi: No.

Interviewer: So he's still a chess piece on the board?

Mazzocchi: Yeah—everybody is . . . I tell you. The minute you get driven into personal animosity, it's distracting. It doesn't mean you have to love the person. But there's no absolute percentage in it at all. And some people are driven to the point where they shoot people, right? . . . I never hated anybody. Strategically, it's crazy to get sucked into that. I never would have gotten back into office if I had gotten into that.

Interviewer: So how do keep from getting angry?

Mazzocchi: Well, I don't know how it actually happens. I think you just say, That's not the issue. The individual's not the issue. If you really believe in historical and dialectical materialism, you say, the person's not the issue. It's all the forces that shape people that make them do what they do.

Mazzocchi did admit the lack of anger was a gift. Part of it came from an abundance of self-confidence. He believed he understood working people and the labor movement as well as anyone. He had no reason to feel threatened personally by those who attacked or betrayed him. Besides, he was a Mazzocchi. He came from a kindhearted family whose diverse members loved each other unconditionally. Mazzocchi's father, his sisters, and his cousins who raised him were unusually positive, gentle souls. As Mazzocchi put it, "My sisters were like that. If you told my sisters, the world is coming to an end, they would say, 'All right, we might make it to the door and watch the sunset.'"

But he was not just any optimistic, kindhearted Mazzocchi. This was the strategic Mazzocchi. In the face of defeat, he immediately turned his concentration to how to out-organize and outmaneuver his opponents the next time around.

Mazzocchi didn't see his 1979 defeat as the end of the world. He wasn't in the mood for any sunsets.

II

Although Goss won by a narrow margin, he gained full control of the union's structure and personnel. And once OCAW had granted its Canadian region autonomy, Goss's margin over Mazzocchi instantly increased from next to nothing to more than sixteen thousand votes. In a public radio interview immediately after the election, Goss's satisfaction slipped through his southwestern drawl. "It was a very close election and that isn't too bad an idea, either," he said. "Because there's a mandate on my part now to put those two pieces together. . . ."[1]

The confident Goss didn't reassign Mazzocchi to North Dakota or Alaska. Instead, he played the uniter and magnanimously appointed Mazzocchi as director of health and safety. Mazzocchi made it easy: After all, he'd never exhibited any personal animosity to Goss, even after his devastating loss.

But Goss's move wasn't altruistic. As health and safety director, Mazzocchi would continue to bring positive acclaim to a Goss administration. And the job placed Mazzocchi in the national Denver office, where Goss and company could see what he was doing. Every trip, every expenditure, could be scrutinized.

Although Goss didn't see it, his most immediate threat came not from Mazzocchi but from upcoming oil bargaining. Still wearing rosy postwar-tinted glasses, Goss believed that business and labor, with a little help from government, would work out their differences—not because they liked each other, but because they desperately needed each other to defeat global communism.

Goss didn't realize that cooperation with the oil industry was now a fantasy. The 1973 OPEC oil embargo, the subsequent quadrupling of oil prices, long lines of cars waiting to fill up, government price controls—all created instability that hadn't registered in Steady Bob's world. Traditional oil bargaining and traditional worker strikes weren't likely to move the oil behemoths and their government allies. As Mazzocchi accurately predicted during his 1979 campaign speeches, business-as-usual bargaining would lead "precisely to what the industry wished to give, not one cent more."[2]

Goss proceeded as if he and the oil industry were still allies fighting communism in Latin America. He tried to bargain quietly. The oil industry stonewalled, daring the union to strike. Goss approved a strike. Automated refineries run by supervisors hummed along as if nothing had happened. The strikers manned their picket lines week after week, unable to stop one ounce of product. Goss truly didn't know what to do.

Mazzocchi could either stand aside and watch Goss implode, taking the union down, or try to salvage the strike, making Goss a hero and the likely winner in the next election. Doing nothing was out of the question. So Tony offered a plan modeled on the Shell Oil campaign: OCAW would rally the public against the oil industry, the most unpopular collection of corporations in America.

Tony argued that Americans had a new view of the oil industry as a "multinational giant" that was "crushing" people. "The most radical piece of literature in America reaches the home of every American each month," Mazzocchi said. "It's called the utility bill. It is escalating the indignation of the American people."[3]

Mazzocchi virtually begged Goss to release him from his responsibilities as health and safety director: "I said I will drop everything I'm doing. I'll organize coalitions with the community groups that I know so well. We'll be in the streets of America. I'll organize a media campaign."[4]

Mazzocchi promised to "gather that public indignation up, focus it against the industry, and rely upon the American public as natural allies in this fight."[5]

But Goss, who had spent nearly a decade in Latin America urging workers to shun such radical unionism, couldn't change his stripes. No, he would soldier along the old-fashioned way, hoping that the oil industry would eventually bail him out. Besides, Goss was not about to let Mazzocchi run around the country raising his profile. Losing an oil strike might be bad. Allowing Mazzocchi to win one might even be worse.

Mazzocchi recalled a conversation with Goss about what constituted power:

> Goss said, "You know, we have a different concept of what power is." I said, "Well, what's your idea of power?" He said, "I'm able to pick up a phone and call any oil company executive and have a conversation." I said, "Well, we definitely have a difference on what power is all about. I believe in building a strong fighting

> organization so that when you do call an oil company executive, you're there as an equal."

Goss stumbled forward without Mazzocchi's aid. The industry pumped out product and kept the workers out for four months. The forty thousand oil workers and the union treasury were drained dry. It was the longest oil strike in OCAW history. Goss's nuts-and-bolts approach had failed. As his assistant Bob Wages put it, "Goss pointed his gun at the oil industry and it blew up in his face. I mean, he really fucked up."[6]

III

Goss was losing his grip on the union, and Mazzocchi, the wild-eyed radical, stood a good chance of defeating him the second time around, in 1981. It was too late to banish Mazzocchi to the hinterland. And no one else could withstand a second Mazzocchi charge any better than Goss.

But Goss had another way to stop Mazzocchi cold: Merge OCAW with a larger conservative union. In a merger agreement, a deal would be struck on who would be the new union's top officers, postponing national elections for several years. What's more, the agreement could eliminate OCAW's rank-and-file executive board and the district councils—annoying springboards for rank-and-file dissent that enabled challenges from people like Mazzocchi.

Almost immediately after getting elected in 1979, Goss set out to merge OCAW, one of the nation's most progressive and democratic unions, with the United Paperworkers of America, one of the most conservative.

Ideology was not the only driving force. For those who saw the union as a business, mergers opened the cookie jar. Union staff could expect a substantial wage and benefit increase. And superfluous officials could land extremely lucrative retirement packages and other sweeteners.

In trying to sell the merger to the rank and file, Goss argued that within ten years of a merger with the Paperworkers, "We could have a union of 700,000 people with more impact than all the rest of the labor movement." Added Goss: "There is, however, no way we can merge with any union with our rank-and-file board."[7]

What Goss meant was that no other union leadership in its right mind would put up with a structure that empowered the ranks to elect their own executive board. It would have to go—and good riddance.

Goss had every reason to believe he could ram this merger through, given his opposition's weakened state after the Canadians' departure. But Mazzocchi jumped into the fray with a fierceness few had ever seen in him. He lambasted the Paperworkers and the proposed merger in union hall after union hall. Before a packed room of local officers and rank-and-filers in New Jersey in 1981, Mazzocchi roared, "The Paperworkers is . . . an amalgamation of four different unions that's never gone anywhere, only down. They lost 50,000 Canadians for lack of democracy. . . . They need us only for our financial viability."[8]

"You don't hear about the Paperworkers unless someone gets in trouble," Mazzocchi continued. "Have you ever heard of anything the Paperworkers did that's been newsworthy?"

What's more, the union "vests all power in the presidency—the power to settle contracts, the power to settle grievances." The president's salary as of January 1982, he said, "will be $92,000 progressing to $165,000 a year," a Cadillac, and "a potential retirement of $119,000 a year." The symbolism of such a union chief, said Mazzocchi, would "turn American workers off generally. It would turn off our own workers."

Mazzocchi took a swing at the paltry services the Paperworkers provided for their members: "The Paperworkers don't have services. Wayne Glenn, the president, appointed his son-in-law to be the head of health and safety. He was an industrial engineer for a company. They don't have a research department."

If Mazzocchi never hated anyone, it seems he came close to hating an institution—the Paperworkers.

> Workers died to build this movement. They didn't die to establish a bureaucracy with those inflated salaries. . . . One of our own members, Karen Silkwood, under my instructions, under our union's directions, was attempting to save her union—and got killed. She was killed in defense of this union—*your* union. What do we tell the memory of Karen Silkwood? "Karen, you died so we could pay

> 119,000 bucks a year for someone who would not be out on the picket line with you?"
>
> Is that what the labor movement is all about?

Mazzocchi rattled poor Karen's bones until he shamed Goss and company to pull out of the merger talks. Goss's failed merger plan had put Mazzocchi back in the limelight, setting the stage for a Goss v. Mazzocchi grudge match in 1981.

IV

Through his two runs for president, Mazzocchi continued his full-scale attack on corporations that sacrificed worker health. Among the dozens of cases he and his staff pursued, one almost defied belief. Mazzocchi called it "flagrant corporate callousness." That was an understatement.

At Dawes Laboratories, a small vitamin and food additive producer in suburban Chicago, fifty production workers had been exposed to diethylstibestrol (DES) while making feed that promoted faster growth in cattle. These workers, all men, developed unsettling symptoms. According to a 1978 feature article written by Bruce Ingersoll in the *Chicago Sun-Times,* one worker, age thirty-one and the father of five, "found himself going through female puberty." He developed breasts. Another young man "had a double mastectomy rather than endure the shame of having a lumpy breast as big as his fist."[9]

Before the union got involved, the workers were sent repeatedly to the nearby company-oriented doctor, Dr. T. J. Bonick, who, according to the *Sun-Times,* "would inject them with a male hormone to counteract the feminization effects of DES." Then they were sent right back to work—without even the bare minimum of a warning or protective equipment. The company shrugged off the problem, claiming that only "a handful of workers" were exposed.

The effects were as painful as they were embarrassing. As one worker reported, "I developed a lump on my left breast. It was so sensitive I couldn't touch it. Wearing a T-shirt was agonizing. Sleeping on my stomach was impossible." Another worker described how "my nipples were discharging this clear, sticky slime. It would wet through my shirt. Finally Dr. Bonick told me he couldn't do anything more for me."

Four years earlier, OCAW had forced Dawes to agree to give workers free annual checkups and install better ventilation equipment. But Rafael Moure, OCAW's health and safety director, later discovered that the company had done nothing. The union filed an "imminent danger" complaint with OSHA, forcing an inspection of the Dawes plant.

The investigation was directly supervised by the new OSHA director, Morton Corn, who was appalled by the conditions at Dawes. According to the *Chicago Sun-Times,* OSHA "found that the complaint understated, if anything, the hazards. The plant was permeated with DES. It was everywhere—inside of a desk, on handrails, ledges and pipes, in the lunch room and locker rooms. They even uncovered DES in a telephone mouth piece."[10]

OSHA forced Dawes to pay twenty-one thousand dollars in fines for "willful and serious violations."[11] The company agreed to clean up the mess and fund special medical monitoring for forty-five workers exposed to DES. However, the union and the company fought over which medical tests were needed and who should do the testing. After rejecting each other's suggestions, the company suggested Dr. Irving Selikoff, of all people, the labor doctor who had uncovered the link between asbestos exposures and disease. As Mazzocchi recalled, "We said, 'Fine, we'll accept him.' And then the company came back and rejected their own nominee! So we said, 'The hell with that.'" The union prevailed, and Selikoff was retained.

In its February 1978 issue, the soft-porn magazine *Hustler* saw humor in the issue—which undoubtedly workers didn't share. It featured a doctored picture of a bald, bearded motorcyclist flashing open his shirt to reveal a pair of ample female breasts. Under the headline "Job Benefits" a short article started with, "You work hard all your life and what do you get? Tits. Don't laugh because a male worker at Dawes Laboratories near Chicago had to have two breasts surgically removed. . . ."

Mazzocchi took several Dawes workers to testify before a congressional committee. When workers were asked if they had received any protective equipment, one worker reached into his bag. Mazzocchi flinched, fearing the worker would pull out a respirator, which would contradict the union's claim that workers hadn't been given such equipment. "He reaches in his bag—pulls out a brassiere! The boss was issuing brassieres to these guys. The committee couldn't *believe* it."

However, the issue at the heart of the Dawes fight was deadly serious, especially for workers like Keith Hess, age twenty-seven, who suffered through more than a dozen of Dr. Bonick's male hormone shots. His marriage collapsed: "My wife and I couldn't make love. Whenever she tried to rub up against me or try to hug me, it hurt. My nipples were that sensitive. After a while she gave up trying to hug me." Finally, he had surgery which left him "with two small hollows in his chest."[12]

The company was unrepentant. Despite the pathetically small fine, company president Vernon Dawes complained that "OSHA regulations are so extensive it's always possible to find violations. We were mistreated by OSHA."[13]

Rafael Moure reported, "Dawes closed down within a year of the OSHA inspection and reopened in Mexico City."[14]

V

Mazzocchi attacked his second OCAW presidential campaign like a man possessed. He was determined to shake the entire labor movement from its stupor as Reagan came to power. In a 1981 press interview, Mazzocchi said: "I think the labor movement is in crisis. For the first time I think it is a crisis of institutional survival. Whereas in the past the corporations were prepared to live with the union, that accommodation has come to an end. Labor leadership in general has failed to understand this new development."

When labor historians look back on the postwar era, many may identify the early 1980s as labor's tipping point. Labor laws were making it harder and harder for unions to organize, and jobs were disappearing from the industrial heartland. Most labor leaders blamed the Republicans for labor's rapid decline. But Mazzocchi believed that labor could no longer organize new workers precisely because it was entwined in a death spiral with the Democrats.

Mazzocchi also pointed to the growing gap between labor leaders and everyday workers. Workers needed see to union officials in the streets again, and living life as their members did. Tony again called for emptying out the union bureaucracy, engaging every labor staffer in organizing—from targeting facilities to making home visits and leafleting at plant gates. (The Service Employees International Union adopted a similar strategy in the mid-1990s.)

But even this would fail, Mazzocchi argued, unless labor pulled free from a failed Democratic Party.

"I don't think we can organize the unorganized in this country unless we have a separate political apparatus," Mazzocchi stated in 1981. "People will look to the labor movement as it is able to develop a public agenda and as it begins to stand for something. This creates a whole different climate, a whole different image. Then it is not just selling an institution—'we can get you a few extra cents an hour.' And a lot of unions can't even do that anymore."[15]

Tony believed the Cold War taboo on third parties had lifted: "Years ago, it was different. You couldn't get a discussion of a labor party within labor. . . . Today, people want to talk about it."[16]

Mazzocchi also didn't buy the excuse that workers were getting more conservative. "I think in the absence of any alternatives, they're frustrated, and if the only articulation in a populist context comes from the right, they'll respond—if they don't hear it from another direction."[17] Using his own campaign as Exhibit A, Mazzocchi showed that OCAW's highly paid rank and file—supposedly the very profile of Reagan Democrats—enthusiastically supported a new party.

Mazzocchi also tested the message with other unions. He learned quickly that while the rank and file loved the idea of a labor party, it did not sit well with labor leaders, even those who were considered progressive.

Ironically, he often found himself at odds with communists-turned-Democrats. He had a comic clash with one during the 1980 presidential primaries, at an education conference at the United Automobile Workers hall in Cranford, New Jersey. Several progressive regional labor leaders, including Archer Cole, treasurer of the International Union of Electrical Workers (IUE), District 3, addressed the two hundred rank-and-file activists. Cole also was the vice president of New Jersey's Industrial Union Council—a collection of former CIO unions that worked tirelessly for the Democratic Party.

A labor intellectual, Archer started out as a CP member in the United Electrical Workers (UE), which had supported the third-party effort of Henry Wallace. After the CIO created the IUE to successfully raid the UE, the Communist Party ordered its remaining UE activists to move their locals into the IUE. Archer complied.

The FBI then publicly labeled Archer the "Red Professor." He was drummed out of the IUE, subsisting by writing newspapers for unions while working for private printing companies. After McCarthyism waned, Archer reentered the New Jersey labor movement. By then, like most former communists, he had become a strong backer of the Democrats and had relegated the idea of a third party to some time in the distant future.

In 1980, Cole faced a conundrum. He knew that rank-and-file workers were disaffected after four years of Jimmy Carter. So Cole looked for a way to tap workers' anger while channeling them to the Democratic Party. At the Cranford conference, he urged "support for Ted Kennedy in the 1980 primaries as a protest vote against Carter."[18] (Once that failed, he would rally labor for Carter against Reagan.)

To grease the skids, Cole threw in a few rabble-rousing applause lines—like calling for the nationalization of the oil industry. (Tony quipped, "They always want to nationalize our industry but not their own.") Archer drew even more applause when he declared, "It's long overdue that labor has to unite and coalesce and think in terms of the third party for the future. . . ." In the meantime, workers had to vote for the Democrats.

Why wait? In his talk, Mazzocchi rejected the idea that workers should be chastised for being politically apathetic. After describing the years he devoted to getting workers to the polls and raising money for Democrats, Mazzocchi admitted to the error of his ways.

"I've learned that the most sophisticated political analyst is the individual who stays home on Election Day," said Mazzocchi. "I realized that in . . . these current times, to implore people to vote is to do a disservice to the American labor movement. Because there is not one legitimate vote an American worker can make today in order to advance his or her interests. . . . We implore people to vote on Election Day. Vote for whom?"

Mazzocchi described the utter failure of labor's "successful" effort to elect Carter in 1976 and then to give him a "veto-proof" Congress. This combo was supposed to deliver badly needed labor law reform. But the Democrats had caved to corporate pressure and passed nothing. Mazzocchi argued that the only pro-labor legislation passed in the entire 1970s was OSHA—under Nixon. Labor's get-out-the-vote strategy was a loser, said Mazzocchi. "If it's to be a Reagan-Carter race, which it appears to be, we fundamentally have no choice."

A labor party, Mazzocchi said, "can't be treated as some abstract nonsense or question that we must wait for in the distant future. There is very little time left. Big Business and government won't let us wait." He went on: "We are going to lose our membership. The cynicism, the disillusionment, will become so pervasive among the rank and file that it will ultimately engulf us." Where other labor leaders saw power, Mazzocchi saw a paper tiger. Where they saw pragmatism, he saw the collapse of the New Deal labor movement and all that it had delivered to the workers.

But a labor party offered hope. "My plea here today is that there must be a starting point. And it might as well start in this union hall and . . . start now, because it is extremely late. Hopefully some future labor historian looking back at this era . . . to determine what turned the American labor movement around—I would hope that someone says, it started on this very warm, spring Sunday in the UAW hall in New Jersey."

All two hundred workers, who had never heard anything like this, jumped to their feet, applauding the hope Mazzocchi had offered.

But the UAW's assistant regional director, who had hosted the event, turned to the conference organizer next to him and whispered angrily, "Didn't anyone tell him what to say?"[19]

VI

Mazzocchi stump speeches described "a common thread of agreement running through our entire union"—that labor needed an "independent political expression. . . . Nowhere, from the deep South to the far West, to the far corners of the nation, did I get one person to stand up in a hall to challenge me on a call for a labor party. They accepted it as a given. . . ."[20]

A labor party offended Goss's deepest conservative sensibilities. Goss's handlers, however, were unabashed opportunists who cared nothing for political ideology. The union was a business, and they ran it. Mazzocchi was the equivalent of a hostile takeover, and they intended to stop him.

If they opposed his labor party nonsense, workers' resentment might carry Mazzocchi right into the presidency. And anyway, what could he really do with the issue? At best he could pass a convention resolution with an unenforceable mandate for the union to do something about it. A resolution from the OCAW, by itself, would hardly be noticed by the rest of the labor movement or by the Democrats. The game was not about visionary politics—it was about who got the power, the jobs, the prestige, and the cash.

So after holding their finger to the wind, the Goss forces jumped on the third-party bandwagon, aiming to turn Mazzocchi's new party campaign into a nonevent.

At the start of the August 1981 convention in Denver, the Goss-dominated District 1 quickly offered a watered-down resolution in favor of an independent workers' party—even though several of the district's local leaders were extremely active in the Democratic Party and detested Mazzocchi's new-party idea. It stated:

> Whereas labor has continued to experience severe political setbacks, including the defeat of all its recent legislative objectives nationally; and
>
> Whereas the presidential election results indicated that the voting strength of labor has diminished because of growing frustration by working people, voting for candidates who do not represent their interests, therefore be it
>
> Resolved that the OCAWIU join the growing number of labor bodies and unions who are examining new strategies and methods in confronting the political crisis that labor faces; and be it further
>
> Resolved that OCAWIU support and participate with other unions in developing a new political strategy for labor in the 1980s that will not rely on the Republican or Democratic Party for success.[21]

That was it. It didn't say *third party,* but left the door open for one.

Goss even wheeled in Ben Schafer, the retired longtime OCAW vice president and secretary-treasurer, to bless the resolution. Schafer, a lifelong anti-communist, concluded that "If we became sort of an independent operation and . . . use our influence with the parties that were willing to work with us, we might find that there might be a stronger implement than we have now in trying to work with the Democratic Party."[22]

Goss's preemptive move left Mazzocchi with two options. The first was to start a floor fight to amend the resolution so that it packed more punch—including, for example, an action plan, a financial commitment, and an obligation that the union's leaders make regular progress reports to the board. Mazzocchi knew most of the delegates would not patiently sit through a debate over these fine points.

Instead Mazzocchi went for option two: He declared victory. Though its wording was weak, he viewed the resolution as a clear mandate to build a new party. If he became a nationally elected official, it would allow him to organize one. This was not the time to get into an editing battle.

And so the resolution passed without opposition, allowing Mazzocchi to spend the next twenty years drumming up support for a new party. Meanwhile, Goss had dodged a powerful Mazzocchi issue at no cost to his position.

VII

The 1981 convention fight was a replay of 1979. Everyone knew that if Goss won, he would clean house, banishing Mazzocchi and his allies from the union. If Mazzocchi lost, people like Steve Wodka would be forced out, and the health and safety department would be eviscerated along with Mazzocchi's organizing experiments.

Although this fierce, open contest for leadership was starting to seem almost normal in OCAW, in the wider labor movement it was extremely rare for an incumbent with full control over the staff to be hanging on for his life. It was a remarkable testimony to OCAW's democratic structure—and Mazzocchi's political skill—that he was in a position not only to challenge, but to win.

With the stakes so high, the candidates' convention speeches took on a new meaning. How would Goss explain the failed strike and the shelved merger?

He immediately tried to eliminate any discussion of the merger:

> I'd like to put one thing to rest right now, the merger question. . . . I do not intend to initiate or resume merger discussions with the Paperworkers, absent any direction from you. . . . Therefore put your mind at ease. As of now, merger with the Paperworkers is a dead issue—anyone, including my opponents, who brings it up will be doing so for their own political purposes.[23]

Next, Goss rapped Mazzocchi for airing the union's dirty laundry:

> I have seen the public criticism of our union. I don't know why it had to be public; they don't have any votes. I feel very strongly that whatever differences and problems we have in this union we can handle in this hall, not anywhere else.[24]

Goss also attacked Mazzocchi for taking funds from outside agitators—much as Goss's ORIT operatives had charged that left-wing Latin American unionists were financed with Moscow gold. Mazzocchi, indeed, had been openly raising money from the broader progressive community to pay for his direct-mail campaign to OCAW's rank and file. "If any other candidate chooses to take money and accepts it from outside this union," Goss charged, "then they will have to answer to who those folks are, why are they contributing to the internal politics of OCAW and what do we owe them?"[25]

Goss proclaimed:

> I am proud of OCAW today. We're a viable union. We're financially responsible. . . . Why do we have all the doom and gloom about OCAW in the public press? I'm proud of OCAW. I don't need to criticize our internal frustrations in public.[26]

He then argued that Mazzocchi's criticism of the failed oil strike was an attack on the workers themselves:

> I sometimes chuckle when people publicly criticize the oil workers' strike and try to make brownie points on that. I consider that a slap in the face to the 40,000 oil workers that were on the bricks

> for ten weeks . . . do not forget that strike was caused by the oil industry. . . . No, I'm proud of the history of the oil strike in this union. . . . We don't apologize to anyone.[27]

Goss also had an answer for Mazzocchi's claim that the strike had failed because the union hadn't organized a public-spirited campaign like the one against Shell: "You can't just put the whole union down the tube because you want to spend it with the public press, who aren't our friends to start with. . . ."[28]

Goss, the consummate bureaucrat, justified why he hadn't used Mazzocchi during the failed oil strike: "My position was I couldn't do that. I had to rule that we have a publicity department . . . Our publicity director runs our publicity campaign."[29]

(One oil corporation executive remarked incredulously, "You chose that guy over Mazzocchi?")

VIII

When Goss attacked Mazzocchi for waging his campaign in the press, he was referring to articles like William Serrin's "Race for Union Post Is a Clash of Styles," which ran in *The New York Times* on June 16, 1981. Goss, through a spokesman, told Serrin that he would "not 'go public' on the 'internal matters of the union.'" This innuendo had deep resonance within OCAW.

"Going public" was a cornerstone of Mazzocchi's anti-corporate campaigns. In a typical health and safety struggle, however, the local leaders and reps often preferred to keep quiet, hoping to resolve the issues behind closed doors. They feared that if the union went public, management would retaliate. At the very least, it would add stress to their jobs.

Paul Renner, then a young Mazzocchi supporter and Merck pharmaceutical worker in Rahway, New Jersey, experienced the tensions of going public. "It was different than going on strike where the worst thing that could happen is that you'd be out a few months," he said. "Some of these health and safety struggles contained within them the threat of a permanent shutdown."[30]

The Merck plant had a vast asbestos problem. Mazzocchi found a young doctor, Mark Nelson, to help workers bargain with management to get the asbestos removed. The company, said Renner, "had a whole army of occupational doctors on site. They tried to bury us, push us off with their experts. So having Mark Nelson in the negotiations was hugely important for us. We had our own expert sitting at the table, and it made it much more difficult for them to refute the asbestos problem."[31]

But the union bargaining committee grew cautious: "When the company agreed only to encapsulate but not remove the asbestos, Mazzocchi gave the story to a friendly media contact who was about to run a major piece. When the bargaining committee got wind of this, they freaked out. They demanded we get Mazzocchi to kill the story, which he did. I was shocked. But the reality was that our workers were scared that Merck would shut us down. They drew the line and we had to abide by it."[32]

"Going public" was like a one-way switch. Once an issue hit the press, it could not be ignored, either by management or the local union. And that was what Mazzocchi wanted, especially when the issue was precedent setting—like the sterility controversy that struck American Cyanamid.

Mazzocchi made sure *The New York Times* knew all about the OCAW-represented American Cyanamid facility in Willow Island, West Virginia. The *Times* reported "women were told they could no longer work in the pigment department at the plant because they would be exposed to trace quantities of lead dust that might injure unborn children." Instead, the company offered to transfer them to another department—at lower pay and with no overtime. In response, "five of the eight women in the department, ranging in age from 26 to 43, then had themselves surgically sterilized."[33]

Mazzocchi fired off a string of press statements warning of this corporate intrusion into workers' lives. As he told the *Times* in its first article on January 4, 1979, "Any company that says it's your job or your life, or as in this case, your job or your offspring—that is a draconian choice."[34]

Mazzocchi believed that this fight was over the most fundamental principle of health and safety: Should the workplace be made safe for the worker or should the worker be adjusted to an unsafe workplace? He worried about the staggering implications of a brave new workplace of sterilized workers. At a time when genetic engineering research was developing quickly, employers might next begin screening workers based on their genetic makeup: If their genes made them susceptible to toxic substances in the workplace, they'd be out of luck. In the not-so-distant future, Mazzocchi could imagine genetically altered workers, like crops, that could better withstand toxic exposures.

Mazzocchi and Wodka fought hard against Cyanamid, and in 1979 they got OSHA to cite and fine the company. Then in September 1980, two administrative judges overturned these OSHA rulings. They said the company's policy of excluding women of childbearing age from the pigment department did not violate the law, even though the law "requires that an employer provide a workplace free of recognized hazards and the threat of serious injury."[35] On technical grounds, they also rejected the argument that if the exposures harmed the women, they also harmed the men. Therefore, the judges did not order the company to make the workplace safe for both men and women. OSHA appealed the ruling and lost.

Mazzocchi told the press, "Ultimately, it will be quite clear that women and men alike suffered from exposure to lead and other toxic chemicals. When that happens, the industry initiative may be to have men sterilized. We will then enter the age of the neutered worker."[36]

In July 1982, *Ms. Magazine* listed Mazzocchi as one of its "Ms. Heros—Men Who've Taken Chances and Made a Difference." The list also included John Lennon, Norman Lear, Alan Alda, and Phil Donahue, among others. Mazzocchi was credited for having "exposed exclusionary fetal protection policies that restrict employment of women of childbearing age and for supporting union women in their campaign to fix the workplace, not the worker."[37]

The case had enormous consequences for women in industrial jobs. Soon one corporation after another adopted policies similar to American Cyanamid's. More immediately, the controversy heightened fear within OCAW that all such public fights would lead, sooner or later, to plant closures. In fact, in the middle of the fight with American Cyanamid, the *Times* reported that the company shut down the pigment department for "economic reasons."[38]

This only reinforced Goss's message. When he charged Mazzocchi with running to the media, he hit a raw nerve. Goss was implying that, if elected president, Mazzocchi would "go public" again and again, and workers would pay with their jobs.

IX

In his speech to the convention, Mazzocchi attacked Goss's failed strategy for tackling Big Oil and his ditched merger with the Paperworkers. But most of his speech was a lecture on how to tackle corporate power. This, Tony later admitted, was a mistake.

Mazzocchi took issue not only with Goss, but with the entire AFL-CIO for backing legislation that made it only marginally more cumbersome for companies to shut down their plants. Such legislation, he said, amounted to a "proposal to negotiate the terms of our burial." Instead, he argued that Americans, like the Europeans, should give workers a say in corporate investment decisions. This right could be won, he believed, if labor allied with the community, which also suffered when a plant closed down.

Mazzocchi's proposal was perceptive in 1981—the early days of US deindustrialization. But the delegates grew restless with his exposition. Undeterred, Mazzocchi cited an informal study by workers at the Mobil local in Paulsboro, New Jersey, which found that on average workers died seven years after retiring (at an average age of seventy-two) rather than the sixteen years projected by the actuaries. Because the union bargained about pensions using the sixteen-year life expectancy figure, Mazzocchi argued they were giving the workers' money away to the company.

Perhaps Mazzocchi's audience understood his argument, since many of them had experience negotiating pension plans. But there was little doubt that he lost them completely when he went on to argue that somehow the premature deaths also posed costs to the American public.

He plunged on, hoping to galvanize workers over the vast genetic tragedy that the union had uncovered:

> We are the only union [to] receive a March of Dimes grant . . . to study what's happening to our children. It's bad enough not to live out your natural life working in the oil and chemical industry. It's the worst sort of indignity however, by virtue of your work, you're condemning your child not yet born.
>
> That's the type of information that not only will cause our own members to be agitated. It's the type of information that can channel the anger of the American people behind our demands.

So far, the speech seemed better suited to the Harvard Public Health School than to restless OCAW delegates. Sensing his audience's discomfort, Mazzocchi returned to a favorite theme: the ill-conceived Paperworkers merger. But this time, he held his ferociousness in check, criticizing only Goss's "set of perceptions that allowed that merger to even be a consideration."

Finally, Mazzocchi took a few swings:

> The proposal to merge with the Paperworkers Union, to accept that undemocratic document, to accept an attitude that said you invest all power at the top, you develop a wage structure that says a president of the union shall be paid ninety-two thousand dollars progressing to a hundred sixty-five thousand dollars, a retirement plan for the president of a hundred nineteen thousand dollars per year, a Cadillac for the president, a cook at union headquarters. That attitude is a rejection of the idealism that was at the very basis of OCAW. The rejection of the democratic process of what this union stands for.

But no applause followed. While Goss's attack on the press and his display of union pride had been interrupted by applause fifteen times, Mazzocchi drew few ovations.

Mazzocchi later admitted he'd dialed down the rhetoric in deference to aides who'd been worried that he might scare off uncommitted delegates if he came on too strong.

But the more passionate Mazzocchi finally emerged as he defended himself against the family curse—not that he was too ethnic or mob-connected or a communist—but that, like his grandfather, he was too much of a dreamer.

Mazzocchi invoked organizer and balladeer Joe Hill, who had dreamed of an industrial union back when the AFL had refused to organize the unskilled. "Without a dream, there is no reality," said Mazzocchi. Then he turned to Martin Luther King Jr., who "died in a labor struggle in Memphis fighting for the rights of sanitation workers. His dream became a reality. He paid with his life, like Joe Hill."

He spoke of Karen Silkwood's dream, the dream of Polish Solidarity, the dreams of mothers who lost their children in wars, the dreams of South American peasants fighting against tyranny, who, like the Lawrence strikers, "cried out for bread and roses . . . this heritage they left us is something we can't forget. We must mean something. We must dream. We must inspire."

Then Mazzocchi described his dream of a labor party, summoning up the workers' alienation, anger, and hope. And when he said, "I would like to see instituted a broad discussion among our rank and file about the possibility of a new labor party," the applause finally came.

At last Mazzocchi attacked Goss's insularity:

> Bob Goss, in his address, said my campaign that reached newspapers and reached the American people is wrong. This is another sharp clash of our philosophical differences. America is our business. Our business is America's concern. The trade union movement is the only hope America has.
>
> Without a free trade union movement there is no free America. We deal with the largest multinational entities on the face of the earth. [We cannot act as if] we are a little social club operating in this convention hall and the decisions we make and the debate we engage in are our property here. If what we do doesn't affect the rest of America, we are ineffective. We must communicate with America.

Would the union be a social club that quietly distributed its goodies to loyal members? Or would it be a cause?

> Yes, I confess. The labor movement should be a crusade. It's a commitment for tomorrow. It's a commitment for the heritage for our children to make it better for them than it was for us. If we fail in that responsibility, we fail the future.

Mazzocchi's final plea defined the choice:

> History is giving each and every one of you in this convention hall a very rare opportunity. Millions of people live their lives without ever being confronted with the opportunity to do something that

can have a profound impact on themselves and the future of all of us, an opportunity to do something that affects that child that's not here yet.

Brothers and sisters, black and brown and white, I'm urging you to join me in a new crusade. I'm urging you to join me to find that rededication that once moved this labor movement—that speaks to the best of the Joe Hills and the Karen Silkwoods and the Martin Luther Kings. I'm asking you for a new spirit, a song to go from this hall that will rebound around America, that will reunite the labor movement. That's what I'm asking you to do.

We can build a new movement and a new movement can build a new America. And in the words of the song we sang at the beginning of the convention, "We *do* have a power mightier than their gold, and we *will* build a new world on the ashes of the old."

X

The 1981 convention took place against the backdrop of the PATCO strike. Members of the Professional Air Traffic Controllers Organization from across the United States went on strike for better working conditions and pay on August 3, 1981. Reagan, citing laws that prohibit strikes by federal employees, fired the more than eleven thousand workers. To honor the strike, every OCAW delegate boycotted the airlines, instead traveling to the Denver convention by car, bus, and train. But many knew they should have been going to a mass mobilization to protest Reagan's attack on labor. The PATCO strike turned out to be a huge turning point for labor—in a dire direction.

Ed Ott, then a convention delegate—who later became head of the New York City Labor Council—noted that if OCAW's Canadian members hadn't left the union, the 1981 convention would have been very different: "It would have been an organizing convention. If we had those sixteen thousand Canadian votes, the other side would have made their peace with us long before and Mazzocchi would have used the convention to put forward a plan for how to mobilize around the PATCO strike. Can you imagine the education sessions he would have held at that convention? He may not have arrested the entire decline of the labor movement, but I think the way labor responded to Reagan would have changed dramatically."[39]

Instead, the OCAW election became another cliffhanger. That a roll-call vote was needed at all signified how far Goss had fallen. Could Mazzocchi really find the sixteen thousand votes lost when the Canadians departed—and another two thousand to go over the top?

Once again, Mazzocchi corralled few votes from the West Coast: 944 to Goss's 12,855. But one of Mazzocchi's supporters, Bruce Clark, the progressive, thirty-three-year-old vice president of Local 1-547 in El Segundo, had his eight hundred Mazzocchi votes and his job stolen away.

"I was organizing for Mazzocchi in California," recalled Clark. "When Goss's crew got wind of it, they told me I would have a bright future if I kept my mouth shut. But I declared for Mazzocchi in June. After I received union leave from Chevron to attend the convention, the local secretary-treasurer, Thom Moss, wrote the company that my credentials were revoked, which he had no right to do. Chevron then revoked my union leave. When I took a calculated risk and went to the convention to make my case to the credentials committee, the company fired me. Then Bob Wages, acting for Goss, put the kibosh on the committee to make sure my credentials were denied."*[40] (Ernie Rouselle, who confirmed the incident, said, "The reps were bragging about it."[41])

Clark remained at the convention and faced considerable hostility:

> . . . A group of Goss international reps started getting belligerent with me and one or two other Mazzocchi people. It came right to the edge of us getting physically pushed around by them. The guys seemed to realize at the last moment that they were going too far and backed off, calming the situation. It was a good thing. They didn't realize it, but one of the other Mazzocchi supporters had a .38 in his pocket.

It wasn't much better in Rocky Mountain District 2, where Mazzocchi got 718 votes and Goss got 8,143.

---

*The 1983 convention sustained the charges that Clark and fellow union activists brought against the local leadership. But it was only a symbolic victory: Mazzocchi did not get the stolen votes, and Clark did not get his job back.

The picture brightened slightly in District 3, which included the border and southern states except for Texas and Louisiana. Last time around, Mazzocchi and Goss had evenly split the district's twenty thousand votes. But in 1981, Mazzocchi won by approximately three thousand votes. Despite the charge that Mazzocchi was anti-nuke, another atomic gaseous diffusion plant moved its 1,041 votes his way.

The race hinged in part on whether oil workers in Texas and Louisiana, District 4, would reject Goss after the failed oil strike. Last time, Goss had received 75 percent of the district's thirty thousand votes. Even if oil leaders didn't think much of Goss anymore, could they stomach Mazzocchi, who had been savagely mob-baited and red-baited?

A seismic shift depended on a handful of very large oil locals, including 4-227 in Houston, home of Phillips Petroleum. This local's more than thirty-eight hundred votes had gone entirely to Goss in 1979. Local leader Joe Campbell had seconded Goss's nomination, calling him, "honest . . . forthright, with integrity beyond reproach." He'd added: "We have no one else with his outstanding attributes that can fill the huge shoes being vacated" by Al Grospiron.

Bob Goss and Joe Campbell were pals. Bob stayed with Joe when in Houston. They liked to play bridge. And Bob had promised Joe a job in his new administration if he wanted one. But Campbell, as full-time officer of his local, had no intention of working for Bob or anyone else. He was quite happy to parlay his union position into a prominent role in Texas politics through appointments to state and county commissions. Campbell did ask Goss to let him know if a spot opened up—he wanted a job for a friend. Goss gave Campbell his solemn pledge that he would.

Campbell didn't like Mazzocchi—or his lady docs, either. At least at first. As Campbell recalled, the first time he and Mazzocchi met was less than pleasant:

> He invited me to a joint health and safety meeting between District 4 and 8 in Washington. I came and I ran right into him in the elevator. He didn't say a word. And then I saw him up on the stage running things and I thought he was an uppity bastard. That's southern for "he should have let someone from District 8

> or 4 chair the sessions." And I felt that his District 8 was kind of leaning on us all the time. No, I didn't like him one bit.[42]

It went from bad to worse.

> I came into the hotel lobby and Mazzocchi was sitting with Al Grospiron, the president. So I come over and Mazzocchi says, "Could you please excuse us a moment?" And I said, "Go fuck yourself. He's my damn president as much as yours."

Later, said Campbell:

> He invited me to a meeting in Washington—some health and safety thing with all those docs. I told him to forget it, that he was wasting his time and money on me, that he should invite someone else. He said, "What's the matter, you afraid or something?" Well, that did it. I go there. I see all those docs. I'm a southern boy and I open the door for this one from Boston, Chris Oliver. She says to me, "Don't open doors for me. I can do it myself." I say, "You can be sure that I won't offer again, and you can kiss my ass."

Later that night at the DC health and safety meeting, Mazzocchi called Campbell to ask him if he would be willing to talk. Reluctantly Campbell agreed to hear him out. Mazzocchi said, "Look, Goss is hiring all kinds of people. He's wasting the union's money for jobs we don't even need."

Campbell was stunned. How could Goss hire anyone without first offering a job to his friend as promised? Goss had given him his word. Maybe, he said, Mazzocchi was lying. No, said Mazzocchi. He listed the people Goss had hired. Campbell was furious.

> I called Goss and I asked him if it were true that he had broken his promise to me—that he had hired new staff without hiring the name I had given him. Well, he started to answer in that slow way of his—like Elmer Fudd. In fact, I was the guy who gave him that nickname. And I said, "You're a no good lying son of a bitch. You made a commitment and you broke it. Besides, you're an embar-

> rassment to the union. As hard as I worked for you, I'm going to work my ass off for Mazzocchi."

Campbell swung his local to Mazzocchi, raised money for the campaign, and traveled to other locals to try to swing them as well. He became one of Mazzocchi's closest campaign allies. By the time of the convention, "I loved him like a brother," Joe said.

But they were the oddest of siblings. Campbell, a wheeler-dealer of the first order, ran his local with a firm hand. He alone would decide whom the local would vote for at the convention. He lived in the nexus connecting hustling business leaders with ambitious politicians, comfortable in the midst of money, politics, and power. He played political hardball, all the time. And just in case he was on the losing end, he kept a loaded .45 in his glove compartment. In short, his culture and Mazzocchi's could hardly have been more different.

It was comical to watch Mazzocchi commune with Joe. Tony would all but put on a cowboy hat as he slipped into a Texas drawl with a clanking Brooklyn undertone. Tony acted tougher around Joe, trying to play the part expected of Texas alpha males. But the important thing to Joe Campbell was that Tony Mazzocchi was a man of his word, which was the axis of Campbell's world.

However odd Joe and Tony were as a couple, together they packed a wallop. Goss's vote total in the Texas-Louisiana district fell from 75 percent in 1979 to 43 percent in 1981. In the union's largest oil district, Mazzocchi beat Goss by nearly four thousand out of twenty-nine thousand votes. After the enormous win in District 4, Mazzocchi was running nine thousand votes ahead of his 1979 total. He needed to gain another seven thousand to make up for the lost Canadians, and then another few votes to win. It was trench warfare, local by local, the rest of the way.

Mazzocchi had considerable hopes for District 5, even though it was home territory to Goss's assistant Bob Wages. In fact, Mazzocchi loved to tell the story about how he "took Wages's local right out from underneath him" during a visit to Wages's home local.

> I went in the union hall, but the local union officers were all opposed to me—they were Wages's people. They got on the stage

> and they wouldn't let me speak. And then, finally, a rank-and-file guy gets up and says, "We want to hear our candidate speak!" And they voted to let me speak. So all the officers walked out of the hall with the rep. They thought the members were going to follow, but not one single member left. So they abandoned all their members to me. When I finished speaking, they mandated their delegation to vote for me—which they didn't.

The convention rules allowed delegates to vote as they pleased. So Wages was able to corral the delegates from his local to vote for Goss—despite the members' mandate. The only sanction available was for local members to vote the delegates out of office when they returned—which they did. But by then, of course, their votes for Goss had been cast.

Mazzocchi still needed fifteen thousand more votes as the election moved into District 8. If Mazzocchi won District 8 by the kind of margin he had received in 1979 (twenty-nine thousand to twenty-five hundred), he would win the election. But just a slight tilt toward Goss would take Mazzocchi down again.

In 1979, Mazzocchi had gotten all 1,665 votes from Local 8-86, a large Philadelphia local. But this time, Goss picked up 1,121 while Mazzocchi only received 559. And another Philly local, 8-397 flipped as well. What happened?

Joe Campbell claimed to be standing next to Mazzocchi when two of the Philly delegates came up and said that Bob Wages had offered one of them a staff job. Did Mazzocchi have any jobs to offer?

"I told Mazzocchi he should promise them the moon," said Campbell. "Then, if he could deliver on it, great. If he couldn't, then he couldn't."

But Campbell ran into the same brick wall that everyone else encountered with Mazzocchi on job promises. "He just told me flat-out no," Campbell recalled. "He said, 'Joe, I ran on a platform that said I wouldn't do that. I'm not going to betray my word.' I mean, how could you not love a guy who stuck to his beliefs like that?"

However, Bob Wages said he believed no one in District 8—or anywhere else—was offered a job, as Campbell had charged. "Frankly, I don't think it was happening from either side."[43]

In any event it was clear that Mazzocchi would not achieve the 92 percent landslide he'd gotten in District 8 in 1979. But he only needed 75.3 percent of the district's vote to win the national election.

What he didn't need was Mike Ricigliano. "Ah, an opportunist extraordinaire!" said Mark Dudzic, an ardent Mazzocchi supporter. "Mike was an incredibly personable guy who specialized in doing favors for people. He was also a fearless son of a bitch who didn't mind walking into the lion's den to advance his career."[44]

The Goss people saw Ricigliano's potential and tapped him to run on their ticket for secretary-treasurer in 1981. Jerry Archuletta, then editor of the OCAW *Union News,* said, "When it was evident to Goss that he and Mazzocchi would run for president to succeed Grospiron, he decided to bring Mike Ricigliano into the Denver headquarters. His strategy was that Ricigliano was Italian, out of District 8, out of the chemical segment of the union, and even out of the cosmetic industry where Mazzocchi had worked. . . . In other words, by bringing Ricigliano aboard, he was going to out-Mazzocchi Mazzocchi."[45]

But what mattered to Goss was that Ricigliano was able to pull from Mazzocchi several large locals in his home district.

And that made all the difference. Instead of the 75.3 percent of District 8 that Mazzocchi needed, he got only 69 percent. He came up short again—this time by 1,884 votes nationwide.

If this had been 1979, Mazzocchi's supporters would have erupted in wild jubilation as District 9, the progressive Canadian district, sauntered to the mike. The district's articulate social democratic leader, Neil Reimer, would have cast all of their sixteen thousand votes for Mazzocchi, giving him a huge fourteen-thousand-vote triumph. The docs, the interns, the radical hangers-on, along with the Joe Campbells, Vern Jensens, and the hundreds of everyday worker-delegates, would have gotten the thrill of their lives at this shot across the bow of corporate America.

But of course, the Canadians were gone, having split from OCAW after the 1979 election to form an independent union in Canada that would soon grow to be almost twice as large as OCAW. The Canadians had their own mission to fulfill and their own labor party to build.

Instead, Mazzocchi got tagged with the most awful sounding words in politics—*two-time loser.*

XI

As the vote ended, Steve Wodka turned to Mazzocchi and said, "What do we do now?" It was a question he had asked many times over the past decade when he and Tony had been such an effective health and safety team. How would they tackle companies that were poisoning workers with asbestos or beryllium? What would they do about the sterilization of female workers? Or the falsification of control rods at Kerr-McGee?

But this time Steve was asking a different kind of question. And Mazzocchi didn't mince words. "Steve, you're on your own. I can't do anything to protect you."

The health and safety operation would be dismantled. Wodka would leave to finish law school and become a successful tort lawyer representing OCAW workers who were poisoned on the job. Goss ended the doc intern program. And Dick McManus, Mazzocchi's longtime partner, was yanked from the promising Boston organizing project and sent to Toledo.

Mazzocchi's own future was murkier. He knew he would be exiled from the union. He hoped he would not be exiled from his family as well. Mazzocchi's family life had nearly collapsed during his incessant campaigning. Right after the convention, Susan had told Tony that she could no longer tolerate living as a de facto single mother, coping alone with their three young children. She, too, wanted a life, a career, but she'd barely been able to get out of the house.

Susan had already made up her mind that she was taking the kids back east to be near her parents and decent day care. After Tony's 1981 defeat, she told him that if he had won the election, she would have left without him, for good.

Tony was horrified. In fact, he was surprised by how horrified he felt. Tony found the prospect of losing yet another family—of losing Susan and the kids—to be overwhelming. He told her that if winning the election would have meant losing her, then he was glad he had lost.

He agreed with Susan that they should move the family to New Jersey, where there would be more support for the children. With more than thirty years of union seniority, Mazzocchi felt he deserved to be assigned the position of international union rep in the New York area. Goss, for obvious reasons, no longer wanted Mazzocchi around. Within twenty-four hours of defeating

Mazzocchi in 1981, Goss "reorganized" the health and safety department and eliminated Tony's job as director of health and safety. He offered Mazzocchi various technical jobs at reduced pay and benefits, and no seniority, including a rep job in North Dakota where he could service the oil local in Mandan.

Mazzocchi put up a fight to get reinstated as health and safety director, thinking that Goss would offer him a staff job in New Jersey or New York as a compromise settlement. The Goss-oriented rank-and-file executive board was the final arbiter, and it concurred with its president, in violation of OCAW Constitutional Rule 5. The rule read: "All eligible and qualified members . . . shall be eligible to be a candidate and . . . shall have the right to support any candidate of their choice without being subject to penalty, discipline, interference or reprisal of any kind."[46]

The board actually used the clause forbidding Tony's ouster to justify his ouster, arguing that if it ruled for Mazzocchi, then anyone who wanted to hold a job for life would just keep running for office. Mazzocchi's only remaining recourse was an appeal to the next convention in 1983.

Tony, reassigned to North Dakota, refused to show up for health reasons. Goss fired him.

In December 1981, the Mazzocchis left Denver for New Jersey. Mazzocchi used another GI Bill loan to buy a home in Maplewood, about fifteen miles from New York. He didn't have any income but didn't seem particularly worried about finding work.

For some progressives, Mazzocchi's move back east took on mythic proportions. They were stunned that such a good man had lost. Tom Geoghegan, in *Which Side Are You On,* used Mazzocchi as the exception to the rule that labor leaders hated democracy because they feared losing and returning to the drudgery of factory work. As Geoghegan wrote:

> Mazzocchi was a legend in labor, as the man who pushed through Congress the Occupational Safety and Health Act (OSHA). He lived in Washington, a professional man, as much as anyone else in that town. Then in the early '80s, when he lost an election, he moved back to Long Island and went back into the plant. No one else at his level of organized labor would have dreamed of it. It still gives me the creeps to think of it. I wonder what it was like to be the foreman of Tony Mazzocchi.[47]

We'll never know, because Mazzocchi wasn't that heroic. He had last worked in a factory in 1952 and didn't ever plan to again. In fact one of his favorite lines was, "Work is an abomination. That's why I became a labor bureaucrat."

So rather than go work in a factory, Tony began doing what he called "redefined work." He waltzed into the Labor Institute on Union Square in New York City, a small research group he'd helped to found in 1975. (The author is a co-founder of the Labor Institute and has been its executive director since 1987.) He offered his services for free, promising to raise his own funds from progressive donors. In addition, he accepted an appointment—for a salary of one dollar per year—as the assistant to the president of the District 8 council. He would be in charge of educational programming for the council, a job he invented. Mazzocchi also urged the ten staff members of the Labor Institute to join him as members of OCAW Local 8-149.

Organizing the sale of one home and the purchase of another, landing at the Labor Institute, and getting the District 8 job helped distract Mazzocchi from his excruciating loss.

If ever he needed his mutant genes—no bitterness, no sulking—it was now. As his allies were swept with depression and shock, Mazzocchi himself seemed somehow shielded from despair, even though, for the first time in his adult life, he was at the fringe of the labor movement, out of power just as the frigid winds of the Reagan era were freezing the heart of the union world.

He faced a new problem: how to be a relevant and respected player from his now marginal position. He was determined never to become a resentful and unaccountable gadfly who showed up at union conventions, petitioning for his rights, attacking the corrupt and anti-democratic leaders, trying to form caucuses that would go nowhere. He didn't want to be confused with left-wing sectarian group members who passed out party newsletters and shouted their lines at the rank and file, hoping to incite upheavals that never came.

Mazzocchi's goal was unchanged: He wanted to build a mass social movement with labor serving at its core. He wanted to win over not just OCAW, but the bulk of the labor movement to this cause. And even in defeat, he believed he could find a way to do it. Meanwhile, he consoled his friends and supporters. His loss just meant he couldn't take that particular shortcut to building a mass movement. As he wrote to a former intern after his second defeat in 1981, "Well, we tried doing it the easy way. I guess we'll have to do it the hard way now."

Had any labor leader ever come back from the hole Mazzocchi was now in? Certainly none had ever been more confident that he could. No matter how many elections the bureaucrats won, Mazzocchi continued to believe that workers would one day again explode into a new social movement. He was certain that Goss and company would be overcome by the corporate assault they faced. He was certain that, given the opportunity, the rank and file would react to that loss by joining a new movement.

And Mazzocchi would build it—or die trying.

FIFTEEN

Lost Battalions

Two-time loser! Two-time loser!

Those who suck up to power looked differently at Mazzocchi. And they treated him differently. The awe was shattered. He was more accessible, less formidable, and less unusual. To some, he seemed not as smart as he had the day before when he had institutional heft. For them, his vision seemed less realistic, less compelling, and maybe even less desirable.

It was evident in the little things—what they said to him, how they said it. Those who once were thrilled to have Vice President Mazzocchi return their calls now treated him with little deference. Those who argued with him were often more dismissive. Vice President Mazzocchi was now a more ordinary Tony, another idealist with pie-in-the-sky ideas.

Never mind that virtually half of the union's convention delegates had embraced Tony's radical platform or that an overwhelming majority of the rank and file believed in his cause. It still looked as if Tony *and* his ideas had been rejected. The common wisdom was that Tony Mazzocchi must be out of touch with political realities. His ideas were over the edge. A dreamer without institutional power was charming, but not particularly relevant.

Furthermore, the way he'd lost haunted him. It looked like he'd been unwilling to make the hardheaded political maneuvers required of winners. Some of his allies suggested that he was too pure, too unwilling to get his hands dirty, too removed from the real world. While his principled stands may have been admirable, some thought he was downright crazy for not trading a few jobs for victory. It looked as if Tony was not suited to wield real power.

Since elective office in OCAW was out of reach, friends and allies hoped he would secure another significant health and safety job. But Tony wasn't interested. He wanted out of what he called "the health and safety box." He wanted to do something to stop what he feared soon would be the total collapse of the industrial labor movement.

His tools were now limited. Mazzocchi knew that his only real power still resided in his precious base of loyalists deep inside OCAW. It had taken years to build it, and he desperately wanted to hold on to it. While he expected that some supporters would fade away, perhaps a solid third of OCAW, he hoped, still shared his ideal of radically reforming the labor movement. This was his life savings of political capital.

He would not squander it by accepting a job that would take him away from OCAW. Instead Mazzocchi had a so-called job at the Labor Institute, where he had to raise his own money and could do as he pleased. He'd helped create it five years earlier when he'd asked a few radical economists to pilot educational programs for workers. Now it became a good home in exile—Tony's version of a golden parachute.

He still worked his base. He spoke at OCAW meetings. He helped out on health and safety and other bargaining issues. He arranged unusual educational sessions for OCAW district councils. And he asked young technicians and activists to assist on local union problems.

That was what he meant by having "to do it the hard way." But for Mazzocchi it wasn't that hard. As he put it, "Hey, it beats working."

II

Mazzocchi seemed to suffer from a joyous form of attention deficit disorder. His creative leaps often sprang from his morning coffee as he read the Sunday *New York Times* sprawled across his antique kitchen table in Maplewood. Something would catch his eye, causing him to grab the phone to call an Institute colleague (usually this author). Mazzocchi would start each conversation with, "I was just reading in the *Times* about . . ." Then he would ask for help in checking out a new notion that had been triggered by something in the news (or in the coffee).

For the next several years, a ringing phone on a Sunday morning produced a Pavlovian response of foreboding. The call inevitably meant that Mazzocchi had another idea that took him about a minute to think up, but would entail months of hard work to bring to fruition. It got to the point at which you would debate whether or not to answer the phone at all on Sunday mornings, knowing that a caffeinated thunderclap was about to puncture the calm.

For starters, Mazzocchi hoped to piece together a coherent anti-concession movement. As Reagan's deindustrialization policies took hold, unions were under enormous pressure to give back many of their collective bargaining gains. Rather than just resist worker concessions, Mazzocchi and the Institute called for management concessions. Mazzocchi argued that concession bargaining was fundamentally about power, not economics. All the worker concessions in the world would not guarantee job security as long as management unilaterally controlled investment decisions. He pointed out that management could (and did) take cash saved through worker concessions to invest all over the globe. Unless that power was curtailed, corporations would keep on slashing high-wage union jobs in the United States.

Mazzocchi made it seem like a mass movement was in the making when he brought a hundred New Jersey labor activists to Edison, New Jersey, in June 1982. As *New York Times* labor correspondent William Serrin reported:

> An effort is underway to create a national movement to resist the concessions on wages, benefits and work rules that are being widely made by American labor unions. The campaign, being led by Anthony Mazzocchi, a former vice president of the Oil, Chemical and Atomic Workers Union, and other union people in the Northeast, would also demand concessions from businesses, management compensation and investment practices.

Serrin described Mazzocchi's new institutional base within District 8—he didn't say it was an unpaid position—as representing "about 35,000 union members in 11 Northeastern states." Mazzocchi told Serrin, "To continue to accede to management demands amounts to surrender."[1]

Mazzocchi got the Institute to produce a series of economic booklets, and to help him write op-ed pieces and articles for newspapers and journals. They conducted anti-Reaganomics workshops at worker conferences around the country, where rump groups within major unions were fighting hard against concessions. Mazzocchi called them "lost battalions" in the class war. Rank-and-file dissidents nearly defeated the 1982 GM concession contract that had been promoted by the UAW leadership. In 1984, the OCAW local at Merck, led by Mazzocchi backers, fought for six months to defeat a pernicious two-tiered wage proposal. A group of worker-activists in the

Twin Cities organized a large "We're Not the Problem" union conference, based on the title of an Institute booklet. But Mazzocchi was too distant from institutional power to meld the lost battalions into a fighting force.

After another Sunday-morning caffeinated call, Mazzocchi revived an idea he had tried successfully in OCAW: producing National Public Radio call-in shows. Soon the Institute became a regular radio production shop, with nearly one hundred stations signing up for its controversial programming on military spending, Social Security, women's rights, and any other topic Mazzocchi could dream up.

The Mazzocchi tornado even spun through his own quiet New Jersey community. When Tony and Susan discovered that Maplewood–South Orange school buildings contained hundreds of pipes insulated with asbestos, they created quite a stir. As the local school board quickly discovered, hell hath no fury like a pair of health and safety troublemakers with three kids enrolled in an asbestos-contaminated school system.

The Mazzocchis found that their public schools were not covered by any government asbestos regulations and that the usual remediation program was a disaster. Knowing that town after town around the country must be facing similar problems, Tony and Susan launched a national organization, Parents Against Asbestos Hazards in Schools.

To the school board's chagrin, *The New York Times* ran a feature, "New Data Find Asbestos a Peril, in Home, at Job." Philip Shabecoff wrote: "Anthony Mazzocchi, a longtime occupational safety and health official for the Oil, Chemical and Atomic Workers Union, who is now a leader of an organization call Parents Against Asbestos Hazards in Schools, said, 'What passes for abatement programs is no more than a patchwork quilt of controls that will absolutely make the situation worse rather than better.'"

In a follow-up piece about the EPA dealing with asbestos in its own building, Shabecoff again went to Mazzocchi for a biting quotation: "I would have thought children deserved at least as much attention and concern as EPA is showing to itself."[2]

Although Tony and Susan were able to provide advice and support for parents in other communities, the organization largely remained a party of two.

Usually, when Mazzocchi showed up in the press, it was to critique labor's meltdown. In Bill Serrin's May 1981 *New York Times* piece "Where Are the

Pickets of Yesteryear?," Tony coined one of the decade's best labor lines when he lamented that unions were "walking backwards into the 1980s."[3]

In "Wage Concessions: Revolt in the Unions," a 1982 article, Mazzocchi told Serrin that the gap between the leadership and the led is "an occupational problem" among top union leaders.[4]

In his extensive October 1983 feature "The Corporate Assault on Wages," *New York Times* reporter Steven Greenhouse relayed Mazzocchi's observation about the negative impact of concession bargaining on organizing: "Workers can see you don't need a union card to hold up a white flag."[5]

The most in-depth piece was Serrin's "The Man Who Is Taking the Labor Movement to Task," a sixteen-hundred-word feature that ran in *The New York Times* in 1983. It described Mazzocchi as "widely respected for energy and intelligence even by people in business or the union movement who do not agree with his philosophies. In particular, many younger, aggressive men and women in the labor movement or those sympathetic to its aims, think highly of him."[6]

The article came out two months before the OCAW convention at which Tony's appeal of his dismissal would be heard. Now out of office for nearly two years, Mazzocchi told Serrin that he didn't have the troops to run again for president: "Mr. Mazzocchi says his supporters do not have the energy or resources for a campaign. But it seems clear that, with time and the loss of union membership, some of Mr. Mazzocchi's support has disappeared and Mr. Mazzocchi realizes that if he lost three times, his political career would be ended."[7]

Yet if Mazzocchi didn't at least fight his dismissal, his supporters argued, a bad precedent would stand unchallenged—that an OCAW president could retaliate against challengers. Even though Mazzocchi felt uneasy about making this a contest about *his* job, seniority, and benefits, he felt obliged to follow his supporters' advice, even if it meant taking another drubbing.

So in 1983, for the third convention in a row, there were speeches from Mazzocchi and Goss, the usual hyperbole from supporters and foes, and a roll-call vote. Goss beat back Mazzocchi's appeal by nearly twenty thousand votes.

The vote revealed two sad truths. The first was that OCAW was getting smaller: The total delegate vote represented only 112,619 workers, a drop of more than 50,000 in just four years. The second was that Mazzocchi's progressive forces within OCAW were declining. The perception on the floor was that Tony's time in the union had come and gone.

III

As industrial jobs vanished, many workers blamed environmental regulations. And many environmentalists were losing sympathy for workers who seemed willing to let their companies trash the environment to protect jobs that would soon disappear anyway. Mazzocchi sensed a major brawl coming.

It happened at the fourteen-thousand-acre Ciba-Geigy facility in Toms River, New Jersey. Only a few miles west of Barnegat Bay's pristine beaches, Ciba-Geigy produced dyes for the textile, paper, and leather industries as well as high-performance lubricants and epoxy resins used as additives for plastics and coatings. During peak operations, it produced more than 220,000 pounds of chemical products per day. It also generated enormous quantities of solid and liquid wastes, which it habitually dumped on the grounds. And it discharged four million gallons a day of supposedly treated wastewater into the ocean via an underground pipeline that extended half a mile out to sea near Ortley Beach, a popular swimming area.

The wastes the company dumped into its holding ponds and rotting fifty-five-gallon drums were a who's who of carcinogenic chemicals—phenols, benzene, chloroform, chromium, trichloroethylene, tetrachloroethylene. They all leached into the groundwater and migrated into the community. Occasionally, an effluent pipe would break, dumping toxic waste underneath nearby homes.

One former employee told *The New York Times* that the waste was dumped "right out into the woods and straight into the ground" and that "tens of thousands of drums were buried four to six deep because no one knew what else to do with them." He also said that "this and other pipelines leading to a wastewater treatment plant were often cracked" and that "stuff oozed into the ground and through the foundations of some of the buildings there."[8]

This potent toxic stew later would be associated with increased childhood cancers in the surrounding community. With more than ninety-two thousand drums of highly toxic waste on site, in 1983 the federal EPA listed the facility as number twenty-seven of the eighty-five worst dumpsites in New Jersey.

Ciba-Geigy was a vast multinational corporation accustomed to having its way with New Jersey regulatory agencies. Faced with the injunction to remediate, it did what most chemical companies did: It stalled. First it negotiated endlessly over a cleanup consent order. Then it refused to sign the one it agreed to. The company even delayed admitting state investigators who arrived to inspect the facility. At the same time, it dangled before the state the prospect that it might build a second facility on the site, providing more jobs and tax dollars.

OCAW Local 8-562 represented the 650 production workers at the Geigy facility. Mazzocchi had helped bring the workers into OCAW in the 1970s by emphasizing the struggle for better health and safety conditions. In 1979, 8-562 had backed Mazzocchi for president. The local actively supported a series of campaigns organized by Rick Engler (a former Mazzocchi intern) for stronger health and safety laws in New Jersey. But in 1981, it switched its support to Goss.

Greenpeace was tracking the problems at Ciba-Geigy's plant. It sent divers to take samples from the end of the ocean effluent pipe. It also surreptitiously gathered soil samples from the Toms River compound. Then, in August 1984, two young Greenpeace activists scaled the top of the Ciba-Geigy water tank and occupied it for three days. Later, Greenpeace divers stoppered the effluent pipeline.

New Jersey's Department of Environmental Protection and the state Division of Criminal Justice both investigated the company. The Ocean County prosecutor's office obtained a sample of effluent and had it analyzed by an independent laboratory.[9]

A group of mothers from the community, many of whose children attended a school adjacent to the Ciba-Geigy compound, protested the pollution.

Mazzocchi expected that the union rep, who had become a Goss ally, would line workers up behind the company and against the environmentalists. But even he was surprised when the rep led a worker counterdemonstration against the mothers. "Marching against mothers?" Mazzocchi said. "Jesus, how stupid can you get?"

Stupider. One of the Greenpeace demonstrators told *The New York Times* that a Ciba-Geigy employee had "run her car off the company road and had beaten her."[10]

This was the stuff of Mazzocchi's proto-fascism nightmares. He had warned environmentalists again and again that workers would "eat them for lunch" if they failed to address the jobs issue. When fundamentally threatened, he told them, workers could go right or left, depending on how they were organized and how the issues were framed. Without alternative leadership and new ideas, they could even march against mothers and beat up environmentalists.

Mazzocchi had been working on a new idea ever since the late 1960s. He had realized then that there was no way to protect workers and society from toxic substances without banning them. But banning would cause OCAW workers to lose their jobs. Mazzocchi's jarring solution was for society to pay workers *not* to make poisons.

Mazzocchi, who had once championed the idea of transforming New York's arms manufacturers into makers of trains and other peaceful products, had come to realize that conversion had its limits. Manufacturing products for peaceful use could be just as damaging to workers' health and the environment as fabricating military products.

> If you make a missile, you're utilizing the same chemical process that you use if you were making a train. And you're processing the metal the same way. You're fabricating it a bit differently—but utilizing the same toxic substances. So you're assaulting the environment, whether you're producing a missile or some product for peaceful uses. So I thought the notion of utilizing these existing facilities no longer had any validity. . . .
>
> I had never thought about that before, because I was not environmentally aware. Like most people, I thought we could beat swords into plowshares. And I know I angered a lot of people when I'd go to a peace meeting or a meeting on plant closings and say that we can't beat swords into plowshares—nor should we even think about it. We should walk away from these facilities. And then we have to take care of the workers.

The idea of paying workers not to work confused many progressives, who felt workers needed jobs for their own self-worth. But what most people saw as "good" blue-collar work, Mazzocchi saw as "an abomination." The very idea of going to work each day and getting exposed to cancer-causing substances, no matter what the pay, was for Tony a violation of human rights. As he put it,

> We were working on so many health and safety problems: coke oven workers, the steel workers, our chemical workers. You start to realize what people went through in these jobs. They died early, or they got sick. What the hell? There really was no future for people who worked in these industries.

For Mazzocchi, the phrase *dignity of work* was corporate-speak, and he flinched whenever progressives used it. Although he thought workers brought enormous dignity *to* the job, he saw little dignity inherent *in* the job. As Mazzocchi put it, "Work is shit. We should do as little of it as possible." After six months on an auto assembly line and another year or two on the line at Helena Rubinstein, he'd had enough work "dignity" to last a lifetime.

He drew a strong distinction between corporate work and what he called "redefined work." Corporate work included traditional factory jobs and menial service jobs. "Redefined" work was getting paid to do creative things, to promote social change, to think and to grow. Ever since Mazzocchi was elected to a full-time union job, he'd been doing redefined work.

Being a social activist, getting paid to go to school, or working in the nonprofit world were all, for Mazzocchi, redefined work. He argued that it made no sense to use the word *work* to include both cleaning toilets and doing research at a place like the Labor Institute. The only common feature, he argued, was that each type of "worker" received an income.

Mazzocchi thought the goal of a just society should be to reduce boring, repetitive, dirty, and dangerous work to a minimum, and to maximize redefined work:

> The employer defines work as, you work for eight hours; you take orders. You're reduced to child status. You leave all your rights

> behind; you've got to raise your hand to get permission to go to the bathroom. I'm saying there are other forms of work where people have social contact as equals.

For Mazzocchi, there was nothing utopian about this quest for a new kind of work. It was precisely what he had experienced after World War II when he received fifty-two weeks of pay (at twenty dollars per week, two-thirds the average take-home pay at that time) from the GI Bill of Rights.

> I tell people about the 52-20 Club—that's when the US redefined work. Society said, *Do what you want to do for fifty-two weeks. All you have to do is go once a week and report for your check.* If you went to the beach, that was considered work. If you went to do anything you want, it's work. If you wanted to go to school, you got paid to go. Your tuition was paid. If you had a wife, you were given an additional benefit. You were given housing.
>
> When someone says to me, "It's pie in the sky," I point out that we've already done it: It was the Servicemen's Readjustment Act of 1944. So this idea, which was considered crazy, was instituted, and it turned out to be wildly successful. Now we know that it didn't cost society anything, because the social investment in GI education generated $6.90 of GDP for every dollar spent.

Mazzocchi first used this idea in the 1970s to tackle what he thought was the obvious fate of nuclear weapons workers. "You're either gonna use this weapon, and none of us will be around, or you're gonna stop making it," he told atomic workers. Sooner or later, he said, "Peace is going to break out. Then what are you going to do, march to demand more hydrogen bombs?"

But instead of paying workers to "go to the beach," why not give nuke workers the job of cleaning up the huge quantities of hazardous waste buried at the weapons complexes? Mazzocchi vehemently objected.

> Humans have never done this type of work since we came on the face of the earth. You cannot clean these places up without giving people whole-body burdens early. And then those workers are going to be cast off, and nobody's going to hire them.

Mazzocchi offered what he believed was a more humane solution. Since atomic cleanup was so dangerous, and since society needed it done, workers should be protected through drastically reduced work time.

> You want it cleaned up? Our position ought to be that you work two hours a day—and get paid for eight. You're fucking around with high levels of plutonium and everything else. And everybody says it's very bad. Those who work there say it's far worse. Two hours on, eight hours pay. You work two years, you get five years off with full pay. In the nuclear industry, there is money for it.

Mazzocchi also believed that both nuclear workers and toxic workers, "because of the danger of their jobs and their service to the country, should be entitled to full income and benefits for life even if their jobs are eliminated."

(After 9/11, Mazzocchi applied these principles to the cleanup at the World Trade Center: "There is no way to protect the workers when you have a catastrophe of that magnitude. We should be on our hind legs screaming, 'No one should have to work on the site more than four hours a day.' And the workers should have sabbaticals: Every four weeks there should be a week or two off. What's wrong with this demand? Thirty-five years from now there's going to be an incredible tragedy for those people who were working extraordinary hours there."[11] Mazzocchi was wrong. The tragedy of sick workers began unfolding within five years.)

To make his idea a bit easier to stomach, Mazzocchi compromised: Instead of getting paid for not working at all, he conceded, dislocated toxic or atomic workers should get full pay, benefits, and tuition for up to four years, just like the GI Bill of Rights after World War II. Education would be redefined as work.

But it still wasn't easy to convince progressives, who were stuck on the old definition of work. Mazzocchi wholeheartedly agreed with Stanley Aronowitz, who observed:

> There's a very strong ethical obligation that comes out of one section of the left. And I don't mean just the communist left—I mean, the socialist left, social democratic left. They really believe in work. They believe in work as redemption; work as obligation;

> work as necessary for personal development; work as giving back to the society.[12]

Rather than manufacture toxic substances or weapons of mass destruction, Mazzocchi said, he'd rather pay workers to go to school and then, if necessary, pay them to "stand on the street corner arguing about Aristotle and Plato."

Mazzocchi knew that, if the left loved work, workers didn't—at least not traditional work. "I always recognized, even in the '50s, that people wanted out of the plant," he said. "I saw that nobody wanted to go back to their facilities. Nobody said, 'Oh, I'm gonna give up this union staff job and go back to where I came from.'"

Mazzocchi wanted every worker, not just chemically exposed workers, to have more free time. He advocated that everyone should, like professors, get a yearlong paid sabbatical once every seven years: "I think people could better tolerate work, as it's now constituted, if there were more sabbaticals where they could refresh themselves. I think there's a lot in life that people aren't exposed to. Sabbaticals would give them the time to try new things."

Mazzocchi also wanted the retirement age set at fifty-five and layoffs based on reverse seniority. During layoffs, he wanted the older, more chemically exposed workers to have the first choice to opt out of the workplace, either to retire or to go to school: "If I'm working in a plant, my seniority should take me out—it shouldn't keep me in. See, I've been arguing we should have the prison concept. You put your time in and you get out. But we do it the other way: You put your time in and you stay in! I'm saying, it's crazy!"

Mazzocchi and the Labor Institute called their proposal for a four-year income and benefit guarantee for chemical and atomic workers the Superfund for Workers. The name played off a new federal bill that established a cleanup fund for hazardous waste sites.

OCAW members caught on quickly. At one protest rally, an atomic worker wrote a placard that read, TREAT WORKERS LIKE DIRT. Since the government was spending billions to reclaim the land at nuclear facilities, these workers cogently argued, shouldn't something be set aside to reclaim the workers by sending them to school? Later, environmentalists complained that the word *superfund* had too many negative connotations, and the name of the plan was changed to Just Transition.

Mazzocchi was powerless to bring this concept to Ciba-Geigy's Toms River plant. "Had I been a national officer, I think I could have made a difference there," he said.

But just in case an opening appeared, Mazzocchi and the Labor Institute's Mike Merrill worked out a proposal for a "University of Reclamation" to be created on the Ciba-Geigy site, a new branch of Rutgers University dedicated to the study of reclamation of chemically contaminated sites. Dislocated chemical workers would get full pay and benefits to attend and contribute to a multidisciplinary program on cleanup.

Instead, the local OCAW leaders at Ciba-Geigy (who didn't want Mazzocchi anywhere near them) became pawns in a predictably degrading game. The government finally clamped down on the company, which decided to cut its losses by shutting down the plant. All the workers were laid off except for a skeleton crew that patrolled the property. Local families sued the company as clusters of children began developing cancer. What remained of the local union and its treasury were used to establish a political action fund to fight environmental regulations in New Jersey.

Mazzocchi used this story to urge progressives to break free from their traditional notions of work and income. As he put, "If we accept the boss's definition of work, we lose before we start."

IV

In the mid-1980s, a lot of people were listening to a whole other kind of boss. Tony Mazzocchi had never heard of him. "Who is Bruce Springfield?" he asked. But once he got the name right, Mazzocchi realized that he might be able to enlist the Boss to promote a new approach to plant closings.

Rocker Bruce Springsteen's song "My Hometown" (on the 1984 album *Born in the USA*) was about Freehold, New Jersey, where he'd been born and raised. The lyrics described the 1964 closing of the local Karagheusian Rug Mill.

When 3M announced in 1985 that it was closing its facility in Freehold, OCAW members approached Springsteen for help. Not only was it his hometown, but the facility produced high-end audio tape for music recording studios.

From the moment he caught wind of 3M's impending shutdown, Stanley Fischer, president of OCAW Local 8-760, was determined to put up a fight. Fischer, who had helped Mazzocchi greatly in his campaigns for union president, shared Tony's sense of struggle and his audacity. He was a native of the scrappy working-class town of West New York, New Jersey, and if he couldn't get 3M to reverse its decision, then he was going to make the company pay for the suffering it caused by closing the plant.

Fischer asked the Labor Institute to write to Springsteen on the workers' behalf. Springsteen's managers responded. Fischer was ecstatic.

Although a bit slow on the rock music uptake, Mazzocchi soon realized that Springsteen's involvement was a great opportunity to popularize the Superfund for Workers idea. Mazzocchi, unlike the Freehold workers, held no illusions about how their struggle with 3M would end. With or without Springsteen, the company would shut the plant down. Nothing short of a new national mass movement and a powerful labor party, Mazzocchi argued, would compel 3M, or any other company, to keep open its doors. But maybe Springsteen would endorse the idea that 3M should provide full pay, benefits, and tuition to all the laid-off workers until they found comparable jobs. They could call it a Plant-Closing Bill of Human Rights.

On December 1, 1985, Springsteen joined Stanley and his wife, Linda, for dinner at their modest home in Bricktown, New Jersey. Their two young boys nearly died as Springsteen posed for pictures and signed everything they handed to him. Then Springsteen asked how he could help. Coached by Mazzocchi, Stanley asked him to sign on to a *New York Times* ad in support of the workers' cause. Springsteen liked the idea and made a twenty-thousand-dollar donation.

Stanley also wanted to hook country singer Willie Nelson into the ad. Didn't Mazzocchi have a good friend, Carolyn Mugar (the former organizing intern), who now headed Farm Aid and who worked closely with Willie? Couldn't she prevail on him? Mugar asked and Willie said yes.

On December 5, 1985, the ad, written and placed by the Labor Institute, appeared in the front section of *The New York Times* national edition, the *St. Paul Pioneer Press* (which served 3M's corporate headquarters), *Variety,* and the *Asbury Park Press* in New Jersey. In it, Springsteen and Nelson said, "We know these decisions are always difficult to make, but we believe that people of good-will should be able to sit down and come up with a humane program that will keep those jobs and those workers in Freehold."

Of course, that wasn't the message Mazzocchi preferred, but for an opening gambit it was good enough.

The ad generated more news coverage than any other story in the union's history, more even than Karen Silkwood's death. Mazzocchi was impressed. That Springfield guy sure was popular.

OCAW agreed to pay for additional ads that featured a petition calling for a worker bill of rights: full pay, health care, day care, and tuition for laid-off workers. Fischer took the petition on tour, visiting labor struggles around the country. He stopped at record stores to pick up signatures and media attention.

Fischer was a busy man. Not only was he negotiating with Springsteen's people for a benefit concert, but he was also trying to connect with black South African 3M workers living under the yoke of apartheid. Miraculously, the pieces fell into place. The Labor Institute found an ally in Amon Msane, a vibrant young leader of workers at a 3M facility near Johannesburg. What appealed most to Msane was the notion of *giving* aid rather than receiving it. This was the era of big multistar rock concerts to raise funds to help impoverished Africans under the banner of "US Aid for Africa." Msane said, "How about this time, we make it 'African Aid for the USA'?"

Through the Labor Institute, Stanley met with radical media activist Danny Schechter, then a producer for ABC's *20/20*. Schechter, who also worked with rock stars to protest apartheid, liked the idea of a piece on the 3M struggle.

Using Springsteen as the hook, Schechter produced a thirty-minute segment for *20/20* that followed Fischer as he traveled across the country drumming up support for his campaign, Hometowns Against Shutdowns. Along the way, Schechter connected Fischer to nearly every labor struggle in the country. The piece concluded with a heart-wrenching collage that flashed between Springsteen singing "My Hometown" and scenes of empty factories around the country. To top it off, the Springsteen people gave *20/20* a taped rendition of "This Land Is Your Land" that had never been aired before.

At the end of Schechter's piece, *20/20* co-host Barbara Walters turned to her colleague and asked, "I understand there was a development today in South Africa?"

Her colleague responded, "We just received a report that hundreds of workers in South Africa that work at 3M—black workers—will go out on a sympathy demonstration tomorrow—a kind of reverse solidarity."[13]

The next morning, February 28, 1986, for more than two hours, two hundred black South African 3M workers joyously chanted and danced out of and around the 3M facility in Johannesburg. They wore OCAW 8-760 T-shirts with logos that played on two Springsteen song titles: the front said NO RETREAT, NO SURRENDER; the back read 3M, DON'T ABANDON FREEHOLD, MY HOMETOWN!

The Labor Institute managed to smuggle out a photograph of the demonstration, and a flock of TV stations descended on Fischer's office as he spoke directly by phone to the South African protesters.

Stanley, who by now could walk on water, next invited Msane to the United States to continue the protest. The picture of a black South African joining a protest in support of largely white American workers made news again. In a lengthy interview on public television's *MacNeil/Lehrer NewsHour* on June 13, Msane debated Hebert Beukes, the South African ambassador to the US, about the state of emergency the apartheid government had declared in anticipation of the anniversary of the 1976 Soweto massacre.* After returning home, Msane was twice jailed for his anti-apartheid comments in America, the second time for six months. Fisher and the Labor Institute organized successful campaigns to free him. After apartheid ended, Msane was elected to Parliament.

The more media attention Stanley Fischer drew, the more flak he received from many progressives fighting against plant closings in other areas of the country. They wanted Fischer to fight only to keep the plants open, not to demand reparations.

Mazzocchi was disappointed that these progressives couldn't understand that working people were entitled to life beyond the factory and to an education that would bring them more possibilities in life. He was certain that the plant-closing movement, as it was called, would fade away. As he put it,

---

*More than 150 black schoolchildren were killed by police on June 16, 1976, during a protest against a decree by the South African government making Afrikaans the official language of all black schools.

"It's funny they call my schemes for full pay and education unrealistic. Yet every plant they fight for has gone down. *That's* realistic?"

Although 3M's Freehold facility got more publicity than any other endangered plant in America, it was ultimately shut down like all the rest. And even with the Boss's support, Mazzocchi's Superfund for Workers did not become reality. But Mazzocchi believed the public airing it received would be valuable in the long run. Fischer used the media attention to gain substantial state training funds for a resource center to help dislocated workers, which he ran for several years after the plant closed on May 29, 1986.

At a benefit concert for the 3M workers at the Stone Pony in Asbury Park, where Springsteen got his start, the singer came pretty close to articulating Mazzocchi's position: "When a company comes and exploits natural resources, there are laws that say they have to replenish those resources," Springsteen told a packed house. "Yet when a company comes into a town and exploits our greatest natural resource, our workers, there are few laws that protect the people. . . ."[14]

V

On the night of December 3, 1984, a Union Carbide plant in Bhopal, India, leaked twenty-seven tons of deadly methyl isocyanate (MIC). The gas, similar to the poison gas used in World War I, affected at least half a million residents. No one is certain how many died that night or in the days after. Union Carbide admitted to about two thousand deaths, but local undertakers thought there were more than fifteen thousand. Other estimates suggested that over twenty thousand died, with tens of thousands suffering lifelong illnesses. It was the worst chemical accident in history—and a US-based company, operating in a developing nation, was responsible.

Because it happened there and not here, Mazzocchi thought American corporations and the media downplayed the disaster, conveying a false sense of security. He immediately began searching for ways to demonstrate that we were no better equipped than India to prevent or respond to such a tragedy. In March 1985, Mazzocchi—together with Labor Institute staff and Ward Morehouse from the Council on International and Public Affairs, a small progressive nonprofit—organized a conference titled, After Bhopal, Implications for Developed and Developing Nations, in Newark, New Jersey. Morehouse, who had traveled widely in India, arranged for several knowledgeable speakers from India, including H. M. Juriwala, the local union secretary at the Bhopal facility; Dr. Ramana Dhara, who helped provide medical aid to the victims; Arun Subramanian, an investigative reporter from *Business India;* and Rasa Kulkarni, a member of the Indian parliament and president of the Chemical Workers Union of India.

In addition to assembling panels of experts for the conference, Mazzocchi arranged to have his Indian guests speak before unionists, journalists, and public health groups. A prominent activist contacted Mazzocchi to ask if the Indian experts could speak at a protest rally at the gates of the Union Carbide plant in Institute, West Virginia. This plant, whose workers were represented by OCAW, also produced the deadly MIC gas.

The demonstration should have provided an ideal venue to unite the workers with community residents who were also worried about MIC. Unfortunately, Mazzocchi discovered, protest organizers had failed to enlist the support of the local OCAW leaders. Without this collaboration, Tony knew workers would side with the company, fearing job loss. A few might even vent their fear with angry words and acts of violence—leading to more division, hostility, and horrendous press.

So Mazzocchi told the organizer that the Indians would not appear at the plant gates.

But the protest organizer wouldn't take no for an answer. He called repeatedly to urge Mazzocchi to change his mind. Didn't Mazzocchi know that the movement for plant safety depended upon him? Didn't he recognize his moral obligations to the Bhopal victims and to the progressive movement? With the chips down, had he become some kind of fair-weather radical?

And then, for the first time in anyone's memory, Mazzocchi snapped. He was utterly outraged to have his thirty-year record of activism impugned by this careless organizer.

"I don't need you to tell me about my moral obligations!" Mazzocchi roared at the phone. He yelled and screamed, and yelled some more.

It was as if all Mazzocchi's frustrations with being out of power had burst onto this one man. If Tony had won the OCAW presidency, he would have been organizing Bhopal demonstrations all over the country—led by the union! The union would have chased Union Carbide around the globe until it made proper restitution to the victims. Mazzocchi would have demanded that the company remove MIC from production and fully compensate any laid-off workers.

But Mazzocchi didn't have the power to do what really needed to be done. Instead, he had to listen to a lecture on his moral responsibilities by an organizer who hadn't done his homework.

After his outburst, Mazzocchi had a brainstorm about how to alert the public that the next Bhopal could be Anytown, USA. As director of the Workers' Policy Project within the Labor Institute, Mazzocchi dreamed up a survey: Could the hospitals in northern New Jersey—home to so many chemical factories—handle a large release of a toxic substance like phosgene or cyanide? Did they have protocols for such treatment? How many beds and staff did they have?

Mazzocchi, of course, had neither the time nor the inclination to conduct a peer-reviewed study. So he asked Dr. Steven Markowitz, an occupational medicine physician from Mount Sinai Medical Center, to help devise a list of questions. And then Tony and Susan, sitting at their kitchen table in Maplewood, New Jersey, started calling the sixty-five hospitals in seven northern New Jersey counties likely to be affected by a Bhopal-like release.

They raced to complete the survey by December 3, 1985, the first Bhopal anniversary. By the press briefing, Tony and Susan had reached only forty-four of the local hospitals. Nevertheless, the results were shocking: More than half had no formal protocols for treating victims of chemical plant accidents. Further, most emergency room personnel had little familiarity with industrial toxic chemicals. In short, the medical system in New Jersey would be totally overwhelmed by a Bhopal-like disaster.

Despite the flimsiness of the study, it was news. Mazzocchi contacted *New York Times* reporter Stuart Diamond to alert him before the press conference. Diamond confirmed the study's basic findings by calling several hospitals and experts. He and his editors agreed the study was noteworthy.

Still, no one quite expected the play the story received. There was the study on page 1 of the *Times:* "Hospitals Found to Be Ill-Prepared for Toxic Spills in New York Area."

"These hospitals hardly know how to handle any of the important toxic chemicals," said Anthony Mazzocchi, the [Workers' Policy Project] director and a former national vice president of the Oil, Chemical and Atomic Workers Union.

"This is one of the most sophisticated areas in the United States for medical treatment," he added. "And yet we found that many of the hospitals could barely deal with five chemical poisoning victims in the middle of the night, let alone with tens of thousands of injuries, as occurred in Bhopal."

Authorities at various hospitals in the survey agreed.[15]

VI

While Mazzocchi was making front-page news based on a study that could fit on the back of a postcard, OCAW was heading for the obituary page.

OCAW membership plummeted as the oil industry consolidated at a furious pace, shutting down hundreds of smaller refineries that didn't merit reinvestment. Old chemical plants also went under as production moved abroad. And feeble union organizing efforts failed to make up for the losses.

The magnitude of the decline could be measured by the drop of votes cast at OCAW conventions. In 1979: 168,000 votes. In 1981, after the Canadians' departure: 142,000. In 1983: 112,600. In 1985: 105,000.

OCAW's glory days were over. Staff members (some of whom, Mazzocchi thought, had been hired in deals aimed at depriving him of votes in the past two elections) would have to go. Like many other declining unions, OCAW looked to merge with a bigger counterpart, and fast.

With Mazzocchi gone, OCAW leaders now had a free hand to merge with the United Paperworkers International Union. The deal could secure and increase officer salaries and provide handsome buyouts for top OCAW officials. All it took was a vote at OCAW's August 1985 convention and a similar one at the Paperworkers meeting in December.

---

*Years later, Mazzocchi claimed he had sat next to a woman on a plane who said she had worked for a labor section of the CIA, which had persuaded Goss to resign.

But first the Goss team had to clean house—and that meant getting rid of Goss, who had grown increasingly incompetent. He resigned on December 9, 1983,* giving way to his vice president Joe Misbrenner. Bob Wages then replaced Misbrenner as vice president. Misbrenner and Wages led a concerted effort to merge with the Paperworkers (still led by Wayne Glenn, whom Mazzocchi had excoriated in 1981). With the OCAW in a nosedive and Mazzocchi forces fading, the merger seemed inevitable.

To pass a merger, the OCAW constitution required a two-thirds delegate vote—about 70,000 of the 105,000 votes. Mazzocchi and many of his supporters still strongly opposed the merger, which would have eliminated the rank-and-file executive board and allowed collective bargaining contracts to be approved by only one-third of the membership. But could Tony's forces still muster thirty-five thousand votes to stop it?

From the convention floor, Vern Jensen, then District 8 council president, exposed the golden parachutes that he believed had motivated OCAW's leaders to go for the merger. As he explained to the convention delegates,

> If we merge, your executive board members will have a hundred fifty thousand dollars in pensions that we have at convention twice denied. Our officers will have a whopping pay increase that you would never give them in conventions, a fatter pension plan than you'd ever give them and a degree of job security none of us will ever see.[16]

Speaker after speaker argued against the merger agreement. But . . . what difference did it make to deny officers these luxuries if the union was destined to die? Wasn't a merger absolutely necessary just to survive?

Mark Dudzic, from Mazzocchi's old local, OCAW 8-149, told the delegates that it was better to be small and visionary than large and dull. "Political clout is more the result of political vision and the ability to build coalitions," he argued. "It wasn't our great numbers that put OCAW in the forefront of the battle to pass the OSHA Act in 1970."[17]

But Dudzic left the obvious unstated. No, it wasn't the size of OCAW—although the union had been nearly twice as large then. Rather, it was that Mazzocchi had been able to nurture a new movement. Now he was out of power, and for some the absence of his vision made the merger not worth fighting.

Misbrenner and Wages twisted countless arms and promised many goodies to achieve the 70,126 votes they needed to pass the merger. And yet, in the end, they came up short by 1,919 votes. Merger supporters were furious. One delegate likened the vote to minority apartheid rule in South Africa. However, Joe Misbrenner kept his cool. Workers gave him a standing ovation when he said, "It is the constitution, it is the requirement, it is what we live by. If you can be good winners, let's be good losers also."[18]

But not dumb losers. Misbrenner, Wages, and their allies hadn't come this far to let the merger slip away. Their first step was to invite Wayne Glenn to address the convention, supposedly to clarify issues and answer questions. The invitation bought time to reconfigure the vote.

Glenn, a polished speaker, nevertheless bored the delegates with a rendition of the great and glorious history of the Paperworkers, starting with "A century ago, [when] a small group of proud, courageous men joined together . . ."

What must have felt like a full century later, Glenn finally addressed the reasons for merger. The best he could do was: the "word 'union' means joined together to create strength."

Along the way, he let slip a revealing metaphor: "The American labor movement must circle the wagons, so to speak, to protect what we already have."[19] For Mazzocchi, Glenn's statement was Exhibit A for a labor movement that had ceased to be a cause. He believed that if you replaced Glenn's reference to "the American labor movement" with "American labor leaders," this would precisely define the real reason for the merger. Only through merger could these leaders hold on to their handsome wage and retirement benefits. They needed that expanded asset base and those golden parachutes.

The next day, Misbrenner and Wages maneuvered a motion to reconsider the merger. In the meantime, the administration had time to perhaps twist one or two more arms with promises they might or might not keep.

With the death of OCAW so near at hand, Mazzocchi, who'd attended its founding convention, rose to the floor to try one last time to argue that instead of a merger, delegates needed to "capture that crusading spirit."[20]

His effort failed. The merger squeaked through by only 479 votes.

At their convention four months later, the Paperworkers were set to vote on the merger document. Given the top-down nature of that union, a revolt was highly unlikely.

And yet, when the time came, Paperworkers members upended the merger. Their delegates were furious that Wayne Glenn had used the merger agreement to slip through new internal procedures that the delegates themselves had rejected in convention only months earlier. "None of the issues were issues that OCAW cared about one way or the other," said Bob Wages. "So there you have it. An arrogant president decided to ram through changes via a merger he could not get otherwise and the membership revolted."[21]

VII

OCAW soon descended into political hell as members of the governing coalition went at one another's throats. Misbrenner and Wages thought Mike Ricigliano, their secretary-treasurer, was a crook. After accumulating what they believed was foolproof evidence of a series of kickbacks, they brought him up on charges before the rank-and-file executive board.

Kip Phillips, a strong Mazzocchi supporter, decided to serve as Ricigliano's defense counsel. "It offended my sense of fairness," said Phillips. "The union was using its lawyers to prosecute Mike before the board, and none of the union's staff was willing to serve in his defense because they feared political retribution from above. So I stepped in."[22]

Despite the damning evidence that Wages, a lawyer, believed he had amassed on Ricigliano, the board deadlocked four-to-four, leaving him in place. After that, Ricigliano grew in stature and mounted a campaign aimed at taking the union away from Misbrenner and Wages at the 1988 OCAW convention.

From the sidelines, Mazzocchi watched with horror. He was convinced that Ricigliano would be a disaster for the union.

For Tony, there was no comparison between the Misbrenner-Wages team and Ricigliano. For one thing, Bob Wages viewed Mazzocchi as an important source of new ideas and had opened up a line of communication with him. Ties between the two deepened during the epic lockout of some 370 OCAW workers at the BASF chemical facility in Geismar, Louisiana. The lockout, one of the longest and most bitter labor disputes in American labor history, spanned five and a half years, from June 1984 to December 1989.

Wages committed the union to fully backing the locked-out workers. He assigned the union's lead researcher, Dick Leonard (a Mazzocchi supporter), to head up a relentless assault on BASF. He also hired Richard Miller (a Labor Institute consultant who had done excellent work on a previous lockout at Merck) to organize on behalf of the BASF workers—which Miller did with dedication for five years. Miller worked closely with Ernie Rouselle, who was back in Louisiana as a field representative after losing the vice presidency to Joe Misbrenner in the hard-fought 1981 election.

Against the backdrop of labor's spectacularly disastrous defeats at Eastern Airlines, Hormel, and International Paper, the BASF campaign may have been OCAW's finest hour. In the tightly interlocked oil and chemical industries, the OCAW membership quickly grasped the terrible consequences that would follow if BASF was allowed to prevail. The company had already decertified or locked out local unions in New York, New Jersey, West Virginia, and Michigan.

Leonard and Miller developed a far-reaching international corporate campaign that became a model for confronting corporate power in the post-PATCO era. They hounded BASF from its boardroom in Germany to Terre Haute, Indiana, where they defeated the company's bid to build a toxic waste incinerator. Environmental groups allied with the union to attack the company.

BASF ended the lockout on December 18, 1989. After the worker victory, the local union demonstrated its solidarity with environmentalists by funding an environmental organizer. The organizer worked out of the union hall for the next decade on projects such as toxic substance cleanups and getting town water to rural African American communities.

Wages's unwavering support for the BASF workers showed that he, like Mazzocchi, thought multinational corporate power needed to be confronted, not appeased. As OCAW rank-and-file leaders and activists came together to support the BASF fight, divisions that had split the union down the middle during the 1979 and 1981 elections began to heal.

"Our success with BASF gave pause to other multinationals that we dealt with, in the oil industry and chemical industry, that we were capable of a pretty destructive fight," said Wages.[23]

Wages and Mazzocchi conferred about the BASF campaign and the union's other challenges. Tony also asked for and received one important favor from Wages: The administration agreed to reassign Mazzocchi's closest ally and friend, Dick McManus, from exile in Ohio back to his home local in the New York area. In 1987, Wages recruited the Labor Institute to apply on behalf of the union for government training grants for hazardous waste workers and to carry out an aggressive worker training program. He also permitted the Institute to put Mazzocchi on the grant to assist.

Meanwhile, Ricigliano was gaining momentum for his presidential run at the 1988 convention. Not only did he corral some of the old Mazzocchi forces, but he made serious inroads into Misbrenner's base as well.

Wages realized that the only way out was to team up with Mazzocchi. He pitched the idea to Joe Misbrenner and to Jack Foley, the District 1 director who had for years opposed Mazzocchi. "Once Joe said yes, I went to New Jersey. Mazzocchi and I met at the Clam Broth House in Hoboken," Wages said. "And that is when we discussed in great detail the plan for the alliance. Later meetings took place as well to get everybody on board and to agree to the broad platform ideas."

Wages struggled to convince his team that Mazzocchi was precisely what they needed. Texas was key. "Joe Campbell let us use his lake house . . . for that meeting and Joe was very supportive and helpful," Wages recalled. "The meeting itself was tough with some very anti-Mazzocchi people in the room. That was the toughest sell I had ever made."[24]

Mazzocchi talked with Mark Dudzic and Mac about whether he would be perceived as an opportunist for joining with those who had opposed him for so long. Dudzic recalled Mac saying to Mazzocchi, "For crying out loud, this is your chance. You can write the program here. Are you going to wander in the wilderness for another forty years?"

Over the course of several meetings, Mazzocchi became convinced that Wages and Misbrenner would agree to his substantive platform for the union. Tony was ready to give it a go. Thus was the Alliance for Progress born: Misbrenner for president, Wages and Calvin Moore for the two vice presidents, and Mazzocchi for the secretary-treasurer, the second most powerful position in the union. It was clearly understood that Mazzocchi would design their platform based on broad principles all had agreed upon. This was no problem for Wages, who already had moved leftward. Also, it was understood clearly that Wages, a generation younger than Mazzocchi, would be the presidential candidate the next time around, after Misbrenner stepped down.

There was one more crucial codicil: an understanding between Tony and Susan Mazzocchi, who had absolutely no intention of moving back to Denver. She didn't like the idea of Tony commuting from New Jersey for the next three years, either. However, she believed she owed him the chance to take the job, because for the sake of the family he had recently made a great sacrifice: At her behest, he had turned down a job as court-appointed trustee of the mobbed-up Tony Provenzano Teamster local union in New Jersey. (Tony had felt that the challenge of reforming the ten-thousand-member local union was worth pursuing even if it took him away from OCAW.) Susan had feared the mob would kill him. It was now understood that Mazzocchi would take the next big union opportunity that came by, assuming it wouldn't get him murdered.

While Susan wanted Tony to contribute again to the national union, she didn't want him separated from the family indefinitely. So they agreed on term limits: Tony would hold office only for one three-year term in Denver, commuting as often as possible back to New Jersey. After this term ended, the plan was for Tony to become an assistant to the president (who then would be Wages) and return home to work on the East Coast. Tony, Susan, and Bob Wages all accepted the deal.

The Alliance for Progress still needed to win the election. First, Misbrenner and Wages had to convince their camp that Mazzocchi didn't have horns—and Mazzocchi had to convince his own team, and himself, that Misbrenner and Wages weren't the enemy, either. Supporters in both camps were perplexed. Mazzocchi recalled overhearing one Wages supporter ask him, "Hey, I thought you told us Mazzocchi was a communist. Now you want us to support him?"

Mazzocchi's allies were convinced that he'd get royally screwed at the convention. They feared that since the vote for president came first, Mazzocchi's forces would put Misbrenner over the top, but then Misbrenner and Wages would collude to deny Mazzocchi the secretary-treasurer spot.

In a May 18, 1988, letter to a Louisiana supporter, Mazzocchi acknowledged, "I know you probably are surprised by my candidacy on the Alliance ticket." But, he argued, "It was time to put the union together. . . . The fact that Mike Ricigliano is running for president is the final straw. Ricigliano possesses not a strand of leadership talent."[25]

The critical point for Mazzocchi was getting Wages and Misbrenner to support the building of a labor party. Even though the OCAW had passed a resolution in 1981 to explore independent politics, Goss and Misbrenner had done nothing about it. Wages had his doubts about it. (In a March 4, 1987, letter, Mazzocchi acknowledged that Wages believed "that such a party is not feasible in the US."[26]) Nevertheless, Misbrenner and Wages agreed that as OCAW leaders, they would back a labor party.

As the voting at the convention proceeded, it became clear that District 8, still the heart of Mazzocchi's support, had the power to swing the presidential race either to Misbrenner or to Ricigliano, a Jersey boy. With Mazzocchi and his allies working hard for the Alliance, Misbrenner won District 8 by almost eight thousand votes, giving him the victory. Mazzocchi had fulfilled his part of the bargain.

Although it took a three-way race and a runoff, Misbrenner and Wages fulfilled their pledges to Mazzocchi as well. Mazzocchi was back, as secretary-treasurer of the union he'd built and twice tried to lead.

Mazzocchi's coveted prize had been devalued greatly during his absence: OCAW, always modest in size, had lost 50 percent of its members since its peak in the 1970s. Unions everywhere were in full-scale retreat. Creating an alternative path for the labor movement from the number two position of a smallish, declining union would be difficult indeed.

Though, as Mac said, it certainly beat forty more years in the wilderness.

SIXTEEN

Party Time

OCAW secretary-treasurer Tony Mazzocchi, at age sixty-two, was hell-bent on pursuing his backlog of ideas and projects. Bring on the coffee!

Mazzocchi had always wanted OCAW members to have their own college. A decade earlier, he had nearly persuaded the union to buy a campus in Denver. Now he started a university without walls called the Alice Hamilton College (in honor of Alice Hamilton, 1869–1970, the first woman professor at Harvard and a founder of occupational medicine).

Mazzocchi also thought that the health and safety movement badly needed a peer-reviewed professional journal to explore worker-oriented safety, health, and environment issues. He pressed OCAW to start and fund *New Solutions,* ably edited by Charles Levenstein, then a professor at the Work Environment Department, University of Massachusetts–Lowell.

And how about a workers' radio network? Mazzocchi had learned from a passenger sitting next to him on a plane that subcarrier radio bands allowed for private communications to designated audiences. For the next several years, he explored ways to build a shop stewards' radio network to provide round-the-clock education for shop-floor leaders.

Mazzocchi recognized that for most of the OCAW delegates, the next convention would be their first. Rather than spending tens of thousands of dollars on hospitality suites and booze, Mazzocchi would use the union's treasury to commission and stage at the convention an original play, *Keepers of the Dream,* on the union's history.

Even as he was packing to return to Denver, Mazzocchi organized the first US union conference on global warming. He then took the show on the road to OCAW districts. He recruited the Institute's Mike Merrill to publish, in 1988, *Global Warming Watch,* certainly the first publication on the implications of climate change for American workers.

With his talented Denver crew, and in particular Phyllis Ohlemacher who a decade before had been his administrative assistant, Mazzocchi launched a campaign to familiarize OCAW members with the "single-payer" national health insurance plan designed by Physicians for a National Health Program (PNHP). Mazzocchi invited PNHP doctors to brief OCAW officers and staff on the need for an American system modeled after Canada's universal, government-provided health care insurance. He also arranged for cross-border trips so that rank-and-file leaders could see firsthand how Canada delivered quality health care to all its citizens for a fraction of the cost of the US private insurance system. OCAW members soon endorsed single-payer health care and pressed it forward within the AFL-CIO.

And bouncing between his staff in Denver and at the Labor Institute in New York, Mazzocchi tried to ignite a new labor insurgency through newsletters, educational materials, conferences, and new alliances.

It certainly felt good to be back from exile.

But what mattered most of all to Tony was building a new labor party.

Mazzocchi had been a loyal Democrat forever, it seemed—an insider. He resurrected the Democratic Party on Long Island, supported its ticket from top to bottom, and even ran for Congress as a Democrat himself. He did it all—get out the vote, fund-raising, voter registration, issue development, media work. No one could accuse him of not giving the Democratic Party a chance. But by the mid-1960s, Mazzocchi's hopes for it had collapsed. He remained a Democrat only to support the party's peace candidates.

Mazzocchi first seriously raised the idea of a new party to OCAW leaders in 1972, after a majority of Democrats supported President Nixon's wage controls. "It's become more and more apparent," Mazzocchi wrote, "that labor will have to recognize the fact that independent political action will be necessary."[1] Four years of Jimmy Carter pushed Mazzocchi into open rebellion.

> When Carter got elected, the AFL-CIO was saying: *We'll make the change we need to make in labor law, health and safety laws, to give us the power we need, by electing a veto-proof Congress.* And we elected a veto-proof Congress. We had a Democratic House, Democratic Senate, and a Democratic president. And we couldn't even get a mild labor reform bill. . . . That's when I left DC—because this was not the way to go. Lobbying your friends was not enough.

But what about the access to top officials Mazzocchi had enjoyed during the Carter administration—like Eula Bingham at OSHA, and his friend

Tony Robbins, who headed NIOSH? Mazzocchi was even appointed himself to serve on the Acid Rain Commission (only to be unappointed when Reagan took over). Weren't these tangible political benefits that made it worth electing Democrats?

"Sure, I'd rather have a friend than an enemy there, for the couple of goodies you can get. But I'm not going to break my back over it." Besides, Mazzocchi noted, Democrats never gave labor its due:

> Only Republicans have given us [the labor movement] the secretary of labor. Under Eisenhower, we got Tobin, president of the Teamsters; under Nixon, we got Brennan, from the building trades. There's never been an appointee of labor from a Democratic president—which I always razzed my fellow unionists about. With all their support for Dems, they can't even get a stinking position that they're entitled to.

Mazzocchi pointed out that labor and environmentalists made their greatest gains under Nixon, who had approved both OSHA and the EPA.

> Nixon was anti-labor, going back to the days of Taft-Hartley. He was a stringent corporate rights sort of guy—he thought workers should listen and be quiet. But we were able to force that administration to do things that they were philosophically opposed to, because the power equation was different.
>
> There was a lot of motion in the streets. There was an antiwar movement. The environmental movement was making a lot of noise, and we were reaching out to them. And we were elevating health and safety into the national consciousness.

The task, Mazzocchi argued, was to rebuild a movement from below. No amount of politicking for tepid Democrats would help.

But why did rekindling a movement mean jettisoning the Democratic Party? Look at the way labor and the Democrats responded to the air traffic controllers strike, Tony responded. After Reagan fired the eleven thousand PATCO workers on August 5, 1981, the AFL-CIO had reluctantly staged a national rally in Washington. They named it Solidarity Day for the anti-communist union movement in Poland, which AFL-CIO Cold Warriors had strongly supported.

Much to the surprise of labor's top leadership, on September 19, 1981, hundreds of thousands poured into Washington. Many were eager to demonstrate their solidarity by marching to the DC National Airport and shutting it down. But this gesture was unacceptable to AFL-CIO president Lane Kirkland. He wrote to state and local AFL-CIO affiliates: "I personally do not think that the trade union movement should undertake anything that would represent punishing, injuring, or inconveniencing the public at large for the sins or transgressions of the Reagan Administration."[2]

Why not? Because the AFL-CIO feared that a disruptive show of force would hurt the Democrats in the 1982 midterm elections. Instead, Kirkland and the throngs of Democratic Party speakers on the podium put forth their battle cry: "The next Solidarity Day is Election Day!"[3]

Mazzocchi was dumbfounded. How could Kirkland and company let the eleven thousand PATCO workers get fired *en masse*? They had to know that this would launch an open season on the entire labor movement. How could these leaders be so out of touch with workers' desire to do something to back up the fired strikers?

For Mazzocchi, this was mass suicide. In a speech to OCAW members seven years later, he said:

> I along with many of you in late 1981 joined 850,000 people and marched on Washington for social justice. We were called there by the leadership of the AFL-CIO. It was the first time in years where we reached out to our rank-and-file. And although we characterized them as being apathetic, they responded—850,000 working people marched to Washington. We stared Ronald Reagan in the eye, and the leadership of our trade union movement blinked. We went in with a bang and left with a whimper. Had we marched to the National Airport, 850,000 strong and joined the picket lines of the PATCO workers, the union movement would have been in different shape today.[4]

Just as disturbing, Mazzocchi saw the Democratic Party stand helpless before the massive corporate restructuring of the 1980s as mergers, acquisitions, and runaway plants scurrying to all corners of the globe slashed millions of manufacturing jobs. No industrial union could possibly bargain effectively under the threat of plant closures. Clearly, America needed to control capital mobility and provide income support for dislocated workers to ameliorate the domestic ravages of globalization. Instead, Mazzocchi watched liberal Democrats like Ted Kennedy call for more deregulation, betting workers' security on even greater corporate freedom.

Tony truly wanted to be wrong. But he had predicted the impending catastrophe with uncanny accuracy. In a few short years, the industrial heartland hollowed out—and so did unions. As union leaders clung more desperately to the corporate-oriented Democrats, Mazzocchi watched legions of workers give up on unions. As Mazzocchi said, "They don't need us to negotiate the terms of their funeral."

But Mazzocchi also offered a more hopeful prophecy: that the rank and file would enthusiastically welcome an anti-corporate political party with the guts to defy the establishment—assuming unions had the guts to build one. This new labor party had to reignite the kind of solidarity Tony had witnessed at the Rubinstein local, where "nobody dared cross a picket line for fear of being ostracized from your neighborhood." And the new class-based party had to help workers see the big picture: There was such a thing as capitalism, and if unchallenged, bosses and politicians would collude against them. It would help workers understand how the problems they faced were connected—from job insecurity, to inadequate health care, to declining public services, to low-wage work, to toxic exposures. Because the Democrats wouldn't dare make such anti-corporate connections, working people needed a party of their own.

But what planet was Mazzocchi on? Wasn't it blatantly obvious that by the 1980s workers no longer had class consciousness—that for most the entire idea of class had become vacuous?

Mazzocchi wasn't a Pollyanna. Workers, he understood, had multiple personas: They also referred to themselves as middle class and consumers and patriots, with religious, race, and gender identities mixed in. But Mazzocchi still believed that working people—meaning those who worked for a boss under strict hierarchies—still had a sense, however ill defined, that they were getting screwed. Mazzocchi believed that class institutions such as unions and political parties could, if they really wanted to, rekindle class awareness. He had seen the CIO do it in the 1930s and '40s. He'd done so at the Rubinstein local. In the supposedly silent 1950s, he'd developed a militant cadre and combated racism. It wasn't mysterious. It took education. It took acts of solidarity. It took more education. Working-class consciousness was a construction, not an act of God.

For Mazzocchi, this was not mushy sloganeering. He'd already pulled off an astonishing national shift in consciousness on occupational health and safety. It didn't fall from the sky—he and a cast of thousands created it, and it's still with us. By setting in motion an army of doctors, technicians, environmentalists, journalists, and local union activists, a new movement changed the way the entire country views the workplace environment. And because of mass education and dramatic anti-corporate campaigns to protect endangered workers and communities, workplaces continue to be policed and cleaned up today—albeit insufficiently. Mazzocchi had learned that a new consciousness could be developed if the conditions were right *and* if enough people could be impelled to work toward it.

With the collapse of the trade union movement, the rise of globalization, the stalling of workers' wages, the redistribution of wealth to the super-rich, and the implosion of industrial America, the conditions, Mazzocchi believed, were ripe for an anti-corporate workers' movement. History had done its part. The rest was up to the thousands of activists in and around the labor movement. Mazzocchi would try again to be their catalyst.

In a 1995 interview with Terry Gross on the public radio show *Fresh Air,* Mazzocchi laid out his project:

> What this effort is all about is the re-creation of a new movement and the rejuvenation of a working-class culture that once existed in this country. Part of this task is creating a party, a class party—we make no bones about it, this is going to be a party of the working class. We'll break down the nonsense that we're the middle class. We are working class. . . . When I grew up, working class meant anyone who worked for a wage and wasn't a manager or a small-business person, whether you're a white-collar or a blue-collar person. In a culture that existed when I came into this workforce, you understood the value of organization, of unions. You supported unions. In those days, if you lived in a neighborhood, it was a working-class

> neighborhood and if you scabbed on a strike, you probably could not come back to that neighborhood. Scabs had to be imported. People understood the nature of their class, and they knew the nature of those who were benefiting at their expense.[5]

II

But how do you build a labor party within a labor movement so firmly entrenched in the Democratic Party? Mazzocchi wrestled with this question for nearly two decades. He was firm on what he *didn't* want.

First, he had no use for fusion parties—those that endorsed Democratic or Republican candidates on a separate ballot line. "I grew up with that in New York," he said. "It was just a vehicle for Democrats. It's nice if what you want are a few appointments in return for your endorsement. But fundamentally it is and always will be a way to steer alienated voters back to the Democrats. It's cynical politics."

And he didn't want a spoiler party, either. He knew a new labor party that tipped elections to the Republicans would be drummed out of the labor movement. "I realized from the start that you could only run candidates if you could win. And that would take years and years of effort."

For Mazzocchi there was only one remaining option: build a labor party that *did not initially run candidates*. Instead, the party would spend its first years educating and mobilizing, building class consciousness and a mass membership large enough to eventually challenge for power.

It was a very tough sell. A political party that stayed out of electoral politics? It did not compute for many progressives, who had no experience with anything like this. They itched to enter the electoral fray, hoping against hope that once they did, masses of workers would follow.

Mazzocchi believed no one could wish away the fact that labor was glued to the Democratic Party and would not leave anytime soon. It was also clear, he argued, that labor leaders would crucify spoiler parties. A labor party could enter electoral politics only when labor unions were ready to endorse it. Until then it was obvious to Mazzocchi (but to few others) that a new labor party had to refrain almost entirely from electoral politics. A labor party had to allow unions to work on two tracks—to support Democrats in elections even while they supported a labor party that set a new agenda and educated for it. The strategy was to slowly win over the labor movement to something it had never done before.

But what would a labor party really do if it didn't run candidates? As Mazzocchi told worker audiences, plenty:

> There's got to be an organization that has a coherent program that makes sense to people. We could get into the streets, but we have to know what we're in the streets for. We need a political party that hammers out a program, and says: This is a program that addresses our needs as working people—not someone else's needs. It's got to be coherent—it's got to resonate. People have to understand it, and people have to be part of formulating it. Most Americans—and most, if not all, working Americans—will tell you, "We want a job; we want to be able to retire with decent pay; we want to be able to retire earlier; we want healthcare; we want education for our kids." These are very simple, fundamental needs and wants of the people.[6]

But why not hook up with a progressive alliance such as Jesse Jackson's Rainbow Coalition, which was founded to support Jackson's 1984 and 1988 presidential campaigns? Although Mazzocchi believed that someday a broad movement coalition would be needed, he thought it was the wrong way to start. Coalition parties like the Rainbow Coalition, Mazzocchi believed, attracted only a thin layer of labor officials and lead activists, leaving the vast majority of workers behind. Besides, he argued, most workers didn't relate to the progressive culture that bound such coalitions together. It didn't seem like their party. Mazzocchi did see the possibility of coalitions down the road, once a labor party—and perhaps other constituent-based parties—had developed their bases and defined their issues. But it had to start with a party of and by working people.

Mazzocchi wanted the labor party's door open to all workers who were fed up with Corporate America, even if they could not pass liberal-left litmus tests on social issues such as gun control or abortion. While he personally supported left social issues, he wanted a labor party to be a home not only for self-defined progressives but also for gun-toting, Bible-thumping workers who supported a pro-worker, anti-corporate program. In fact, he believed one of the most important functions of a labor party would be to attract a broad spectrum of workers to an arena where they could learn about and debate issues beyond class—including race, gender, and social issues of all kinds. He hoped the labor party would inspire a new generation of working-class radicals, as had the Rubinstein local, where workers learned about racism and fought for civil rights. As Mazzocchi would remind progressives, "Look, most workers don't even know what progressive is."

He also was pragmatic about resources. Only trade unions had sufficient economic and institutional heft to make a labor party real in America. And they would only support a labor party that *they* ran. That was political reality.

Lingering just below the surface was Mazzocchi's perpetual fear of an emerging right-wing working-class movement. If workers were not organized along class lines, Mazzocchi believed, others might organize them around xenophobic issues—race, immigration, nationalism. As he told Alexander Cockburn in *The Nation,* progressive purists unwittingly could drive workers into the arms of the right.

> We aren't organizing around a "progressive" agenda. We're trying to organize the working class around their economic interests, and many of them [for instance, hunters] are opposed to a "progressive" agenda. If we don't fill this political void something much uglier could take over. This is a dangerous moment.[7]

Mazzocchi also believed that the self-defined progressive community was just too small to seriously influence the national agenda. "If we just went out and recruited everyone who agreed with us," he told *The Nation,* "we could hold [our founding] convention in a telephone booth."[8]

To further confound progressives, Mazzocchi questioned the value of holding isolated elective offices:

> Look, if some progressive wants to run for local office because he needs a job, I can understand that. But don't tell me it's going to fundamentally change anything important. You become mayor of

> Detroit or Newark, then what are you going to do? What can you really do with an entire economy stacked against you from top to bottom?

Neither appointments, nor elective office, nor narrow policy reforms constituted real power in Tony's mind. Rather, power came from what he called "shifting the terms of debate"—a difficult concept for ambitious progressives to grasp or stomach.

For Mazzocchi, power meant defining what gets debated even more than what comes out of the debate. If you set up the terms of the public debate, you can win a good deal before you start. He argued that the right understood this as it fearlessly launched what at first seemed like outrageous, unacceptable ideas. Starting with Senator Barry Goldwater, the right had argued against the mainstream understanding that government could help people. Margaret Thatcher even argued that there was no such thing as "society," only families and individuals.

Mazzocchi respected how those on the right stuck to their positions for years and years until the tide turned their way. They knew about the power of ideas. They knew how to control the debate. As Mazzocchi observed, "Once you get into a debate on saying: 'The rich deserve a tax cut. Now, let's argue about how much they should get'—you've lost the fight. Whoever sets the parameters of the debate wins."

Mazzocchi wanted a new labor party to set those parameters. He wanted it to stand for universal public health coverage, not Democrats' Band-Aids to the dysfunctional system of employer-based private insurance. He wanted free higher education at all public institutions, not the Democrats' complex patchwork of Pell grants to the poor, and burdensome student loans. He wanted full income for workers who lose their jobs due to globalization and environmental protection, not the Democrats' paltry Trade Adjustment Assistance Act. He wanted publicly guaranteed paid sabbaticals for workers, not just unpaid parental leave.

Mazzocchi believed such radical demands could reframe the debate and put the other side on the defensive. What's wrong with universal health care, free higher education, and a stable income? Who says that we have to live in constant fear of unemployment, while pundits tell us to retrain for a never-ending series of disappearing jobs? (Remember when workers were being retrained as keypunch operators?) Who says we don't deserve more time off, or that society can't afford it?

III

As the number two leader of a union with nearly a hundred thousand members, Mazzocchi came under pressure to turn his labor party talk into action. So what was he going to do about it? Both Tony and his new union partner, Bob Wages, knew that OCAW wasn't ready to launch a labor party on its own. Mazzocchi asked his friend Rick Massingil, a levelheaded OCAW activist from Michigan, what he would need to promote a labor party in his local union. Rick thought that it would help to have a poll showing what workers thought about the idea.

Rick was right, thought Mazzocchi. But OCAW wasn't ready to spring for a major poll, so Mazzocchi leaned on the Labor Institute. Back in 1979, Institute instructors had passed out a simple questionnaire at the end of a "labor and politics" course for UAW Local 259 led by the local president, Sam Meyers, Tony's friend and an outspoken socialist. The poll asked whether the class favored the Democrats, the Republicans, or the building of a new Labor Party. By a vote of twenty-two to one, they favored a labor party. (The "one" was Sam Meyers, who rushed to the front of the class to implore his workers to support the Democrats.)

Now, at Mazzocchi's urging, the Institute designed a nine-question survey that could be administered quickly by shop stewards, local by local. It included such questions as "Who best represents the interests of working people: Democratic Party? Republican Party? Neither Party?" The poll also questioned workers about the influence of big business on the two parties and about strategy: should unions support the Democrats, the Republicans, or was it "time for labor to build a new independent party of working people?"

The poll eventually reached 1,589 OCAW members—about 1.5 percent of the membership. While not a scientific sample, it was nevertheless a serious effort to get an honest reading of workers' opinions. According to Mark Dudzic (who would become the Labor Party's national organizer), "I was told to give out the surveys in plant lunchrooms rather than at union meetings so the results wouldn't be skewed in favor of more active members."

The survey found that half of the workers thought neither party represented the best interests of working people. Two-thirds thought that "both parties care more about the interests of big business than they do about the interests of working people."

However, many workers had obvious loyalties to the Democratic Party: More than 46 percent agreed that "Unions should do all they can to support the Democratic Party." At the same time, nearly 53 percent agreed that it was time to build a new labor party, while only 18.5 percent disagreed.

This only confirmed Mazzocchi's iconoclastic idea of a party. Yes, there was widespread support for a new labor party. But the party needed an initial "no candidates" strategy because workers still felt close to the Democrats.

The poll highlighted a split between the leadership and the rank and file. The fifty-six full-time OCAW officers and staff who filled out the survey showed significantly greater support for the Democrats and much less support for a labor party. It was clear that it would take a long time to wean labor officials from the Democratic Party.

The survey gave Mazzocchi a multipurpose tool he could take on the road to challenge skeptical labor leaders and activists. "If you don't believe me," he argued, "run the poll on your own members." Over the next year, twenty unions did. Inevitably, the rank and file favored the idea of a labor party. Union staff members, no matter which union, were always far less enthusiastic. It also became apparent that public-sector unions (because they prefer to negotiate with Democratic elected officials) were somewhat less favorable toward a labor party.

Mazzocchi was perfectly content to continue the polling process for years. There were still eighty thousand local unions out there. It was a productive activity that for the next decade or two could help build a base wide and deep enough to support a viable labor party. During his 1988 OCAW convention speech, Mazzocchi admitted, "It won't happen in my lifetime, but I see my role here . . . as a . . . bridge to another generation of union leadership."[9]

Laura McClure (who later became editor of the *Labor Party Press*) watched Mazzocchi win over skeptics with his pitch:

> Repeatedly unionists would stand up and make these quite smart if whiny observations about all the obstacles that stood in the way of a labor party—basically, why it couldn't work. I loved the way Tony responded. He said, "Very sharp critique there—you're probably absolutely right. But what do you propose instead?"
>
> There would be no response. Then Mazzocchi would continue, "Besides, it's fun trying to change things. A lot more fun than standing by and letting the bosses walk all over us."

The more of these encounters Mazzocchi had, the more supporters of the idea urged him to start the labor party now. Wasn't that what he'd been elected to do? The voices for action came from so many sides that Mazzocchi founded Labor Party Advocates to serve as a halfway house on the road to a full-fledged party.

IV

It was a delicious moment for Mazzocchi. Everything in OCAW was coming together. Bob Wages had adopted a militant agenda, making it feel like progressives had captured full control of the union. Mazzocchi soon realized that he could hold on to the secretary-treasurer's job for as long as he wished. He had so consolidated his base within OCAW that no one could defeat him. He loved the independence his office provided. Unlike every other position in the union, his was not directly controlled by the president, who almost certainly would be Bob Wages in 1991. Mazzocchi could work on whatever he wished, subject only to the union's executive board and to the constitution. He could make the labor party the center of his life. He had a loving family back in New Jersey, whom he visited often. He had a strong staff in Denver and another in New York. And he worked well with Wages. He could build for a labor party until he dropped.

But he had promises to keep. He had promised Susan that after one term he would step down as secretary-treasurer and return home. During his 1988 campaign, Mazzocchi also had promised the rank and file he would step down in 1991. And he had promised Wages to become his presidential assistant, at reduced pay and stature, to work on the labor party.

Normally such pledges were sacrosanct to Mazzocchi. But this time, he was ready to break not one, but all three promises. He had come too far. Wages would win the presidency. But Wages could also see that if Mazzocchi ran for reelection as secretary-treasurer, he would win hands-down. (He would agree to run with Tony.) Mazzocchi also was certain the rank and file didn't want him to retire, no matter what he'd said during his previous campaign.

That left Susan. Tony assumed that Susan, as always, would accommodate his political aspirations—though he was aware that his life as an organizer clashed with the needs of his family. In his 1988 victory speech, he said:

> My family isn't here—my six children, my wife, and the countless others in my family who have been supportive of my efforts at great pain over the years. Every individual in this room who is a parent knows what it is to leave a child behind in order to be out with a trade union. Over the past six years when my children greeted me at night, I realized how much I had missed in my former trade union incarnation, when I had been gone much of the time. We all sacrifice a great deal.
>
> I think that sacrifice is ennobling. . . .[10]

Ennobling for whom?

Tony failed to see that Susan had been "ennobled" to the breaking point. She'd had to raise three children completely on her own. A review of Mazzocchi's 1991 calendar reveals how little she saw of him. In the first six months alone, Tony was away from home 120 nights.[11] Kristina, who was fifteen at the time, knew it was hard on her mom: "I always had the sense that she was sailing the ship. She was obviously a bit depressed being alone most of the time and probably felt disconnected from my father."[12]

When Tony told Susan of his new ambitions, Susan instantly realized that he was deadly serious about breaking his promise. It was who he was. It was what he really wanted, and there was no changing him. She snapped. She'd had enough. She called it quits.

Mazzocchi had been so oblivious to her pain that he was flat-out stunned. He realized this wasn't just a little spat. Susan wasn't kidding. She was gone emotionally, and Tony stared at another broken family—the strained visits with the kids on weekends, the cantankerous negotiations with a bitter wife, the shards of broken love scarring his kids, his wife, and himself.

Mazzocchi, for the first time in his life, broke down. His unflappable self-assurance deserted him. He was a mess. His kids saw him moaning in grief, sleeping on their living room couch, trying to hang on, trying to reconcile the marriage. He even got completely drunk once in their presence, something he had never done before. "It wasn't pretty," said Anthony, who was in his senior year in high school.

Mazzocchi, a genius at understanding the flow of complicated events, lost all control over what was happening to him. He dragged himself from friend to friend spilling his guts in a looped tape of self-pity: "I'm just a working-class stiff with no education. I'm not worthy of someone so refined as Susan. I'm no good. She was right to toss me out. I'm just a working-class stiff. . . ."

In desperation, Mazzocchi tried to reverse history. He told Susan and Wages he would fulfill his earlier pledges and not run again. He would take the job as presidential assistant and work from home in New Jersey. He would be the good father and husband Susan needed.

But it was far too late to save the marriage. As Tony floundered and grieved, Wages cut his losses, replacing Tony for secretary-treasurer on his ticket with the popular Ernie Rouselle, Mazzocchi's good friend.

Mazzocchi was left with the worst of both worlds: He'd lost both Susan *and* his job as secretary-treasurer. Now he could barely function. Through the fall and winter of 1990–1991 he bordered on total collapse. For the first time ever, his friends feared for him.

Mazzocchi later confirmed that he had never before experienced depression. Not even in the army, during combat. Not even when his first marriage broke up or when his brother had been killed in a car crash.

Emotional crisis was all new to him, and he stumbled his way through it. As spring came, Mazzocchi's lifelong armor slowly re-formed around his losses. He began to talk about his crisis with more detachment. He began to acknowledge simply that his marriage had ended and that his job had changed. Slowly, his senses again pointed forward and outward.

Tony soon learned to live with what he could not change. He rented an apartment in Hoboken, New Jersey, and then, in the fall of 1992, moved into an attic apartment in Montclair, New Jersey (our home). Fortunately, Tony and Susan didn't rip each other apart. They worked reasonably well on the divorce and a never-ending series of kids' issues, and remained friends. Tony would always wonder whether, given his lifestyle, he should have ever had a family, let alone two. And Susan said she worried each day whether she had wrecked Tony's career.

The children didn't take sides. Rather, they developed great insight into their parents, especially their father. As Kristina put it, "I never felt unloved or not an important part of my father's life. But I felt I was not granted access to him as a full person. I see a complicated man who loved his family in the best way he could, but loved his work even more."

V

That work grew even more enticing after Bill Clinton and the New Democrats slipped into power in 1992. Mazzocchi's no-election, no-coalition labor party idea gained momentum as the Democrats flew their true corporate colors. First came the Clintons' disastrous health care reform proposal, an attempt to salvage the wasteful health insurance industry through an unintelligible Rube Goldberg contraption of a plan. Then Clinton tried to outflank the Republicans by balancing the budget and slashing welfare benefits that primarily supported low-income, women-led families. (Even Robert Rubin, Clinton's Wall Street treasury secretary, opposed pummeling those women and children.) Clinton admitted that his administration resembled Eisenhower Republicans.

Mainstream labor Democrats woke up when Clinton rammed through the North American Free Trade Agreement. All Clinton's talk about how NAFTA would lower prices and increase American jobs overall could not hide the fact that it would make good-paying US manufacturing jobs disappear. It was not clear that it would help Mexican workers and farmers, either. What's more, NAFTA was all any employer needed to scare manufacturing workers out of organizing or bargaining hard. It was another death knell for industrial labor, and labor leaders knew it. The AFL-CIO failed to stop the pact as Clinton and the New Democrats cut the few remaining strings restraining American capital.

Meanwhile, the changing of the guard at the AFL-CIO and the Teamsters increased expectations of labor activists. John Sweeney, who had replaced

Lane Kirkland as head of the AFL-CIO in 1995, moved the federation away from its Cold War legacy. Sweeney brought with him a boatload of progressives, many of whom had warm ties with Mazzocchi (including two who had formerly worked at the Labor Institute). In the hallowed AFL-CIO executive conference room overlooking the White House, Sweeney was meeting with radical economics educators to create a working-class education initiative much like the one Mazzocchi had tried to launch twenty years earlier.

Rich Trumka, the former Mine Worker president, was elected as AFL-CIO secretary-treasurer. Trumka shared Mazzocchi's and Bob Wages's militant unionism, and supported the labor party idea. His election gave Mazzocchi an open door to top AFL-CIO leadership.

It was a heady time outside the federation as well. Ron Carey, a candidate associated with the progressive Teamsters for a Democratic Union, won the presidency of the Teamsters in 1991. With him, another group of progressives gained positions of power within the labor movement.

Andy Stern, a '60s progressive, succeeded Sweeney as president of Service Employees International Union in 1996. Immediately, he began a virtual Cultural Revolution, radically increasing spending on organizing to more than half of the union's entire budget. He made it clear to the union's staff that every activity and everyone would be evaluated on how they helped organize new members. Stern's strategies captured the spirit of Mazzocchi's mass organizing experiments in OCAW fifteen years before.

The New Democrats and the prospect of a labor renaissance emboldened those who wanted to launch a new labor party. Yes, the AFL-CIO was still locked to the Democrats. But the space for a carefully designed labor party seemed to have grown. Maybe now was the time.

As Mazzocchi spoke around the country, he picked up support from several significant unions. The innovative and fast-growing California Nurses Association came out strongly for a new labor party and affiliated with Labor Party Advocates. So did the Farm Labor Organizing Committee, which represented migrant workers in the Ohio area. The United Mine Workers, the United Electrical Workers, and the West Coast Longshore Workers, all small but vociferous unions, also joined. (The American Federation of Government Employees and the Brotherhood of Maintenance of Way Employees would join later.) Several important districts in the United

Needle, Industrial and Textile Employees, the Communications Workers of America, the Teamsters, the Carpenters, the United Steelworkers, and the Service Employees International Union affiliated with Labor Party Advocates, along with many smaller local unions.

Mazzocchi attracted some excellent organizers. Adolph Reed Jr., the brilliant politics professor and public intellectual, became a close adviser. Jerry Gordon and Leo Seidlitz, radical organizers with strong labor backgrounds, volunteered, along with United Electrical Worker activist Bob Brown. Many OCAW local leaders became very active, especially Dave Campbell in California, Don Holmstrom in Colorado, and Mark Dudzic in New Jersey. And crucially important, Bob Wages made it clear that OCAW now was ready to pay and play.

Another major boost came in 1992, when Bob Kasen signed on as a Labor Party Advocates organizer. A veteran of the civil rights movement, Kasen had been a lead organizer for the International Chemical Workers. For nearly a decade, he had organized low-wage workers, including Sanderson Farms poultry workers in Laurel, Mississippi. In 1980, he brought together thousands of civil rights, labor, women, and church activists to show their support for the poultry workers in the largest labor demonstration in Mississippi history.

Still, Mazzocchi was reluctant to call a founding convention. The new mood in labor didn't fool him. He wanted Labor Party Advocates to continue advocating until it drew in many more unions and at least a hundred thousand dues-paying members. Mazzocchi thought this base-building work would keep everyone busy for the better part of a decade.

Patience, comrades, patience.

VI

"The comrades," in fact, posed a vexing problem. What was to be done with the sectarian radicals who were itching to latch onto a labor party?

Left sectarianism, especially since the mid-1960s, had metastasized along the fault lines of international Marxist movements. There were followers of Trotsky who no longer had the Soviets to hate. There were unrepentant Stalinists who still hated the Trotskyists. There were Maoists who hated them both. There was even a handful who cherished the words of Enver Hoxha, the founder of Albania's Communist Party. And there were more sophisticated sects with connections to current leftist tendencies in England and Ireland. What these narrow partisans lacked in numbers (most groups had only a few hundred members concentrated in New York and the Bay Area), they made up for in zeal.

Most of these groups detested one another, but they all wanted to be in on a labor party. What a great place to make your political statement! A labor party would greatly improve their marginal position within the labor movement. No way were they going to miss out on anything that Mazzocchi was organizing.

Unfortunately, when sectarian radicals mingled with nonradical workers, disaster often followed. If sectarians dominated a worker meeting with their statements and calls to action, the workers would soon leave. And the battles among the different sectarian groups were generally incomprehensible to outsiders.

Mazzocchi's advisers feared that if the labor party became a haven for sectarians, it might well become nothing more than a collection of tiny bickering factions who would fight it out until they devoured one another as well as the organization.

One option was to shut these groups out. Mazzocchi could, if he wanted, encourage rules that would ban individual membership and limit labor party membership to local, regional, and national unions as well as central labor bodies. Working-class community groups could be considered on a case-by-case basis. Sectarian groups need not apply. Several of Mazzocchi's closest allies strongly advocated such rules, but Tony refused. He wanted the labor party to be open to non-union as well as union members, which required open individual memberships.

Tony understood that this open door would leave a labor party with no principled way to weed out sectarians—you couldn't screen members for ideological beliefs. So if the party allowed individuals at large, it would have to prepare for an invasion of sectarians. Nevertheless, Mazzocchi was supremely confident that he and his core activists could reason with, and if necessary outmaneuver, the sectarian groups. Also, Mazzocchi had met many decent activists in and around these groups. He could lead the best of them toward good work for the labor party.

"We were certain that their influence would fade as more and more workers joined and became active," Mark Dudzic said. "Perhaps Mazzocchi's experiences with reds and radicals in the '40s made him feel that they could help leaven the bread of the new Labor Party."[13]

VII

With the Clinton debacle unfolding and with the progressive shift within the AFL-CIO, a collection of very serious trade union leaders and activists in Labor Party Advocates told Mazzocchi that five years of advocating was long enough. They wanted the real thing.

Meetings like the one at the Carpenters' Hall in Haywood, California, in January 1995 made it seem like the labor movement was deliciously ripe for the picking. As Alexander Cockburn wrote in *The Nation,*

> It was not just the capacity crowd of 500 on a Saturday afternoon. Or the presence of Jack Henning, executive secretary-treasurer of California's Labor Federation, branding the Democrats the "party of compromise" and calling for "political liberation." Or the speech by former Governor Jerry Brown denouncing "the unofficial Clinton doctrine" of keeping 10 million out of work so inflation stays down.
>
> For Mazzocchi and Leo Seidlitz, the Advocates' organizer in Northern California, the most rousing sight was the solid working class presence, people who would normally flee from mutinous political assemblies on a wet weekend: plenty of local union officials from labor councils in and around San Francisco, as well as activists from across the Bay Area.[14]

Even Mazzocchi expressed amazement when he reportedly said, "I've been active since 1946, and I've never seen a moment like this one."[15]

Yet his doubts lingered. He could count. The international unions ready to endorse a new labor party were small. UE and the Mine Workers together had fewer than sixty thousand working members. OCAW was down below ninety thousand. Organizing a founding convention was an enormous hassle that would fall entirely on Mazzocchi and his staff. And it was costly. How many people would really pay to attend? Since facilities had to be booked and payment guaranteed in advance, a poor showing would be financially ruinous. What's more, a founding convention would raise expectations for action, especially electoral activity. If, in its exuberance, the convention gave the green light to electioneering, Mazzocchi was sure the party would be ostracized from mainstream labor—dead on arrival.

But the pressure still mounted. "I really thought we were on the brink of something very important," Dudzic said. "Sweeney, Carey, the UPS strike—it seemed like the right time for a bold move. I thought it could work."

But Dudzic also sensed Mazzocchi's doubts. "I could tell," Mark said. "Usually before meetings he would let me know where he wanted it to go—not giving marching orders, but giving me a sense of direction. But in the meetings leading up to the labor party founding convention, he gave none at all."[16]

Mazzocchi realized that unless he vociferously opposed it, the momentum would carry everyone toward a founding convention. It was one of those rare moments when his misgivings were overwhelmed by the enthusiasm of others. The union leaders and activists assembled in Labor Party Advocates thought they could make a labor party work. They pledged themselves to make it work. Wages pledged OCAW's support and finances, as did the UE.

At best LPA had perhaps ten thousand, not a hundred thousand, individual members. But Mazzocchi was swayed by organizers' favorable reports about the growth of local LPA chapters and well-attended LPA meetings such as the one in California. Most important, he was influenced by his own sense that if he tried to halt the process, the organization would collapse. He was stuck with the success of his "agitation." Now his job was to make it work.

And work was what it would take—lots of it. Fortunately, by this time Mazzocchi had formed a highly productive political, organizational and social partnership with Katherine Isaac, whom he met through one of Nader's projects. Katherine, perhaps even more than Tony, was addicted to nonstop organizational work. Better yet, she complemented Tony's many work deficiencies. She had just written a high school textbook encouraging active citizenship, and could write quickly and well. She was highly organized and never forgot to follow through. She mastered ways of responding to the spaghetti bowl of ideas that Mazzocchi liked to present at every opportunity. Although more than a generation younger than him, she managed Mazzocchi's work life wisely. They greatly enjoyed each other's company and worked incessantly together, rarely, if ever, taking a day off. That the convention stood any chance at all depended on Katherine Isaac's brains and thoroughness.

Cleveland was selected as the site for the 1996 convention. After signing hotel contracts for at least five hundred attendees, Mazzocchi focused on the turnout. He convinced key OCAW district leaders to hold their council meetings directly before the start of the convention, and then to stay on for the event. This, Mazzocchi hoped, would attract about two hundred OCAW delegates, who would form the core of the convention.

Mazzocchi set up a committee structure to ensure that the convention ran properly (although, as Dudzic pointed out, it was the usual "Mazzocchi free-form jazz style of committee building"[17]). He asked Dudzic to chair a rules committee to set up good procedures for the convention and the party. He asked Don Holmstrom from OCAW and Mike Munoz from the California Carpenters to chair the constitution committee along with Andrea DeUrquiza, from the Farm Labor Organizing Committee. Also a platform committee (chaired by OCAW's Dave Campbell and Kit Costello, president of the California Nurses Association) was set up to develop the party's visionary program. All of these leaders agreed with Mazzocchi that making the party electoral at the outset would spell disaster. As Mazzocchi argued repeatedly,

> We're not about dividing Democrats. The Labor Party will tell people to vote for who they want to vote for. However, the Labor Party has to agree on an agenda. Our task is to decide what our agenda is, how we implement it, and how we insert it into the consciousness of the American people. . . .

As the convention approached, Mazzocchi's attendance fears faded. Rather than a delegate shortage, the requests for rooms started to push a thousand. More hotels were needed. Katherine's totals hit eleven hundred, then twelve hundred. They called local colleges for dorm rooms. Then the number reached thirteen hundred. What was going on? Then fourteen, fifteen hundred!

Substantive convention activities began several months before the delegates arrived. The Dudzic rules committee held regional meetings on the labor party constitution and rules to govern the convention. A week before the convention, all the committees convened to finalize what rules, constitution, and platform would be proposed to the delegates.[18] The committees also sought input from individuals and unions who had sent in resolutions: Some even showed up early to make their case. The platform committee broke into teams to triage two hundred or so resolutions. Several items concerning mass transportation, reform of the military budget, and environmental protection were added to their draft platform. They also incorporated new language on abortion rights presented by Kit Costello of the California Nurses. "Our members have seen firsthand the results of back-alley abortions," she said.[19] Language in favor of legal and safe abortion was added.

To double-check their work, the platform committee sent its final draft platform to the rules and constitutional committees. It was a very smart move. As soon as the draft circulated, Andrea DeUrquiza from the Farm Labor Organizing Committee raised a most serious objection to the abortion plank.

The real convention had started.

VIII

The Farm Labor Organizing Committee (FLOC), led by Baldemar Velasquez, had formed out of a long and difficult campaign by migrant workers who picked crops for the Campbell's Soup Company, mostly in Ohio. After years of struggle, FLOC workers secured a remarkable union contract. With five thousand members, FLOC became a political force in Toledo, Ohio, and now its eyes were set on organizing Mount Olive pickle workers in the South (a campaign that succeeded a decade later).

Under Velasquez's leadership, FLOC fought to secure rights and services for immigrant workers, whether they were FLOC members or not. It supported progressive causes and labor struggles all over the world while continually educating its own members on political issues. It was among the brightest stars in the labor movement.

Baldemar brought quite a package to the table. He'd grown up working in the fields, but had also managed to work his way through college and then divinity school. Along the way, he developed a fierce dedication to social justice as well as a talent for the guitar, vocals, and TexMex music. To raise money for FLOC, his excellent band played (and sold their CDs) at movement events. He received a MacArthur Foundation genius award (but not a Grammy) for his tireless work. He and Mazzocchi were clearly movement brothers.

However, the abortion issue raised enormous difficulties for the many devout Catholics in FLOC. As Baldemar put it, "Scripture says, 'Life is in the blood . . . that He knew us from the time we were in our mother's womb, and created us to live.'"

Once the platform committee added the abortion rights plank sponsored by the California Nurses Association, the issue was joined. If the plank stayed in the platform, FLOC delegates threatened to walk out of the convention waving their bright red flags of struggle for all the world to see.

The tension between class and this social issue ensnarled the convention. How could you have a labor party that didn't have room for devout Hispanic migrant workers?

Then again, how could you have a labor party that didn't have the courage to support women's right to abortion? Which was it, a class-based party that ducked social issues, or a progressive party that had no room for immigrant farmworkers?

What would Mazzocchi do?

Nothing—nothing at all.

When the problem emerged, his aides rushed to him for guidance. Surely, he had some way to reconcile the problem. Did he want to intervene? Mazzocchi just smiled and said, "Let them work it out. Isn't that what we're here to do?"

They certainly tried. Without any interference or guidance from Mazzocchi, drafts of compromise language were shuttled back and forth between Costello of the California Nurses and the FLOC staff. As they met and discussed various words and meanings, it was obvious how much each side respected the other for trying to accommodate the conflicting principles. There was no rancor as they carefully worked through the needs of their committed constituencies. After much discussion, the issue bore down to the word *abortion.* Was there some way to rephrase the plank without using that word? asked FLOC. If so, FLOC could accept the plank, though they weren't happy about it.

"We saw the original language in the abortion plank as audacious sloganeering," said Baldemar. Those who disagreed with FLOC's position on abortion, he said, didn't realize that the union's "risk-taking commitment to organizing is based on the very idea of a God of Life. We opposed all interference to the life God gives us, in or out of our mother's womb. We oppose mistreatment of men and women, working and living conditions, that shortens lives."[20]

But Baldemar and most of FLOC did not oppose all abortions, especially in cases of rape, incest, and endangering of the mother's life. "This is why we reluctantly agreed to the compromise language although we would have preferred to stay away from this issue altogether and stick strictly to class issues. There are many other forums to take up these social issues," he said.

After hours of shuttle diplomacy, the parties agreed on new language in the platform's health care section. It called for "unimpeded access to a full range of family planning and reproductive services for men and women, including the right to continue or terminate a pregnancy."[21]

It didn't say *abortion,* but it did support a woman's right to choose. It seemed to satisfy both camps, and each promised to sell it to their respective delegates when they arrived the next day. Easier said than done.

IX

As the convention opened, Mazzocchi left the stage to the convention chairs: OCAW president Bob Wages, California Nurses Association executive director Rose Ann DeMoro, and UE secretary-treasurer Bob Clark. There would be no speeches from Mazzocchi.

However, at one point early in the proceedings Tony had to make a pedestrian announcement about convention arrangements. As delegates spotted him walking to the podium, a rolling applause rippled through the hall. Soon fifteen hundred delegates rose to their feet to give a thunderous ovation for the man who had brought them there.

But as soon as the rules committees reported its planks to the convention, the fight began. While considerable floor debate was generated by the non-sectarian majority, it was greatly amplified by members of sectarian groups who wanted to amend the platform in ways they felt were more radical. How would votes be allocated on the convention floor? The sects wanted one delegate, one vote, no matter how large the group or union that delegate represented. Should the labor party run candidates? Yes, immediately. Should it control chapters that are set up locally in its name? No, the chapters should be autonomous.

Again and again, the sectarians challenged the proposed procedures and stance of the new party, even when it was obvious they would lose. They seemed not to care (or in some cases even realize) that they would lose.

But they kept at it. They had come to the convention with the view that politics was not about offering a program and winning others over to it. Rather, it was about testimony, about getting up and demonstrating your conviction—whether or not anyone else could be convinced. It didn't even matter that more and more people became alienated by their behavior. What mattered was shaking things up.

The leader of the Bay Area's Golden Gate chapter repeatedly rose to the microphone to scream until he was red in the face. It was as if he was begging for the chair to cut him off and make him a martyr. There wasn't the faintest possibility that the majority of the delegates would accept his message. Yet he continued to bay at the moon.

It wasn't easy for the rotating chairs to handle the chaos. But no one was more skilled and poised at it than Rose Ann DeMoro, executive director of the California Nurses Association (CNA). With tact, composure and acute intelligence, she would calmly cajole the contentious delegates and keep the convention moving forward as if it were a gathering of fifteen rather than fifteen hundred. Her serene demeanor on stage was misleading. Rose Ann, in fact, was a live wire.

Rose Ann grew up in a working-class neighborhood in St. Louis. "Social injustice was in my face," she said. "I learned early on that I lived in a war zone. And my Irish mother taught me to fight and stand up for what you believe in."[22]

When she hit the University of Illinois in 1968 to study psychology, Rose Ann "believed then that social change could come from empowering the individual to fight the good fight." She switched to sociology for graduate work at the University of California–Santa Barbara, then a hotbed of intellectual radicalism. "I saw the role of the collective, social structures, and political economy. You'd have to turn your back not to learn at that time. And when I read about feminism, it was like getting a new set of eyes to see the world."

What Rose Ann perhaps learned best was how to be analytic and strategic. "I was curious about trade unions and I thought I could use my education to teach young people in a working-class college."

But while conducting "participant research" on sexism among retail clerks, Rose Ann got caught up in union work. "I looked around and saw that the young women who were cashiers stayed cashiers, and the young men became the office managers. There was a union there, but there were no female organizers. And I realized then that I loved getting people in motion to improve things."

For the next seven years, she tried out organizing for several different unions and found life stressful for a forceful woman. "Except for AFSCME [the American Federation of State, County, and Municipal Employees], in every union where I worked, the fact that I was a woman was ever-present. They never let me forget it," recalled Rose Ann.

After her husband, Don DeMoro, took a teaching job at Cal State Northridge, Rose Ann accepted what she thought would be a temporary job at the California Nurses Association in Oakland. "It had about sixteen thousand members and was run as a professional association that reproduced the hospital's class structure and struggles between administrative nurses and the nurses on the wards. It had no organizers and cared only about individual advancement and credentialing," she said.

But not for long. Rose Ann bonded quickly with a group of activist nurses who had absorbed the Bay Area's progressive energy. And off they went. "I realized the union had everything I valued. Its members were working class, union-oriented, cared for people everyday, and worked for society's health and well-being. And they were women in a woman's culture. I finally could breathe."

The union grew rapidly, reaching seventy-five thousand members by 2007. And it changed the way hospitals did business. Under DeMoro's direction, CNA organized a mass movement to win a state law that mandated no more than five patients per nurse, down from twelve when she first arrived. In 2005, Governor Arnold Schwarzenegger said he would strike down the law. And, as for CNA, he would "kick their butts." But it was the other way around. CNA built a statewide grassroots coalition that pushed Schwarzenegger's approval ratings from 65 to 35 percent.

Part of their offensive was to auction the governor off on eBay. "We wanted people to be able to buy him just like the big corporations do," Rose Ann said. (The bidding hit $3.6 million before eBay noticed and stopped the auction.) CNA had wrapped the governor's corporate backers around his neck until he surrendered. At the same time, CNA also became one of the loudest voices in America for single-payer health care.

Much earlier, Don and Rose Ann had spotted Mazzocchi. "We had heard about him in college. He was quite an icon in the progressive press. I finally met him at a meeting in the Bay Area around 1990, and he was the complete package—a real trade unionist, a social unionist, he cared about the public good and he was hopeful and optimistic."

"Also, we loved his idea of a labor party," said Rose Ann. "I mean, if you're working class, you just know that the two parties don't speak for you."

Baldemar and the farmworkers, Rose Ann and the nurses: Mazzocchi had recruited to the labor party two of the most dynamic labor leaders—and two of the fastest-growing unions—in the country.

Mazzocchi urged Rose Ann to play a prominent role at the convention, and now she had her hands full as delegates hotly debated the question of whether or not to run candidates—an issue that divided not just the individuals but the endorsing unions as well.

There were many delegates, especially from UE and the Longshore Workers, who wanted to run candidates as soon as possible. They believed that without swift electoral activity, workers would lose interest in a labor party. They also had little sympathy with the spoiler argument since they saw little difference between the two parties. If you're going to be a real labor party, they argued, you needed to pick a few races and strut your stuff.

As the issue played out, Mazzocchi's position was cast as the more conservative one while the "elections-now" advocates were the radicals. Adolph Reed marveled at this flip in political posturing. "Since when have radicals been so interested in the bourgeois electoral process?" Adolph said. "I thought they believed in direct action."[23]

The elections-now faction had sufficient backing to force a significant compromise. After overnight meetings, the UE, Longshore Workers, and OCAW leaders came up with a proposal to create a commission to set up rules for electoral activity. The commission, which would report back in two years at the next labor party convention, was to carefully consider under what conditions the party would engage in electoral activity. The proposal seemed reasonably satisfactory to everyone except some sectarian groups that cried foul.

But the most contentious debate was over the abortion plank. The carefully worded compromise unraveled before the ink was even dry. Despite Kit Costello's and Rose Ann's best efforts, their fellow nurses opposed it. They wanted the platform to overtly endorse a women's right to chose and to use the word *abortion*. They were joined by a wide variety of progressive unionists (and every sectarian). On the other side, a significant number of delegates, not just the Catholic migrant workers, believed that a plank using the word *abortion* would make it harder to draw more conservative workers to the labor party.

Again Mazzocchi's aides prodded him to intervene. Again he declined. This debate, he believed, had to be decided by the delegates. No matter what the results, he hoped it would demonstrate to all that a class organization could debate such issues and make its own decisions. In fact, Mazzocchi welcomed the debate on abortion precisely because it was out in the open, under democratic rules, and involved workers who held differing views. The results would never be perfect, but for Mazzocchi, this was as good as it got. He expected the party "to function more like the big family dinners of his youth," Mark Dudzic observed, "loud, raucous, and loving."[24]

As the debate heated up, Rose Ann and the other chairs called a time-out so that the delegations could gather among themselves for further discussions. The OCAW caucus turned into a case study of abortion politics. During a suspension of rules, the OCAW delegates (absent Mazzocchi) gathered around Bob Wages, their president, to debate the plank. (It was common practice for them to take a straw vote after such deliberations and then agree to vote as a bloc for whatever the majority of the caucus decided.)

Wages climbed on a chair to address the two hundred or so delegates. Wages had developed serious misgivings about the milder abortion plank and was ready to join the nurses in pushing for overt abortion language. He knew that if the OCAW delegates agreed with him, they would cast enough votes to put the stronger plank in the platform. As he put it, "I'll be damned if we take a position weaker than the goddamn Democrats."[25] He was willing to call the cards on FLOC. If they wanted to walk out, let them.

But as soon as he staked out his position, Wages was besieged by local OCAW leaders who greatly preferred the compromise language. As one delegate said, "That compromise language is just about perfect. Look, I don't want to encourage anti-abortion sentiment, but I also don't want to stick the word *abortion* up the noses of our Baptist members back home."[26]

As Dudzic recalled, "Others of us felt personally supportive of the CNA position but we didn't want to jeopardize the unity on this issue that we had carefully built with other union delegations."[27]

Red in the face, Wages made the case as strongly as he could from his perch on the chair. But he didn't prevail. The OCAW delegates voted to remain firm on the original compromise language as presented by the platform committee and to vote as a bloc against all amendments to strengthen or weaken it.

With the OCAW delegation's full support, the compromise language passed. Baldemar Velasquez rose to say, "Some of you inquired whether FLOC would leave the Party over this issue. The decision is not whether FLOC leaves the Labor Party over the abortion issue—a party which apart from this issue is a worthwhile and necessary initiative for the American working class. The real issue is whether you want us to stay in the face of us constantly reminding you that we think you are wrong on this issue."[28]

And the convention roared, "Stay! Stay! Stay!"

No one walked out, and the delegates proceeded to adopt the entire platform, which was named the Call for Economic Justice. It was a victory for Mazzocchi's conception of how a class-based party could openly debate hot-button social issues.

But the dust would barely settle on the convention before some on the left starting taking potshots at the labor party for its abortion compromise. They implied that the party's failure to use the word *abortion* proved that it was just another conservative, male-dominated labor organization. Alexander Cockburn, who did not attend but relied on a colleague for information, used his potent pen to paint an entirely fictitious portrait of Mazzocchi, standing "on the stage biting his nails [while] delegates debated the wisdom" of adding "a simple declaration that "the Labor Party supports safe and legal abortion."[29]

Cockburn and others chose not to see the abortion debate as genuine and free from manipulation from convention leaders. They didn't notice the remarkable OCAW revolt against Wages and his pro-abortion position. They didn't report that it was migrant farmworkers, not Wages or Mazzocchi, who hadn't wanted the word *abortion* in *their* platform. It wasn't worth noting how these devout farmworkers, sitting front and center at the convention, waved proudly their bright red flags when their compromise language finally passed. Their strong stance and their power to influence the convention had been invisible.

But while Cockburn was ridiculing the labor party, he did stick a needle into its Achilles' heel: What does a labor party do if it doesn't run candidates?

X

Mazzocchi wanted a labor party that resembled a working-class party during the popular front era—but without the rigidity, secrecy, hero worship, and subservience to a foreign power. Then, elections were but a small part of party life. Local Communist Party chapters, for example, had been a hub of movement activity that attracted union and non-union workers, the employed and the unemployed, young and old, black and white. They engaged in strike support, rent strikes, and demonstrations of all kinds along with a vast array of cultural and educational efforts. They were never at a loss for things to do.

Mazzocchi was taken aback by how difficult it was for Labor Party chapters to develop a plan for, and then begin, mass recruiting. It was so obvious to him that the Labor Party needed to recruit, recruit, and then recruit some more—at work, at house parties, and at union meetings.

But the chapters pined for more action and got high from the very thought of electioneering. To satisfy this craving, Mazzocchi and his colleagues on the Labor Party's "national council" (the leadership body created under the constitution) dreamed up a new campaign for a "28th Amendment." This constitutional amendment would guarantee all Americans the right to a job at a living wage—or a guaranteed income when no jobs were available.

This non-electoral campaign could reframe the issue of low-wage work and unemployment by raising the idea that everyone should have work or income (starting at ten dollars an hour in 1997 and then indexed to inflation). They saw it as the Labor Party's alternative to minimum-wage legislation, a response to the explosive rise of low-wage service work and the impact of globalization on industrial workers.

Several party chapters really did try. They met at shopping centers to collect signatures. They even went door-to-door. But while many people signed the petitions, there was a generalized pie-in-the-sky dreaminess to it. Although some local activists persisted for many months, the campaign never gained traction.

Recruiting new Labor Party members wasn't easy, either. Labor Party organizer Bob Kasen believed that at least for some of the chapters, the problem was a lack of deep conviction and will. "They complain about not getting more members but they seem incapable of 'making the ask.' You've got to *ask* someone to join—one at a time—not wait around for new members to come running to you."[30]

Mazzocchi had seen just how Kasen did it. "If you walked with Bob down any street in a city in this country, you'd meet somebody and Bob would literally have them by the lapels and would not let go, attempting to convince them that they should participate in this struggle. . . ."[31]

Some chapters did grow and became a steady local presence with good support from local unions. These chapters—spanning the country from Los Angeles to southern Maine, central Florida to Cleveland—did what they could to recruit and build support for the Labor Party's program.

The New York Metro chapter was the largest in the country, in part because a positive buzz about the Labor Party temporarily engulfed New York's liberal-left community. The New York chapter quickly grew to over a thousand members, making it one of the largest political entities in the city. If it continued to grow, it could become a serious political force.

But instead, two fringe ideological sects went to war with each other. And each set out to capture the chapter. Because votes in the chapter's elections were based on individual membership, each group went on a mad dash to recruit their comrades and friends. In one case, a faction was accused of signing up toddlers to pad its vote totals.

Charges and countercharges soon dominated every chapter meeting.

One side ran off with the books. The other side locked the office. When chapter elections were held, the results were contested. Chaos reigned. As the battling factions duked it out, everyone else ran for the exits. Mazzocchi and his national council had a mess on their hands.

As the party's national organizer, Mazzocchi was empowered to settle such disputes. He listened to both factions. He tried reason. He finally imposed a semblance of order onto the chapter. But the damage was done, and its membership dwindled. Some other Labor Party chapters around the country experienced similar problems that drove unionists and other nonsectarian workers away.

The Labor Party's national council was forced to discontinue the chapter system. With Mazzocchi's concurrence, they replaced it with chartered organizing committees. You could only get a charter if you developed a concrete organizing plan complete with time lines.

Fortunately, union recruiting, especially within the OCAW, had accelerated a bit. "OCAW made consistent and conscious attempts to integrate the Labor Party into all of their work," Dudzic recalled. "They required the reps to raise it with every local they served. Locals all over the country had vibrant member-based committees engaged in creative activities. My favorite was the BP Alaska group raffling off a hunting rifle to support the LP. And hundreds of individual members participated in payroll checkoff" to support the party.[32]

Meanwhile, the electoral commission established during the first convention opened the door to electoral activity, but only if it could be done credibly with strong union support. To run candidates, a state or local Labor Party group first had to apply to a special national election committee for permission. The committee would apply rigorous criteria to ensure that the campaign would not divide the labor movement. For instance, to run a candidate, the local Labor Party had to secure sufficient local labor endorsements so that the candidate would be seen as a labor candidate. It had to submit a detailed financing plan. Candidates had to run on the Labor Party line and adhere to its platform. No fusion endorsements would be permitted. The message was: If you want to engage in electoral politics, get serious. No sectarian play-acting permitted.

With the chapter fires doused and the election policies settled, the Labor Party survived its initial shocks. Its second convention ratified the new electoral rules and further refined its platform. In the coming years, several Labor Party groups discovered effective non-electoral activities, including organizing successful popular ballot initiatives calling for universal health insurance in Ohio, Florida, Massachusetts, and Maine. And Mazzocchi continued to speak before scores of union groups each year, urging them to cover their bets by supporting the Labor Party even while they continued to labor for the Democrats.

But something wasn't right. The Labor Party wasn't growing as Mazzocchi had expected, and it wasn't spreading to larger unions. Even the unions that were committed to the party struggled to find time and resources to support it. The UE assigned staff members, including its energetic former organizing director, Ed Bruno, to work on the party; other unions, including CNA, committed staff time as well. But even for those unions, many other more immediate needs took priority—like winning decent contracts, fighting job loss, and trying to organize new union members.

There were some bright spots. The fifteen-thousand-member South Carolina AFL-CIO, led by Donna Dewitt, affiliated in 1998. "I got disgusted with the southern Democratic Party," she said. "I was looking for something that represented who we really are. Then Mazzocchi came down here. He joined us in a demonstration protesting in behalf of firefighters in Myrtle Beach. He loved the diversity of our organization—so many women and minorities—and we loved the idea of a labor party."[33]

But nationally, the initial rush of enthusiasm was fading fast, and Mazzocchi struggled to understand why. As he'd feared, labor's mid-1990s revival turned out to be short-lived. "It was nothing more than a temporary blip on labor's steady decline and had pretty much played itself out by the late 1990s," Dudzic said. "It was finally extinguished by the Gore debacle and post-9/11 politics. An expansive project like the Labor Party could only flourish at a time of upsurge."[34]

Why was it so difficult to create a party that could flourish in any season? Mazzocchi wondered. Why didn't more unions sign on? Why didn't they dedicate to a labor party even a fraction of the resources they devoted to Democrats? Why weren't Labor Party supporters—both inside and outside unions—able to build a vibrant organization? Why were people so caught up in elections? Why did the chapters implode? Why couldn't they make "the ask," as Bob Kasen had observed?

When it came to this kind of visionary politics, there was a noticeable gap between Tony's expectations and those of most activists. Part of it may have stemmed from the vast purges of the labor movement in the late 1940s and early '50s. As historians have pointed out, most radicals like Mazzocchi either had been drummed out of the labor movement, or silenced. And with them went the movement's memory of how parties functioned outside the two-party system and what they did day-to-day to build commitment and enthusiasm. Mark Dudzic expressed that loss well:

> I think the LP chapter problem points to a deeper crisis in working class culture that the LP was never able to overcome. Mazzocchi, more than almost anyone else connected with the LP movement, wanted to build these class-based memberships that transcended union, occupations, racial and ethnic boundaries. Most of the younger generation of activists (including me) had no such experience, and had trouble seeing how a non-electoral LP chapter could work. So when we realized that the entire concept of the chapters was ill-conceived, it was really an admission of a (hopefully temporary) defeat in his original vision of the LP.[35]

But of all those involved, Mazzocchi worried the least about the lull. He lived for solving such complex puzzles. He was certain that given enough time, he would attract sufficient union support and weave together the right mix of activities to succeed. Sooner or later, events would move his way.

Not for a moment did Mazzocchi lose confidence in his analysis. After all, the Democrats were in bed with corporations. They were no longer even embarrassed by it. But what really kept Mazzocchi going was the response he still received from everyday workers. No matter where he spoke, working people lit up when he argued for a new labor politics. Their energy refueled his. He could lead on indefinitely, provided he had sufficient resources. As long as OCAW supported the Labor Party, Mazzocchi believed he had time to crack the puzzle. And since Mazzocchi's personal base within OCAW was rock solid, time was on his side. Or so he hoped.

SEVENTEEN

Stepping-Stones

With Bob Wages as president and Tony Mazzocchi as his special assistant, OCAW blossomed. "I went to DC and built the Labor Party, and Bob supported it," said Mazzocchi. "Don't forget when we ran together, I wrote out our agenda and he bought into it 100 percent."

As Wages championed every radical cause in sight, he looked very much like the militant president that Mazzocchi never had a chance to become. Wages had already led the union into several fierce anti-corporate battles, including the five-year BASF campaign (modeled after Mazzocchi's 1973 Shell assault) that deployed powerful labor-environmental alliances. Wages now promoted Mazzocchi's Superfund for Workers/Just Transition concept to deal with the jobs-versus-environment conundrum. He became the first union president to negotiate partnerships with Greenpeace and the environmental justice communities. He collaborated with the Labor Institute to develop worker-run educational programs on health and safety, the environment, and economics. Wages joined Mazzocchi in pushing OCAW into the forefront of the battle for single-payer health care. And he even opposed the first Gulf war.

"Once Bob was exposed to this other world, he did very well in it," Tony said. "He became a darling of the progressive community, because he's smart—and, I think, genuinely progressive."

But what made Wages so powerfully effective also made him dangerous. Mazzocchi knew that an ambitious and talented leader like Wages would never settle for presiding over a declining enterprise. By 1990, OCAW had fewer than ninety thousand members—and falling. It wasn't clear any longer if it had the resources to take on global corporations or successfully organize new members. Mazzocchi believed that Wages needed a larger stage, and if Tony didn't help him find one, OCAW and the Labor Party would be in serious trouble.

The best solution, Mazzocchi thought, was to merge OCAW with a group of small progressive unions, starting with the United Mine Workers.

In 1989, while Tony was secretary-treasurer, he almost pulled it off, in a deal that would have given UMW president Richard Trumka the presidency of the new union, and installed Bob Wages as vice president. And Tony?

> I was going to be secretary. They asked me, "What do you want?" And I told them I'd write up my own job description. So I took the preamble of the mine workers' union. It's still the old preamble that was written in the days when they wanted to overthrow the government, and everything else. I said: "My job will be to carry out the intent of the preamble." And they said, fine. What a friggin' job I could have had. They had loads of money. I could have done anything I wanted for the Labor Party, all over the country.

Mazzocchi believed, "Wages didn't want that deal. He wanted to be president of the new merged union. But Rich Trumka was going to get that job, because the UMW had a huge treasury."

The deal breaker came from OCAW's merger committee, which believed that the Mine Workers union was covering up a massive membership decline by counting all of its retirees as full members. When the union refused to give OCAW the active-member totals, the merger talks collapsed.

Mazzocchi continued to hunt for other suitors, but finding a match wasn't easy. "With Bob's aggressiveness, he could have carried OCAW into a merger with a number of unions," Tony said. "But with some unions, we were concerned about corruption. If we merged with a smaller union, there wouldn't have been as many goodies for the staff. In a merger with a larger, more conservative union, some people would end up doing very well."

Mazzocchi even considered a merger with the Teamsters, then the largest union in the country with a membership more than ten times OCAW's. At least in the International Brotherhood of Teamsters, OCAW would be able to retain its name—OCAW, a Division of the IBT. Mazzocchi sketched out a scheme in which OCAW would ally with dissidents in the Teamsters for a Democratic Union and other progressive Teamsters. Together they could create a base for Wages to run for high office. Although it was a long shot, Mazzocchi believed Wages had the drive to pull it off.

Wages didn't bite. "I think it was more fantasy than anything else," he said. "I met with Mazzocchi and [a Teamster leader] over drinks at the

Tabard Inn in DC and we talked about it but it was only talk and I was only involved in the one discussion."[1]

Instead, like a homing pigeon, Wages flew right back to the Paperworkers.

II

Bob Wages, a generation younger than Mazzocchi, was a powder keg of conflicting emotions. Like Tony, he came from a CIO family. But during the twenty-three years in age that separated them, the CIO tradition had faded. Gone were nearly all of the socialists and communists who had given the labor movement its conscience. Gone, too, were so many of the utopian dreams about alternatives to corporate capitalism. Even the dream of an ever-expanding labor movement that could control the political agenda was fading fast. Although the Wages family subscribed to CIO anti-corporatism, it was also in tune with the broader American culture, which put a premium on individualism and rising prosperity.

Like Tony, Bob had absorbed unionism from his parents. Even as a pre-schooler, he liked to hang out with his dad at the union hall. Bob's father, like Tony's, was a devoted shop steward. He worked in a Kansas City refinery and was an active player in many strikes. But while Mazzocchi's family was part of the New York left's antiracist culture, the Wages family was shaped by Cold War unionism.

"They were a conservative people by their nature, and I grew up in a racist environment," said Wages. "Blacks were relegated to second-tier jobs in the refineries. They were segregated into their own local unions." Bob also "grew up learning that the company people were bastards, evil. Supervisors who came up from the ranks were suck-asses.[2] On the Vietnam War, Bob went his own way. "Dad and I had bitter, bitter fights about it," Bob recalled. "He was 'kill the pinkos, shoot the gooks.'"

Perhaps the most glaring difference between Mazzocchi and Wages was their sense of avocation. It was quite natural for Mazzocchi, given where he came from and the strength of New York's left, to view union organizing as a noble calling above all others. But by the time Wages grew up, it was natural for him to value personal achievement and material success along with service to the union.

After starting work with his father in the refinery, Wages, like Mazzocchi, realized he could rise within the union. Along with a strong, quick mind, he had a will to succeed that distinguished him among the refinery workers. Within two years, Wages won the presidency of the local. At the same time, he finished college, went to law school, got married, and had a child.

All this made for a tightly coiled personality—and Bob had already inherited a short fuse from his father. He never backed away from a fight. When he led his local on an illegal wildcat strike, he told OCAW president Al Grospiron to screw himself.

After Wages finished law school, a solid Kansas City firm recruited him. Soon he was out of the plant, out of the labor movement, and earning a good living as a lawyer. But OCAW's national legal department wanted to hire him—despite his earlier fight with Grospiron. They liked his combination of aggression, union experience, and addiction to hard work. They made Wages an offer in July 1975.

The draw for Wages was that OCAW "had really established itself in health and safety. You could just go anywhere and people knew you. It was a lot of Steve Wodka's work. It was meeting Jeanne Stellman. It was the Silkwood stuff. It was a big deal."

It didn't take long for Wages to recognize that Mazzocchi was probably his closest match in the union. "I thought he was, hands-down, the smartest guy there. He was the genuine article," Wages said.

He may also have suspected that Mazzocchi, someday, would become his ultimate competitor for power. The pair had their prickly moments. Tony's old friend George Roach had built an unwieldy amalgamated OCAW local based in Baltimore. President Grospiron didn't like its finances and instructed Wages to "fix that fucking mess." When Mazzocchi tried to defend Roach's project, Wages blew up. "I took it wrong," he said. "I just looked at him and said, 'If you got a fucking problem with what I do in Baltimore, you go see Grospiron, otherwise I don't want to fucking hear it.'" Wages said later: "In retrospect, I now know he was protecting George. But it was a very testy exchange. I don't know that it ever bothered Tony after that, but it always bothered me."

Wages, clearly, was never going to become a Mazzocchi acolyte, and in the battle of 1979 he went with Goss. "So many of the deeper friendships that I had were with people on the oil side of the union," Wages said.

"They worked me pretty hard to be more supportive of Goss, even before the campaign. I had sat with Bob in bargaining. He wasn't a dumb-ass. He was solid in his fundamental knowledge of collective bargaining. And I thought he had a real steely character."

Wages also didn't like the way Mazzocchi's gang treated him. He remembers that Tony never asked him for his support in the 1979 campaign, "which I found odd. But no big deal." On the night that Al Grospiron declined to run for president, a pro-Mazzocchi board member from District 8's Niagara Falls area, Angelo Augustino, buttonholed Wages, demanding he support Mazzocchi:

> Angie worshiped the ground Tony walked on. So Angie grabs me and he was almost threatening the way he approached it. He said, "If you know what's good for you, that's what you're gonna do . . ."—you know, New York Italian shit. That really pissed me off. I told him to go fuck himself.
>
> I don't know that anything would have changed if Tony had come to me that night, but I always had doubts about my decision from the day I made it. I don't know that I would have gone back and reversed it but I always had doubts about what I thought each of them brought to the table.

Those doubts wouldn't stop Wages from using his talents to play a decisive role in defeating Mazzocchi in 1979 and again in 1981.

And all Wages's progressive accomplishments as president wouldn't stop him from merging OCAW into oblivion.

III

By the late 1990s, Wages said, he was "convinced that OCAW would not be able to maintain its viability over the long term. We were losing members and not organizing in sufficient numbers to give me any hope that we could reverse our fortunes through organizing."[3]

After searching for merger partners, Wages concluded that the United Paperworkers International Union was "the only player in town because they were willing to create a new structure that would accommodate some of OCAW's key interests. No other union with whom I spoke was willing to really undertake a structure change and embrace some of our programs."

Mazzocchi still didn't want to merge with the conservative Paperworkers. But he was trapped. He was convinced that fighting the merger would fatally injure the Labor Party. OCAW had been picking up the tab for Mazzocchi's salary and that of Katherine Isaac, the Labor Party's secretary-treasurer—as well as travel costs and other expenses. The Labor Party depended upon this considerable subsidy. Although it took only one-third of the delegates to defeat the merger, it would take a majority to protect the Labor Party, and winning an anti-merger majority was out of the question. If he defeated the merger with a mere plurality, Mazzocchi was certain the pro-merger majority would retaliate by disaffiliating OCAW from the Labor Party, ending its subsidy. Wages meant business, and Tony knew it.

Tony held his fire over the merger because his primary allegiance had already shifted from OCAW to the Labor Party. He knew the difference between a vibrant labor movement and what he now saw around him. He'd grown up with an expanding, hope-filled movement that dominated political events. A shrunken OCAW couldn't re-create that reality on its own. For Tony, the only hope lay in the party.

The merger went into effect in January 1999 through the last democratic vote OCAW members would ever make. To the very end, most of the rank-and-file executive board didn't protest. Most of the independent district councils didn't oppose it. No one put a gun to the heads of those OCAW activists who put up a halfhearted fight. Instead, there was a whirlwind of deal cutting as leaders, large and small, tried to extract whatever they could from the merger, like vultures over a carcass.

Now Mazzocchi focused on how to maintain, for as long as possible, the new union's support for the Labor Party. He was realistic. He told his colleagues, "Three more years. Three more years of support is the most we can get after the merger." That, he hoped, would be long enough to recruit more unions to replace the loss of OCAW's institutional support.

The merger would mark the end of OCAW's raucous democratic traditions. It eliminated the rank-and-file executive board. It also eliminated the name *OCAW* within the new merged entity, which would be called PACE (Paper, Allied, Chemical and Energy International Union).

The merger seriously set back labor-environment collaborations that OCAW had championed for decades, since the Paperworkers took decidedly pro-corporate environmental positions. The Paperworkers had permitted—even encouraged—the industry to set up a joint labor-management anti-environmental lobbying organization, the Pulp and Paper Resource Council, complete with dozens of full-time union members armed with company credit cards. This company-union phalanx lobbied on behalf of the industry and against nearly every environmental regulation imaginable. It was the antithesis of everything Mazzocchi (and Wages) stood for.

Still, hope sprang eternal among OCAW progressives. Some thought that the merger would bring more resources for organizing and strike campaigns. Others believed Wages would use his prodigious talents to become the real power behind the throne. No one could imagine Wages losing at palace politics; surely he'd find a way to the top, just as he had in OCAW. After a beer or two, it was even possible to conjure up an outraged Wages unleashing his scathing temper to crush the Pulp and Paper Resource Council in the name of green unionism.

Then reality hit. After the merger, PACE was not a happy place for progressive OCAW staffers. As one said,

> The entire goal of PACE is opposite from OCAW's. In OCAW, we were about raising expectations to encourage militant action by the rank and file. PACE deliberately wants to lower expectations. They don't want the members demanding anything from the international."[4]

PACE also showed little reverence for OCAW's traditions of open communications and debate. It refused to give local union officers its national list of names and phone numbers so that the officers could communicate directly with one another. The union's environmental activists were told, "If you wanted to do environmental work, you shouldn't have merged with us." PACE even ended OCAW's toll-free health and safety hotline, saying, "If the membership wants to bug us, let them call on their own dime."[5]

Even as the big chill set in, some OCAW progressives still hoped Wages would lead them forward. But as he put it, "If I ever harbored ambitions to become president of PACE, they were short-lived. As the gavel went down on the merger convention and certainly after the first staff meeting the following day, I knew we were all fucked."[6]

Over the next two years, Wages said he became certain "that there was no way to change the course of the union, and I was persuaded that to run for the PACE presidency was an exercise in futility."

To the great shock of OCAW progressives, Wages retired from the union in April 2001, a little over two years after the merger. "I left because of a combination of disillusionment and, quite frankly, powerlessness. There was no way to change the course of the union. For my own sanity, I had to leave," he said.

For OCAW progressives, it felt like a betrayal. As grief turned to anger, many wanted Mazzocchi to exact revenge. Tony refused.

> Look, it's a tragedy and it's lamentable. It is a tragedy like Shakespeare. I can't turn it around by being bitter. I can't affect the outcome. So you try to think about, how do you make the best of it? To seek retribution would be destructive. Nothing could be gained, except for somebody who was interested in personal revenge for the moment. But personal revenge only further embitters you, because it never has the results you want it to have. Sometimes you just got to swallow hard and say, "How do I make something out of this?"

Mazzocchi knew that the roots of OCAW's demise went deeper than the actions of one man, and he still saw Wages as an ally. The industrial labor movement was in free fall, with private-sector union membership each year sinking to record lows. Younger unionized workers were sparse as companies consolidated, shut down, or moved abroad. Many of the brightest union activists, seeing no future in declining industrial unions, fled to service sector unions or left the labor movement.

So rather than get even or wallow in OCAW's demise, Mazzocchi maneuvered carefully to get PACE to support the Labor Party for a few more years. He encouraged the new PACE leaders to spearhead the fight for single-payer health care. And he quietly reconvened his OCAW troops to build a new rank-and-file caucus called Change of PACE, which Wages and his contacts could assist. Mazzocchi hoped that in time, progressives could challenge for leadership in a few districts. He was prepared to help organize yet another grassroots revolt—especially if it could buy some more time for the Labor Party.

But without Wages running interference for the progressive agenda, time ran out. PACE cut off the subsidy to the Labor Party in March 2001, and Mazzocchi had to retire from PACE. He and Katherine Isaac were forced to scramble for funds. Yet Mazzocchi still believed that if he could keep the Labor Party in motion for another decade or so, it would take off.

That was asking a great deal of history . . . and, at age seventy-four, of biology.

IV

First OCAW died. Then the 2000 presidential election nearly killed the Labor Party. For Mazzocchi, Ralph Nader's run for the presidency was, as he put it, "problematic." He greatly admired Nader's anti-corporate stance, but feared the electoral foray would be a major setback for third-party efforts. If Nader was perceived as tipping the balance to the Republicans, then the Labor Party would be toast.

Nader believed he was not a spoiler: His voters, he argued, wouldn't vote at all if it were not for his campaign. He really didn't care which lousy corporate party won, and didn't care about organized labor's romance with the Democrats. Anyway, Nader believed Mazzocchi's prospects for success were slim to none after the demise of OCAW—the foundation for the Labor Party.[7]

Mazzocchi certainly had great sympathy for Nader. Laura McClure, who was editor of the *Labor Party Press* at that time, recalled:

> We ran a piece—and Tony helped conceive of and reviewed everything we ran in *Labor Party Press*—that laid out the stances of Gore, Bush, Buchanan and Nader on one of our core issues, healthcare. Nader's stance was by far the closest to the Labor Party's. But we didn't endorse—in fact, at the 1998 LP convention, we'd voted that we could not endorse any non–Labor Party candidates. However, both the California Nurses Association and the United Electrical Workers endorsed Nader in 2000. Our *Labor Party Press* article got an ally in PACE in trouble, and Tony felt some heat too. He also

> took heat for speaking at the Green convention that nominated Nader. It seems to me Tony himself pushed the limits toward supporting Nader. And I don't remember a radical change of heart even after he took some criticism for it.[8]

Dick McManus, Mazzocchi's closest political ally, wished Mazzocchi had talked to him before going to the Green Party convention: "I would have told him, 'What are you, crazy? You don't need to be a hero to the Greens. You've got all these reactionary assholes in the union just laying for you and you're going to hand them an issue like this?'"[9]

Most of the labor movement would never forgive Nader for 2000. And the Labor Party would suffer collateral damage for years to come. Mazzocchi's close association with Nader added to the hit the Labor Party took from some union leaders, especially in PACE, which moved to cut off its subsidy. The record was clear: Tony Mazzocchi and Ralph Nader had been anti-corporate partners since the 1960s, with Nader repeatedly lending his prestige to Mazzocchi's causes.

If anyone wanted to wrap the two together, they had only to read the remarkable passage Nader wrote about Mazzocchi in *Crashing the Party* (2002):

> Tony Mazzocchi, founder of the Labor Party, and in my judgment the most visionary, accomplished, and steadfast leader in the nation, has traveled the most and spoken the most with more union members in small gatherings around the country than anyone else. One of his conclusions is that without a concrete agenda of action for working people, forged, discussed and backed by them, there will be no turnaround for organized labor. Mazzocchi and I have worked together for many years on occupational health and safety, on health insurance, on corporate globalization. This World War II veteran has brought scientists together with workers, as far back as the sixties, blazed the way for the asbestos litigation, pushed for more worker say on the shop floor, brought witnesses from the rank and file to testify before Congress in situations that led to the natural gas pipeline safety law and OSHA, and helped make the Oil, Chemical and Atomic Workers Union one of the most progressive, as OCAW's

> vice president. When Mazzocchi speaks, I listen, and someday the media may discover this honest, selfless, ever curious patriot. Someday may the leaders of the AFL-CIO listen to him. It is not that they disagree with him. It is that the times never seem ripe for doing today what should have been done forty years ago.[10]

The Labor Party and Nader's 2000 bid were both viewed by many labor leaders as reckless and dangerous.

"And things didn't get any better after the Bush administration proved to be the most anti-labor administration in modern American history," observed Dudzic. "Desperate to stop the bleeding, many progressives inside and outside the labor movement abandoned any pretense of an independent agenda as the mantra of 'anybody but Bush' became the accepted political wisdom."[11]

V

With events running against him, Mazzocchi found solace in books. He stumbled upon a historical soul mate, the abolitionist William Lloyd Garrison, as portrayed in *All on Fire* by Henry Mayer. Mazzocchi rarely identified with historical figures (though he read about them furiously, often in the middle of the night), but something about Garrison struck a chord. Mazzocchi could have been reading about himself in the book's passages, which he highlighted with brightly colored markers:

> His career is a landmark in the American dissenting tradition and exemplifies the fault line that in democratic politics separates the insiders, who think progress comes from quiet lobbying within the halls of power, from outsiders, who insist that only public manifestations of dissatisfaction can overcome institutional inertia.[12]

Garrison's role as visionary continually placed him out of step both with the powerful and with reformers who strived to be "practical." In one telling passage Mazzocchi highlighted, Meyer describes Garrison as a movement catalyst who "refused to weigh the impact of his views upon the quest for political power—a refusal that infuriated his critics at the time as well as subsequent historians who find it difficult to fathom public discussion that is not keyed to the tactical constraints of the two-party system."[13]

Breaking free of those damn two-party constraints defined Mazzocchi to the core. As Tony put it: "Show me the gains from your realism. Realism—all these compromises—got us where we are now. Look where we were and look where we are now. Demonstrate to me where your realism has ever paid off."

Informed by history, Mazzocchi soberly took stock of his fledgling Labor Party. He knew it was a long shot. It had survived the sectarian wars, false starts, and failed campaigns. By focusing on free higher education and single-payer health care, the party's platform was gaining traction. One or two local electoral campaigns had emerged in which Labor Party candidates stood a fighting chance. Mazzocchi believed the Labor Party just had to hang on. If history taught him anything, it was that "the laws of capitalism cannot be repealed." Instability for working people was written into the game. At some point, a crisis would hit and workers would seek alternatives. The Labor Party needed to be there with an analysis, a program, a vision. (In 2006 the South Carolina Labor Party formed in a state largely abandoned by the national Democratic Party. It was widely embraced by the state's labor movement and secured a ballot line.)

Mazzocchi also continued to hope that those in the labor movement would finally grow disenchanted with handing their support to corporate Democrats who betrayed them. As he told *The Nation,* "This is the only movement where they'll give you money, you can kick them in the ass, and they'll give you more money."[14]

But Mazzocchi wasn't counting on a sudden economic collapse or a rapidly spreading epidemic of labor enlightenment. He was ruthlessly honest about the Labor Party's chances of success:

> I just look at it as something that has got to be done. I think the chances of defeat are greater than the chances of success—appreciably greater. What's the expression? To have loved and lost is better than never to have loved? And not to have tried would have been more tragic than to have tried and been defeated. I mean, the chances of defeat are overwhelming no matter what you do,

> unless you count as success these little pinpricks in the wall of a system.

Mazzocchi made a conscious choice not to work on the "little pinpricks." It wasn't that he thought such work wasn't worth doing. It was that he could do something else, something most people could not and would not do:

> I'm not saying people shouldn't work on reforms, because they're important. I mean, there's some poor slob working for four bucks an hour, and then a living-wage campaign succeeds and he's getting seven. That's nothing to sneeze at. That's social work, and social work is important. But I want to go beyond that. I choose not to do social work.

Like William Lloyd Garrison, Mazzocchi focused on his ultimate goal: human liberation. He was able to stand apart and see a city on the hill where working people were freed from demeaning labor. It seemed so obvious to him that the relationship between work and society was fundamentally flawed and deeply inhumane:

> Look at how life is defined today in this society. You should toil, almost all your waking hours, and you should toil for as many years as you can—longer and longer. Why not a vision of society where people are able to enjoy the arts, relaxation, interaction with other people, free time? They shouldn't have to be out there working to enrich other people, even though it may get them some material things that make their lives more comfortable than their parents' lives. You listen to any TV financial program and they'll say, "Well, you should be saving today for tomorrow. In other words, you should be scrimping so that in your old age, you can pay for that long-term nursing care, where somebody's going to be spoonfeeding you, so you're not laying in the gutter."

Mazzocchi just knew that life could be reorganized so that everyone could be liberated from such a constricted human existence.

> It's incredible, when you think about it—life is really short—really friggin' short! Humans just don't live that long. I think it's ridiculous that anybody has to work over twenty hours a week in a time when we've got the ability to produce everything we need. Instead of some guy at the top skimming millions of dollars, you could pay for health care for a hell of a lot of people, for a lot of years—just one guy. You know, there's an awful lot of wealth out there. If it was distributed appropriately, everyone could have a fairly decent life—I think globally. And people could be happy transforming the way we live. Just rebuilding, not having anyone live in a crappy place. Not everyone has to live in a mansion, but everyone can live in a decent environment. It's all possible.

Mazzocchi wasn't just after a redistribution of wealth. He was after human fulfillment. His highest calling was to demand human freedom—freedom from demeaning and dangerous work, freedom to learn, freedom to live a life full of ideas, engagement, beauty, and friends—and of course excellent food, preferably involving pasta. The Labor Party was his vehicle to promote such a vision. That it might fail was irrelevant, in the same way that the possible failure of abolition was never an issue for Garrison. What mattered was trying until you could try no more.

VI

Tony Mazzocchi's biological clock was winding down. A severe case of kidney stones left him writhing on the floor in the middle of the night and landed him in the emergency room. Then his enlarged prostate became cancerous. Fortunately, the treatment worked, with only a few nagging side effects. When Tony felt pain in his back and pressure around his stomach, it was originally diagnosed as a pinched nerve. It persisted, and he got an MRI, which located a mass the size of a tennis ball on the tail portion of his pancreas. The bad news was that it was pancreatic cancer, which often proves fatal and may have been what killed his mother. The good news was that, because it was on the organ's tail, it would likely be operable.

On October 25, 2001, at New York's Memorial Sloan-Kettering hospital, a surgical team performed a laparoscopy—inserting a tube through a small incision to visually check the area, take biopsies, and make certain the tumor could be removed. It could not. It had metastasized to two places on the liver. It was Stage IV, and experimental chemotherapy was the recommended course of action. Tony knew he'd be lucky to survive another year.

His life split in two. One part became consumed by chemotherapy and the search for treatments to prolong his life. That part also accommodated a stream of visitors—family, friends, comrades who wanted to see him again, maybe for the last time.

The other part of him focused on building a Labor Party as though nothing were amiss. The next convention needed to be planned, and new organizing themes developed. He needed to do what he could to help the party survive the enormous rightward tide of post-9/11 politics. He couldn't and wouldn't quit.

Tony's illness seemed to kick him into overdrive at times. A typical weekend on the Mazzocchi Express would exhaust a fully healthy human. His swing through New York on a cold January weekend in 2002 was enough to take your breath away.

Throughout that weekend, like a Bible-thumper seeking converts, Mazzocchi clutched in his right hand another favored book, *When Dreams Came True: The GI Bill and the Making of Modern America* by Michael J. Bennett. Mazzocchi was on a revival mission to reintroduce free higher education onto the national political agenda. He called it Free for All, modeled on the Serviceman's Readjustment Act of 1944—the GI Bill of Rights. Mazzocchi took his message this winter weekend to the media and key associates in New York City.

It started as he and Katherine Isaac barreled up I-95 in record time—three hours and forty-five minutes from DC to the New York side of the Lincoln Tunnel. They then headed over to Madison Avenue, to the *Newsweek* building.

Mazzocchi, looking very fit for a seventy-five-year-old, stood about five foot seven, with a slight paunch and dressed more or less as he usually was—crisply self-ironed gray slacks, brown soft leather shoes, black merino wool turtleneck, a brown suede jacket, and a gray fedora with a black band that covered a nearly bald head. Isaac, much younger, diminutive, with fine features and high cheekbones, wore a simple black dress, because they were also going to see *La Bohème* at Lincoln Center after their interview with Jonathan Alter, *Newsweek* columnist.

Alter escorted them to a small conference area in the cluttered *Newsweek* offices, where he queried Mazzocchi about the decline of the labor movement and what could be done about it. Mazzocchi, as usual, spoke forcefully, as if to a larger audience. It didn't take him long to swing the topic to his latest cause. "Right now the Labor Party's coming up with a notion of free education in public colleges, graduate, post-graduate," he told Alter. "You know, the total bill for tuition today is $23 billion—that's a drop in the bucket."[15]

Mazzocchi then explained how the GI Bill of Rights passed despite the objections of the Roosevelt administration, through the efforts of a coalition led by the American Legion and William Randolph Hearst. "I was just reading a statement by Peter Drucker—you know, the management guru," he told Alter. "In 1946, he said, 'Years from now, people will look back and say that this was the most revolutionary piece of legislation in the 20th century.'"

While Alter, a devout, born-and-bred liberal Democrat from Chicago, admired Mazzocchi's accomplishments and character, he fundamentally disagreed with his dismissal of two-party politics, and was skeptical at best about the need for a Labor Party. But he was intrigued by the free higher education proposal. He challenged Mazzocchi on it: Why did the entire population deserve free higher education without "earning" it? "There was a reciprocal social responsibility," Alter suggested. "You had just served in the Army. Isn't the reciprocal thing now national service?"

Alter's question stayed with Mazzocchi during the evening of *La Bohème,* and the next morning he worked it through. He previewed his solution at lunch in a noisy Italian restaurant in Greenwich Village with his longtime friend Laura McClure, the former editor of the Labor Party's newspaper who was now a freelance labor writer. "When people are in trouble, like now, they don't say 'I don't deserve it,'" Tony said over the clanging of dishes. "If you went to the corner and said, 'You want to go to Rutgers? Here's nine grand'—nobody's going to say, 'I don't deserve it.'" Then he produced some supporting evidence, from the work of professor and labor activist Frank Emspak.

> Look. Emspak has this class of carpenters in a weeklong school at the University of Wisconsin. First he asks them, "How many of you would be willing to pay more taxes to improve social programs in this state?" Not one single hand went up. Then he asked, "How many of you are willing to pay higher taxes so that everyone could attend this university for free?" They all raised their hands.[16]

Leaving most of his pasta untouched—he could have made a far better clam sauce at home!—Tony redeployed his troops around the corner to the Labor Institute, which after thirty years still served as his informal think tank. There he met with Rick McArthur, the publisher of *Harper's Magazine,* and Adolph Reed Jr., then on the New School's graduate faculty, who would soon be leading the Free for All higher education campaign.

Mazzocchi strategically sat in the black leather armchair that rested between his guests, blocking their avenue of escape. He sensed a twofer in the making. Not only could he further inspire the already committed Reed in his organizing efforts, but together they might also interest *Harper's* in the subject. The hook was history.

"I mean this American Legion guy Colmery, former commander, an Oberlin guy, sits in the Mayflower Hotel on the weekend and writes the GI Bill out on a yellow pad," Tony told them. "Today you got sixty people on the staff—takes them six months to come up with some asshole proposal, right?"[17]

"That's because they have to make sure it doesn't help anyone," Isaac deadpanned, to laughter around the room.

Flipping through Michael Bennett's GI Bill book, Mazzocchi set the scene in 1944.

"I think a movie could be made out of this. The bill is in committee, and Rankin has arranged to stalemate the bill because it provided the same unemployment benefits for blacks as whites—twenty dollars a week, which was more than blacks made in much of the South. So they're one vote shy of reading the bill out of committee. And they have the vote. It was Representative John Gipson of Georgia who happened to be out fishing in some backwater swamp back home. And they figured out that if they got him to a commercial airliner, he'd never get back in time. So they convinced the army to lend him a plane. They called ahead and they got the state police to help them find him and get him to the transport."

"Is this all in the book?" McArthur interrupted.

"Yeah. And they find him and the army flies him back. He gets in one minute before the bill is to be reported out. If they can get it out, no one is going to vote against it, right? You know, who's gonna vote against the GIs? But Rankin's idea was to keep it in committee. And this guy walks in one minute before the vote. The bill comes out and passes. And people now see it as one of the greatest pieces of legislation ever. Even Peter Drucker, the management guru, says 'Future historians may consider it the most important event of the twentieth century.'"

Tony was just warming up. He gleefully thumbed through the book looking for a passage.

"I'm trying to break out of the historical amnesia. We did it then, when the deficit was more than half the GNP. And a congressional study in 1988 showed that it paid for itself six times over. Here it is, listen to this. This conservative guy ends up agreeing with lefty Howard Zinn: 'If history is to be creative, to anticipate a possible future'—and that's what we want to do, right?—'it should, I believe, emphasize such possibilities by disclosing those hidden episodes of the past'—like this hidden GI Bill story—'when even if in brief flashes, people showed their ability to resist, to join together, occasionally to win.'"

Mazzocchi looked up from the book and said to McArthur, "That's us."

VII

Like others with terminal illnesses, Tony had good days, and other days when he just wanted to die. He needled those who commended him for handling terminal cancer so nobly: "Hey, they say I'm being heroic. What else am I going to do? Show me a coward's way out and I'll take it."

During his raucous GI Bill seminar at the Institute (and when Katherine was out of earshot), he'd reached down to probe a spot high on his stomach and said, "Amazing, you can feel it here. It's growing." With no trace of sadness he added, "The tumor has spread up here, where they removed some malignant tissue during the laparoscopy. We'll see what happens, but I have no illusions."

As his whirlwind mission through editorial New York demonstrated, Tony still had a lot he intended to accomplish. In 2002, in the age of terrorism, a plummeting stock market, reduced economic expectations, the demise of social programs, and the collapse of the trade union movement, Mazzocchi was calling for a twenty-three-billion-dollar-a-year program for higher education. He truly believed that a mass movement could be built to support it—a very inclusive movement.

"Here's what I'd like to do during the Labor Party convention," Mazzocchi, grinning, told his astonished Institute guests and aides. "You know our hotel, the Hilton, is kitty-corner from the American Legion and right next door to the Mayflower, where Colmery wrote the GI Bill in his hotel room. I'd like to get the American Legion to join with our Labor Party delegates and march to the Roosevelt Memorial on the Mall and deliver a plaque there commemorating what Colmery did. He's an unsung hero. And then get the legion officially to endorse our campaign for free higher ed."

"Jesus," flashed the atheistic Reed. "The American Legion?"

"Hey," said Mazzocchi, "History makes strange bedfellows."

In his last months, Tony tried to convince workers, activists, the media, and just about everyone else he met that now was the time for free higher education. His friends and colleagues got a fresh taste of his passion for human freedom, the likes of which they knew they might never experience again.

If only he could reach enough people personally, the idea would catch on, Mazzocchi was sure. The view he presented was expansive. Here, in this marvelous piece of social legislation, were the seeds of the good life. We all needed sabbaticals. We all needed a break from the unfree and uncreative nature of corporate employment. We all needed to participate in continuing education. It should be part of our work life, and it should be free.

Why do we deserve it? Because we're alive and that's what life's about. Because education makes our lives more fulfilling. Because it's fun to play, to relax, to create, to engage in work defined by human need, not the corporate order. Because it's good to have enough money to live decently and enjoy the fleeting gift of life. We are not born to be slaves to the corporate order. We are meant to be free, with time to stroll on the beach, talking about Aristotle. *All* of us.

VIII

Once freed from the tyranny of the Ford assembly line in Edgewater, New Jersey, Tony Mazzocchi developed an insatiable lust for what he did each day—the meetings, the visits, and the organizing. He could not distinguish work from play. He liked nothing more than to cook an elaborate meal for a houseful of friends and prospective friends. Amid the cooking, the drinking, and the talking, Tony created an upbeat harmony that was the soul of his work and the spirit of the movement he was trying to build.

Around Tony, you didn't fight too much. You could argue among yourselves—but gently. You knew he didn't want to hear your petty resentments and grievances. If you were angry, it had better be against the corporate structure and not comrades, including those who might be your enemies at the moment. Tony pulled people together while always reaching out to more and more possible supporters for the cause. It was obvious that he was in love with what he did and with whom he did it.

As the pain of the spreading tumors grew, Mazzocchi took comfort from the sounds of political chatter among his friends, even when he no longer possessed the energy to participate fully. As these voices engulfed him, he was carried back to his childhood, surrounded by family and friends talking politics into the night in Bensonhurst and Blairstown, the cacophony of debate that had been his bedtime security blanket. It was again now as his body ran down.

One particularly painful afternoon, Tony lay on his couch waiting for the morphine to kick in from a portable IV drip. He dozed in and out as friends around the nearby dining room table indulged in some political griping.

They condemned the many labor activists they knew who had opted for the so-called good life—the six-figure union paychecks, the perks, the early retirements. Why hadn't Mazzocchi gone for those goodies when they were in reach? How could he resist such obvious temptations? It was an old refrain, sung by friends who were, on this day, trying to distract themselves from the immediate and unthinkable.

Like a jazz artist sensing the need to pick up the tempo, Tony joined in. Time to cut through this maudlin hero worship. He raised his head slowly from the couch pillow. A wry smile that could melt your heart spread across his gaunt face. "Hey, that wouldn't have been any fun," Tony said, his voice raspy. "I had a ball."

Bibliography

Anderson, Terry. *The Sixties*. New York: Addison Wesley Longman, 1999.

Aronowitz, Stanley. *False Promises: The Shaping of American Working Class Consciousness*. New York: McGraw-Hill, 1973.

Attewell, Paul. *Radical Political Economy Since the Sixties: A Sociology of Knowledge Analysis*. New Brunswick, NJ: Rutgers University Press, 1984.

Barnard, Harry. *Eagle Forgotten: The Biography of John Peter Altgeld*. Secaucus, NJ: Lyle Stuart, 1973.

Bayor, Ronald H. *Neighbors in Conflict: The Irish, Germans, Jews and Italians of New York City, 1929–1941*. Baltimore and London: Johns Hopkins University Press, 1978.

Bennett, Michael J. *When Dreams Come True: The GI Bill and the Making of Modern America*. Washington, DC: Brassey's, 2000.

Berman, Dan. *Death on the Job: Occupational Health and Safety Struggles in the United States*. New York: Monthly Review Press, 1978.

Berman, Dan, and John O'Connor, *Who Owns the Sun? People, Politics, and the Struggle for a Solar Economy*. White River Junction, VT: Chelsea Green Publishing, 1996.

Boyer, Richard O., and Herbert M. Morais. *Labor's Untold Story*. New York: United Electrical, Radio and Machine Workers of America, 1955.

Brodeur, Paul, *Asbestos and Enzymes*. New York: Ballantine Books, 1972.

———. *Expendable Americans*. New York: Viking Press, 1974.

———. *Outrageous Misconduct*. New York: Pantheon Books, 1985.

———. *Secrets*. Boston: Faber and Faber, 1997.

Carson, Rachel, *Silent Spring*. 1962. Reprint, New York: Houghton Mifflin, 2002.

Cohen, Gary, and John O'Connor, editors, with a foreword by Barry Commoner. *Fighting Toxics: A Manual for Protecting Your Family, Commmunity, and Workplace*. Washington, DC: Island Press, 1990.

Committee of Concerned Asian Scholars. *China! Inside the People's Republic*. New York: Bantam Books, 1972.

Commoner, Barry. *The Closing Circle*. New York: Alfred A. Knopf, 1971.

———. *Science and Survival*. New York: Ballantine Books, 1970.

Coye, Molly Joel, and Jon Livingston, editors. *China: Yesterday and Today*. New York: Bantam Books, 1973.

Culver, John C., and John Hyde. *American Dreamer: A Life of Henry A. Wallace*. New York: W. W. Norton, 2000.

Davidson, Ray. *Challenging the Giants: A History of the Oil, Chemical and Atomic Workers International Union*. Denver: Oil, Chemical and Atomic Workers International Union, 1988.

———. *Peril on the Job*. Washington, DC: Public Affairs Press, 1970.

De Bell, Garrett, editor. *The Environmental Handbook, Prepared for the First National Environmental Teach-In,* April 22, 1970. New York: Ballantine Books, 1970.

De Caux, Len. *Labor Radical*. Boston: Beacon Press, 1970.

Diggins, John P. *The American Left in the Twentieth Century*. New York: Harcourt Brace Jovanovich, 1973.

Draper, Ellen. *Risky Business: Genetic Testing and Exclusionary Practices in the Hazardous Workplace*. Cambridge: Cambridge University Press, 1991.

Draper, Theodore. *The Roots of American Communism*. Chicago: Evan R. Dee, 1989.

Eichstaedt, Peter H. *If You Poison Us: Uranium and Native Americans*. Santa Fe, NM: Red Crane Books, 1994.

Fabe, Maxine. *Beauty Millionaire: The Life of Helena Rubinstein*. New York: Thomas Y. Crowell Company, 1972.

Fast, Howard. *The American*. New York: Duell, Sloan and Pearce, 1946.

———. *Being Red: A Memoir*. Armonk, NY: M. E. Sharpe, 1990.

———. *Spartacus*. New York: Bantam Books, 1960.

———. *The Unvanquished*. New York: Bantam Books, 1967.

Federal Writers Project. *The WPA Guide to New York City*. New York: Pantheon Books, 1982.

Foner, Philip S. *History of the Labor Movement in the United States*, Vol. 9: *The T.U.E.L. to the End of the Gompers Era*. New York: International Publishers, 1991.

———. *History of the Labor Movement in the United States*, Vol. 10: *The T.U.E.L, 1925–1929*. New York: International Publishers, 1994.

Fosl, Catherine. *Subversive Southerner: Anne Braden and the Struggle for Racial Justice in the Cold War South*. New York: Palgrave Macmillan, 2002.

Franklin, H. Bruce. *Vietnam and Other American Fantasies*. Amherst: University of Massachusetts Press, 2000.

Fraser, Steven. *Labor Will Rule: Sidney Hillman and the Rise of American Labor*. Ithaca, NY: Cornell University Press, 1991.

Freeland, Richard M. *The Truman Doctrine and the Origins of McCarthyism*. New York: Alfred A. Knopf, 1972.

Freeman, Joshua B. *In Transit: The Transport Workers Union in New York City, 1933–1966*. Philadelphia: Temple University Press, 2001.

———. *Working Class New York: Life and Labor Since World War II*. New York: New Press, 2000.

Fuller, John G. *We Almost Lost Detroit*. New York: Ballantine Books, 1975.

Gabaccia, Donna Rae. *Militants and Migrants: Rural Sicilians Become American Workers*. New Brunswick, NJ: Rutgers University Press, 1988.

Garson, Barbara. *All the Livelong Day: The Meaning and Demeaning of Routine Work*. Garden City, NY: Doubleday and Company, 1972.

Geoghegan, Thomas. *Which Side Are You On?: Trying to Be for Labor When It's Flat on Its Back*. New York: New Press, 1991.

Gitlin, Todd. *The Sixties: Years of Hope, Days of Rage*. New York: Bantam Books, 1993.

Gortz, Andre. *Ecology as Politics*. Boston: South End Press, 1980.

Gottlieb, Robert. *Forcing the Spring: The Transformation of the American Environmental Movement*. Washington, DC: Island Press, 1993.

Goulden, Joseph C. *The Best Years, 1945–1950*. New York: Atheneum, 1976.

Griffith, Robert, and Athan Theoharis. *The Specter: Original Essays on the Cold War and the Origins of McCarthyism*. New York: Franklin Watts, 1974.

Hechler, Ken. *The Bridge at Remagen*. Missoula, MT: Pictorial Histories Publishing Company, 1957.

Howe, Irving, and Lewis Cosner. *The American Communist Party: A Critical History (1919–1957).* Boston: Beacon Press, 1957.

Jacobs, Paul. *Is Curly Jewish? A Political Self-Portrait Illuminating Three Turbulent Decades of Social Revolt 1935–1965.* New York: Atheneum, 1965.

Jenkins, Roy. *Churchill.* London: Pan Books, 2001.

Kazin, Michael. *The Populist Persuasion.* New York: Basic Books, 1995.

Kazis, Richard, and Richard L. Grossman. *Fear at Work: Job Blackmail, Labor and the Environment.* New York: Pilgrim Press, 1982.

Kennedy, David M. *Freedom from Fear: The American People in Depression and War, 1929–1945.* New York: Oxford University Press, 1999.

Kohn, Howard. *Who Killed Karen Silkwood?* New York: Summit Books, 1981.

Kryder, Daniel. *Divided Arsenal: Race and the American State During World War II.* Cambridge: Cambridge University Press, 2000.

Kurlansky, Mark. *1968: The Year That Rocked the World.* New York: Ballantine Books, 2004.

La Puma, Salvatore. *The Boys of Bensonhurst.* Athens: University of Georgia Press, 1987.

Lichtenstein, Nelson. *The Most Dangerous Man in Detroit: Walter Reuther and the Fate of American Labor.* New York: Basic Books, 1995.

London, Jack. *The Iron Heel.* Chicago: Lawrence Hill Books, 1907.

Mantsios, Gregory, editor. *A New Labor Movement for the New Century.* New York: Garland Publishing, 1998.

Markowitz, Gerald, and Rosner, David. *Deceit and Denial: The Deadly Politics of Industrial Pollution.* Berkeley: University of California Press, 2002.

Marks, Jonathan. *Human Biodiversity: Genes, Race and History.* New York: Aldine De Gruyter, 1995.

Matusow, Allen J. *The Unraveling of America: A History of Liberalism in the 1960s.* New York: Harper and Row, 1984.

Mayer, Henry. *All on Fire: William Lloyd Garrison and the Abolition of Slavery.* New York: St. Martin's Press, 1998.

Marzani, Carl. *The Education of a Reluctant Radical: Roman Childhood, Book 1.* New York: Topical Books, 1992.

McCullough, David. *Truman.* New York: Touchstone, Simon and Schuster, 1992.

———. *Brooklyn . . . And How It Got That Way.* New York: Dial Press, 1983.

Merriam, Robert E. *The Battle of the Bulge: Hitler's Last Desperate Gamble to Win the War.* New York: Ballantine Books, 1957.

Meyer, Gerald. *Vito Marcantonio: Radical Politician 1902–1954.* Albany: State University of New York Press, 1989.

Miller, James. *Democracy in the Streets: From Port Huron to the Siege of Chicago.* New York: Simon and Schuster, 1987.

Minchin, Timothy J. *Forging A Common Bond: Labor and Environmental Activism During the BASF Lockout.* Tallahassee: University of Florida Press, 2003.

Nader, Ralph. *Crashing the Party: How to Tell the Truth and Still Run for President.* New York: Thomas Dunne Books, St. Martin's Press, 2002.

Neel, J.V., and W. J. Schull. *The Effect of Exposure to the Atomic Bombs on Pregnancy Termination in Hiroshima and Nagasaki.* Washington, DC: National Academy of Sciences—National Research Council, 1956.

Nelson, Bruce. *Workers on the Waterfront: Seamen, Longshoremen, and Unionism in the 1930s.* Urbana and Chicago: University of Illinois Press, 1990.

Obach, Brian K. *Labor and the Environmental Movement: The Quest for Common Ground.* Cambridge, MA: MIT Press, 2004.

O'Connor, Harvey. *History of Oil Workers International Union–CIO.* Denver: A. B. Hirschfeld Press, 1950.

Ottanelli, Fraser M. *The Communist Party of the United States: From the Depression to World War II.* New Brunswick, NJ: Rutgers University Press, 1991.

Page, Joseph A., and Mary-Win O'Brian. *Bitter Wagers: Ralph Nader's Study Group Report on Disease and Injury on the Job.* New York: Grossman Publishers, 1973.

Perrow, Charles. *Normal Accidents.* New York: Basic Books, 1984.

Putnam, Robert D. *Making Democracy Work: Civic Traditions in Modern Italy.* Princeton, NJ: Princeton University Press, 1993.

Rashke, Richard. *The Killing of Karen Silkwood: The Story Behind the Kerr-McGee Plutonium Case.* Ithaca, NY: Cornell University Press, 2000.

Richter, Irving. *Labor's Struggles, 1945–1950.* Cambridge: Cambridge University Press, 1994.

Rogin, Michael Paul. *The Intellectuals and McCarthy: The Radical Specter.* Cambridge, MA: MIT Press, 1967.

Rucker, Allen. *The Sopranos Family Cookbook.* New York: Warner Books, 2002.

Sale, Kirkpatrick. *The Green Revolution: The American Environmental Movement 1962–1992.* New York: Hill and Wang, 1993.

Sayres, Sohnya, Anders Stephanson, Stanley Aronowitz, and Fredric Jameson. *The 60s Without Apology.* Minneapolis: University of Minnesota Press, 1984.

Schrecker, Ellen. *Many Are the Crimes: McCarthyism in America.* Boston: Little Brown and Company, 1998.

Schweitzer, Albert. *Peace or Atomic War?* New York: Henry Holt and Company, 1958.

Shabecoff, Philip. *A Fierce Green Fire: The American Environmental Movement.* New York: Hill and Wang, 1993.

Silver, Larry B. *The Misunderstood Child.* New York: Random House, 1998.

Spretnak, Charlene, and Fritjof Capra. *Green Politics: The Global Promise.* Santa Fe, NM: Bear and Company, 1986.

Stellman, Jeanne M., and Susan M. Daum. *Work Is Dangerous to Your Health.* New York: Pantheon Books, 1973.

Valerio, Anthony. *Valentino and the Great Italian.* New York: Freundlich Books, 1986.

Werfel, Franz. *The Forty Days of Musa Dagh.* New York: Carroll and Graf Publishers, 1983.

Weisberg, Barry. *Beyond Repair: The Ecology of Capitalism.* Boston: Beacon Press, 1972.

West, Thomas G. *In the Mind's Eye.* Amherst, NY: Prometheus Books, 1997.

Worster, Donald. *Nature's Economy: The Roots of Ecology.* Garden City, NY: Anchor Books, 1979.

Yellen, Samuel. *American Labor Struggles, 1877–1934.* New York: A Pathfinder Book, 1974.

Zieger, Robert H. *The CIO: 1935–1955.* Chapel Hill: University of North Carolina Press, 1995.

Notes

Prologue

1. All quotations from Tony Mazzocchi, unless otherwise noted, are from taped interviews and discussions with the author from January 2002 to September 2002.
2. *Hoople* for Mazzocchi came from a 1940s cartoon series, *Our Boarding House . . . with Major Hoople,* originated by Gene Ahern, which featured a rotund, stuffed-shirt buffoon.

1. The Prince of Shallow Junior High

1. David W. McCullough, *Brooklyn . . . And How It Got That Way* (New York: Dial Press, 1983), 10–13.
2. Anthony Valerio, *Valentino and the Great Italians According to Anthony Valerio* (New York: Freundlich Books, 1986), 48.
3. Harry Hearder, *Italy in the Age of Risorgimento: 1790–1870* (New York: Longman, 1983), 126. As cited in Robert D. Putnam, *Making Democracy Work: Civic Traditions in Modern Italy* (Princeton, NJ: Princeton University Press, 1993), 136.
4. All quotations from Connie Tozzi are from taped interviews with the author in November 2002.
5. Ronald H. Bayor, *Neighbors in Conflict: The Irish, Germans, Jews and Italians of New York City, 1929–1941* (Baltimore and London: Johns Hopkins University Press, 1978), 14.
6. Steven Fraser, *Labor Will Rule: Sidney Hillman and the Rise of American Labor* (Ithaca and London: Cornell University Press, 1991), 204.
7. Ibid., 86.
8. Ibid., 151. The union was powerful enough to curtail child labor, win the eight-hour day and the forty-eight-hour week, and achieve wages that were 25 to 50 percent higher than earned by workers in non-union facilities.
9. Ibid., 150.
10. Ibid., 140.
11. Ibid., 182.
12. As a union activist, Joe Mazzocchi might also have taken part in the union's educational and cultural programs and subscribed to radical political journals. Like all shop stewards, he also would be expected to attend the union's educational lectures—which, as Fraser describes (page 221), included such topics as "Russia's New Economic Policy (NEP)," "What Is Doing in Europe?," "American Imperialism," "The Paris Commune," and "Must We Change Human Nature?" As many as twenty-five hundred workers would attend such lectures. The union also sponsored courses on the arts, music, and great literature, as well as English classes for new immigrants.
13. Aileen S. Kraditor, *Jimmy Higgins: The Mental World of the American Rank-and-File Communist, 1930–1958* (Westport, CT: Greenwood Press, 1988), 2.
14. Felix Frankfurter, "The Case of Sacco and Vanzetti," *Atlantic Monthly,* March 1927, 50.

"By systematic exploitation of the defendants' alien blood, their imperfect knowledge of English, their unpopular social views, and their opposition to [World War I], the District Attorney invoked against them a riot of political passion and patriotic sentiment," wrote Harvard professor (and later Supreme Court chief justice) Frankfurter.

15. Fraser, *Labor Will Rule,* 228.
16. Mary Josephine D'Alvia, *The History of the New Croton Dam* (1976), 126.
17. Eric Foner, *The Story of American Freedom* (New York: W. W. Norton, 1998), 131.
18. In the decades around Tony's birth, Italian immigrants understood that the public thought of them not only as racially inferior, but very often as anarchist "bomb-throwing Italians." A very few *were* anarchists, and they came in many flavors: libertarians, who advocated for small self-governing social units; syndicalists, who believed unions would replace the government; and communists of various stripes. Only a handful advocated violence.
19. www.msu.edu/course/mc/112/1920s/Sacco-Vanzetti. The rallies and protests did not succeed: Sacco and Vanzetti were executed on August 23, 1927. Half a century later, they were pardoned by Massachusetts governor Michael Dukakis.
20. Fraser, *Labor Will Rule,* 206. In the 1920s, the clothing industry contracted as consumer spending shifted away from clothing and toward new big-ticket items such as radios, kitchen appliances, and automobiles. Joe Mazzocchi's employer, Rogers Peet, survived, but the pressure to cut costs mounted.
21. Ibid., 240.
22. Kristina Mazzocchi, e-mail to the author, February 26, 2007.
23. FDR inaugural address, March 4, 1933, http://newdeal.feri.org/timeline/1933e2.htm.
24. www2.census.gov/prod2/statcomp/documents/CT1970p1-05.pdf, 178.
25. www.bls.gov/news.release/union2.nr0.htm.
26. David M. Kennedy, *Freedom from Fear* (New York and Oxford: Oxford University Press, 1999), 282.
27. Bayor, *Neighbors in Conflict,* 78.
28. Fraser, *Labor Will Rule,* 229.
29. In 1933, Coughlin could still be heard saying, "We are determined once and for all to attack and overpower the enemy of financial slavery; to oppose and to defeat those who still support the ancient heresy of the concentration of wealth in the hands of the few. . . ." From Michael Kazin, *The Populist Persuasion* (New York: Basic Books, 1995), 114.
30. In 1938, Coughlin used his national newspaper, *Social Justice,* to publish the "Protocols of the Elders of Zion," a czarist forgery that purported to reveal the Jewish plot to rule the world.
31. Bayor, *Neighbors in Conflict,* 95.
32. Ibid., 97–98.
33. Ibid., 98.
34. Thomas G. West, *In the Mind's Eye* (Amherst, NY: Prometheus Books, 1997), 108.
35. R. R. Palmer, *A History of the Modern World* (New York: Alfred A. Knopf, 1960), 837.
36. Also in January 1942, unbeknownst to the American public, at the Wannsee Conference in Berlin, Reinhard Heydrich, a subordinate of SS leader Heinrich Himmler, presided over a meeting that laid out in detail, country by country, the plan to kill eleven million European Jews. On March 21, 1942, the first Jews arrived at Auschwitz and Birkenau for gassing.

2. Basic Training

1. *The History of the 563rd Anti-Aircraft Artillery Automatic Weapons Battalion* (New York: Comet Press, date and author unknown), 9.
2. Daniel Kryder, *Divided Arsenal: Race and the American State During World War II* (New York: Cambridge University Press, 2000), 135.
3. Ibid., 181.
4. Ibid., 182.
5. Ibid., 186.
6. Ibid., 178.
7. Ibid., 176.
8. Ibid., 194.
9. Ibid., 197.
10. Ibid., 204.
11. Ibid., 203.
12. David M. Oshinsky, "Only the Accused Were Innocent," http://nytimes.com, April 3, 1994.
13. Kryder, *Divided Arsenal,* 18.
14. *History of the 563rd,* 20.
15. Ibid.
16. Ibid., 34.
17. Ibid., 35.
18. Ibid., 36.
19. "Abandoned pregnant and penniless on the teeming streets of London, sixteen-year-old Amber St. Clare uses her wits, beauty and courage to climb to the highest position a woman could achieve in Restoration England—that of favorite mistress of the Merry Monarch, Charles II. From whores and highwaymen to courtiers and noblemen, from the Great Plague and the Fire of London to the intimate passions of ordinary—and extraordinary—men and women, Amber experiences it all. . . ." The book sold a hundred thousand copies in the first week of 1944.
20. Ken Hechler, *The Bridge at Remagen* (Missoula, MT: Pictorian Histories Publishing, 2001), 115.
21. *History of the 563rd,* 46.
22. Hechler, *Bridge at Remagen,* 160.
23. *History of the 563rd,* 44.
24. Ibid.
25. www.scrapbookpages.com/Buchenwald/Ovens.html.
26. Buchenwald was a horrific work camp. Professional criminals supervised by the SS ran and maintained the crematorium. Prisoners who were skilled craftsmen constructed the facility and ran an assortment of workshops to produce luxuries for the SS. When more children began to arrive, the Jewish children and Gypsy boys were culled out and sent to Auschwitz for gassing. David A. Hackett, editor, *The Buchenwald Report* (Boulder, CO: Westview Press, 1995), 32–97.
27. Joseph C. Goulden, *The Best Years, 1945–1950* (New York: Atheneum, 1976), 31.
28. Ibid., 30.
29. Ibid.

30. Ibid., 29.
31. Ibid., 32.
32. Ibid.
33. Joseph Clark, "GI's Brig Gripe," *Daily Worker,* February 3, 1946.

3. Running with the Reds

1. All quotations from Jerry and Ruth Fine are from taped interviews with the author on November 1, 2002.
2. Irving Richter, *Labor's Struggles, 1945–1950* (Cambridge: Cambridge University Press, 1994), 48.
3. Joshua B. Freeman, *Working Class New York* (New York: New Press, 2000), 4.
4. Bruce Nelson, *Workers on the Waterfront: Seaman, Longshoremen, and Unionism in the 1930s* (Urbana: University of Illinois Press, 1990), 215.
5. Ibid., 83.
6. Freeman, *Working Class New York,* 4.
7. Irving Howe and Lewis Cosner, *The American Communist Party* (Boston: Beacon Press, 1957), 375.
8. John C. Culver and John Hyde, *American Dreamer: A Life of Henry Wallace* (New York: W.W. Norton, 2000), 414.
9. Ibid., 421.
10. Ibid., 415.
11. Ibid., 459.
12. Freeman, *Working Class New York,* 77.
13. Culver and Hyde, *American Dreamer,* 474.
14. Ibid., 500–501.
15. Gerald Meyer, *Vito Marcantonio, Radical Politician, 1902–1954* (Albany: State University of New York, 1989), 23.
16. Ibid., 36.
17. Ibid., 39.
18. Howard Fast, *Being Red: A Memoir* (Armonk, NY: M. E. Sharpe, 1994), 231.
19. Freeman, *Working Class New York,* 81.
20. Ibid.
21. Howe and Cosner, *American Communist Party,* 478.
22. www.korean-war.com/TimeLine/1950/06-25to08-03-50.html.
23. Freeman, *Working Class New York,* 91.
24. Ibid., 93.
25. This negative depiction belies the fact that for much of the period between the two world wars, many CP members and sympathizers were the driving force in America for union democracy, organizing the unorganized, building CIO industrial unionism, and fighting for the rights of African Americans.

4. Infiltrator

1. *The New York Times,* March 16, 1944, 21.
2. www.helenarubinsteinfdn.org/about.html.
3. Maxine Fabe, *Beauty Millionaire* (New York: Thomas Y. Crowell Company, 1972), 134.

4. All citations in the book from George Roach are from author interviews, May 17, 2002, and July 8, 2003.
5. Ray Davidson, *Challenging the Giants* (Denver: Oil, Chemical and Atomic Workers International Union, 1988), 135.
6. Ibid., 168.
7. Jack Curran interview by Publications Production Group, 900 2nd Street, NE, Washington, DC, December 21, 1995, tapes 1 and 2.
8. All citations referring to local union minutes come from USW Local 149 archives on loan to the author.
9. Davidson, *Challenging the Giants,* 166.
10. Ibid., 166.
11. Jack Curran interview, Publications Production Group, December 12, 1995.
12. Ibid.
13. *New York Times,* March 27, 1948.
14. Ibid.
15. *Union Leader,* April 14, 1948.
16. Ibid., April 15, 1948.
17. Davidson, *Challenging the Giants,* 171.
18. Robert H. Zieger, *The CIO, 1935–1955* (Chapel Hill: University of North Carolina Press, 1995), 341.
19. All citations in the book from Bobby Guinta are from author interviews, April 15 and May 15, 2003.
20. E-mail to author, January 2, 2007.

5. Subversive Suburbs

1. Freeman, *Working Class New York,* 55.
2. Goulden, *The Best Years,* 139.
3. Ellen Schrecker, *Many Are the Crimes: McCarthyism in America* (Boston: Little Brown, 1998), 208.
4. Ibid., 209.
5. Ibid., 395.
6. Ibid., 412.
7. Local 149 union minutes, March 20, 1953.
8. *The Militant,* August 27, 1957.
9. Howard Fast, *Freedom Road* (New York: Amsco School Publications, 1970), 92.
10. Howard Fast, *Spartacus* (New York: Bantam Books, 1960), 229.
11. Schrecker, *Many Are the Crimes,* 152.
12. *The Militant,* August 16, 1955.
13. Ibid., September, 27, 1955.
14. Ibid., December 20, 1955.
15. Ibid., February 5, 1957.
16. Ibid., April 30, 1957.
17. Ibid., February 19, 1957.
18. Ibid., August 27, 1957.
19. Ibid., August 16, 1955.

20. Ibid., November 9, 1955.
21. Ibid., May 22, 1956.
22. Ibid., January 22, 1957.

6. From Bombs to Broadway

1. Barbara Garson, *All the Livelong Day: The Meaning and Demeaning of Routine Work* (New York: Doubleday, 1975), 64.
2. Ibid., 71.
3. Ibid., 69.
4. Ibid., 72.
5. http://nuketesting.enviroweb.org/atmosphr/ustest.htm.
6. "The Biological Effects of Ionizing Radiation: A Report to the Public, from a Study by the National Academy of Sciences" (Washington: National Academy of Sciences—National Research Council, 1956), 4–6.
7. Milton S. Katz, *Ban the Bomb* (New York: Greenwood Press, 1986), 84.
8. *The Militant,* May 6, 1958.
9. www.mcs.drexel.edu/~gbrandal/Illum_html/Day.html.
10. Author interview with George Roach, July 22, 2003.
11. See the President's Commission on Organized Crime, April 2, 1986, at www.laborers.org/Commission_IBT.html, and United States Court of Appeals for the Second Circuit, No. 1609 August Term 1992, argued May 25, 1993, decided July 13, 1993, Docket No. 93-6030, at www.ipsn.org/court_cases/adelstein_v_investigation_officer_appeal.htm.
12. *The Militant,* December 10, 1957.
13. Leonard Baker, "LI Unionists See LBJ, Ask Industry Aid," and Paul Leventhal, "Labor Seeks Non-Defense Jobs for LI," *Newsday,* February 17–23, 1964.
14. Author interview with Morty Bahr, May 23, 2003.

7. From CIO to CIA

1. Thomas W. Braden, "I'm Glad the CIA Is 'Immoral,'" *Saturday Evening Post,* May 20, 1967, 10.
2. Davidson, *Challenging the Giants,* 123.
3. Ibid., 123–124.
4. Ibid., 230.
5. Phil Agee, *Inside the Company: CIA Diary* (New York: Bantam Books, 1975), 632.
6. Davidson, *Challenging the Giants,* 240.
7. "Global Force in Oil Bargaining," *Business Week,* February, 13, 1960.
8. "Helping Labor Grow Overseas," *Business Week,* September 8, 1962.
9. Ibid.
10. Harvey O'Connor, *History of Oil Workers International Union–CIO* (Denver: Oil Workers International Union, 1950), 43.
11. E-mail from Mark Dudzic to the author, January 3, 2007.
12. Albert Schweitzer, "The Schweitzer Declaration" *Saturday Review,* May 18, 1957, 19.
13. James Carey, "Message to the OCAW Constitutional Convention," August 12, 1967.
14. Davidson, *Challenging the Giants,* 235.

15. *Proceedings of the Fifth Constitutional Convention* (Denver: Oil, Chemical and Atomic Workers International Union, 1959), 19.
16. Davidson, *Challenging the Giants,* 270.
17. Author interview with Stanley Aronowitz, March 12, 2003.
18. *Proceedings of the Sixth Constitutional Convention* (Denver: Oil, Chemical and Atomic Workers International Union, 1961), 140.
19. Agee, *Inside the Company,* 631.
20. Ibid., 130–131.
21. Davidson, *Challenging the Giants,* 293.
22. *New York Times,* September, 1, 1964.
23. Davidson, *Challenging the Giants,* 295.
24. Ibid.
25. Aronowitz e-mail to the author, December 2006.
26. *Proceedings of the Eighth Constitutional Convention* (Denver: Oil, Chemical and Atomic Workers International Union, 1965), 209–210.
27. Ibid., 211.
28. Author interview with Geraldine Amitin, March 14, 2003.

8. Masters of War

1. Terry Anderson, *The Sixties* (New York: Addison Wesley Longman, 1999), 54.
2. Ibid., 52.
3. Ibid., 66.
4. Full disclosure: For two years in the early 1960s, Aronowitz was married to my sister Evelyn Leopold, who introduced him to Tom Hayden and SDS. I met Mazzocchi through Aronowitz and my sister. I have remained friends with Aronowitz ever since.
5. Aronowitz interview with the author, March 12, 2003.
6. Sohnya Sayres, Andres Stephanson, Stanley Aronowitz, and Frederic Jameson, editors, *The 60s Without Apology* (Minneapolis: University of Minnesota Press, 1984), 31.
7. Sol Stern, *Ramparts,* March 1967, 35–36.
8. Neil Sheehan, "CIA Men Aided Strikes in Guiana Against Dr. Jagan," *New York Times,* February, 22, 1967, A1.
9. "CIA Money Use Linked to 2 Denver Labor Units," *Denver Post,* February, 24, 1967, 1.
10. Marjorie Hunger, "Kennedy Lays CIA Financing to Executive Branch Decisions," *New York Times,* February 22, 1967, 17.
11. Ibid.
12. "Meany Will Study CIA–Labor Ties; Opposes Subsidies," *New York Times,* February 25, 1967.
13. Fern Ingersoll, "Leo Goodman, Helen Gahagan Douglas and Her Work with Labor on Housing and Atomic Energy" (Berkeley: University of California, Regional Oral History Office, Bancroft Library, Women in Politics Oral History Project, 1981), 60.
14. John G. Fuller, *We Almost Lost Detroit* (New York: Ballantine Books, 1975), 128.
15. Ibid., 26.
16. Ibid., 47.
17. Ibid., 127.

18. Peter Eichstaedt, *If You Poison Us* (Santa Fe, NM: Red Crane Books, 1994), 81.
19. Ibid., 83.
20. Ibid., 89.
21. Jack Sheehan interview with the author, February 1, 2007.
22. Hearings, US Congress, Subcommittee on Research, Development, and Radiation, Joint Committee on Atomic Energy, 90th Congress, 1st session, May 9, 1967–August 10, 1967, 424.
23. Ibid.
24. Ibid., 425.
25. Ibid.
26. Ibid., 426.
27. Ibid.
28. Ibid., 427.
29. Ibid., 431.
30. Ibid., 432.
31. Ibid.
32. Those words became the title of the book *If You Poison Us,* written by Peter H. Eichstaedt in 1994, that offers the definitive account of the long sordid history of the poisoning of the Navajo uranium miners and their fight for just compensation.
33. Ibid., 433.
34. Ibid., 437.
35. J.V. Reistrup, "Industry Attacks, Labor Defends New Limit on Radiation in Mines," *Washington Post,* Friday, June 9, 1967, A23.

9. Stars in Their Vision

1. Rachel Carson, *Silent Spring* (Boston: Houghton Mifflin Company, 1962), 22.
2. Ibid., 25.
3. Ibid., 31.
4. Barry Commoner interview with the author, April 27, 2004.
5. Paul Brodeur, *Expendable Americans* (New York: Viking Press, 1974), 142.
6. Allen J. Matusow, *The Unraveling of America* (New York: Harper and Row, 1984), 363.
7. *Ninth Constitutional Convention Proceedings* (Denver: Oil, Chemical and Atomic Workers International Union, 1967), 28.
8. Ibid., 31.
9. Ibid., 92.
10. Ibid.
11. Ibid., 92–93.
12. Ibid., 93.
13. Ibid., 94.
14. *New York Times,* April 29, 1966, 27.
15. Ibid., October 4, 1966, 75.
16. Ibid..
17. Ibid.
18. *New York Times,* August 3, 1967.
19. Ralph Nader, "Tony Mazzocchi, Top Union Leader," syndicated column, July 1981.

20. *Ninth Constitutional Convention Proceedings,* 58.
21. Ibid., 60.
22. Ibid., 61.
23. Ibid.
24. Ibid., 62.
25. Ibid., 64–65.
26. H. Bruce Franklyn, *Vietnam and Other American Fantasies* (Amherst: University of Massachusetts Press, 2000), 94.
27. Anderson, *The Sixties,* 104.
28. Ibid.
29. Ibid., 106.
30. Glenn Paulson interview with the author, May 14, 2004.
31. James Miller, *Democracy in the Streets* (New York: Simon and Schuster, 1987), 21.
32. Brodeur, *Expendable Americans,* 78.
33. Ibid., 100.
34. Hazards in the Industrial Environment, A Conference Sponsored by District 8 Council OCAW, Holiday Inn, Kenilworth, New Jersey, March 29, 1969, Conference Organized by Citizenship Legislative Department, OCAW, 1126 16th Street, NW, Washington, DC, 20036, 1–2.
35. Ibid., 5–6.
36. Ibid., 31.
37. Ibid.
38. Ibid., 32.
39. Ibid., 33.
40. Ibid., 35–39.
41. Ibid., 46.
42. Ibid., 57–58.
43. Ibid., 58–59.
44. Ibid., 39.
45. Ibid., 40.
46. Ibid., 43.
47. Ibid., 58.
48. Ibid., 70.
49. Ibid.
50. Ibid., 71.
51. Ibid., 72.
52. Ibid.
53. Ibid., 71.
54. Ibid.
55. Ibid., 72.
56. Ruth Heifetz e-mail to the author, February 16, 2007.
57. Joe Anderson interview with the author, May 5, 2004.
58. Susan Mazzocchi interview with the author, April 2004.

10. The Mad Rush

1. Steve Wodka interview with the author, February 8, 2007.
2. Marjorie Baron, Carol Eckart, Gary Fujimoto, Robert Harrison, and Joanne Koslofsky, *Merck Is Not a Candy Factory,* Medical Electives Report, A Special Education Program for Medical Students and Residents in Relevant Occupational Safety and Health, Sponsored by the Citizenship-Legislative Department, Oil, Chemical and Atomic Workers Union, 1126 16th Street, NW, Washington, DC 20026, August, 16, 1976, 59.
3. Pyser Edelsack interview with the author, March 3, 2005.
4. Vern Jensen interview with Gail Bateson, January 24, 2002, 2.
5. Susan Mazzocchi, "Training Occupational Physicians: Suppose They Gave a Profession and Nobody Came," *Health/PAC Bulletin* 75 (March–April 1997), 7.
6. David Zinman, Bob Wyrick, and Dennis Kevesi, "Once-Deadly Plant Cleaned Up," *Newsday,* January 22, 1977, 47R.
7. Homer Bigart, "Lung-Disease Problem, Traced to Beryllium Refinery, Plagues Hazelton, Pa.," *New York Times,* October 29, 1972, 58.
8. Ibid.
9. Ibid.
10. Bob Salitza, "Kawecki Berylco, Union Disagree on Safety," *Hazelton Standard Speaker,* December 1, 1972, 32.
11. Nevertheless, many of these workers would die from beryllium exposures. Two decades later, Mazzocchi ran into the son of one who was struggling unsuccessfully with the company and the state to get medical and financial help for retired Kawecki Berylco workers, especially medical screening that could prevent the disease if caught early. Mazzocchi connected these workers with Richard Miller, an OCAW consultant, who was lobbying the Clinton administration to provide automatic workers' compensation to exposed nuclear workers. Miller, working closely with OCAW president Robert Wages and David Michaels, assistant secretary of the Department of Energy, succeeded in securing medical screening and financial compensation from the DOE in 1999—since these workers had produced beryllium for the nuclear weapons industry.
12. Hazards in the Industrial Environment, A Conference Sponsored by District 3 Council OCAW, Henry Grady Hotel, Atlanta, Georgia, January 23–25, 1970, Conference Organized by Citizenship Legislative Department, OCAW, 1126 16th Street, NW, Washington, DC, 20036, 39.
13. Joseph Lelyveld, "Mood Is Joyful as City Gives Its Support," *New York Times,* April 23, 1970, 30.
14. Ibid.
15. Bill Dodds interview with the author, February 2, 2004.
16. Bill Bywater interview with the author, July 8, 2003.
17. Albert Vetere Lannon and Marvin Rogoff, "Building the Anti–Vietnam War Movement in the House of Labor," *Science and Society* 66, no. 4 (winter 2002–2003), 537.
18. Ibid., 538.
19. Bernard Rapoport interview with the author, February 2, 2004.
20. Ralph Nader interview with the author, February 28, 2007.
21. Jack Sheehan interview with the author, February 1, 2007.

22. David Foster, "Steel Magnolias: Steelworkers and the Sierra Club Tie the Knot," *New Labor Forum* 16, no. 1 (winter 2007), 60.
23. Ibid.
24. *Weekly Compilation of Presidential Documents,* January 2, 1971, 5.
25. Jack Sheehan e-mail to the author, March 8, 2007.
26. The OCAW heavily used these agencies. By 1979, for example, Steve Wodka alone had eighteen active cases pending simultaneously before the OSHRC.
27. Judson MacLaury, "The Job Safety Law of 1970: Its Passage Was Perilous," www.dol.gov/oasam/programs/history/osha.htm, originally published in the *Monthly Labor Review,* March 1981.
28. Susan Mazzocchi, "The First Complaint Filed and the First Citation Issued Under the Occupational Safety and Health Act, 1970, Filed by the Oil, Chemical and Atomic Workers International Union, AFL-CIO, on behalf of Local 3-586 Involving Allied Chemical Corporation, Moundsville, West Virginia," unpublished manuscript, 1978, 4.
29. Ibid., 5.
30. Ibid., 6.
31. Ibid., 11–12.
32. Ibid., 13.
33. Ibid., 15.
34. Ibid., 17.
35. Robert Sherrill, "What's Behind the Failure to Protect the Health of America's Workers," *Today's Health,* August 1972, 66.
36. Susan Mazzocchi, "The First Complaint Filed," 22.
37. Ibid., 36.

11. Catalytic Converter

1. Hal Willard, "Long Live Mazzocchi!" *Washington Post,* February 10, 1972.
2. Jeanne Stellman interview with the author, December 13, 2004.
3. Paul Brodeur, *Secrets: A Writer in the Cold War* (Boston: Faber and Faber, 1997), 149.
4. Ibid., 82.
5. Paul Brodeur, *Asbestos and Enzymes* (New York: Ballantine Books, 1972), 81.
6. Brodeur, *Secrets,* 151–152.
7. Steve Wodka, "Confidential Report: Occupational Health Tragedy, Pittsburgh Corking Corporation, Tyler, Texas, OCAWIU Local 4-202," January 28, 1972, 4.
8. Ibid., 5
9. Brodeur, *Expendable Americans,* 35.
10. Steve Wodka, "Confidential Report," 7.
11. Ibid., 9.
12. Ibid., 15.
13. Ibid., 22.
14. Brodeur, *Expendable Americans,* 55.
15. Ibid., 5–6.
16. Ibid., 72.
17. Brodeur, *Secrets,* 155.

18. Brodeur, *Expendable Americans,* 124.
19. Ibid.
20. Ibid., 245.
21. Paul Brodeur, *Secrets,* 153–154.
22. Cathy Lerza interview with the author, March 13, 2005.
23. Sam Love interview with the author, February 9, 2007.
24. Cathy Lerza, "Giving Shell Some Gas: Environmental Issues Reach the Bargaining Table," *Environmental Action* 4, no. 20 (March 3, 1973), 6.
25. "11 Groups Back Strike at Shell," *Washington Post,* January 31, 1973.
26. Samuel S. Epstein, MD, "The Shell Strike for Workers Health and Safety," April 13, 1973, Collected Health and Safety Papers, Oil, Chemical and Atomic Workers International Union, on file at the Labor Institute, New York.
27. Stuart Auerbach, "The First Strike Over Potential Hazards to Health," *San Francisco Chronicle,* March 3, 1973, 21.
28. Robert Gordon, "Shell No!: OCAW and the Labor–Environmental Alliance," *Environmental History* 3, no. 4 (October 1998), 474.
29. Ibid.
30. Ibid.
31. Ibid.
32. Ibid.
33. Ibid., 475.
34. Dale Champion, "A Labor Warning on Environment," *San Francisco Chronicle,* March 8, 1973.
35. John Herling, "Labor and Ecology," *Washington Post,* February 24, 1973.
36. *Twelfth Constitutional Convention Proceedings: Oil, Chemical and Atomic Workers International Union,* Toronto, Ontario, August 7, 1973.
37. Ibid.
38. Ibid.
39. Ibid.

12. Crash

1. Steven Wodka interview with the author, April 30, 2004.
2. "The Grants Strike: Uranium Workers Fight Historic Battle," *Lifelines, OCAW Health and Safety News* 1, no. 2 (November 1973).
3. Richard Rashke, *The Killing of Karen Silkwood: The Story Behind the Kerr-McGee Plutonium Case* (Ithaca, NY: Cornell University Press, 2000), 35–42.
4. James Finch, "Uranium Mining Revival in New Mexico Through Solution Mining," http://EzineArticles.com/?expert=James_Finch, 2007.
5. Martin Walden, "Nuclear Fuel Plant Disturbs Its Neighbors," *New York Times,* January 7, 1975.
6. "Policing Deviance in Business," www.ucalgary.ca/~branniga/biz96.html.
7. Recordings of this phone conversations between Steve Wodka and Karen Silkwood are in the possession of Steve Wodka and were reviewed by the author.
8. Recordings of these workshops are in the possession of Steve Wodka and were reviewed by the author.

9. "Death of Karen Silkwood," *Harry Reasoner Report,* ABC TV, March 2, 1975.
10. Rashke, *Killing of Karen Silkwood,* 55–59.
11. Ibid., 235.
12. Ibid., 77.
13. "Problems in the Accounting for and Safeguarding of Special Nuclear Materials," Hearing Before the Subcommittee on Energy and Environment of the Committee on Small Business, House of Representatives, 94th Congress, 2nd session, Washington, DC, April 26, May 7, and May 20, 1976, 63.
14. David Burnham, "Death of Plutonium Worker Questioned by Union Official," *New York Times,* November 19, 1974, 28.
15. Rashke, *Killing of Karen Silkwood,* 96.
16. Steve Wodka interview with the author, February 8, 2007.
17. Letter from Tony Mazzocchi to John G. Davis, deputy director for field operations, US Nuclear Regulatory Commission, Washington, DC, January 21, 1975, and sworn affidavit from Jack Tice, filed with the National Labor Relations Board, case number 1b-CA-5905.
18. Ibid.
19. "Death of Karen Silkwood."
20. David Burnham, "Plutonium Plant Under Scrutiny," *New York Times,* November 20, 1974.
21. David Burnham, "Atom Aide's Death Ruled Accidental," *New York Times,* November 22, 1974.
22. Rashke, *Killing of Karen Silkwood,* 105–106.
23. David Burnham, "AEC Can't Say How Worker Swallowed Plutonium," *New York Times,* January 7, 1975.
24. David Burnham, "AEC Studies 3 Accidents at One Plant," *New York Times,* December 19, 1974.
25. Rashke, *Killing of Karen Silkwood,* 112.
26. Ibid., 123.
27. Ibid., 124.
28. Steve Wodka interview with the author, February 8, 2007.
29. *Proceedings, Oil Chemical and Atomic Workers International Union, 15th Constitutional Convention,* Diplomat Hotel, Hollywood Beach, Florida, August 13–17, 1979, 30.
30. Bob Woodward, "Watergate Unit to Probe Plot on Columnist," *Washington Post,* September 30, 1975, A13.
31. Ibid.

13. The Heart of the Deal

1. Cliff Welch, "Labor Internationalism: US Involvement in Brazilian Unions, 1945–1965," *Latin American Research Review* 30, no. 2 (spring 1995), 72–73.
2. Anthony Carew, "Free Trade Unionism in the International Context," 2002, 12 (21), www.arbark.se/pdf_wrd/Carew_int.pdf.
3. Welch, "Labor Internationalism," 72.
4. Philip Agee, *Inside the Company* (New York: Bantam Books, 1975), 632.
5. Ibid., 566.

6. "[T]he Secretary-General of ORIT, Arturo Juaregui, was fully recruited so that now he can be guided more effectively," wrote Agee. "Before our control of ORIT in Mexico City was exercised through Morris Paladino, the Assistant Secretary-General and the principal AFL-CIO representative on the staff." *Inside the Company,* 302.
7. Davidson, *Challenging the Giants,* 294.
8. Agee, *Inside the Company,* 131.
9. "Global Force in Oil Bargaining," *Business Week,* February 13, 1960.
10. Peter Gribbin, "Brazil and the CIA," *CounterSpy,* April–May 1979, 4–23.
11. Davidson, *Challenging the Giants,* 294.
12. Anthony Mazzocchi interview with the author, March 2007.
13. *Proceedings, Oil Chemical and Atomic Workers International Union, 15th Constitutional Convention,* 31.
14. Ibid.
15. Ibid., 68.
16. Carolyn Mugar interview with the author, June 22, 2002.
17. Mark Dudzic e-mail to the author, February 13, 2007.
18. Helen Dewar, "Energy Workers: New vs. Old, Militant Challenges 'Nuts and Bolts' Man for Presidency," *Washington Post,* August 6, 1979, A2.
19. Ibid.
20. From Tony Mazzocchi for President 1979 campaign literature.
21. Bob Wages interview with the author, April 28, 2004.
22. *Striking Nuclear Workers Take Their Fight to Washington,* booklet published by the Oil, Chemical and Atomic Workers International Union, July 1979.
23. Bob Wages e-mail to the author, May 6, 2005.
24. Sharon Itaya interview with the author, March 15, 2005.
25. Bob Wages interview with the author, April 28, 2004.
26. Eula Bingham interview with the author, March 29, 2005.
27. *Proceedings, Oil Chemical and Atomic Workers International Union, 15th Constitutional Convention,* 30.
28. Christine Oliver interview with the author, February 28, 2005.
29. L. C. Oliver and R. P. Weber, "Chest Pain in Rubber Chemical Workers Exposed to Carbon Disulfide and Methemoglobin Formers," *British Journal of Industrial Medicine* 41 (1984), 296–304.
30. Ruth Heifetz interview with the author, March 7, 2005.
31. Molly Coye interview with the author, March 28, 2005.
32. Linda Rudolph interview with the author, February 28, 2007.
33. Ralph Nader interview with the author, February 27, 2007.
34. Speeches of the Candidate for International Office, August 15, 1979, *Proceedings, Oil, Chemical and Atomic Workers International Union, 15th Constitutional Convention,* 112–113.
35. Ernie Rouselle interview with the author, March 24, 2005.
36. Rafael Moure interview with the author, March 9, 2005.
37. Sharon Itaya interview with the author, March 15, 2005.
38. Speeches of the Candidate for International Office, August 15, 1979, *Proceedings, Oil, Chemical and Atomic Workers International Union, 15th Constitutional Convention,* 101–105.

39. Ibid., 105–108.
40. Doug Stevens interview with the author, February 2, 2007.
41. Doug Stevens interview with the author, March 24, 2007.
42. Sylvia Kieding interview with the author, March 23, 2005.
43. *Proceedings, Oil, Chemical and Atomic Workers International Union, 15th Constitutional Convention,* 216.
44. Ibid., 218.
45. Ibid., 239.
46. Interview with Harold Edwards, March 31, 2005.
47. *Proceedings, Oil, Chemical and Atomic Workers International Union, 15th Constitutional Convention,* 239–240.
48. "Anatomy of a Labor Convention," KPFA Radio, August 17, 1979.

14. Round Two

1. "Anatomy of a Labor Convention," KPFA Radio, August 17, 1979.
2. *Proceedings, Oil, Chemical and Atomic Workers International Union, 15th Constitutional Convention,* 107.
3. *Proceedings, Oil, Chemical and Atomic Workers International Union, 16th Constitutional Convention,* Denver Hilton Hotel, Denver, Colorado, August 10–14, 1981, 124.
4. Tony Mazzocchi's Compendium of Campaign Literature, 1981, 8.
5. *Proceedings, Oil, Chemical and Atomic Workers International Union, 16th Constitutional Convention,* 124.
6. Bob Wages e-mail to the author, September 15, 2005.
7. "Merger Could Mean 700,000 Members Within 10 Years," *Union News,* Oil, Chemical and Atomic Workers, Denver, Colorado, July 1980, 8.
8. Address by Tony Mazzocchi to the OCAW District 8 council, Kenilworth, New Jersey, July 1981.
9. Bruce Ingersoll, "The Place Where Men Grew Breasts," *Chicago Sun-Times,* June 19, 1978, 8.
10. Ibid.
11. Eddie McNeil, "DES Tests Mapped Out," *Suburban Tribune,* September 10, 1979.
12. Ingersoll, "Where Men Grew Breasts," 8.
13. Ibid.
14. Rafael Moure e-mail to the author, March 2, 2007.
15. David Moberg, "Tony Mazzocchi Has a Different Idea," *In These Times,* April 29–May 5, 1981, 2.
16. Ibid.
17. Ibid.
18. Comments by Cole and Mazzocchi from Labor Institute Conference Transcripts, May 27, 1980, UAW Region 9, Cranford, New Jersey.
19. Comment by Tom Natchuras, assistant regional director, UAW Region 9.
20. Labor Institute Conference Transcripts, May 27, 1980.
21. *Proceedings, Oil, Chemical and Atomic Workers International Union, 16th Constitutional Convention,* 85–86.

22. Ibid., 87.
23. Ibid., 116.
24. Ibid., 116–117.
25. Ibid., 117.
26. Ibid., 118.
27. Ibid., 119.
28. Ibid.
29. Ibid.
30. Paul Renner interview with the author, March 4, 2005.
31. Paul Renner interview with Gail Bateson, 2002.
32. Paul Renner interview with the author, March 4, 2005.
33. "Company and Union in Dispute as Women Undergo Sterilization," *New York Times,* January 4, 1979, A7.
34. Ibid.
35. "Pigment Plant Wins Fertility-Risk Case: Government's Challenge Rejected on Policy Excluding Women for a 'Hazardous' Area," *New York Times,* September 8, 1980, A14.
36. Ricard Severo, "Should Firms Screen the Workplace or the Worker?," *New York Times,* September 28, 1980, E22.
37. Ellen Sweet, "Men Who've Taken Chances and Made a Difference," *Ms Magazine,* July–August, 1982, 104.
38. "Pigment Plant Wins Fertility-Risk Case."
39. Ed Ott interview with the author, November 2, 2006.
40. Bruce Clark interview with the author, February 24, 2007.
41. Ernie Rouselle interview with the author, March 24, 2005.
42. Joe Campbell interview with the author, March 24, 2005.
43. Bob Wages e-mail to the author, September 15, 2005.
44. Mark Dudzic e-mail to the author, February 23, 2007.
45. Jerry Archuletta e-mail to the author, February 28, 2007.
46. *Proceedings, Oil, Chemical and Atomic Workers International Union, 17th Constitutional Convention,* San Francisco Hilton, San Francisco, California, August 1–5, 1983, 157.
47. Thomas Geoghegan, *Which Side Are You On?: Trying to Be for Labor When It's Flat on Its Back* (New York: Penguin Press, 1992), 197.

15. Lost Battalions

1. William Serrin, "Labor Is Resisting More Concessions," *New York Times,* June 13, 1982.
2. Philip Shabecoff, "New Data Find Asbestos a Peril, in Home, at Job," *New York Times,* August 7, 1984; Philip Shabecoff, "EPA; Asbestos, Asbestos, Who's Got Asbestos," *New York Times,* September 11, 1984.
3. William Serrin, "Where Are the Pickets of Yesteryear," *New York Times,* May 31, 1981.
4. William Serrin, "Wage Concessions: Revolt in the Unions; New Analysis," *New York Times,* November 22, 1982.
5. Steven Greenhouse, "The Corporate Assault on Wages," *New York Times,* October 9, 1983.
6. William Serrin, "The Man Who Is Taking the Labor Movement to Task," *New York Times,* May 15, 1983.

7. Ibid.
8. Leo H. Carney, "Ciba-Geigy Accord Eludes Negotiators," *New York Times,* September 9, 1984.
9. Ibid.
10. Ibid.
11. Tony Mazzocchi address to the New York Committee for Occupational Safety and Health meeting, April 2002.
12. Author interview with Mazzocchi and Aronowitz, April 7, 1988, 853 Broadway, New York.
13. ABC *20/20,* February 27, 1986.
14. OCAW 8-760 Benefit Concert, Stone Pony, Asbury Park, New Jersey, June 19, 1986.
15. Stuart Diamond, "Hospitals Found to Be Ill-Prepared for Toxic Spills in New York Area," *New York Times,* December 4, 1985.
16. *Proceedings, Oil, Chemical and Atomic Workers International Union, 18th Constitutional Convention,* Radisson Hotel, Denver, Colorado, August 19–23, 1985, 135.
17. Ibid., 128.
18. Ibid., 168.
19. Ibid., 233.
20. Ibid., 284.
21. Bob Wages e-mail to the author, October 6, 2005.
22. Author interview with Kip Phillips, March 6, 2007.
23. Tim Minchin, *Forging a Common Bond: Labor and Environmental Activism During the BASF Lockout* (Tallahassee: University of Florida Press, 2003), 175.
24. Bob Wages e-mail to the author, March 10, 2007.
25. Tony Mazzocchi letter to Nedas Gauthreaux, OCAW Local 4-447, Gretna, Louisiana, May 18, 1998.
26. Tony Mazzocchi letter to Robert Wages, vice president, OCAW International Union, Denver, Colorado, March 4, 1987.

16. Party Time

1. Oil, Chemical and Atomic Workers International Union intra-organization communication from Tony Mazzocchi to Al Grospiron, March 24, 1972.
2. Jeremy Brecher, "American Labor on the Eve of the Millennium: A Review of Rank and File Struggles," www.zmag.org/instructionals/rtinstruc/id91_m.htm.
3. Slogan heard by author while attending Solidarity Day rally, September 19, 1981, Washington Mall, Washington, DC.
4. *Proceedings, Oil, Chemical and Atomic Workers International Union, 19th Constitutional Convention,* Diplomat Resort and Country Club, Hollywood, Florida, August 15–19, 1988, 135.
5. Mazzocchi interview with Terry Gross, *Fresh Air,* National Public Radio, replayed on October 10, 2002. It came from a previous interview by Terry Gross that she said was recorded in 1995, just before the Labor Party founding convention.
6. Tony Mazzocchi address to OCAW Occupational Safety and Health Coordinators, October 16, 1998, Cape May, New Jersey.
7. Alexander Cockburn, "Beat the Devil," *The Nation,* February 6, 1995, 156.

8. David Bacon, "Will the Labor Party Work?" *The Nation,* July 8, 1996, 22.
9. *Proceedings, Oil, Chemical and Atomic Workers International Union, 19th Constitutional Convention,* 136.
10. Ibid., 334.
11. Tony Mazzocchi, "1991 OCAW Monthly Calendar," April–June.
12. Kristina Mazzocchi e-mail to the author, March 5, 2007.
13. Mark Dudzic e-mail to the author, December 10, 2006.
14. Cockburn, "Beat the Devil."
15. Ibid.
16. Mark Dudzic e-mail to the author, December 10, 2006.
17. Mark Dudzic e-mail to the author, March 1, 2006.
18. The constitution that eventually passed established a "national council" to set labor party policy. The council included local chapter representatives as well as representatives from every major endorsing union: OCAW, the United Mine Workers, the United Electrical Workers, the Brotherhood of Maintenance of Way Employees (a rail union), the American Federation of Government Employees, the Farm Labor Organizing Committee, the International Longshore Workers Union, and the California Nurses Association. The dynamic Kensington Welfare Rights Organization also gained a seat on the council.
19. As heard by the author, who attended the platform committee meetings.
20. Baldemar Velasquez quotations in this section from e-mail to the author, February 27, 2007.
21. Labor Party "Call for Economic Justice," www.thelaborparty.org/a_progra.html#5.
22. Rose Ann DeMoro quotations in this section are from an interview with the author, February 27, 2007.
23. Adolph Reed Jr. to the author during the labor party convention, June 7, 1995.
24. Mark Dudzic e-mail to the author, December 10, 2006.
25. Bob Wages to the author during the labor party convention, June 7, 1995.
26. As heard by the author, who attended the OCAW labor party convention caucus.
27. Mark Dudzic e-mail to the author, March 1, 2007.
28. Baldemar Velasquez e-mail to the author, February 27, 2007.
29. Alexander Cockburn, "Beat the Devil."
30. Bob Kasen to the author on many occasions.
31. Tony Mazzocchi address at Bob Kasen's memorial service, February 17, 1999.
32. Mark Dudzic e-mail to the author, December 10, 2006.
33. Donna Dewitt interview with the author, March 8, 2007.
34. Mark Dudzic e-mail to the author, December 10, 2006.
35. Ibid.

17. Stepping-Stones

1. Bob Wages e-mail to the author, February 24, 2007.
2. Bob Wages interview with the author, April 28, 2004 for all citations in this section.
3. Bob Wages e-mail to the author, January 22, 2007.
4. Richard Leonard to the author, March 30, 2005.
5. Anonymous PACE staff members to the author, 2000.

6. Bob Wages e-mail to the author, January 22, 2007.
7. Ralph Nader interview with the author, February 27, 2007.
8. Laura McClure e-mail to the author, February 24, 2007.
9. Richard MacManus to Mark Dudzic, January 25, 2001.
10. Ralph Nader, *Crashing the Party: How to Tell the Truth and Still Run for President* (New York: Thomas Dunne Books, St. Martin's Press, 2002), 196–197.
11. Mark Dudzic e-mail to the author, March 1, 2007.
12. Henry Mayer, *All on Fire: William Lloyd Garrison and the Abolition of Slavery* (New York: St. Martin's Press, 1998), xiv.
13. Ibid., 251.
14. Bacon, "Will the Labor Party Work?," 23.
15. Jonathan Alter interview with Tony Mazzocchi, taped by the author, January 8, 2002.
16. Laura McClure discussion with Tony Mazzocchi, taped by the author, January 9, 2002.
17. Tony Mazzocchi discussion with Rick McArthur, Adolph Reed Jr., and Katherine Isaac, taped by the author, January 9, 2002.

Index

Note: Page numbers for the Photo Section are entered as *PS:* followed by the page number, also in italics.